Rethinking the Western Tradition

*The volumes in this series
seek to address the present debate
over the Western tradition
by reprinting key works of
that tradition along with essays
that evaluate each text from
different perspectives.*

Selected Writings of Thomas Paine

Edited by
Ian Shapiro and
Jane E. Calvert
with an Introduction by
Ian Shapiro
with essays by
J. C. D. Clark
Jane E. Calvert
Eileen Hunt Botting

Yale
UNIVERSITY PRESS

New Haven and London

Published with assistance from the Annie Burr Lewis Fund.
Published with assistance from the foundation established in
memory of Amasa Stone Mather of the Class of 1907, Yale College.

Yale University Press books may be purchased in quantity for
educational, business, or promotional use. For information,
please e-mail sales.press@yale.edu (U.S. office) or
sales@yaleup.co.uk (U.K. office).

Set in Times Roman and Perpetua types by Newgen North America.
Printed in the United States of America.

Library of Congress Cataloging-in-Publication Data
Paine, Thomas, 1737–1809.
[Works. Selections. 2014]
Selected writings of Thomas Paine / edited by Ian Shapiro and
Jane E. Calvert ; with an introduction by Ian Shapiro ; with essays
by J. C. D. Clark, Jane E. Calvert, Eileen Hunt Botting.
pages cm. – (Rethinking the western tradition)
Includes bibliographical references and index.
ISBN 978-0-300-16745-0 (pbk. : alk. paper) 1. Political science—Early works
to 1800. I. Shapiro, Ian, editor. II. Calvert, Jane E., 1970– editor. III. Title.
JC177.A5 2014
320.51'2092—dc23
2014005794

A catalogue record for this book is available from the British Library.
This paper meets the requirements of ANSI/NISO Z39.48–1992
(Permanence of Paper).

10 9 8 7 6 5 4 3 2 1

Contributors

Eileen Hunt Botting is Associate Professor of Political Science at the University of Notre Dame.

Jane E. Calvert is Associate Professor of History at the University of Kentucky.

J. C. D. Clark is an historian of Britain and America in the long eighteenth century.

Ian Shapiro is Sterling Professor of Political Science and Henry R. Luce Director of the MacMillan Center at Yale University.

A 1793 cartoon by James Gillray showing Thomas Paine tightening Britannia's corset. The tape protruding from his pocket is inscribed "Rights of Man," and the cottage behind them is inscribed "Thomas Pain, Staymaker from Thetford." Library of Congress, Prints & Photographs Division.

Contents

Acknowledgments

The editors would like to thank David Armitage, R. B. Bernstein, and Rogers Smith, as well as two anonymous readers for Yale University Press for their helpful comments and suggestions on the selections from Paine's writings, the introduction, and the interpretive essays. Gaye Ilhan Demiryol also deserves thanks for her diligent proofreading of the transcribed documents.

Introduction

Thomas Paine, America's First Public Intellectual

IAN SHAPIRO

Thomas Paine died in 1809 at the age of seventy-two, by coincidence the year in which both Charles Darwin and Abraham Lincoln were born. Lincoln would turn out to be a great Paine admirer.[1] He was strongly influenced by Paine's rhetorical style and in 1835 even wrote a defense of Paine's deism, which a friend, Samuel Hill, destroyed before it could be published, out of concern for Lincoln's political future.[2] Deism, the doctrine that humans can know that there is a creator who, like a watchmaker, set the world in motion but nothing further about him, was among the most incendiary of Paine's convictions—defended at length in *The Age of Reason*, published in two parts in 1794 and 1795. The threat that it posed to organized religion attracted vitriolic opprobrium from many quarters, which he never managed to shed, despite his once-exalted status as the philosopher of the American Revolution, whose pamphlets and books had sold in the hundreds of thousands and been read by millions. The fact that Theodore Roosevelt would feel the need to dismiss Paine, incorrectly, as a "filthy little atheist" many decades after his—and Lincoln's—deaths suggests that Hill's action had been prudent.[3] Darwin had no direct connection with Paine, but his discovery of natural selection led him to reject Christianity in favor of a similar kind of deism to Paine's—though Darwin would eventually become a fully fledged agnostic. Unlike Lincoln, Darwin did not need to be saved from himself by his friends. He generally remained circumspect about what he knew would be unpopular views. In 1873, he cautioned his son George against publishing a diatribe against prayer and belief in the afterlife, to avoid "injuring your own power & usefulness."[4]

Paine would have been incapable of heeding—perhaps even of hearing—such advice. Whatever he was, Thomas Paine was not circumspect. Convinced that life is "a daring adventure, or nothing,"[5] he lived with astounding directness, optimism, and confidence—in himself, in others, and in his ideas. This is all the more remarkable in view of the many setbacks and failures he experienced throughout his life. He lost numerous jobs and all his assets several times. His first wife died in childbirth, and his second marriage ended following a humiliating business failure and personal bankruptcy. He suffered from severe illnesses – including typhoid, which almost killed him on his first transatlantic voyage in 1774. He was betrayed by erstwhile friends and associates, with devastating consequences for his liberty and his reputation. He was convicted of seditious libel and burned in effigy for his attack on the British monarchy in his *Rights of Man*. Though he escaped to France, where he was named a French citizen and elected as a deputy to the National Convention, in 1793 he was imprisoned and narrowly escaped execution by the Jacobins for trying to save the life of Louis XVI. The American Federalists attacked him relentlessly for his defense of the French Revolution. He had to scrape together an ignoble living during his declining years. He was buried on his farm in New Rochelle, New York, with a mere six mourners in attendance, having been denied interment in a Quaker cemetery. Even in death Paine was shunned. William Cobbett, who had overcome earlier antipathy to become one of Paine's great devotees, exhumed his body in 1819 for reburial in England. But permission was denied. His bones were subsequently lost; they have been the subject of macabre speculation ever since.[6]

Yet Paine bounced back from his many catastrophes, sometimes with astonishing panache. Indeed, inventiveness and resilience marked him from the beginning. He would never have amounted to anything more than a regional excise collector in Lewes, East Sussex, England, were it not for his audacious self-confidence leavened by a capacity for bootstrapping, which has seldom, if ever, been matched. For all practical purposes self-educated and lacking any advantages of birth, Paine would become a major figure in elite circles in Britain, France, and the United States and a confidant of three American presidents as well as Napoleon Bonaparte. His mother was the daughter of a relatively well-to-do lawyer, but she married down, with the result that Paine had to leave school at the age of twelve and apprentice in his father's trade of stay-making.

In 1756 the Seven Years War gave him his ticket out. Rejecting his father's counsel, he enlisted as a privateer and earned a thirty-pound commission. This small fortune enabled Paine to move to London and talk his way into the bustling world of intellectual clubs and cafés spawned by the new intelligentsia, where he came to know – among others – Benjamin Franklin. This would turn out to be a fortuitous connection. In late 1774, following the death of his wife and child, his failed stay-making business and second marriage, and his dismissal from the excise service prompted by a quixotic attempt to get Parliament to improve conditions for tax collectors, Paine left for America at the age of thirty-seven. A letter of introduction from Franklin gave him his entrée into Philadelphia society.[7]

Even armed with Franklin's letter, which recommended Paine only for a modest teaching or clerical position, he faced an uphill battle in the New World. No one could have guessed then that this underachieving middle-aged misfit was soon to become a household name; that *Common Sense* (1776) and his sixteen pamphlets on *The Crisis*[8] (1776–1783) would widely be heralded for galvanizing Americans to demand full independence and sustaining the Revolution's army through the worst days of the war, "when nothing but hope and virtue could survive";[9] that his *Rights of Man* (1791–1792) would become the definitive critical response to Edmund Burke's *Reflections on the Revolution in France* – provoking enough unrest throughout England to convince William Pitt's government to ban it, burn it, and declare war on its author; that *The Age of Reason* would be a blockbuster on both sides of the Atlantic, selling hundreds of thousands of copies and provoking dozens of responses – including from such leading theologians as Joseph Priestley and Richard Watson; or that his case for redistribution in *Agrarian Justice* (1797) would still be in currency more than two centuries after its publication.[10] When the shivering, delirious Paine was carried off the deck of the *London Packet* in Philadelphia's harbor in December of 1774, that all lay in the future.

Soon after Paine had recovered from the rigors of his transatlantic voyage, he persuaded one Robert Aitken, the owner of a bookstore and printing press, to start publishing *The Pennsylvania Magazine* under Paine's editorship. It was an overnight success, in a few months attracting fifteen hundred paid subscribers. This made it the most widely read periodical in the New World.[11] Paine wrote much of the magazine himself under various pseudonyms, honing the skills that would soon make him the best-selling author of his generation. He fell out with Aitken, however, while trying to renegotiate the terms of his employment, reflecting a dynamic that would repeat itself throughout his life: Paine fought not only with his adversaries but also with allies and even friends. Combining unusually large doses of generosity, courage, and vanity, he frustrated his supporters, goaded his enemies, and took enormous risks – sometimes without seeming even to be aware of them. Among the reasons why Paine is a figure of enduring fascination is that he defies easy classification as a thinker or as a human being.

Paine was, first and always, an intellectual. Today he would be called a public intellectual. Among other things, this means that he was no politician.

This is not to deny that Paine sought – and achieved – remarkable political influence. *Common Sense* is widely credited for galvanizing disaffected American colonists to demand independence from Britain. His *Crisis* letters garnered comparable acclaim for sustaining American forces through the darkest days of the Revolutionary War – when defeat seemed all but inevitable. The Declaration of Independence mimics Paine's style and arguments so thoroughly that some claimed him as its ghost author – even though Paine denied this.[12] The rousing effects of his *Rights of Man* on Britain's lower orders were sufficiently alarming to elites that the government poured great effort into discrediting him and, when that failed, into prosecuting him. In France he served as one of nine deputies on the committee that drafted the post-Revolution constitution (and one of only three who survived the Reign of Terror), and he supplied Napoleon with plans for a proposed invasion of Britain along the Lincolnshire coast – whose contours he knew well from his years as an excise man.[13] President Jefferson often sought his advice, most notably to resolve the crisis that led to the Louisiana Purchase in 1803 – even if he was by then so great a liability that Jefferson would not acknowledge him publicly.[14]

Influence is one thing; politics, another. Paine wielded one of the most inspiring pens of the century, but this was not matched by a facility for persuasive public speaking. Few letters or other direct sources of evidence about his character have survived, yet it seems clear that, despite an arresting twinkle in his eyes, he was devoid of personal charisma. He could be engaging in conversation but was often withdrawn in company. Though tall and reputedly handsome, he had a bulbous nose that deteriorated with age, possibly due to chronic rosacea. This helped his enemies exaggerate his drinking, denigrating him as an alcoholic.[15] He had a searingly acute analytical intellect, but he always wrote from the heart with uncompromising passion – scorning those who pulled punches or sought the middle ground. He heaped vitriol on his critics, particularly if they had once been friends. *Rights of Man* was at least as famous for its contemptuous derision of Burke as for the substance of Paine's arguments. George Washington, who had helped him greatly as a young man and whose prowess as a general he had defended against critics during the war, would eventually be trashed by Paine not only as an incompetent soldier who had been bailed out by the French, but as "treacherous in private friendship" and so hypocritical that "the world will be puzzled to decide whether you are an apostate or an imposter."[16] Paine's ravenous need always to have the last word, as in the escalating venom that marked his replies to critics of *The Age of*

Reason, meant that even the like-minded would often sidestep association with him.

Common Sense was well crafted to win support for Paine's revolutionary cause, but in this it was exceptional. For the most part he was clueless about how to build political coalitions, when to keep his powder dry, or even why it might sometimes be wise to avoid giving unnecessary offense. As a result, most of his direct interventions in politics were disastrous flops. His petition to Parliament on behalf of the excise collectors achieved nothing but his firing. His service to the American Revolution should have secured him lifetime positions of honor and financial security in the new order, but he seldom held on to appointments for long, and political adversaries easily ran rings round him. Even when Paine was in the right (as in his accusations that Silas Deane had been an opportunistic traitor who secretly worked for the British during the war), Paine managed to come off as the political loser. His revolutionary credentials secured him French citizenship and invitations to represent no fewer than four constituencies at the National Convention in 1792 (he opted for Calais), but his censorious style soon alienated potential allies. His speech to save Louis XVI's life the following January was a noble gambit, but it fell on deaf ears and predictably finished Paine as a significant figure at the convention. By the time Maximilien de Robespierre and Jean-Paul Marat turned on him, driving him first from the convention, then from French public life, and finally into prison, no one who could help him was willing to take up his cause. That he avoided the guillotine seems to have been due mainly to the incompetence of his captors.

Nor was Paine a scholar. He was voraciously curious and widely read – impressively so by any measure but especially given his lack of formal education. Like the other American founders, he wrote in conversation with major thinkers from the past, but he absorbed ideas from them and those around him more like a sponge than a student or a participant in disciplined intellectual exchange. He seldom rewrote or even revised his work, which was uncluttered by references and other scholarly paraphernalia. No doubt this contributed to its accessibility. He scoffed at the suggestion that his ideas were derived from John Locke, whom he dismissed as too speculative and impractical to be worth his time.[17] He blended the analytical and the polemical in ways that are reminiscent of Jean-Jacques Rousseau and Karl Marx. For Paine, ideas were rocks to be hurled at adversaries and to provide the motivating foundations for political action. He had an unerring faith in the power of reason to move people, which meant that he had more in common with the European rationalist tradition, from René Descartes to Immanuel Kant, than with the British empiricists, from Thomas Hobbes to David Hume, for whom reason is, as Hume put it, the slave of the passions.[18] But Paine's rationalism was for Everyman.[19] As R. B. Bernstein puts it, Paine democratized political language, transforming it "from a medium restricted to the intellectual elite" into a medium that "any intelligent person could use."[20] It was not the prerogative of political elites "to begin the world over again," as Paine declared in the conclusion to *Common Sense*.[21] He saw mankind through the lens of his own bootstrapped biography, convinced that vivid depictions of people's interests and the ways in which they were frustrated by corrupt and exploitative arrangements would move people to tear down the instruments of their oppression.

This is what made him dangerous. Craig Nelson points out that what distinguished the second part of *Rights of Man,* published in 1792, from the first (1791) – and moved the attorney general to prosecute Paine – was not its message but its likely audience. *Part the Second* immediately became widely and cheaply available, spurring fears that it would be the kind of catalyst to rebellion in England that *Common Sense* had been in America.[22] Likewise, Nelson observes that *The Age of Reason* provoked fury among American elites, who often did not dispute Paine's deist message but opposed sharing it with the middle and lower classes, which were Paine's natural audience. The worry was what today might be called a Straussian anxiety, that if their children "were not Sunday schooled in notions of good and evil, of striving for the rewards of heaven and fearing the punishments of hell, they would become as immoral as apes."[23] Paine was a true believer in the rational capacities of the common man. His vocation was to excite them to action which would be unmediated by self-appointed guardians of prudent political evolution. This is why his work has always appealed to intellectual activists. Paine was anti-elitist to the core.

Paine's anti-elitism colored his enthusiasm for the scientific revolution that accelerated around him over the course of his life. His relentless curiosity bespoke a Renaissance intellect, fueled, no doubt, by his association with such brilliant figures as Franklin, Washington, Jefferson, Antoine-Nicolas de Caritat (Condorcet), Mary Wollstonecraft, Benjamin Rush, William Blake, Richard Price, and William Godwin. Whether he was trying to account for the origins of flammable methane, building a pierless bridge that could span freezing rivers (a lifelong obsession at which he eventually succeeded), or opining about the need for independent banks and international political institutions, Paine exuded confidence that every facet of nature and every human contrivance could be thoroughly under-

stood and tamed for benevolent ends. Yet he was not in the least drawn to
the kinds of technocratic elitism or vanguardism that would – in different
ways – appeal to Enlightenment thinkers like Jeremy Bentham and Karl
Marx. He also had no time for the neo-Aristotelian political science of
institutional design, based on metaphors – if not theories – of balance, separation, and equilibrium, which motivated others in America's founding
generation.[24] Paine was a pragmatist about institutions, and his views about
them evolved with his experience. His strongly egalitarian instincts, combined with his contempt for European monarchs – dead and living – many
of whom struck him as little better than imbeciles, inclined him initially to
bet on strong democracy expressed through unfettered unicameral legislatures. But he eventually changed his mind. In 1786 he attacked the Pennsylvania legislature's revocation to the Bank of North America's charter
(the bank had opposed the government's inflationary printing of money),
during the course of which he endorsed bicameralism and robust courts as
checks on "the despotism of numbers."[25] No doubt his subsequent experience at the hands of the French National Convention reinforced his worries
about majoritarianism.

Part of the reason that Paine did not reify particular political arrangements is that he did not harbor an elevated view of politics. To be sure, he
believed that government had a major role to play in preventing domination
and redistributing wealth. The second part of Rights of Man argued for progressive taxation to fund the rudiments of a welfare state. Agrarian Justice,
composed in 1795 and 1796, called for estate taxes to reduce inequality
by providing substantial payments to young adults and lifetime pensions
for the elderly. These attacks on the privileges of property engendered pre-
dictable excoriation, particularly from those who identified the ownership
of property as a natural right or a precursor for citizenship. Paine's arguments in these works have often led progressives to portray him as a kind
of proto-socialist. The shoe does not fit, partly, as Nelson notes, because
Paine was an admirer of Adam Smith's arguments in support of commerce
and market economics.[26] But the shoe is also a bad fit because Paine had
a strong anti-statist streak. Although he declared at the outset of Common
Sense that "society in every state is a blessing," he was adamant that "gov
ernment even in its best state is but a necessary evil." Typically, it is no
better than a monument to the human propensity for sin. Government "is
the badge of lost innocence."[27] In what might have been James Madison's
inspiration for Federalist No. 51, Paine lamented that if only "the impulses
of conscience" were "clear, uniform, and irresistibly obeyed, man would
need no other lawgiver."[28] As it is, our propensity to do evil to one another

makes government essential. Lacking the lofty view of government and politics that so often accompanies socialist worldviews, Paine would not have lost much sleep over changing his mind about particular institutional arrangements in light of his experience.

At times such changes of mind enabled Paine's enemies to dismiss him as an opportunist. It is true that he was not above taking polemical stands that contradicted his professed beliefs and commitments, as Jane Calvert details in her contribution to the present volume with respect to his dealings with the Pennsylvania Quakers. But it would be difficult to pin opportunism on Paine as a general or summary charge of flawed character. For one thing, he held steadfast to core moral convictions throughout his life: on the existence of a supreme being, on the injustice of slavery, and on the wrongness of the death penalty. Moreover, he stuck to these convictions through thick and thin – even, as we saw with his deism and his effort to save Louis XVI – when this threatened his own livelihood or indeed his life. It is hard to imagine Paine dismissing consistency as the hobgoblin of little minds; his faith in reason was too powerful for that. By the same token, however, he was reluctant to reify political tactics, strategies, or institutions. Paine was a man of action who recalibrated many of his beliefs in light of his experience and changing circumstances, but he did not want for a moral compass. Indeed, one reason for his defense of deism in *The Age of Reason* was his conviction that without it there would be no anchor for moral imperatives geared toward the possibility of human improvement. It seems that he anticipated – and feared – the nihilist conclusion that if there is no god, then anything is permitted.[29] Mere humanism, for Paine, was not enough.

Joyce Appleby notes that Paine was not an especially profound thinker and that his political theorizing could sometimes be rambling.[30] But there is, nonetheless, an arresting quality to his best writing that stemmed from his impulse to drive ideas to the hilt: to defend them without qualification and to take them to extremes that would not occur to others – let alone garner their endorsement. In this – if nothing other than the bizarre subsequent histories of their physical remains – he is reminiscent of Jeremy Bentham.[31] Appleby describes Paine as "a vector for the radical theorizing about the origins of government" begun by Hobbes and Locke in the seventeenth century; modified by such eighteenth-century anti-absolutists as Montesquieu, Voltaire, and Rousseau; and repatriated to England as Paine was finding his intellectual feet; that he soaked up these ideas along with the other anti-elitist currents that were swirling around him; mixed them "with his rage at the way English institutions thwarted the ambitions of ordinary men, and discovered in the American struggle 'the cause of all mankind.'"[32] To this it should be added that just as he pushed common complaints about Britain's overbearing colonial administration into a full-throated roar for American independence in *Common Sense,* so he revamped contractual understanding of the relations between the people and their governments into a relentless denunciation of every last vestige of monarchical or aristocratic authority in his *Rights of Man.*

Though Paine was not a profound theoretician, there are two ways in which he was strikingly novel. One is that his underlying disposition was democratic to the core. Paine did not actually say that much about democracy. The term does not even appear in *Common Sense,* which, judging from his choice of epitaph, he regarded as his greatest work.[33] Nor is democracy a major motif in *Rights of Man,* though his assumptions and assertions about it in the book are revealing. In the course of heaping scorn on Burke's reverence for aristocrats, whom Paine dismisses as little more than inbred degenerates, he insists that "the greatest characters the world have known, have rose on the democratic floor."[34] Just as Paine never doubted his own understanding or capabilities, he saw no reason that others should prostrate themselves before those who had arbitrarily been privileged by birth. This illuminates what might otherwise seem like an odd mixture of arrogance and humility: he was conceited in that he saw no reason ever to defer to anyone because of wealth, status, or rank; but he was humble in that he never expected deference from anyone else. The core of his disposition was egalitarian, reflected, as I noted earlier, in his appeal to unadorned reason. To be sure, people sometimes disappointed him – as when Congress denied him a pension. But this was about what he perceived as ingratitude for his service to the nation, not a failure to acknowledge his importance.

That heredity could be the source of anything valuable in politics struck Paine as ludicrous. He thought the notion of a hereditary legislator "as absurd as an hereditary mathematician, or an hereditary wise man; and as ridiculous as an hereditary poet-laureat."[35] The natural thing is for people to govern themselves. Thus while most ancient governments "present to us a miserable picture of the condition of man," Athens was the exception. "We see more to admire, and less to condemn, in that great, extraordinary people, than in any thing which history affords." Paine speculated that had Athens not been small enough for the people to govern themselves directly, the Athenians might have come up with the idea of representative government as the natural response to the challenges of scale, saving mankind from centuries of grief. Had that occurred, there is no reason to suppose that monarchy or aristocracy, "those unnatural modes of government," would ever have been instituted.[36]

Paine's enthusiasm for Athenian democracy gives him the rare distinction of being one of democracy's earliest modern supporters. The democratic idea was not, of course, new in the eighteenth century, but it had few categorical defenders. In this, it was distinctive. The other major political ideologies of the Enlightenment have been made famous by their champions. Hobbes and Locke were advocates for the social contract. Jeremy Bentham and John Stuart Mill were the animated architects of utilitarianism. Karl Marx and Friedrich Engels were communism's apostles. Democracy, by contrast, had for centuries been made famous by its critics – the most famous of whom had been Plato and Aristotle. The American founders were keenly aware of their antipathy for the Athenian model, which they blamed for the mob mentality that had led to the death of Socrates. This was partly why the founding generation saw their enterprise as a neo-Roman venture to create what Madison would describe in *Federalist No. 10* as a nontyrannical republic as distinct from a "pure democracy." And it is why the founders drew on Aristotle's mix of the one, the few, and the many, rather than any variant of the Athenian model. Paine had no time for the one or the few, as we have seen. For him, the great modern invention was representative government. It was sufficient to address the challenges of size, adapting the Athenian ideal to the modern world.

As this last observation suggests, Paine was a novel thinker also in that his central preoccupations were remarkably prescient. He was one of the very first to realize, more than four decades before Alexis de Tocqueville wrote *Democracy in America,* that in the big sweep of history, monarchy and aristocracy were finished as sources of political legitimacy.[37] In the future, legitimacy would flow from the people. He was more confident than the other American founders (with the possible exception of Madison toward the end of his life) that majoritarian politics had arrived to stay and that it must ultimately constrain republican institutions.[38] He saw that, despite its limitations – and he was keenly aware of at least some of them – representative government would have to be the engine by which the moral authority of democracy was reconciled with realities of modern mass politics. John Stuart Mill would take up the subject in definitive detail seven decades after the appearance of *Rights of Man,* but in a noteworthy sense, Paine set the table for Mill's discussion.[39]

Paine's writings about taxation, redistribution, and pensions were also remarkably forward-looking. As I noted earlier, they prefigured debates about the twentieth-century welfare state long before anything resembling modern nation states were even dimly in view. Paine's populist inclinations notwithstanding, he also exhibited a surprisingly sophisticated grasp of markets, banking, and public finance – including at least some of the institutions they were going to require. And, more than half a century before nationalism would begin sweeping the world in ways that would transpose commerce and international conflict into new keys, Paine was thinking about the need for international institutions based on a global convention of delegates, along the lines of the United Nations.[40] He insisted against Abbé Guillaume-Thomas Raynal that all countries, whatever their internal political forms, "are relatively republics with each other," and that there should be international agreements limiting the size of navies to ensure the "future tranquillity of mankind" – a precursor to modern arms-reduction agreements.[41]

In short, as Jonathan Clark notes in his essay in this volume, Paine defies attempts to slot him into the usual pigeonholes. This partly accounts for why, just as many have found things to despise in his writings, a remarkably diverse assemblage of successors has subsequently claimed Paine's mantle. For Philip Foner and Harvey Kaye, he was a kind of proto-Marxist whose ideas have inspired socialist and working-class movements since the eighteenth century.[42] Teddy Roosevelt's antipathy notwithstanding, Paine was indeed a stalwart of the progressive movement. Yet, as J. G. A. Pocock has noted, Paine never fit neatly into the mold of radical politics.[43] His libertarian streak has also appealed to iconoclastic anti-statists like Christopher Hitchens.[44] Paine has been embraced by conservatives like Ronald Reagan, who turned to him for the proposition that "we have it in our power to begin the world over again" in accepting his party's presidential nomination in 1980, not to mention Glenn Beck – who surely deserves an Olympic gold medal in chutzpah for declaring Paine to be "the me of his generation."[45] Romantic nationalists like Walt Whitman credited Paine with substantial responsibility for America's independence, for "severing the nation from ecclesiastical and superstitious domination," and embracing a constitution that incorporates a "radical" respect for human rights.[46] But Paine has appealed to writers and poets of many stripes, including Ralph Waldo Emerson, Henry David Thoreau, Theodore Parker, Samuel Clemens (Mark Twain), and Herman Melville.[47] In 1925 Thomas Edison declared Paine to be "our greatest political thinker" whose "sagacious reasoning" was "surpassed nowhere else in American letters" and "seldom in any school of writing."[48]

Militarists have also found alluring strands in his writings. General George Patton turned to the opening paragraph of Paine's first *Crisis* pamphlet to rally European troops against Hitler, declaring that "tyranny, like hell, is not easily conquered."[49] David Frum and Richard Perle began their neo-conservative tract on counterterrorism after the September 11, 2001, attacks with "These are the times that try men's souls" – the oft-repeated line also deployed by FDR following the Japanese attack on Pearl Harbor.[50] Not to be forgotten, on the topic of trying times, is Barack Obama's first inaugural declaration in January of 2009 at the height of the global financial crisis, that future generations would learn that "in the depth of winter, when nothing but hope and virtue could survive . . . the city and the country, alarmed at one common danger, came forth to meet it."[51]

It is true that the aphoristic character of many of Paine's writings makes them readily available to people of many stripes. When Frum and Perle took aim at "the summer soldier and the sunshine patriot" who "will, in this crisis, shrink from the service of his country," they no doubt had rather different people in mind from those Paine was thinking about when he crafted his first *Crisis* pamphlet in December of 1776 – not to mention the scores of people who have called on these words in multiple settings in the years since. And while Paine's enthusiasm for America has often garnered the attention of romantic nationalists, we should not lose sight of the reality that this self-described citizen of the world saw the human condition in unremittingly cosmopolitan terms. "The cause of America is in a great measure the cause of all mankind" he declared in *Common Sense,*[52] a view Lincoln would repeatedly echo eight decades later in his universalist depictions of the Union cause in the Civil War.[53]

Paine bet on America as the harbinger of democratic change throughout the world, as he would later bet on France, though both would subsequently disappoint him. In this he is reminiscent of Alexis de Tocqueville, who also thought American democracy a model for France and would also be doubly disappointed – if for illuminatingly different reasons. Whereas Paine hoped America would be an exporter of leveling egalitarianism, for Tocqueville it offered the best model of how to domesticate that ideology via republican practices and institutions. The French inability to heed what Tocqueville took to be America's lessons had played itself out not only after 1789 but also in the revolutions of 1830 and, as he would remind readers in the preface to the twelfth edition of *Democracy in America,* in 1848.[54] Tocqueville would eventually despair of the American experiment. He lost his earlier confidence that American individualism could be inhibited by "self-interest rightly understood" or sequestered from politics, which struck him as increasingly dominated by people lacking in "moderation, sometimes probity, above all education."[55] He had always been troubled by American slavery, but when he wrote *Democracy in America,* he thought it was dying out.[56] With the passage of the Kansas-Nebraska Act in 1854, the election of James Buchanan two years later, and the *Dred Scott* decision and the dress-rehearsal for the Civil War in Kansas prompted by the adoption of a pro-slavery constitution there the year after that, Tocqueville decided that he had also been wrong about slavery and that its looming expansion into the territories would destroy what remained of America's decaying moral authority in Europe.[57] He never lived to see the Civil War erupt, but the distress manifest in his last letters to American friends suggests that he would not have been surprised.[58]

By the time the war arrived, Paine had been dead for half a century. America was on its sixteenth president, the man who had been an infant in rural Kentucky when Paine died and who would come eventually to admire Paine's theology and imitate his rhetorical style. But what would Paine have made of Lincoln? Surely he would have admired Lincoln after January of 1863. The Emancipation Proclamation would have resonated with Paine's antipathy for slavery, as would the theological reticence that infused Lincoln's second inaugural address.[59] But it is hard to imagine Paine embracing Lincoln's earlier political stance. The 1860 Republican platform, famously set forth in Lincoln's Cooper Union speech and reiterated in his first inaugural address, opposed extending slavery into the territories but accepted it in the South. In effect, Lincoln sought to reinstate the status-quo ante that had collapsed when the Kansas-Nebraska Act upended the Missouri Compromise of 1820.[60] It is difficult to see Paine endorsing Lincoln's pragmatic willingness to accept Southern slavery in hopes of saving the Union. Had he been willing to join the party at all, he would likely have sided with more-radical Republicans who wanted emancipation as a war aim from the start. For the same reason, he would have looked askance at Lincoln's preliminary Emancipation Proclamation of September 1862, which threatened emancipation of slaves only in rebel states that did not return to the Union by the year's end.[61]

Paine would likely have resisted Lincoln's underlying logic that, in order for American democracy to be a beacon to the world, preserving the Union was more important than abolishing slavery right away.[62] That view might have been tenable in the late eighteenth century, perhaps as late as the end of the Napoleonic Wars.[63] Indeed, the fact that Paine never attacked the compromises with slavery built into the Constitution might be invoked as ballast for the suggestion that it might have been his view – even though Paine never explicitly said so. Moreover, it now seems unlikely that Paine wrote "African Slavery in America," published in *The Pennsylvania Journal; and Weekly Advertiser* in March of 1775 and often attributed to him, and it is certain that his participation in anti-slavery societies has been exaggerated.[64]

But the world was a very different place by 1860. The Atlantic slave trade had been illegal for more than half a century – stamped out by the British navy everywhere except Cuba, where it would end in a few years. Slavery itself had been illegal throughout the great bulk of the British Empire for nearly three decades.[65] Surely someone with Paine's sensibilities would by then have shared the lens through which the aging Tocqueville had come to view slavery as the defining moral issue of the age – and Paine would probably have rendered a verdict similar to Tocqueville's. After all, even James Lynch, who has set the record straight concerning the exaggeration of Paine's role as an abolitionist, concludes that perhaps no one hated "the concept" of slavery more than Paine did; that he "found it repulsive and sincerely hoped for its eradication"; that he warned Jefferson of the "immorality" of extending slavery into Louisiana; and that in 1791 he described the Haitian Revolution in Saint-Dominique as the "natural consequence of slavery."[66] It is hard to imagine someone with these sentiments dragging his feet over the slavery issue by 1860.

Some of Lincoln's other compromises, in particular his willingness to compensate slave states for emancipation along the lines that the British had pursued in the West Indies, might have appealed to Paine more.[67] Paine was no pacifist. He thought that war is at times necessary and indeed desirable in pursuit of a righteous cause; this belief lay at the heart of his differences with the Pennsylvania Quakers explored by Jane Calvert in this volume. Nor was Paine merely a humanist, as I have noted; but he was a humanist. He valued life and disliked gratuitous killing. His manifest idealism notwithstanding, he was not above tactical or strategic compromise to vindicate his ideals – even if he sometimes lacked the judgment to know which compromises would likely be effective. Nor did Paine think money or property sacrosanct; he often forwent royalties to promote the diffusion of his ideas, and he gave away most of his assets to support the army during the Revolutionary War. Had the South been willing to buckle, for a price, as Lincoln hoped they would in 1862, Paine might have agreed with him that it was worth it to the Union to end the war. Indeed, when Lincoln returned to the issue of compensation in the war's waning days, to stop what had become senseless killing by any measure now that the outcome was beyond all doubt, he might well have received a more indulgent hearing from Paine than he did from his cabinet colleagues.[68]

If Paine's beliefs defy easy classification, so does his personality. This is partly due to the dearth of direct evidence about his personal life, already mentioned. Nelson, among others, speculates that he might have been something of a manic-depressive.[69] Paine's intense confidence, not to say obsessive single-mindedness, together with a disregard for his personal and financial security, which many would judge reckless, might arguably be evidence of manic "highs." But his bouts of depression were situational, not endogenous. There were good reasons for them: personal losses and betrayals, the failure of professional and political projects, and physical illness and decline.[70] Indeed, what is remarkable about Paine is how frequently he triumphed over adversities that would have overwhelmed most people. Still, to classify Paine merely as a conventional – if tough, resourceful, and intense – personality, would miss important dimensions of his temperament. His extreme literal-mindedness and rigidness in the face of criticism, together with his imperviousness to how others saw him, suggest that in some fundamental way he was a loner.

The fact that Paine had virtually no personal emotional life, so far as anyone has been able to discover, after the death of his first wife in 1760 (when he was twenty-four years old) lends credence to this suspicion. Keane notes that there is serious doubt as to whether Paine's second marriage was ever consummated. Certainly he and Elizabeth Ollive spent virtually no time together even before their separation, and he was uncharacteristically evasive and defensive when asked about it.[71] Eileen Hunt Botting notes in her contribution to the present volume that enemies like George Chalmers and James Cheetham accused Paine of fathering an illegitimate child during an affair he was alleged to have engaged in with Marguerite de Bonneville. They also accused him of worse, but though the charges remained in currency, sullying Paine's name for many decades after his death, none of them withstands scrutiny.[72] And although contemporaries sometimes commented on the dearth of Paine's interest in women and his preference for male company, no one has adduced evidence that he had homosexual inclinations – or, at any rate, that he acted on them, if he did. Paine seems, rather, to have been someone who was uncomfortable with close personal connection. Certainly his brief experience of marriage did not endear him to the institution, which he dismissed as enervating in one of his few pronouncements on the subject.[73] He seems to have been free of the loneliness that often drives people into unsatisfactory relationships when satisfying ones are unavailable, preferring solitude and platonic friendships to the rewards, risks, and demands of human intimacy.

Paine's lack of deep human connection might have been reinforced by the fact that his sense of belonging was so often compromised. He must have felt like an interloper among the richer children in the local Thetford

Grammar School, and as a young man when he muscled his way into London's elite intellectual circles. He can scarcely have known America when *Common Sense* catapulted him to prominence little more than a year after his arrival there; for most people it would have been a surreal experience. He was feted as a national hero after the Revolutionary War, and later he would receive a hero's welcome in France after what would turn out to be his permanent exile from Britain in 1792. But neither of his adopted homes would be sanctuaries, at least not unambiguous ones. His French citizenship and status as a National Convention deputy could not save him from the Luxembourg Prison at the height of the Terror in late 1793.[74] They did, however, enable his sometime antagonist Gouverneur Morris (then George Washington's minister plenipotentiary to France) to declare that Paine had forfeited his American citizenship and let him languish in prison without diplomatic help for months – severely ill with typhus and under perpetual threat of execution. And when he finally returned to America in 1802, Paine found that the reaction to *The Age of Reason* was decidedly bimodal. It had its voluble admirers, but he was also viciously attacked by the religious establishment and relentlessly pilloried in the press as a debauched and traitorous malcontent. He was summarily ostracized by longtime friends, including Benjamin Rush, Patrick Henry, John Jay, and, perhaps most painfully of all, his old revolutionary ally Samuel Adams.[75] It is likely that Paine never felt fully at home anywhere, and notable that one of his biographers identified him as history's greatest exile.[76]

Part of the enduring fascination with Paine is that he is enigmatic and difficult to peg, both as a historical figure and as a human being. To some extent this has been aggravated by distortions promoted or tolerated by his enemies, not a few of whom wielded considerable influence and power. Some, like John Adams, were jealous of his skills and success as a writer. Others, like Robert Aitken, James Cheetham, and William Carver, harbored resentments borne of personal conflicts – often over money, recognition, or both. His political intemperance antagonized people like John Jay, Samuel Adams, Gouverneur Morris, and George Washington. His visceral antipathy for deference combined with his impulse to speak directly to the common man infuriated establishment figures. Nowhere was this more manifest than with Paine's deism, which stood as an unvarnished rebuke to people and institutions whose legitimacy depended on claiming knowledge of God's word and access to the Divine plan.[77] If Paine was right, they were nothing better than deluded fools or charlatans – and he never tired of saying so. Many people who talked about democracy had no interest in practicing it as thoroughly and as personally as Paine insisted on doing. For this, he paid a significant price.

If Paine's detractors had the upper hand when he died, and retained it for generations due to slanderous biographies commissioned or written by his enemies, it does seem that a more-measured and accurate picture of him and his ideas has triumphed over the past half century. Biographers, notably Keane and Nelson, have successfully scotched the worst calumnies.[78] Monuments, libraries, and societies have immortalized his contributions on both sides of the Atlantic. American presidents of every ideological stripe now reach for his name in times of crisis, underscoring his normalization as one of the nation's inspirational architects. To some extent this has been helped along, as Kaye notes, by the de-idealization of America's other founding fathers—as historians have discovered and written more about their flaws and limitations.[79] Whatever the reason, Paine has taken his rightful place in the American historical pantheon. He will never be recognized in the same way as Washington, Madison, Jefferson, or Jay, because he never held major political office in the United States. Indeed, the only political office of any consequence that he ever held was his improbable stint as the deputy for Calais to the French National Convention in 1792–1793, where he could not even speak the language in which business was being transacted. But as a political thinker and public intellectual, he was every bit their equal, and in some ways he bettered them.

Some will, perhaps, contest that judgment; but what is beyond debate is that Paine was one of modern democracy's earliest and most articulate champions. His democratic commitments shaped his personal dealings as much as his views of politics; indeed the two flowed into and reinforced one another. Paine despised pomposity and pretense as much as he did domination and arbitrary power, skewering both—often in the same paragraph—with the withering contempt that flowed so effortlessly from his pen. This bought him enemies and cost him recognition. But for all his prickliness and pride, Paine's writings and actions radiated a commitment to a democratic cause that he never doubted was larger than himself. He worked for it, fought for it, and, on more than one occasion, showed himself willing to die for it. That is the essence of his legacy, and it is the chief reason he commands enduring respect.

NOTES

1. Roy P. Basler, ed. *Abraham Lincoln: His Speeches and Writings* (Cleveland and New York: World Publishing, 1946), p. 6.

2. Michael Burlingame, *Abraham Lincoln: A Life,* 2 vols. (Baltimore, MD: Johns Hopkins University Press, 2008), vol. 2, p 83.

3. Theodore Roosevelt, *Gouverneur Morris* (Boston: Houghton Mifflin, 1898), p. 289.

4. Darwin continued: "Remember that an enemy might ask who is this man . . . that he should give to the world his opinions on the deepest subjects? . . . but my advice is to pause, pause, pause." "Darwin C. R. to Darwin G. H.," Letter 9105, October 21, 1873, Darwin Correspondence Project, http://www.darwinproject .ac.uk/letter/entry-9105 [accessed 01-09-2014].

5. John Keane, *Tom Paine: A Political Life* (New York: Grove Press, 1995), p. ix.

6. David Chen, "Rehabilitating Thomas Paine, Bit by Bony Bit," *The New York Times,* March 30, 2001, http://www.nytimes.com/2001/03/30/nyregion/ rehabilitating-thomas-paine-bit-by-bony-bit.html [accessed 6-11-2012]. "Thomas Paine's Remains Are Still a Bone of Contention," http://articles.latimes.com/2001/ apr/01/news/mn-45431 [accessed 01-16-2014]. See also Paul Collins, *The Trouble with Tom: The Strange Afterlife and Times of Thomas Paine* (New York: Bloomsbury, 2005).

7. Craig Nelson, *Thomas Paine: Enlightenment, Revolution, and the Birth of Modern Nations* (New York: Penguin, 2006), pp. 12–50.

8. *The Crisis* (also known as *The American Crisis)* eventually appeared as a series of sixteen pamphlets, the first thirteen published between 1776 and 1777, and the last three between 1777 and 1783.

9. Paine, *The Crisis,* "Number I," this volume, p. 58.

10. See, for example, Bruce Ackerman and Anne Alstott, *The Stakeholder Society* (New Haven, CT: Yale University Press, 2000), who turn to Paine's argument in *Agrarian Justice* as inspiration for their proposal that eighteen-year-old high school graduates should receive an $80,000 stake from the state, funded by a 2 percent annual wealth tax on households with assets in excess of $1.5 million. Paine's variant had called for a £15 stake to be given every twenty-one-year-old, paid for by a 10 percent estate tax on inheritances passed to close relatives (and somewhat higher rate on other bequests), which would also fund a pension scheme for the elderly and disabled.

11. Nelson, *Thomas Paine,* pp. 60–62.

12. Keane, *Tom Paine,* pp. 135–137.

13. Nelson, *Thomas Paine,* pp. 38–39, 298–304.

14. Keane, *Tom Paine,* pp. 472–482.

15. Nelson, *Thomas Paine,* pp. 20–21, 327.

16. Ibid., pp. 292–294.

17. Ibid., p. 320.

18. David Hume, *A Treatise of Human Nature*, bk. II, pt. III, § 3 (Oxford, UK: Clarendon, 1896 [1739]), p. 415.

19. See Eric Foner, *Tom Paine and Revolutionary America* (New York: Oxford University Press, 2005), pp. 71–106.

20. R. B. Bernstein, "Rediscovering Thomas Paine," *New York Law School Law Review* 39 (1994), p. 919.

21. Paine, *Common Sense*, this volume, p. 46.

22. Nelson, *Thomas Paine*, p. 227.

23. Ibid., pp. 265–266. The twentieth-century political theorist Leo Strauss believed that the esoteric knowledge that we know nothing was too dangerous to be put into common political currency, so it had to be hidden in philosophical nuance that was accessible only to the cognoscenti. For the masses, a more-benign exoteric message was in order, designed to ensure that they would not upset the political order that made life safe for the intellectual elite. See Leo Strauss, "Persecution and the Art of Writing," in *Strauss, Persecution and the Art of Writing and other Essays* (Chicago: University of Chicago Press, 1952), pp. 22–37; "On a Forgotten Kind of Writing," in Strauss, *What Is Political Philosophy? and Other Studies* (Chicago: University of Chicago Press, 1959), pp. 221–232; and Strauss, "Exoteric Teaching," in *The Rebirth of Classical Rationalism: Essays and Lectures by Leo Strauss*, ed. Thomas Pangle (Chicago: University of Chicago Press, 1989), pp. 63–71. See also Laurence Lampert, "Strauss's Recovery of Esotericism," in Steven B. Smith, *The Cambridge Companion to Leo Strauss* (Cambridge: Cambridge University Press, 2009), pp. 63–92.

24. Bernard Bailyn, *The Ideological Origins of the American Revolution* (Cambridge, MA: Harvard University Press, 1992). See Gordon Wood, *The Creation of the American Republic 1776–1787* (Chapel Hill, NC: University of North Carolina Press, 1998), and J. G. A. Pocock, *The Machiavellian Moment: Florentine Political Thought and the Atlantic Republican Tradition* (Princeton, NJ: Princeton University Press, 1974), pp. 462–532.

25. Nelson, *Thomas Paine*, pp. 149, 170–171.

26. Ibid., p. 290.

27. Paine, *Common Sense*, this volume, p. 8.

28. Madison's formulation was "If men were angels, no government would be necessary. If angels were to govern men, neither external nor internal controls on government would be necessary." Alexander Hamilton, James Madison, and John Jay, *The Federalist Papers*, ed. Ian Shapiro (New Haven, CT: Yale University Press, 2009), No. 51, p. 264.

29. The aphorism sometimes misattributed to Nietzsche, "If God does not exist, everything is permitted," occurs in Fyodor Dostoyevsky's *The Brothers Karamazov*. Nietzsche's formulation is "Nothing is true, everything is allowed."

Fredrich Nietzsche, *Genealogy of Morals* (Mineola, NY: Dover Thrift, 2003), p. 109.

30. See Joyce Appleby, "Introduction," in Thomas Paine, *Common Sense and Other Writings* (New York: Barnes and Noble Classics, 2005), pp. xv–xxxviii.

31. After Bentham's body had been dissected in a public anatomy lecture, as stipulated in his will, his remains were embalmed and donated to University College London – where they are on permanent display. However, the mummification of Bentham's head left it looking grotesque, so the display instead contains a wax replica into which some of Bentham's hair has been implanted. Because the real head was famously used in student pranks, it has now been locked away. See "Auto-Icon," The UCL Bentham Project, http://www.ucl.ac.uk/Bentham-Project/who/autoicon [accessed 08-09-2012]; C. F. R. Marmoy, "The 'Auto-Icon' of Jeremy Bentham at University College, London," UCL Bentham Project, http://web.archive.org/web/20070210065136/http://www.ucl.ac.uk/Bentham-Project/info/marmoy.htm [accessed 08-09-2012]. Ironically but not surprisingly, Bentham despised Paine. He dismissed the "rotten" *Rights of Man* on the grounds that "it is written on the wrong principle; it never so much as mentions the greatest happiness principle." The account is from a dinner with Bentham reported by George Wheatley in "Letters Written to My Sister during a Visit to Jeremy Bentham in the Beginning of the Year 1850," pp. 51–52. Unrecorded copy made available to me by Philip Schofield, director of the UCL Bentham Project, September 8, 2012.

32. Appleby, "Introduction," pp. xxi–xxii.

33. The tombstone reads "On this site was buried Thomas Paine, Author of Common Sense."

34. Paine, *Rights of Man (first part),* this volume, p. 211.

35. Ibid. p. 211.

36. Paine, *Rights of Man, Part the Second,* this volume, p. 283.

37. Tocqueville visited America with Gustave de Beaumont in mid-1831, initially to study the prison system. They traveled widely over the ensuing nine months, during which time Tocqueville gathered the materials for his magnum opus *Democracy in America,* which would appear in two volumes published in 1835 and 1840.

38. On the evolution of Madison's views about majority rule, see my introduction to *The Federalist Papers* (New Haven, CT: Yale University Press, 2009), pp. ix–xxii, and *The Real World of Democratic Theory* (Princeton, NJ: Princeton University Press, 2011), pp. 68–71.

39. Mill's *Considerations on Representative Government* was first published in 1861.

40. Nelson, *Thomas Paine*, p. 161.

41. Paine, "Letter to the Abbé Raynal, on the Affairs of North America in which the Mistakes in the Abbé's Account of the Revolution of America are Corrected and Cleared Up," reprinted in Daniel Wheeler, ed., *Life and Writings of Thomas Paine*, History of Economic Thought Books, McMaster University Archive for the History of Economic Thought, vol. 8, no. paine1908g (1908), pp. 245, 281, http://ideas.repec.org/h/hay/hetcha/paine1908-99.html [accessed 08-16-2012].

42. Philip Foner, "Thomas Paine: World Citizen and Democrat," introduction to Philip Foner, ed., *The Complete Writings of Thomas Paine*, 2 vols. (New York: Citadel Press, 1945), vol. 1, pp. ix–xlvi; Harvey Kaye, *Thomas Paine and the Promise of America* (New York: Hill and Wang, 2005).

43. J. G. A. Pocock, "The Varieties of Whiggism from Exclusion to Reform," reprinted in J. G. A. Pocock, *Virtue, Commerce, and History* (Cambridge: Cambridge University Press, 1985), p. 276. Pocock points out that despite the hatred of English governing institutions that infuses *Common Sense*, "It does not consistently echo any established radical vocabulary; Paine had no real place in the club of Honest Whigs to which Franklin had introduced him in London, and his use of anti-Normanism to insist that Britain did not have a constitution but rather a tyranny does not permit us to think of him (as contemporaries might have) as a New Model soldier risen from the grave. Moreover, when the Revolutionary War was over Paine returned to live under 'the Royal brute of Great Britain' as if nothing much had happened, nor was he pursued by the authorities until the very different circumstances of 1791. One of the few practicing revolutionaries in English history, he performed no independent revolutionary action in England."

44. Christopher Hitchens, *Thomas Paine's Rights of Man: A Biography* (New York: Atlantic Monthly Press, 2006).

45. Ronald Reagan, Acceptance Speech at the 1980 Republican National Convention, http://www.nationalcenter.org/ReaganConvention1980.html [accessed 08-03-2012]; "Glenn Beck Calls Himself Thomas Paine," YouTube, http://www.youtube.com/watch?v=j5qEkWF7HBo [accessed 08-03-2012].

46. Walt Whitman, "In Memory of Thomas Paine," in Walt Whitman, *Prose Works* (1892), http://www.bartleby.com/229/1122.html [accessed 12-18-2013].

47. Michael A. Lawrence, *Radicals in Their Own Time: Four Hundred Years of Struggle for Liberty and Equal Justice in America* (Cambridge: Cambridge University Press, 2011), p. 125.

48. Thomas Edison, "The Philosophy of Paine" (1925), The Campaign for Philosophical Freedom, http://www.cfpf.org.uk/articles/scientists/tp/edison-tp.html [accessed 02-02-2103].

49. Nelson, *Thomas Paine,* p. 335.

50. Lawrence, Radicals in Their Own Time, p. 334. David Frum and Richard Perle, *An End to Evil: How to Win the War on Terror* (New York: Random House, 2004), p. 1. FDR drew on Thomas Paine (*The Crisis*) in the most difficult of times; the Roosevelt Institute online archive, http://www.rooseveltinstitute.org/new -roosevelt/fdr-drew-thomas-paine-most-difficult-times [accessed 01–09-2014].

51. Barack Obama's First Inaugural Address, Washington, D.C., (January 21, 2009), transcript in *The New York Times,* http://www.nytimes.com/2009/01/20/us/politics/20text-obama.html?src=tp&pagewanted=all [accessed 08-15-2012]. This quote is also from *The Crisis.*

52. Paine, *Common Sense,* this volume, p. 7.

53. This was perhaps most poignant in Lincoln's annual message to Congress in 1862: "We say we are for the Union. The world will not forget that we say this. We know how to save the Union. The world knows we do know how to save it. We–even we here–hold the power, and bear the responsibility. In giving freedom to the slave, we assure freedom to the free–honorable alike in what we give, and what we preserve. We shall nobly save, or meanly lose, the last best hope of earth." Abraham Lincoln, "Annual Message to Congress–Concluding Remarks," December 1, 1862, http://showcase.netins.net/web/creative/lincoln/speeches/congress .htm [accessed 08–17-2012].

54. "American institutions, which for France under the monarchy were simply a subject of curiosity, ought now [1848] to be studied by Republican France. . . . While all the nations of Europe have been ravaged by war or torn by civil strife, the American people alone in the civilized world have remained pacific. Almost the whole of Europe has been convulsed by revolutions; America has not even suffered from riots. Private property is better guaranteed there than in any other land on earth. Anarchy is as unknown as despotism. . . . Where else can we find greater cause of hope or more valuable lessons?" Alexis de Tocqueville, Author's Preface to the 12th ed. in *Democracy in America,* ed. J. P. Mayer (New York: Anchor Books, 1969), pp. xiii–xiv. For further discussion, see my *Democratic Justice* (New Haven, CT: Yale University Press, 1999 [1848]), pp. 238–240.

55. Alexis de Tocqueville, *Oeuvres complètes VII: Correspondance étrangere d'Alexis de Tocqueville,* ed. François Mélonio, Lisa Queffélec, and Anthony Pleasance (Paris: Gallimard, 1986), p. 277.

56. Tocqueville, *Democracy in America,* pp. 340–363.

57. David Goldfield, *America Aflame: How the Civil War Created a Nation* (New York: Bloomsbury Press, 2011), p. 156.

58. See Aurelian Craiutu and Jeremy Jennings, "The Third Democracy: Tocqueville's Views of America after 1840," *American Political Science Review* 98, no. 3 (August, 2004), pp. 391–404.

59. Lincoln was criticized in the Northern press for demurring divine support for the Union cause, noting that both sides "read the same Bible and pray to the same God, and each invokes His aid against the other. It may seem strange that any men should dare to ask a just God's assistance in wringing their bread from the sweat of other men's faces, but let us judge not, that we be not judged. . . . The Almighty has His own purposes." Abraham Lincoln, Second Inaugural Address, Washington, D.C., March 4, 1865, http://www.bartleby.com/124/pres32 .html [accessed 08-18-2012].

60. "I have no purpose, directly or indirectly, to interfere with the institution of slavery in the States where it exists." Abraham Lincoln, First Inaugural Address, March 4, 1861, http://www.bartleby.com/124/pres31.html [accessed 08-18-2012]. See also Goldfield, *America Aflame*, pp. 158–179.

61. Preliminary Emancipation Proclamation, September 22, 1862, http://www .archives.gov/exhibits/american_originals_iv/sections/transcript_preliminary _emancipation.html [accessed 08-13-2012]; Allan Nevins, *Ordeal of the Union*, vol. 6, *War Becomes Revolution, 1862-1863* (New York: Scribner's, 1960), pp. 231–245.

62. Lincoln believed that so long as slavery was restricted to the existing slave states and kept out of the territories, it would eventually die out. See Goldfield, *America Aflame*, pp. 158–204.

63. In this connection it is worth noting that by the time Tocqueville published the first volume of *Democracy in America* in 1835, his was actually a contrarian voice in the French debate about America. Most commentators had by then shed their earlier enthusiasm for the new regime as a model for France, partly because of the persistence of American slavery when it was being abolished elsewhere. See Craiutu and Jennings, "The Third Democracy," pp. 393–394.

64. See James V. Lynch, "The Limits of Revolutionary Radicalism: Tom Paine and Slavery," *The Pennsylvania Magazine of History and Biography* 123, no. 3 (July 1999), pp. 181–182, 183–188. Lynch also notes (p. 183) that there is no evidence that Paine wrote the preamble to Pennsylvania's Emancipation Act, as is often supposed.

65. In 1833 the British Parliament abolished slavery throughout the empire except for Ceylon, St. Helena, and some territories possessed by the British East India Company. Slavery would not finally be abolished in Puerto Rico until 1873, and it hung on in Brazil until 1888.

66. Lynch, "The Limits of Revolutionary Radicalism," pp. 188, 194, 179.

67. On the emancipation with compensation plans that Lincoln floated in the first half of 1862, see Goldfield, *America Aflame*, p. 248. On the British £20,000,000 indemnity (a colossal sum when it was authorized as part of the Emancipation Act of 1833) to West Indian planters who would lose their slaves

over the next seven years, see Chaim D. Kaufman and Robert A. Pape, "Explaining Costly International Moral Action," *International Organization* 53, no. 4 (Autumn 1999), pp. 639, 657.

68. After Congress had passed the Thirteenth Amendment in January of 1865, when Lincoln still expected the war (which was costing $3 million a day) to continue for at least three months, he proposed offering the Southern states $400 million in government bonds, half payable by April 1 if they had by then surrendered to the Union army, and the other half upon their ratification of the amendment. No Cabinet member supported the proposal. Goldfield, *America Aflame*, p. 253.

69. Nelson, *Thomas Paine*, p. 138.

70. See Keane, *Tom Paine*, pp. 215, 230, 373, 382, 524, 531.

71. Keane, *Tom Paine*, pp. 51–52; 77–78, 229.

72. See Nelson, *Thomas Paine*, pp. 326–330. Bonneville and her husband, Nicolas, were friends with whom Paine had lived for several years after his release from prison in Paris. Paine supported her and several of her children in America in his later years and named her family in his will (she and one of her sons were among the few mourners at his funeral), but there is no evidence of a romantic involvement between them.

73. See Nelson, *Thomas Paine*, pp. 46–47. Nelson notes that Paine did write a letter with a softer judgment about marriage to a newlywed friend in 1879, noting wistfully that the possibility had passed him by when he had been consumed with politics and revolution.

74. Ironically he was imprisoned on the (groundless) accusation that he was a British spy.

75. Nelson, *Thomas Paine*, pp. 269–270.

76. See David Powell, *Tom Paine: The Greatest Exile* (London: Hutchinson, 1985).

77. It especially stung Gouverneur Morris, who, rather than exert any effort to get Paine released from the Luxembourg Prison in 1794, wrote Jefferson: ". . . Lest I should forget it, I must mention, that Thomas Paine is in prison, where he amuses himself with publishing a pamphlet against Jesus Christ." Gouverneur Morris letter to Thomas Jefferson, January 21, 1794, http://www.familytales.org/dbDisplay.php?id=ltr_gom4690 [accessed 02-02-2013].

78. The first sympathetic biography did not appear until more than eight decades after his death. Moncure D. Conway, *The Life of Thomas Paine: With a History of His Literary, Political, and Religious Career in America, France, and England,* 2 vols. (New York: G. P. Putnam's Sons, 1892, 1893).

79. Kaye, *Thomas Paine and the Promise of America*, pp. 11–12.

Note on the Texts

Two features of this collection distinguish it from other volumes of Paine's writings. Whereas most are silent about where and how the texts were acquired and reproduced, the editors of this collection aim for transparency. Here the documents were transcribed directly from first editions (except where noted), the citations for which are given with each document. In at least one case, drawing from the original has corrected a significant collective error. Paine's provocative little essay, "Of the Religion of Deism Compared with the Christian Religion . . . ," has been reproduced many times in print and on the Web. But every reproduction omits two paragraphs in the middle of the essay, thus perpetuating a single mistake (or arbitrary editorial decision) committed decades earlier. Here, for perhaps the first time, this essay is reproduced in full. Also, according to best documentary editing practice, all documents were tandem oral proofread (one person reading aloud from the original and another correcting the transcription against it) for accuracy. These two features make this collection one of the most reliable sources of Paine's works currently available to scholars.

In order to preserve the original textual atmosphere, the editors have interfered only minimally with the transcriptions. Idiosyncratic eighteenth-century spelling, punctuation, and capitalization have been preserved. Obvious printers' errors have been silently corrected when the correction did not interfere with the meaning of the passage in question. If a correction for clarity was necessary, the change is indicated in brackets. The only significant alteration made throughout was to render the long s (ſ, as in Pennſylvania) as a modern s.

Texts

THOUGHTS ON DEFENSIVE WAR.[1]

COULD the peaceable principle of the Quakers be universally established, arms and the art of war would be wholly extirpated. But we live not in a world of angels. The reign of Satan is not ended; neither are we to expect to be defended by miracles. The pillar of the cloud existed only in the wilderness. In the nonage of the Israelites. It protected them in their retreat from Pharoah, while they were destitute of the natural means of defence, for they brought no arms from Egypt, but it neither fought their battles nor shielded them from dangers afterwards.

I am thus far a Quaker, that I would gladly agree with all the world to lay aside the use of arms, and settle matters by negociation; but unless the whole will, the matter ends, and I take up my musket and thank heaven he has put it in my power.

Whoever considers the unprincipled enemy we have to cope with, will not hesitate to declare that nothing but arms or miracles can reduce them to reason and moderation. They have lost sight of the limits of humanity. The portrait of a parent red with the blood of her children is a picture fit only for the gallaries of the infernals. From the House of Commons the troops of Britain have been exhorted to fight, not for the defence of their natural rights, not to repel the invasion or the insult of enemies; but on the vilest of all pretences, gold. "Ye fight for solid revenue" was vociferated in the House. Thus America *must suffer* because she has something to lose. Her crime is property. That which allures the highwayman has allured the ministry under a gentler name. But the position laid down, by Lord Sandwich, is a clear demonstration of the justice of defensive arms. The Americans, quoth this Quixotte of modern days, *will not fight;* therefore we will. His Lordship's plan when analized amounts to this. These people are either too superstitiously religious, or too cowardly for arms; they either *cannot*

"Thoughts on Defensive War," in *The Pennsylvania Magazine: or, American Monthly Museum,* July 1775, p. 313.

1. [Editors' note:] We include this document in the volume advisedly. It has long been attributed to Paine by editors and biographers, and, unlike many documents once attributed to Paine but now proven not to be his, its attribution has never been questioned. Yet neither has it been proven through digital linguistic analysis to be his. Therefore, because the circumstantial evidence of topic and tone admits the strong possibility of it being Paine's work, we include it with this qualifying note.

or *dare not* defend; their property is open to any one who has the courage
to attack them. Send but your troops and the prize is ours. Kill a few and
take the whole. Thus the peaceable part of mankind will be continually
over run by the vile and abandoned, while they neglect the means of self
defence. The supposed quietude of a good man allures the ruffian: while
on the other hand, arms like laws discourage and keep the invader and
the plunderer in awe, and preserve order in the world as well as property.
The balance of power is the scale of peace. The same balance would be
preserved were all the world destitute of arms, for all would be alike; but
since some *will not,* others *dare not* lay them aside. And while a single
nation refuses to lay them down, it is proper that all should keep them up.
Horrid mischief would ensue were one half the world deprived of the use
of them; for while avarice and ambition have a place in the heart of man,
the weak will become a prey to the strong. The history of every age and
nation establishes these truths, and facts need but little arguments when
they prove themselves.

But there is a point to view this matter in of superior consequence to
the defence of property; and that point is *Liberty* in all its meanings. In the
barbarous ages of the world, men in general had no liberty. The strong governed the weak at will; 'till the coming of Christ there was no such thing
as political freedom in any known part of the earth. The Jewish Kings were
in point of government as absolute as the Pharoahs. Men were frequently
put to death without trial at the will of the Sovereign. The Romans held the
world in slavery, and were themselves the slaves of their emperors. The
madman of Macedon governed by caprice and passion, and strided as arro-
gantly over the world as if he had made and peopled it; and it is needless to
imagine that other nations at that time were more refined. Wherefore political as well as spiritual freedom is the gift of God through Christ. The second
in the catalogue of blessings; and so intimately related, so sympathetically
united with the first, that the one cannot be wounded without communicat-
ing an injury to the other. Political liberty is the visible pass, which guards
the religious. It is the outwork by which the church militant is defended,
and the attacks of the enemy are frequently made through this fortress. The
same power which has established a restraining Port Bill in the Colonies,
has established a restraining Protestant Church Bill in Canada.

I had the pleasure and advantage of hearing this matter wisely investigated, by a gentleman, in a sermon to one of the battalions of this city; and
am fully convinced, that spiritual freedom is the root of political liberty.

First, Because till spiritual freedom was made manifest, political liberty
did not exist.

Secondly, Because in proportion that *spiritual freedom* has been manifested, *political liberty* has encreased.

Thirdly, Whenever the visible church has been oppressed, political freedom has suffered with it. Read the history of Mary and the Stuarts. The popish world at this day by not knowing the full manifestation of spiritual freedom, enjoy but a shadow of political liberty. – Though I am unwilling to accuse the present government of popish principles, they cannot, I think, be clearly acquitted of popish practices; the facility with which they perceive the dark and ignorant are governed, in popish nations, will always be a temptation to the lovers of arbitrary power to adopt the same methods.

As the union between spiritual freedom and political liberty seems nearly inseperable, it is our duty to defend both. And defence in the first instance is best. The lives of hundreds of both countries had been preserved had America been in arms a year ago. Our enemies have mistaken our peace for cowardice, and supposing us unarmed have begun the attack.

– A LOVER OF PEACE.

COMMON SENSE;

ADDRESSED TO THE

INHABITANTS OF AMERICA,

On the following interesting

SUBJECTS.[1]

I. Of the Origin and Design of Government in general, with concise Remarks on the English Constitution.
II. Of Monarchy and Hereditary Succession.
III. Thoughts on the present State of American Affairs.
IV. Of the present Ability of America, with some miscellaneous Reflections.

A NEW EDITION, with several Additions in the Body of the Work. To which is added an APPENDIX; together with an Address to the People called QUAKERS.

N. B. The New Addition here given increases the Work upwards of one Third.

> Man knows no Master save creating HEAVEN,
> Or those whom Choice and common Good ordain.

THOMSON.

Common Sense, 3rd ed. (Philadelphia: William and Thomas Bradford, 1776).

1. [Editors' note:] *Common Sense* was first published on January 9, 1776, by Robert Bell. After a falling out with Bell, for the next edition, which appeared in February, Paine switched to the publishers Thomas and William Bradford and added the appendix and the "Address to the Quakers." The editors have chosen to reproduce the Bradford edition here.

Introduction.

PERHAPS the sentiments contained in the following pages, are not *yet* sufficiently fashionable to procure them general favor; a long habit of not thinking a thing *wrong*, gives it a superficial appearance of being *right*, and raises at first a formidable outcry in defence of custom. But the tumult soon subsides. Time makes more converts than reason.

As a long and violent abuse of power, is generally the Means of calling the right of it in question (and in Matters too which might never have been thought of, had not the Sufferers been aggravated into the inquiry) and as the King of England hath undertaken in his *own Right,* to support the Parliament in what he calls *Theirs,* and as the good people of this country are grievously oppressed by the combination, they have an undoubted privilege to enquire into the pretensions of both, and equally to reject the usurpation of either.

In the following sheets, the author hath studiously avoided every thing which is personal among ourselves. Compliments as well as censure to individuals make no part thereof. The wise, and the worthy, need not the triumph of a pamphlet; and those whose sentiments are injudicious, or unfriendly, will cease of themselves unless too much pains are bestowed upon their conversion.

The cause of America is in a great measure the cause of all mankind. Many circumstances hath, and will arise, which are not local, but universal, and through which the principles of all Lovers of Mankind are affected, and in the Event of which, their Affections are interested. The laying a Country desolate with Fire and Sword, declaring War against the natural rights of all Mankind, and extirpating the Defenders thereof from the Face of the Earth, is the Concern of every Man to whom Nature hath given the Power of feeling; of which Class, regardless of Party Censure, is the

– AUTHOR.

P. S. The Publication of this new Edition hath been delayed, with a View of taking notice (had it been necessary) of any Attempt to refute the Doctrine of Independance: As no Answer hath yet appeared, it is now presumed that none will, the Time needful for getting such a Performance ready for the Public being considerably past.

Who the Author of this Production is, is wholly unnecessary to the Public, as the Object for Attention is the *Doctrine itself,* not the *Man.* Yet it may not be unnecessary to say, That he is unconnected with any Party, and under no sort of Influence public or private, but the influence of reason and principle.

Philadelphia, February 14, 1776.

Common Sense.

OF THE ORIGIN AND DESIGN OF GOVERNMENT IN GENERAL. WITH CONCISE REMARKS ON THE ENGLISH CONSTITUTION.

SOME writers have so confounded society with government, as to leave little or no distinction between them; whereas they are not only different, but have different origins. Society is produced by our wants, and government by our wickedness; the former promotes our happiness *positively* by uniting our affections, the latter *negatively* by restraining our vices. The one encourages intercourse, the other creates distinctions. The first is a patron, the last a punisher.

Society in every state is a blessing, but government even in its best state is but a necessary evil; in its worst state an intolerable one: for when we suffer, or are exposed to the same miseries *by a government,* which we might expect in a country *without government,* our calamity is heightened by reflecting that we furnish the means by which we suffer. Government, like dress, is the badge of lost innocence; the palaces of kings are built on the ruins of the bowers of paradise. For were the impulses of conscience clear, uniform, and irresistibly obeyed, man would need no other lawgiver; but that not being the case, he finds it necessary to surrender up a part of his property to furnish means for the protection of the rest; and this he is induced to do by the same prudence which in every other case advises him out of two evils to choose the least. *Wherefore,* security being the true design and end of government, it unanswerably follows that whatever *form* thereof appears most likely to ensure it to us, with the least expence and greatest benefit, is preferable to all others.

In order to gain a clear and just idea of the design and end of government, let us suppose a small number of persons settled in some sequestered part of the earth, unconnected with the rest, they will then represent the first peopling of any country, or of the world. In this state of natural liberty, society will be their first thought. A thousand motives will excite them thereto, the strength of one man is so unequal to his wants, and his mind so unfitted for perpetual solitude, that he is soon obliged to seek assistance and relief of another, who in his turn requires the same. Four or five united would be able to raise a tolerable dwelling in the midst of a wilderness, but *one* man might labour out the common period of life without accomplishing any thing; when he had felled his timber he could not remove it, nor erect it after it was removed; hunger in the mean time would urge him from his work, and every different want call him a different way. Disease, nay even misfortune would be death, for though neither might be mortal, yet either would disable him from living, and reduce him to a state in which he might rather be said to perish than to die.

Thus necessity, like a gravitating power, would soon form our newly arrived emigrants into society, the reciprocal blessings of which, would supersede, and render the obligations of law and government unnecessary while they remained perfectly just to each other; but as nothing but heaven is impregnable to vice, it will unavoidably happen, that in proportion as they surmount the first difficulties of emigration, which bound them together in a common cause, they will begin to relax in their duty and attachment to each other; and this remissness, will point out the necessity, of establishing some form of government to supply the defect of moral virtue.

Some convenient tree will afford them a State-House, under the branches of which, the whole colony may assemble to deliberate on public matters. It is more than probable that their first laws will have the title only of REGULATIONS, and be enforced by no other penalty than public disesteem. In this first parliament every man, by natural right, will have a seat.

But as the colony increases, the public concerns will increase likewise, and the distance at which the members may be separated, will render it too inconvenient for all of them to meet on every occasion as at first, when their number was small, their habitations near, and the public concerns few and trifling. This will point out the convenience of their consenting to leave the legislative part to be managed by a select number chosen from the whole body, who are supposed to have the same concerns at stake which those have who appointed them, and who will act in the same manner as the whole body would act were they present. If the colony continue increasing, it will become necessary to augment the number of the representatives, and that the interest of every part of the colony may be attended to, it will be found best to divide the whole into convenient parts, each part sending its proper number; and that the *elected* might never form to themselves an interest separate from the *electors,* prudence will point out the propriety of having elections often; because as the *elected* might by that means return and mix again with the general body of the *electors* in a few months, their fidelity to the public will be secured by the prudent reflexion of not making a rod for themselves. And as this frequent interchange will establish a common interest with every part of the community, they will mutually and naturally support each other, and on this (not on the unmeaning name of king) depends the *strength of government, and the happiness of the governed.*

Here then is the origin and rise of government; namely, a mode rendered necessary by the inability of moral virtue to govern the world; here too is the design and end of government, viz. freedom and security. And however our eyes may be dazzled with show, or our ears deceived by sound; however prejudice may warp our wills, or interest darken our understanding, the simple voice of nature and of reason will say, it is right.

I draw my idea of the form of government from a principle in nature, which no art can overturn, viz. that the more simple any thing is, the less liable it is to be disordered, and the easier repaired when disordered; and with this maxim in view, I offer a few remarks on the so much boasted constitution of England. That it was noble for the dark and slavish times in which it was erected, is granted. When the world was over run with tyranny the least remove therefrom was a glorious rescue. But that it is imperfect, subject to convulsions, and incapable of producing what it seems to promise, is easily demonstrated.

Absolute governments (tho' the disgrace of human nature) have this advantage with them, that they are simple; if the people suffer, they know the head from which their suffering springs, know likewise the remedy, and are not bewildered by a variety of causes and cures. But the constitution of England is so exceedingly complex, that the nation may suffer for years together without being able to discover in which part the fault lies, some will say in one and some in another, and every political physician will advise a different medicine.

I know it is difficult to get over local or long standing prejudices, yet if we will suffer ourselves to examine the component parts of the English constitution, we shall find them to be the base remains of two ancient tyrannies, compounded with some new republican materials.

First. – The remains of monarchical tyranny in the person of the king.

Secondly. – The remains of aristocratical tyranny in the persons of the peers.

Thirdly. – The new republican materials, in the persons of the commons, on whose virtue depends the freedom of England.

The two first, by being hereditary, are independent of the people; wherefore in a *constitutional sense* they contribute nothing towards the freedom of the state.

To say that the constitution of England is a *union* of three powers reciprocally *checking* each other, is farcical, either the words have no meaning, or they are flat contradictions.

To say that the commons is a check upon the king, presupposes two things.

First.—That the king is not to be trusted without being looked after, or in other words, that a thirst for absolute power is the natural disease of monarchy.

Secondly.—That the commons, by being appointed for that purpose, are either wiser or more worthy of confidence than the crown.

But as the same constitution which gives the commons a power to check the king by withholding the supplies, gives afterwards the king a power to check the commons, by empowering him to reject their other bills; it again supposes that the king is wiser than those whom it has already supposed to be wiser than him. A mere absurdity!

There is something exceedingly ridiculous in the composition of monarchy; it first excludes a man from the means of information, yet empowers him to act in cases where the highest judgment is required. The state of a king shuts him from the world, yet the business of a king requires him to know it thoroughly; wherefore, the different parts, by unnaturally opposing and destroying each other, prove the whole character to be absurd and useless.

Some writers have explained the English constitution thus, the king, say they, is one, the people another; the peers are an house in behalf of the king; the commons in behalf of the people; but this hath all the distinctions of an house divided against itself; and though the expressions be pleasantly arranged, yet when examined they appear idle and ambiguous; and it will always happen, that the nicest construction that words are capable of, when applied to the description of some thing which either cannot exist, or is too incomprehensible to be within the compass of description, will be words of sound only, and though they may amuse the ear, they cannot inform the mind, for this explanation includes a previous question, viz. *How came the king by a power which the people are afraid to trust, and always obliged to check?* Such a power could not be the gift of a wise people, neither can any power, *which needs checking,* be from God; yet the provision, which the constitution makes, supposes such a power to exist.

But the provision is unequal to the task; the means either cannot or will not accomplish the end, and the whole affair is a felo de se; for as the greater weight will always carry up the less, and as all the wheels of a machine are put in motion by one, it only remains to know which power in the constitution has the most weight, for that will govern; and though the others, or a part of them, may clog, or, as the phrase is, check the rapidity of its motion, yet so long as they cannot stop it, their endeavors will be ineffectual; the first moving power will at last have its way, and what it wants in speed is supplied by time.

That the crown is this overbearing part in the English constitution needs not be mentioned, and that it derives its whole consequence merely from being the giver of places and pensions is self-evident, wherefore, though we have been wise enough to shut and lock a door against absolute monarchy, we at the same time have been foolish enough to put the crown in possession of the key.

The prejudice of Englishmen, in favour of their own government by king, lords and commons, arises as much or more from national pride than reason. Individuals are undoubtedly safer in England than in some other countries, but the *will* of the king is as much the *law* of the land in Britain as in France, with this difference, that instead of proceeding directly from his mouth, it is handed to the people under the more formidable shape of an act of parliament. For the fate of Charles the First, hath only made kings more subtle – not more just.

Wherefore, laying aside all national pride and prejudice in favour of modes and forms, the plain truth is, that *it is wholly owing to the constitution of the people, and not to the constitution of the government* that the crown is not as oppressive in England as in Turkey.

An inquiry into the *constitutional errors* in the English form of government is at this time highly necessary, for as we are never in a proper condition of doing justice to others, while we continue under the influence of some leading partiality, so neither are we capable of doing it to ourselves while we remain fettered by any obstinate prejudice. And as a man, who is attached to a prostitute, is unfitted to choose or judge of a wife, so any prepossession in favour of a rotten constitution of government will disable us from discerning a good one.

OF MONARCHY AND HEREDITARY SUCCESSION.

MANKIND being originally equals in the order of creation, the equality could only be destroyed by some subsequent circumstance; the distinctions of rich, and poor, may, in a great measure be accounted for, and that without having recourse to the harsh ill sounding names of oppression and avarice. Oppression is often the *consequence,* but seldom or never the *means* of riches; and though avarice will preserve a man from being necessitously poor, it generally makes him too timorous to be wealthy.

But there is another and greater distinction for which no truly natural or religious reason can be assigned, and that is, the distinction of men into KINGS and SUBJECTS. Male and female are the distinctions of nature, good and bad the distinctions of heaven; but how a race of men came into the world so exalted above the rest, and distinguished like some new species, is worth enquiring into, and whether they are the means of happiness or of misery to mankind.

In the early ages of the world, according to the scripture chronology, there were no kings; the consequence of which was there were no wars; it is the pride of kings which throws mankind into confusion. Holland without a king hath enjoyed more peace for this last century than any of the monarchical governments in Europe. Antiquity favors the same remark; for the quiet and rural lives of the first patriarchs hath a happy something in them, which vanishes away when we come to the history of Jewish royalty.

Government by kings was first introduced into the world by the Heathens, from whom the children of Israel copied the custom. It was the most prosperous invention the Devil ever set on foot for the promotion of idolatry. The Heathens paid divine honors to their deceased kings, and the christian world hath improved on the plan by doing the same to their living ones. How impious is the title of sacred majesty applied to a worm, who in the midst of his splendor is crumbling into dust!

As the exalting one man so greatly above the rest cannot be justified on the equal rights of nature, so neither can it be defended on the authority of scripture; for the will of the Almighty, as declared by Gideon and the prophet Samuel, expressly disapproves of government by kings. All anti-monarchical parts of scripture have been very smoothly glossed over in monarchical governments, but they undoubtedly merit the attention of countries which have their governments yet to form. *"Render unto Cæsar the things which are Cæsar's"* is the scripture doctrine of courts, yet it is no support of monarchical government, for the Jews at that time were without a king, and in a state of vassalage to the Romans.

Near three thousand years passed away from the Mosaic account of the creation, till the Jews under a national delusion requested a king. Till then, their form of government (except in extraordinary cases, where the Almighty interposed) was a kind of republic administred by a judge and the elders of the tribes. Kings they had none, and it was held sinful to acknowledge any Being under that title but the Lord of Hosts. And when a man seriously reflects on the idolatrous homage which is paid to the persons of Kings, he need not wonder, that the Almighty ever jealous of his honor, should disapprove of a form of government which so impiously invades the prerogative of heaven.

Monarchy is ranked in scripture as one of the sins of the Jews, for which a curse in reserve is denounced against them. The history of that transaction is worth attending to.

The children of Israel being oppressed by the Midianites, Gideon marched against them with a small army, and victory, thro' the Divine interposition, decided in his favour. The Jews elate with success, and attributing it to the generalship of Gideon, proposed making him a king, saying, *Rule thou over us, thou and thy son and thy son's son.* Here was temptation in its fullest extent; not a kingdom only, but an hereditary one, but Gideon in the piety of his soul replied, *I will not rule over you, neither shall my son rule over you,* THE LORD SHALL RULE OVER YOU. Words need not be more explicit; Gideon doth not *decline* the honor, but denieth their right to give it; neither doth he compliment them with invented declarations of his thanks, but in the positive stile of a prophet charges them with disaffection to their proper Sovereign, the King of heaven.

About one hundred and thirty years after this, they fell again into the same error. The hankering which the Jews had for the idolatrous customs of the Heathens, is something exceedingly unaccountable; but so it was, that laying hold of the misconduct of Samuel's two sons, who were entrusted with some secular concerns, they came in an abrupt and clamorous manner to Samuel, saying, *Behold thou art old, and thy sons walk not in thy ways, now make us a king to judge us like all the other nations.* And here we cannot but observe that their motives were bad, viz. that they might be *like* unto other nations, i. e. the Heathens, whereas their true glory laid in being as much *unlike* them as possible. *But the thing displeased Samuel when they said, Give us a king to judge us; and Samuel prayed unto the Lord, and the Lord said unto Samuel, Hearken unto the voice of the people in all that they say unto thee, for they have not rejected thee, but they have rejected me,* THAT I SHOULD NOT REIGN OVER THEM. *According to all the works which they have done since the day that I brought them up out of Egypt, even unto this day; wherewith they have forsaken me and served other Gods; so do they also unto thee. Now therefore hearken unto their voice, howbeit, protest solemnly unto them and shew them the manner of the king that shall reign over them,* i. e. not of any particular king, but the general manner of the kings of the earth, whom Israel was so eagerly copying after. And notwithstanding the great distance of time and difference of manners, the character is still in fashion, *And Samuel told all the words of the Lord unto the people, that asked of him a king. And he said, ["]This shall be the manner of the king that shall reign over you; he will take your sons and appoint them for himself, for his chariots, and to be his horsemen, and some shall run before his chariots* (this description agrees with the present mode of impressing men) *and he will appoint him captains over thousands and captains over fifties, and will set them to ear his ground and to reap his harvest, and to make his instruments of war, and instruments of his chariots; and he will take your daughters to be confectionaries, and to be cooks and to be bakers* (this describes the expence and luxury as well as the oppression of kings) *and he will take your fields and your olive yards, even the best of them, and give them to his servants; and he will take the tenth of your seed, and of your vineyards, and give them to his officers and to his servants* (by which we see that bribery, corruption and favoritism are the standing vices of kings) *and he will take the tenth of your men servants, and your maid servants, and your goodliest young men and your asses, and put them to his work; and he will take the tenth of your sheep, and ye shall be his servants, and ye shall cry out in that day because of your king which ye shall have chosen,* AND THE LORD WILL NOT HEAR YOU IN THAT DAY." This accounts for the continuation of monarchy; neither do the characters of the few good kings which have lived since, either sanctify the title, or blot out the sinfulness of the origin; the high encomium given of David takes no notice of him *officially as a king,* but only as a *man* after God's own heart. *Nevertheless the People refused to obey the voice of Samuel, and they said, Nay, but we will have a king over us, that we may be like all the nations, and that our king may judge us, and go out before us, and fight our battles.* Samuel continued to reason with them, but to no purpose; he set before them their ingratitude, but all would not avail; and seeing them fully bent on their folly, he cried out, *I will call unto the Lord, and he shall send thunder and rain* (which then was a punishment, being in the time of wheat harvest) *that ye may perceive and see that your wickedness is great which ye have done in the sight of the Lord,* IN ASKING YOU A KING. *So Samuel called unto the Lord, and the Lord sent thunder and rain that day, and all the people greatly feared the Lord and Samuel. And all the people said unto Samuel, Pray for thy servants unto the Lord thy God that we die not, for* WE HAVE ADDED UNTO OUR SINS THIS EVIL, TO ASK A KING. These portions of scripture are direct and positive. They admit of no equivocal construction. That the Almighty hath here entered his protest against monarchical government is true, or the scripture is false. And a man hath good reason to believe that there is as much of king-craft, as priest-craft, in withholding the scripture from the public in Popish countries. For monarchy in every instance is the Popery of government.

To the evil of monarchy we have added that of hereditary succession; and as the first is a degradation and lessening of ourselves, so the second, claimed as a matter of right, is an insult and an imposition on posterity. For all men being originally equals, no *one* by *birth* could have a right to set up his own family in perpetual preference to all others for ever, and though himself might deserve *some* decent degree of honors of his cotemporaries, yet his descendants might be far too unworthy to inherit them. One of the strongest *natural* proofs of the folly of hereditary right in kings, is, that nature disapproves it, otherwise she would not so frequently turn it into ridicule by giving mankind an *ass for a lion.*

Secondly, as no man at first could possess any other public honors than were bestowed upon him, so the givers of those honors could have no power to give away the right of posterity, and though they might say "We choose you for *our* head," they could not, without manifest injustice to their children, say "that your children and your childrens children shall reign over *ours* for ever.["] Because such an unwise, unjust, unnatural compact might (perhaps) in the next succession put them under the government of a rogue or a fool. Most wise men, in their private sentiments, have ever treated hereditary right with contempt; yet it is one of those evils, which when once established is not easily removed; many submit from fear, others from superstition, and the more powerful part shares with the king the plunder of the rest.

This is supposing the present race of kings in the world to have had an honorable origin; whereas it is more than probable, that could we take off the dark covering of antiquity, and trace them to their first rise, that we should find the first of them nothing better than the principal ruffian of some restless gang, whose savage manners or pre-eminence in subtility obtained him the title of chief among plunderers; and who by increasing in power, and extending his depredations, over-awed the quiet and defence-less to purchase their safety by frequent contributions. Yet his electors could have no idea of giving hereditary right to his descendants, because such a perpetual exclusion of themselves was incompatible with the free and unrestrained principles they professed to live by. Wherefore, hereditary succession in the early ages of monarchy could not take place as a matter of claim, but as something casual or complimental; but as few or no records were extant in those days, and traditionary history stuffed with fables, it was very easy, after the lapse of a few generations, to trump up some superstitious tale, conveniently timed, Mahomet like, to cram hereditary right down the throats of the vulgar. Perhaps the disorders which threatened, or seemed to threaten, on the decease of a leader and the choice of a new one (for elections among ruffians could not be very orderly) induced many at first to favor hereditary pretensions; by which means it happened, as it hath happened since, that what at first was submitted to as a convenience, was afterwards claimed as a right.

England, since the conquest, hath known some few good monarchs, but groaned beneath a much larger number of bad ones; yet no man in his senses can say that their claim under William the Conqueror is a very honorable one. A French bastard landing with an armed banditti, and establishing himself king of England against the consent of the natives, is in plain terms a very paltry rascally original.—It certainly hath no divinity in it. However, it is needless to spend much time in exposing the folly of hereditary right, if there are any so weak as to believe it, let them promiscuously worship the ass and lion, and welcome. I shall neither copy their humility, nor disturb their devotion.

Yet I should be glad to ask how they suppose kings came at first? The question admits but of three answers, viz. either by lot, by election, or by usurpation. If the first king was taken by lot, it establishes a precedent for the next, which excludes hereditary succession. Saul was by lot, yet the succession was not hereditary, neither does it appear from that transaction there was any intention it ever should. If the first king of any country was by election, that likewise establishes a precedent for the next; for to say, that the *right* of all future generations is taken away, by the act of the first electors, in their choice not only of a king, but of a family of kings for ever, hath no parallel in or out of scripture but the doctrine of original sin, which supposes the free will of all men lost in Adam; and from such comparison, and it will admit of no other, hereditary succession can derive no glory. For as in Adam all sinned, and as in the first electors all men obeyed; as in the one all mankind were subjected to Satan, and in the other to Sovereignty; as our innocence was lost in the first, and our authority in the last; and as both disable us from reassuming some former state and privilege, it unanswerably follows that original sin and hereditary succession are parallels. Dishonorable rank! Inglorious connexion! Yet the most subtile sophist cannot produce a juster simile.

As to usurpation, no man will be so hardy as to defend it; and that William the Conqueror was an usurper is a fact not to be contradicted. The plain truth is, that the antiquity of English monarchy will not bear looking into.

But it is not so much the absurdity as the evil of hereditary succession which concerns mankind. Did it ensure a race of good and wise men it would have the seal of divine authority, but as it opens a door to the *foolish,* the *wicked,* and the *improper,* it hath in it the nature of oppression. Men who look upon themselves born to reign, and others to obey, soon grow insolent; selected from the rest of mankind their minds are early poisoned by importance; and the world they act in differs so materially from the world at large, that they have but little opportunity of knowing its true interests, and when they succeed to the government are frequently the most ignorant and unfit of any throughout the dominions.

Another evil which attends hereditary succession is, that the throne is subject to be possessed by a minor at any age; all which time the regency, acting under the cover of a king, have every opportunity and inducement to betray their trust. The same national misfortune happens, when a king worn out with age and infirmity, enters the last stage of human weakness. In both these cases the public becomes a prey to every miscreant, who can tamper successfully with the follies either of age or infancy.

The most plausible plea, which hath ever been offered in favour of hereditary succession, is, that it preserves a nation from civil wars; and were this true, it would be weighty; whereas, it is the most barefaced falsity ever imposed upon mankind. The whole history of England disowns the fact. Thirty kings and two minors have reigned in that distracted kingdom since the conquest, in which time there have been (including the Revolution) no less than eight civil wars and nineteen rebellions. Wherefore instead of making for peace, it makes against it, and destroys the very foundation it seems to stand on.

The contest for monarchy and succession, between the houses of York and Lancaster, laid England in a scene of blood for many years. Twelve pitched battles, besides skirmishes and sieges, were fought between Henry and Edward. Twice was Henry prisoner to Edward, who in his turn was prisoner to Henry. And so uncertain is the fate of war and the temper of a nation, when nothing but personal matters are the ground of a quarrel, that Henry was taken in triumph from a prison to a palace, and Edward obliged to fly from a palace to a foreign land; yet, as sudden transitions of temper are seldom lasting, Henry in his turn was driven from the throne, and Edward recalled to succeed him. The parliament always following the strongest side.

This contest began in the reign of Henry the Sixth, and was not entirely extinguished till Henry the Seventh, in whom the families were united. Including a period of 67 years, viz. from 1422 to 1489.

In short, monarchy and succession have laid (not this or that kingdom only) but the world in blood and ashes. 'Tis a form of government which the word of God bears testimony against, and blood will attend it.

If we inquire into the business of a king, we shall find that in some countries they have none; and after sauntering away their lives without pleasure to themselves or advantage to the nation, withdraw from the scene, and leave their successors to tread the same idle round. In absolute monarchies the whole weight of business, civil and military, lies on the king; the children of Israel in their request for a king, urged this plea "that he may judge us, and go out before us and fight our battles." But in countries where he is neither a judge nor a general, as in England, a man would be puzzled to know what *is* his business.

The nearer any government approaches to a republic the less business there is for a king. It is somewhat difficult to find a proper name for the government of England. Sir William Meredith calls it a republic; but in its present state it is unworthy of the name, because the corrupt influence of the crown, by having all the places in its disposal, hath so effectually swallowed up the power, and eaten out the virtue of the house of commons (the republican part in the constitution) that the government of England is nearly as monarchical as that of France or Spain. Men fall out with names without understanding them. For it is the republican and not the monarchical part of the constitution of England which Englishmen glory in, viz. the liberty of choosing an house of commons from out of their own body – and it is easy to see that when republican virtue fails, slavery ensues. Why is the constitution of England sickly, but because monarchy hath poisoned the republic, the crown hath engrossed the commons?

In England a king hath little more to do than to make war and give away places; which in plain terms, is to impoverish the nation and set it together by the ears. A pretty business indeed for a man to be allowed eight hundred thousand sterling a year for, and worshipped into the bargain! Of more worth is one honest man to society and in the sight of God, than all the crowned ruffians that ever lived.

THOUGHTS ON THE PRESENT STATE OF AMERICAN AFFAIRS.

IN the following pages I offer nothing more than simple facts, plain arguments, and common sense; and have no other preliminaries to settle with the reader, than that he will divest himself of prejudice and prepossession, and suffer his reason and his feelings to determine for themselves; that he will put *on,* or rather that he will not put *off,* the true character of a man, and generously enlarge his views beyond the present day.

Volumes have been written on the subject of the struggle between England and America. Men of all ranks have embarked in the controversy, from different motives, and with various designs; but all have been ineffectual, and the period of debate is closed. Arms, as the last resource, decide the contest; the appeal was the choice of the king, and the continent hath accepted the challenge.

It hath been reported of the late Mr. Pelham (who tho' an able minister was not without his faults) that on his being attacked in the house of commons, on the score, that his measures were only of a temporary kind, replied ["]*they will last my time.*" Should a thought so fatal and unmanly possess the colonies in the present contest, the name of ancestors will be remembered by future generations with detestation.

The sun never shined on a cause of greater worth. 'Tis not the affair of a city, a county, a province, or a kingdom, but of a continent – of at least one eighth part of the habitable globe. 'Tis not the concern of a day, a year, or an age; posterity are virtually involved in the contest, and will be more or less affected, even to the end of time, by the proceedings now. Now is the seed time of continental union, faith and honor. The least fracture now will be like a name engraved with the point of a pin on the tender rind of a young oak; the wound will enlarge with the tree, and posterity read it in full grown characters.

By referring the matter from argument to arms, a new æra for politics is struck; a new method of thinking hath arisen. All plans, proposals, &c. prior to the nineteenth of April, *i. e.* to the commencement of hostilities, are like the almanacks of the last year; which, though proper then, are superceded and useless now. Whatever was advanced by the advocates on either side of the question then, terminated in one and the same point, viz. a union with Great-Britain; the only difference between the parties was the method of effecting it; the one proposing force, the other friendship; but it hath so far happened that the first hath failed, and the second hath withdrawn her influence.

As much hath been said of the advantages of reconciliation, which, like an agreeable dream, hath passed away and left us as we were, it is but right, that we should examine the contrary side of the argument, and inquire into some of the many material injuries which these colonies sustain, and always will sustain, by being connected with, and dependant on Great-Britain. To examine that connexion and dependance on the principles of nature and common sense, to see what we have to trust to, if separated, and what we are to expect, if dependant.

I have heard it asserted by some, that as America hath flourished under her former connexion with Great-Britain, that the same connexion is necessary towards her future happiness, and will always have the same effect. Nothing can be more fallacious than this kind of argument. We may as well assert that because a child hath thrived upon milk, that it is never to have meat, or that the first twenty years of our lives is to become a precedent for the next twenty. But even this is admitting more than is true, for I answer roundly, that America would have flourished as much, and probably much more, had no European power had any thing to do with her. The commerce, by which she hath enriched herself are the necessaries of life, and will always have a market while eating is the custom of Europe.

But she has protected us, say some. That she hath engrossed us is true, and defended the continent at our expence as well as her own is admitted, and she would have defended Turkey from the same motive, viz. the sake of trade and dominion.

Alas, we have been long led away by ancient prejudices, and made large sacrifices to superstition. We have boasted the protection of Great-Britain, without considering, that her motive was *interest* not *attachment;* that she did not protect us from *our enemies* on *our account,* but from *her enemies* on *her own account,* from those who had no quarrel with us on any *other account, and who will always be our enemies on the *same accounts.* Let Britain wave her pretensions to the continent, or the continent throw off the dependance, and we should be at peace with France and Spain were they at war with Britain. The miseries of Hanover last war ought to warn us against connexions.

It hath lately been asserted in parliament, that the colonies have no relation to each other but through the parent country, *i. e.* that Pennsylvania and the Jerseys, and so on for the rest, are sister colonies by the way of England; this is certainly a very round-about way of proving relationship, but it is the nearest and only true way of proving enemyship, if I may so call it. France and Spain never were, nor perhaps ever will be our enemies as *Americans,* but as our being the *subjects of Great-Britain.*

But Britain is the parent country, say some. Then the more shame upon her conduct. Even brutes do not devour their young, nor savages make war upon their families; wherefore the assertion, if true, turns to her reproach; but it happens not to be true, or only partly so, and the phrase *parent* or *mother country* hath been jesuitically adopted by the king and his parasites, with a low papistical design of gaining an unfair bias on the credulous weakness of our minds. Europe, and not England, is the parent country of America. This new world hath been the asylum for the persecuted lovers of civil and religious liberty from *every part* of Europe. Hither have they fled, not from the tender embraces of the mother, but from the cruelty of the monster; and it is so far true of England, that the same tyranny which drove the first emigrants from home, pursues their descendants still.

In this extensive quarter of the globe, we forget the narrow limits of three hundred and sixty miles (the extent of England) and carry our friendship on a larger scale; we claim brotherhood with every European christian, and triumph in the generosity of the sentiment.

It is pleasant to observe by what regular gradations we surmount the force of local prejudice, as we enlarge our acquaintance with the world. A man born in any town in England divided into parishes, will naturally associate most with his fellow parishioners (because their interests in many cases will be common) and distinguish him by the name of *neighbour;* if he meet him but a few miles from home, he drops the narrow idea of a street, and salutes him by the name of *townsman;* if he travel out of the county, and meet him in any other, he forgets the minor divisions of street and town, and calls him *countryman,* i. e. *county-man;* but if in their foreign excursions they should associate in France, or any other part of *Europe,* their local remembrance would be enlarged into that of *Englishmen.* And by a just parity of reasoning, all Europeans meeting in America, or any other quarter of the globe, are *countrymen;* for England, Holland, Germany, or Sweden, when compared with the whole, stand in the same places on the larger scale, which the divisions of street, town, and county do on the smaller ones; distinctions too limited for continental minds. Not one third of the inhabitants, even of this province, are of English descent. Wherefore I reprobate the phrase of parent or mother country applied to England only, as being false, selfish, narrow and ungenerous.

But admitting, that we were all of English descent, what does it amount to? Nothing. Britain, being now an open enemy, extinguishes every other name and title: And to say that reconciliation is our duty, is truly farcical. The first king of England, of the present line (William the Conqueror) was a Frenchman, and half the Peers of England are descendants from the same country; wherefore, by the same method of reasoning, England ought to be governed by France.

Much hath been said of the united strength of Britain and the colonies, that in conjunction they might bid defiance to the world. But this is mere presumption; the fate of war is uncertain, neither do the expressions mean any thing; for this continent would never suffer itself to be drained of inhabitants, to support the British arms in either Asia, Africa, or Europe.

Besides, what have we to do with setting the world at defiance? Our plan is commerce, and that, well attended to, will secure us the peace and friendship of all Europe; because, it is the interest of all Europe to have America a *free port*. Her trade will always be a protection, and her barrenness of gold and silver secure her from invaders.

I challenge the warmest advocate for reconciliation, to shew, a single advantage that this continent can reap, by being connected with Great Britain. I repeat the challenge, not a single advantage is derived. Our corn will fetch its price in any market in Europe, and our imported goods must be paid for buy them where we will.

But the injuries and disadvantages we sustain by that connection, are without number; and our duty to mankind at large, as well as to ourselves, instruct us to renounce the alliance: Because, any submission to, or dependance on Great-Britain, tends directly to involve this continent in European wars and quarrels; and sets us at variance with nations, who would otherwise seek our friendship, and against whom, we have neither anger nor complaint. As Europe is our market for trade, we ought to form no partial connection with any part of it. It is the true interest of America to steer clear of European contentions, which she never can do, while by her dependance on Britain, she is made the make-weight in the scale of British politics.

Europe is too thickly planted with kingdoms to be long at peace, and whenever a war breaks out between England and any foreign power, the trade of America goes to ruin, *because of her connection with Britain.* The next war may not turn out like the last, and should it not, the advocates for reconciliation now will be wishing for separation then, because, neutrality in that case, would be a safer convoy than a man of war. Every thing that is right or natural pleads for separation. The blood of the slain, the weeping voice of nature cries, 'TIS TIME TO PART. Even the distance at which the Almighty hath placed England and America, is a strong and natural proof, that the authority of the one, over the other, was never the design of Heaven. The time likewise at which the continent was discovered, adds weight to the argument, and the manner in which it was peopled encreases the force of it. The reformation was preceded by the discovery of America, as if the Almighty graciously meant to open a sanctuary to the persecuted in future years, when home should afford neither friendship nor safety.

The authority of Great-Britain over this continent, is a form of government, which sooner or later must have an end: And a serious mind can draw no true pleasure by looking forward, under the painful and positive conviction, that what he calls "the present constitution" is merely temporary. As parents, we can have no joy, knowing that *this government* is not sufficiently lasting to ensure any thing which we may bequeath to posterity: And by a plain method of argument, as we are running the next generation into debt, we ought to do the work of it, otherwise we use them meanly and pitifully. In order to discover the line of our duty rightly, we should take our children in our hand, and fix our station a few years farther into life; that eminence will present a prospect, which a few present fears and prejudices conceal from our sight.

Though I would carefully avoid giving unnecessary offence, yet I am inclined to believe, that all those who espouse the doctrine of reconciliation, may be included within the following descriptions. Interested men, who are not to be trusted; weak men, who *cannot* see; prejudiced men, who *will not* see; and a certain set of moderate men, who think better of the European world than it deserves; and this last class, by an ill-judged deliberation, will be the cause of more calamities to this continent, than all the other three.

It is the good fortune of many to live distant from the scene of sorrow; the evil is not sufficiently brought to *their* doors to make *them* feel the precariousness with which all American property is possessed. But let our imaginations transport us for a few moments to Boston, that seat of wretchedness will teach us wisdom, and instruct us for ever to renounce a power in whom we can have no trust. The inhabitants of that unfortunate city, who but a few months ago were in ease and affluence, have now, no other alternative than to stay and starve, or turn out to beg. Endangered by the fire of their friends if they continue within the city, and plundered by the soldiery if they leave it. In their present condition they are prisoners without the hope of redemption, and in a general attack for their relief, they would be exposed to the fury of both armies.

Men of passive tempers look somewhat lightly over the offences of Britain, and, still hoping for the best, are apt to call out, "*Come, come, we shall be friends again, for all this.*" But examine the passions and feelings of mankind, Bring the doctrine of reconciliation to the touchstone of nature, and then tell me, whether you can hereafter love, honour, and faithfully serve the power that hath carried fire and sword into your land? If you cannot do all these, then are you only deceiving yourselves, and by your delay bringing ruin upon posterity. Your future connection with Britain, whom you can neither love nor honour, will be forced and unnatural, and being formed only on the plan of present convenience, will in a little time fall into a relapse more wretched than the first. But if you say, you can still pass the violations over, then I ask, Hath your house been burnt? Hath your property been destroyed before your face? Are your wife and children destitute of a bed to lie on, or bread to live on? Have you lost a parent or a child by their hands, and yourself the ruined and wretched survivor? If you have not, then are you not a judge of those who have. But if you have, and still can shake hands with the murderers, then are you unworthy the name of husband, father, friend, or lover, and whatever may be your rank or title in life, you have the heart of a coward, and the spirit of a sycophant.

This is not inflaming or exaggerating matters, but trying them by those feelings and affections which nature justifies, and without which, we should be incapable of discharging the social duties of life, or enjoying the felicities of it. I mean not to exhibit horror for the purpose of provoking revenge, but to awaken us from fatal and unmanly slumbers, that we may pursue determinately some fixed object. It is not in the power of Britain or of Europe to conquer America, if she do not conquer herself by *delay* and *timidity*. The present winter is worth an age if rightly employed, but if lost or neglected, the whole continent will partake of the misfortune; and there is no punishment which that man will not deserve, be he who, or what, or where he will, that may be the means of sacrificing a season so precious and useful.

It is repugnant to reason, to the universal order of things to all examples from former ages, to suppose, that this continent can longer remain subject to any external power. The most sanguine in Britain does not think so. The utmost stretch of human wisdom cannot, at this time, compass a plan short of separation, which can promise the continent even a year's security. Reconciliation is *now* a fallacious dream. Nature hath deserted the connexion, and Art cannot supply her place. For, as Milton wisely expresses, "never can true reconcilement grow where wounds of deadly hate have pierced so deep."

Every quiet method for peace hath been ineffectual. Our prayers have been rejected with disdain; and only tended to convince us, that nothing flatters vanity, or confirms obstinacy in Kings more than repeated petitioning – and nothing hath contributed more than that very measure to make the Kings of Europe absolute: Witness Denmark and Sweden. Wherefore, since nothing but blows will do, for God's sake, let us come to a final separation, and not leave the next generation to be cutting throats, under the violated unmeaning names of parent and child.

To say, they will never attempt it again is idle and visionary, we thought so at the repeal of the stamp-act, yet a year or two undeceived us; as well may we suppose that nations, which have been once defeated, will never renew the quarrel.

As to government matters, it is not in the power of Britain to do this continent justice: The business of it will soon be too weighty, and intricate, to be managed with any tolerable degree of convenience, by a power, so distant from us, and so very ignorant of us; for if they cannot conquer us, they cannot govern us. To be always running three or four thousand miles with a tale or a petition, waiting four or five months for an answer, which when obtained requires five or six more to explain it in, will in a few years be looked upon as folly and childishness—There was a time when it was proper, and there is a proper time for it to cease.

Small islands not capable of protecting themselves, are the proper objects for kingdoms to take under their care; but there is something very absurd, in supposing a continent to be perpetually governed by an island. In no instance hath nature made the satellite larger than its primary planet, and as England and America, with respect to each other, reverses the common order of nature, it is evident they belong to different systems: England to Europe, America to itself.

I am not induced by motives of pride, party, or resentment to espouse the doctrine of separation and independance; I am clearly, positively, and conscientiously persuaded that it is the true interest of this continent to be so; that every thing short of *that* is mere patchwork, that it can afford no lasting felicity,—that it is leaving the sword to our children, and shrinking back at a time, when, a little more, a little farther, would have rendered this continent the glory of the earth.

As Britain hath not manifested the least inclination towards a compromise, we may be assured that no terms can be obtained worthy the acceptance of the continent, or any ways equal to the expence of blood and treasure we have been already put to.

The object, contended for, ought always to bear some just proportion to the expence. The removal of North, or the whole detestable junto, is a matter unworthy the millions we have expended. A temporary stoppage of trade, was an inconvenience, which would have sufficiently ballanced the repeal of all the acts complained of, had such repeals been obtained; but if the whole continent must take up arms, if every man must be a soldier, it is scarcely worth our while to fight against a contemptible ministry only. Dearly, dearly, do we pay for the repeal of the acts, if that is all we fight for; for in a just estimation, it is as great a folly to pay a Bunker-hill price for law, as for land. As I have always considered the independancy of this continent, as an event, which sooner or later must arrive, so from the late rapid progress of the continent to maturity, the event could not be far of[f]. Wherefore, on the breaking out of hostilities, it was not worth the while to have disputed a matter, which time would have finally redressed, unless we meant to be in earnest; otherwise, it is like wasting an estate on a suit at law, to regulate the trespasses of a tenant, whose lease is just expiring. No man was a warmer wisher for reconciliation than myself, before the fatal nineteenth of April 1775[2], but the moment the event of that day was made known, I rejected the hardened, sullen tempered Pharoah of England for ever; and disdain the wretch, that with the pretended title of FATHER OF HIS PEOPLE can unfeelingly hear of their slaughter, and composedly sleep with their blood upon his soul.

But admitting that matters were now made up, what would be the event? I answer, the ruin of the continent. And that for several reasons.

First. The powers of governing still remaining in the hands of the king, he will have a negative over the whole legislation of this continent. And as he hath shewn himself such an inveterate enemy to liberty, and discovered such a thirst for arbitrary power; is he, or is he not, a proper man to say to these colonies, *"You shall make no laws but what I please."* And is there any inhabitant in America so ignorant, as not to know, that according to what is called the *present constitution,* that this continent can make no laws but what the king gives leave to; and is there any man so unwise, as not to see, that (considering what has happened) he will suffer no law to be made here, but such as suit *his* purpose. We may be as effectually enslaved by the want of laws in America, as by submitting to laws made for us in England. After matters are made up (as it is called) can there be any doubt, but the whole power of the crown will be exerted, to keep this continent as low and humble as possible? Instead of going forward we shall go backward, or be perpetually quarrelling or ridiculously petitioning. – We are already greater than the king wishes us to be, and will he not hereafter endeavour to make us less? To bring the matter to one point. Is the power who is jealous of our prosperity, a proper power to govern us? Whoever says *No* to this question is an *independant,* for independancy means no more, than, whether we shall make our own laws, or, whether the king, the greatest enemy this continent hath, or can have, shall tell us *"there shall be no laws but such as I like."*

But the king you will say has a negative in England; the people there can make no laws without his consent. In point of right and good order, there is something very ridiculous, that a youth of twenty-one (which hath

2. Massacre at Lexington.

often happened) shall say to several millions of people, older and wiser than himself, I forbid this or that act of yours to be law. But in this place I decline this sort of reply, though I will never cease to expose the absurdity of it, and only answer, that England being the King's residence, and America not so, makes quite another case. The king's negative *here* is ten times more dangerous and fatal than it can be in England, for *there* he will scarcely refuse his consent to a bill for putting England into as strong a state of defence as possible, and in America he would never suffer such a bill to be passed.

America is only a secondary object in the system of British politics, England consults the good of *this* country, no farther than it answers her *own* purpose. Wherefore, her own interest leads her to suppress the growth of *ours* in every case which doth not promote her advantage, or in the least interferes with it. A pretty state we should soon be in under such a second-hand government, considering what has happened! Men do not change from enemies to friends by the alteration of a name: And in order to shew that reconciliation *now* is a dangerous doctrine, I affirm, *that it would be policy in the king at this time, to repeal the acts for the sake of reinstating himself in the government of the provinces;* in order, that HE MAY ACCOM-PLISH BY CRAFT AND SUBTILTY, IN THE LONG RUN, WHAT HE CANNOT DO BY FORCE AND VIOLENCE IN THE SHORT ONE. Reconciliation and ruin are nearly related.

Secondly. That as even the best terms, which we can expect to obtain, can amount to no more than a temporary expedient, or a kind of government by guardianship, which can last no longer than till the colonies come of age, so the general face and state of things, in the interim, will be unsettled and unpromising. Emigrants of property will not choose to come to a country whose form of government hangs but by a thread, and who is every day tottering on the brink of commotion and disturbance: and numbers of the present inhabitants would lay hold of the interval, to dispose of their effects, and quit the continent.

But the most powerful of all arguments, is, that nothing but independance, i. e. a continental form of government, can keep the peace of the continent and preserve it inviolate from civil wars. I dread the event of a reconciliation with Britain now, as it is more than probable, that it will be followed by a revolt somewhere or other, the consequences of which may be far more fatal than all the malice of Britain.

Thousands are already ruined by British barbarity; (thousands more will probably suffer the same fate)[.] Those men have other feelings than us who having nothing suffered. All they *now* possess is liberty, what they before enjoyed is sacrificed to its service, and having nothing more to lose, they disdain submission. Besides, the general temper of the colonies, towards a British government, will be like that of a youth, who is nearly out of his time; they will care very little about her. And a government which cannot preserve the peace, is no government at all, and in that case we pay our money for nothing; and pray what is it that Britain can do, whose power will be wholly on paper, should a civil tumult break out the very day after reconciliation? I have heard some men say, many of whom I believe spoke without thinking, that they dreaded an independance, fearing that it would produce civil wars. It is but seldom that our first thoughts are truly correct, and that is the case here; for there are ten times more to dread from a patched up connexion than from independance. I make the sufferers case my own, and I protest, that were I driven from house and home, my property destroyed, and my circumstances ruined, that as man, sensible of injuries, I could never relish the doctrine of reconciliation, or consider myself bound thereby.

The colonies have manifested such a spirit of good order and obedience to continental government, as is sufficient to make every reasonable person easy and happy on that head. No man can assign the least pretence for his fears, on any other grounds, than such as are truly childish and ridiculous, viz. that one colony will be striving for superiority over another.

Where there are no distinctions there can be no superiority; perfect equality affords no temptation. The republics of Europe are all (and we may say always) in peace. Holland and Swisserland are without wars, foreign or domestic: Monarchical governments, it is true, are never long at rest; the crown itself is a temptation to enterprizing ruffians at *home;* and that degree of pride and insolence ever attendant on regal authority, swells into a rupture with foreign powers, in instances, where a republican government, by being formed on more natural principles, would negociate the mistake.

If there is any true cause of fear respecting independance, it is because no plan is yet laid down. Men do not see their way out–Wherefore, as an opening into that business, I offer the following hints; at the same time modestly affirming, that I have no other opinion of them myself, than that they may be the means of giving rise to something better. Could the straggling thoughts of individuals be collected, they would frequently form materials for wise and able men to improve into useful matter.

LET the assemblies be annual, with a President only. The representation more equal. Their business wholly domestic, and subject to the authority of a Continental Congress.

Let each colony be divided into six, eight, or ten, convenient districts, each district to send a proper number of delegates to Congress, so that each colony send at least thirty. The whole number in Congress will be at least 390. Each Congress to sit and to choose a president by the following method. When the delegates are met, let a colony be taken from the whole thirteen colonies by lot, after which, let the whole Congress choose (by ballot) a president from out of the delegates of *that* province. In the next Congress, let a colony be taken by lot from twelve only, omitting that colony from which the president was taken in the former Congress, and so proceeding on till the whole thirteen shall have had their proper rotation. And in order that nothing may pass into a law but what is satisfactorily just, not less than three fifths of the Congress to be called a majority. – He that will promote discord, under a government so equally formed as this, would have joined Lucifer in his revolt.

But as there is a peculiar delicacy, from whom, or in what manner, this business must first arise, and as it seems most agreeable and consistent, that it should come from some intermediate body between the governed and the governors, that is, between the Congress and the people, let a CONTINEN-TAL CONFERENCE be held, in the following manner, and for the following purpose.

A committee of twenty-six members of Congress, viz. two for each colony. Two members from each House of Assembly, or Provincial Convention; and five representatives of the people at large, to be chosen in the capital city or town of each province, for, and in behalf of the whole province, by as many qualified voters as shall think proper to attend from all parts of the province for that purpose; or, if more convenient, the representatives may be chosen in two or three of the most populous parts thereof. In this conference, thus assembled, will be united, the two grand principles of business, *knowledge* and *power.* The members of Congress, Assemblies, or Conventions, by having had experience in national concerns, will be able and useful counsellors, and the whole, by being empowered by the people, will have a truly legal authority.

The conferring members being met, let their business be to frame a CONTINENTAL CHARTER, or Charter of the United Colonies; (answering to what is called the Magna Charta of England) fixing the number and manner of choosing members of Congress, members of Assembly, with their date of sitting, and drawing the line of business and jurisdiction between them: (Always remembering, that our strength is continental not provincial:) Securing freedom and property to all men, and above all things, the free exercise of religion, according to the dictates of conscience; with such other matter as is necessary for a charter to contain. Immediately after which, the said Conference to dissolve, and the bodies which shall be chosen conformable to the said charter, to be the legislators and governors of this continent for the time being: Whose peace and happiness, may God preserve, Amen.

Should any body of men be hereafter delegated for this or some similar purpose, I offer them the following extracts from that wise observer on governments *Dragonetti.* "The science" says he "of the politician consists in fixing the true point of happiness and freedom. Those men would deserve the gratitude of ages, who should discover a mode of government that contained the greatest sum of individual happiness, with the least national expence.

– DRAGONETTI ON VIRTUES AND REWARDS."

But where says some is the King of America? I'll tell you Friend, he reigns above, and doth not make havoc of mankind like the Royal Brute of Britain. Yet that we may not appear to be defective even in earthly honors, let a day be solemnly set apart for proclaiming the charter; let it be brought forth placed on the divine law, the word of God; let a crown be placed thereon, by which the world may know, that so far as we approve of monarchy, that in America THE LAW IS KING. For as in absolute governments the King is law, so in free countries the law *ought* to be King; and there ought to be no other. But lest any ill use should afterwards arise, let the crown at the conclusion of the ceremony be demolished, and scattered among the people whose right it is.

A government of our own is our natural right: And when a man seriously reflects on the precariousness of human affairs, he will become convinced, that it is infinitely wiser and safer, to form a constitution of our own in a cool deliberate manner, while we have it in our power, than to trust such an interesting event to time and chance. If we omit it now, some[3] Massanello may hereafter arise, who laying hold of popular disquietudes, may collect together the desperate and the discontented, and by assuming to themselves the powers of government, may sweep away the liberties of the continent like a deluge. Should the government of America return again into the hands of Britain, the tottering situation of things, will be a temptation for some desperate adventurer to try his fortune; and in such a case, what relief can

3. Thomas Anello, otherwise Massanello, a fisherman of Naples, who after spiriting up his countrymen in the public market place, against the oppression of the Spaniards, to whom the place was then subject, prompted them to revolt, and in the space of a day became King.

Britain give? Ere she could hear the news, the fatal business might be done; and ourselves suffering like the wretched Britons under the oppression of the Conqueror. Ye that oppose independance now, ye know not what ye do; ye are opening a door to eternal tyranny, by keeping vacant the seat of government. There are thousands, and tens of thousands, who would think it glorious to expel from the continent, that barbarous and hellish power, which hath stirred up the Indians and Negroes to destroy us, the cruelty hath a double guilt, it is dealing brutally by us, and treacherously by them.

To talk of friendship with those in whom our reason forbids us to have faith, and our affections wounded through a thousand pores instruct us to detest, is madness and folly. Every day wears out the little remains of kindred between us and them, and can there be any reason to hope, that as the relationship expires, the affection will increase, or that we shall agree better, when we have ten times more and greater concerns to quarrel over than ever?

Ye that tell us of harmony and reconciliation, can ye restore to us the time that is past? Can ye give to prostitution its former innocence? Neither can ye reconcile Britain and America. The last cord now is broken, the people of England are presenting addresses against us. There are injuries which nature cannot forgive; she would cease to be nature if she did. As well can the lover forgive the ravisher of his mistress, as the continent forgive the murders of Britain. The Almighty hath implanted in us these unextinguishable feelings for good and wise purposes. They are the guardians of his image in our hearts. They distinguish us from the herd of common animals. The social compact would dissolve, and justice be extirpated the earth, or have only a casual existence were we callous to the touches of affection. The robber, and the murderer, would often escape unpunished, did not the injuries which our tempers sustain, provoke us into justice.

O ye that love mankind! Ye that dare oppose, not only the tyranny, but the tyrant, stand forth! Every spot of the old world is overrun with oppression. Freedom hath been hunted round the globe. Asia, and Africa, have long expelled her. – Europe regards her like a stranger, and England hath given her warning to depart. O! receive the fugitive, and prepare in time an asylum for mankind.

OF THE PRESENT ABILITY OF AMERICA, WITH SOME MISCELLANEOUS REFLEXIONS.

I Have never met with a man, either in England or America, who hath not confessed his opinion, that a separation between the countries, would take place one time or other: And there is no instance, in which we have shewn less judgment, than in endeavouring to describe, what we call, the ripeness or fitness of the Continent for independance.

As all men allow the measure, and vary only in their opinion of the time, let us, in order to remove mistakes, take a general survey of things, and endeavour, if possible, to find out the *very* time. But we need not go far, the inquiry ceases at once, for, the *time hath found us.* The general concurrence, the glorious union of all things prove the fact.

It is not in numbers but in unity, that our great strength lies; yet our present numbers are sufficient to repel the force of all the world. The Continent hath, at this time, the largest body of armed and disciplined men of any power under Heaven; and is just arrived at that pitch of strength, in which, no single colony is able to support itself, and the whole, when united, can accomplish the matter, and either more, or, less than this, might be fatal in its effects. Our land force is already sufficient, and as to naval affairs, we cannot be insensible, that Britain would never suffer an American man of war to be built, while the continent remained in her hands. Wherefore, we should be no forwarder an hundred years hence in that branch, than we are now; but the truth is, we should be less so, because the timber of the country is every day diminishing, and that, which will remain at last, will be far off and difficult to procure.

Were the continent crowded with inhabitants, her sufferings under the present circumstances would be intolerable. The more sea port towns we had, the more should we have both to defend and to loose. Our present numbers are so happily proportioned to our wants, that no man need be idle. The diminution of trade affords an army, and the necessities of an army create a new trade.

Debts we have none; and whatever we may contract on this account will serve as a glorious memento of our virtue. Can we but leave posterity with a settled form of government, an independant constitution of [its] own, the purchase at any price will be cheap. But to expend millions for the sake of getting a few vile acts repealed, and routing the present ministry only, is unworthy the charge, and is using posterity with the utmost cruelty; because it is leaving them the great work to do, and a debt upon their backs, from which, they derive no advantage. Such a thought is unworthy a man of honor, and is the true characteristic of a narrow heart and a p[i]dling politician.

The debt we may contract doth not deserve our regard if the work be but accomplished. No nation ought to be without a debt. A national debt is a national bond; and when it bears no interest, is in no case a grievance. Britain is oppressed with a debt of upwards of one hundred and forty millions sterling, for which she pays upwards of four millions interest. And as a compensation for her debt, she has a large navy; America is without a debt, and without a navy; yet for the twentieth part of the English national debt, could have a navy as large again. The navy of England is not worth, at this time, more than three millions and an half sterling.

The first and second editions of this pamphlet were published without the following calculations, which are now given as a proof that the above estimation of the navy is a just one. *See Entic's naval history, intro.* page 56.

The charge of building a ship of each rate, and furnishing her with masts, yards, sails and rigging, together with a proportion of eight months boatswain's and carpenter's sea-stores, as calculated by Mr. Burchett, Secretary to the navy.

			£.
For a ship of a 100 guns	–	–	35,553
90	–	–	29,886
80	–	–	23,638
70	–	–	17,785
60	–	–	14,197
50	–	–	10,606
40	–	–	7,558
30	–	–	5,846
20	–	–	3,710

And from hence it is easy to sum up the value, or cost rather, of the whole British navy, which in the year 1757, when it was at its greatest glory consisted of the following ships and guns.

Ships.		Guns.		Cost of one.		Cost of all.
6	–	100	–	35,553 *l.*	– – –	213,318 *l.*
12	–	90	–	29,886	– – –	358,632
12	–	80	–	23,638	– – –	283,656
43	–	70	–	17,785	– – –	764,755
35	–	60	–	14,197	– – –	496,895
40	–	50	–	10,606	– – –	424,240
45	–	40	–	7,558	– – –	340,110
58	–	20	–	3,710	– – –	215,180

85 Sloops, bombs, and fireships, one with another, at	2,000	170,000
	Cost	3,266,786
Remains for guns,	– –	233,214
		3,500000

No country on the globe is so happily situated, or so internally capable of raising a fleet as America. Tar, timber, iron, and cordage are her natural produce. We need go abroad for nothing. Whereas the Dutch, who make large profits by hiring out their ships of war to the Spaniards and Portuguese, are obliged to import most of the materials they use. We ought to view the building a fleet as an article of commerce, it being the natural manufactory of this country. It is the best money we can lay out. A navy when finished is worth more than it cost. And is that nice point in national policy, in which commerce and protection are united. Let us build; if we want them not, we can sell; and by that means replace our paper currency with ready gold and silver.

In point of manning a fleet, people in general run into great errors; it is not necessary that one fourth part should be sailors. The Terrible privateer, Captain Death, stood the hottest engagement of any ship last war, yet had not twenty sailors on board, though her complement of men was upwards of two hundred. A few able and social sailors will soon instruct a sufficient number of active landmen in the common work of a ship. Wherefore, we never can be more capable to begin on maritime matters than now, while our timber is standing, our fisheries blocked up, and our sailors and shipwrights out of employ. Men of war, of seventy and eighty guns were built forty years ago in New-England, and why not the same now? Ship-building is America's greatest pride, and in which, she will in time excel the whole world. The great empires of the east are mostly inland, and consequently excluded from the possibility of rivalling her. Africa is in a state of barbarism; and no power in Europe, hath either such an extent of coast, or such an internal supply of materials. Where nature hath given the one, she has withheld the other; to America only hath she been liberal of both. The vast empire of Russia is almost shut out from the sea; wherefore, her boundless forests, her tar, iron, and cordage are only articles of commerce.

In point of safety, ought we to be without a fleet? We are not the little people now, which we were sixty years ago; at that time we might have trusted our property in the streets, or fields rather; and slept securely without locks or bolts to our doors or windows. The case now is altered, and our methods of defence, ought to improve with our increase of property. A common pirate, twelve months ago, might have come up the Delaware, and laid the city of Philadelphia under instant contribution, for what sum he pleased; and the same might have happened to other places. Nay, any daring fellow, in a brig of fourteen or sixteen guns, might have robbed the whole Continent, and carried off half a million of money. These are circumstances which demand our attention, and point out the necessity of naval protection.

Some, perhaps, will say, that after we have made it up with Britain, she will protect us. Can we be so unwise as to mean, that she shall keep a navy in our harbours for that purpose? Common sense will tell us, that the power which hath endeavoured to subdue us, is of all others, the most improper to defend us. Conquest may be effected under the pretence of friendship; and ourselves, after a long and brave resistance, be at last cheated into slavery. And if her ships are not to be admitted into our harbours, I would ask, how is she to protect us? A navy three or four thousand miles off can be of little use, and on sudden emergencies, none at all. Wherefore, if we must hereafter protect ourselves, why not do it for ourselves? Why do it for another?

The English list of ships of war, is long and formidable, but not a tenth part of them are at any one time fit for service, numbers of them not in being; yet their names are pompously continued in the list, if only a plank be left of the ship: and not a fifth part, of such as are fit for service, can be spared on any one station at one time. The East, and West Indies, Mediterranean, Africa, and other parts over which Britain extends her claim, make large demands upon her navy. From a mixture of prejudice and inattention, we have contracted a false notion respecting the navy of England, and have talked as if we should have the whole of it to encounter at once, and for that reason, supposed, that we must have one as large; which not being instantly practicable, have been made use of by a set of disguised Tories to discourage our beginning thereon. Nothing can be farther from truth than this; for if America had only a twentieth part of the naval force of Britain, she would be by far an over match for her; because, as we neither have, nor claim any foreign dominion, our whole force would be employed on our own coast, where we should, in the long run, have two to one the advantage of those who had three or four thousand miles to sail over, before they could attack us, and the same distance to return in order to refit and recruit. And although Britain by her fleet hath a check over our trade to Europe, we have as large a one over her trade to the West-Indies, which, by laying in the neighbourhood of the Continent, is entirely at its mercy.

Some method might be fallen on to keep up a naval force in time of peace, if we should not judge it necessary to support a constant navy. If premiums were to be given to merchants to build and employ in their service, ships mounted with twenty, thirty, forty, or fifty guns, (the premiums to be in proportion to the loss of bulk to the merchants) fifty or sixty of those ships, with a few guard ships on constant duty, would keep up a sufficient navy, and that without burdening ourselves with the evil so loudly complained of in England, of suffering their fleet, in time of peace to lie rotting in the docks. To unite the sinews of commerce and defence is sound policy; for when our strength and our riches, play into each other's hand, we need fear no external enemy.

In almost every article of defence we abound. Hemp flourishes even to rankness, so that we need not want cordage. Our iron is superior to that of other countries. Our small arms equal to any in the world. Cannon we can cast at pleasure. Saltpetre and gunpowder we are every day producing. Our knowledge is hourly improving. Resolution is our inherent character, and courage hath never yet forsaken us. Wherefore, what is it that we want? Why is it that we hesitate? From Britain we can expect nothing but ruin. If she is once admitted to the government of America again, this Continent will not be worth living in. Jealousies will be always arising; insurrections will be constantly happening; and who will go forth to quell them? Who will venture his life to reduce his own countrymen to a foreign obedience? The difference between Pennsylvania and Connecticut, respecting some unlocated lands, shews the insignificance of a British government, and fully proves, that nothing but Continental authority can regulate Continental matters.

Another reason why the present time is preferable to all others, is, that the fewer our numbers are, the more land there is yet unoccupied, which instead of being lavished by the king on his worthless dependants, may be hereafter applied, not only to the discharge of the present debt, but to the constant support of government. No nation under heaven hath such an advantage as this.

The infant state of the Colonies, as it is called, so far from being against, is an argument in favor of independance. We are sufficiently numerous, and were we more so, we might be less united. It is a matter worthy of observation, that the more a country is peopled, the smaller their armies are. In military numbers the ancients far exceeded the moderns: and the reason is evident, for trade being the consequence of population, men become too much absorbed thereby to attend to any thing else. Commerce diminishes the spirit, both of patriotism and military defence. And history sufficiently informs us, that the bravest atchievements were always accomplished in the non-age of a nation. With the increase of commerce, England hath lost its spirit. The city of London, notwithstanding its numbers, submits to continued insults with the patience of a coward. The more men have to lose, the less willing are they to venture. The rich are in general slaves to fear, and submit to courtly power with the trembling duplicity of a Spaniel.

Youth is the seed time of good habits, as well in nations as in individuals. It might be difficult, if not impossible, to form the Continent into one government half a century hence. The vast variety of interests, occasioned by an increase of trade and population, would create confusion. Colony would be against colony. Each being able might scorn each other's assistance: and while the proud and foolish gloried in their little distinctions, the wise would lament, that the union had not been formed before. Wherefore, the *present time* is the *true time* for establishing it. The intimacy which is contracted in infancy, and the friendship which is formed in misfortune, are, of all others, the most lasting and unalterable. Our present union is marked with both these characters: we are young, and we have been distressed; but our concord hath withstood our troubles, and fixes a memorable æra for posterity to glory in.

The present time, likewise, is that peculiar time, which never happens to a nation but once, *viz.* the time of forming itself into a government. Most nations have let slip the opportunity, and by that means have been compelled to receive laws from their conquerors, instead of making laws for themselves. First, they had a king, and then a form of government; whereas, the articles or charter of government, should be formed first, and men delegated to execute them afterward: but from the errors of other nations, let us learn wisdom, and lay hold of the present opportunity—*To begin government at the right end.*

When William the Conqueror subdued England, he gave them law at the point of the sword; and until we consent, that the seat of government, in America, be legally and authoritatively occupied, we shall be in danger of having it filled by some fortunate ruffian, who may treat us in the same manner, and then, where will be our freedom? where our property?

As to religion, I hold it to be the indispensible duty of all government, to protect all conscientious professors thereof, and I know of no other business which government hath to do therewith, Let a man throw aside that narrowness of soul, that selfishness of principle, which the niggards of all professions are so unwilling to part with, and he will be at once delivered of his fears on that head. Suspicion is the companion of mean souls, and the bane of all good society. For myself, I fully and conscientiously believe, that it is the will of the Almighty, that there should be diversity of religious opinions among us: It affords a larger field for our Christian kindness. Were we all of one way of thinking, our religious dispositions would want matter for probation; and on this liberal principle, I look on the various denominations among us, to be like children of the same family, differing only, in what is called, their Christian names.

In page [thirty], I threw out a few thoughts on the propriety of a Continental Charter, (for I only presume to offer hints, not plans) and in this place, I take the liberty of re-mentioning the subject, by observing, that a charter is to be understood as a bond of solemn obligation, which the whole enters into, to support the right of every separate part, whether of religion, personal freedom, or property. A firm bargain and a right reckoning make long friends.

In a former page, I likewise mentioned the necessity of a large and equal representation; and there is no political matter which more deserves our attention. A small number of electors, or a small number of representatives, are equally dangerous. But if the number of the representatives be not only small, but unequal, the danger is increased. As an instance of this, I mention the following; when the Associators petition was before the House of Assembly of Pennsylvania, twenty-eight members only were present, all the Bucks county members, being eight, voted against it, and had seven of the Chester members done the same, this whole province had been governed by two counties only, and this danger it is always exposed to. The unwarrantable stretch likewise, which that house made in their last sitting, to gain an undue authority over the Delegates of that province, ought to warn the people at large, how they trust power out of their own hands. A set of instructions for the Delegates were put together, which in point of sense and business would have dishonored a schoolboy, and after being approved by a *few,* a *very few* without doors, were carried into the House, and there passed *in behalf of the whole colony;* whereas, did the whole colony know, with what ill-will that House hath entered on some necessary public measures, they would not hesitate a moment to think them unworthy of such a trust.

Immediate necessity makes many things convenient, which if continued would grow into oppressions. Expedience and right are different things. When the calamities of America required a consultation, there was no method so ready, or at that time so proper, as to appoint persons from the

several Houses of Assembly for that purpose; and the wisdom with which
they have proceeded hath preserved this continent from ruin. But as it is
more than probable that we shall never be without a CONGRESS, every well
wisher to good order, must own, that the mode for choosing members of
that body, deserves consideration. And I put it as a question to those, who
make a study of mankind, whether *representation and election* is not too
great a power for one and the same body of men to possess? When we are
planning for posterity, we ought to remember, that virtue is not hereditary.

It is from our enemies that we often gain excellent maxims, and are
frequently surprised into reason by their mistakes. Mr. Cornwall (one of
the Lords of the Treasury) treated the petition of the New-York Assembly
with contempt, because *that* House, he said, consisted but of twenty-six
members, which trifling number, he argued, could not with decency be put
for the whole. We thank him for his involuntary honesty[4].

To CONCLUDE, however strange it may appear to some, or however unwilling they may be to think so, matters not, but many strong and striking
reasons may be given, to shew, that nothing can settle our affairs so expedi-
tiously as an open and determined declaration for independance. Some of
which are,

First. – It is the custom of nations, when any two are at war, for some
other powers, not engaged in the quarrel, to step in as mediators, and bring
about the preliminaries of a peace: but while America calls herself the Subject of Great-Britain, no power, however well disposed she may be, can
offer her mediation. Wherefore, in our present state we may quarrel on
for ever.

Secondly. – It is unreasonable to suppose, that France or Spain will give
us any kind of assistance, if we mean only, to make use of that assistance
for the purpose of repairing the breach, and strengthening the connection
between Britain and America; because, those powers would be sufferers by
the consequences.

Thirdly. – While we profess ourselves the subjects of Britain, we must in
the eye of foreign nations, be considered as rebels. The precedent is somewhat dangerous to *their peace,* for men to be in arms under the name of
subjects; we, on the spot, can solve the paradox: but to unite resistance and
subjection, requires an idea much too refined for common understanding.

Fourthly. – Were a manifesto to be published, and despatched to foreign
courts, setting forth the miseries we have endured, and the peaceable meth-

---

4. Those who would fully understand of what great consequence a large and
equal representation is to a state, should read Burgh's political Disquisitions.

ods we have ineffectually used for redress; declaring, at the same time, that not being able, any longer, to live happily or safely under the cruel disposition of the British court, we had been driven to the necessity of breaking off all connections with her; at the same time, assuring all such courts of our peaceable disposition towards them, and of our desire of entering into trade with them: Such a memorial would produce more good effects to this Continent, than if a ship were freighted with petitions to Britain.

Under our present denomination of British subjects, we can neither be received nor heard abroad: The custom of all courts is against us, and will be so, until, by an independance, we take rank with other nations.

These proceedings may at first appear strange and difficult; but, like all other steps which we have already passed over, will in a little time become familiar and agreeable; and, until an independance is declared, the Continent will feel itself like a man who continues putting off some unpleasant business from day to day, yet knows it must be done, hates to set about it, wishes it over, and is continually haunted with the thoughts of its necessity.

Appendix.

SINCE the publication of the first edition of this pamphlet, or rather, on the same day on which it came out, the King's Speech made its appearance in this city. Had the spirit of prophecy directed the birth of this production, it could not have brought it forth, at a more seasonable juncture, or a more necessary time. The bloody mindedness of the one, shew the necessity of pursuing the doctrine of the other. Men read by way of revenge. And the Speech, instead of terrifying, prepared a way for the manly principles of Independance.

Ceremony, and even, silence, from whatever motive they may arise, have a hurtful tendency, when they give the least degree of countenance to base and wicked performances; wherefore, if this maxim be admitted, it naturally follows, that the King's Speech, as being a piece of finished villainy, deserved, and still deserves, a general execration both by the Congress and the people. Yet, as the domestic tranquillity of a nation, depends greatly, on the *chastity* of what may properly be called NATIONAL MANNERS, it is often better, to pass some things over in silent disdain, than to make use of such new methods of dislike, as might introduce the least innovation, on that guardian of our peace and safety. And, perhaps, it is chiefly owing to this prudent delicacy, that the King's Speech, hath not, before now, suffered a public execution. The Speech if it may be called one, is nothing better than a wilful audacious libel against the truth, the common good, and the existence of mankind; and is a formal and pompous method of offering up human sacrifices to the pride of tyrants. But this general massacre of mankind, is one of the privileges, and the certain consequence of Kings; for as nature knows them *not,* they know *not her,* and although they are beings of our *own* creating, they know not *us,* and are become the Gods of their creators. The Speech hath one good quality, which is, that it is not calculated to deceive, neither can we, even if we would, be deceived by it. Brutality and tyranny appear on the face of it. It leaves us at no loss: And every line convinces, even in the moment of reading, that He, who hunts the woods for prey, the naked and untutored Indian, is less a Savage than the King of Britain.

Sir John Dalrymple, the putative father of a whining jesuitical piece, fallaciously called, *"The Address of the people of* ENGLAND, *to the inhabitants of* AMERICA," hath, perhaps, from a vain supposition, that the people *here* were to be frightened at the pomp and description of a king, given, (though very unwisely on his part) the real character of the present one: "But," says this writer, "if you are inclined to pay compliments to an administration, which we do not complain of," (meaning the Marquis of Rockingham's at the repeal of the Stamp Act) "it is very unfair in you to withhold them from that prince, *by whose* NOD ALONE *they were permitted to do any thing."* This is toryism with a witness! Here is idolatry even without a mask: And he who can calmly hear, and digest such doctrine, hath forfeited his claim to rationality – an apostate from the order of manhood; and ought to be considered – as one, who hath not only given up the proper dignity of man, but sunk himself beneath the rank of animals, and contemptibly crawl through the world like a worm.

However, it matters very little now, what the king of England either says or does; he hath wickedly broken through every moral and human obligation, trampled nature and conscience beneath his feet; and by a steady and constitutional spirit of insolence and cruelty, procured for himself an universal hatred. It is *now* the interest of America to provide for herself. She hath already a large and young family, whom it is more her duty to take care of, than to be granting away her property, to support a power who is become a reproach to the names of men and christians – YE, whose office it is to watch over the morals of a nation, of whatsoever sect or denomination ye are of, as well as ye, who, are more immediately the guardians of the public liberty, if ye wish to preserve your native country uncontaminated by European corruption, ye must in secret wish a separation – But leaving the moral part to private reflection, I shall chiefly confine my farther remarks to the following heads.

First. That it is the interest of America to be separated from Britain.

Secondly. Which is the easiest and most practicable plan, RECONCILIATION or INDEPENDANCE? with some occasional remarks.

In support of the first, I could, if I judged it proper, produce the opinion of some of the ablest and most experienced men on this continent; and whose sentiments, on that head, are not yet publicly known. It is in reality a self-evident position: For no nation, in a state of foreign dependance, limited in its commerce, and cramped and fettered in its legislative powers, can ever arrive at any material eminence. America doth not yet know what opulence is; and although the progress which she hath made stands unparalleled in the history of other nations, it is but childhood, compared with what she would be capable of arriving at, had she, as she ought to have, the legislative powers in her own hands. England is, at this time, proudly coveting what would do her no good, were she to accomplish it; and the Continent hesitating on a matter, which will be her final ruin if neglected. It is the commerce and not the conquest of America, by which England is to be benefited, and that would in a great measure continue, were the countries as independant of each other as France and Spain; because in many articles, neither can go to a better market. But it is the independance of this country on Britain or any other, which is now the main and only object worthy of contention, and which, like all other truths discovered by necessity, will appear clearer and stronger every day.

First. Because it will come to that one time or other.

Secondly. Because, the longer it is delayed the harder it will be to accomplish.

I have frequently amused myself both in public and private companies, with silently remarking, the specious errors of those who speak without reflecting. And among the many which I have heard, the following seems the most general, viz. that had this rupture happened forty or fifty years hence, instead of *now*, the Continent would have been more able to have shaken off the dependance. To which I reply, that our military ability, *at this time,* arises from the experience gained in the last war, and which in forty or fifty years time, would have been totally extinct. The Continent, would not, by that time, have had a General, or even a military officer left; and we, or those who may succeed us, would have been as ignorant of martial matters as the ancient Indians: And this single position, closely attended to, will unanswerably prove, that the present time is preferable to all others: The argument turns thus – at the conclusion of the last war, we had experience, but wanted numbers; and forty or fifty years hence, we should have numbers, without experience; wherefore, the proper point of time, must be some particular point between the two extremes, in which a sufficiency of the former remains, and a proper increase of the latter is obtained: And that point of time is the present time.

The reader will pardon this digression, as it does not properly come under the head I first set out with, and to which I again return by the following position, viz.

Should affairs be patched up with Britain, and she to remain the governing and sovereign power of America, (which, as matters are now circumstanced, is giving up the point intirely) we shall deprive ourselves of the very means of sinking the debt we have, or may contract. The value of the back lands, which some of the provinces are clandestinely deprived of, by the unjust extention of the limits of Canada, valued only at five pounds sterling per hundred acres, amount to upwards of twenty-five millions, Pennsylvania currency; and the quit-rents at one penny sterling per acre, to two millions yearly.

It is by the sale of those lands that the debt may be sunk, without burthen to any, and the quit-rent reserved thereon, will always lessen, and in time, will wholly support the yearly expence of government. It matters not how long the debt is in paying, so that the lands when sold be applied to the discharge of it, and for the execution of which, the Congress for the time being, will be the continental trustees.

I proceed now to the second head, viz. Which is the easiest and most practicable plan, RECONCILIATION or INDEPENDANCE; with some occasional remarks.

He who takes nature for his guide is not easily beaten out of his argument, and on that ground, I answer *generally – That* INDEPENDANCE *being a* SINGLE SIMPLE LINE, *contained within ourselves; and reconciliation, a matter exceedingly perplexed and complicated, and in which, a treacherous capricious court is to interfere, gives the answer without a doubt.*

The present state of America is truly alarming to every man who is capable of reflexion. Without law, without government, without any other mode of power than what is founded on, and granted by courtesy. Held together by an unexampled concurrence of sentiment, which, is nevertheless subject to change,[5] and which, every secret enemy is endeavouring to dissolve. Our present condition, is, Legislation without law; wisdom without

---

5. [Editors' note:] This word was printed as *charge,* but an "erata" note was added after the introduction that it should be read as *change.*

a plan; a constitution without a name; and, what is strangely astonishing, perfect Independance contending for dependance. The instance is without a precedent; the case never existed before; and who can tell what may be the event? The property of no man is secure in the present unbraced system of things. The mind of the multitude is left at random, and seeing no fixed object before them, they pursue such as fancy or opinion starts. Nothing is criminal; there is no such thing as treason; wherefore, every one thinks himself at liberty to act as he pleases. The Tories dared not have assembled offensively, had they known that their lives, by that act, were forfeited to the laws of the state. A line of distinction should be drawn, between, English soldiers taken in battle, and inhabitants of America taken in arms. The first are prisoners, but the latter traitors. The one forfeits his liberty, the other his head.

Notwithstanding our wisdom, there is a visible feebleness in some of our proceedings which gives encouragement to dissentions. The Continental Belt is too loosely buckled. And if something is not done in time, it will be too late to do any thing, and we shall fall into a state, in which, neither *Reconciliation* nor *Independance* will be practicable. The king and his worthless adherents are got at their old game of dividing the Continent, and there are not wanting among us, Printers, who will be busy in spreading specious falsehoods. The artful and hypocritical letter which appeared a few months ago in two of the New-York papers, and likewise in two others, is an evidence that there are men who want either judgment or honesty.

It is easy getting into holes and corners and talking of reconciliation: But do such men seriously consider, how difficult the task is, and how dangerous it may prove, should the Continent divide thereon. Do they take within their view, all the various orders of men whose situation and circumstances, as well as their own, are to be considered therein. Do they put themselves in the place of the sufferer whose *all* is *already* gone, and of the soldier, who hath quitted *all* for the defence of his country. If their ill judged moderation be suited to their own private situations *only,* regardless of others, the event will convince them, that "they are reckoning without their Host."

Put us, says some, on the footing we were on in sixty-three: To which I answer, the request is not *now* in the power of Britain to comply with, neither will she propose it; but if it were, and even should be granted, I ask, as a reasonable question, By what means is such a corrupt and faithless court to be kept to its engagements? Another parliament, nay, even the present, may hereafter repeal the obligation, on the pretence of its being violently obtained, or unwisely granted; and in that case, Where is our redress?—No going to law with nations; cannon are the barristers of Crowns; and the sword, not of justice, but of war, decides the suit. To be on the footing of sixty-three, it is not sufficient, that the laws only be put on the same state, but, that our circumstances, likewise, be put on the same state; Our burnt and destroyed towns repaired or built up, our private losses made good, our public debts (contracted for defence) discharged; otherwise, we shall be millions worse than we were at that enviable period. Such a request, had it been complied with a year ago, would have won the heart and soul of the Continent – but now it is too late, "The Rubicon is passed."

Besides, the taking up arms, merely to enforce the repeal of a pecuniary law, seems as unwarrantable by the divine law, and as repugnant to human feelings, as the taking up arms to enforce obedience thereto. The object, on either side, doth not justify the means; for the lives of men are too valuable to be cast away on such trifles. It is the violence which is done and threatened to our persons; the destruction of our property by an armed force; the invasion of our country by fire and sword, which conscientiously qualifies the use of arms: And the instant, in which such a mode of defence became necessary, all subjection to Britain ought to have ceased; and the independancy of America, should have been considered, as dating its æra from, and published by, *the first musket that was fired against her.* This line is a line of consistency; neither drawn by caprice, nor extended by ambition; but produced by a chain of events, of which the colonies were not the authors.

I shall conclude these remarks, with the following timely and well intended hints[.] We ought to reflect, that there are three different ways, by which an independancy may hereafter be effected; and that *one* of those *three,* will one day or other, be the fate of America, viz. By the legal voice of the people in Congress; by a military power; or by a mob: It may not always happen that our soldiers are citizens, and the multitude a body of reasonable men; virtue, as I have already remarked, is not hereditary, neither is it perpetual. Should an independancy be brought about by the first of those means, we have every opportunity and every encouragement before us, to form the noblest purest constitution on the face of the earth. We have it in our power to begin the world over again. A situation, similar to the present, hath not happened since the days of Noah until now. The birth-day of a new world is at hand, and a race of men, perhaps as numerous as all Europe contains, are to receive their portion of freedom from the event of a few months. The Reflexion is awful – and in this point of view, How trifling, how ridiculous, do the little, paltry cavellings, of a few weak or interested men appear, when weighed against the business of a world.

Should we neglect the present favorable and inviting period, and an Independance be hereafter effected by any other means, we must charge the consequence to ourselves, or to those rather, whose narrow and prejudiced souls, are habitually opposing the measure, without either inquiring or reflecting. There are reasons to be given in support of Independance, which men should rather privately think of, than be publicly told of. We ought not now to be debating whether we shall be independant or not, but, anxious to accomplish it on a firm, secure, and honorable basis, and uneasy rather that it is not yet began upon. Every day convinces us of its necessity. Even the Tories (if such beings yet remain among us) should, of all men, be the most solicitous to promote it; for, as the appointment of committees at first, protected them from popular rage, so, a wise and well established form of government, will be the only certain means of continuing it securely to them. *Wherefore*, if they have not virtue enough to be WHIGS, they ought to have prudence enough to wish for Independance.

In short, Independance is the only BOND that can tye and keep us together. We shall then see our object, and our ears will be legally shut against the schemes of an intriguing, as well, as a cruel enemy. We shall then too, be on a proper footing, to treat with Britain; for there is reason to conclude, that the pride of that court, will be less hurt by treating with the American states for terms of peace, than with those, whom she denominates, "rebellious subjects," for terms of accommodation. It is our delaying it that encourages her to hope for conquest, and our backwardness tends only to prolong the war. As we have, without any good effect therefrom, withheld our trade to obtain a redress of our grievances, let us *now* try the alternative, by *independantly* redressing them ourselves, and then offering to open the trade. The mercantile and reasonable part in England, will be still with us; because, peace *with* trade, is preferable to war *without* it. And if this offer be not accepted, other courts may be applied to.

On these grounds I rest the matter. And as no offer hath yet been made to refute the doctrine contained in the former editions of this pamphlet, it is a negative proof, that either the doctrine cannot be refuted, or, that the party in favour of it are too numerous to be opposed. WHEREFORE, instead of gazing at each other with suspicious or doubtful curiosity, let each of us, hold out to his neighbour the hearty hand of friendship, and unite in drawing a line, which, like an act of oblivion shall bury in forgetfulness every former dissention. Let the names of Whig and Tory be extinct; and let none other be heard among us, than those of *a good citizen, an open and resolute friend, and a virtuous supporter of the* RIGHTS *of* MANKIND *and of the* FREE AND INDEPENDANT STATES OF AMERICA.

To the Representatives of the Religious Society of the People called Quakers, or to so many of them as were concerned in publishing a late piece, entitled "The ANCIENT TESTIMONY and PRINCIPLES of the People called QUAKERS renewed, with Respect to the KING and GOVERNMENT, and touching the COMMOTIONS now prevailing in these and other parts of AMERICA addressed to the PEOPLE IN GENERAL."

THE Writer of this, is one of those few, who never dishonors religion either by ridiculing, or cavilling at any denomination whatsoever. To God, and not to man, are all men accountable on the score of religion. Wherefore, this epistle is not so properly addressed to you as a religious, but as a political body, dabbling in matters, which the professed Quietude of your Principles instruct you not to meddle with.

As you have, without a proper authority for so doing, put yourselves in the place of the whole body of the Quakers, so, the writer of this, in order to be on an equal rank with yourselves, is under the necessity, of putting himself in the place of all those, who, approve the very writings and principles, against which, your testimony is directed: And he hath chosen this singular situation, in order, that you might discover in him that presumption of character which you cannot see in yourselves. For neither he nor you can have any claim or title to *Political Representation.*

When men have departed from the right way, it is no wonder that they stumble and fall. And it is evident from the manner in which ye have managed your testimony, that politics, (as a religious body of men) is not your proper Walk; for however well adapted it might appear to you, it is, nevertheless, a jumble of good and bad put unwisely together, and the conclusion drawn therefrom, both unnatural and unjust.

The two first pages, (and the whole doth not make four) we give you credit for, and expect the same civility from you, because the love and desire of peace is not confined to Quakerism, it is the *natural,* as well as the religious wish of all denominations of men. And on this ground, as men laboring to establish an Independant Constitution of our own, do we exceed all others in our hope, end, and aim. *Our plan is peace for ever.* We are tired of contention with Britain, and can see no real end to it but in a final separation. We act consistently, because for the sake of introducing an endless and uninterrupted peace, do we bear the evils and burthens of the present day. We are endeavoring, and will steadily continue to endeavor, to separate and dissolve a connexion which hath already filled our land with blood; and which, while the name of it remains, will be the fatal cause of future mischiefs to both countries.

We fight neither for revenge nor conquest; neither from pride nor passion; we are not insulting the world with our fleets and armies, nor ravaging the globe for plunder. Beneath the shade of our own vines are we attacked; in our own houses, and on our own lands, is the violence committed against us. We view our enemies in the character of Highwaymen and Housebreakers, and having no defence for ourselves in the civil law, are obliged to punish them by the military one, and apply the sword, in the very case, where you have before now applied the halter —— Perhaps we feel for the ruined and insulted sufferers in all and every part of the continent, with a degree of tenderness which hath not yet made its way into some of your bosoms. But be ye sure that ye mistake not the cause and ground of your testimony. Call not coldness of soul, religion; nor put the *Bigot* in the place of the *Christian.*

O ye partial ministers of your own acknowledged principles. If the bearing arms be sinful, the first going to war must be more so, by all the difference between wilful attack and unavoidable defence. Wherefore, if ye really preach from conscience, and mean not to make a political hobbyhorse of your religion, convince the world thereof, by proclaiming your doctrine to our enemies, *for they likewise hear* ARMS. Give us proof of your sincerity by publishing it at St. James's, to the commanders in chief at Boston, to the Admirals and Captains who are piratically ravaging our coasts, and to all the murdering miscreants who are acting in authority under HIM whom ye profess to serve. Had ye the honest soul of[6] *Barclay* ye would preach repentance to *your* king; Ye would tell the Royal Wretch his sins, and warn him of eternal ruin. Ye would not spend your partial invectives against the injured and the insulted only, but, like faithful ministers, would cry aloud and *spare none.* Say not that ye are persecuted, neither endeavour to make us the authors of that reproach, which, ye are bringing upon yourselves; for we testify unto all men, that we do not complain against you because ye are *Quakers,* but because ye pretend to *be* and are NOT Quakers.

6. "Thou hast tasted of prosperity and adversity; thou knowest what it is to be banished thy native country, to be over-ruled as well as to rule, and sit upon the throne; and being oppressed thou hast reason to know how *hateful* the *oppressor* is both to God and man: If after all these warnings and advertisements, thou dost not turn unto the Lord with all thy heart, but forget him who remembered thee in thy distress, and give up thyself to follow lust and vanity, surely great will be thy condemnation.—Against which snare, as well as the temptation of those who may or do feed thee, and prompt thee to evil, the most excellent and prevalent remedy will be, to apply thyself to that light of Christ which shineth in thy conscience, and which neither can, nor will flatter thee, nor suffer thee to be at ease in thy sins."

Barclay's Address to Charles II.

Alas! it seems by the particular tendency of some part of your testimony, and other parts of your conduct, as if, all sin was reduced to, and comprehended in, *the act of bearing arms,* and that by the *people only.* Ye appear to us, to have mistaken party for conscience; because, the general tenor of your actions wants uniformity: And it is exceedingly difficult to us to give credit to many of your pretended scruples; because, we see them made by the same men, who, in the very instant that they are exclaiming against the mammon of this world, are nevertheless, hunting after it with a step as steady as Time, and an appetite as keen as Death.

The quotation which ye have made from Proverbs, in the third page of your testimony, that, "when a man's ways please the Lord, he maketh even his enemies to be at peace with him"; is very unwisely chosen on your part; because, it amounts to a proof, that the king's ways (whom ye are so desirous of supporting) do *not* please the Lord, otherwise, his reign would be in peace.

I now proceed to the latter part of your testimony, and that, for which all the foregoing seems only an introduction, viz.

"It hath ever been our judgment and principle, since we were called to profess the light of Christ Jesus, manifested in our consciences unto this day, that the s[e]tting up and putting down kings and governments, is God's peculiar prerogative; for causes best known to himself: And that it is not our business to have any hand or contrivance therein; nor to be busy bodies above our station, much less to plot and contrive the ruin, or overturn of any of them, but to pray for the king, and safety of our nation, and good of all men: That we may live a peaceable and quiet life, in all godliness and honesty; *under the government which God is pleased to set over us.*" – If these are *really* your principles, why do you not abide by them? Why do ye not leave that, which ye call God's Work, to be managed by himself? These very principles instruct you to wait with patience and humility, for the event of all public measures, and to receive *that event* as the divine will towards you. *Wherefore,* what occasion is there for your *political testimony* if you fully believe what it contains? And the very publishing it proves, that either, ye do not believe what ye profess, or have not virtue enough to practise what ye believe.

The principles of Quakerism have a direct tendency to make a man the quiet and inoffensive subject of any, and every government *which is set over him.* And if the setting up and putting down of kings and governments is God's peculiar prerogative, he most certainly will not be robbed thereof by us; wherefore, the principle itself leads you to approve of every thing, which ever happened, or may happen to kings as being his work. OLIVER

CROMWELL thanks you. CHARLES, then, died not by the hands of man; and should the present Proud Imitator of him, come to the same untimely end, the writers and publishers of the Testimony, are bound, by the doctrine it contains, to applaud the fact. Kings are not taken away by miracles, neither are changes in governments brought about by any other means than such as are common and human; and such as we are now using. Even the dispersion of the Jews, though foretold by our Saviour, was effected by arms. Wherefore, as ye refuse to be the means on one side, ye ought not to be meddlers on the other; but to wait the issue in silence; and unless ye can produce divine authority, to prove, that the Almighty who hath created and placed this *new* world, at the greatest distance it could possibly stand, east and west, from every part of the old, doth, nevertheless, disapprove of its being independent of the corrupt and abandoned court of Britain, unless I say, ye can shew this, how can ye on the ground of your principles, justify the exciting and stirring up the people "firmly to unite in the *abhorrence* of all such *writings,* and *measures,* as evidence a desire and design to break off the *happy* connexion we have hitherto enjoyed, with the kingdom of Great-Britain, and our just and necessary subordination to the king, and those who are lawfully placed in authority under him." What a slap of the face is here! the men, who in the very paragraph before, have quietly and passively resigned up the ordering, altering, and disposal of kings and governments, into the hands of God, are now, recalling their principles, and putting in for a share of the business. Is it possible, that the conclusion, which is here justly quoted, can any ways follow from the doctrine laid down? The inconsistency is too glaring not to be seen; the absurdity too great not to be laughed at; and such as could only have been made by those, whose understandings were darkened by the narrow and crabby spirit of a despairing political party; for ye are not to be considered as the whole body of the Quakers but only as a factional and fractional part thereof.

Here ends the examination of your testimony; (which I call upon no man to abhor, as ye have done, but only to read and judge of fairly;) to which I subjoin the following remark; "That the setting up and putting down of kings," most certainly mean, the making him a king, who is yet not so, and the making him no king who is already one. And pray what hath this to do in the present case? We neither mean to *set up* nor to *put down,* neither to *make* nor to *unmake,* but to have nothing to *do* with them. Wherefore, your testimony in whatever light it is viewed serves only to dishonor your judgement, and for many other reasons had better have been let alone than published.

First, Because it tends to the decrease and reproach of all religion what-ever, and is of the utmost danger to society, to make it a party in political disputes.

Secondly, Because it exhibits a body of men, numbers of whom dis-avow the publishing political testimonies, as being concerned therein and approvers thereof.

Thirdly, Because it hath a tendency to undo that continental harmony and friendship which yourselves by your late liberal and charitable dona-tions hath lent a hand to establish; and the preservation of which, is of the utmost consequence to us all.

And here without anger or resentment I bid you farewell. Sincerely wishing, that as men and christians, ye may always fully and uninterrupt-edly enjoy every civil and religious right; and be, in your turn, the means of securing it to others; but that the example which ye have unwisely set, of mingling religion with politics, *may be disavowed and reprobated by every inhabitant of* AMERICA.

FINIS.

[Selections from]

THE

CRISIS:

IN THIRTEEN NUMBERS.

WRITTEN DURING THE LATE WAR, [1]

By the AUTHOR of COMMON SENSE.

The Crisis.

NUMBER I.

December 23, 1776.

THESE are the times that try men's souls: The summer soldier and the sunshine patriot will, in this crisis, shrink from the service of his country; but he that stands it NOW, deserves the love and thanks of man and woman. Tyranny, like hell, is not easily conquered; yet we have this consolation with us, that the harder the conflict, the more glorious the triumph. What we obtain too cheap, we esteem too lightly: 'Tis dearness only that gives every thing its value. Heaven knows how to put a proper price upon its goods; and it would be strange indeed, if so celestial an article as FREEDOM

The Crisis: In Thirteen Numbers. Written During the Late War (Albany, NY: Charles R. & George Webster, 1792).

1. [Editors' note:] *The American Crisis,* as Paine originally titled his letters, was published as a series of sixteen individual pamphlets, the first thirteen between 1776 and 1777, and the last three between 1777 and 1783. Because of the difficulty in obtaining all the numbers from one publisher, for the sake of uniformity, the editors have chosen to use the first stand-alone collected edition of the letters, published in 1792, to reproduce numbers I–IV, IX, "The Crisis, Extraordinary," and XIII.

should not be highly rated. Britain, with an army to enforce her tyranny, has declared that she has a right (*not only to* TAX) but "*to* BIND *us in* ALL CASES WHATSOEVER," and if being *bound in that manner,* is not slavery, then is there not such a thing as slavery upon earth. Even the expression is impious, for so unlimited a power can belong only to GOD.

Whether the independence of the continent was declared too soon, or delayed too long, I will not now enter into as an argument; my own simple opinion is, that had it been eight months earlier, it would have been much better. We did not make a proper use of last winter, neither could we, while we were in a dependant state. However, the fault, if it were one, was all our own; we have none to blame but ourselves. But no great deal is lost yet; all that Howe has been doing for this month past is rather a ravage than a conquest, which the spirit of the Jerseys a-year ago would have quickly repulsed, and which time and a little resolution will soon recover.

I have as little superstition in me as any man living, but my secret opinion has ever been, and still is, that God Almighty will not give up a people to military destruction, or leave them unsupportedly to perish, who had so earnestly and so repeatedly sought to avoid the calamities of war, by every decent method which wisdom could invent. Neither have I so much of the infidel in me, as to suppose that HE has relinquished the government of the world, and given us up to the care of devils; and as I do not, I cannot see on what grounds the king of Britain can look up to Heaven for help against us: A common murderer, a highwayman, or a house-breaker has as good a pretence as he.

'Tis surprising to see how rapidly a panic will sometimes run through a country. All nations and ages have been subject to them: Britain has trembled like an ague at the report of a French fleet of flat bottomed boats; and in the fourteenth century the whole English army, after ravaging the kingdom of France, was driven back like men petrified with fear; and this brave exploit was performed by a few broken forces collected and headed by a woman, Joan of Arc. Would, that Heaven might inspire some Jersey maid to spirit up her countrymen, and save her fair fellow sufferers from ravage and ravishment! Yet panics, in some cases, have their uses, they produce as much good as hurt. Their duration is always short; the mind soon grows through them, and acquires a firmer habit than before. But their peculiar advantage is, that they are the touchstones of sincerity and hypocrisy, and bring things and men to light, which might otherwise have lain for ever undiscovered. In fact, they have the same effect on secret traitors, which an imaginary apparition would have upon a private murderer. They sift out the hidden thoughts of man, and hold them up in public to the world. Many a disguised tory has lately shewn his head, that shall penitentially solemnize with curses the day on which Howe arrived upon the Delaware.

As I was with the troops at Fort-Lee, and marched with them to the edge of Pennsylvania, I am well acquainted with many circumstances, which those, who lived at a distance, know but little or nothing of. Our situation there was exceedingly cramped, the place being on a narrow neck of land between the North-River and the Hackensack. Our force was inconsiderable, being not one fourth so great as Howe could bring against us. We had no army at hand to have relieved the garrison, had we shut ourselves up and stood on the defence. Our ammunition, light artillery, and the best part of our stores, had been removed upon the apprehension that Howe would endeavor to penetrate the Jerseys, in which case Fort-Lee could be of no use to us; for it must occur to every thinking man, whether in the army or not, that these kind of field forts are only for temporary purposes, and last in use no longer than the enemy directs his force against the particular object, which such forts are raised to defend. Such was our situation and condition at Fort-Lee on the morning of the 20th of November, when an officer arrived with information that the enemy with 200 boats had landed about seven or eight miles above: Major General Greene, who commanded the garrison, immediately ordered them under arms, and sent express to his Excellency General Washington at the town of Hackensack, distant by the way of the ferry six miles. Our first object was to secure the bridge over the Hackensack, which laid up the river between the enemy and us, about six miles from us, and three from them. General Washington arrived in about three quarters of an hour, and marched at the head of the troops towards the bridge, which place I expected we should have a brush for; however they did not choose to dispute it with us, and the greatest part of our troops went over the bridge, the rest over the ferry, except some which passed at a mill on a small creek, between the bridge and the ferry, and made their way through some marshy grounds up to the town of Hackensack, and there passed the river. We brought off as much baggage as the waggons could contain, the rest was lost. The simple object was to bring off the garrison, and to march them on till they could be strengthened by the Jersey or Pennsylvania militia, so as to be enabled to make a stand. We staid four days at Newark, collected in our out-posts with some of the Jersey militia, and marched out twice to meet the enemy on information of their being advancing, though our numbers were greatly inferior to theirs. Howe, in my little opinion, committed a great error in generalship in not throwing a body of forces off from Staten-Island through Amboy, by which means he might have seized all our stores at Brunswick, and intercepted our march into

Pennsylvania: But if we believe the power of hell to be limited, we must likewise believe that their agents are under some providential controul.

I shall not now attempt to give all the particulars of our retreat to the Delaware; suffice it for the present to say, that both officers and men, though greatly harrassed and fatigued, frequently without rest, covering, or provision, the inevitable consequences of a long retreat, bore it with a manly and a martial spirit. All their wishes were one, which was, that the country would turn out and help them to drive the enemy back. Voltaire has remarked that King William never appeared to full advantage but in difficulties and in action; the same remark may be made on General Washington, for the character fits him. There is a natural firmness in some minds which cannot be unlocked by trifles, but which, when unlocked, discovers a cabinet of fortitude; and I reckon it among those kind of public blessings, which we do not immediately see, that GOD hath blest him with uninterrupted health, and given him a mind that can even flourish upon care.

I shall conclude this paper with some miscellaneous remarks on the state of our affairs; and shall begin with asking the following question, Why is it that the enemy have left the New-England provinces, and made these middle ones the seat of war? The answer is easy: New-England is not infested with tories, and we are. I have been tender in raising the cry against these men, and used numberless arguments to shew them their danger, but it will not do to sacrifice a world to either their folly or their baseness. The period is now arrived, in which either they or we must change our sentiments, or one or both must fall. And what is a tory? Good GOD! what is he? I should not be afraid to go with an hundred whigs against a thousand tories, were they to attempt to get into arms. Every tory is a coward, for a servile, slavish, self-interested fear is the foundation of toryism; and a man under such influence, though he may be cruel, never can be brave.

But, before the line of irrecoverable separation be drawn between us, let us reason the matter together: Your conduct is an invitation to the enemy, yet not one in a thousand of you has heart enough to join him. Howe is as much deceived by you as the American cause is injured by you. He expects you will all take up arms, and flock to his standard with muskets on your shoulders. Your opinions are of no use to him, unless you support him personally, for 'tis soldiers, and not tories, that he wants.

I once felt all that kind of anger, which a man ought to feel, against the mean principles that are held by the tories: A noted one, who kept a tavern at Amboy, was standing at his door with as pretty a child in his hand, about eight or nine years old, as most I ever saw, and after speaking his mind as freely as he thought was prudent, finished with this unfatherly expression,

"*Well! give me peace in my day.*" Not a man lives on the continent but fully believes that a separation must some time or other finally take place, and a generous parent should have said, "*If there must be trouble, let it be in my day that my child may have peace;*" and this single reflection, well applied, is sufficient to awaken every man to duty. Not a place upon earth might be so happy as America. Her situation is remote from all the wrangling world, and she has nothing to do but to trade with them. A man may easily distinguish in himself between temper and principle, and I am as confident, as I am that GOD governs the world, that America will never be happy till she gets clear of foreign dominion. Wars, without ceasing, will break out till that period arrives, and the continent must in the end be conqueror; for though the flame of liberty may sometimes cease to shine, the coal never can expire.

America did not, nor does not want force; but she wanted a proper application of that force. Wisdom is not the purchase of a day, and it is no wonder that we should err at first setting off. From an excess of tenderness, we were unwilling to raise an army, and trusted our cause to the temporary defence of a well-meaning militia. A summer's experience has now taught us better; yet with those troops, while they were collected, we were able to set bounds to the progress of the enemy, and, thank GOD! they are again assembling. I always considered a militia as the best troops in the world for a sudden exertion, but they will not do for a long campaign. Howe, it is probable, will make an attempt on this city, should he fail on this side the Delaware, he is ruined; If he succeeds, our cause is not ruined. He stakes all on his side against a part on ours; admitting he succeeds, the consequence will be, that armies from both ends of the continent will march to assist their suffering friends in the middle states; for he cannot go every where, it is impossible. I consider Howe as the greatest enemy the tories have; he is bringing a war into their country, which, had it not been for him and partly for themselves, they had been clear of. Should he now be expelled, I wish with all the devotion of a Christian, that the names of whig and tory may never more be mentioned; but should the tories give him encouragement to come, or assistance if he come, I as sincerely wish that our next year's arms may expel them from the continent, and the congress appropriate their possessions to the relief of those who have suffered in well-doing. A single successful battle next year will settle the whole. America could carry on a two years war by the confiscation of the property of disaffected persons, and be made happy by their expulsion. Say not that this is revenge, call it rather the soft resentment of a suffering people, who, having no object in view but the GOOD of ALL, have staked their OWN ALL upon a seemingly doubtful event. Yet it is folly to argue against determined hardness; eloquence may strike the ear, and the language of sorrow draw forth the tear of compassion, but nothing can reach the heart that is steeled with prejudice.

Quitting this class of men, I turn with the warm ardor of a friend to those who have nobly stood, and are yet determined to stand the matter out: I call not upon a few, but upon all; not on THIS state or THAT state, but on EVERY state; up and help us; lay your shoulders to the wheel; better have too much force than too little, when so great an object is at stake. Let it be told to the future world, that in the depth of winter, when nothing but hope and virtue could survive, that the city and the country, alarmed at one common danger, came forth to meet and to repulse it. Say not, that thousands are gone, turn out your tens of thousands; throw not the burden of the day upon Providence, but *"shew your faith by your works,"* that God may bless you. It matters not where you live, or what rank of life you hold, the evil or the blessing will reach you all. The far and the near, the home counties and the back, the rich and the poor, will suffer or rejoice alike. The heart that feels not now, is dead: The blood of his children will curse his cowardice, who shrinks back at a time when a little might have saved the whole, and made *them* happy. I love the man that can smile in trouble, that can gather strength from distress, and grow brave by reflection. 'Tis the business of little minds to shrink; but he whose heart is firm, and whose conscience approves his conduct, will pursue his principles unto death. My own line of reasoning is to myself as strait and clear as a ray of light. Not all the treasures of the world, so far as I believe, could have induced me to support an offensive war, for I think it murder; but if a thief break into my house, burn and destroy my property, and kill or threaten to kill me, or those that are in it, and to *"bind me in all cases whatsoever,"* to his absolute will, am I to suffer it? What signifies it to me, whether he who does it, is a king or a common man; my countryman or not my countryman? whether it is done by an individual villain, or an army of them? If we reason to the root of things we shall find no difference; neither can any just cause be assigned why we should punish in the one case and pardon in the other. Let them call me rebel, and welcome, I feel no concern from it; but I should suffer the misery of devils, were I to make a whore of my soul by swearing allegiance to one whose character is that of a sottish, stupid, stubborn, worthless, brutish man. I conceive likewise a horrid idea in receiving mercy from a being, who at the last day shall be shrieking to the rocks and mountains to cover him, and fleeing with terror from the orphan, the widow, and the slain of America.

There are cases which cannot be overdone by language, and this is one. There are persons too who see not the full extent of the evil which threatens them, they solace themselves with hopes that the enemy, if they succeed, will be merciful. It is the madness of folly to expect mercy from those who have refused to do justice; and even mercy, where conquest is the object, is only a trick of war: The cunning of the fox is as murderous as the violence of the wolf; and we ought to guard equally against both. Howe's first object is partly by threats and partly by promise, to terrify or seduce the people to deliver up their arms, and receive mercy. The ministry recommended the same plan to Gage, and this is what the tories call making their peace; *"a peace which passeth all understanding" indeed!* A peace which would be the immediate forerunner of a worse ruin than any we have yet thought of. Ye men of Pennsylvania, do reason upon these things! Were the back counties to give up their arms, they would fall an easy prey to the Indians, who are all alarmed: This perhaps is what some tories would not be sorry for. Were the home counties to deliver up their arms, they would be exposed to the resentment of the back counties, who would then have it in their power to chastise their defection at pleasure. And were any one state to give up its arms, THAT state must be garrisoned by all Howe's army of Britons and Hessians to preserve it from the anger of the rest. Mutual fear is a principal link in the chain of mutual love, and woe be to that state that breaks the compact. Howe is mercifully inviting you to barbarous destruction, and men must be either rogues or fools that will not see it. I dwell not upon the powers of imagination, I bring reason to your ears; and in language as plain as A, B, C, hold up truth to your eyes.

I thank GOD that I fear not. I see no real cause for fear. I know our situation well, and can see the way out of it. While our army was collected, Howe dared not risk a battle, and it is no credit to him that he decamped from the White Plains, and waited a mean opportunity to ravage the defenceless Jerseys; but it is great credit to us, that, with a handful of men, we sustained an orderly retreat for near an hundred miles, brought off our ammunition, all our field-pieces, the greatest part of our stores, and had four rivers to pass. None can say that our retreat was precipitate, for we were near three weeks in performing it, that the country might have time to come in. Twice we marched back to meet the enemy and remained out till dark. The sign of fear was not seen in our camp, and had not some of the cowardly and disaffected inhabitants spread false alarms through the country, the Jerseys had never been ravaged. Once more we are again collected and collecting; our new army at both ends of the continent is recruiting fast, and we shall be able to open the next campaign with sixty thousand men, well armed and cloathed. This is our situation, and who will may know it. By perseverance and fortitude we have the prospect of a glorious issue; by cowardice and submission, the sad choice of a variety of evils – a ravaged country – a depopulated city – habitations without safety, and slavery without hope – our homes turned into barracks and bawdy-houses for Hessians, and a future race to provide for whose fathers we shall doubt of. Look on this picture and weep over it! and if there yet remains one thoughtless wretch who believes it not, let him suffer it unlamented.

The Crisis.

NUMBER II.

Philadelphia, January 13, 1777.

To Lord Howe.

"What's in the name of LORD that I should fear,
To bring my grievance to the public ear."

CHURCHILL.

UNIVERSAL empire is the prerogative of a writer. His concerns are with all mankind, and though he cannot command their obedience, he can assign them their duty. The Republic of Letters is more ancient than monarchy, and of far higher character in the world, than the vassal court of Britain; he that rebels against reason is a real rebel, but he that in defence of reason, rebels against tyranny, has a better title to "DEFENDER OF THE FAITH," than George the third.

As a military man your lordship may hold out the sword of war, and call it the *"Ultima Ratio Regum:" The last reason of kings;* we in return can show you the sword of justice, and call it, "The best scourge of tyrants." The first of these two may threaten, or even frighten, for a while, and cast a sickly langor over an insulted people, but reason will soon recover the debauch, and restore them again to tranquil fortitude. Your lordship, I find, has now commenced author, and published a proclamation; I have published a crisis; as they stand, they are the antipodes of each other; both cannot rise at once, and one of them must descend:–And so quick is the revolution of things, that your lordship's performance, I see, has already fallen many degrees from its first place, and is now just visible on the edge of the political horizon.

It is surprising to what pitch of infatuation blind folly and obstinacy will carry mankind, and your lordship's drowsy proclamation is a proof that it does not even quit them in their sleep. Perhaps you thought America too was taking a nap, and therefore chose, like satan to Eve, to whisper the delusion softly, lest you should awaken her. This continent, sir, is too extensive to sleep all at once, and too watchful, even in its slumbers, not to startle at the unhallowed foot of an invader. You may issue your proclamations, and welcome, for we have learned to "reverence ourselves," and scorn the insulting ruffian that employs you. America, for your deceased brother's sake, would gladly have shown you respect, and it is a new aggravation to her feelings, that Howe should be forgetful, and raise his sword against those, who at their own charge raised a monument to his brother. But your master has commanded, and you have not enough of nature left to refuse. Surely! there must be something strangely degenerating in the love of monarchy, that can so completely wear a man down to an ingrate, and make him proud to lick the dust that kings have trod upon. A few more years, should you survive them, will bestow on you the title of 'an old man.' And in some hour of future reflection you may probably find the fitness of Woolsey's desparing penitence–"had I served my God as faithfully as I have served my king, he would not thus have forsaken me in my old age."

The character you appear to us in is truly ridiculous. Your friends, the tories, announced your coming with high descriptions of your unlimited powers; but your proclamation has given them the lie, by shewing you to be a commissioner without authority. Had your powers been ever so great, they were nothing to us, farther than we pleased; because we had the same right which other nations had, to do what we thought was best. "*The* UNITED STATES *of* AMERICA" will sound as pompously in the world or in history, as "The kingdom of Great Britain;" the character of *general Washington,* will fill a page with as much lustre as that of lord Howe: and the *congress* have as much right to command the *king and parliament* of London, to desist from legislation, as *they* or *you* have to command the congress. Only suppose how laughable such an edict would appear from us, and then, in that merry mood, do but turn the tables upon yourself, and you will see how your proclamation is received here. Having thus placed you in a proper position in which you may have a full view of folly, and learn to despise it, I hold up to you, for that purpose, the following quotation from your own lunarian proclamation – "And we (lord Howe and general Howe) do command (and in his majesty's name forsooth) all such persons as are assembled together, under the name of general or provincial congressess, committees, conventions or other associations, by whatever name or names known or distinguished, to desist and cease from all such treasonable actings and doings."

You introduce your proclamation by referring to your declarations of the 14th of July and 19th of September. In the last of these, you sunk yourself below the character of a private gentleman. That I may not seem to accuse you unjustly, I shall state the circumstance: By a verbal invitation of yours, communicated to congress by general Sullivan, then a prisoner on his parole, you signified your desire of conferring with some members of that body as private gentlemen. It was beneath the dignity of the American Congress to pay any regard to a message that at best was but a genteel afront, and had too much of the ministerial complection of tampering with private persons; and which might probably have been the case, had the gentlemen who were deputed on the business, possessed that kind of easy virtue which an English courtier is so truly distinguished by. Your request however was complied with, for honest men are naturally more tender of their civil than their political fame. The interview ended as every sensible man thought it would; for your lordship knows, as well as the writer of the Crisis, that it is impossible for the king of England to promise the repeal, or even the revisal of any acts of parliament; wherefore, on your part, you had nothing to say, more than to request, in the room of demanding, the entire surrender of the continent; and then, if that was complied with, to promise that the inhabitants should escape with their lives. This was the upshot of the conference. You informed the conferees that you were two months in soliciting these powers. We ask, What powers? for as commissioner you have none. If you mean the power of pardoning, it is an oblique proof that your master was determined to sacrifice all before him; and that you were two months in dissuading him from his purpose. Another evidence of his savage obstinacy! From your own account of the matter we may justly draw these two conclusions: first, that you serve a monster; and secondly, that never was a commissioner sent on a more foolish errand than yourself. This plain language may perhaps sound uncouthly to an ear vitiated by courtly refinements; but words were made for use, and the fault lies in deserving them, or the abuse in applying them unfairly.

Soon after your return to New-York, you published a very illiberal and unmanly hand bill against the congress; for it was certainly stepping out of the line of common civility first to screen your national pride by soliciting an interview with them as private gentlemen, and in the conclusion to endeavor to deceive the multitude by making an hand bill attack on the whole body of the congress; you got them together under one name, and abused them under another. But the king you serve, and the cause you support, afford you so few instances of acting the gentleman, that out of pity to your situation the congress pardoned the insult by taking no notice of it.

You say in that hand bill, "that they, the congress, disavowed every purpose for reconciliation not consonant with their extravagant and inadmissible claim of independence." Why, God bless me! what have you to do with our independence? We ask no leave of yours to set it up; we ask no money of yours to support it; we can do better without your fleets and armies than with them; you may soon have enough to do to protect yourselves without being burdened with us. We are very willing to be at peace with you, to buy of you and sell to you, and, like young beginners in the world, to work for our own living; therefore, why do you put yourselves out of cash, when we know you cannot spare it, and we do not desire you to run into debt? I am willing, sir, you should see your folly in every view I can place it, and for that reason descend sometimes to tell you in jest what I wish you to see in earnest. But to be more serious with you, why do you say, "their independence?" To set you right, sir, we tell you, that the independency is ours, not theirs. The congress were authorised by every state on the continent to publish it to all the world, and in so doing are not to be considered as the inventors, but only as the heralds that proclaimed it, or the office from which the sense of the people received a legal form; and it was as much as any or all their heads were worth, to have treated with you on the subject of submission under any name whatever. But we know the men in whom we have trusted; can England say the same of her parliament?

I come now more particularly to your proclamation of the 30th of November last. Had you gained an entire conquest over all the armies of America, and then put forth a proclamation, offering (what you call) mercy, your conduct would have had some specious show of humanity; but to creep by surprise into a province, and there endeavor to terrify and seduce the inhabitants from their just allegiance to the rest by promises, which you neither meant, nor were able to fulfil, is both cruel and unmanly: Cruel in its effects; because, unless you can keep all the ground you have marched over, how are you, in the words of your proclamation to secure to your proselytes "the enjoyment of their property?" What are to become either of your new adopted subjects, of your old friends the tories, in Burlington, Bordentown, Trenton, Mountholly, and many other places, where you proudly lorded it for a few days, and then fled with the precipitation of a pursued thief? What, I say, are to become of those wretches? What are to become of those who went over to you from this city and state? What more can you say to them than "Shift for yourselves?" Or what more can they hope for than to wander like vagabonds over the face of the earth? You may now tell them to take their leave of America, and all that once was theirs. Recommend them, for consolation, to your master's court; there perhaps they may make a shift to live on the scraps of some dangling parasite, and choose companions among thousands like themselves. A traitor is the foulest fiend on earth!

In a political sense we ought to thank you for thus bequeathing estates to the continent; we shall soon, at this rate, be able to carry on a war without expence, and grow rich by the ill policy of lord Howe, and the generous defection of the tories. Had you set your foot into this city you would have bestowed estates upon us which we never thought of, by bringing forth traitors we were unwilling to suspect. But these men, you'll say, "are his majesty's most faithful subjects;" let that honor then be all their fortune, and let his majesty take them to himself.

I am now thoroughly disgusted with them; they live in ungrateful ease, and bend their whole minds to mischief. It seems as if God had given them over to a spirit of infidelity, and that they are open to conviction in no other line but that of punishment. It is time to have done with taring, feathering, carting, and taking securities for their future good behaviour; every sensible man must feel a conscious shame at seeing a poor fellow hawked for a show about the streets, when it is known he is only the tool of some principal villain, biased into his offence by the force of false reasoning, or bribed thereto through sad necessity. We dishonor ourselves by attacking such trifling characters, while greater ones are suffered to escape; 'tis our duty to find *them* out, and their proper punishment would be to exile them from the continent for ever. The circle of them is not so great as some imagine; the influence of a few have tainted many who are not naturally corrupt. A continual circulation of lies among those who are not much in the way of hearing them contradicted, will in time pass for truth; and the crime lies not in the believer but the inventor. I am not for declaring war against every man that appears not so warm as myself: Difference of constitution, temper, habit of speaking, and many other things will go a great way in fixing the outward character of a man, yet simple honesty may remain at bottom. Some men have naturally a military turn, and can brave hardships and the risk of life with a cheerful face; others have not; no slavery appears to them so great as the fatigue of arms, and no terror so powerful as that of personal danger: What can we say? We cannot alter nature, neither ought we to punish the son because the father begot him in a cowardly mood. However, I believe most men have more courage than they know of, and that a little at first is enough to begin with. I knew the time when I thought that the whistling of a cannon ball would have frightened me almost to death: but I have since tried it, and find I can stand it with as little discomposure, and, I believe, with a much easier conscience than your lordship. The same dread would return to me again were I in your situation, for my solemn belief of your cause is, that it is hellish and damnable, and under that conviction every thinking man's heart *must* fail him.

From a concern that a good cause should be dishonored by the least disunion among us, I said in my former paper, No. I. "That should the enemy now be expelled, I wish, with all the sincerity of a Christian, that the names of whig and tory might never more be mentioned," but there is a knot of men among us of such a venomous cast, that they will not admit even one's good wishes to act in their favor. Instead of rejoicing that Heaven had, as it were, providentially preserved this city from plunder and destruction, by delivering so great a part of the enemy into our hands with so little effusion of blood, they stubbornly affected to disbelieve it till within an hour, nay, half an hour, of the prisoners arriving; and the Quakers put forth a testimony, dated the 20th of December, signed "John Pemberton," declaring their attachment to the British government[2]. These men are continually harping on the great sin of *our* bearing arms, but the king of Britain may lay waste the world in blood and famine, and they, poor fallen souls, have nothing to say.

In some future paper I intend to distinguish between the different kind of persons who have been denominated tories; for this I am clear in, that all are not so who have been called so, nor all men whigs who were once thought so; and as I mean not to conceal the name of any true friend when there shall be occasion to mention him, neither will I that of an enemy who ought to be known, let his rank, station or religion be what it may. Much pains have been taken by some to set your lordship's private character in an amiable light, but as it has chiefly been done by men who know nothing

---

2. I have ever been careful of charging offences upon whole societies of men, but as the paper referred to is put forth by an unknown set of men, who claim to themselves the right of representing the whole; and while the whole society of Quakers admit its validity by a silent acknowledgment, it is impossible that any distinction can be made by the public; and the more so, because the New-York paper of the 30th of December, printed by permission of our enemies, says that "the Quakers begin to speak openly of their attachment to the British constitution." We are certain that we have many friends among them, and wish to know them.

about you, and who are no ways remarkable for their attachment to us, we
have no just authority for believing it. George the third was imposed upon
us by the same arts, but TIME, at length, has done him justice, and the
same fate may probably attend your lordship. Your avowed purpose here, is
to kill, conquer, plunder, pardon, and enslave; and the ravages of your army
through the Jerseys have been marked with as much barbarism as if you
had openly professed yourself the prince of ruffians; not even the appearance of humanity has been preserved either on the march or the retreat of
your troops; no general order that I could ever learn, has ever been issued to
prevent or even forbid your troops from robbery, wherever they came, and
the only instance of justice, if it can be called such, which has distinguished
you for impartiality, is, that you treated and plundered all alike; what could
not be carried away has been destroyed, and mahogany furniture has been
deliberately laid on the fire for fuel, rather than the men should be fatigued
with cutting wood[3]. There was a time when the whigs confided much in
your supposed candor, and the tories rested themselves in your favor; the
experiments have now been made, and failed; in every town, nay every cottage, in the Jerseys, where your arms have been, is a testimony against you.
How you may rest under this sacrifice of character I know not, but this I
know, that you sleep and rise with the daily curses of thousands upon you;
perhaps the misery which the tories have suffered by your proffered mercy
may give them some claim to their country's pity, and be in the end the best
favor you could shew them.

In a folio general-order book belonging to colonel Rhol's battalion,
taken at Trenton, and now in the possession of the council of safety for
this state, the following barbarous order is frequently repeated, "His excellency the COMMANDER IN CHIEF orders, that all inhabitants who shall
be found with arms, not having an officer with them, shall be immediately
taken and hung up." How many you may thus have privately sacrificed we
know not, and the account can only be settled in another world. Your treatment of prisoners, in order to distress them to enlist into your infernal service, is not to be equalled by any instance in Europe. Yet this is the humane
lord Howe and his brother, whom the tories and their three quarter kindred
the Quakers, or some of them at least, have been holding up for patterns of
justice and mercy!

3. As some people may doubt the truth of such wanton destruction, I think it
necessary to inform, that one of the people called Quakers, who lives at Trenton,
gave me this information at the house of Mr. Michael Hutchinson (one of the same
profession) who lives near to Trenton ferry, on the Pennsylvania side, Mr. Hutchinson being present.

A bad cause will ever be supported by bad means, and bad men, and whoever will be at the pains of examining strictly into things, will find that one and the same spirit of oppression and impiety, more or less, governs through your whole party in both countries: Not many days ago I accidentally fell in company with a person of this city, noted for espousing your cause, and on my remarking to him, "that it appeared clear to me, by the late providential turn of affairs, that GOD Almighty was visibly on our side," he replied, "We care nothing for that, you may have HIM, and welcome; if we have but enough of the devil on our side we shall do." However carelessly this might be spoken matters not, 'tis still the insensible principle that directs all your conduct, and will at last most assuredly deceive and ruin you.

If ever a nation was mad and foolish, blind to its own interest and bent on its own destruction, it is Britain. There are such things as national sins, and though the punishment of individuals may be reserved to *another* world, national punishment can only be inflicted in *this* world. Britain, as a nation, is in my inmost belief the greatest and most ungrateful offender against GOD on the face of the whole earth: Blessed with all the commerce she could wish for, and furnished by a vast extension of dominion, with the means of civilizing both the eastern and western world, she has made no other use of both than proudly to idolize her own, "Thunder," and rip up the bowels of whole countries for what she could get; – like Alexander she has made war her sport, and inflicted misery for prodigality sake. The blood of India is not yet repaid, nor the wretchedness of Africa yet requited. Of late she has enlarged her list of national cruelties, by her butcherly destruction of the Caribbs of St. Vincents, and in returning an answer by the sword to the meek prayer for *"Peace, liberty and safety."* These are serious things, and whatever a foolish tyrant, a debauched court, a trafficking legislature or a blinded people may think, the national account with Heaven must some day or other be settled: All countries have sooner or later been called to their reckoning; the proudest empires have sunk when the balance was struck; and Britain, like an individual penitent, must undergo her day of sorrow, and the sooner it happens to her the better. As I wish it over, I wish it to come, but withal wish that it may be as light as possible.

Perhaps your lordship has no taste for serious things; by your connections in England I should suppose not: Therefore I shall drop this part of the subject, and take it up in a line in which you will better understand me.

By what means, may I ask, do you expect to conquer America? If you could not effect it in the summer, when our army was less than yours, nor in the winter when we had none, how are you to do it? In point of generalship you have been outwitted, and in point of fortitude outdone; your advantages turn out to your loss, and show us that it is in our power to ruin you by gifts: Like a game of drafts, we can move out of *one* square to let you come in, in order that we may afterwards take two or three for one; and as we can always keep a double corner for ourselves, we can always prevent a total defeat. You cannot be so insensible, as not to see that we have two to one the advantage of you, because we conquer by a drawn game, and you lose by it. Burgoyne might have taught your lordship this knowledge; he has been long a student in the doctrine of chances.

I have no other idea of conquering countries than by subduing the armies which defend them: Have you done this, or can you do this? If you have not, it would be civil in you to let your proclamations alone for the present; otherwise, you will ruin more tories by your grace and favor than you will whigs by your arms.

Were you to obtain possession of this city, you would not know what to do with it more than to plunder it. To hold it in the manner you hold New-York, would be an additional dead weight upon your hands; and if a general conquest is your object, you had better be without the city than with it. When you have defeated all our armies, the cities will fall into your hands of themselves; but to creep into them in the manner you got into Princetown, Trenton, &c. is like robbing an orchard in the night before the fruit be ripe, and running away in the morning. Your experiment in the Jerseys is sufficient to teach you that you have something more to do than barely to get into other people's houses; and your new converts, to whom you promised all manner of protection, and seduced into new guilt by pardoning them from their former virtues, must begin to have a very contemptible opinion both of your power and your policy. Your authority in the Jerseys is now reduced to the small circle which your army occupies, and your proclamation is no where else seen unless it be to be laughed at. The mighty subduers of the continent are retreated into a nutshell, and the proud forgivers of our sins are fled from those they came to pardon; and all this at a time when they were dispatching vessel after vessel to England with the great news of every day. In short, you have managed your Jersey expedition so very dextrously that the dead only are conquerors, because none will dispute the ground with them.

In all the wars you have formerly been concerned in, you had only armies to contend with; in this case you have both an army and a country to combat with. In former wars, the countries followed the fate of their capitals; Canada fell with Quebec, and Minorca with Port Mahon or St. Philips; by subduing those, the conquerors opened a way into, and became masters of the country: Here it is otherwise; if you get possession of a city here, you are obliged to shut yourselves up in it, and can make no other use of it, than to spend your country's money in. This is all the advantage you have drawn from New-York; and you would draw less from Philadelphia, because it requires more force to keep it, and is much farther from the sea. A pretty figure you and the tories would cut in this city, with a river full of ice, and a town full of fire; for the immediate consequence of your getting here would be, that you would be cannonaded out again and the tories be obliged to make good the damage; and this, sooner or later, will be the fate of New-York.

I wish to see the city saved, not so much from military as from natural motives. 'Tis the hiding-place of women and children, and lord Howe's proper business is with our armies. When I put all the circumstances together which ought to be taken, I laugh at your notion of conquering America. Because you lived in a little country, where an army might run over the whole in a few days, and where a single company of soldiers might put a multitude to the route, you expected to find it the same here. It is plain that you brought over with you all the narrow notions you were bred up with, and imagined that a proclamation in the king's name was to do great things; but Englishmen always travel for knowledge, and your lordship, I hope, will return, if you return at all, much wiser than you came.

We may be surprised by events we did not expect, and in that interval of recollection you may gain some temporary advantage: Such was the case a few weeks ago, but we soon ripen again into reason, collect our strength, and while you are preparing for a triumph we come upon you with a defeat. Such it has been, and such it would be were you to try it an hundred times over. Were you to garrison the places you might march over, in order to secure their subjection, (for remember you can do it by no other means) your army would be like a stream of water running to nothing. By the time you reached from New-York to Virginia, you would be reduced to a string of drops not capable of hanging together; while we, by retreating from state to state, like a river turning back upon itself, would acquire strength in the same proportion as you lost it, and in the end be capable of overwhelming you. The country in the meantime would suffer, but 'tis a day of suffering, and we ought to expect it. What we contend for is worthy the affliction we may go through. If we get but bread to eat, and any kind of raiment to put on, we ought not only to be contented, but thankful. More than *that* we ought not to look for, and less than *that* Heaven has not yet suffered us to want. He that would sell his birthright for a little *salt,* is as worthless as he who sold it for *porridge* without salt. And he that would part with it for a gay coat, or a *plain* coat, ought for ever to be a slave in buff. What are salt, sugar and finery to the inestimable blessings of "Liberty and safety?" Or what are the inconveniencies of a few months to the tributary bondage of ages? The meanest peasant in America, blest with these sentiments, is a happy man compared with a New-York tory; he can eat his morsel without repining, and when he has done, can sweeten it with a repast of wholesome air; he can take his child by the hand and bless it without feeling the conscious shame of neglecting a parent's duty.

In publishing these remarks I have several objects in view.

On your part they are, to expose the folly of your pretended authority as a commissioner; the wickedness of your cause in general; and the impossibility of your conquering us at any rate. On the part of the public my meaning is, to shew them their true and solid interest; to encourage them to their own good, to remove the fears and falsities which bad men had spread, and weak men had encouraged; and to excite in all men a love for union, and a cheerfulness for duty.

I shall submit one more case to you respecting your conquest of this country, and then proceed to new observations:

Suppose our armies in every part of the continent were immediately to disperse, every man to his home, or where else he might be safe, and engage to re-assemble again on a certain future day; it is clear that you would then have no army to contend with, yet you would be as much at a loss in that case as you are now; you would be afraid to send your troops in parties over the continent, either to disarm, or prevent us from assembling, lest they should not return; and while you kept them together, having no army of ours to dispute with, you could not call it a conquest; you might furnish out a pompous page in the London gazette or the New-York paper, but when we returned at the appointed time, you would have the same work to do you had at first.

It has been the folly of Britain to suppose herself more powerful than she really is, and by that means has arrogated to herself a rank in the world she is not entitled to: for more than this century past she has not been able to carry on a war without foreign assistance. In Marlborough's campaigns, and from that day to this, the number of German troops and officers assisting her have been about equal with her own; ten thousand Hessians were sent to England last war to protect her from a French invasion; and she would have cut but a poor figure in her Canadian and West-Indian expeditions, had not America been lavish both of her money and men to help her along. The only instance in which she was engaged singly, that I can recollect, was against the rebellion in Scotland in forty-five and forty-six, and in that, out of three battles, she was twice beaten, till by thus reducing their numbers (as we shall yours) and taking a supply ship that was coming to Scotland with cloaths, arms and money (as we have often done) she was at last enabled to defeat them. England was never famous by land; her officers have generally been suspected of cowardice, have more of the air of a dancing-master than a soldier, and by the sample we have taken prisoners we give the preference to ourselves. Her strength of late has laid in her extravagance; but as her finances and her credit are now low, her sinews in that line begin to fail fast. As a nation she is the poorest in Europe; for were the whole kingdom, and all that is in it, to be put up to sale like the estate of a bankrupt, it would not fetch as much as she owes; yet this thought-less wretch must go to war, and with the avowed design too of making us beasts of burden, to support her in riot and debauchery, and to assist her afterwards in distressing those nations who are now our best friends. This ingratitude may suit a tory, or the unchristian peevishness of a fallen Quaker, but none else.

'Tis the unhappy temper of the English to be pleased with any war, right or wrong, be it but successful; but they soon grow discontented with ill fortune, and it is an even chance that they are as clamorous for peace next summer, as the king and his ministers were for war last winter. In this natural view of things, your lordship stands in a very ugly critical situation: Your whole character is staked upon your laurels; if they wither you wither with them; if they flourish, you cannot live long to look at them; and at any rate, the black account hereafter is not far off. What lately appeared to us misfortunes, were only blessings in disguise; and the seeming advantages on your side have turned out to our profit. Even our loss of this city, as far as we can see, might be a principal gain to us: The more surface you spread over, the thinner you will be, and the easier wiped away; and our consolation under that apparent disaster would be, that the estates of the tories would become securities for the repairs. In short, there is no old ground we can fail upon, but some new foundation rises again to support us. "We have put, sir, our hands to the plough, and cursed be he that looketh back."

Your king, in his speech to parliament last spring, declared to them, "That he had no doubt but the great force they had enabled him to send to America, would effectually reduce the rebellious colonies." It has not, neither can it; but it has done just enough to lay the foundation of its own next year's ruin. You are sensible that you left England in a divided dis-tracted state of politics, and, by the command you had here, you became a principal prop in the court party; their fortunes rest on yours; by a single express you can fix their value with the public, and the degree to which their spirits shall rise or fall; they are in your hands as stock, and you have the secret of the ally with you. Thus situated and connected, you become the unintentional mechanical instrument of your own and their overthrow. The king and his ministers put conquest out of doubt, and the credit of both depended on the proof. To support them in the interim, it was necessary you should make the most of every thing; and we can tell by Hugh Gaine's New-York paper what the complexion of the London gazette is. With such a list of victories the nation cannot expect you will ask new supplies; and to confess your want of them, would give the lie to your triumphs, and impeach the king and his ministers of treasonable deception. If you make the necessary demand at home, your party sinks; if you make it not you sink yourself; to ask it now is too late, and to ask it before was too soon, and unless it arrive quickly will be of no use. In short, the part you have to act, cannot be acted; and I am fully persuaded that all you have to trust to is, to do the best you can with what force you have got, or little more. Though we have greatly exceeded you in point of generalship and bravery of men, yet, as a people, we have not entered into the full soul of enterprize; for I, who know England and the disposition of the people well, am confident, that it is easier for us to effect a revolution there, than you a conquest here; a few thousand men landed in England with the declared design of deposing the present king, bringing his ministers to trial, and setting up the duke of Gloucester in his stead, would assuredly carry their point, while you were groveling here ignorant of the matter. As I send all my papers to England, this, like COMMON SENSE, will find its way there; and tho' it may put one party on their guard, it will inform the other and the nation in general of our design to help them.

Thus far, sir, I have endeavored to give you a picture of present affairs: You may draw from it what conclusions you please. I wish as well to the true prosperity of England as you can, but I consider *Independence as America's natural right and interest,* and never could see any real disservice it would be to Britain. If an English merchant receives an order, and is paid for it, it signifies nothing to him who governs the country. This is my creed of politics. If I have any where expressed myself overwarmly, 'tis from a fixt immovable hatred I have, and ever had, to cruel men and cruel measures. I have likewise an aversion to monarchy, as being too debasing to the dignity of man; but I never troubled others with my notions till very lately, nor ever published a syllable in England in my life. What I write is pure nature, and my pen and my soul have ever gone together. My writings I have always given away, reserving only the expence of printing and paper, and sometimes not even that. I never courted either fame or interest, and my manner of life, to those who know it, will justify what I say. My study is to be useful, and if your lordship loves mankind as well as I do, you would, seeing you cannot conquer us, cast about and lend your hand towards accomplishing a peace. Our independence, with God's blessing, we will maintain against all the world; but as we wish to avoid evil ourselves, we wish not to inflict it on others. I am never over inquisitive into the secrets of the cabinet, but I have some notion, that if you neglect the present opportunity, that it will not be in our power to make a separate peace with you afterwards; for whatever treaties or alliances we form, we shall most faithfully abide by; wherefore you may be deceived if you think you can make it with us at any time. A lasting independent peace is my wish, end and aim; and to accomplish that, "*I pray God the*" Americans "*may never be defeated, and I trust while they have good officers, and are well commanded,*" and willing to be commanded, "*that they* NEVER WILL."

The Crisis.

NUMBER III.

Philadelphia, April 19, 1777.

IN the progress of politics, as in the common occurrences of life, we are not only apt to forget the ground we have travelled over, but frequently neglect to gather up experience as we go. We expend, if I may so say, the knowledge of every day on the circumstances that produce it, and journey on in search of new matter and new refinements: But as it is pleasant, and sometimes useful, to look back, even to the first periods of infancy, and trace the turns and windings through which we have passed, so we may likewise derive many advantages by halting a while in our political career, and taking a review of the wondrous complicated labyrinth of little more than yesterday.

Truly, may we say, that never did man grow old in so short a time! We have crowded the business of an age into the compass of a few months, and have been driven through such a rapid succession of things, that, for the want of leisure to think, we unavoidably wasted knowledge as we came, and have left nearly as much behind us as we brought with us: But the road is yet rich with the fragments, and, before we fully lose sight of them, will repay us for the trouble of stopping to pick them up.

Were a man to be totally deprived of memory, he would be incapable of forming any just opinion; every thing about him would seem a chaos; he would have even his own history to ask from every one; and by not knowing how the world went on in his absence, he would be at a loss to know how it *ought* to go on when he recovered, or rather, returned to it again. In like manner, though in a less degree, a too great inattention to past occurrences retards and bewilders our judgment in every thing; while on the contrary, by comparing what is past with what is present, we frequently hit on the true character of both, and become wise with very little trouble. It is a kind of countermarch, by which we get into the rear of time, and mark the movements and meaning of things as we make our return. There are certain circumstances, which, at the time of their happening, are kind of riddles, and as every riddle is to be followed by its answer, so those kind of circumstances will be followed by their events, and those events are always the true solution. A considerable space of time may lapse between, and unless we continue our observations from the one to the other, the harmony of them will pass away unnoticed: But the misfortune is, that partly from the pressing necessity of some instant things, and partly from the impatience of our own tempers, we are frequently in such a hurry to make out the meaning of every thing as fast as it happens, that we thereby never truly understand it; and not only start new difficulties to ourselves by so doing, but, as it were, embarrass Providence in her good designs.

I have been civil in stating this fault on a large scale, for, as it now stands, it does not appear to be levelled against any particular set of men; but were it to be refined a little farther, it might afterwards be applied to the tories with a degree of striking propriety: Those men have been remarkable for drawing sudden conclusions from single facts. The least apparent mishap on our side, or the least seeming advantage on the part of the enemy, have determined with them the fate of a whole campaign. By this hasty judgment they have converted a retreat into a defeat; mistook generalship for error; while every little advantage purposely given the enemy, either to weaken their strength by dividing it, embarrass their councils by multiplying their objects, or to secure a greater post by the surrender of a less, has been instantly magnified into a conquest. Thus, by quartering ill policy upon ill principles, they have frequently promoted the cause they designed to injure, and injured that which they intended to promote.

It is probable the campaign may open before this number comes from the press. The enemy have long lain idle and amused themselves with carrying on the war by proclamations only. While they continue their delay our strength increases, and were they to move to action now, it is a circumstantial proof they have no reinforcement coming; wherefore, in either case, the comparative advantage will be ours. Like a wounded disabled whale, they want only time and room to die in; and though in the agony of their exit, it may be unsafe to live within the flapping of their tail, yet every hour shortens their date and lessens their power of mischief. If any thing happens while this number is in the press, it will afford me a subject for the last pages of it. At present I am tired of waiting; and as neither the enemy, nor the state of politics, have *yet* produced any thing new, I am thereby left in the field of general matter undirected by any striking or particular object. This Crisis, therefore, will be made up rather of variety than novelty, and consist more of things useful than things wonderful.

The success of the cause, the union of the people, and the means of supporting and securing both, are points which cannot be too much attended to. He who doubts of the former is a desponding coward, and he who wilfully disturbs the latter is a traitor. Their characters are easily fixt, and under these short descriptions I leave them for the present.

One of the greatest degrees of sentimental union which America ever knew, was in denying the right of the British parliament "*to bind the colonies in all cases whatsoever.*" The declaration is in its form an almighty one, and is the loftiest stretch of arbitrary power that ever one set of men, or one country claimed over another. Taxation was nothing more th[a]n the putting the declared right into practice; and this failing, recourse was had to arms, as a means to establish both the right *and* the practice, or to answer a worse purpose, which will be mentioned in the course of this number. And in order to repay themselves the expence of an army, and to profit by their own injustice, the colonies were, by another law, declared to be in a state of actual rebellion, and of consequence all property therein would fall to the conquerors.

The colonies, on their part, FIRST, denied the right; SECONDLY, they suspended the use of taxable articles, and petitioned against the practice of taxation: and these failing, they THIRDLY, defended their property by force, as soon as it was forcibly invaded, and in answer to the declaration of rebellion and non-protection, published their declaration of independence and right of self-protection.

These, in a few words, are the different stages of the quarrel; and the parts are so intimately and necessarily connected with each other as to admit of no separation. A person, to use a trite phrase, must be a whig or a tory in the lump. His feeling, as a man, may be wounded; his charity, as a Christian, may be moved; but his political principles must go through all the cases on one side or the other. He cannot be a whig in *this* stage, and a tory in *that.* If he says he is against the united independence of the continent, he is to all intents and purposes against her in all the rest; because THIS LAST comprehends the whole. And he may just as well say, that Britain was right in declaring us rebels; right in taxing us; and right in declaring her *"right to bind the colonies in all cases whatsoever."* It signifies nothing what neutral ground, of his own creating, he may skulk upon for shelter, for the quarrel in no stage of it hath afforded any such ground; and either we or Britain are absolutely right or absolutely wrong through the whole.

Britain, like a gamester nearly ruined, hath now put all her losses into one bet, and is playing a desparate game for the total. If she wins it, she wins from *me* my life; she wins the continent as the forfeited property of rebels; the right of taxing those that are left as reduced subjects; and the power of binding them slaves: And the single die which determines this unparalled event is, whether we support our independence or she overturn it. This is coming to the point at once. Here is the touch-stone to try men by. *He that is not a supporter of the independent states of America, in the same degree that his religious and political principles would suffer him to support the government of any other country, of which he called himself a subject, is, in the American sense of the word,* A TORY; *and the instant that he endeavors to bring his toryism into practice, he becomes* A TRAITOR. The first can only be detected by a general test, and the law hath already provided for the latter.

It is unnatural and impolitic to admit men who would root up our independence to have any share in our legislation, either as electors or representatives; because the support of our independence rests in a great measure on the vigor and purity of our public bodies. Would Britain, even in time of peace, much less in war, suffer an election to be carried by men who professed themselves to be her subjects, or allow such to sit in parliament? Certainly not.

But there are a certain species of tories with whom conscience or principle hath nothing to do, and who are so from avarice only. Some of the first fortunes in the continent, on the part of the whigs, are staked on the issue of our present measures. And shall disaffection only be rewarded with security? Can any thing be a greater inducement to a miserly man, than the hope of making his mammon safe? And though the scheme be fraught with every character of folly, yet, so long as he supposes, that by doing nothing materially criminal against America on one part, and by expressing his private disapprobation against independence, as palliative with the enemy on the other part, he stands thereby in a safe line between both, while, I say, this ground be suffered to remain, craft and the spirit of avarice will point it out, and men will not be wanting to fill up this most contemptible of all characters.

These men, ashamed to own the sordid cause from whence their disaffection springs, add thereby meanness to meanness, by endeavoring to shelter themselves under the mask of hypocrisy; that is, they had rather be thought to be tories from *some kind of principle,* than tories by having *no principle at all.* But till such time as they can show some real reason, natural, political or conscientious, on which their objections to independence are founded, we are not obliged to give them credit for being tories of the first stamp, but must set them down as tories of the last.

In the second number of the Crisis I endeavored to shew the impossibility of the enemy making any conquest of America, that nothing was wanting on our part but patience and perseverance, and that, with these virtues, our success, as far as human speculation could discern, seemed as certain as fate. But as there are many among us, who, influenced by others, have regularly gone back from the principles they once held, in proportion as we have gone forward; and as it is the unfortunate lot of many a good man to live within the neighborhood of disaffected ones; I shall therefore, for the sake of confirming the one and recovering the other, endeavor, in the space of a page or two, to go over some of the leading principles in support of independence. It is a much pleasanter task to prevent vice than to punish it; and however our tempers may be gratified by resentment, or our national expences eased by forfeited estates, harmony and friendship is nevertheless the happiest condition a country can be blest with.

The principal arguments in support of independence may be comprehended under the four following heads.

First, – The natural right of the continent to independence.
Secondly, – Her interest in being independent.
Thirdly, – The necessity, – and
Fourthly, – The moral advantages arising therefrom.

I. The natural right of the continent to independence, is a point which never yet was called in question. It will not even admit of a debate. To deny such a right, would be a kind of atheism against nature: And the best answer to such an objection would be, *"The fool hath said in his heart, there is no God."*

II. The interest of the continent in being independent is a point as clearly right as the former. America, by her own internal industry, and unknown to all the powers of Europe, was at the beginning of the dispute, arrived at a pitch of greatness, trade and population, beyond which it was the interest of Britain not to suffer her to pass, lest she should grow too powerful to be kept subordinate. She began to view this country with the same uneasy malicious eye, with which a covetous guardian would view his ward whose estate he had been enriching himself by for twenty years, and saw him just arriving at manhood. And America owes no more to Britain for her present maturity, than the ward would to his guardian for being twenty-one years of age. That America hath flourished *at the time* she was under the government of Britain, is true; but there is every natural reason to believe, that had she been an independent country from the first settlement thereof, uncontrouled by any foreign power, free to make her own laws, regulate and encourage her own commerce, she had by this time been of much greater worth than now. The case is simply this, The first settlers in the different colonies were left to shift for themselves, unnoticed and unsupported by any European government; but as the tyranny and persecution of the old world daily drove numbers to the new, and, as by the favor of Heaven on their industry and perseverance, they grew into importance, so, in a like degree, they became an object of profit to the greedy eyes of Europe. It was impossible in this state of infancy, however thriving and promising, that they could resist the power of any armed invader that should seek to bring them under his authority. In this situation Britain thought it worth her while to claim them, and the continent received and acknowledged the claimer. It was, in reality, of no very great importance who was her master, seeing, that from the force and ambition of the different powers of Europe she must, till she acquired strength enough to assert her own right, acknowledge some one. As well, perhaps, Britain as another; and it might have been as well to have been under the states of Holland as any. The same hopes of engrossing and profiting by her trade, by not oppressing it too much, would have operated alike with any master, and produced to the colonies the same effects. The clamor of protection, likewise, was all a farce; because, in order to make *that* protection necessary, she must first, by her own quarrels create us enemies. Hard terms, indeed!

To know whether it be the interest of the continent to be independent, we need only ask this easy, simple question: Is it the interest of a man to be a boy all his life? The answer to one will be the answer to both. America hath been one continued scene of legislative contention from the first king's representative to the last; and this was unavoidably founded in the natural opposition of interest between the old country and the new. A governor sent from England, or receiving his authority therefrom, ought never to have been considered in any other light than that of a genteel commissioned spy, whose private business was information, and his public business a kind of civilized oppression. In the first of these characters he was to watch the tempers, sentiments and disposition of the people, the growth of trade, and the increase of private fortunes; and in the latter, to suppress all such acts of the assemblies, however beneficial to the people, which did not directly or indirectly throw some increase of power or profit into the hands of those who sent him.

America, till now, could never be called a *free country,* because her legislation depended on the will of a man three thousand miles distant, whose interest was in opposition to ours, and who, by a single "no," could forbid what law he pleased.

The freedom of trade, likewise, is, to a trading country, an article of such vast importance, that the principal source of wealth depends upon it; and it is impossible that any country can flourish, as it otherwise might do, whose commerce is engrossed, cramped and fettered by the laws and mandates of another—yet these evils, and more than I can here enumerate, the continent has suffered by being under the government of Great-Britain. By an independence we clear the whole at once—put an end to the business of unanswered petitions and fruitless remonstrances—exchange Britain for Europe—shake hands with the world—live at peace with mankind—and trade to any market where we best can buy and sell.

III. The necessity, likewise, of being independent, even before it was declared, became so evident and important, that the continent ran the risk of being ruined every day she delayed it. There were reasons to believe that Britain would endeavor to make an European matter of it, and rather than lose the whole, would dismember it like Poland, and dispose of her several claims to the highest bidder. Genoa, failing in her attempts to reduce Corsica, made a sale of it to the French, and such traffics have been common in the old world. We had at that time no Ambassador in any part of Europe, to counteract her negociations, and by that means she had the range of every foreign court uncontradicted on our part. We even knew nothing of the treaty for the Hessians till it was concluded, and the troops ready to embark. Had we been independent before, we had probably prevented her obtaining them. We had no credit abroad, because of our rebellious dependency. Our ships could claim no protection in foreign ports, because we afforded them no justifiable reason for granting it to us. The calling ourselves subjects, and at the same time fighting against the power we acknowledged, was a dangerous precedent to all Europe. If the grievances justified our taking up arms, they justified our separation; if they did not justify our separation, neither could they justify our taking up arms. All Europe was interested in reducing us as rebels, and all Europe (or the greatest part at least) is interested in supporting us as independent states. At home our condition was still worse: Our currency had no foundation, and the fall of it would have ruined whig and tory alike. We had no other law than a kind of moderated passion; no other civil power than an honest mob; and no other protection than the temporary attachment of one man to another. Had independence been delayed a few months longer, this continent would have been plunged into irrecoverable confusion: Some violent for it, some against it, till in the general cabal the rich would have been ruined, and the poor destroyed. It is to independence that every tory owes the present safety he lives in; for by *that,* and *that only,* we emerged from a state of dangerous suspense, and became a regular people.

The necessity likewise of being independent, had there been no rupture between Britain and America, would in a little time have brought one on. The encreasing importance of commerce, the weight and perplexity of legislation, and the entangled state of European politics, would daily have shewn to the continent the impossibility of continuing subordinate; for, after the coolest reflections on the matter, *this must* be allowed, that Britain was too jealous of America, to govern it justly; too ignorant of it, to govern it well; and too distant from it, to govern it at all.

IV. But, what weigh most with all men of serious reflection are the MORAL ADVANTAGES arising from independence: War and desolation are become the trades of the old world; and America neither could, nor can be under the government of Britain without becoming a sharer of her guilt, and a partner in all the dismal commerce of death. The spirit of duelling, extended on a national scale, is a proper character for European wars. They have seldom any other motive than pride, or any other object than fame. The conquerors and the conquered are generally ruined alike, and the chief difference at last is, that the one marches home with his honors, and the other without them. 'Tis the natural temper of the English to fight for a feather, if they suppose *that feather* to be an affront; and America, without the right of asking why, must have abetted in every quarrel and abided by its fate. It is a shocking situation to live in, that one country must be brought into all the wars of another, whether the measure be right or wrong, or whether she will or not; yet this, in the fullest extent, was, and ever would be, the unavoidable consequence of the connection. Surely! the Quakers forgot their own principles, when in their late testimony they called *this connection* with these military and miserable appendages hanging to it, *"The happy constitution."*

Britain, for centuries past, has been nearly fifty years out of every hundred at war with some power or other. It certainly ought to be a conscientious as well as political consideration with America, not to dip her hands in the bloody work of Europe. Our situation affords us a retreat from their cabals, and the present happy union of the states bids fair for extirpating the future use of arms from one quarter of the world; yet such have been the ir-religious politics of the present leaders of the Quakers, that, for the sake of they scarce knew what, they would cut off every hope of such a blessing by tying this continent to Britain, like Hector to the chariot-wheel of Achilles, to be dragged through all the miseries of endless European wars.

The connection, viewed from this ground, is distressing to every man who has the feelings of humanity. By having Britain for our master, we be-came enemies to the greatest part of Europe, and they to us; and the conse-quence was war inevitable. By being our own masters, independent of any foreign one, we have Europe for our friends, and the prospect of an endless peace among ourselves. Those who were advocates for the British govern-ment over these colonies, were obliged to limit both their arguments and their ideas to the period of an European peace only: The moment Britain became plunged in war, every supposed convenience to us vanished away, and all we could hope for was *not to be ruined*. Could this be a desirable condition for a young country to be in?

Had the French pursued their fortune immediately after the defeat of Braddock last war this city and province had then experienced the woful calamities of being a British subject. A scene of the same kind might hap-pen again; for America, considered as a subject to the crown of Britain, would ever have been the seat of war and the bone of contention between the two powers.

On the whole, if the future expulsion of arms from one quarter of the world be a desirable object to a peaceable man; – if the freedom of trade to every part of it can engage the attention of a man of business; – if the sup-port or fall of millions of currency can affect our interest; – if the entire possession of estates, by cutting off the lordly claims of Britain over the soil, deserves the regard of landed property; – and if the right of making our own laws, uncontrouled by royal or ministerial spies or mandates, be worthy our care as freemen; – then are all men interested in the support of independence; and may he that supports it not, be driven from the blessing, and live unpitied beneath the servile sufferings of scandalous subjection!

We have been amused with the tales of ancient wonders; we have read, and wept over, the histories of other nations; applauded, censured or pitied, as their cases affected us. – The fortitude and patience of the sufferers – the justness of their cause – the weight of their oppressions and oppressors – the object to be saved or lost – with all the consequences of a defeat or a conquest – have, in the hour of sympathy, bewitched our hearts and chained it to their fate: But where is the power that ever made war upon petitioners? Or where is the war on which a world was staked till now?

We may not, perhaps, be wise enough to make all the advantages we ought of our independence; but they are, nevertheless, marked and presented to us with every character of GREAT and GOOD, and worthy the hand of Him who sent them. I look through the present trouble to a time of tranquility, when we shall have it in our power to set an example of peace to all the world. Were the Quakers really impressed and influenced by the quiet principles they profess to hold, they would, however they might disapprove the means, be the first of all men to approve of INDEPENDENCE, because, by separating from the cities of Sodom and Gomorrah, it affords an opportunity, never given to man before, of carrying their favorite principle of peace into general practice, by establishing governments that shall hereafter exist without wars. Oh ye fallen, cringing priest and Pemberton-ridden people! what more can we say of ye than that a religious Quaker is a valuable character, and a political Quaker a real Jesuit.

Having thus gone over some of the principal points in support of independence, I must now request the reader to return back with me to the period when it first began to be a public doctrine, and to examine the progress it has made among the various classes of men. The era I mean to begin at, is the breaking out of hostilities, April 19th, 1775. Until this event happened, the continent seemed to view the dispute as a kind of law-suit for a matter of right, litigating between the old country and the new; and she felt the same kind and degree of horror, as if she had seen an oppressive plaintiff, at the head of a band of ruffians, enter the court, while the cause was before it, and put the judge, the jury, the defendant and his council to the sword. Perhaps a more heart-felt convulsion never reached a country with the same degree of power and rapidity before, and never may again. Pity for the sufferers, mixt with indignation at the violence and heightened with apprehensions of undergoing the same fate, made the affair of Lexington the affair of the continent. Every part of it felt the shock, and all vibrated together. A general promotion of sentiment took place: Those who had drank deeply into whiggish principles, that is, the right and necessity not only of opposing, but wholly setting aside the power of the crown as soon as it became practically dangerous (for in theory it was always so) stept into the first stage of independence; while another class of whigs, equally sound in principle, but not so sanguine in enterprize, attached themselves the stronger to the cause and fell close in with the rear of the former; their partition was a mere point. Numbers of the moderate men, whose chief fault, *at that time,* arose from their entertaining a better opinion of Britain than she deserved, convinced now of their mistake, gave her up and publicly declared themselves good whigs. While the tories, seeing it was no longer a laughing matter, either sunk into silent obscurity, or contented themselves with coming forth and abusing General Gage: Not a single advocate appeared to justify the action of that day; it seemed to appear to every one with the same magnitude, struck every one with the same force, and created in every one the same abhorrence. From this period we may date the growth of independence.

If the many circumstances, which happened at this memorable time, be taken in one view, and compared with each other, they will justify a conclusion which seems not to be attended to, I mean a fixt design in the king and ministry of driving America into arms, in order that they might be furnished with a pretence for seizing the whole continent, as the immediate property of the crown. A noble plunder for hungry courtiers!

It ought to be remembered, that the first petition from the congress was at this time unanswered on the part of the British king. That the motion, called lord North's motion, of the 20th of February, 1775, arrived in America the latter end of March. This motion was to be laid by the several governors, then in being, before the assembly of each province; and the first assembly before which it was laid, was the assembly of Pennsylvania in *May* following. This being a just state of the case, I then ask, why were hostilities commenced between the time of passing the resolve in the house of commons, of the 20th of February, and the time of the assemblies meeting to deliberate upon it? Degracing and infamous as that motion was, there is, nevertheless, reason to believe that the king and his adherents were afraid the colonies would agree to it, and lest they should, took effectual care they should not, by provoking them with hostilities in the interim. They had not the least doubt at that time of conquering America at one blow; and what they expected to get by a conquest being infinitely greater than any thing they could hope to get either by taxation or accommodation, they seemed determined to prevent even the possibility of hearing each other, lest America should disappoint their greedy hopes of the whole, by listening even to their own terms. On the one hand they refused to hear the petition of the continent, and on the other hand took effectual care the continent should not hear them.

That the motion of the 20th of February and the orders for commencing hostilities were both concerted by the same person or persons, and not the latter by General Gage, as was falsely imagined at first, is evident from an extract of a letter of his to administration, read among other papers in the house of commons; in which he informs his masters, *That though their idea of his disarming certain counties was a right one, yet it required him to be master of the country, in order to enable him to execute it.* This was prior to the commencement of hostilities, and consequently before the motion of the 20th of February could be deliberated on by the several assemblies.

Perhaps it may be asked, why was the motion past, if there was at the same time a plan to aggravate the Americans not to listen to it? Lord North assigned one reason himself, which was, *a hope of dividing them.* This was publicly tempting them to reject it; that if, in case, the injury of arms should fail of provoking them sufficiently, the insult of such a declaration might fill it up. But by passing the motion and getting it afterwards rejected in America, it enabled them, in their wretched idea of politics, among other things, to hold up the colonies to foreign powers with every possible mark of disobedience and rebellion. They had applied to those powers not to supply the continent with arms, ammunition, &c. and it was necessary they should incense them against us, by assigning on their own part some seeming reputable reason why. By dividing, it had a tendency to weaken the states, and likewise to perplex the adherents of America in England. But the principal scheme, and that which has marked their character in every part of their conduct, was a design of precipitating the colonies into a state which they might afterwards deem rebellion, and under that pretence put an end to all future complaints, petitions or remonstrances, by seizing the whole at once. They had ravaged one part of the globe, till it could glut them no longer; their prodigality required new plunder, and through the East-India article TEA they hoped to transfer their rapine from that quarter of the world to this. – Every designed quarrel has its pretence; and the same barbarian avarice accompanied the *plant* to America, which ruined the country which produced it.

That men never turn rogues without turning fools, is a maxim, sooner or later, universally true. The commencement of hostilities, being in the beginning of April, was, of all times the worst chosen: The congress were to meet the tenth of May following, and the distress the continent felt at this unparalleled outrage gave a stability to *that body,* which no other circumstance could have done. It suppressed too, all inferior debates, and bound them together by a necessitous affection, without giving them time to differ upon trifles. The suffering likewise, softened the whole body of the people into a degree of pliability, which laid the principal foundation-stone of union, order and government; and which, at any other time, might only have fretted and then faded away unnoticed and unimproved: But Providence, who best knows how to time her misfortunes as well as her immediate favors, chose this to be the time: And who dares dispute it?

It did not seem the disposition of the people at this crisis to heap petition upon petition, while the former remained unanswered: The measure, however, was carried in congress, and a second petition was sent; of which I shall only remark, that it was submissive even to a dangerous fault, because the prayer of it appealed solely to, what it called, the prerogative of the crown, while the matter in dispute was confessed to be constitutional. But even this petition, flattering as it was, was still not so harmonious as the chink of cash, and consequently not sufficiently grateful to the tyrant and his ministry. From every circumstance it is evident, that it was the determination of the British court to have nothing to do with America but to conquer it fully and absolutely. They were certain of success, and the field of battle was to be the only place of treaty. I am confident there are thousands and tens of thousands in America who wonder *now* they should ever think otherwise; but the sin of that day was the sin of civility, yet it operated against our present good in the same manner that a civil opinion of the devil would against our future peace.

Independence was a doctrine scarce and rare even towards the conclusion of the year seventy-five: All our politics had been founded on the hope or expectation of making the matter up—a hope, which, though general on the side of America, had never entered the head or heart of the British court. Their hope was conquest and confiscation. Good Heavens! what volumes of thanks does America owe to Britain! What infinite obligations to the tool, that fills, with paradoxical vacancy, the throne! Nothing but the sharpest essence of villany, compounded with the strongest distillation of folly, could have produced a menstruum that would have effected a separation. The congress in seventy-four administered an abortive medicine to independence, by prohibiting the importation of goods, and the succeeding congress rendered the dose still more dangerous by continuing it. Had independence been a settled system with America (as Britain has advanced) she ought to have *doubled* her importation, and prohibited in some degree her exportation. And this single circumstance is sufficient to acquit America before any jury of nations of having a continental plan of independence in view: A charge, which had it been true, would have been honorable, but is so grossly false, that either the amazing ignorance, or the wilful dishonesty, of the British court is effectually proved by it.

The second petition like the first produced no answer; it was scarcely acknowledged to be received; the British court were too determined in their villany even to act it artfully, and in their rage for conquest neglected the necessary subtilties for obtaining it. They might have divided, distracted and played a thousand tricks with us, had they been as cunning as they were cruel.

This last indignity gave a new spring to independence. Those who knew the savage obstinacy of the king and the jobbing gambling spirit of the court predicted the fate of the petition, as soon as it was sent from America; for the men being known, their measures were easily foreseen. As politicians we ought not so much to ground our hope on the reasonableness of the thing we ask, as on the reasonableness of the person of whom we ask it; Who would expect discretion from a fool, candor from a tyrant, or justice from a villain?

As every prospect of accommodation seemed now to fail fast, men began to think seriously on the matter; and their reason being thus stript of the false hope which had long encompassed it, became approachable by fair debate; yet still the bulk of the people hesitated; they startled at the novelty of independence, without once considering that our getting into arms at first was a more extraordinary novelty, and that all other nations had gone through the work of independence before us. They doubted, likewise, the ability of the continent to support it, without reflecting, that it required the same force to obtain an accommodation by arms as an independence. If the one was acquirable, the other was the same; because, to accomplish either, it was necessary that our strength should be too great for Britain to subdue; and it was too unreasonable to suppose, that with the power of being masters, we should submit to be servants[4]. Their caution at this

4. In this state of political suspense the pamphlet *Common Sense* made its appearance, and the success it met with does not become me to mention. Dr. Franklin, Mr. Samuel and John Adams were severally spoken of as the supposed author. I had not, at that time, the pleasure either of personally knowing or being known to the two last gentlemen. The favor of Dr. Franklin's friendship I possessed in England, and my introduction to this part of the world was through his patronage. I happened, when a school boy, to pick up a pleasing natural history of Virginia, and my inclination from that day of seeing the western side of the Atlantic never left me. In October, seventy-five, Dr. Franklin proposed giving me such materials as were in his hands, towards completing a history of the present transactions, and seemed desirous of having the first volume out the next spring. I had then formed the outlines of Common Sense, and finished nearly the first part; and as I supposed the Doctor's design in getting out a history, was to open the new year with a new system, I expected to surprise him with a production on that subject, much earlier than he thought of; and without informing him of what I was doing, got it ready for the press as fast as I conveniently could, and sent him the first pamphlet that was printed off.

time, was exceedingly misplaced; for if they were able to defend their property and maintain their rights by arms, they consequently were able to defend and support their independence; and in proportion as these men saw the necessity and rightness of the measure, they honestly and openly declared and adopted it, and the part they have acted since, has done them honor, and fully established their characters. Error in opinion has this peculiar advantage with it, that the foremost point of the contrary ground may at any time be reached by the sudden exertion of a thought; and it frequently happens in sentimental differences that some striking circumstance, or some forcible reason, quickly conceived, will effect in an instant what neither argument nor example could produce in an age.

I find it impossible in the small compass I am limited to, to trace out the progress which independence has made on the minds of the different classes of men, and the several reasons by which they were moved. With some, it was a passionate abhorrence against the king of England and his ministry, as a set of savages and brutes; and these men, governed by the agony of a wounded mind, were for trusting every thing to hope and Heaven, and bidding defiance at once. With others, it was a growing conviction that the scheme of the British court was to create, ferment and drive on a quarrel for the sake of confiscated plunder: Men of this cast ripened into independence in proportion as the evidence increased. While a third class, conceived it was the true interest of America, internally and externally, to be her own master, gave their support to independence, step by step, as they saw her abilities to maintain it enlarge. With many, it was a compound of all these reasons; while those who were too callous to be reached by either, remained, and still remain tories.

The *legal necessity* of being independent, with several collateral reasons, is pointed out in an elegant, masterly manner, in a charge to the grand jury for the district of Charlestown, by the hon. William Henry Drayton, esq. chief justice of South-Carolina. The performance, and the address of the convention of New-York, are pieces, in my humble opinion, of the first rank in America.

The principal causes why independence has not been so universally supported as it ought, are *fear* and *indolence,* and the causes why it has been opposed, are, *avarice, downright villany,* and *lust of personal power.* There is not such a being in America, as a tory from conscience; some secret defect or other is interwoven in the character of all those, be they men or women, who can look with patience on the brutality, luxury and debauchery of the British court, and the violations of their army here. A woman's virtue must fit very lightly on her who can even hint a favorable sentiment in their behalf. It is remarkable that the whole race of prostitutes in New-York were tories; and the schemes for supporting the tory cause, in this city, for which several are now in gaol, and one hanged, were concerted and carried on in common baudy-houses, assisted by those who kept them.

The connection between vice and meanness is a fit object for satire, but when the satire is a fact, it cuts with the irresistible power of a diamond. If a Quaker, in defence of his just rights, his property and the chastity of his house, takes up a musket, he is expelled the meeting; but the present king of England, who seduced and took into keeping a sister of their society, is reverenced and supported with repeated testimonies, while the friendly noodle from whom she was taken (and who is now in this city) continues a drudge in the service of his rival, as if proud of being cuckolded by a creature called a king.

Our support and success depend on such a variety of men and circumstances, that every one, who does but wish well, is of some use: There are men who have a strange awkwardness to arms, yet have hearts to risk every shilling in the cause, or in support of those who have better talents for defending it. Nature, in the arrangement of mankind, has fitted some for every service in life: Were all soldiers, all would starve and go naked, and were none soldiers, all would be slaves. As *disaffection* to independence is the badge of a tory, so *affection* to it is the mark of a whig; and the different services of the whigs down from those who nobly contribute every thing, to those who have nothing to render but their wishes, tend all to the same centre, though with different degrees of merit and ability. The larger we make the circle, the more we shall harmonize, and the stronger we shall be. All we want to shut out, is disaffection, and, *that excluded,* we must accept from each other such duties as we are best fitted to bestow. A narrow system of politics, like a narrow system of religion, is calculated only to sour the temper, and live at variance with mankind.

All we want to know in America is simply this, who is for independence, and who is not? Those who are for it, will support it, and the remainder will undoubtedly see the reasonableness of their paying the charges; while those who oppose or seek to betray it, must expect the more rigid fate of the gaol and the gibbit. There is a bastard kind of generosity, which, by being extended to all men, is as fatal to society, on one hand, as the want of true generosity is on the other. A lax manner of administering justice, falsely termed moderation, has a tendency both to dispirit public virtue, and promote the growth of public evils. Had the late committee of safety taken cognizance of the last testimony of the Quakers, and proceeded against such delinquents as were concerned therein, they had, probably prevented the treasonable plans which have been concerted since. When one villain is suffered to escape, it encourages another to proceed, either from a hope of escaping likewise, or an apprehension that we dare not punish. It has been a matter of general surprise, that no notice was taken of the incendiary publication of the Quakers, of the 20th of November last: A publication evidently intended to promote sedition and treason, and encourage the enemy, who were then within a day's march of this city, to proceed on and possess it. I here present the reader with a memorial, which was laid before the board of safety a few days after the testimony appeared. Not a member of that board, that I conversed with, but expressed the highest detestation of the perverted principles and conduct of the Quaker junto, and that the board would take the matter up; notwithstanding which, it was suffered to pass away unnoticed, to the encouragement of new acts of treason, the general danger of the cause, and the disgrace of the state.

To the honorable the council of safety of the state of Pennsylvania.

At a meeting of a reputable number of the inhabitants of the city of Philadelphia, impressed with a proper sense of the justice of the cause which this continent is engaged in, and animated with a generous fervor for supporting the same, it was resolved, that the following be laid before the board of safety:

"We profess liberality of sentiment to all men; with this distinction *only,* that those who do *not* deserve it, would become wise and *seek* to deserve it. We hold the pure doctrine of universal liberty of conscience, and conceive it our duty to endeavor to secure that sacred right to others, as well as to defend it for ourselves; for we undertake not to judge of the religious rectitude of tenets, but leave the whole matter to Him who made us.

"We persecute no man, neither will we abet in the persecution of any man for religion sake; our common relation to others, being that of fellow-citizens and fellow-subjects of one civil community; and in this line of connection we hold out the right hand of fellowship to all men. But we should conceive ourselves to be unworthy members of the FREE AND IN-DEPENDENT STATES OF AMERICA, were we unconcernedly to see or suffer any treasonable wound, public or private, directly or indirectly, to be given against the peace and safety of the same. We enquire not into the rank of the offenders, nor their religious persuasion; we have no business with either, our part being only to find them out, and exhibit them to justice.

"A printed paper, dated the 20th of November, and signed "*John Pemberton,*" whom we suppose to be an inhabitant of this city, has lately been dispersed abroad, a copy of which accompanies this. Had the framers and publishers of that paper conceived it their duty, to exhort the youth, and others, of their society, to a patient submission under the present trying visitations, and humbly to wait the event of Heaven towards them, they had therein shewn a Christian temper, and we had been silent; but the anger and political virulence with which their instructions are given, and the abuse with which they stigmatize all ranks of men, not thinking like themselves, leave no doubt on our minds from what spirit their publication proceeded: And it is disgraceful to the pure cause of truth, that men can dally with words of the most sacred import, and play them as mechanically off as if religion consisted only in contrivance. We know of no instance in which the Quakers have been compelled to bear arms, or do any thing which might strain their conscience; wherefore their advice, "to withstand and refuse to submit to the arbitrary instructions and ordinances of men," appear to us a false alarm, and could only be treasonably calculated to gain favor with our enemies, when they were seemingly on the brink of invading this state, or, what is still worse, to weaken the hands of our defence, that their entrance into this city might be made practical and easy.

"We disclaim all tumult and disorder in the punishment of offenders; and wish to be governed, not by temper but by reason, in the manner of treating them. We are sensible that our cause has suffered by the two following errors; first, by ill-judged lenity to traiterous persons in some cases; and secondly, by only a passionate treatment of them in others. For the future we disown both, and wish to be steady in our proceedings, and serious in our punishments.

"Every state in America has by the repeated voice of its inhabitants, directed and authorised the continental congress to publish a formal declaration of independence of, and separation from, the oppressive king and parliament of Great Britain; and we look on every man an enemy who does not in some line or other give his assistance towards supporting the same; at the same time we consider the offence to be heightened to a degree of unpardonable guilt, when such persons, under the shew of religion, endeavor, either by writing, speaking, or otherwise, to subvert, overturn, or bring reproach upon the independence of this continent as declared by congress.

"The publishers of the paper, signed "John Pemberton," have called in a loud and passionate manner on their friends and connections, "to withstand and refuse" obedience to whatever "instructions or ordinances" may be published, not warranted by (what they call) "that happy constitution under which they and others long enjoyed tranquility and peace." If this be not treason, we know not what may properly be called by that name.

"To us it is a matter of surprise and astonishment, that men with the word *"peace, peace"* continually on their lips should be so fond of living under, and supporting a government, and at the same time calling it *"happy,"* which is never better pleased than when at war–that hath filled India with carnage and famine–Africa with slavery–and tampered with Indians and Negroes to cut the throats of the freemen of America. We conceive it a disgrace to this state to harbor or wink at such palpable hypocrisy. But as we seek not to hurt the hair of any man's head, when we can make ourselves safe without, we wish such persons to restore peace to themselves and us, by removing themselves to some part of the king of Great Britain's dominions, as by that means they may live unmolested by us or we by them; for our fixt opinion is, that those who do not deserve a place among us, ought not to have one.

"We conclude, with requesting the council of safety to take into their consideration the paper signed *"John Pemberton;"* and if it shall appear to them to be of a dangerous tendency, or of a treasonable nature, that they would commit the signer, together with such other persons as they can discover were concerned therein, into custody, until such time as some mode of trial shall ascertain the full degree of their guilt and punishment; in the doing of which, we wish their judges, whoever they may be, to disregard the man, his connections, interest, riches, poverty or principles of religion, and to attend to the nature of his offence only."

THE most cavilling sectarian cannot accuse the foregoing with containing the least ingredient of persecution. The free spirit on which the American cause is founded, disdains to mix with such an impurity, and leave it a rubbish fit only for narrow and suspicious minds to grovel in: Suspicion and persecution are weeds of the same dunghill, and flourish best together. Had the Quakers minded their religion and their business, they might have lived through this dispute in enviable ease, and none would have molested them. The common phrase with these people is, *"Our principles are peace."* To which may be replied, *and your practices are the reverse;* for never did the conduct of men oppose their own doctrine more notoriously than the present race of the Quakers. They have artfully changed themselves into a different sort of people to what they used to be, and yet have the address to pursuade each other they are not altered; like antiquated virgins they see not the havoc deformity hath made upon them, but pleasantly mistaking wrinkles for dimples, conceit themselves yet lovely, and wonder at the stupid world for not admiring them.

Did no injury arise to the public by this apostacy of the Quakers from themselves, the public would have nothing to do with it; but as both the design and consequences are pointed against a cause in which the whole community are interested, it is therefore no longer a subject confined to the cognizance of the meeting only, but comes as a matter of criminality before either the authority of the particular state *in which* it is acted, or of the continent *against which* it operates. Every attempt now to support the authority of the king and parliament of Great Britain over America, is treason against *every* state; therefore it is impossible that any *one* can pardon or screen from punishment an offender against *all*.

But to proceed: While the infatuated tories of this and other states were last spring talking of commissioners, accommodation, making the matter up, and the Lord knows what stuff and nonsense, their *good* king and ministry were glutting themselves with the revenge of reducing America to *unconditional submission,* and solacing each other with the certainty of conquering it in *one campaign.* The following quotations are from the parliamentary register of the debates of the house of lords, March 5th, 1776.

"The Americans," says lord *Talbot,*[5] "have been obstinate, undutiful and ungovernable from the very beginning, from their first early and infant settlements; and I am every day more and more convinced that this people will never be brought back to their duty, and the subordinate relation they stand in to this country, till *reduced to an unconditional effectual submission; no concession on our part, no lenity, no endurance,* will have any other effect but that of increasing their insolence."

"The struggle," says lord *Townsend,*[6] "is now a struggle for power; the die is cast, and the ONLY POINT which now remains to be determined, is, in what manner the war can be most effectually prosecuted and speedily finished, in order to procure that *unconditional submission,* which has been so ably stated by the noble Earl with the white staff" (meaning lord Talbot); "and I have no reason to doubt that the measures now pursuing will put an end to the war in the course of a SINGLE CAMPAIGN." "Should

5. Steward of the king's houshold.
6. Formerly general Townsend at Quebec, and late lord-lieutenant of Ireland.

it linger longer, we shall then have reason to expect that some foreign power will interfere, and take advantage of our domestic troubles and civil distractions."

Lord *Littleton,* "My sentiments are pretty well known. I shall only observe now, that lenient measures have had no other effect than to produce insult after insult; that the more we conceded, the higher America rose in her demands, and the more insolent she has grown. It is for this reason that I am now for the most effective and decisive measures; and am of opinion, that no alternative is left us, but to relinquish America forever, or finally determine to compel her to acknowledge the legislative authority of this country; and it is the principle of an *unconditional submission* I would be for maintaining."

Can words be more expressive than these. Surely the tories will believe the tory lords! The truth is, *they do believe them,* and know as fully as any whig on the continent knows, that the king and ministry never had the least design of an accommodation with America, but an absolute unconditional conquest. And the part which the tories were to act, was, by downright lying, to endeavor to put the continent off its guard, and to divide and sow discontent in the minds of such whigs as they might gain an influence over. In short, to keep up a distraction here, that the force sent from England might be able to conquer in *"one campaign."* They and the ministry were, by a different game, playing into each others hands. The cry of the tories in England was, *"No reconciliation, no accommodation,"* in order to obtain the greater military force; while those in America were crying nothing but *"reconciliation and accommodation,"* that the force sent might conquer with the less resistance.

But *this "single campaign"* is over, and America not conquered. The whole work is yet to do, and the force much less to do it with. Their condition is both despicable and deplorable: Out of cash – out of heart, and out of hope. A country furnished with arms and ammunition, as America now is, with three millions of inhabitants, and three thousand miles distant from the nearest enemy that can approach her, is able to look and laugh them in the face.

Howe appears to have two objects in view, either to go up the North-river, or come to Philadelphia.

By going up the North-river, he secures a retreat for his army through Canada, but the ships must return if they return at all, the same way they went; and as our army would be in the rear, the safety of their passage down is a doubtful matter. By such a motion he shuts himself from all supplies from Europe but thro' Canada, and exposes his army and navy to the danger of perishing. The idea of his cutting off the communication between the Eastern and Southren states, by means of the North-river, is merely visionary. He cannot do it by his shipping; because no ship can lay long at anchor in any river within reach of the shore; a single gun would drive a first rate from such a station. This was fully proved last October at fort Washington and Lee, where one gun only, on each side the river, obliged two frigates to cut and be towed off in an hour's time. Neither can he cut it off by his army; because the several posts they must occupy, would divide them almost to nothing, and expose them to be picked up by ours like pebbles on a river's bank; but admitting he could, where is the injury? Because while his whole force is cantoned out, as centries over the water, they will be very innocently employed, and the moment they march into the country, the communication opens.

The most probable object is Philadelphia, and the reasons are many. Howe's business in America is to conquer it, and in proportion as he finds himself unable to the task, he will employ his strength to distress women and weak minds, in order to accomplish thro' *their* fears what he cannot effect by his *own* force. His coming or attempting to come to Philadelphia is a circumstance that proves his weakness: For no general, that felt himself able to take the field and attack his antagonist, would think of bringing his army into a city in the summer time; and this mere shifting the scene from place to place, without effecting any thing, has feebleness and cowardice on the face of it, and holds him up in a contemptible light to any one who can reason justly and firmly. By several informations from New-York, it appears that their army in general, both officers and men, have given up the expectation of conquering America; their eye, now is fixt upon the spoil. They suppose Philadelphia to be rich with stores, and as they think to get more by robbing a town than by attacking an army, their movement to-wards this city is probable. We are not now contending against an army of soldiers, but against a band of thieves, who had rather plunder than fight, and have no other hope of conquest than by cruelty.

They expect to get a mighty booty and strike another general panic by making a sudden movement and getting possession of this city, but unless they can march *out* as well as *in,* or get the entire command of the river, to remove off their plunder, they may probably be stopt with the stolen goods upon them. They have never yet succeeded wherever they have been opposed but at fort Washington. At Charleston their defeat was effectual. At Ticonderoga they ran away. In every skirmish at Kingsbridge and the White-Plains they were obliged to retreat, and the instant our arms were turned upon them in the Jerseys, they turned likewise, and those that turned not were taken.

The necessity of always fitting our internal police to the circumstances of the times we live in, is something so strikingly obvious that no sufficient objection can be made against it. The safety of all societies depend upon it; and where this point is not attended to, the consequences will either be a general languor or a tumult. The encouragement and protection of the good subjects of any state, and the suppression and punishment of bad ones, are the principal objects for which all authority is instituted, and the line in which it ought to operate. We have in this city a strange variety of men and characters, and the circumstances of the times require they should be publicly known; it is not the number of tories that hurt us, so much, as the not finding out who they are; men must now take one side or the other, and abide by the consequences: The Quakers, trusting to their short-sighted sagacity, have, most unluckily for them, made their declaration in their last testimony, and we ought *now* to take them at their word. They have voluntarily read themselves out of the continental meeting, and cannot hope to be restored to it again, but by payment and penitence. Men whose political principles are founded on avarice, are beyond the reach of reason, and the only cure of toryism of this cast, is to tax it. A substantial good drawn from a real evil, is of the same benefit to society, as if drawn from a virtue; and where men have not public spirit to render themselves serviceable, it ought to be the study of government to draw the best use possible from their vices. When the governing passion of any man or set of men is once known, the method of managing them is easy; for even misers, whom no public virtue can impress, would become generous, could a heavy tax be laid upon covetousness.

The tories have endeavored to insure their property with the enemy, by forfeiting their reputation with us; from which may be justly inferred, that their governing passion is avarice. Make them as much afraid of losing on one side as the other, and you stagger their toryism; make them more so, and you reclaim them; for their principle is to worship any power they are most afraid of.

This method of considering men and things together opens into a large field for speculation, and affords me opportunity of offering some observations on the state of our currency, so as to make the support of it go hand in hand, with the suppression of disaffection and the encouragement of public spirit.

The thing which first presents itself in inspecting the state of the currency, is, that we have too much of it, and that there is a necessity of reducing the quantity, in order to encrease the value. Men are daily growing poor by the very means they take to get rich, for in the same proportion that the prices of all goods on hand are raised, the value of all money laid by is reduced. A simple case will make this clear: Let a man have one hundred pounds cash, and as many goods on hand as will to-day sell for £20 but not content with the present market price, he raises them to 40, and by so doing, obliges others in their own defence to raise cent per cent likewise; in this case, it is evident that his hundred pound laid by is reduced fifty pounds in value; whereas, had the markets dropt cent per cent, his goods would have sold but for ten, but his hundred pounds would have risen in value to two hundred; because it would then purchase as many goods again, or support his family as long again as before. And strange as it may seem, he is one hundred and fifty pounds the poorer for raising his goods, to what he would have been had he lowered them; because the forty pounds his goods sold for, is by the general rise of the markets, cent per cent, rendered of no more value than the ten pounds would be had the market fallen in the same proportion; and consequently the whole difference of gain or loss is on the different values of the hundred pounds laid by, viz. from fifty to two hundred. This rage for raising goods is for several reasons much more the fault of the tories than the whigs; and yet the tories (to their shame and confusion ought they to be told of it) are by far the most noisy and discontented. The greatest part of the whigs, by being now either in the army or employed in some public service, are *buyers* only and not *sellers,* and as this evil has its origin in trade, it cannot be charged on those who are out of it.

But the grievance is now become too general to be remedied by partial methods, and the only effectual cure is to reduce the quantity of money; with half the quantity we should be richer than we are now, because the value of it would be doubled, and consequently our attachment to it increased; for it is not the number of dollars a man has, but how far they will go, that makes him either rich or poor.

These two points being admitted, viz. that the quantity of money is too great, and that the prices of goods can only be effectually reduced by reducing the quantity of the money, the next point to be considered is, The method how to reduce it?

The circumstances of the times, as before observed, require that the public characters of all men should *now* be fully understood, and the only general method of ascertaining it is by an oath or affirmation, renouncing all allegiance to the king of Great Britain, and to support the independency of the United States as declared by congress. Let at the same time, a tax of ten, fifteen or twenty per cent per annum, to be collected quarterly, be levied on all property. These alternatives, by being perfectly voluntary, will take in all sorts of people. Here is the test; here is the tax. He who takes the former, conscientiously proves his affection to the cause, and binds himself to pay his quota by the best *services* in his power, and is thereby justly exempt from the latter; and those who chuse the latter, pay their quota in money, to be excused from taking the former, or rather 'tis the price paid to us for their supposed, though mistaken, insurance with the enemy.

But this is only a part of the advantage which would arise by knowing the different characters of men. The whigs stake every thing on the issue of their arms, while the tories, by their disaffection, are sapping and under-mining their strength, and, of consequence, the property of the whigs is the more exposed thereby; and whatever injury their estates may sustain by the movements of the enemy, must either be borne by themselves, who have done every thing which has *yet* been done, or by the tories, who have not only done nothing, but have by their disaffection, invited the enemy on.

In the present crisis we ought to know square by square, and house by house, who are in real alleglance with the United Independent States, and who are not. Let but the line be made clear and distinct, and all men will then know what they are to trust to. It would not only be good policy, but strict justice, to raise fifty or a hundred thousand pounds, or more, if it is necessary, out of the estates and property of the king of England's votaries, resident in Philadelphia, to be distributed, as a reward to those inhabitants of the city and state, who should turn out and repulse the enemy, should they attempt their march this way; and likewise, to bind the property of all such persons to make good the damages which that of the whigs might sustain. In the undistinguishable mode of conducting a war, we frequently make reprisals at sea, on the vessels of persons in England who are friends to our cause compared with the residentary tories among us.

In every former publication of mine, from Common Sense down to the last Crisis, I have generally gone on the charitable supposition, that the tories were rather a mistaken than a criminal people, and have applied ar-gument after argument with all the candor and temper I was capable of, in order to set every part of the case clearly and fairly before them, and if possible to reclaim them from ruin to reason. I have done my duty by them and have now done with that doctrine, taking it for granted, that those who yet hold their disaffection, are, either a set of avaricious miscreants, who would sacrifice the continent to save themselves, or a banditti of hungry traitors, who are hoping for a division of the spoil. To which may be added, a list of crown or proprietary dependants, who, rather than go without a portion of power, would be content to share it with the devil. Of such men there is no hope; and their obedience will only be according to the danger that is set before them, and the power that is exercised over them.

A time will shortly arrive, in which, by ascertaining the characters of persons now, we shall be guarded against their mischiefs then; for in proportion as the enemy despair of conquest, they will be trying the arts of seduction and the force of fear by all the mischiefs they can inflict. But in war we may be certain of these two things, viz. that cruelty in an enemy, and motions made with more than usual parade, are always signs of weakness. He that can conquer, finds his mind too free and pleasant to be brutish; and he that intends to conquer, never makes too much show of his strength.

We now know the enemy we have to do with. While drunk with the certainty of victory they disdained to be civil; and in proportion as disappointment makes them sober, and their apprehensions of an European war alarm them, they will become cringing and artful; honest they cannot be. But our answer to them, in either condition they may be in, is short and full, "As free and independent states we are willing to make peace with you tomorrow, but we can neither hear nor reply in any other character."

If Britain cannot conquer us, it proves, that she is neither able to govern or protect us, and our particular situation now is such, that any connection with her would be unwisely exchanging a half defeated enemy for two powerful ones. Europe, by every appearance and information, is now on the eve, nay, on the morning twilight of a war, and any alliance with *George the third* brings *France* and *Spain* upon our backs; a separation from him attach them to our side; therefore, the only road to *peace, honor* and commerce is INDEPENDENCE.

Written this fourth year of the UNION, *which GOD preserve!*

The Crisis.

NUMBER IV.

Philadelphia, Sept. 12, 1777.

THOSE who expect to reap the blessings of freedom, must, like men, undergo the fatigues of supporting it. The event of yesterday is one of those kind alarms which is just sufficient to rouse us to duty, without being of consequence enough to depress our fortitude. It is not a field of a few acres of ground, but a cause that we are defending, and whether we defeat the enemy in one battle, or by degrees, the consequence will be the same.

Look back at the events of last winter and the present year, there you will find that the enemy's successes have always contributed to reduce them. What they have gained in ground, they paid so dearly for in numbers, that their victories have in the end amounted to defeats. We have always been masters at the last push, and always shall while we do our duty. Howe has been once on the banks of the Delaware, and from thence driven back with loss and disgrace; and why not be again driven from the Schuylkill? His condition and ours are very different. He has every body to fight, we have only his *one* army to cope with, and which wastes away at every engagement; we can not only reinforce, but can redouble our numbers; he is cut off from all supplies, and must sooner or later inevitably fall into our hands.

Shall a band of ten or twelve thousand robbers, who are this day fifteen hundred or two thousand men less in strength than they were yesterday, conquer America, or subdue even a single state? The thing cannot be, unless we sit down and suffer them to do it. Another such a brush, notwithstanding we lost the ground, would, by still reducing the enemy, put them in a condition to be afterwards totally defeated.

Could our whole army have come up to the attack at one time, the consequences had probably been otherwise; but our having different parts of the Brandywine-creek to guard, and the uncertainty which road to Philadelphia, the enemy would attempt to take, naturally afforded them an opportunity of passing with their main body at a place where only a part of ours could be posted; for it must strike every thinking man with conviction, that it requires a much greater force to oppose an enemy in several places, than is sufficient to defeat in any one place.

Men who are sincere in defending their freedom, will always feel concern at every circumstance which seems to make against them; it is the natural and honest consequence of all affectionate attachments, and the want of it is a vice. But the dejection lasts only for a moment; they soon rise out of it with additional vigor; the glow of hope, courage and fortitude, will, in a little time supply the place of every inferior passion and kindle the whole heart into heroism.

There is a mystery in the countenance of some causes, which we have not always present judgment enough to explain. It is distressing to see an enemy advancing into a country, but it is the only place in which we can beat them, and in which we have always beaten them, whenever they made the attempt. The nearer any disease approaches to a crisis, the nearer it is to a cure. Danger and deliverance make their advances together, and it is only the last push, that one or the other takes the lead.

There are many men who will do their duty when it is not wanted; but a genuine public spirit always appears most when there is most occasion for it. Thank God! our army though fatigued, is yet entire. The attack made by us yesterday, was under many disadvantages, naturally arising from the uncertainty of knowing which route the enemy would take; and from that circumstance, the whole of our force could not be brought up together time enough to engage all at once. Our strength is yet reserved; and it is evident that Howe does not think himself a gainer by the affair, otherwise he would this morning have moved down and attacked General Washington.

Gentlemen of the city and country, it is in your power, by a spirited improvement of the present circumstance, to turn it to a real advantage. Howe is now weaker than before, and every shot will contribute to reduce him. You are more immediately interested than any other part of the continent; your all is at stake; it is not so with the general cause; you are devoted by the enemy to plunder and destruction: It is the encouragement which Howe, the chief of plunderers, has promised his army. Thus circumstanced, you may save yourselves by a manly resistance, but you can have no hope in any other conduct. I never yet knew our brave general, or any part of the army, officers or men, out of heart, and I have seen them in circumstances a thousand times more trying than the present. It is only those that are not in action, that feel langor and heaviness, and the best way to rub it off is to turn out, and make sure work of it.

Our army must undoubtedly feel fatigue, and want a reinforcement of rest, though not of valor. Our own interest and happiness call upon us to give them every support in our power, and make the burden of the day, on which the safety of this city depends, light as possible. Remember, gentlemen, that we have forces both to the northward and southward of Philadelphia, and if the enemy be but stopt till those can arrive, this city will be saved, and the enemy finally routed. You have too much at stake to hesitate. You ought not to think an hour upon the matter, but to spring to action at once. Other states have been invaded, have likewise driven off the invaders. Now our time and turn is come, and perhaps the finishing stroke is reserved for us. When we look back on the dangers we have been saved from, and reflect on the success we have been blessed with, it would be sinful either to be idle or despair.

I close this paper with a short address to gen. Howe. You, sir, are only lingering out the period that shall bring with it your defeat[.] You have yet scarce began upon the war, and the farther you enter, the faster will your troubles thicken. What you now enjoy is only a respite from ruin; an invitation to destruction: something that will lead on to our deliverance at your expence. We know the cause we are engaged in, and though a passionate fondness for it may make us grieve at every injury that threatens it, yet, when the moment of concern is over, the determination to duty returns. We are not moved by the gloomy smile of a worthless king, but by the ardent glow of generous patriotism. We fight not to enslave, but to set a country free, and to make room upon the earth for honest men to live in. In such a cause we are sure we are right; and we leave to you the despairing reflection of being the tool of a miserable tyrant.

The Crisis.

NUMBER IX.

Philadelphia, June 9, 1780.

HAD America pursued her advantages with half the spirit she resisted her misfortunes, she would before now, have been a conquering and a peaceful people; but lulled in the lap of soft tranquility, she rested on her hopes, and adversity only has convulsed her into action. Whether subtlety or sincerity, at the close of the last year, induced the enemy to an appearance for peace, is a point not material to know; it is sufficient that we see the effects it has had on our politics, and that we sternly rise to resent the delusion.

The war, on the part of America, has been a war of natural feelings. Brave in distress; serene in conquest; drowsey while at rest; and in every situation generously disposed to peace. A dangerous calm, and a most heightened zeal, have, as circumstances varied, succeeded each other. Every passion, but that of dispair, has been called to a tour of duty; and so mistaken has been the enemy, of our abilities and disposition, that when she supposed us conquered, we rose the conquerors. The extensiveness of the United States, and the variety of their resources; the universality of their cause, the quick operation of their feelings, and the similarity of their sentiments, have, in every trying situation, produced a *something* which favored by Providence, and pursued with ardor, has accomplished in an instant the business of a campaign. We have never deliberately sought victory, but snatched it; and bravely undone in an hour, the plotted operations of a season.

The reported fate of Charlestown, like the misfortunes of seventy-six, has at last called forth a spirit, and kindled up a flame, which perhaps no other event could have produced. If the enemy has circulated a falsehood, they have unwisely aggravated us into life, and if they have told us a truth, they have unintentionally done us a service. We were returning with folded arms from the fatigues of war, and thinking and setting leisurely down to enjoy repose. The dependance that has been put upon Charlestown threw a drowsiness over America. We looked on the business done – the conflict over – the matter settled – or that all which remained unfinished would follow of itself. In this state of dangerous relax, exposed to the poisonous infusions of the enemy, and having no common danger to attract our attention, we were extinguishing by stages the ardor we began with, and surrendering by peace-meals the virtue that defended us.

Afflicting as the loss of Charlestown may be, yet if it universally rouse us from the slumber of a twelve-months past, and renew in us the spirit of former days, it will produce an advantage more important than its loss. America ever *is* what she *thinks* herself to be. Governed by sentiment, and acting her own mind, she becomes, as she pleases, the victor or the victim.

It is not the conquest of towns, nor the accidental capture of garrisons, that can reduce a country so extensive as this. The sufferings of one part can ever be relieved by the exertions of another, and there is no situation the enemy can be in, that does not afford to us the same advantages she seeks herself. By dividing her force, she leaves every post attackable. It is a mode of war that carries with it a confession of weakness, and goes on the principle of distress, rather than conquest.

The decline of the enemy is visible not only in their operations, but in their plans; Charlestown originally made but a secondary object in the system of attack, and it is now become their principal one, because they have not been able to succeed elsewhere. It would have carried a cowardly appearance in Europe had they formed their grand expedition in seventy-six, against a part of the continent where there was no army, or not a sufficient one to oppose them; but failing year after year in their impressions here, and to the eastward and northward, they deserted their first capital design, and prudently contenting themselves with what they can get, give a flourish of honor to conceal disgrace.

But this peace-meal work is not conquering the continent. It is a discredit in them to attempt it, and in us to suffer it. It is now full time to put an end to a war of aggravations, which, on one side, has no possible object, and on the other, has every inducement which honor, interest, safety and happiness can inspire. If we suffer them much longer to remain among us, we shall become as bad as themselves. An association of vices will reduce us more than the sword. A nation hardened in the practice of iniquity knows better how to profit by it, than a young country newly corrupted. We are not a match for them in the line of advantageous guilt, nor they to us on the principles we bravely set out with. Our first days were our days of honor. They have marked the character of America wherever the story of her wars are told; and convinced of this, we have nothing to do, but wisely and unitedly to tread the well known track.

The progress of a war is often as ruinous to individuals, as the issue of it is to a nation; and it is not only necessary that our forces be such, that we be conquerors in the end, but that by timely exertions we be secure in the interim. The present campaign will afford an opportunity which has never presented itself before, and the preparations for it are equally nec essary, whether Charlestown stand or fall. Suppose the first, it is in that case only a failure of the enemy, not a defeat. All the conquest a besieged town can hope for is, not to be conquered; and compelling an enemy to raise the siege, is to the besieged a victory. But there must be a probability amounting almost to certainty, that would justify a garrison marching out to attack a retreat. Therefore should Charlestown not be taken, and the en- emy abandon the siege, every other part of the continent should prepare to meet them; and on the contrary, should it be taken, the same preparations are necessary, to balance the loss, and put ourselves in a condition to co- operate with our allies, immediately on their arrival.

We are not now fighting our battles alone, as we were in seventy-six. England, from a malicious disposition to America, has not only not declared war against France and Spain, but the better to prosecute her passions here, has afforded those powers no military object, and avoids them, to distress us. She will suffer her West-India islands to be over-run by France, and her southern settlements taken by Spain, rather than quit the object that grati- fies revenge. This conduct, on the part of Britain, has pointed out the pro- priety of France sending a naval and land force to co-operate with America on the spot. Their arrival cannot be very distant, nor the ravages of the enemy long. In the mean time the part necessary to us needs no illustration. The recruiting the army, and procuring the supplies, are the two things needful, and a capture of either of the enemy's divisions will restore to America peace and plenty.

At a crisis, big, like the present, with expectation and events, the whole country is called to unanimity and exertion. Not an ability ought now to sleep, that can produce but a mite to the general good, nor even a whisper to pass that militates against it. The necessity of the case, and the importance of the consequences, admit no delay from a friend, no apology from an enemy. To spare now, would be the height of extravagance, and to consult present ease, would be to sacrifice it, perhaps, for ever.

America, rich in patriotism and produce, can want neither men nor supplies, when a serious necessity calls them forth. The slow operation of taxes, owing to the extensiveness of collection, and their depreciated value before they arrived in the treasury, have, in many instances, thrown a burthen upon government, which has been artfully interpreted by the enemy into a general decline throughout the country. Yet this, inconvenient as it may at first appear, is not only remediable, but may be turned to an immediate advantage; for it makes no real difference, whether a certain number of men, or company of militia (and in this country every man is a militiaman) are directed by law to send a recruit at their own expence, or whether a tax is laid on them for that purpose, and the man hired by government afterwards. The first, if there is any difference, is both cheapest and best, because it saves the expence which would attend collecting it as a tax, and brings the man sooner into the field than the modes of recruiting formerly used: And on this principle, a law has been passed in this state for recruiting two men from each company of militia, which will add upwards of a thousand to the force of the country.

But the flame, which has broke forth in this city since the report from New-York of the loss of Charlestown, not only does honor to the place, but, like the blaze of seventy-six, will kindle into action the scattered sparks throughout America. – The valor of a country may be learned by the bravery of its soldiery, and the general cast of its inhabitants, but confidence of success is best discovered by the active measures pursued by men of property; and when the spirit of enterprize becomes so universal, as to act at once on all ranks of men, a war may then and not till then, be stiled truly popular.

In seventy-six the ardor of the enterprising part was considerably checked by the real revolt of some, and the coolness of others. But in the present case there is a firmness in the substance and property of the country to the public cause. An association has been entered into by the merchants, tradesmen and principal inhabitants of this city, to receive and support the new state money at the value of gold and silver; a measure which, while it does them honor, will likewise contribute to their interest, by rendering the operations of the campaign convenient and effectual.

Neither has the spirit of exertion stopt here. A voluntary subscription is likewise began to raise a fund of hard money, to be given as bounties to fill up the full quota of the Pennsylvania line. It has been the remark of the enemy, that every thing in America has been done by the force of government; but when she sees the individuals throwing in their voluntary aids, and facilitating the public measures in concert with the established powers of the country, it will convince her that the cause of America stands not on the will of a few, but on the broad foundation of property and popularity.

Thus aided, and thus supported, disaffection will decline, and the withered head of tyranny expire in America. The ravages of the enemy will be short and limited, and like all their former ones will produce a victory over themselves.

– COMMON SENSE.

☞At the time of writing this number of the Crisis, the loss of Charlestown, though believed by some, was more confidently disbelieved by others. But there ought to be no longer a doubt on the matter. Charlestown is gone, and I believe for the want of a sufficient supply of provisions. The man that does not now feel for the honor of the best and noblest cause that ever a country engaged in, and exert himself accordingly, is no longer worthy a peaceable residence among a people determined to be free.

– C. S.

The Crisis,
extraordinary.

(ON THE SUBJECT OF TAXATION.)

Philadelphia, October 6, 1780.

IT is impossible to sit down and think seriously on the affairs of America, but the original principles on which she resisted, and the glow and ardor they inspired, will occur like the undefaced remembrance of a lovely scene. To trace over in imagination the purity of the cause, the voluntary sacrifices made to support it, and all the various turnings of the war in its defence, is at once both paying and receiving respect. The principles deserve to be remembered, and to remember them rightly is repossessing them. In this indulgence of generous recollection we become gainers by what we seem to give, and the more we bestow the richer we become.

So extensively right was the ground on which America proceeded, that it not only took in every just and liberal sentiment which could impress the heart, but made it the direct interest of every class and order of men to defend the country. The war, on the part of Britain, was originally a war of covetousness. The sordid and not the splendid passions gave it being. The fertile fields and prosperous infancy of America appeared to her as mines for tributary wealth. She viewed the hive, and disregarding the industry that had enriched it, thirsted for the honey. But in the present stage of her affairs, the violence of temper is added to the rage of avarice; and therefore, that which at the first setting out proceeded from purity of principle and public interest, is now heightened by all the obligations of necessity; for it requires but little knowledge of human nature to discern what would be the consequence, were America again reduced to the subjection of Britain. Uncontrouled power, in the hands of an incensed, imperious and rapacious conqueror, is an engine of dreadful execution, and woe be to that country over which it can be exercised. The names of whig and tory would then be sunk in the general term of rebel, and the oppression, whatever it might be, would, with very few instances of exception, light equally on all.

Britain did not go to war with America for the sake of dominion, because she was then in possession; neither was it for the extension of trade and commerce, because she had monopolized the whole and the country had yielded to it; neither was it to extinguish what *she* might call rebellion, because before she began no resistance existed. It could then be from no other motive than avarice, or a design of establishing, in the first instance, the same taxes in America as are paid in England (which, as I shall presently show, are above eleven times heavier than the taxes we now pay for the present year 1780) or, in the second instance, to confiscate the whole property of America, in case of resistance and conquest of the latter, of which she had then no doubt.

I shall now proceed to show what the taxes in England are, and what the yearly expence of the present war is to her – What the taxes of this country amount to, and what the annual expence of defending it effectually will be to us; and shall endeavor concisely to point out the cause of our difficulties, and the advantages on one side, and the consequences on the other, in case we do, or do not, put ourselves in an effectual state of defence. I mean to be open, candid and sincere. I see a universal wish to expel the enemy from the country, a murmuring because the war is not carried on with more vigor, and my intention is to show as shortly as possible both the reason and the remedy.

The number of souls in England (exclusive of Scotland and Ireland) is seven millions[7], and the number of souls in America is three millions.

The amount of the taxes in England (exclusive of Scotland and Ireland) was, before the present war commenced, eleven millions six hundred and

7. This is taking the highest number that the people of England have been, or can be rated at.

forty-two thousand six hundred and fifty-three pounds sterling, which on an average is no less a sum than one pound thirteen shillings and three-pence sterling per head per annum, men, women and children; besides county taxes, taxes for the support of the poor, and a tenth of all the produce of the earth for the support of the bishops and clergy[8]. Nearly five millions of this sum went annually to pay the interest of the national debt contracted by former wars, and the remaining sum of six millions six hundred and forty-two thousand six hundred pounds was applied to defray the yearly expence of government, the peace establishment of the army and navy, placemen, pensioners, &c. consequently the whole of her enormous taxes being thus appropriated she had nothing to spare out of them towards defraying the expences of the present war or any other. Yet had she not been in debt at the beginning of the war as we were not, and like us had only a land and not a naval war to carry on, her then revenue of eleven millions and a half pounds sterling would defray all her annual expences of war and government within each year.

But this not being the case with her, she is obliged to borrow about ten million pounds sterling yearly, to prosecute the war she is now engaged in

8. The following is taken from Dr. Price's state of the taxes of England, pages 96, 97, 98.
An account of the money drawn from the public by taxes annually, being the medium of three years before the year 1776.

Amount of customs in England,	£. 2,528,275
Amount of the excise in England,	4,649,892
Land tax at 3s.	1,300,000
Land tax at 1s. in the pound,	450,000
Salt duties,	218,739
Duties on stamps, cards, dice, advertisements, bonds, leases, indentures, newspapers, almanacks, &c.	280,788
Duties on houses and windows,	385,369
Post office, seizures, wine licences, hackney coaches, &c.	250,000
Annual profits from lotteries,	150,000
Expence of collecting the excises in England,	297,887
Expence of collecting the customs in England,	468,703
Interest of loans on the land tax at 4s. expences of collection, militia, &c.	250,000
Perquisites, &c. on custom house officers, &c. supposed	250,000
Expence of collecting the salt duties in England 10½ per cent.-	27,000
Bounties on fish exported,	18,000
Expence of collecting the duties on stamps, cards, advertisements, &c. at 5 and 1–4 per cent.	18,000

Total, £. 11,642,653

(this year she borrowed twelve) and lay on new taxes to discharge the interest; and allowing that the present war has cost her only fifty millions sterling, the interest thereon at five per cent. will be two millions and an half, therefore the amount of her taxes now must be fourteen millions, which on an average is no less than forty shillings sterling per head, men, women and children throughout the nation. Now as this expence of fifty millions was borrowed on the hopes of conquering America, and as it was avarice which first induced her to commence the war, how truly wretched and deplorable would the condition of this country be, were she, by her own remissness, to suffer an enemy of such a disposition, and so circumstanced, to reduce her to subjection.

I now proceed to the revenues of America.

I have already stated the number of souls in America to be three millions, and by a calculation I have made, which I have every reason to believe is sufficiently right, the whole expence of the war, and the support of the several governments, may be defrayed for two million pounds sterling, annually; which on an average is thirteen shillings and four pence per head, men, women and children, and the peace establishment at the end of the war, will be but three quarters of a million, or five shillings sterling per head. Now, throwing out of the question every thing of honor, principle, happiness, freedom and reputation in the world, and taking it up on the simple ground of interest, I put the following case.

Suppose Britain was to conquer America, and as conquerors was to lay her under no other conditions than to pay the same proportions towards her annual revenue which the people of England pay; our share in that case, would be six million pounds sterling yearly; can it then be a question, whether it is best to raise two millions to defend the country, and govern it ourselves, and only three quarters of a million afterwards, or pay six millions to have it conquered, and let the enemy govern it.

Can it be supposed that conquerors would chuse to put themselves in a worse condition than what they granted to the conquered. In England, the tax on rum is five shillings and one penny sterling per gallon, which is one silver dollar and fourteen coppers. Now would it not be laughable to imagine, that after the expence they have been at, they would let either whig or tory in America drink it cheaper than themselves. Coffee which is so considerable an article of consumption and support here, is there loaded with a duty, which makes the price between five and six shillings sterling a pound, and a penalty of fifty pounds sterling on any person detected in roasting it in his own house. There is scarce an article of life you can eat, drink, wear, or enjoy, that is not there loaded with a tax; even the light from heaven is only permited to shine into their dwellings by paying eighteen pence sterling per window annually; and the humblest drink of life, small beer, cannot there be purchased without a tax of nearly two coppers a gallon, besides a heavy tax upon the malt, and another on the hops before it is brewed, exclusive of a land tax on the earth which produces them. In short, the condition of that country in point of taxation is so oppressive, the number of her poor so great, and the extravagance and rapaciousness of the court so enormous, that were they to effect a conquest of America, it is then only that the distresses of America would begin. Neither would it signify any thing to a man whether he be whig or tory. The people of England and the ministry of that country know us by no such distinctions. What they want is clear solid revenue, and the modes they would take to procure it, would operate alike on all. Their manner of reasoning would be short, because they would naturally infer that if we were able to carry on a war of five or six years against them, we were able to pay the same taxes which they do.

I have already stated that the expence of conducting the present war, and the government of the several states, may be done for two millions sterling and the establishment in time of peace, for three quarters of a million.[9]

As to navy matters, they flourish so well, and are so well attended in the hands of individuals; that I think it consistent on every principle of real use and œconomy, to turn the navy into hard money (keeping only three or four packets) and apply it to promote the service of the army We shall not have a ship the less; the use of them, and the benefit from them, will be greatly increased, and their expence saved. We are now allied with a formidable naval power, from whom we derive the assistance of a navy. And the line in which we can prosecute the war, so as to reduce the common enemy and benefit the alliance most effectually, will be by attending closely to the land service.

I estimate the charge of keeping up and maintaining an army, officering them, and all expences included, sufficient for the defence of the country, to be equal to the expence of forty thousand men at thirty pounds sterling per head, which is one million two hundred thousand pounds.

I likewise allow four hundred thousand pounds for continental expences at home and abroad.

9. I have made the calculations in sterling, because it is a rate generally known in all the states, and because likewise, it admits of an easy comparison between our expences to support the war and those of the enemy. Four silver dollars and an half is one pound sterling, and three pence over.

And four hundred thousand pounds for the support of the several state governments, the amount will then be,

For the army,	1,200,000
Continental expences at home and abroad,	400,000
Government of the several states,	400,000
Total,	2,000,000

I take the proportion of this state, Pennsylvania, to be an eighth part of the thirteen United States, the quota then for us to raise will be two hundred and fifty thousand pounds sterling; two hundred thousand of which will be our share for the support and pay of the army and continental expences at home and abroad, and fifty thousand pounds for the support of state government.

In order to gain an idea of the proportion in which the raising such a sum will fall, I make the following calculation.

Pennsylvania contains three hundred and seventy-five thousand inhabitants, men, women and children, which is likewise an eighth of the whole inhabitants of the whole United States: therefore two hundred and fifty thousand pounds sterling to be raised among three hundred and seventy-five thousand persons, is, on an average, thirteen shillings and four pence sterling per head, per annum, or something more than one shilling sterling per month. And our proportion of three quarters of a million for the government of the country, in time of peace, will be ninety-three thousand seven hundred and fifty pounds sterling, fifty thousand of which will be for the government expences of the state, and forty-three thousand seven hundred and fifty pounds for continental expences at home and abroad.

The peace establishment then will, on an average, be five shillings sterling per head. Whereas was England now to stop, and the war cease, her peace establishment would continue the same as it is now, viz. forty shillings per head; therefore was our taxes necessary for carrying on the war as much per head as hers now is, and the difference to be only whether we should, at the end of the war, pay at the rate of five shillings per head, or forty shillings per head, the case needs no thinking of. But as we can securely defend and keep the country for one third less than what our burthen would be if it was conquered, and support the governments afterward for one eighth of what Britain would levy on us, and could I find a miser whose heart never felt the emotion of a spark of principle, even that man, uninfluenced by every love but the love of money, and capable of no attachment but to his interest, would and must, from the frugality which governs him contribute to the defence of the country, or he ceases to be a miser and becomes an ideot. But when we take in with it every thing that can ornament mankind; when the line of our interest becomes the line of our happiness; when all that can cheer and animate the heart; when sense of honor, fame, character, at home and abroad, are interwoven not only with the security but the increase of property, there exists not a man in America, unless he be a hired emissary, who does not see that his good is connected with keeping up a sufficient defence.

I do not imagine that an instance can be produced in the world of a country putting herself to such an amazing charge to conquer and enslave another as Britain has done. The sum is too great for her to think of with any tolerable degree of temper; and when we consider the burthen she sustains as well as the disposition she has shewn, it would be the height of folly in us to suppose that she would not reimburse herself by the most rapid means, had she once more America within her power. With such an oppression of expence, what would an empty conquest be to her! what relief under such circumstances could she derive from a victory without a prize? It was money, it was revenue she first went to war for, and nothing but *that* would satisfy her. It is not the nature of avarice to be satisfied with any thing else. Every passion that acts upon mankind has a peculiar mode of operation. Many of them are temporary and fluctuating; they admit of cessation and variety. But avarice is a fixed uniform passion. It neither abates of its vigor nor changes its object; and the reason why it does not is founded in the nature of things, for wealth has not a rival where avarice is a ruling passion. One beauty may excel another, and extinguish from the mind of a man the pictured remembrance of a former one: But wealth is the phœnix of avarice, and therefore cannot seek a new object, because there is not another in the world.

I now pass on to shew the value of the present taxes, and compare them with the annual expence; but this I shall preface with a few explanatory remarks.

There are two distinct things which make the payment of taxes difficult; the one is the large and real value of the sum to be paid, and the other is the scarcity of the thing in which the payment is to be made; and although these appear to be one and the same, they are in several instances not only different, but the difficulty springs from different causes.

Suppose a tax was to be laid equal to one half of what a man's yearly income is, such a tax could not be paid because the property could not be spared; and on the other hand, suppose a very trifling tax was laid to be collected in *pearls,* such a tax likewise could not be paid, because it could not be had. Now any person may see that these are distinct cases, and the latter of them is a representation of ours.

That the difficulty cannot proceed from the former, that is, from the real value or weight of the tax is evident at first view to any person who will consider it.

The amount of the quota of taxes for this state for the present year, 1780 (and so on in proportion for every other state) is twenty millions of dollars, which at seventy for one is but sixty four thousand two hundred and eighty pounds three shillings sterling, and on an average is no more than three shillings and five pence sterling per head per annum per man, woman and child, or 3 2/5 pence per head per month. Now here is a clear positive fact, that cannot be contradicted, and which proves that the difficulty cannot be in the weight of the tax, for in itself it is a trifle and far from being adequate to our quota of the expence of the war. The quit-rents of one penny sterling per acre on only one half the state, come to upwards of fifty thousand pounds, which is almost as much as all the taxes of the present year, and as those quit-rents made no part of the taxes then paid, and are now discontinued, the quantity of money drawn for public service this year, exclusive of the militia fines, which I shall take notice of in the process of this work, is less than what was paid and payable in any year preceding the revolution, and since the last war; what I mean is that the quit-rents and taxes taken together came to a larger sum then, than the present taxes without the quit-rents do now.

My intention by these arguments and calculations is to place the difficulty to the right cause, and shew that it does not proceed from the weight or worth of the tax, but from the scarcity of the medium in which it is paid; and to illustrate this point still farther, I shall now shew, that if the tax of twenty millions of dollars was of four times the real value it now is or nearly so, which would be about two hundred and fifty thousand pounds sterling, and would be our full quota, that this sum would have been raised with more ease, and less felt, than the present sum of only sixty-four thousand two hundred and eighty pounds.

The convenience or inconvenience of paying a tax in money arises from the quantity of money that can be spared out of trade.

When the emissions stopt, the continent was left in possession of two hundred millions of dollars, perhaps as equally dispersed as it was possible for trade to do it. And as no more was to be issued, the rise or fall of prices could neither increase nor diminish the quantity. It therefore remained the same through all the fluctuations of trade and exchange.

Now had the exchange stood at twenty for one, which was the rate congress calculated upon when they quoted the states the latter end of last year, trade would have been carried on for nearly four times less money than it is now, and consequently the twenty millions would have been spared with much greater ease, and when collected would have been of almost four times the value they now are. And on the other hand, was the depreciation to be ninety or one hundred for one, the quantity required for trade would be more than at sixty or seventy for one, and though the value of them would be less, the difficulty of sparing the money out of trade would be greater. And on these facts and arguments I rest the matter, to prove that it is not the want of property, but the scarcity of the medium by which the proportion of property for taxation is to be measured out, that makes the embarrassment we lie under. There is not money enough, and what is equally as true, the people will not let there be money enough.

While I am on the subject of the currency, I shall offer one remark which will appear true to every body, and can be accounted for by nobody, which is, that the better the times were, the worse the money grew; and the worse the times were, the better the money stood. It never depreciated by any advantage obtained by the enemy. The troubles of seventy-six, and the loss of Philadelphia in seventy-seven, made no sensible impression on it, and every one knows that the surrender of Charlestown did not produce the least alteration in the rate of exchange, which for long before, and for more than three months after, stood at sixty for one. It seems as if the certainty of its being our own, made us careless of its value, and that the most distant thoughts of losing it made us hug it the closer, like something we were loth to part with; or that we depreciate it for our pastime, which, when called to seriousness by the enemy, we leave off to renew again at our leisure. In short our good luck seems to break us, and our bad make us whole.

Passing on from this digression, I shall now endeavor to bring into one view the several parts I have already stated, and form thereon some propositions, and conclude.

I have placed before the reader, the average tax per head paid by the people in England; which is forty shillings sterling.

And I have shewn the rate on an average per head, which will defray all the expence of the war to us, and support the several governments without running the country into debt, which is thirteen shillings and four pence.

I have shewn what the peace establishment may be conducted for, viz. an eighth part of what it would be, if under the government of Britain.

And I have likewise shewn what the average per head of the present taxes are, namely, three shillings and five pence sterling, or 3 2/5 pence per month; and that their whole yearly value, in sterling, is only sixty-four thousand two hundred and eighty pounds. Whereas our quota, to keep the payments equal with the expences, is two hundred and fifty thousand pounds. Consequently, there is a deficiency of one hundred and eighty-five thousand seven hundred and twenty pounds, and the same proportion of defect, according to the several quotas, happens in every other state. And this defect is the cause why the army has been so indifferently fed, cloathed and paid. It is the cause, likewise, of the nerveless state of the campaign, and the insecurity of the country. Now, if a tax equal to thirteen and four pence per head, will remove all these difficulties, make people secure in their homes, leave them to follow the business of their stores and farms unmolested, and not only keep out, but drive out the enemy from the country; and if the neglect of raising this sum will let them in, and produce the evils which might be prevented – on which side, I ask, does the wisdom, interest and policy lie? Or, rather, would it not be an insult to reason to put the question? The sum, when proportioned out according to the several abilities of the people, can hurt no one, but an inroad from the enemy ruins hundreds of families.

Look at the destruction done in this city. The many houses totally destroyed, and others damaged; the waste of fences in the country round it, besides the plunder of furniture, forage and provision. I do not suppose that half a million sterling would reinstate the sufferers; and, does this, I ask, bear any proportion to the expence that would make us secure. The damage, on an average, is at least ten pounds sterling per head, which is as much as thirteen shillings and four pence per head comes to for fifteen years. The same has happened on the frontiers, and in the Jerseys, New-York, and other places where the enemy has been – Carolina and Georgia are likewise suffering the same fate.

That the people generally do not understand the insufficiency of the taxes to carry on the war, is evident, not only from common observation, but from the construction of several petitions, which were presented to the assembly of this state, against the recommendation of Congress of the 18th of March last, for taking up and funding the present currency at forty for one, and issuing new money in its stead. The prayer of the petition was, *That the currency might be appreciated by taxes* (meaning the present taxes) *and that part of the taxes be applied to the support of the army, if the army could not be otherwise supported.* Now it could not have been possible for such a petition to have been presented, had the petitioners known, that so far from *part* of the taxes being sufficient for the support of the army, the *whole* of them falls three-fourths short of the year's expences.

Before I proceed to propose methods by which a sufficiency of money may be raised, I shall take a short view of the general state of the country.

Notwithstanding the weight of the war, the ravages of the enemy, and the obstructions she has thrown in the way of trade and commerce, so soon does a young country outgrow misfortune, that America has already surmounted many that once heavily oppressed her. For the first year or two of the war, we were shut up within our ports, scarce venturing to look towards the ocean. Now our rivers are beautified with large and valuable vessels, our stores filled with merchandize, and the produce of the country has a ready market, and an advantageous price. Gold and silver, that for a while seemed to have retreated again within the bowels of the earth, is once more risen into circulation, and every day adds new strength to trade, commerce, and agriculture. In a pamphlet written by Sir John Dalrymple, and dispersed in America in the year 1775, he asserted, that, *two twenty gun ships, nay,* says he, *tenders of those ships, stationed between Albermarle sound and Chesapeake bay would shut up the trade of America for 600 miles.* How little did Sir John Dalrymple know of the abilities of America!

While under the government of Britain, the trade of this country was loaded with restrictions. It was only a few foreign ports we were allowed to sail to. Now it is otherwise; and allowing that the quantity of trade is but half what it was before the war, the case must shew the vast advantage of an open trade, because the present quantity under her restrictions could not support itself; from which I infer, that if half the quantity without the restrictions can bear itself up nearly, if not quite, as well as the whole when subject to them, how prosperous must the condition of America be when the whole shall return open with all the world. By trade I do not mean the employment of a merchant only, but the whole interest and business of the country taken collectively.

It is not so much my intention, by this publication, to propose particular plans for raising money, as it is to shew the necessity and the advantages to be derived from it. My principal design is to form the disposition of the people to such measures which I am fully persuaded is their interest and duty to adopt, and which needs no other force to accomplish them than the force of being felt. But as every hint may be useful, I shall throw out a sketch, and leave others to make such improvements upon it as to them may appear reasonable.

The annual sum wanted is two millions, and the average rate in which it falls is thirteen shillings and four pence per head.

Suppose then that we raise half the sum and sixty thousand pounds over. The average rate thereof will be seven shillings per head.

In this case we shall have half the supply we want and an annual fund of sixty thousand pounds whereon to borrow the other million; because sixty thousand pounds is the interest of a million at six per cent, and if at the end of another year we should be obliged, by the continuance of the war, to borrow another million, the taxes will be increased to seven shillings and six pence; and thus for every million borrowed, an additional tax equal to six pence per head must be levied.

The sum then to be raised next year will be one million and sixty thousand pounds: One half of which I would propose should be raised by duties on imported goods and prize goods, and the other half by a tax on landed property and houses, or such other means as each state may devise.

But as the duties on imports and prize goods must be the same in all the states, therefore the rate per cent. or what other form the duty shall be laid, must be ascertained and regulated by Congress, and ingrafted in that form into the law of each state; and the monies arising therefrom carried into the treasury of each state. The duties to be paid in gold or silver.

There are many reasons why a duty on imports is the most convenient duty or tax that can be collected; one of which is, because the whole is payable in a few places in a country, and it likewise operates with the greatest ease and equality, because as every one pays in proportion to what he consumes, so people in general consume in proportion to what they can afford, and therefore the tax is regulated by the abilities which every man supposes himself to have, or in other words every man becomes his own assessor, and pays by a little at a time when it suits him to buy. Besides, it is a tax which people may pay or let alone by not consuming the articles; and though the alternative may have no influence on their conduct, the power of choosing is an agreeable thing to the mind. For my own part, it would be a satisfaction to me, was there a duty on all sorts of liquors during the war, as in my idea of things, it would be an addition to the pleasure of society, to know, that when the health of the army goes round, a few drops from every glass become theirs. How often have I heard an imphatical wish almost accompanied with a tear, *"Oh, that our poor fellows in the field had some of this!"* Why then need we suffer under a fruitless sympathy, when there is a way to enjoy both the wish and the entertainment at once?

But the great national policy of putting a duty upon imports is, that it either keeps the foreign trade in our own hands or draws something for the defence of the country from every foreigner who participates it with us.

Thus much for the first half of the taxes, and as each state will best devise means to raise the other half, I shall confine my remarks to the resources of this state.

The quota then of this state of one million and sixty thousand pounds will be one hundred and thirty-three thousand two hundred and fifty pounds, the half of which is sixty-six thousand six hundred and twenty-five pounds; and supposing one fourth part of Pennsylvania inhabited, then a tax of one bushel of wheat on every twenty acres of land, one with another, would produce the sum, and all the present taxes to cease. Whereas the tythes of the bishops and clergy in England, exclusive of the taxes, are upwards of half a bushel of wheat on *every single* acre of land, good and bad, throughout the nation.

In the former part of this paper I mentioned the militia fines, but reserved speaking to the matter, which I shall now do: The ground I shall put it upon is, that two millions sterling a-year will support a sufficient army, and all the expences of war and government, without having recourse to the inconvenient method of continually calling men from their employments, which of all others is the most expensive and the least substantial. I consider the revenues created by taxes as the first and principal thing, and fines only as secondary and accidental things. It was not the intention of the militia law to apply the militia fines to anything else but the support of the militia, neither do they produce any revenue to the state, yet these fines amount to more than all the taxes; for taking the muster-roll to be sixty thousand men, the fine on forty thousand who may not attend, will be sixty thousand pounds sterling, and those who muster, will give up a portion of time equal to half that sum, and if the eight classes should be called within the year, and one third turn out, the fine on the remaining forty thousand would amount to seventy-two millions of dollars, besides the fifteen shillings on every hundred pounds property, and the charge of seven and an half per cent for collecting in certain instances, which on the whole would be upwards of two hundred and fifty thousand pounds sterling.

Now if those very fines disable the country from raising a sufficient revenue without producing an equivalent advantage, would it not be to the ease and interest of all parties to encrease the revenue, in the manner I have proposed, or any better, if a better can be devised, and cease the operation of the fines? I would still keep the militia as an organized body of men, and should there be a real necessity to call them forth, pay them out of the proper revenues of the state, and encrease the taxes a third or fourth per cent, on those who do not attend. My limits will not allow me to go farther into this matter, which I shall therefore close with this remark; that fines are, of all modes of revenue, the most unsuited to the mind of a free country. When a man pays a tax, he knows the public necessity requires it, and therefore feels a pride in discharging his duty; but a fine seems an atonement for neglect of duty, and of consequence is paid with discredit, and frequently levied with severity.

I have now only one subject more to speak to, with which I shall conclude, which is, the resolve of congress of the 18th of March last, for taking up and funding the present currency at forty for one, and issuing new money in its stead.

Every one knows I am not the flatterer of congress, but in this instance *they are right;* and if that measure is supported, the currency will acquire a value, which without it, it will not. But this is not all: It will give relief to the finances until such time as they can be properly arranged, and save the country from being immediately double taxed under the present mode. In short, support that measure, and it will support you.

I have now waded through a tedious course of difficult business, and over an untrodden path. The subject on every point it could be viewed was entangled with perplexities, and enveloped in obscurity, yet such are the resources of America, that she wants nothing but system to insure success.

– COMMON SENSE.

The Crisis,

NUMBER XIII.

Philadelphia, April 19, 1783.

"THE times that tried mens souls,"[10] are over – and the greatest and completest revolution the world ever knew, gloriously and happily accomplished.

But to pass from the extremes of danger to safety – from the tumult of war, to the tranquility of peace, though sweet in contemplation, requires a gradual composure of the senses to receive it. Even calmness has the power of stunning, when it opens too instantly upon us. The long and raging hurricane that should cease in a moment, would leave us in a state rather of wonder than enjoyment; and some moments of recollection must pass, before we could be capable of tasting the full felicity of repose. There are but few instances, in which the mind is fitted for sudden transitions: It takes in its pleasures by reflection and comparison, and those must have time to act, before the relish for new scenes is complete.

10. "These are the times that try mens souls." Crisis No. I. published December 19, 1776.

In the present case – the mighty magnitude of the object – the various uncertainties of fate it has undergone – the numerous and complicated dangers we have suffered or escaped – the eminence we now stand on, and the vast prospect before us, must all conspire to impress us with contemplation.

To see it in our power to make a world happy – to teach mankind the art of being so – to exhibit on the theatre of the universe, a character hitherto unknown – and to have, as it were, a new creation entrusted to our hands, are honors that command reflection, and can neither be too highly estimated, nor too gratefully received.

In this pause then of recollection – while the storm is ceasing, and the long agitated mind vibrating to a rest, let us look back on the scenes we have passed, and learn from experience what is yet to be done.

Never, I say, had a country so many openings to happiness as this. Her setting out into life, like the rising of a fair morning, was unclouded and promising. Her cause was good. Her principles just and liberal. Her temper serene and firm. Her conduct regulated by the nicest steps, and every thing about her wore the mark of honor.

It is not every country (perhaps there is not another in the world) that can boast so fair an origin. Even the first settlement of America corresponds with the character of the revolution. Rome, once the proud mistress of the universe, was originally a band of ruffians. Plunder and rapine made her rich, and her oppression of millions made her great. But America needs never be ashamed to tell her birth, nor relate the stages by which she rose to empire.

The remembrance then of what is past, if it operates rightly, must inspire her with the most laudable of all ambition, that of adding to the fair fame she began with. The world has seen her great in adversity. Struggling without a thought of yielding beneath accumulated difficulties. Bravely, nay proudly, encountering distress, and rising in resolution as the storm encreased. All this is justly due to her, for her fortitude has merited the character. Let then the world see that she can bear prosperity: and that her honest virtue in time of peace, is equal to the bravest virtue in time of war.

She is now descending to the scenes of quiet and domestic life. Not beneath the cypress shade of disappointment, but to enjoy in her own land, and under her own vine, the sweet of her labors, and the reward of her toil – In this situation, may she never forget that a fair national reputation, is of as much importance as independence. That it possesses a charm which wins upon the world, and makes even enemies civil. That it gives a dignity which is often superior to power, and commands a reverence where pomp and splendor fail.

It would be a circumstance ever to be lamented and never to be forgotten, were a single blot, from any cause whatever, suffered to fall on a revolution, which to the end of time must be an honor to the age that accomplished it: and which has contributed more to enlighten the world, and diffuse a spirit of freedom and liberality among mankind, than any human event (if this may be called one) that ever preceded it.

It is not among the least of the calamities of a long continued war, that it unhinges the mind from those nice sensations which at other times appear so amiable. The continual spectacle of woe, blunts the finer feelings, and the necessity of bearing with the sight, renders it familiar. In like manner, are many of the moral obligations of society weakened, till the custom of acting by necessity, becomes an apology where it is truly a crime. Yet let but a nation conceive rightly of its character, and it will be chastly just in protecting it. None ever began with a fairer than America, and none can be under a greater obligation to preserve it.

The debt which America has contracted, compared with the cause she has gained, and the advantages to flow from it, ought scarcely to be mentioned. She has it in her choice to do, and to live, as happily, as she pleases. The world is in her hands. She has no foreign power to monopolize her commerce, perplex her legislation, or controul her prosperity. The struggle is over, which must one day have happened, and, perhaps, never could have happened at a better time.[11]

11. That the revolution began at the exact period of time best fitted to the purpose, is sufficiently proved by the event–But the great hinge on which the whole machine turned is the UNION OF THE STATES: and this union was naturally produced by the inability of any one state to support itself against any foreign enemy without the assistance of the rest.

Had the states severally been less able than they were when the war began, their united strength would not have been equal to the undertaking, and they must, in all human probability, have failed–And on the other hand, had they severally been more able, they might not have seen, or, what is more, might not have felt the necessity of uniting; and either by attempting to stand alone, or in small confederacies, would have been separately conquered.

Now, as we cannot see a time (and many years must pass away before it can arrive) when the strength of any one state, or several united, can be equal to the whole of the present United States, and as we have seen the extreme difficulty of collectively prosecuting the war to a successful issue, and preserving our national importance in the world, therefore, from the experience we have had, and the knowledge we have gained, we must, unless we make a waste of wisdom, be strongly impressed with the advantage, as well as the necessity of strengthening that happy union which has been our salvation, and without which we should have been a ruined people.

While I was writing this note, I cast my eye on the pamphlet COMMON SENSE, from which I shall make an extract, as it applies exactly to the case. It is as follows:

And instead of a domineering master, she has gained an *ally*, whose exemplary greatness, and universal liberality, have extorted a confession even from her enemies.

With the blessings of peace, independence, and an universal commerce, the states individually and collectively, will have leisure and opportunity to regulate and establish their domestic concerns, and to put it beyond the power of calumny to throw the least reflection on their honor. Character is much easier kept than recovered, and that man, if any such there be, who, from any sinister views, or littleness of soul, lends unseen his hand to injure it, contrives a wound it will never be in his power to heal.

As we have established an inheritance for posterity, let that inheritance descend, with every mark of an honorable conveyance. The little it will cost, compared with the worth of the states, the greatness of the object, and the value of national character, will be a profitable exchange.

But that which must more forcibly strike a thoughtful penetrating mind, and which includes and renders easy all inferior concerns, is the UNION OF THE STATES. On this, our great national character depends. It is this which must give us importance abroad and security at home. It is through this only that we are, or can be nationally known in the world. It is the flag of the United States which renders our ships and commerce safe on the seas, or in a foreign port. Our Mediterranean passes must be obtained under the same stile. All our treaties whether of alliance, peace or commerce, are formed under the sovereignty of the United States, and Europe knows us by no other name or title.

The division of the empire into states is for our own convenience, but abroad this distinction ceases. The affairs of each state are local. They can go no farther than to itself. And were the whole worth of even the richest of

---

"I have never met with a man, either in England or America, who hath not confessed his opinion that a separation between the countries would take place one time or other: And there is no instance in which we have shewn less judgment, than in endeavoring to describe, what we call, the ripeness or fitness of the continent for independence.

"As all men allow the measure, and differ only in their opinion of the time, let us, in order to remove mistakes, take a general survey of things, and endeavor, if possible, to find out the VERY TIME. But we need not go far, the enquiry ceases at once, for, THE TIME HATH FOUND US. The general concurrence, the glorious union of all things prove the fact.

"It is not in numbers, but in a union, that our great strength lies. The continent is just arrived at that pitch of strength, in which no single colony is able to support itself, and the whole, when united, can accomplish the matter; and either more or less than this, might be fatal in its effects."

them expended in revenue, it would not be sufficient to support sovereignty against a foreign attack. In short, we have no other national sovereignty than as United States. It would even be fatal for us if we had – too expensive to be maintained, and impossible to be supported. Individuals or individual states may call themselves what they please; but the world, and especially the world of enemies, is not to be held in awe by the whistling of a name. Sovereignty must have power to protect all the parts that compose and constitute it: and as UNITED STATES we are equal to the importance of the title, but otherwise we are not. Our union well and wisely regulated and cemented, is the cheapest way of being great – the easiest way of being powerful, and the happiest invention in government which the circumstances of America can admit of – Because it collects from each state, that which, by being inadequate, can be of no use to it, and forms an aggregate that serves for all.

The states of Holland are an unfortunate instance of the effects of individual sovereignty. Their disjointed condition exposes them to numerous intrigues, losses, calamities and enemies; and the almost impossibility of bringing their measures to a decision, and that decision into execution, is to them, and would be to us, a source of endless misfortune.

It is with confederated states as with individuals in society; something must be yielded up to make the whole secure. In this view of things we gain by what we give, and draw an annual interest greater than the capital. – I ever feel myself hurt when I hear the union, that great palladium of our liberty and safety, the least irreverently spoken of. It is the most sacred thing in the constitution of America, and that which every man should be most proud and tender of. Our citizenship in the United States is our national character. Our citizenship in any particular state is only our local distinction. By the latter we are known at home, by the former to the world. Our great title is, AMERICANS – our inferior one varies with the place.

So far as my endeavors could go, they have all been directed to conciliate the affections, unite the interests and draw and keep the mind of the country together; and the better to assist in this foundation-work of the revolution, I have avoided all places of profit or office, either in the state I live in, or in the United States; kept myself at a distance from all parties and party connections, and even disregarded all private and inferior concerns: and when we take into view the great work we have gone through, and feel, as we ought to feel, the just importance of it, we shall then see, that the little wranglings and indecent contentions of personal parly, are as dishonorable to our characters, as they are injurious to our repose.

It was the cause of America that made me an author. The force with which it struck my mind, and the dangerous condition the country appeared to me in, by courting an impossible and an unnatural reconciliation with those who were determined to reduce her, instead of striking out into the only line that could cement and save her, A DECLARATION OF INDE-PENDENCE, made it impossible for me, feeling as I did, to be silent: and if, in the course of more than seven years, I have rendered her any service, I have likewise added something to the reputation of literature, by freely and disinterestedly employing it in the great cause of mankind, and shewing there may be genius without prostitution.

Independence always appeared to me practicable and probable; provided the sentiment of the country could be formed and held to the object: and there is no instance in the world, where a people so extended, and wedded to former habits of thinking, and under such a variety of circumstances, were so instantly and effectually pervaded, by a turn in politics, as in the case of independence, and who supported their opinion, undiminished, through such a succession of good and ill fortune, till they crowned it with success.

But as the scenes of war are closed, and every man preparing for home and happier times, I therefore take my leave of the subject. I have most sincerely followed it from beginning to end, and through all its turns and windings; and whatever country I may hereafter be in, I shall always feel an honest pride at the part I have taken and acted, and a gratitude to Nature and Providence for putting it in my power to be of some use to mankind.

– COMMON SENSE.

END.

TO THE

PEOPLE OF AMERICA.

[A Supernumerary Crisis]

IN *"Rivington's New-York Gazette,"* of Dec. 6th, is a publication, under the appearance of a letter from London, dated Sept. 30th; and is on a subject which demands the attention of the United States.

The Public will remember, that a Treaty of Commerce between the United States and England was set on foot last Spring, and that until the said Treaty could be compleated, a Bill was brought into the British Parliament, by the then Chancellor of the Exchequer, Mr. Pitt, to admit and legalize (as the case then required) the Commerce of the United States into the British ports and dominions. But neither the one nor the other has been compleated. The Commercial Treaty is either broken off, or remains as it began; and the Bill in Parliament has been thrown aside. And in lieu thereof, a selfish system of English politics has started up, calculated to fetter the Commerce of America, by engrossing to England the carrying trade of the American produce to the West India Islands.

Among the advocates for this last measure, is Lord Sheffield, a Member of the British Parliament, who has published a Pamphlet, entitled, *"Observations on the Commerce of the American States."* The pamphlet has two objects; the one is, to allure the Americans to purchase British manufactures; and the other, to spirit up the British Parliament to prohibit the Citizens of the United States from trading to the West-India Islands.

Viewed in this light, the pamphlet, though in some parts dextrously written, is an absurdity. It offends, in the very act of endeavouring to ingratiate; and his Lordship, as a politician, ought not to have suffered the two objects to have appeared together. The letter alluded to contains extracts from the pamphlet, with high encomiums on Lord Sheffield, for laboriously endea-

"To the People of America" [A Supernumerary Crisis], in *Rivington's New-York Gazette*, December 10, 1783.

vouring (as the letter stiles it) "to shew the mighty advantages of retaining the carrying trade."

Since the publication of this pamphlet in England, the Commerce of the United States to the West-Indies, in American vessels, has been prohibited; and all intercourse, except in British bottoms, the property of, and navigated by British subjects, cut off.

That a country has a right to be as foolish as it pleases, has been proved by the practice of England for many years past: In her island-situation, sequestered from the world, she forgets that her whispers are heard by other nations; and in her plans of politics and commerce, she seems not to know, that other votes are necessary besides her own. America would be equally as foolish as Britain, were she to suffer so great a degradation on her flag, and such a stroke on the freedom of her Commerce, to pass without a balance.

We admit the right of any nation to prohibit the Commerce of another into its own dominions, where there are no treaties to the contrary; but as this right belongs to one side, as well as to the other, there is always a way left to bring avarice and insolence to reason.

But the ground of security which Lord Sheffield has chosen to erect his policy upon, is of a nature which ought, and I think must awaken, in every American, a just and strong sense of national dignity. Lord Sheffield appears to be sensible that in advising the British Nation and Parliament to engross to themselves so great a part of the Carrying Trade of America, he is attempting a measure which cannot succeed, if the Politics of the United States be properly directed to counteract the assumption.

But, says he, in his pamphlet, "*It will be a long time before the American States can be brought to act as a Nation, neither are they to be feared as such by us.*"

What is this more or less than to tell us, that while we have no National System of Commerce, the British will govern our trade by their own Laws and Proclamations as they please. The quotation discloses a truth too serious to be overlooked, and too mischievous not to be remedied.

Among other circumstances which led them to this discovery, none could operate so effectually, as, the injudicious, uncandid, and indecent opposition made by sundry persons in a certain State, to the recommendations of Congress last Winter, for an import duty of five percent. It could not but explain to the British a weakness in the National Power of America, and encourage them to attempt restrictions on her trade, which otherwise they would not have dared to hazard. Neither is there any State in the Union, whose policy was more mis directed to its interest than the State I allude to, because her principal support is the Carrying Trade, which Britain, induced by the want of a well-centered Power in the United States to protect and secure, is now attempting to take away. It fortunately happened (and to no State in the Union more than the State in question) that the Terms of Peace were agreed on before the Opposition appeared, otherwise, there needs not a doubt, that if the same idea of the diminished authority of America, had occurred to them at that time as has occurred to them since, but they would have made the same grasp at the Fisheries, as they have done at the Carrying Trade.

It is surprising that an authority which can be supported with so much ease, and so little expence, and capable of such extensive advantages to the country, should be cavelled at by those whose duty it is to watch over it, and whose existence, as a people depends upon it. But this, perhaps, will ever be the case, till some misfortune awaken us into reason, and the instance now before us is but a gentle beginning of what America must expect, unless she guards her Union with nicer care and stricter honour. United, she is formidable, and that with the least possible charge, a Nation can be so: Separated, she is a medley of individual nothings, subject to the sport of foreign Nations.

It is very probable that the ingenuity of Commerce may have found out a method to evade and supercede the intentions of the British in interdicting the Trade with the West-India Islands. The language of both being the same, and their customs well understood, the vessels of one country may, by deception, pass for those of another. But this would be a practice too debasing for a Sovereign people to stoop to, and too profligate not to be discountenanced. An illicit Trade, under any shape it can be placed, cannot be carried on without a violation of truth. America is now Sovereign and Independent, and ought to act all her affairs in a regular stile of character. She has the same right to say that no British vessel shall enter her ports, or that no British manufactures shall be imported but in American bottoms, the property of, and navigated by American subjects, as Britain has to say the same thing respecting the West-Indies. Or she may lay a duty of ten, fifteen, or twenty shillings per ton (exclusive of other duties) on every British vessel coming from any port of the West-Indies where she is not admitted to trade, the said tonnage to continue as long on her side as the prohibition continues on the other.

But it is only by acting in Union, that the usurpations of foreign Nations on the freedom of trade, can be counteracted, and security extended to the Commerce of America. And when we view a Flag, which to the eye is beautiful, and to contemplate its rise and origin, inspires a sensation of sublime delight, our National Honour must unite with our Interest to prevent injury to the one, or insult to the other.

– COMMON SENSE.

New-York, Dec. 9, 1783.

DISSERTATIONS

ON

GOVERNMENT,

THE

AFFAIRS OF THE BANK,

AND

PAPER-MONEY.

By The Author of COMMON SENSE.

Preface.

I HERE present the Public with a new performance. Some parts of it are more particularly adapted to the State of Pennsylvania, on the present state of its affairs: But there are others which are on a larger scale. The time bestowed on this work has not been long, the whole of it being written and printed during the short recess of the Assembly.

As to parties, merely considered as such, I am attached to no particular one. There are such things as right and wrong in the world, and so far as these are parties against each other, the signature of COMMON SENSE *is properly employed.*

– THOMAS PAINE.

Philadelphia, Feb. 18, 1786.

Dissertations on Government, the Affairs of the Bank, and Paper-Money (Philadelphia: Charles Cist, 1786).

Dissertations
on
Government,
the
Affairs of the Bank,
and
Paper-Money.

EVERY Government, let its form be what it may, contains within itself a principle common to all, which is, that of a sovereign power, or a power over which there is no controul, and which controuls all others: And as it is impossible to construct a form of government in which this power does not exist, so there must of necessity be a place, if it may be so called, for it to exist in.

IN Despotic Monarchies this power is lodged in a single person, or sovereign. His Will is law; which he declares, alters, or revokes as he pleases, without being accountable to any power for so doing. Therefore, the only modes of redress, in countries so governed, are by petition or insurrection. And this is the reason we so frequently hear of insurrections in despotic governments; for as there are but two modes of redress, this is one of them.

PERHAPS it may be said that as the united resistance of the people is able, by force, to controul the Will of the sovereign, that, therefore, the controuling power lodged in them: but it must be understood that I am speaking of such powers only as are constituent parts of the government, not of those powers which are externally applied to resist and overturn it.

IN Republics, such as those established in America, the sovereign power, or the power over which there is no controul and which controuls all others, remains where nature placed it; in the people; for the people in America are the fountain of power. It remains there as a matter of right, recognized in the constitutions of the country, and the exercise of it is constitutional and legal.——This sovereignty is exercised in electing and deputing a certain number of persons to represent and act for the whole, and who, if they do not act right, may be displaced by the same power that placed them there, and others elected and deputed in their stead, and the wrong measures of former representatives corrected and brought right by this means. Therefore the republican form and principle leaves no room for insurrection, because it provides and establishes a rightful means in its stead.

IN countries under a despotic form of government, the exercise of this power is an assumption of sovereignty; a wresting it from the person in whose hand their form of government has placed it, and the exercise of it there is stiled rebellion. Therefore the despotic form of government knows no intermediate space between being slaves and being rebels.

I shall in this place offer an observation which, though not immediately connected with my subject, is very naturally deduced from it, which is, That the nature, if I may so call it, of a government over any people may be ascertained from the modes which the people pursue to obtain redress; for like causes will produce like effects. And therefore the government which Britain attempted to erect over America could be no other than a despotism, because it left to the Americans no other modes of redress than those which are left to people under despotic governments, petition and resistance: and the Americans, without ever attending to a comparison on the case, went into the same steps which such people go into, because no other could be pursued: and this similarity of effects leads up to, and ascertains, the similarity of the causes or governments which produced them.

BUT to return——The repository where the sovereign power is placed is the first criterion of distinction between a country under a despotic form of government and a free country. In a country under a despotic government, the sovereign is the only free man in it.——In a republic, the people retaining the sovereignty in themselves, naturally and necessarily retain freedom with it: for, wherever the sovereignty is, there must the freedom be; the one cannot be in one place and the other in another.

As the repository where the sovereign power is lodged is the first criterion of distinction; the second is the principles on which it is administered.

A despotic government knows no principle but WILL. Whatever the sovereign wills to do, the government admits him the inherent right, and the uncontrouled power of doing. He is restrained by no fixed rule of right and wrong, for he makes the right and wrong himself and as he pleases. – If he happens (for a miracle may happen) to be a man of consummate wisdom, justice and moderation, of a mild affectionate disposition, disposed to business, and understanding and promoting the general good, all the beneficial purposes of government will be answered under his administration, and the people so governed may, while this is the case, be prosperous and easy. But as there can be no security that this disposition will last, and this administration continue, and still less security that his successor shall have the same qualities and pursue the same measures; therefore no people exercising their reason and understanding their rights, would, of their own choice, invest any one man with such a power.

NEITHER is it consistent to suppose the knowledge of any one man competent to the exercise of such a power. A Sovereign of this sort, is brought up in such a distant line of life, and lives so remote from the people, and from a knowledge of every thing which relates to their local situations and interests, that he can know nothing from experience and observation, and all which he does know he must be told. Sovereign power without sovereign knowledge, that is, a full knowledge of all the matters over which that power is to be exercised, is a something which contradicts itself.

THERE is a species of sovereign power in a single person, which is very proper when applied to a commander in chief over an army, so far as relates to the military government of an army, and the army constitute the reason why it is so.

IN an army every man is of the same profession, that is, he is a soldier, and the commander in chief is a soldier too: therefore the knowledge necessary to the exercise of the power is within himself. By understanding what a soldier is, he comprehends the local situation, interest and duty of every man within, what may be called, the dominion of his command; and therefore the condition and circumstances of an army make a fitness for the exercise of the power.

THE purpose likewise, or object of an army, is another reason: for this power in a commander in chief, though exercised over the army, is not exercised against it; but is exercised thro' or over the army against the enemy. Therefore the enemy, and not the people, is the object it is directed to. Neither is it exercised over an army, for the purpose of raising a revenue from it, but to promote its combined interest, condense its powers, and give it capacity for action.

BUT all these reasons cease when sovereign power is transferred from the commander of an army to the commander of a nation, and entirely loses its fitness when applied to govern subjects following occupations, as it governs soldiers following arms. A nation is quite another element, and every thing in it differs not only from each other, but all of them differ from those of an army. A nation is composed of distinct unconnected individuals, following various trades, employments and pursuits; continually meeting, crossing, uniting, opposing and separating from each other as accident, interest and circumstance shall direct.—An army has but one occupation and but one interest.

ANOTHER very material matter in which an army and a nation differ, is that of temper. An army may be said to have but one temper; for, however the *natural* temper of the persons composing the army may differ from each other, there is a second temper takes place of the first: a temper formed by discipline, mutuality of habits, union of objects and pursuits, and the stile of military manners: but this can never be the case among all the individuals of a nation. Therefore the fitness, arising from those circumstances, which disposes an army to the command of a single person, and the fitness of a single person to that command, is not to be found either in one or the other, when we come to consider them as a sovereign and a nation.

HAVING already shewn what a despotic government is, and how it is administered, I now come to shew what the administration of a republic is.

THE administration of a republic is supposed to be directed by certain fundamental principles of right and justice, from which there cannot, because there ought not to, be any deviation; and whenever any deviation appears, there is a kind of stepping out of the republican principle, and an approach towards the despotic one. This administration is executed by a select number of persons, periodically chosen by the people, and act as representatives and in behalf of the whole, and who are supposed to enact the same laws, and pursue the same line of administration, as the whole of the people would do were they assembled together.

THE PUBLIC GOOD is to be their object. It is therefore necessary to understand what Public Good is.

PUBLIC Good is not a term opposed to the good of individuals; on the contrary, it is the good of every individual collected. It is the good of all, because it is the good of every one: for as the public body is every individual collected, so the public good is the collected good of those individuals.

THE foundation-principle of Public Good is justice, and wherever justice is impartially administered the public good is promoted; for as it is to the good of every man that no injustice be done to him, so likewise it is to his good that the principle which secures him should not be violated in the person of another, because such a violation weakens *his* security, and leaves to chance what ought to be to him a rock to stand on.

BUT in order to understand more minutely, how the Public Good is to be promoted, and the manner in which the representatives are to act to promote it, we must have recourse to the original or first principles, on which the people formed themselves into a republic.

WHEN a people agree to form themselves into a republic (for the word REPUBLIC means the PUBLIC GOOD, or the good of the whole, in contradistinction to the despotic form, which makes the good of the sovereign, or of one man, the only object of the government) when, I say, they agree to do this, it is to be understood, that they mutually resolve and pledge themselves to each other, rich and poor alike, to support and maintain this rule of equal justice among them. They therefore renounce not only the despotic form, but the despotic principle, as well of governing as of being governed by mere Will and Power, and substitute in its place a government of justice.

BY this mutual compact the citizens of a republic put it out of their power, that is, they renounce, as detestable, the power of exercising, at any future time, any species of despotism over each other, or doing a thing, not right in itself, because a majority of them may have strength or numbers sufficient to accomplish it.

IN this pledge and compact[1] lies the foundation of the republic: and the security to the rich and the consolation to the poor is, that what each man

1. This pledge and compact is contained in the declaration of Rights prefixed to the constitution, and is as follows–

I. THAT all men are born equally free and independent, and have certain natural, inherent and unalienable rights, amongst which are the enjoying and defending life and liberty, acquiring, possessing and protecting property, and pursuing and obtaining happiness and safety.

II. THAT all men have a natural and unalienable right to worship Almighty God, according to the dictates of their own consciences and understanding: And that no man ought or of right can be compelled to attend any religious worship, or erect or support any place of worship, or maintain any ministry, contrary to, or against, his own free will and consent: Nor can any man, who acknowledges the being of a God, be justly deprived or abridged of any civil right as a citizen, on account of his religious sentiments or peculiar mode of religious worship, And that no authority can or ought to be vested in, or assumed by any power whatever, that shall in any case interfere with, or in any manner controul, the right of conscience in the free exercise of religious worship.

III. THAT the people of this state have the sole, exclusive and inherent right of governing and regulating the internal police of the same

IV THAT all power being originally inherent in, and consequently derived from, the people; therefore all officers of government, whether legislative or executive, are their trustees and servants, and at all times accountable to them.

V. THAT government is, or ought to be, instituted for the common benefit, protection and security of the people, nation or community; and not for the particular emolument or advantage of any single man, family or set of men who are a part only of that community: And that the community hath an indubitable, unalienable and indefeasible right to reform, alter or abolish government in such manner as shall be by that community judged most conducive to the public weal.

VI. THAT those who are employed in the legislative and executive business of the state may be restrained from oppression, the people have a right, at such periods as they may think proper, to reduce their public officers to a private station, and supply the vacancies by certain and regular elections.

VII. THAT all elections ought to be free; and that all free men having a sufficient evident common interest with, and attachment to the community, have a right to elect officers, or be elected into office.

VIII. THAT every member of society hath a right to be protected in the enjoyment of life, liberty and property, and therefore is bound to contribute his proportion towards the expence of that protection, and yield his personal service when necessary, or an equivalent thereto: But no part of a man's property can be justly taken from him, or applied to public uses, without his own consent, or that of his has is his own; that no despotic sovereign can take it from him, and that the common cementing principle which holds all the parts of a republic together, secures him likewise from the despotism of numbers: For despotism may be more effectually acted by many over a few than by one man over all.

---

legal representatives: Nor can any man who is conscientiously scrupulous of bearing arms, be justly compelled thereto, if he will pay such equivalent: Nor are the people bound by any laws, but such as they have in like manner assented to, for their common good.

IX. THAT in all prosecutions for criminal offences, a man hath a right to be heard by himself and his council, to demand the cause and nature of his accusation, to be confronted with the witnesses, to call for evidence in his favour, and a speedy public trial, by an impartial jury of the country, without the unanimous consent of which jury he cannot be found guilty: Nor can he be compelled to give evidence against himself: Nor can any man be justly deprived of his liberty, except by the laws of the land, or the judgment of his peers.

X. THAT the people have a right to hold themselves, their houses, papers, and possessions free from search or seizure; and therefore warrants without oaths or affirmations first made, affording a sufficient foundation for them, and whereby any officer or messenger may be commanded or required to search suspected places, or to seize any person or persons, his or their property not particularly described, are contrary to that right and ought not to be granted.

XI. THAT in controversies respecting property, and in suits between man and man, the parties have a right to trial by jury, which ought to be held sacred.

XII. THAT the people have a right to freedom of speech, and of writing, and publishing their sentiments; therefore the freedom of the press ought not to be restrained.

XIII. THAT the people have a right to bear arms for the defence of themselves and the state; and as standing armies in the time of peace, are dangerous to liberty, they ought not to be kept up: And that the military should be kept under strict subordination to, and governed by, the civil power.

XIV. THAT a frequent recurrence to fundamental principles, and a firm adherence to justice, moderation, temperance, industry and frugality are absolutely necessary to preserve the blessings of liberty and keep a government free: The people ought therefore to pay particular attention to these points in the choice of officers and representatives, and have a right to exact a due and constant regard to them, from their legislators and magistrates, in the making and executing such laws as are necessary for the good government of the state.

XV. THAT all men have a natural inherent right to emigrate from one state to another that will receive them, or to form a new state in vacant countries, or in such countries as they can purchase, whenever they think that thereby they may promote their own happiness.

XVI. THAT the people have a right to assemble together, to consult for their common good, to instruct their representatives, and to apply to the legislature for redress of grievances by address, petition, or remonstrance.

THEREFORE, in order to know how far the power of an Assembly, or a house of representatives can act in administering the affairs of a republic, we must examine how far the power of the people extends under the original compact they have made with each other; for the power of the representatives is in many cases less, but never can be greater than that of the people represented; and whatever the people in their mutual original compact have renounced the power of doing towards, or acting over each other, the representatives can not assume the power to do, because, as I have already said, the power of the representatives cannot be greater than that of the people whom they represent.

IN this place it naturally presents itself that the people in their original compact of equal justice or first principles of a republic, renounced, as despotic, detestable and unjust, the assuming a right of breaking and violating their engagements, contracts and compacts with, or defrauding, imposing or tyrannizing over, each other, and therefore the representatives can not make an Act to do it for them, and any such an Act would be an attempt to depose, not the personal sovereign, but the sovereign principle of the republic, and to introduce despotism in its stead.

IT may in this place be proper to distinguish between that species of sovereignty which is claimed and exercised by despotic monarchs, and that sovereignty which the citizens of a republic inherit and retain.——The sovereignty of a despotic monarch assumes the power of making wrong right, or right wrong, as he pleases or as it suits him. The sovereignty in a republic is exercised to keep right and wrong in their proper and distinct places, and never to suffer the one to usurp the place of the other. A republic, properly understood, is a sovereignty of justice in contradistinction to a sovereignty of Will.

OUR experience in republicanism is yet so slender, that it is much to be doubted, whether all our public Laws and Acts are consistent with, or can be justified on, the principles of a republican government.

WE have been so much habited to act in committees at the commencement of the dispute, and during the interregnum of government, and in many cases since, and to adopt expedients warranted by necessity, and to permit to ourselves a discretionary use of power suited to the spur and exigency of the moment, that a man transferred from a committee to a seat in the Legislature imperceptibly takes with him the ideas and habits he has been accustomed to, and continues to think like a committee-man instead of a legislator, and to govern by spirit rather than by the rule of the constitution and the principles of the Republic.

HAVING already stated that the power of the representatives can never exceed the power of the people whom they represent, I now proceed to examine more particularly, what the power of the representatives is.

IT is, in the first place, the power of acting as legislators in making laws,—and in the second place, the power of acting in certain cases, as agents or negociators for the Commonwealth, for such purposes as the circumstances of the Commonwealth require.

A VERY strange confusion of ideas dangerous to the credit, stability, and the good and honor of the Commonwealth has arisen by confounding those two distinct powers and things together, and blending every Act of the Assembly, of whatever kind it may be, under one general name of *"Laws of the Commonwealth,"* and thereby creating an opinion (which is truly of the despotic kind) that every succeeding Assembly has an equal power over every transaction, as well as law, done by a former Assembly.

ALL laws are Acts, but all Acts are not laws. Many of the Acts of the Assembly are Acts of agency or negociation, that is, they are Acts of contract and agreement, on the part of the State, with certain persons therein mentioned, and for certain purposes therein recited. An Act of this kind, after it has passed the House, is of the nature of a deed or contract, signed, sealed and delivered; and subject to the same general laws and principles of justice as all other deeds and contracts are: for in a transaction of this kind the State stands as an individual, and can be known in no other character in a court of justice.

By "LAWS" as distinct from the agency transactions, or matters of negociation, are to be comprehended all those public Acts of the Assembly or Commonwealth, which have a universal operation, or apply themselves to every individual of the Commonwealth. Of this kind are the laws for the distribution and administration of justice, for the preservation of the peace, for the security of property, for raising the necessary revenue by just proportions, &c. &c.

ACTS of this kind are properly LAWS, and they may be altered and amended or repealed, or others substituted in their places, as experience shall direct, for the better effecting the purpose for which they were intended: and the right and power of the Assembly to do this, is derived from the right and power which the people, were they all assembled together, instead of being represented, would have to do the same thing: because, in Acts or laws of this kind, there is no other party than the public. The law, or the alteration, or the repeal, is for themselves;—and whatever the effects may be, it falls on themselves;—if for the better, they have the benefit of it—if for the worse, they suffer the inconvenience. No violence to any one is here offered——no breach of faith is here committed. It is therefore one of these rights and powers which is within the sense, meaning and limits of the original compact of justice which they formed with each other as the foundation principle of the Republic, and being one of those rights and powers, it devolves on their representatives by delegation.

As it is not my intention (neither is it within the limits assigned to this work) to define every species of what may be called LAWS, (but rather to distinguish that part in which the representatives act as agents or negociators for the State, from the legislative part,) I shall pass on to distinguish and describe those Acts of the Assembly which are Acts of agency or negociation, and to shew that as they are different in their nature, construction and operation from legislative Acts, so likewise the power and authority of the Assembly over them, after they are passed, is different.

IT must occur to every person on the first reflection, that the affairs and circumstances of a Commonwealth require other business to be done besides that of making laws, and consequently, that the different kinds of business cannot all be classed under one name, or be subject to one and the same rule of treatment.——But to proceed——

BY agency transactions, or matters of negociation, done by the Assembly, are to be comprehended all that kind of public business, which the Assembly, as representatives of the Republic, transact in its behalf, with certain person or persons, or part or parts of the Republic, for purposes mentioned in the Act, and which the Assembly confirm and ratify on the part of the Commonwealth, by affixing to it the seal of the State.

AN Act of this kind, differs from a law of the before mentioned kind; because here are two parties and there but one, and the parties are bound to perform different and distinct parts: whereas, in the before mentioned law, every man's part was the same.

THESE Acts, therefore, though numbered among the laws, are evidently distinct therefrom, and are not of the legislative kind. The former are laws for the government of the Commonwealth; these are transactions of business, such as, selling and conveying an estate belonging to the public, or buying one; Acts for borrowing money, and fixing with the lender the terms and mode of payment; Acts or agreement and contract, with certain person or persons, for certain purposes; and, in short, every kind of Act in which two parties, the State being one, are particularly mentioned or described, and in which the form and nature of a bargain or contract is comprehended.——These, if for custom and uniformity sake we call by the name of LAWS, they are not laws for the government of the Commonwealth, but for the government of the contracting parties, as all deeds and contracts are; and are not, properly speaking, Acts of the Assembly, but joint Acts, or Acts of the Assembly in behalf of the Commonwealth on one part, and certain persons therein mentioned on the other part.

ACTS of this kind are distinguishable into two classes. –

FIRST, those wherein the matters inserted in the Act have already been settled and adjusted between the State on one part, and the persons therein mentioned on the other part. In this case the Act is the completion and ratification of the contract or matters therein recited. It is in fact a deed signed, sealed and delivered.

SECONDLY, those Acts wherein the matters have not been already agreed upon, and wherein the Act only holds forth certain propositions and terms to be accepted of and acceded to.

I SHALL give an instance of each of those Acts. First – The State wants the loan of a sum of money – certain persons make an offer to Government to lend that sum, and send in their proposals: the Government accept these proposals and all the matters of the loan and the payment are agreed on; and an Act is passed, according to the usual form of passing Acts, ratifying and confirming this agreement. This Act is final.

IN the second case, – The State, as in the preceding one, wants a loan of money – the Assembly passes an Act holding forth the terms on which it will borrow and pay: this Act has no force, until the propositions and terms are accepted of and acceded to by some person or persons, and when those terms are accepted of and complied with the Act is binding on the State.——But if at the meeting of the next Assembly, or any other, the whole sum intended to be borrowed, should not be borrowed, that Assembly may stop where they are, and discontinue proceeding with the loan, or make new propositions and terms for the remainder; but so far as the subscriptions have been filled up, and the terms complied with, it is, as in the first case, a signed deed: and in the same manner are all Acts, let the matters in them be what they may, wherein, as I have before mentioned, the State on one part, and certain individuals on the other part, are parties in the Act.

IF the State should become a bankrupt, the creditors, as in all cases of bankruptcy, will be sufferers; they will have but a dividend for the whole: but this is not a dissolution of the contract, but an accommodation of it, arising from necessity. And so in all cases of Acts of this kind, if an inability takes place on either side, the contract cannot be performed, and some accommodation must be gone into or the matter falls thro' of itself.

IT may likewise happen, tho' it ought not to happen, that in performing the matters, agreeably to the terms of the Act, inconveniencies, unforeseen at the time of making the Act, may arise to either or both parties: in this case, those inconveniencies may be removed by the mutual consent and agreement of the parties, and each find its benefit in so doing: for in a Republic it is the harmony of its parts that constitutes their several and mutual Good.

BUT the Acts themselves are legally binding, as much as if they had been made between two private individuals. The greatness of one party cannot give it a superiority of advantage over the other. The State, or its representatives the Assembly, has no more power over an Act of this kind, after it is passed, than if the State was a private person. It is the glory of a Republic to have it so, because it secures the individual from becoming the prey of power, and prevents MIGHT overcoming RIGHT.

IF any difference or dispute arise afterwards between the State and the individuals with whom the agreement is made, respecting the contract, or the meaning, or extent of any of the matters contained in the Act, which may affect the property or interest of either, such difference or dispute must be judged of, and decided upon, by the laws of the land, in a court of justice and trial by jury; that is, by the laws of the land already in being at the time such Act and contract was made.——No law made afterwards can apply to the case, either directly, or by construction or implication: For such a law would be a retrospective law, or a law made after the fact, and cannot even be produced in court as applying to the case before it for judgment.

THAT this is justice, that it is the true principle of republican government, no man will be so hardy as to deny: – If, therefore, a lawful contract or agreement, sealed and ratified, cannot be affected or altered by any Act made afterwards, how much more inconsistent and irrational, despotic and unjust would it be, to think of making an Act with the professed intention of breaking up a contract already signed and sealed.

THAT it is possible an Assembly, in the heat and indiscretion of party, and meditating on power rather than on the principle by which all power in a republican government is governed, that of equal justice, may fall into the error of passing such an Act, is admitted; – but it would be an actless Act, an Act that goes for nothing, an Act which the courts of justice, and the established laws of the land, could know nothing of.

BECAUSE such an Act would be an Act of one party only, not only without, but against the consent of the other; and, therefore, cannot be produced to affect a contract made between the two.——That the violation of a contract should be set up as a justification to the violator, would be the same thing as to say, that a man by breaking his promise is freed from the

140 Dissertations on Government

obligation of it, or that by transgressing the laws he exempts himself from the punishment of them.

BESIDES the constitutional and legal reasons why an Assembly cannot, of its own Act and authority, undo or make void a contract made between the State, (by a former Assembly,) and certain individuals, may be added, what may be called, the natural reasons, or those reasons which the plain rules of common sense point out to every man. Among which are the following.

THE Principals, or real parties, in the contract, are the State and the persons contracted with. The Assembly is not a party, but an Agent in behalf of the State, authorised and empowered to transact its affairs.

THEREFORE it is the State that is bound on one part and certain individuals on the other part, and the performance of the contract, according to the conditions of it, devolves on succeeding Assemblies, not as Principals, but as Agents.

THEREFORE for the next or any other Assembly to undertake to dissolve the State from its obligation is an assumption of power of a novel and extraordinary kind – It is the Servant attempting to free his Master.

THE election of new Assemblies following each other makes no difference in the nature of the thing. The State is still the same State. – The public is still the same body. These do not annually expire though the time of an Assembly does. These are not new-created every year, nor can they be displaced from their original standing; but are a perpetual permanent body, always in being and still the same.

BUT if we adopt the vague inconsistent idea that every new Assembly has a full and complete authority over every Act done by the State in a former Assembly, and confound together laws, contracts and every species of public business, it will lead us into a wilderness of endless confusion and unsurmountable difficulties. It would be declaring an Assembly despotic for the time being.——Instead of a government of established principles administered by established rules, the authority of Government by being strained so high, would, by the same rule, be reduced proportionably as low, and would be no other than that of a Committee of the State acting with discretionary powers for one year. Every new election would be a new revolution, or it would suppose the public of the former year dead and a new public risen in its place.

HAVING now endeavoured to fix a precise idea to, and distinguish between, Legislative Acts and Acts of Negociation and Agency, I shall proceed to apply this distinction to the case now in dispute, respecting the charter of the Bank.

THE charter of the Bank, or what is the same thing, the Act for incorporating it, is to all intents and purposes an Act of Negociation and Contract, entered into, and confirmed, between the State on one part, and certain persons mentioned therein on the other part. The purpose for which the Act was done on the part of the State is therein recited, viz. the support which the finances of the country would derive therefrom. The incorporating clause is the condition or obligation on the part of the State; and the obligation on the part of the Bank, is, "that nothing contained in that Act shall be construed to authorise the said Corporation to exercise any powers in this State repugnant to the laws or constitution thereof."

HERE are all the marks and evidences of a Contract. The Parties——the Purport——and the reciprocal Obligations.

THAT it is a Contract, or a joint Act, is evident from its being in the power of either of the parties to have forbidden or prevented its being done. The State could not force the stockholders of the Bank to be a corporation, and therefore as their consent was necessary to the making the Act, their dissent would have prevented its being made; so on the other hand, as the Bank could not force the State to incorporate them, the consent or dissent of the State would have had the same effect to *do,* or to prevent its being done; and as neither of the parties could make the Act alone, for the same reason can neither of them dissolve it alone: But this is not the case with a law or Act of legislation, and therefore the difference proves it to be an Act of a different kind.

THE Bank may forfeit the charter by delinquency, but the delinquency must be proved and established by a legal process in a court of justice and trial by jury: for the State, or the Assembly, is not to be a judge in its own case, but must come to the laws of the land for judgment; for that which is law for the individual, is likewise law for the State.

BEFORE I enter farther into this affair, I shall go back to the circumstances of the country and the condition the Government was in, for some time before, as well as at the time it entered into this engagement with the Bank, and this Act of incorporation was passed: for the Government of this State, and I suppose the same of the rest, were then in want of two of the most essential matters which governments could be destitute of.——Money and Credit.——

IN looking back to those times, and bringing forward some of the circumstances attending them, I feel myself entering on unpleasant and disagreeable ground; because some of the matters which the attack on the Bank now make necessary to state, in order to bring the affair fully before the Public, will not add honor to those who have promoted that measure, and carried it through the late House of Assembly; and for whom, tho' my own judgment and opinion on the case oblige me to differ from, I retain my esteem, and the social remembrance of times past. But, I trust, those Gentlemen will do me the justice to recollect my exceeding earnestness with them, last spring, when the attack on the Bank first broke out; for it clearly appeared to me one of those overheated measures, which, neither the country at large, nor their own constituents, would justify them in when it came to be fully and clearly understood; for however high a party-measure may be carried in an Assembly, the people out of doors are all the while following their several occupations and employments, minding their farms and their business, and take their own time and leisure to judge of public measures; the consequence of which is that they often judge in a cooler spirit than their representatives act in.

IT may be easily recollected that the present Bank was preceded by, and rose out, of a former one, called the Pennsylvania Bank, which began a few months before; the occasion of which I shall briefly state.

IN the spring [of] 1780, the Pennsylvania Assembly was composed of many of the same Members, and nearly all of the same connection, which composed the late House that began the attack on the Bank. I served as Clerk of the Assembly of 1780, which station I resigned at the end of the year and accompanied a much lamented friend the late Colonel John Laurens on an embassy to France.

THE spring of 1780 was marked with an accumulation of misfortunes. The reliance placed on the defence of Charlestown failed and exceedingly lowered or rather depressed the spirits of the country. The measures of Government, from the want of money, means and credit, dragged on like a heavy loaded carriage without wheels, and were nearly got to what a countryman would understand by a dead pull.

THE Assembly of that year met by adjournment at an unusual time, the tenth of May, and what particularly added to the affliction, was, that so many of the Members, instead of spiriting up their constituents to the most nervous exertions, came to the Assembly furnished with petitions to be exempt from paying taxes. How the public measures were to be carried on, the country defended, and the army recruited, clothed, fed, and paid, when the only resource, and that not half sufficient, that of taxes, should be relaxed to almost nothing, was a matter too gloomy to look at. A language very different from that of petitions ought at this time to have been the language of every one. A declaration to have stood forth with their lives and fortunes, and a reprobation of every thought of partial indulgence would have sounded much better than petitions.

WHILE the Assembly was sitting a letter from the Commander in chief was received by the Executive Council and transmitted to the House. The doors were shut and it fell officially to me to read.

IN this letter the naked truth of things was unfolded. Among other informations the General said, that notwithstanding his confidence in the attachment of the army to the cause of the country, the distresses of it, from the want of every necessary which men could be destitute of, were arisen to such a pitch, that the appearance of mutiny and discontent were so strongly marked on the countenance of the army that he dreaded the event of every hour.

WHEN the letter was read I observed a despairing silence in the House. No body spoke for a considerable time. At length a Member of whose fortitude to withstand misfortunes I had a high opinion, rose: "If," said he, "the account in that letter is a true state of things, and we are in the situation there represented, it appears to me in vain to contend the matter any longer. We may as well give up at first as at last."

THE Gentleman who spoke next, was (to the best of my recollection) a Member from Bucks county, who, in a cheerful note, endeavoured to dissipate the gloom of the House——"Well, well," said he, "don't let the House despair, if things are not so well as we wish, we must endeavour to make them better." And on a motion for adjournment, the conversation went no farther.

THERE was now no time to lose, and something absolutely necessary to be done, which was not within the immediate power of the House to do: for what with the depreciation of the Currency, the slow operation of taxes, and the petitions to be exempt therefrom, the treasury was moneyless, and the Government creditless.

IF the Assembly could not give the assistance which the necessity of the case immediately required, it was very proper the matter should be known by those who either could or would endeavour to do it. To conceal the information within the House, and not provide the relief which that information required, was making no use of the knowledge and endangering the Public Cause. The only thing that now remained, and was capable of reaching the case, was private credit, and the voluntary aid of individuals; and under this impression, on my return from the House, I drew out the salary due to me as Clerk, enclosed five hundred dollars in a letter to a Gentleman in this City, in part of the whole, and wrote fully to him on the subject of our affairs.

THE Gentleman to whom this letter was addressed is Mr. Blair M'Clenaghan. I mentioned to him, that notwithstanding the current opinion that the enemy were beaten from before Charlestown, there were too many reasons to believe the place was then taken and in the hands of the enemy; the consequence of which would be, that a great part of the British force would return, and join that at New-York. That our own army required to be augmented, ten thousand men, to be able to stand against the combined force of the enemy. I informed Mr. M'Clenaghan of General Washington's letter, the extreme distresses he was surrounded with, and the absolute occasion there was for the citizens to exert themselves at this time, which there was no doubt they would do, if the necessity was made known to them; for that the ability of Government was exhausted. I requested Mr. M'Clenaghan, to propose a voluntary subscription among his friends, and added, that I had enclosed five hundred dollars as my mite thereto, and that I would encrease it as far as the last ability would enable me to go.[2]

THE next day Mr. M'Clenaghan informed me, he had communicated the contents of the letter at a meeting of Gentlemen at the Coffee-house, and that a subscription was immediately began – that Mr. Robert Morris and himself had subscribed two hundred pounds each, in hard money, and that the subscription was going very successfully on. – This subscription was intended as a donation, and to be given in bounties to promote the recruiting service. It is dated June 8th, 1780. The original subscription list is now in my possession – it amounts to four hundred pounds hard money, and one hundred and one thousand three hundred and sixty pounds continental.

WHILE this subscription was going forward, information of the loss of Charlestown arrived,[3] and on a communication from several Members of Congress to certain Gentlemen of this city, of the encreasing distresses and dangers then taking place, a meeting was held of the subscribers, and such other Gentlemen who chose to attend, at the City Tavern. This meeting was on the 17th of June, nine days after the subscriptions had began.

AT this meeting it was resolved to open a security subscription, to the amount of three hundred thousand pounds, Pennsylvania currency, in real money; the subscribers to execute bonds to the amount of their subscriptions, and to form a Bank thereon for supplying the army. This being resolved on and carried into execution the plan of the first subscriptions was discontinued, and this extended one established in its stead.

BY means of this Bank the army was supplied thro' the campaign, and being at the same time recruited, was enabled to maintain its ground: And

2. Mr. M'Clenaghan being now returned from Europe, has my consent to shew the letter to any Gentleman who may be inclined to see it.

3. Col. Tennant, Aid to General Lincoln, arrived the 14th of June, with despatches of the capitulation of Charlestown.

on the appointment of Mr. Morris to be Superintendant of the finances the spring following, he arranged the system of the present Bank, stiled the Bank of North-America, and many of the subscribers of the former Bank transferred their subscriptions into this.

TOWARDS the establishment of this Bank, Congress passed an ordinance of incorporation December 21st 1781, which the Government of Pennsylvania recognized by sundry matters: And afterwards, on an application from the President and Directors of the Bank, thro' the mediation of the Executive Council, the Assembly agreed to, and passed the State Act of Incorporation April 1st 1782.

THUS arose the Bank——produced by the distress of the times and the enterprising spirit of patriotic individuals.——Those individuals furnished and risked the money, and the aid which the Government contributed was that of incorporating them.——It would have been well if the State had made all its bargains and contracts with as much true policy as it made this; for a greater service for so small a consideration, that only of an Act of incorporation, has not been obtained since the Government existed.

HAVING now shewn how the Bank originated, I shall proceed with my remarks.

THE sudden restoration of public and private credit, which took place on the establishment of the Bank is an event as extraordinary in itself as any domestic occurrence during the progress of the Revolution.

How far a spirit of envy might operate to produce the attack on the Bank during the sitting of the late Assembly, is best known and felt by those who began or promoted that attack. The Bank had rendered services which the Assembly of 1780 could not, and acquired an honor which many of its Members might be unwilling to own, and wish to obscure.

BUT surely every wise Government acting on the principles of patriotism and Public Good would cherish an Institution capable of rendering such advantages to the Community. The establishment of the Bank in one of the most trying vicissitudes of the war, its zealous services in the public cause, its influence in restoring and supporting credit, and the punctuality with which all its business has been transacted, are matters, that so far from meriting the treatment it met with from the late Assembly, are an honor to the State, and what the body of her citizens may be proud to own.

BUT the attack on the Bank, as a Chartered Institution, under the protection of its violators, however criminal it may be as an error of Government, or impolitic as a measure of party, is not to be charged on the constituents of those who made the attack. It appears from every circumstance that has come to light to be a measure which that Assembly contrived of itself.

The Members did not come charged with the affair from their constituents. There was no idea of such a thing when they were elected or when they met. The hasty and precipitate manner in which it was hurried through the House, and the refusal of the House to hear the Directors of the Bank in its defence, prior to the publication of the repealing Bill for public consideration, operated to prevent their constituents comprehending the subject: Therefore, whatever may be wrong in the proceedings lies not at the door of the Public. The House took the affair on its own shoulders, and whatever blame there is lies on them.

THE matter must have been prejudged and predetermined by a majority of the Members out of the House, before it was brought into it. The whole business appears to have been fixed at once, and all reasoning or debate on the case rendered useless.

PETITIONS from a very *inconsiderable* number of persons suddenly procured, and so privately done, as to be a secret among the few that signed them, were presented to the House and read twice in one day, and referred to a Committee of the House to *inquire* and report thereon. I here subjoin the Petition[4] and the Report, and shall exercise the right and privilege

4.   Minutes of the Assembly, March 21, 1785.
Petitions from a considerable number of the inhabitants of *Chester* county were read, representing that the bank established at *Philadelphia* has fatal effects upon the Community; that whilst men are enabled, by means of the bank, to receive near three times the rate of common interest, and at the same time to receive their money at very short warning, whenever they have occasion for it, it will be impossible for the husbandman or mechanic to borrow on the former terms of legal interest and distant payments of the principal; that the best security will not enable the person to borrow; that experience clearly demonstrates the mischievous consequences of this institution to the fair trader; that impostors have been enabled to support themselves in a fictitious credit, by means of a temporary punctuality at the bank, until they have drawn in their honest neighbours to trust them with their property, or to pledge their credit as sureties, and have been finally involved in ruin and distress; that they have repeatedly seen the stopping of discounts at the bank, operate on the trading part of the Community, with a degree of violence scarcely inferior to that of a stagnation of the blood in the human body, hurrying the wretched merchant who hath debts to pay into the hands of griping usurers; that the Directors of the bank may give such preference in trade, by advances of money, to their particular favorites, as to destroy that equality which ought to prevail in a commercial country; that paper-money has often proved beneficial to the state, but the bank forbids it, and the people must acquiesce: therefore, and in order to restore public confidence and private security, they pray that a bill may be brought in and passed into a law for repealing the law for incorporating the bank.

of a citizen in examining their merits, not for the purpose of opposition, but with a design of making an intricate affair more generally and better understood.

So far as my private judgment is capable of comprehending the subject, it appears to me, that the Committee were unacquainted with, and have

---

March 28.

The report of the committee, read March 25, on the petitions from the counties of *Chester* and *Berks,* and the city of *Philadelphia* and its vicinity, praying the act of Assembly, whereby the bank was established at *Philadelphia,* may be repealed, was read the second time as follows, viz.

The committee to whom were referred the petitions concerning the bank established at *Philadelphia,* and who were instructed to inquire whether the said bank be compatible with the public safety, and that equality which ought ever to prevail between the individuals of a republic, beg leave to report, That it is the opinion of this committee, that the said bank, as at present established, is in every view incompatible with the public safety: that in the present state of our trade, the said bank has a direct tendency to banish a great part of the specie from the country, so as to produce a scarcity of money, and to collect into the hands of the stockholders of the said bank almost the whole of the money which remains amongst us. That the accumulation of enormous wealth in the hands of a society, who claim perpetual duration, will necessarily produce a degree of influence and power, which cannot be entrusted in the hands of any set of men whatsoever, without endangering the public safety. That the said bank, in its corporate capacity, is empowered to hold estates to the amount of ten millions of dollars, and by the tenor of the present charter, is to exist forever, without being obliged to yield any emolument to the government, or to be at all dependent upon it. That the great profits of the bank, which will daily encrease as money grows scarcer, and which already far exceed the profits of European banks, have tempted foreigners to vest their money in this bank, and thus to draw from us large sums for interest.

That foreigners will doubtless be more and more induced to become stockholders, until the time may arrive when this enormous engine of power may become subject to foreign influence; this country may be agitated with the politics of European courts, and the good people of *America* reduced once more into a state of subordination, and dependence upon some one or other of the European powers. That at best, if it were even confined to the hands of Americans, it would be totally destructive of that equality which ought to prevail in a republic. We have nothing in our free and equal government capable of balancing the influence which this bank must create; and we see nothing which in the course of a few years, can prevent the directors of the bank, from governing Pennsylvania. Already we have felt its influence indirectly interfering in the measures of the legislature. Already the house of Assembly, the representatives of the people have been threatened, that the credit of our paper currency will be blasted by the bank; and if this growing evil continues, we fear the time is not very distant, when the bank will be able to dictate to the legislature, what laws to pass and what to forbear.

totally mistaken, the nature and business of a Bank, as well as the matter committed to them, considered as a proceeding of Government.

THEY were instructed by the House to *inquire* whether the Bank established at Philadelphia was compatible with the public safety.

IT is scarcely possible to suppose the instructions meant no more than that they were to inquire of one another. It is certain they made no inquiry at the Bank, to inform themselves of the situation of its affairs, how they were conducted, what aids it had rendered the public cause, or whether any; nor do the Committee produce in their report a single fact or circumstance to shew they made any inquiry at all, or whether the rumors then circulated were true or false; but content themselves with modelling the insinuations of the petitions into a report and giving an opinion thereon.

IT would appear from the report, that the Committee either conceived that the House had already determined how it would act without regard to the case, and that they were only a Committee for form sake, and to give a color of inquiry without making any, or that the case was referred to them, *as law-questions are sometimes referred to law-officers, for an opinion only.*

THIS method of doing public business serves exceedingly to mislead a country.——When the constituents of an Assembly hear that an enquiry into any matter is directed to be made, and a Committee appointed for that purpose, they naturally conclude that the inquiry *is made,* and that the future proceedings of the House are in consequence of the matters, facts, and information obtained by means of that inquiry.——But here is a Committee of inquiry making no inquiry at all, and giving an opinion on a case without inquiring into it. This proceeding of the Committee would justify an opinion that it was not their wish to *get,* but to *get over* information, and lest the enquiry should not suit their wishes, omitted to make any. The subsequent conduct of the House, in resolving not to hear the Directors of the Bank on their application for that purpose, prior to the publication of the Bill for the consideration of the people, strongly corroborates this opinion: For why should not the House hear them, unless it was apprehensive, that the Bank,

---

Your committee therefore beg leave further to report the following resolution to be adopted by the house, *viz.*

Resolved, that a committee be appointed to bring in a bill to repeal the act of Assembly, passed the first day of *April* 1782, entitled, "*An act to incorporate the subscribers to the bank of* North-America;" and also to repeal one other act of Assembly, passed the 18th of *March,* 1782, entitled, "*An act for preventing and punishing the counterfeiting of the common seal, bank-bills and bank-notes of the president, directors and company, of the bank of* North-America, *and for the other purposes therein mentioned.*"

by such a public opportunity, would produce proofs of its services and use-fulness, that would not suit the temper and views of its opposers?

BUT if the House did not wish or chuse to hear the defence of the Bank, it was no reason their constituents should not. The Constitution of this State, in lieu of having two branches of Legislature, has substituted, that "To the end that laws before they are enacted may be more *maturely considered*, and the inconvenience of *hasty determinations* as much as possible prevented, all Bills of a public nature shall be printed for the consideration of the people[5]."——The people, therefore, according to the Constitution, stand in the place of another House; or, more properly speaking, are a House in their own right.——But in this instance the Assembly arrogates the whole power to itself, and places itself as a bar to stop the necessary information spreading among the people.——The application of the Bank to be heard before the Bill was published for public consideration had two objects.——First, to the House,—and secondly, thro' the House to the people, who are as another House. It was as a defence in the first instance, and as an appeal in the second. But the Assembly absorbs the right of the people to judge; because, by refusing to hear the defence, they barred the appeal.——Were there no other cause which the constituents of that Assembly had for censuring its conduct, than the exceeding unfairness, partiality, and arbitrariness with which this business was transacted, it would be cause sufficient.

LET the constituents of Assemblies differ, as they may, respecting certain peculiarities in the *form* of the Constitution, they will all agree in supporting its *principles,* and in reprobating unfair proceedings and despotic measures. Every constituent is a member of the Republic, which is a station of more consequence to him than being a member of a party, and tho' they may differ from each other in their choice of persons to transact the public business, it is of equal importance to all parties that the business be done on right principles: otherwise our laws and Acts, instead of being founded in justice, will be founded in party, and be laws and Acts of retaliation; and instead of being a Republic of free citizens, we shall be alternately tyrants and slaves.—But to return to the Report.——

THE Report begins by stating that, "The Committee to whom were referred the petitions concerning the Bank established at Philadelphia, and who were instructed to *inquire* whether the said Bank be compatible with the public safety, and that equality which ought ever to prevail between the individuals of a Republic, beg leave to report," (not that they have made

5. Constitution, section the 15th.

any *inquiry,* but) "That it is the *opinion* of this Committee, that the said Bank, as at present established, is, in every view, incompatible with the public safety."——But why is it so? Here is an opinion unfounded and unwarranted. The Committee have began their Report at the wrong end; for an opinion, when given as a matter of judgment, is an action of the mind which follows a fact, but here it is put in the room of one.

THE Report then says, "That in the present state of our trade the said Bank has a direct tendency to banish a great part of the specie from the country, and to collect into the hands of the stockholders of the Bank almost the whole of the money which remains among us."

HERE is another mere assertion, just like the former, without a single fact or circumstance to shew why it is made or whereon it is founded.——Now the very reverse, of what the Committee asserts, is the natural consequence of a Bank.——Specie may be called the stock in trade of the Bank, it is therefore its interest to prevent it from wandering out of the country, and to keep a constant standing supply to be ready for all domestic occasions and demands. Were it true that the Bank has a direct tendency to banish the specie from the country, there would soon be an end to the Bank; and, therefore, the Committee have so far mistaken the matter, as to put their fears in the place of their wishes: for if it is to happen as the Committee states, let the Bank alone and it will cease of itself, and the repealing Act need not have been passed.

IT is the interest of the Bank that people should keep their cash there, and all commercial countries find the exceeding great convenience of having a general repository for their cash. – But so far from banishing it, there are no two classes of people in America who are so much interested in preserving hard money in the country as the Bank and the Merchant. Neither of them can carry on their business without it. Their opposition to the paper-money of the late Assembly was because it has a direct effect, as far as it is able, to banish the specie and that without providing any means for bringing more in. The Committee must have been aware of this, and therefore chose to spread the first alarm, and groundless as it was to trust to the delusion.

As the keeping the specie in the country is the interest of the Bank, so it has the best opportunities of preventing its being sent away, and the earliest knowledge of such a design. While the Bank is the general repository of cash no great sums can be obtained without getting it from thence, and as it is evidently prejudicial to its interest to advance money to be sent abroad, because in this case, the money can not by circulation return again, the Bank, therefore, is interested in preventing what the Committee would have it suspected of promoting.

IT is to prevent the exportation of cash and to retain it in the country that the Bank has on several occasions stopt the discounting notes till the danger has been passed.[6] The first part, therefore, of the assertion, that of banishing the specie, contains an apprehension as needless as it is ground-less, and which, had the Committee understood, or been the least informed of the nature of a Bank, they could not have made. It is very probable that some of the opposers to the Bank are those persons who have been disap-pointed in their attempt to obtain specie for this purpose and now cloak their opposition under other pretences.

I NOW come to the second part of the assertion, which is, that when the Bank has banished a great part of the specie from the country, "it will collect into the hands of the stockholders almost the whole of the money which remains among us."—But how, or by what means, the Bank is to ac-

---

6. The petitions say "That they have repeatedly seen the stopping of discounts at the bank, operate on the trading part of the Community, with a degree of violence scarcely inferior to that of a stagnation of the blood in the human body, hurrying the wretched merchant who hath debts to pay into the hands of griping usurers."

As the persons who say or signed this live somewhere in Chester county, they are not, from situation, certain of what they say. Those petitions have every appear-ance of being contrived for the purpose of bringing the matter on. The petition and the report have strong evidence in them of being both drawn up by the same person: for the report is as clearly the echo of the petition as ever the address of the British Parliament was the echo of the King's speech.

Besides the reason I have already given for occasionally stopping discounting notes at the bank, there are other necessary reasons. It is for the purpose of settling accounts. Short reckonings make long friends. The bank lends its money for short periods, and by that means assists a great many different people: and if it did not sometimes stop discounting as a means of settling with the persons it has already lent its money to, those persons would find a way to keep what they had borrowed longer than they ought, and prevent others being assisted. It is a fact, and some of the Committee know it to be so, that sundry of those persons who then opposed the Bank acted this part.

The stopping the discounts do not, and cannot, operate to call in the loans sooner than the time for which they were lent, and therefore the charge is false that "it hur-ries men into the hands of griping usurers":—and the truth is, that it operates to keep them from thence.

If petitions are to be contrived to cover the designs of a house of Assembly and give a pretence for its conduct, or if a house is to be led by the nose by the idle tale of any fifty or sixty signers to a petition, it is time for the public to look a little closer into the conduct of its representatives.

complish this wonderful feat the Committee have not informed us. Whether people are to give their money to the Bank for nothing, or whether the Bank is to charm it from them as a rattlesnake charms a squirrel from a tree, the Committee have left us as much in the dark about [it] as they were themselves.

Is it possible the Committee should know so very little of the matter, as not to know that no part of the money which at any time may be in the Bank belongs to the stockholders; not even the original capital which they put in is any part of it their own until every person who has a demand upon the Bank is paid, and if there is not a sufficiency for this purpose on the balance of loss and gain, the original money of the stockholders must make up the deficiency.

THE money which at any time may be in the Bank is the property of every man who holds a Bank-note, or deposits cash there, or who has a just demand upon it from the city of Philadelphia up to fort Pitt, or to any part of the United States; and he can draw the money from it when he pleases. Its being in the Bank, does not in the least make it the property of the stockholders, any more than the money in the State Treasury is the property of the State Treasurer. They are only stewards over it for those who please to put it, or let it remain there: and, therefore, this second part of the assertion is somewhat ridiculous.

THE next paragraph in the Report is, "That the accumulation of *enormous wealth* in the hands of a *society* who claim perpetual duration will necessarily produce a degree of influence and power which cannot be entrusted in the hands of any set of men whatsoever" (the Committee I presume excepted) "without endangering the public safety."——There is an air of solemn fear in this paragraph which is somewhat like introducing a ghost in a play to keep people from laughing at the players.

I HAVE already shewn that whatever wealth there may be, at any time, in the Bank, is the property of those who have demands upon the Bank, and not the property of the stockholders. As a Society they hold no property, and most probably never will, unless it should be a house to transact their business in, instead of hiring one. Every half year the Bank settles its accounts and each individual stockholder takes his dividend of gain or loss to himself, and the Bank begins the next halfyear in the same manner it began the first, and so on. This being the nature of a Bank, there can be no accumulation of wealth among them as a society.

FOR what purpose the word "*society*" is introduced into the Report I do not know, unless it be to make a false impression on people's minds. It has no connection with the subject, for the Bank is not a society, but a company, and denominated so in the Charter. There are several religious societies incorporated in this State, which hold property as the right of those societies, and to which no person can belong that is not of the same religious profession. But this is not the case with the Bank. The Bank is a company for the promotion and convenience of commerce, which is a matter in which all the State is interested, and holds no property in the manner which those societies do.

BUT there is a direct contradiction in this paragraph to that which goes before it. The Committee, there, accuses the Bank of banishing the specie, and here, of accumulating enormous sums of it.———So here are two enormous sums of specie; one enormous sum going out, and another enormous sum remaining.———To reconcile this contradiction, the Committee should have added to their Report, *that they suspected the Bank had found out the Philosopher's stone, and kept it a secret,*

THE next paragraph is, "That the said Bank, in its corporate capacity, is empowered to hold estates to the amount of ten millions of dollars, and by the tenor of the present Charter is to exist for ever, without being obliged to yield any emolument to the Government, or be at least dependent on it."

THE Committee have gone so vehemently into this business, and so completely shewn their want of knowledge in every point of it, as to make, in the first part of this paragraph, a fear of what, the greater fear is, will never happen. Had the Committee known anything of Banking, they must have known, that the objection against Banks has been, (not that they held great estates, but) that they held none; that they had no real, fixed, and visible property, and that it is the maxim and practice of Banks not to hold any.

THE Honorable Chancellor Livingston, late Secretary for foreign affairs, did me the honor of shewing, and discoursing with me on, a plan of a Bank he had drawn up for the State of New-York. In this plan it was made a condition or obligation, that whatever the capital of the Bank amounted to in specie, there should be added twice as much in real estates. But the mercantile interest rejected the proposition.

IT was a very good piece of policy in the Assembly which passed the Charter Act, to add the Clause to impower the Bank to purchase and hold real estates. It was as an inducement to the Bank to do it, because such estates being held as the property of the Bank would be so many mortgages to the Public in addition to the money capital of the Bank.

BUT the doubt is that the Bank will not be induced to accept the opportunity. The Bank has existed five years and has not purchased a shilling of real property: and as such property or estates can not be purchased by the Bank but with the interest money which the stock produces, and as that is divided every half year among the stockholders, and each stockholder chuses to have the management of his own dividend, and if he lays it out in purchasing an estate to have that estate his own private property, and under his own immediate management, there is no expectation, so far from being any fear, that the Clause will be accepted.

WHERE knowledge is a duty, ignorance is a crime; and the Committee are criminal in not understanding this subject better. Had this Clause not been in the Charter, the Committee might have reported the want of it as a defect, in not empowering the Bank to hold estates as a real security to its creditors: but as the complaint now stands, the accusation of it is, that the Charter empowers the Bank to *give real security* to its creditors. A complaint never made, heard of, or thought of before.

THE second article in this paragraph is, "That the Bank according to the tenor of the present Charter is to exist for ever"——Here I agree with the Committee, and am glad to find that among such a list of errors and contradictions there is one idea which is not wrong, altho' the Committee have made a wrong use of it.

As we are not to live for ever ourselves, and other generations are to follow us, we have neither the power nor the right to govern them, or to say how they shall govern themselves. It is the summit of human vanity, and shews a covetousness of power beyond the grave, to be dictating to the world to come. It is sufficient that we do that which is right in our own day and leave them with the advantage of good examples.

As the generations of the world are every day both commencing and expiring, therefore, when any public Act of this sort is done it naturally supposes the age of that generation to be then beginning, and the time contained between coming of age, and the natural end of life, in the extent of time it has a right to go to, which may be about thirty years; for tho' many may die before, others will live beyond; and the mean time is equally fair for all generations.

IF it was made an article in the Constitution, that all laws and Acts should cease of themselves in thirty years, and have no legal force beyond that time, it would prevent their becoming too numerous and voluminous, and serve to keep them within view and in a compact compass. Such as were proper to be continued, would be enacted again, and those which were not, would go into oblivion. There is the same propriety that a nation should fix a time for a full settlement of its affairs, and begin again from a new date, as that an individual should, and to keep within the distance of thirty years would be a convenient period.

THE British, from the want of some general regulation of this kind, have a great number of obsolete laws; which, tho' out of use and forgot, are not out of force, and are occasionally brought up for sharping purposes, and innocent unwary persons trepanned thereby.

To extend this idea still further, – it would probably be a considerable improvement in the political system of nations, to make all treaties of peace for a limited time. It is the nature of the mind to feel uneasy under the idea of a condition perpetually existing over it, and to excite in itself apprehensions that would not take place were it not from that cause.

WERE treaties of peace made for, and renewable every, seven or ten years, the natural effect would be, to make peace continue longer than it does under the custom of making peace for ever. If the parties felt or apprehended any inconveniencies under the terms already made, they would look forward to the time when they should be eventually relieved there from, and might renew the treaty on improved conditions. This opportunity periodically occurring, and the recollection of it always existing, would serve as a chimney to the political fabric, to carry off the smoke and fume of national fire. It would naturally abate, and honorably take off, the edge and occasion for fighting; and however the parties might determine to do it, when the time of the treaty should expire, it would then seem like fighting in cool blood: The fighting temper would be dissipated before the fighting time arrived, and negociation supply its place. To know how probable this may be, a man need do no more than observe the progress of his own mind on any private circumstance similar in its nature to a public one.——But to return to my subject——

To give Limitation is to give Duration: and tho' it is not a justifying reason, that because an Act or Contract is not to last for ever, that it shall be broken or violated to day, yet, where no time is mentioned, the omission affords an opportunity for the abuse. When we violate a contract on this pretence, we assume a right that belongs to the next generation; for tho' they, as a following generation, have the right of altering or setting it aside, as not being concerned in the making it, or not being done in their day, we, who made it, have not that right; and, therefore, the Committee, in this part of their report, have made a wrong use of a right principle; and as this Clause in the Charter might have been altered by the consent of the parties, it cannot be produced to justify the violation.——And were it not altered there would be no inconvenience from it. The term "for ever" is an absurdity that would have no effect. The next age will think for itself by the same rule of right that we have done, and not admit any assumed authority of ours to encroach upon the system of their day. Our *for ever* ends where their *for ever* begins.

THE third article in this paragraph is, that the Bank holds its Charter "without being obliged to yield any emolument to the Government."

INGRATITUDE has a short memory. It was on the failure of the Government, to support the Public Cause, that the Bank originated. It stept in as a support when some of the persons then in the Government, and who now oppose the Bank, were apparently on the point of abandoning the cause, not from disaffection, but from despair. While the expences of the war were carried on by emissions of continental money, any set of men, in Government, might carry it on. The means being provided to their hands, required no great exertions of fortitude or wisdom: but when this means failed, they would have failed with it, had not a public spirit awakened itself with energy out of doors. It was easy times to the Governments while continental money lasted. The dream of wealth supplied the reality of it; but when the dream vanished, the Government did not awake.

BUT what right has the Government to expect any emolument from the Bank? Does the Committee mean to set up Acts and Charters for sale, or what do they mean? Because it is the practice of the British Ministry to grind a toll out of every public institution they can get a power over, is the same practice to be followed here?

THE war being now ended, and the Bank having rendered the service expected, or rather hoped for, from it, the principal public use of it, at this time, is for the promotion and extension of commerce. The whole community derives benefit from the operation of the Bank. It facilitates the commerce of the country. It quickens the means of purchasing and paying for country-produce, and hastens on the exportation of it. The emolument, therefore, being to the Community, it is the office and duty of Government to give protection to the Bank.

AMONG many of the principal conveniencies arising from the Bank, one of them is, that it gives a kind of life to, what would otherwise be, dead money. Every merchant and person in trade, has always in his hands some quantity of cash, which constantly remains with him; that is, he is never entirely without: This remnant money, as it may be called, is of no use to him till more is collected to it. He can neither buy produce nor merchandize with it, and this being the case with every person in trade, there will be (tho' not all at the same) as many of those sums lying uselessly by, and scattered throughout the city, as there are persons in trade, besides many that are not in trade.

I SHOULD not suppose the estimation overrated, in conjecturing, that half the money in the city, at any one time, lies in this manner. By collecting those scattered sums together, which is done by means of the Bank, they become capable of being used, and the quantity of circulating cash is doubled, and by the depositors alternately lending them to each other, the commercial system is invigorated; and as it is the interest of the Bank to preserve this money in the country for domestic uses only, and as it has the best opportunity of doing so, the Bank serves as a sentinel over the specie.

IF a farmer, or a miller, comes to the city with produce, there are but few merchants that can individually purchase it with ready money of their own; and those few would command nearly the whole market for country produce: But, by means of the Bank, this monopoly is prevented, and the chance of the market enlarged. It is very extraordinary that the late Assembly should promote monopolizing; yet such would be the effect of suppressing the Bank; and it is much to the honor of those merchants, who are capable, by their fortunes, of becoming monopolizers, that they support the Bank. In this case, honor operates over interest. They were the persons who first set up the Bank, and their honor is now engaged to support what it is their interest to put down.

IF merchants, by this means, or farmers, by similar means, among themselves, can mutually aid and support each other, what has the Government to do with it? What right has it to expect emolument from associated industry, more than from individual industry? It would be a strange sort of a Government, that should make it illegal for people to assist each other, or pay a tribute for doing so.

BUT the truth is, that the Government has already derived emoluments, and very extraordinary ones. It has already received its full share, by the services of the Bank during the war; and it is every day receiving benefits, because whatever promotes and facilitates commerce, serves likewise to promote and facilitate the revenue.

THE last article in this paragraph is: "That the Bank is not the least dependent on the Government."

HAVE the committee so soon forgot the principles of Republican Government and the Constitution, or are [they] so little acquainted with them, as not to know, that this article in their Report partakes of the nature of treason? Do they not know, that freedom is destroyed by dependence, and the safety of the state endangered thereby? Do they not see that to hold any part of the citizens of the State, as yearly pensioners on the favor of an Assembly, is striking at the root of free elections? If other parts of their Report discover a want of knowledge on the subject of Banks, this shews a want of principle in the science of Government.

ONLY let us suppose this dangerous idea carried into practice, and then see what it leads to. If corporate Bodies are, after their incorporation, to be annually dependent on an Assembly for the continuance of their Charter, the citizens, which compose those corporations, are not free. The Government holds an authority and influence over them, in a manner different from what it does over other citizens, and by this means destroys that equality of freedom, which is the bulwark of the Republic and the Constitution.

BY this scheme of Government any party, which happens to be uppermost in a State, will command all the corporations in it, and may create more for the purpose of extending that influence. The dependent Borough-Towns in England are the rotten part of their Government, and this idea of the Committee has a very near relation to it.

"IF you do not do so and so," expressing what was meant, "take care of your Charter," was a threat thrown out against the Bank. But as I do not wish to enlarge on a disagreeable circumstance, and hope that what is already said, is sufficient to shew the Anti-Constitutional conduct and principles of the Committee, I shall pass on to the next paragraph in the Report.——Which is——

"THAT the great profits of the Bank, which will daily encrease as money grows scarcer, and which already far exceed the profits of European Banks, have tempted foreigners to vest their money in this Bank, and thus to draw from us large sums for interest."

HAD the Committee understood the subject, some dependence might be put on their opinion which now cannot. Whether money will grow scarcer, and whether the profits of the Bank will increase, are more than the Committee know, or are judges sufficient to guess at. The Committee are not so capable of taking care of commerce, as commerce is capable of taking care of itself. The farmer understands farming, and the merchant understands commerce; and as riches are equally the object of both, there is no occasion that either should fear that the other will seek to be poor. The more money the merchant has, so much the better for the farmer, who has produce to sell: and the richer the farmer is, so much the better for the merchant, when he comes to his store.

As to the profits of the Bank, the stockholders must take their chance for it. It may some years be more and others less, and upon the whole may not be so productive as many other ways that money may be employed. It is the convenience which the stockholders, as commercial men, derive from the establishment of the Bank, and not the mere interest they receive, that is the inducement to them. It is the ready opportunity of borrowing alternately of each other that forms the principal object: And as they pay as well as receive a great part of the interest among themselves, it is nearly the same thing, both cases considered at once, whether it is more or less.

THE stockholders are occasionally depositors and sometimes borrowers of the Bank. They pay interest for what they borrow, and receive none for what they deposit; and were a stockholder to keep a nice account of the interest he pays for the one and loses upon the other, he would find, at the year's end, that ten per cent upon his stock would probably not be more than common interest upon the whole, if so much.

As to the Committee complaining "that foreigners by vesting their money in the Bank will draw large sums from us for interest," it is like a miller complaining in a dry season, that so much water runs into his Dam that some of it runs over.

COULD those foreigners draw this interest without putting in any capital the complaint would be well founded; but as they must first put money in before they can draw any out, and as they must draw many years before they can draw even the numerical sum they put in at first, the effect, for at least twenty years to come, will be directly contrary to what the Committee states: Because we draw *capitals* from them and they only *interest* from us, and as we shall have the use of the money all the while it remains with us, the advantage will always be in our favor.——In framing this part of the Report, the Committee must have forgot which side of the Atlantic they were on, for the case would be as they state it if we put money into their Bank instead of they putting it into ours.

I HAVE now gone thro', line by line, every objection against the Bank, contained in the first half of the Report; what follows may be called, *The Lamentations of the Committee,* and a lamentable pusillanimous degrading affair it is.—It is a public affront, a reflection upon the sense and spirit of the whole country. I shall give the remainder together as it stands in the Report, and then my remarks.

THE Lamentations are, "That foreigners will doubtless be more and more induced to become stockholders, until the time may arrive when this *enormous* engine of power may become subject to foreign influence, this country may be agitated by the politics of European Courts, and the good people of America reduced once more into a state of subordination and dependence upon some one or other of the European Powers. That at best, if it were even confined to the hands of Americans, it would be totally destructive of that equality which ought to prevail in a Republic. We have nothing in our free and equal Government capable of balancing the influence which this Bank must create; and we see nothing which in the course of a few years can prevent the Directors of the Bank from governing Pensylvania. Already we have felt its influence indirectly interfering in the measures of the Legislature. Already the House of Assembly, the representatives of the people, have been threatened, that the credit of our paper currency will be blasted by the Bank; and if this growing evil continues, we fear the time is not very distant when the Bank will be able to dictate to the Legislature, what laws to pass and what to forbear."

WHEN the sky falls we shall be all killed. There is something so ridiculously grave, so wide of probability, and so wild, confused and inconsistent in the whole composition of this long paragraph that I am at a loss how to begin upon it.——It is like a drowning man crying fire! fire!

THIS part of the Report is made up of two dreadful predictions. The first is, that if foreigners purchase Bank stock we shall be all ruined:–The second is, that if the Americans keep the Bank to themselves we shall be also ruined.

A COMMITTEE of fortune-tellers is a novelty in Government; and the Gentlemen by giving this specimen of their art, have ingeniously saved their honor on one point, which is, that tho' people may say they are not Bankers, nobody can say they are not Conjurers.–There is, however, one consolation left, which is, that the Committee do not know *exactly* how long it may be; so there is some hope that we may all be in heaven when this dreadful calamity happens upon earth.

BUT to be serious, if any seriousness is necessary on so laughable a subject.–If the state should think there is any thing improper in foreigners purchasing Bank stock, or any other kind of stock or funded property, (for I see no reason why Bank stock should be particularly pointed at) the Legislature have authority to prohibit it. It is a mere political opinion that has nothing to do with the Charter or the Charter with that; and therefore the first dreadful prediction vanishes.

IT has always been a maxim in politics founded on, and drawn from, natural causes and consequences, that the more foreign countries which any nation can interest in the prosperity of its own so much the better. Where the treasure is there will the heart be also; and therefore when foreigners vest their money with us, they naturally invest their good wishes with it, and it is we that obtain an influence over them, not they over us.——But the Committee sat out so very wrong at first that the further they travelled the more they were out of their way; and now they are got to the end of their Report they are at the utmost distance from their business.

As to the second dreadful part, that of the Bank overturning the Government, perhaps the Committee meant that at the next general election themselves might be turned out of it, which has partly been the case; not by the influence of the Bank, for it had none, not even enough to obtain the permission of a hearing from Government, but by the influence of reason and the choice of the people, who most probably resent the undue and unconstitutional influence which that House and the Committee were assuming over the privileges of citizenship.

THE Committee might have been so modest as to have confined themselves to the Bank, and not thrown a general odium on the whole country. Before the events can happen which the Committee predict, the electors of Pennsylvania must become dupes, dunces and cowards, and therefore when the Committee predict the dominion of the Bank they predict the disgrace of the people.

THE Committee having finished their Report proceed to give their advice, which is,

"That a Committee be appointed to bring in a bill to repeal the Act of Assembly passed the first day of April 1782, entitled, *"An Act to incorporate the subscribers to the Bank of North-America,"* and also to repeal one other Act of the Assembly passed the 18th of March 1782, entitled, *"An Act for preventing and punishing the counterfeiting of the common seal, Bank bills, and Bank notes of the President, Directors and Company of the Bank of North-America, and for other purposes therein mentioned."* ["]

THERE is something in this sequel to the Report that is perplexed and obscure.

HERE are two Acts to be repealed. One is, the incorporating Act. – The other, the Act for preventing and punishing the counterfeiting of the common seal, Bank bills, and Bank notes of the President, Directors and Company of the Bank of North-America.

IT would appear from the Committee's manner of arranging them, (were it not for the difference of their dates) that the Act for punishing the counterfeiting the common seal, &c. of the Bank, followed the Act of incorporation, and that the common seal there referred to is a common seal which the Bank held in consequence of the aforesaid incorporating Act. – But the case is quite otherwise. The Act for punishing the counterfeiting the common seal, &c. of the Bank, was passed prior to the incorporating Act, and refers to the common seal which the Bank held in consequence of the Charter of Congress, and the stile which the Act expresses, of President, Directors and Company of the Bank of North-America, is the corporate stile which the Bank derives under the Congress Charter.

THE punishing Act, therefore, hath two distinct legal points. The one is, an authoritative public recognition of the Charter of Congress. The second is, the punishment it inflicts on counterfeiting.

THE Legislature may repeal the punishing part but it cannot undo the recognition, because no repealing Act can say that the State *has not* recognized. The recognition is a mere matter of fact, and no law or Act can undo a fact or put it, if I may so express it, in the condition it was before it existed. The repealing Act therefore does not reach the full point the Committee had in view; for even admitting it to be a repeal of the State Charter, it still leaves another Charter recognized in its stead. – The Charter of Congress, standing merely on itself, would have a doubtful authority, but the recognition of it by the State gives it legal ability. The repealing Act, it is true, sets aside the punishment but does not bar the operation of the Charter of Congress as a Charter recognized by the State, and therefore the Committee did their business but by halves.

I HAVE now gone entirely through the Report of the Committee, and a more irrational inconsistent contradictory Report will scarcely be found on the journals of any Legislature in America.

How the repealing Act is to be applied, or in what manner it is to operate, is a matter yet to be determined. For admitting a question of law to arise, whether the Charter, which that Act attempts to repeal, is a law of the land in the manner which laws of universal operation are, or of the nature of a contract made between the Public and the Bank (as I have already explained in this work) the repealing Act does not and cannot decide the question, because it is the repealing Act that makes the question, and its own fate is involved in the decision. It is a question of law and not a question of legislation, and must be decided on in a court of justice and not by a House of Assembly.

BUT the repealing Act by being passed prior to the decision of this point assumes the power of deciding it, and the Assembly in so doing erects itself unconstitutionally into a tribunal of judicature, and absorbs the authority and right of the courts of justice into itself.

THEREFORE the operation of the repealing Act, in its very outset, requires injustice to be done. For it is impossible on the principles of a republican government and the Constitution, to pass an Act to forbid any of the citizens the right of appealing to the courts of justice on any matter in which his or property is affected; but the first operation of this Act goes to shut up the courts of justice, and holds them subservient to the Assembly. It either commands or influences them not to hear the case, or to give judgment on it on the mere will of one party only.

I WISH the citizens to awaken themselves on this subject. – Not because the Bank is concerned, but because their own constitutional rights and privileges are involved in the event. It is a question of exceeding great magnitude; for if an Assembly is to have this power the laws of the land and the courts of justice are but of little use.

HAVING now finished with the Report, I proceed to the third and last subject – that of Paper-Money. –

I REMEMBER a German farmer expressing as much in a few words as the whole subject requires: *"Money is Money and Paper is Paper."*——All the invention of man cannot make them otherwise. The alchymist may cease his labours, and the hunter after the philosopher's stone go to rest, if paper can be metamorphosed into gold and silver, or made to answer the same purpose in all cases.

GOLD and silver are the emissions of nature; paper is the emission of art. The value of gold and silver is ascertained by the quantity which nature has made in the earth. We cannot make that quantity more or less than it is, and therefore the value being dependent upon the quantity, depends not on man.——Man has no share in making gold or silver; all that his labours and ingenuity can accomplish is, to collect it from the mine, refine it for use and give it an impression, or stamp it into coin.

ITS being stamped into coin adds considerably to its convenience but nothing to its value. It has then no more value than it had before. Its value is not in the impression but in itself. Take away the impression and still the same value remains. Alter it as you will, or expose it to any misfortune that can happen, still the value is not diminished. It has a capacity to resist the accidents that destroy other things. It has, therefore, all the requisite qualities that money can have, and is a fit material to make money of; and nothing, which has not all those properties, can be fit for the purpose of money.

PAPER, considered as a material whereof to make money, has none of the requisite qualities in it. It is too plentiful, and too easily come at. It can be had any where, and for a trifle.

THERE are two ways in which I shall consider paper.

THE only proper use for paper, in the room of money, is to write promissory notes and obligations of payment in specie upon. A piece of paper, thus written and signed, is worth the sum it is given for, if the person who gives it is able to pay it; because, in this case, the law will oblige him. But if he is worth nothing, the paper-note is worth nothing. The value, therefore, of such a note, is not in the note itself, for that is but paper and promise, but in the man who is obliged to redeem it with gold or silver.

PAPER, circulating in this manner, and for this purpose, continually points to the place and person where, and of whom, the money is to be had, and at last finds its home; and, as it were, unlocks its master's chest and pays the bearer.

BUT when an Assembly undertake to issue paper *as* money, the whole system of safety and certainty is overturned, and property set afloat.

Paper-notes given and taken between individuals as a promise of payment is one thing, but paper issued by an Assembly *as* money is another thing. It is like putting an apparition in the place of a man; it vanishes with looking at and nothing remains but the air.

MONEY, when considered as the fruit of many years industry, as the reward of labour, sweat and toil, as the widow's dowry and the children[']s portion, and as the means of procuring the necessaries, and alleviating the afflictions of life, and making old age a scene of rest, has something in it sacred that is not to be sported with, or trusted to the airy bubble of paper-currency.

BY what power or authority an Assembly undertake to make paper-money is difficult to say. It derives none from the Constitution, for that is silent on the subject. It is one of those things which the people have not delegated, and which, were they at any time assembled together, they would not delegate. It is, therefore, an assumption of power which an Assembly is not warranted in, and which may, one day or other, be the means of bringing some of them to punishment.

I SHALL enumerate some of the evils of paper-money and conclude with offering means for preventing them.

ONE of the evils of paper-money is, that it turns the whole country into stock-jobbers. The precariousness of its value and the uncertainty of its fate continually operate, night and day, to produce this destructive effect. Having no real value in itself it depends for support upon accident, caprice and party, and as it is the interest of some to depreciate and of others to raise its value, there is a continual invention going on that destroys the morals of the country.

IT was horrid to see and hurtful to recollect how loose the principles of justice were let by means of the paper-emissions during the war. The experience then had should be a warning to any Assembly how they venture to open such a dangerous door again.

As to the romantic if not hypocritical tale, that a virtuous people need no gold and silver and that paper will do as well, requires no other contradiction than the experience we have seen. Though some well-meaning people may be inclined to view it in this light, it is certain that the sharper always talks this language.

THERE are a set of men who go about making purchases upon credit, and buying estates they have not wherewithal to pay for; and having done this, their next step is to fill the news-papers with paragraphs of the scarcity of money and the necessity of a paper-emission, then to have it made a legal tender under the pretence of supporting its credit; and when out, to depreciate it as fast as they can, get a deal of it for a little price and cheat their creditors; and this is the concise history of Paper-money schemes.

BUT why since the universal custom of the world has established money as the most convenient medium of traffic and commerce, should paper be set up in preference to gold and silver? The productions of nature are surely as innocent as those of art; and in the case of money, are abundantly, if not infinitely, more so. The love of gold and silver may produce covetousness, but covetousness, when not connected with dishonesty, is not properly a vice. It is frugality run to an extreme.

BUT the evils of paper-money have no end. Its uncertain and fluctuating value is continually awakening or creating new schemes of deceit. Every principle of justice is put to the rack and the bond of society dissolved: The suppression therefore of paper-money might very properly have been put into the Act for preventing Vice and Immorality.

THE pretence for paper-money has been, that there was not a sufficiency of gold and silver. This, so far from being a reason for paper emissions, is a reason against them.

As gold and silver are not the productions of North-America, they are, therefore, articles of importation; and if we set up a paper-manufactory of money, it amounts, as far as it is able, to prevent the importation of Hard money, or to send it out again as fast as it comes in; and by following this practice we shall continually banish the specie, till we have none left, and be continually complaining of the grievance instead of remedying the cause.

CONSIDERING gold and silver as articles of importation, there will in time, unless we prevent it by paper-emissions, be as much in the country as the occasions of it require, for the same reasons there are as much of other imported articles. But as every yard of cloth manufactured in the country occasions a yard the less to be imported, so it is by money, with this difference, that in the one case we manufacture the thing itself and in the other we do not. We have cloth for cloth, but we have only paper-dollars for silver ones.

As to the assumed authority of any Assembly in making paper-money, or paper of any kind, a legal tender, or in other language, a compulsive payment, it is a most presumptuous attempt at arbitrary power. There can be no such power in a Republican government: The people have no freedom, and property no security where this practice can be acted: And the Committee who shall bring in a report for this purpose, or the Member who moves for it, and he who seconds it merit impeachment, and sooner or later may expect it.

OF all the various sorts of base coin, paper-money is the basest. It has the least intrinsic value of any thing that can be put in the place of gold and silver. A hobnail or a piece of wampum far exceeds it. And there would be more propriety in making those articles a legal tender than to make paper so.

IT was the issuing base coin and establishing it as a tender, that was one of the principal means of finally overthrowing the power of the Stewart family in Ireland. The article is worth reciting as it bears such a resemblance to the progress practised on paper-money.

"Brass and copper of the basest kind, old cannon, broken bells, household utensils were assiduously collected; and from every pound weight of such vile materials, valued at four-pence, pieces were coined and circulated to the amount of five pounds nominal value. By the first proclamation they were made current in all payments to and from the King and the subjects of the realm, except in duties on the importation of foreign goods, money left in trust, or due by mortgage, bills or bonds; and *James* promised that when the money should be decried, he would receive it in all payments or make full satisfaction in gold and silver. The nominal value was afterwards raised by subsequent proclamations, the original restrictions removed, and this base money was ordered to be received in all kinds of payments. As brass and copper grew scarce it was made of still viler materials, of tin and pewter, and old debts of one thousand pounds were discharged by pieces of vile metal, amounting to thirty shillings in intrinsic value."[7] – Had King James thought of paper he needed not to have been at the trouble or expence of collecting brass and copper, broken bells and household utensils.

THE laws of a country ought to be the standard of equity, and calculated to impress on the mind of the people the moral as well as the legal obligation of reciprocal justice. But tender-laws, of any kind, operate to destroy morality, and to dissolve by the pretence of law what ought to be the principle of law to support, reciprocal justice between man and man: And the punishment of a member who should move for such a law ought to be DEATH.

WHEN the recommendation of Congress in the year 1780 for repealing the tender-laws was before the Assembly of Pennsylvania, on casting up the votes, for and against bringing in a bill to repeal those laws, the numbers were equal, and the casting vote rested on the Speaker, Colonel Bayard. "I give my vote" said he, "for the repeal from a consciousness of

7. Leland's history of Ireland, vol. iv, page 265.

justice; the tender-laws operate to establish iniquity by law." – But when the Bill was brought in, the House rejected it, and the tender-laws continued to be the means of fraud.

IF any thing had, or could have, a value equal to gold and silver it would require no tender-law; and if it had not that value it ought not to have such a law; and, therefore, all tender-laws are tyrannical and unjust, and calculated to support fraud and oppression.

MOST of the advocates for tender-laws are those who have debts to discharge, and who take refuge in such a law, to violate their contracts and cheat their creditors. But as no law can warrant the doing an unlawful act, therefore, the proper mode of proceeding, should any such laws be enacted in future, will be to impeach and execute the Members who moved for and seconded such a Bill, and put the debtor and the creditor in the same situation they were in, with respect to each other, before such a law was passed. Men ought to be made to tremble at the idea of such a barefaced act of injustice. It is in vain to talk of restoring credit, or to complain that money cannot be borrowed at legal interest, until every idea of tender-laws is totally and publicly reprobated and extirpated from among us.

As to paper-money, in any light it can be viewed, it is at best a bubble. Considered as property it is inconsistent to suppose that the breath of an Assembly, whose authority expires with the year, can give to paper the value and duration of gold. They cannot even engage that the next Assembly shall receive it in taxes And by the precedent (for authority there is none) that any one Assembly makes paper-money, another may do the same, until confidence and credit are totally expelled, and all the evils of depreciation acted over again. The amount, therefore, of Paper-Money is this, That it is the illegitimate offspring of Assemblies, and when their year expire they leave it a vagrant on the hands of the Public.

HAVING now gone thro' the three subjects proposed in the title to this work, I shall conclude with offering some thoughts on the present affairs of the State.

MY idea of a single Legislature was always founded on a hope, that whatever personal parties there might be in the State, they would all unite and agree in the general principles of good government – that these party differences would be dropt at the threshold of the state-house, and that the Public Good or the good of the whole, would be the governing principle of the Legislature within it.

PARTY dispute, taken on this ground, would only be, who should have the honor of making the laws; not what the laws should be. But when party operates to produce party laws, a single House is a single person, and subject to the haste, rashness and passion of individual sovereignty. At least, it is an aristocracy.

THE form of the present Constitution is now made to trample on its principles, and the constitutional Members are anti-constitutional Legislators. They are fond of supporting the form for the sake of the power, and they dethrone the principle to display the sceptre.

THE attack of the late Assembly on the Bank discovers such a want of moderation and prudence, of impartiality and equity, of fair and candid enquiry and investigation, of deliberate and unbiassed judgment, and such a rashness of thinking and vengeance of power as is inconsistent with the safety of the Republic. It was judging without hearing and execution without trial.

BY such rash, injudicious and violent proceedings the interest of the State is weakened, its prosperity diminished and its commerce and its specie banished to other places. – Suppose the Bank had not been in an immediate condition to have stood such a sudden attack, what a scene of instant distress would the rashness of that Assembly have brought upon this city and State. The holders of Bank-notes, whoever they might be, would have been thrown into the utmost confusion and difficulties. It is no apology to say the House never thought of this, for it was their duty to have thought of every thing.

BUT by the prudent and provident management of the Bank (tho' unsuspicious of the attack) it was enabled to stand the run upon it without stopping payment a moment, and to prevent the evils and mischiefs taking place which the rashness of the Assembly had a direct tendency to bring on; a trial that scarcely a Bank in Europe, under a similar circumstance, could have stood through.

I CANNOT see reason sufficient to believe that the hope of the House to put down the Bank was placed on the withdrawing the Charter, so much as on the expectation of producing a bankruptcy on the Bank, by starting a run upon it. If this was any part of their project it was a very wicked one, because hundreds might have been ruined to gratify a party-spleen.

BUT this not being the case, what has the attack amounted to, but to expose the weakness, and rashness, the want of judgment as well as justice, of those who made it, and to confirm the credit of the Bank more substantially than it was before.

THE attack, it is true, has had one effect, which is not in the power of the Assembly to remedy, it has banished many thousand hard dollars from the state. – By the means of the Bank, Pennsylvania had the use of a great deal of hard money belonging to citizens of other States, and that without any interest, for it laid here in the nature of a deposit, the depositors taking Bank-notes in its stead. But the alarm called those notes in and the owners drew out their cash.

THE banishing the specie served to make room for the paper-money of the Assembly, and we have now paper dollars where we might have had silver ones. So that the effect of the paper-money has been to make less money in the state than there was before. Paper-money is like dram-drinking, it relieves for the moment by a deceitful sensation, but gradually diminishes the natural heat, and leaves the body worse than it found it. Were not this the case, and could money be made of paper at pleasure, every Sovereign in Europe would be as rich as he pleased. But the truth is, that it is a bubble and the attempt vanity. Nature has provided the proper materials for money, gold and silver, and any attempt of ours to rival her is ridiculous.

BUT to conclude——If the Public will permit the opinion of a friend who is attached to no party, and under obligations to none, nor at variance with any, and who through a long habit of acquaintance with them has never deceived them, that opinion shall be freely given.

THE Bank is an Institution capable of being made exceedingly beneficial to the State, not only as the means of extending and facilitating its commerce, but as a means of increasing the quantity of hard money in the State. The Assembly's paper-money serves directly to banish or croud out the hard, because it is issued *as* money and put in the place of hard money. But Bank-notes are of a very different kind, and produce a contrary effect. They are promissory notes payable on demand, and may be taken to the Bank and exchanged for gold or silver without the least ceremony or difficulty.

THE Bank, therefore, is obliged to keep a constant stock of hard money sufficient for this purpose; which is what the Assembly neither does, nor can do by their paper; because the quantity of hard money collected by taxes into the Treasury is trifling compared with the quantity that circulates in trade and through the Bank.

THE method, therefore, to increase the quantity of hard money would be to combine the security of the Government and the Bank into one. And instead of issuing paper-money that serves to banish the specie, to borrow the sum wanted of the Bank in Bank-notes on the condition of the Bank exchanging those notes at stated periods and quantities with hard money.

PAPER issued in this manner, and directed to this end, would, instead of banishing, work itself into, gold and silver; because it will then be both the advantage and duty of the Bank, and of all the mercantile interest connected with it, to procure and import gold and silver from any part of the world it can be got, to exchange the notes with. The English Bank is restricted to the dealing in no other articles of importation than gold and silver, and we may make the same use of our Bank if we proceed properly with it.

THOSE notes will then have a double security, that of the Government and that of the Bank; and they will not be issued *as* money, but as hostages to be exchanged for hard money, and will, therefore, work the contrary way to what the paper of the Assembly, uncombined with the security of the Bank, produces: And the interest allowed the Bank will be saved to Government by a saving of the expences and charges attending paper-emissions.

IT is, as I have already observed in the course of this work, the harmony of all the parts of a Republic, that constitutes their several and mutual good. A Government, that is constructed only to govern, is not a Republican Government. It is combining authority with usefulness that in a great measure distinguishes the Republican system from others.

PAPER-MONEY appears, at first sight, to be a great saving, or rather that it costs nothing; but it is the dearest money there is. The ease with which it is emitted by an Assembly at first, serves as a trap to catch people in at last. It operates as an anticipation of the next year's taxes. If the money depreciates, after it is out, it then, as I have already remarked, has the effect of fluctuating stock, and the people become stock-jobbers to throw the loss on each other. – If it does not depreciate, it is then to be sunk by taxes at the price of *hard money;* because the same quantity of produce, or goods, that would procure a paper-dollar to pay taxes with would procure a silver one for the same purpose. Therefore in any case of paper-money it is dearer to the country than hard money by all the expence which the paper, printing, signing and other attendant charges come to, and at last goes into the fire.

SUPPOSE one hundred thousand dollars in paper-money to be emitted every year by the Assembly, and the same sum to be sunk every year by taxes, there will then be no more than one hundred thousand dollars out at any one time. If the expence of paper and printing, and of persons to attend the press while the sheets are striking off, signers, &c. be five per cent. it is evident that in the course of twenty years emissions, the one hundred thousand dollars will cost the country two hundred thousand dollars. Because the papermaker's and printer's bills, and the expence of supervisors and signers, and other attendant charges, will in that time amount to as much as the money amounts to; for the successive emissions are but a recoinage of the same sum.

BUT gold and silver require to be coined but once, and will last a hundred years, better than paper will one year, and at the end of that time be still gold and silver. Therefore the saving to Government, in combining its aid and security with that of the Bank in procuring hard money, will be an advantage to both, and to the whole community.

THE case to be provided against, after this, will be, that the Government do not borrow too much of the Bank, nor the Bank lend more notes than it can redeem; and, therefore, should any thing of this kind be undertaken, the best way will be to begin with a moderate sum, and observe the effect of it. The interest given the Bank operates as a bounty on the importation of hard money, and which may not be more than the money expended in making paper-emissions.

BUT nothing of this kind, nor any other public undertaking, that requires security and duration beyond the year, can be gone upon under the present mode of conducting Government. The late Assembly, by assuming a sovereign power over every Act and matter done by the State in former Assemblies, and thereby setting up a precedent of overhauling and overturning, as the accident of elections shall happen or party prevail, have rendered Government incompetent to all the great objects of the State. They have eventually reduced the Public to an annual body like themselves; whereas the Public are a standing permanent body, holding annual elections.

THERE are several great improvements and undertakings, such as inland navigation, building bridges, opening roads of communication thro' the State, and other matters of a public benefit, that might be gone upon, but which now cannot, until this governmental error or defect is remedied. The faith of Government, under the present mode of conducting it, cannot be relied on. Individuals will not venture their money, in undertakings of this kind, on an Act that may be made by one Assembly and broken by another. When a man can say that he cannot trust the Government, the importance and dignity of the Public is diminished, sapped and undermined; and, therefore, it becomes the Public to restore their own honor, by setting these matters to rights.

PERHAPS this cannot be effectually done until the time of the next Convention, when the principles, on which they are to be regulated and fixed, may be made a part of the Constitution.

IN the mean time the Public may keep their affairs in sufficient good order, by substituting prudence in the place of authority, and electing men into the Government, who will at once throw aside the narrow prejudices of party, and make the Good of the Whole the ruling object of their conduct.——
And with this hope, and a sincere wish for their prosperity, I close my book.

RIGHTS OF MAN:

BEING AN

ANSWER TO MR. BURKE's ATTACK

ON THE

FRENCH REVOLUTION.

BY **THOMAS PAINE,**

SECRETARY FOR FOREIGN AFFAIRS TO CONGRESS IN THE
AMERICAN WAR, AND AUTHOR OF THE WORK INTITLED
"COMMON SENSE."

To
George Washington,
PRESIDENT OF THE UNITED STATES OF AMERICA.

SIR,
I PRESENT you a small Treatise in defence of those Principles of Free-
dom which your exemplary Virtue hath so eminently contributed to estab-
lish. – That the Rights of Man may become as universal as your Benevo-
lence can wish, and that you may enjoy the Happiness of seeing the New
World regenerate the Old, is the Prayer of
Sir,
Your much obliged, and
Obedient humble Servant,
THOMAS PAINE.

Rights of Man: Being an Answer to Mr. Burke's Attack on the French Revolution
(London: J. S. Jordan, 1791).

Preface
To The
English Edition.

FROM the part Mr. Burke took in the American Revolution, it was natural that I should consider him a friend to mankind; and as our acquaintance commenced on that ground, it would have been more agreeable to me to have had cause to continue in that opinion, than to change it.

At the time Mr. Burke made his violent speech last winter in the English Parliament against the French Revolution and the National Assembly, I was in Paris, and had written him, but a short time before, to inform him how prosperously matters were going on. Soon after this, I saw his advertisement of the Pamphlet he intended to publish: As the attack was to be made in a language but little studied, and less understood, in France, and as every thing suffers by translation, I promised some of the friends of the Revolution in that country, that whenever Mr. Burke's Pamphlet came forth, I would answer it. This appeared to me the more necessary to be done, when I saw the flagrant misrepresentations which Mr. Burke's Pamphlet contains; and that while it is an outrageous abuse on the French Revolution, and the principles of Liberty, it is an imposition on the rest of the world.

I am the more astonished and disappointed at this conduct in Mr. Burke, as (from the circumstance I am going to mention), I had formed other expectations.

I had seen enough of the miseries of war, to wish it might never more have existence in the world, and that some other mode might be found out to settle the differences that should occasionally arise in the neighbourhood of nations. This certainly might be done if Courts were disposed to set honestly about it, or if countries were enlightened enough not to be made the dupes of Courts. The people of America had been bred up in the same prejudices against France, which at that time characterized the people of England; but experience and an acquaintance with the French Nation have most effectually shown to the Americans the falsehood of those prejudices; and I do not believe that a more cordial and confidential intercourse exists between any two countries than between America and France.

When I came to France in the Spring of 1787, the Archbishop of Thoulouse was then Minister, and at that time highly esteemed. I became much acquainted with the private Secretary of that Minister, a man of an enlarged benevolent heart; and found, that his sentiments and my own perfectly agreed with respect to the madness of war, and the wretched impolicy of two nations, like England and France, continually worrying each other, to no other end than that of a mutual increase of burdens and taxes. That I might be assured I had not misunderstood him, nor he me, I put the substance of our opinions into writing, and sent it to him; subjoining a request, that if I should see among the people of England, any disposition to cultivate a better understanding between the two nations than had hitherto prevailed, how far I might be authorized to say that the same disposition prevailed on the part of France? He answered me by letter in the most unreserved manner, and that not for himself only, but for the Minister, with whose knowledge the letter was declared to be written.

I put this letter into the hands of Mr. Burke almost three years ago, and left it with him, where it still remains; hoping, and at the same time naturally expecting, from the opinion I had conceived of him, that he would find some opportunity of making a good use of it, for the purpose of removing those errors and prejudices, which two neighbouring nations, from the want of knowing each other, had entertained, to the injury of both.

When the French Revolution broke out, it certainly afforded to Mr. Burke an opportunity of doing some good, had he been disposed to it; instead of which, no sooner did he see the old prejudices wearing away, than he immediately began sowing the seeds of a new inveteracy, as if he were afraid that England and France would cease to be enemies. That there are men in all countries who get their living by war, and by keeping up the quarrels of Nations, is as shocking as it is true; but when those who are concerned in the government of a country, make it their study to sow discord, and cultivate prejudices between Nations, it becomes the more unpardonable.

With respect to a paragraph in this Work, alluding to Mr. Burke's having a pension, the report has been some time in circulation, at least two months; and as a person is often the last to hear what concerns him the most to know, I have mentioned it, that Mr. Burke may have an opportunity of contradicting the rumour, if he thinks proper.

– THOMAS PAINE.

Rights of Man, &c.

AMONG the incivilities by which nations or individuals provoke and irritate each other, Mr. Burke's pamphlet on the French Revolution is an extraordinary instance. Neither the people of France, nor the National Assembly, were troubling themselves about the affairs of England, or the English Parliament; and why Mr. Burke should commence an unprovoked attack upon them, both in parliament and in public, is a conduct that cannot be pardoned on the score of manners, nor justified on that of policy.

There is scarcely an epithet of abuse to be found in the English language, with which Mr. Burke has not loaded the French nation and the National Assembly. Every thing which rancour, prejudice, ignorance or knowledge could suggest, are poured forth in the copious fury of near four hundred pages. In the strain and on the plan Mr. Burke was writing, he might have wrote on to as many thousands. When the tongue or the pen is let loose in a phrenzy of passion, it is the man, and not the subject, that becomes exhausted.

Hitherto Mr. Burke has been mistaken and disappointed in the opinions he had formed of the affairs of France; but such is the ingenuity of his hope, or the malignancy of his despair, that it furnishes him with new pretences to go on. There was a time when it was impossible to make Mr. Burke believe there would be any revolution in France. His opinion then was, that the French had neither spirit to undertake it, nor fortitude to support it; and now that there is one, he seeks an escape by condemning it.

Not sufficiently content with abusing the National Assembly, a great part of his work is taken up with abusing Dr. Price (one of the best-hearted men that lives), and the two societies in England known by the name of the Revolution and the Constitutional Societies.

Dr. Price had preached a sermon on the 4th of November, 1789, being the anniversary of what is called in England the Revolution which took place 1688. Mr. Burke, speaking of this sermon, says, 'The political Divine proceeds dogmatically to assert, that, by the principles of the Revolution, the people of England have acquired three fundamental rights:

1. To chuse our own governors.
2. To cashier them for misconduct.
3. To frame a government for ourselves.'

Dr. Price does not say that the right to do these things exists in this or in that person, or in this or in that description of persons, but that it exists in the *whole;* that it is a right resident in the nation. – Mr. Burke, on the contrary, denies that such a right exists in the nation, either in whole or in part, or that it exists any where; and what is still more strange and marvellous, he says, 'that the people of England utterly disclaim such a right, and that they will resist the practical assertion of it with their lives and fortunes.'

That men should take up arms, and spend their lives and fortunes, *not* to maintain their rights, but to maintain they have *not* rights, is an entire new species of discovery, and suited to the paradoxial genius of Mr. Burke.

The method which Mr. Burke takes to prove that the people of England have no such rights, and that such rights do not now exist in the nation, either in whole or in part, or any where at all, is of the same marvellous and monstrous kind with what he has already said; for his arguments are, that the persons, or the generation of persons, in whom they did exist, are dead, and with them the right is dead also. To prove this, he quotes a declaration made by parliament about a hundred years ago, to William and Mary, in these words: – "The Lords Spiritual and Temporal, and Commons, do, in the name of the people aforesaid – (meaning the people of England then living) – most humbly and faithfully *submit* themselves, their *heirs* and *posterities,* for EVER." He also quotes a clause of another act of parliament made in the same reign, the terms of which, he says, "binds us["] – (meaning the people of that day) – "our *heirs* and our *posterity,* to *them,* their *heirs* and *posterity,* to the end of time."

Mr. Burke conceives his point sufficiently established by producing those clauses, which he enforces by saying that they exclude the right of the nation for *ever:* and not yet content with making such declarations, repeated over and over again, he further says, 'that if the people of England possessed such a right before the Revolution, (which he acknowledges to have been the case, not only in England, but throughout Europe, at an early period 'yet that the *English nation* did, at the time of the Revolution, most solemnly renounce and abdicate it, for themselves, and for *all their posterity for ever.*'

As Mr. Burke occasionally applies the poison drawn from his horrid principles (if it is not a profanation to call them by the name of principles) not only to the English nation, but to the French Revolution and the National Assembly, and charges that august, illuminated and illuminating body of men with the epithet of *usurpers,* I shall, *sans ceremonie,* place another system of principles in opposition to his.

The English Parliament of 1688 did a certain thing, which, for themselves and their constituents, they had a right to do, and which it appeared right should be done: but, in addition to this right, which they possessed by delegation, *they set up another right by assumption,* that of binding and controuling posterity to the end of time. The case, therefore, divides itself into two parts; the right which they possessed by delegation, and the right which they set up by assumption. The first is admitted; but, with respect to the second, I reply –

There never did, there never will, and there never can exist a parliament, or any description of men, or any generation of men, in any country, possessed of the right or the power of binding and controuling posterity to the *"end of time,"* or of commanding for ever how the world shall be governed, or who shall govern it: and therefore, all such clauses, acts or declarations, by which the makers of them attempt to do what they have neither the right nor the power to do, nor the power to execute, are in themselves null and void.—— Every age and generation must be as free to act for itself, *in all cases,* as the ages and generations which preceded it. The vanity and presumption of governing beyond the grave, is the most ridiculous and insolent of all tyrannies. Man has no property in man; neither has any generation a property in the generations which are to follow. The parliament or the people of 1688, or of any other period, had no more right to dispose of the people of the present day, or to bind or to controul them *in any shape whatever,* than the parliament or the people of the present day have to dispose of, bind or controul those who are to live a hundred or a thousand years hence. Every generation is and must be competent to all the purposes which its occasions require. It is the living, and not the dead, that are to be accommodated. When man ceases to be, his power and his wants cease with him; and having no longer any participation in the concerns of this world, he has no longer any authority in directing who shall be its governors, or how its government shall be organized, or how administered.

I am not contending for, nor against, any form of government, nor for, nor against, any party here or elsewhere. That which a whole nation chooses to do, it has a right to do. Mr. Burke says, No. Where then *does* the right exist? I am contending for the right of the *living,* and against their being willed away, and controuled and contracted for, by the manuscript assumed authority of the dead; and Mr. Burke is contending for the authority of the dead over the rights and freedom of the living. There was a time when kings disposed of their crowns by will upon their death-beds, and consigned the people, like beasts of the field, to whatever successor they appointed. This is now so exploded as scarcely to be remembered, and so monstrous as hardly to be believed: But the parliamentary clauses upon which Mr. Burke builds his political church, are of the same nature.

The laws of every country must be analogous to some common principle. In England, no parent or master, nor all the authority of parliament, omnipotent as it has called itself, can bind or controul the personal freedom even of an individual beyond the age of twenty-one years: On what ground of right then could the parliament of 1688, or any other parliament, bind all posterity for ever?

Those who have quitted the world, and those who are not yet arrived at it, are as remote from each other as the utmost stretch of mortal imagination can conceive: What possible obligation then can exist between them, what rule or principle can be laid down, that two non-entities, the one out of existence, and the other not in, and who never can meet in this world, that the one should controul the other to the end of time?

In England, it is said that money cannot be taken out of the pockets of the people without their consent: But who authorized, and who could authorize the parliament of 1688 to controul and take away the freedom of posterity, and limit and confine their rights of acting in certain cases for ever, who were not in existence to give or to with-hold their consent?

A greater absurdity cannot present itself to the understanding of man, than what Mr. Burke offers to his readers. He tells them, and he tells the world to come, that a certain body of men, who existed a hundred years ago, made a law, and that there does not now exist in the nation, nor ever will, nor ever can, a power to alter it. Under how many subtilties, or absurdities, has the divine right to govern been imposed on the credulity of mankind! Mr. Burke has discovered a new one, and he has shortened his journey to Rome by appealing to the power of this infallible parliament of former days; and he produces what it has done, as of divine authority: for that power must certainly be more than human, which no human power to the end of time can alter.

But Mr. Burke has done some service, not to his cause, but to his country, by bringing those clauses into public view. They serve to demonstrate how necessary it is at all times to watch against the attempted encroachment of power, and to prevent its running to excess. It is somewhat extraordinary, that the offence for which James II. was expelled, that of setting up power by *assumption,* should be re-acted, under another shape and form, by the parliament that expelled him. It shews, that the rights of man were but imperfectly understood at the Revolution; for certain it is, that the right which that parliament set up by *assumption* (for by delegation it had it not, and could not have it, because none could give it) over the persons and freedom of posterity for ever, was of the same tyrannical unfounded kind which James attempted to set up over the parliament and the nation, and for which he was expelled. The only difference is, (for in principle they differ not) that the one was an usurper over the living, and the other over the unborn; and as the one has no better authority to stand upon than the other, both of them must be equally null and void, and of no effect.

From what, or from whence, does Mr. Burke prove the right of any human power to bind posterity for ever? He has produced his clauses; but he must produce also his proofs, that such a right existed, and shew how it existed. If it ever existed, it must now exist; for whatever appertains to the nature of man, cannot be annihilated by man. It is the nature of man to die, and he will continue to die as long as he continues to be born. But Mr. Burke has set up a sort of political Adam, in whom all posterity are bound for ever; he must therefore prove that his Adam possessed such a power, or such a right.

The weaker any cord is, the less will it bear to be stretched, and the worse is the policy to stretch it, unless it is intended to break it. Had a person contemplated the overthrow of Mr. Burke's positions, he would have proceeded as Mr. Burke has done. He would have magnified the authorities, on purpose to have called the *right* of them into question; and the instant the question of right was started, the authorities must have been given up.

It requires but a very small glance of thought to perceive, that altho' laws made in one generation often continue in force through succeeding generations, yet that they continue to derive their force from the consent of the living. A law not repealed continues in force, not because it *cannot* be repealed, but because it *is not* repealed; and the non-repealing passes for consent.

But Mr. Burke's clauses have not even this qualification in their favour. They become null, by attempting to become immortal. The nature of them precludes consent. They destroy the right which they *might* have, by grounding it on a right which they *cannot* have. Immortal power is not a human right, and therefore cannot be a right of parliament. The parliament of 1688 might as well have passed an act to have authorised themselves to live for ever, as to make their authority live for ever. All therefore that can be said of them is, that they are a formality of words, of as much import, as if those who used them had addressed a congratulation to themselves, and, in the oriental stile of antiquity, had said, O Parliament, live for ever!

The circumstances of the world are continually changing, and the opinions of men change also; and as government is for the living, and not for the dead, it is the living only that has any right in it. That which may be thought right and found convenient in one age, may be thought wrong and found inconvenient in another. In such cases, Who is to decide, the living, or the dead?

As almost one hundred pages of Mr. Burke's book are employed upon these clauses, it will consequently follow, that if the clauses themselves, so far as they set up an *assumed, usurped* dominion over posterity for ever, are unauthoritative, and in their nature null and void, that all his voluminous inferences and declamation drawn therefrom, or founded thereon, are null and void also: and on this ground I rest the matter.

We now come more particularly to the affairs of France. Mr. Burke's book has the appearance of being written as instruction to the French nation; but if I may permit myself the use of an extravagant metaphor, suited to the extravagance of the case, It is darkness attempting to illuminate light.

While I am writing this, there [are] accidentally before me some proposals for a declaration of rights by the Marquis de la Fayette (I ask his pardon for using his former address, and do it only for distinction's sake) to the National Assembly on the 11th of July 1789, three days before the taking of the Bastille; and I cannot but be struck how opposite the sources are from which that Gentleman and Mr. Burke draw their principles. Instead of referring to musty records and mouldy parchments to prove that the rights of the living are lost, "renounced and abdicated for ever," by those who are now no more, as Mr. Burke has done, M. de la Fayette applies to the living world, and emphatically says, "Call to mind the sentiments which Nature has engraved in the heart of every citizen, and which take a new force when they are solemnly recognized by all:–For a nation to love liberty, it is sufficient that she knows it; and to be free, it is sufficient that she wills it." How dry, barren, and obscure, is the source from which Mr. Burke labours; and how ineffectual, though gay with flowers, are all his declamation and his argument, compared with these clear, concise, and soul-animating sentiments! Few and short as they are, they lead on to a vast field of generous and manly thinking, and do not finish, like Mr. Burke's periods, with music in the ear, and nothing in the heart.

As I have introduced the mention of M. de la Fayette, I will take the liberty of adding an anecdote respecting his farewel address to the Congress of America in 1783, and which occurred fresh to my mind when I saw Mr. Burke's thundering attack on the French Revolution.–M. de la Fayette went to America at an early period of the war, and continued a volunteer in her service to the end. His conduct through the whole of that enterprise is one of the most extraordinary that is to be found in the history of a young man, scarcely then twenty years of age. Situated in a country that was like the lap of sensual pleasure, and with the means of enjoying it, how few are there to be found who would exchange such a scene for the woods and wilderness of America, and pass the flowery years of youth in unprofitable danger and hardship! but such is the fact. When the war ended, and he was on the point of taking his final departure, he presented himself to Congress, and contemplating, in his affectionate farewel, the revolution he had seen, expressed himself in these words: *"May this great monument, raised to Liberty, serve as a lesson to the oppressor, and an example to the oppressed!"* – When this address came to the hands of Doctor Franklin, who was then in France, he applied to Count Vergennes to have it inserted in the French Gazette, but never could obtain his consent. The fact was, that Count Vergennes was an aristocratical despot at home, and dreaded the example of the American revolution in France, as certain other persons now dread the example of the French revolution in England; and Mr. Burke's tribute of fear (for in this light his book must be considered) runs parallel with Count Vergennes' refusal. But, to return more particularly to his work –

"We have seen (says Mr. Burke) the French rebel against a mild and lawful Monarch, with more fury, outrage, and insult, than any people has been known to rise against the most illegal usurpers, or the most sanguinary tyrant." – This is one among a thousand other instances, in which Mr. Burke shews that he is ignorant of the springs and principles of the French revolution.

It was not against Louis the XVIth, but against the despotic principles of the government, that the nation revolted. These principles had not their origin in him, but in the original establishment, many centuries back; and they were become too deeply rooted to be removed, and the augean stable of parasites and plunderers too abominably filthy to be cleansed, by any thing short of a complete and universal revolution. When it becomes necessary to do a thing, the whole heart and soul should go into the measure, or not attempt it. That crisis was then arrived, and there remained no choice but to act with determined vigour, or not to act at all. The King was known to be the friend of the nation, and this circumstance was favourable to the enterprise. Perhaps no man bred up in the stile of an absolute King, ever possessed a heart so little disposed to the exercise of that species of power as the present King of France. But the principles of the government itself still remained the same. The Monarch and the Monarchy were distinct and separate things; and it was against the established despotism of the latter, and not against the person or principles of the former, that the revolt commenced, and the revolution has been carried.

Mr. Burke does not attend to the distinction between *men* and *principles,* and therefore, he does not see that a revolt may take place against the despotism of the latter, while there lies no charge of despotism against the former.

The natural moderation of Louis XVI. contributed nothing to alter the hereditary despotism of the monarchy. All the tyrannies of former reigns, acted under that hereditary despotism, were still liable to be revived in the hands of a successor. It was not the respite of a reign that would satisfy France, enlightened as she was then become. A casual discontinuance of the *practice* of despotism, is not a discontinuance of its *principles;* the former depends on the virtue of the individual who is in immediate possession of the power; the latter, on the virtue and fortitude of the nation. In the case of Charles I. and James II. of England, the revolt was against the personal despotism of the men; whereas in France, it was against the hereditary despotism of the established government. But men who can consign over the rights of posterity for ever on the authority of a mouldy parchment, like Mr. Burke, are not qualified to judge of this revolution. It takes in a field too vast for their views to explore, and proceeds with a mightiness of reason they cannot keep pace with.

But there are many points of view in which this revolution may be considered. When despotism has established itself for ages in a country, as in France, it is not in the person of the King only that it resides. It has the appearance of being so in show, and in nominal authority; but it is not so in practice, and in fact. It has its standard every where. Every office and department has its despotism, founded upon custom and usage. Every place has its Bastille, and every Bastille its despot. The original hereditary despotism resident in the person of the King, divides and subdivides itself into a thousand shapes and forms, till at last the whole of it is acted by deputation. This was the case in France; and against this species of despotism, proceeding on through an endless labyrinth of office till the source of it is scarcely perceptible, there is no mode of redress. It strengthens itself by assuming the appearance of duty, and tyrannises under the pretence of obeying.

When a man reflects on the condition which France was in from the nature of her government, he will see other causes for revolt than those which immediately connect themselves with the person or character of Louis XVI. There were, if I may so express it, a thousand despotisms to be reformed in France, which had grown up under the hereditary despotism of the monarchy, and became so rooted as to be in a great measure independent of it. Between the monarchy, the parliament, and the church, there was a *rivalship* of despotism; besides the feudal despotism operating locally, and the ministerial despotism operating every-where. But Mr. Burke, by considering the King as the only possible object of a revolt, speaks as if France was a village, in which every thing that passed must be known to its commanding officer, and no oppression could be acted but what he could immediately controul. Mr. Burke might have been in the Bastille his whole

life, as well [as] under Louis XVI. as Louis XIV. and neither the one nor
the other have known that such a man as Mr. Burke existed. The despotic
principles of the government were the same in both reigns, though the dispositions of the men were as remote as tyranny and benevolence.

What Mr. Burke considers as a reproach to the French Revolution (that
of bringing it forward under a reign more mild than the preceding ones),
is one of its highest honours. The revolutions that have taken place in
other European countries, have been excited by personal hatred. The rage
was against the man, and he became the victim. But, in the instance of
France, we see a revolution generated in the rational contemplation of the
rights of man, and distinguishing from the beginning between persons and
principles.

But Mr. Burke appears to have no idea of principles, when he is contemplating governments. "Ten years ago (says he) I could have felicitated
France on her having a government, without enquiring what the nature of
that government was, or how it was administered." Is this the language of a
rational man? Is it the language of a heart feeling as it ought to feel for the
right and happiness of the human race? On this ground, Mr. Burke must
compliment every government in the world, while the victims who suffer
under them, whether sold into slavery, or tortured out of existence, are
wholly forgotten. It is power, and not principles, that Mr. Burke venerates,
and under this abominable depravity, he is disqualified to judge between
them.—Thus much for his opinion as to the occasions of the French Revolution. I now proceed to other considerations.

I know a place in America called Point-no-Point; because as you proceed along the shore, gay and flowery as Mr. Burke's language, it continually recedes and presents itself at a distance a head; and when you have got
as far as you can go, there is no point at all. Just thus it is with Mr. Burke's
three hundred and fifty-six pages. It is therefore difficult to reply to him.
But as the points he wishes to establish may be inferred from what he
abuses, it is in his paradoxes that we must look for his arguments.

As to the tragic paintings by which Mr. Burke has outraged his own
imagination, and seeks to work upon that of his readers, they are very well
calculated for theatrical representation, where facts are manufactured for
the sake of show, and accommodated to produce, through the weakness of
sympathy, a weeping effect. But Mr. Burke should recollect that he is writing History, and not *Plays;* and that his readers will expect truth, and not
the spouting rant of high-toned exclamation.

When we see a man dramatically lamenting in a publication intended to
be believed, that, "*The age of chivalry is gone!* that *The glory of Europe is*

extinguished for ever! that *The unbought grace of life,* (if any one knows what it is), *the cheap defence of nations, the nurse of manly sentiment and heroic enterprize, is gone!"* and all this because the Quixote age of chivalry nonsense is gone, What opinion can we form of his judgment, or what regard can we pay to his facts? In the rhapsody of his imagination, he has discovered a world of wind-mills, and his sorrows are, that there are no Quixotes to attack them. But if the age of aristocracy, like that of chivalry, should fall, and they had originally some connection, Mr. Burke, the trumpeter of the Order, may continue his parody to the end, and finish with exclaiming, *"Othello's occupation's gone!"*

Notwithstanding Mr. Burke's horrid paintings, when the French Revolution is compared with that of other countries, the astonishment will be, that it is marked with so few sacrifices; but this astonishment will cease when we reflect that it was *principles,* and not *persons,* that were the meditated objects of destruction. The mind of the nation was acted upon by a higher stimulus than what the consideration of persons could inspire, and sought a higher conquest than could be produced by the downfal of an enemy. Among the few who fell, there do not appear to be any that were intentionally singled out. They all of them had their fate in the circumstances of the moment, and were not pursued with that long, cold-blooded, unabated revenge which pursued the unfortunate Scotch in the affair of 1745.

Through the whole of Mr. Burke's book I do not observe that the Bastille is mentioned more than once, and that with a kind of implication as if he were sorry it is pulled down, and wished it were built up again. "We have rebuilt Newgate (says he), and tenanted the mansion; and we have prisons almost as strong as the Bastille for those who dare to libel the Queens of France[1]." As to what a madman, like the person called Lord George Gordon, might say, and to whom Newgate is rather a bedlam than a prison, it is unworthy a rational consideration. It was a madman that libelled – and that is sufficient apology; and it afforded an opportunity for confining him, which was the thing that was wished for: But certain it is that Mr. Burke, who does not call himself a madman, whatever other people may do, has

1. Since writing the above, two other places occur in Mr. Burke's pamphlet, in which the name of the Bastille is mentioned, but in the same manner. In the one, he introduces it in a sort of obscure question, and asks – "Will any ministers who now serve such a king, with but a decent appearance of respect, cordially obey the orders of those whom but the other day, *in his name,* they had committed to the Bastille?" In the other, the taking it is mentioned as implying criminality in the French guards who assisted in demolishing it. – "They have not (says he) forgot the taking the king's castles at Paris."——This is Mr. Burke, who pretends to write on constitutional freedom.

libelled, in the most unprovoked manner, and in the grossest stile of the most vulgar abuse, the whole representative authority of France; and yet Mr. Burke takes his seat in the British House of Commons! From his violence and his grief, his silence on some points, and his excess on others, it is difficult not to believe that Mr. Burke is sorry, extremely sorry, that arbitrary power, the power of the Pope, and the Bastille, are pulled down.

Not one glance of compassion, not one commiserating reflection, that I can find throughout his book, has he bestowed on those who lingered out the most wretched of lives, a life without hope, in the most miserable of prisons. It is painful to behold a man employing his talents to corrupt himself. Nature has been kinder to Mr. Burke than he is to her. He is not affected by the reality of distress touching his heart, but by the showy resemblance of it striking his imagination. He pities the plumage, but forgets the dying bird. Accustomed to kiss the aristocratical hand that hath purloined him from himself, he degenerates into a composition of art, and the genuine soul of nature forsakes him. His hero or his heroine must be a tragedy-victim expiring in show, and not the real prisoner of misery, sliding into death in the silence of a dungeon.

As Mr. Burke has passed over the whole transaction of the Bastille (and his silence is nothing in his favour), and has entertained his readers with reflections on supposed facts distorted into real falsehoods, I will give, since he has not, some account of the circumstances which preceded that transaction. They will serve to shew, that less mischief could scarcely have accompanied such an event, when considered with the treacherous and hostile aggravations of the enemies of the Revolution.

The mind can hardly picture to itself a more tremendous scene than what the city of Paris exhibited at the time of taking the Bastille, and for two days before and after, nor conceive the possibility of its quieting so soon. At a distance, this transaction has appeared only as an act of heroism, standing on itself; and the close political connection it had with the Revolution is lost in the brilliancy of the atchievement. But we are to consider it as the strength of the parties, brought man to man, and contending for the issue. The Bastille was to be either the prize or the prison of the assailants. The downfal of it included the idea of the downfal of Despotism; and this compounded image was become as figuratively united as Bunyan's Doubting Castle and giant Despair.

The National Assembly, before and at the time of taking the Bastille, was sitting at Versailles, twelve miles distant from Paris. About a week before the rising of the Parisians, and their taking the Bastille, it was discovered that a plot was forming, at the head of which was the Count d'Artois,

the King's youngest brother, for demolishing the National Assembly, seizing its members, and thereby crushing, by a *coup de main,* all hopes and
prospects of forming a free government. For the sake of humanity, as well
as of freedom, it is well this plan did not succeed. Examples are not wanting to shew how dreadfully vindictive and cruel are all old governments,
when they are successful against what they call a revolt.

    This plan must have been some time in contemplation; because, in order
to carry it into execution, it was necessary to collect a large military force
round Paris, and to cut off the communication between that city and the
National Assembly at Versailles. The troops destined for this service were
chiefly the foreign troops in the pay of France, and who, for this particular
purpose, were drawn from the distant provinces where they were then stationed. When they were collected, to the amount of between twenty-five and
thirty thousand, it was judged time to put the plan into execution. The ministry who were then in office, and who were friendly to the Revolution, were
instantly dismissed, and a new ministry formed of those who had concerted
the project; – among whom was Count de Broglio, and to his share was given
the command of those troops. The character of this man, as described to me
in a letter which I communicated to Mr. Burke before he began to write his
book, and from an authority which Mr. Burke well knows was good, was
that of "an high-flying aristocrat, cool, and capable of every mischief."

    While these matters were agitating, the National Assembly stood in the
most perilous and critical situation that a body of men can be supposed to
act in. They were the devoted victims, and they knew it. They had the hearts
and wishes of their country on their side, but military authority they had
none. The guards of Broglio surrounded the hall where the assembly sat,
ready, at the word of command, to seize their persons, as had been done the
year before to the parliament of Paris. Had the National Assembly deserted
their trust, or had they exhibited signs of weakness or fear, their enemies
had been encouraged, and the country depressed. When the situation they
stood in, the cause they were engaged in, and the crisis then ready to burst
which should determine their personal and political fate, and that of their
country, and probably of Europe, are taken into one view, none but a heart
callous with prejudice, or corrupted by dependance, can avoid interesting
itself in their success.

    The archbishop of Vienne was at this time president of the National
Assembly; a person too old to undergo the scene that a few days, or a few
hours, might bring forth. A man of more activity, and bolder fortitude, was
necessary; and the National Assembly chose (under the form of a vice-

president, for the presidency still resided in the archbishop) M. de la Fayette; and this is the only instance of a vice-president being chosen. It was at the moment that this storm was pending (July 11.) that a declaration of rights was brought forward by M. de la Fayette, and is the same which is alluded to in page [180]. It was hastily drawn up, and makes only a part of a more extensive declaration of rights, agreed upon and adopted afterwards by the National Assembly. The particular reason for bringing it forward at this moment, (M. de la Fayette has since informed me) was, that if the National Assembly should fall in the threatened destruction that then surrounded it, some traces of its principles might have the chance of surviving the wreck.

Every thing now was drawing to a crisis. The event was freedom or slavery. On one side, an army of nearly thirty thousand men; on the other, an unarmed body of citizens; for the citizens of Paris, on whom the National Assembly must then immediately depend, were as unarmed and as undisciplined as the citizens of London are now. – The French guards had given strong symptoms of their being attached to the national cause; but their numbers were small, not a tenth part of the force that Broglio commanded, and their officers were in the interest of Broglio.

Matters being now ripe for execution, the new ministry made their appearance in office. The reader will carry in his mind, that the Bastille was taken the 14th of July: the point of time I am now speaking to, is the 12th. Immediately on the news of the change of ministry reaching Paris in the afternoon, all the play-houses and places of entertainment, shops and houses, were shut up. The change of ministry was considered as the prelude of hostilities, and the opinion was rightly founded.

The foreign troops began to advance towards the city. The Prince de Lambesc, who commanded a body of German cavalry, approached by the Place of Lewis XV. which connects itself with some of the streets. In his march, he insulted and struck an old man with his sword. The French are remarkable for their respect to old age, and the insolence with which it appeared to be done, uniting with the general fermentation they were in, produced a powerful effect, and a cry of *To arms! to arms!* spread itself in a moment over the city.

Arms they had none, nor scarcely any who knew the use of them: but desperate resolution, when every hope is at stake, supplies, for a while, the want of arms. Near where the Prince de Lambesc was drawn up, were large piles of stones collected for building the new bridge, and with these the people attacked the cavalry. A party of the French guards, upon hearing the firing, rushed from their quarters and joined the people; and night coming on the cavalry retreated.

The streets of Paris, being narrow, are favourable for defence; and the loftiness of the houses, consisting of many stories, from which great annoyance might be given, secured them against nocturnal enterprises; and the night was spent in providing themselves with every sort of weapon they could make or procure: Guns, swords, black-smiths hammers, carpenters axes, iron crows, pikes, halberts, pitchforks, spits, clubs, &c. &c.

The incredible numbers with which they assembled the next morning, and the still more incredible resolution they exhibited, embarrassed and astonished their enemies. Little did the new ministry expect such a salute. Accustomed to slavery themselves, they had no idea that Liberty was capable of such inspiration, or that a body of unarmed citizens would dare to face the military force of thirty thousand men. Every moment of this day was employed in collecting arms, concerting plans, and arranging themselves into the best order which such an instantaneous movement could afford. Broglio continued lying round the city, but made no further advances this day, and the succeeding night passed with as much tranquillity as such a scene could possibly produce.

But defence only was not the object of the citizens. They had a cause at stake, on which depended their freedom or their slavery. They every moment expected an attack, or to hear of one made on the National Assembly; and in such a situation, the most prompt measures are sometimes the best. The object that now presented itself, was the Bastille; and the eclat of carrying such a fortress in the face of such an army, could not fail to strike a terror into the new ministry, who had scarcely yet had time to meet. By some intercepted correspondence this morning, it was discovered, that the Mayor of Paris, M. Defflesselles, who appeared to be in their interest, was betraying them; and from this discovery, there remained no doubt that Broglio would reinforce the Bastille the ensuing evening. It was therefore necessary to attack it that day; but before this could be done, it was first necessary to procure a better supply of arms than they were then possessed of.

There was adjoining to the city a large magazine of arms deposited at the Hospital of the Invalids, which the citizens summoned to surrender; and as the place was not defensible, nor attempted much defence, they soon succeeded. Thus supplied, they marched to attack the Bastille; a vast mixed multitude of all ages, and of all degrees, and armed with all sorts of weapons. Imagination would fail in describing to itself the appearance of such a procession, and of the anxiety for the events which a few hours or a few minutes might produce. What plans the ministry was forming, were as unknown to the people within the city, as what the citizens were doing was unknown to them; and what movements Broglio might make for the support or relief of the place, were to the citizens equally as unknown. All was mystery and hazard.

That the Bastille was attacked with an enthusiasm of heroism, such only as the highest animation of liberty could inspire, and carried in the space of a few hours, is an event which the world is fully possesed of. I am not undertaking a detail of the attack, but bringing into view the conspiracy against the nation which provoked it, and which fell with the Bastille. The prison to which the new ministry were dooming the National Assembly, in addition to its being the high altar and castle of despotism, became the proper object to begin with. This enterprise broke up the new ministry, who began now to fly from the ruin they had prepared for others. The troops of Broglio dispersed, and himself fled also.

Mr. Burke has spoken a great deal about plots, but he has never once spoken of this plot against the National Assembly, and the liberties of the nation; and that he might not, he has passed over all the circumstances that might throw it in his way. The exiles who have fled from France, whose case he so much interests himself in, and from whom he has had his lesson, fled in consequence of the miscarriage of this plot. No plot was formed against them: it were they who were plotting against others; and those who fell, met, not unjustly, the punishment they were preparing to execute. But will Mr. Burke say, that if this plot, contrived with the subtlety of an ambuscade, had succeeded, the successful party would have restrained their wrath so soon? Let the history of all old governments answer the question.

Whom has the National Assembly brought to the scaffold? None. They were themselves the devoted victims of this plot, and they have not retaliated; why then are they charged with revenge they have not acted? In the tremendous breaking forth of a whole people, in which all degrees, tempers and characters are confounded, and delivering themselves, by a miracle of exertion, from the destruction meditated against them, is it to be expected that nothing will happen? When men are sore with the sense of oppressions, and menaced with the prospect of new ones, is the calmness of philosophy, or the palsy of insensibility, to be looked for? Mr. Burke exclaims against outrage; yet the greatest is that which himself has committed. His book is a volume of outrage, not apologized for by the impulse of a moment, but cherished through a space of ten months; yet Mr. Burke had no provocation, no life, no interest at stake.

More citizens fell in this struggle than of their opponents: but four or five persons were seized by the populace, and instantly put to death; the Governor of the Bastille, and the Mayor of Paris, who was detected in the act of betraying them; and afterwards Foulon, one of the new ministry, and Berthier his son-in-law, who had accepted the office of intendant of Paris. Their heads were stuck upon spikes, and carried about the city; and it is upon this mode of punishment that Mr. Burke builds a great part of his tragic scenes. Let us therefore examine how men came by the idea of punishing in this manner.

They learn it from the governments they live under, and retaliate the punishments they have been accustomed to behold. The heads stuck upon spikes, which remained for years upon Temple-bar, differed nothing in the horror of the scene from those carried about upon spikes at Paris: yet this was done by the English government. It may perhaps be said, that it signifies nothing to a man what is done to him after he is dead; but it signifies much to the living: it either tortures their feelings, or hardens their hearts; and in either case, it instructs them how to punish when power falls into their hands.

Lay then the axe to the root, and teach governments humanity. It is their sanguinary punishments which corrupt mankind. In England the punishment in certain cases, is by *hanging, drawing,* and *quartering;* the heart of the sufferer is cut out, and held up to the view of the populace. In France, under the former goverment, the punishments were not less barbarous. Who does not remember the execution of Damien, torn to pieces by horses? The effect of those cruel spectacles exhibited to the populace, is to destroy tenderness, or excite revenge; and by the base and false idea of governing men by terror, instead of reason, they become precedents. It is over the lowest class of mankind that government by terror is intended to operate, and it is on them that it operates to the worst effect. They have sense enough to feel they are the objects aimed at; and they inflict in their turn the examples of terror they have been instructed to practise.

There are in all European countries, a large class of people of that description which in England are called the *"mob."* Of this class were those who committed the burnings and devastations in London in 1780, and of this class were those who carried the heads upon spikes in Paris. Foulon and Berthier were taken up in the country, and sent to Paris, to undergo their examination at the Hotel de Ville; for the National Assembly, immediately on the new ministry coming into office, passed a decree, which they communicated to the King and Cabinet, that they (the National Assembly) would hold the ministry, of which Foulon was one, responsible for the measures they were advising and pursuing; but the mob, incensed at the appearance of Foulon and Berthier, tore them from their conductors before they were carried to the Hotel de Ville, and executed them on the spot. Why then does Mr. Burke charge outrages of this kind on a whole people? As well may he charge the riots and outrages of 1780 on all the people of London, or those in Ireland on all his country.

But every thing we see or hear offensive to our feelings, and derogatory to the human character, should lead to other reflections than those of reproach. Even the beings who commit them have some claim to our consideration. How then is it that such vast classes of mankind as are distinguished by the appellation of the vulgar, or the ignorant mob, are so numerous in all old countries? The instant we ask ourselves this question, reflection feels an answer. They arise, as an unavoidable consequence, out of the ill construction of all old governments in Europe, England included with the rest. It is by distortedly exalting some men, that others are distortedly debased, till the whole is out of nature. A vast mass of mankind are degradedly thrown into the back-ground of the human picture, to bring forward, with greater glare, the puppet-show of state and aristocracy. In the commencement of a Revolution, those men are rather the followers of the *camp* than of the *standard* of liberty, and have yet to be instructed how to reverence it.

I give to Mr. Burke all his theatrical exaggerations for facts, and I then ask him, if they do not establish the certainty of what I here lay down? Admitting them to be true, they shew the necessity of the French Revolution, as much as any one thing he could have asserted. These outrages were not the effect of the principles of the Revolution, but of the degraded mind that existed before the Revolution, and which the Revolution is calculated to reform. Place them then to their proper cause, and take the reproach of them to your own side.

It is to the honour of the National Assembly, and the city of Paris, that during such a tremendous scene of arms and confusion, beyond the controul of all authority, they have been able, by the influence of example and exhortation, to restrain so much. Never were more pains taken to instruct and enlighten mankind, and to make them see that their interest consisted in their virtue, and not in their revenge, than what have been displayed in the Revolution of France.—I now proceed to make some remarks on Mr. Burke's account of the expedition to Versailles, October 5th and 6th.

I cannot consider Mr. Burke's book in scarcely any other light than a dramatic performance; and he must, I think, have considered it in the same light himself, by the poetical liberties he has taken of omitting some facts, distorting others, and making the whole machinery bend to produce a stage effect. Of this kind is his account of the expedition to Versailles. He begins this account by omitting the only facts which as causes are known to be true; every thing beyond these is conjecture even in Paris: and he then works up a tale accommodated to his own passions and prejudices.

It is to be observed throughout Mr. Burke's book, that he never speaks of plots *against* the Revolution; and it is from those plots that all the mischiefs have arisen. It suits his purpose to exhibit the consequences without their causes. It is one of the arts of the drama to do so. If the crimes of men were exhibited with their sufferings, the stage effect would sometimes be lost, and the audience would be inclined to approve where it was intended they should commiserate.

After all the investigations that have been made into this intricate affair, (the expedition to Versailles), it still remains enveloped in all that kind of mystery which ever accompanies events produced more from a concurrence of awkward circumstances, than from fixed design. While the characters of men are forming, as is always the case in revolutions, there is a reciprocal suspicion, and a disposition to misinterpret each other; and even parties directly opposite in principle, will sometimes concur in pushing forward the same movement with very different views, and with the hopes of its producing very different consequences. A great deal of this may be discovered in this embarrassed affair, and yet the issue of the whole was what nobody had in view.

The only things certainly known, are, that considerable uneasiness was at this time excited at Paris, by the delay of the King in not sanctioning and forwarding the decrees of the National Assembly, particularly that of the *Declaration of the rights of Man,* and the decrees of the *fourth of August,* which contained the foundation principles on which the constitution was to be erected. The kindest, and perhaps the fairest conjecture upon this matter is, that some of the ministers intended to make remarks and observations upon certain parts of them, before they were finally sanctioned and sent to the provinces; but be this as it may, the enemies of the revolution derived hopes from the delay, and the friends of the revolution, uneasiness.

During this state of suspense, the *Garde du Corps,* which was composed, as such regiments generally are, of persons much connected with the Court, gave an entertainment at Versailles (Oct. 1,) to some foreign regiments then arrived; and when the entertainment was at the height, on a signal given, the *Garde du Corps* tore the national cockade from their hats, trampled it under foot, and replaced it with a counter cockade prepared for the purpose. An indignity of this kind amounted to defiance. It was like

declaring war; and if men will give challenges, they must expect consequences. But all this Mr. Burke has carefully kept out of sight. He begins
his account by saying, "History will record, that on the morning of the 6th
of October 1789, the King and Queen of France, after a day of confusion,
alarm, dismay, and slaughter, lay down under the pledged security of public
faith, to indulge nature in a few hours of respite, and troubled melancholy
repose." This is neither the sober stile of history, nor the intention of it. It
leaves every thing to be guessed at, and mistaken. One would at least think
there had been a battle; and a battle there probably would have been, had it
not been for the moderating prudence of those whom Mr. Burke involves
in his censures. By his keeping the *Garde du Corps* out of sight, Mr. Burke
has afforded himself the dramatic licence of putting the King and Queen
in their places, as if the object of the expedition was against them. – But, to
return to my account –

This conduct of the *Garde du Corps,* as might well be expected, alarmed
and enraged the Parisians. The colours of the cause, and the cause itself,
were become too united to mistake the intention of the insult, and the Parisians were determined to call the *Garde du Corps* to an account. There
was certainly nothing of the cowardice of assassination in marching in the
face of day to demand satisfaction, if such a phrase may be used, of a body
of armed men who had voluntarily given defiance. But the circumstance
which serves to throw this affair into embarrassment is, that the enemies of
the revolution appear to have encouraged it, as well as its friends. The one
hoped to prevent a civil war by checking it in time, and the other to make
one. The hopes of those opposed to the revolution, rested in making the
King of their party, and getting him from Versailles to Metz, where they
expected to collect a force, and set up a standard. We have therefore two
different objects presenting themselves at the same time, and to be accomplished by the same means; the one, to chastise the *Garde du Corps,* which
was the object of the Parisians; the other, to render the confusion of such a
scene an inducement to the King to set off for Metz.

On the 5th of October, a very numerous body of women, and men in
the disguise of women, collected round the Hotel de Ville or town-hall at
Paris, and set off for Versailles. Their professed object was the *Garde du
Corps;* but prudent men readily recollect that mischief is easier begun than
ended; and this impressed itself with the more force, from the suspicions
already stated, and the irregularity of such a cavalcade. As soon therefore
as a sufficient force could be collected, M. de la Fayette, by orders from the
civil authority of Paris, set off after them at the head of twenty thousand
of the Paris militia. The revolution could derive no benefit from confusion,

and its opposers might. By an amiable and spirited manner of address, he had hitherto been fortunate in calming disquietudes, and in this he was extraordinarily successful; to frustrate, therefore, the hopes of those who might seek to improve this scene into a sort of justifiable necessity for the King's quitting Versailles and withdrawing to Metz, and to prevent at the same time the consequences that might ensue between the *Garde du Corps* and this phalanx of men and women, he forwarded expresses to the King, that he was on his march to Versailles, at the orders of the civil authority of Paris, for the purpose of peace and protection, expressing at the same time the necessity of restraining the *Garde du Corps* from firing upon the people[2].

He arrived at Versailles between ten and eleven at night. The *Garde du Corps* was drawn up, and the people had arrived some time before, but every thing had remained suspended. Wisdom and policy now consisted in changing a scene of danger into a happy event. M. de la Fayette became the mediator between the enraged parties; and the King, to remove the uneasiness which had arisen from the delay already stated, sent for the President of the National Assembly, and signed the *Declaration of the rights of Man,* and such other parts of the constitution as were in readiness.

It was now about one in the morning. Every thing appeared to be composed, and a general congratulation took place. At the beat of drum a proclamation was made, that the citizens of Versailles would give the hospitality of their houses to their fellow-citizens of Paris. Those who could not be accommodated in this manner, remained in the streets, or took up their quarters in the churches; and at two o'clock the King and Queen retired.

In this state matters passed till the break of day, when a fresh disturbance arose from the censurable conduct of some of both parties, for such characters there will be in all such scenes. One of the *Garde du Corps* appeared at one of the windows of the palace, and the people who had remained during the night in the streets accosted him with reviling and provocative language. Instead of retiring, as in such a case prudence would have dictated, he presented his musket, fired, and killed one of the Paris militia. The peace being thus broken, the people rushed into the palace in quest of the offender. They attacked the quarters of the *Garde du Corps* within the palace, and pursued them throughout the avenues of it, and to the apartments of the King. On this tumult, not the Queen only, as Mr. Burke

2. I am warranted in asserting this, as I had it personally from M. de la Fayette, with whom I have lived in habits of friendship for fourteen years.

has represented it, but every person in the palace, was awakened and alarmed; and M. de la Fayette had a second time to interpose between the parties, the event of which was, that the *Garde du Corps* put on the national cockade, and the matter ended as by oblivion, after the loss of two or three lives.

During the latter part of the time in which this confusion was acting, the King and Queen were in public at the balcony, and neither of them concealed for safety's sake, as Mr. Burke insinuates. Matters being thus appeased, and tranquillity restored, a general acclamation broke forth, of *Le Roi à Paris – Le Roi à Paris* – The King to Paris. It was the shout of peace, and immediately accepted on the part of the King. By this measure, all future projects of trapanning the King to Metz, and setting up the standard of opposition to the constitution, were prevented, and the suspicions extinguished. The King and his family reached Paris in the evening, and were congratulated on their arrival by M. Bailley the Mayor of Paris, in the name of the citizens. Mr. Burke, who throughout his book confounds things, persons, and principles, has in his remarks on M. Bailley's address, confounded time also. He censures M. Bailley for calling it, "*un bon jour,*" a good day. Mr. Burke should have informed himself, that this scene took up the space of two days, the day on which it began with every appearance of danger and mischief, and the day on which it terminated without the mischiefs that threatened; and that it is to this peaceful termination that M. Bailley alludes, and to the arrival of the King at Paris. Not less than three hundred thousand persons arranged themselves in the procession from Versailles to Paris, and not an act of molestation was committed during the whole march.

Mr. Burke, on the authority of M. Lally Tollendal, a deserter from the National Assembly, says, that on entering Paris, the people shouted, "*Tous les eveques à la lanterne.*" All Bishops to be hanged at the lanthorn or lamp-posts. – It is surprising that nobody should hear this but Lally Tollendal, and that nobody should believe it but Mr. Burke. It has not the least connection with any part of the transaction, and is totally foreign to every circumstance of it. The bishops had never been introduced before into any scene of Mr. Burke's drama; Why then are they, all at once, and altogether, *tout à coup et tous ensemble,* introduced now? Mr. Burke brings forward his bishops and his lanthorn like figures in a magic lanthorn, and raises his scenes by contrast instead of connection. But it serves to shew, with the rest of his book, what little credit ought to be given, where even probability is set at defiance, for the purpose of defaming; and with this reflection, instead of a soliloquy in praise of chivalry, as Mr. Burke has done, I close the account of the expedition to Versailles[3].

I have now to follow Mr. Burke through a pathless wilderness of rhapsodies, and a sort of descant upon governments, in which he asserts whatever he pleases, on the presumption of its being believed, without offering either evidence or reasons for so doing.

Before any thing can be reasoned upon to a conclusion, certain facts, principles, or data, to reason from, must be established, admitted, or denied. Mr. Burke with his usual outrage, abuses the *Declaration of the rights of Man,* published by the National Assembly of France as the basis on which the constitution of France is built. This he calls "paltry and blurred sheets of paper about the rights of man."–Does Mr. Burke mean to deny that *man* has any rights? If he does, then he must mean that there are no such things as rights any where, and that he has none himself; for who is there in the world but man? But if Mr. Burke means to admit that man has rights, the question then will be, What are those rights, and how came man by them originally?

The error of those who reason by precedents drawn from antiquity, respecting the rights of man, is, that they do not go far enough into antiquity. They do not go the whole way. They stop in some of the intermediate stages of an hundred or a thousand years, and produce what was then done as a rule for the present day. This is no authority at all. If we travel still farther into antiquity, we shall find a direct contrary opinion and practice prevailing; and if antiquity is to be authority, a thousand such authorities may be produced, successively contradicting each other: But if we proceed on, we shall at last come out right; we shall come to the time when man came from the hand of his Maker. What was he then? Man. Man was his high and only title, and a higher cannot be given him.——But of titles I shall speak hereafter.

We are now got at the origin of man, and at the origin of his rights. As to the manner in which the world has been governed from that day to this, it is no farther any concern of ours than to make a proper use of the errors or the improvements which the history of it presents. Those who lived a hundred or a thousand years ago, were then moderns as we are now. They had *their* ancients, and those ancients had others, and we also shall be ancients in our turn. If the mere name of antiquity is to govern in the affairs of life, the people who are to live an hundred or a thousand years hence, may as well take

3. An account of the expedition to Versailles may be seen in No. 13. of the *Revolution de Paris,* containing the events from the 3d to the 10th of October 1789.

us for a precedent, as we make a precedent of those who lived an hundred or a thousand years ago. The fact is, that portions of antiquity, by proving every thing, establish nothing. It is authority against authority all the way, till we come to the divine origin of the rights of man at the creation. Here our enquiries find a resting-place, and our reason finds a home. If a dispute about the rights of man had arose at the distance of an hundred years from the creation, it is to this source of authority they must have referred, and it is to the same source of authority that we must now refer.

Though I mean not to touch upon any sectarian principle of religion, yet it may be worth observing, that the genealogy of Christ is traced to Adam. Why then not trace the rights of man to the creation of man? I will answer the question. Because there have been an upstart of governments, thrusting themselves between, and presumptuously working to *un-make* man.

If any generation of men ever possessed the right of dictating the mode by which the world should be governed for ever, it was the first generation that existed; and if that generation did not do it, no succeeding generation can shew any authority for doing it, nor set any up. The illuminating and divine principle of the equal rights of man, (for it has its origin from the Maker of man) relates, not only to the living individuals, but to generations of men succeeding each other. Every generation is equal in rights to the generations which preceded it, by the same rule that every individual is born equal in rights with his cotemporary.

Every history of the creation, and every traditionary account, whether from the lettered or unlettered world, however they may vary in their opinion or belief of certain particulars, all agree in establishing one point, *the unity of man;* by which I mean that man is all of *one degree,* and consequently that all men are born equal, and with equal natural rights, in the same manner as if posterity had been continued by *creation* instead of *generation,* the latter being only the mode by which the former is carried forward; and consequently, every child born into the world must be considered as deriving its existence from God. The world is as new to him as it was to the first man that existed, and his natural right in it is of the same kind.

The Mosaic account of the creation, whether taken as divine authority, or merely historical, is fully up to this point, *the unity or equality of man.* The expressions admit of no controversy. "And God said, Let us make man in our own image. In the image of God created he him; male and female created he them." The distinction of sexes is pointed out, but no other distinction is even implied. If this be not divine authority, it is at least historical authority, and shews that the equality of man, so far from being a modern doctrine, is the oldest upon record.

It is also to be observed, that all the religions known in the world are founded, so far as they relate to man, on the *unity of man,* as being all of one degree. Whether in heaven or in hell, or in whatever state man may be supposed to exist hereafter, the good and the bad are the only distinctions. Nay, even the laws of governments are obliged to slide into this principle, by making degrees to consist in crimes, and not in persons.

It is one of the greatest of all truths, and of the highest advantage to cultivate. By considering man in this light, and by instructing him to consider himself in this light, it places him in a close connection with all his duties, whether to his Creator, or to the creation, of which he is a part; and it is only when he forgets his origin, or, to use a more fashionable phrase, his *birth and family,* that he becomes dissolute. It is not among the least of the evils of the present existing governments in all parts of Europe, that man, considered as man, is thrown back to a vast distance from his Maker, and the artificial chasm filled up by a succession of barriers, or a sort of turnpike gates, through which he has to pass. I will quote Mr. Burke's catalogue of barriers that he has set up between man and his Maker. Putting himself in the character of a herald, he says – "We fear God – we look with *awe* to kings – with affection to parliaments – with duty to magistrates – with reverence to priests, and with respect to nobility." Mr. Burke has forgot to put in *"chivalry."* He has also forgot to put in Peter.

The duty of man is not a wilderness of turnpike gates, through which he is to pass by tickets from one to the other. It is plain and simple, and consists but of two points. His duty to God, which every man must feel; and with respect to his neighbour, to do as he would be done by. If those to whom power is delegated do well, they will be respected; if not, they will be despised: and with regard to those to whom no power is delegated, but who assume it, the rational world can know nothing of them.

Hitherto we have spoken only (and that but in part) of the natural rights of man. We have now to consider the civil rights of man, and to shew how the one originates out of the other. Man did not enter into society to become *worse* than he was before, nor to have less rights than he had before, but to have those rights better secured. His natural rights are the foundation of all his civil rights. But in order to pursue this distinction with more precision, it will be necessary to mark the different qualities of natural and civil rights.

A few words will explain this. Natural rights are those which appertain to man in right of his existence. Of this kind are all the intellectual rights, or rights of the mind, and also all those rights of acting as an individual for his own comfort and happiness, which are not injurious to the natural rights of

others.———Civil rights are those which appertain to man in right of his being a member of society. Every civil right has for its foundation some natural right pre-existing in the individual, but to which his individual power
is not, in all cases, sufficiently competent. Of this kind are all those which
relate to security and protection.

From this short review, it will be easy to distinguish between that class
of natural rights which man retains after entering into society, and those
which he throws into common stock as a member of society.

The natural rights which he retains, are all those in which the *power*
to execute is as perfect in the individual as the right itself. Among this
class, as is before mentioned, are all the intellectual rights, or rights of
the mind: consequently, religion is one of those rights. The natural rights
which are not retained, are all those in which, though the right is perfect
in the individual, the power to execute them is defective. They answer not
his purpose. A man, by natural right, has a right to judge in his own cause;
and so far as the right of the mind is concerned, he never surrenders it. But
what availeth it him to judge, if he has not power to redress? He therefore
deposits this right in the common stock of society, and takes the arm of society, of which he is a part, in preference and in addition to his own. Society
grants him nothing. Every man is a proprietor in society, and draws on the
capital as a matter of right.

From those premises, two or three certain conclusions will follow.

First; That every civil right grows out of a natural right; or, in other
words, is a natural right exchanged.

Secondly, That civil power, properly considered as such, is made up
of the aggregate of that class of the natural rights of man, which becomes
defective in the individual in point of power, and answers not his purpose; but when collected to a focus, becomes competent to the purpose of
every one.

Thirdly, That the power produced from the aggregate of natural rights,
imperfect in power in the individual, cannot be applied to invade the natural rights which are retained in the individual, and in which the power to
execute is as perfect as the right itself.

We have now, in a few words, traced man from a natural individual to a
member of society, and shewn, or endeavoured to shew, the quality of the
natural rights retained, and of those which are exchanged for civil rights.
Let us now apply those principles to governments.

In casting our eyes over the world, it is extremely easy to distinguish the
governments which have arisen out of society, or out of the social compact,
from those which have not: but to place this in a clearer light than what a

single glance may afford, it will be proper to take a review of the several sources from which governments have arisen, and on which they have been founded.

They may be all comprehended under three heads. First, Superstition. Secondly, Power. Thirdly, the common interest of society, and the common rights of man.

The first was a government of priestcraft, the second of conquerors, and the third of reason.

When a set of artful men pretended, through the medium of oracles, to hold intercourse with the Deity, as familiarly as they now march up the backstairs in European courts, the world was completely under the government of superstition. The oracles were consulted, and whatever they were made to say, became the law; and this sort of government lasted as long as this sort of superstition lasted.

After these a race of conquerors arose, whose government, like that of William the Conqueror, was founded in power, and the sword assumed the name of a scepter. Governments thus established, last as long as the power to support them lasts; but that they might avail themselves of every engine in their favour, they united fraud to force, and set up an idol which they called *Divine Right,* and which, in imitation of the Pope, who affects to be spiritual and temporal, and in contradiction to the Founder of the Christian religion, twisted itself afterwards into an idol of another shape, called *Church and State.* The key of St. Peter, and the key of the Treasury, became quartered on one another, and the wondering cheated multitude worshipped the invention.

When I contemplate the natural dignity of man; when I feel (for Nature has not been kind enough to me to blunt my feelings) for the honour and happiness of its character, I become irritated at the attempt to govern mankind by force and fraud, as if they were all knaves and fools, and can scarcely avoid disgust at those who are thus imposed upon.

We have now to review the governments which arise out of society, in contradistinction to those which arose out of superstition and conquest.

It has been thought a considerable advance towards establishing the principles of Freedom, to say, that government is a compact between those who govern and those who are governed: but this cannot be true, because it is putting the effect before the cause; for as man must have existed before governments existed, there necessarily was a time when governments did not exist, and consequently there could originally exist no governors to form such a compact with. The fact therefore must be, that the *individu-*

als themselves, each in his own personal and sovereign right, *entered into a compact with each other* to produce a government: and this is the only mode in which governments have a right to arise, and the only principle on which they have a right to exist.

To possess ourselves of a clear idea of what government is, or ought to be, we must trace it to its origin. In doing this, we shall easily discover that governments must have arisen, either *out* of the people, or *over* the people. Mr. Burke has made no distinction. He investigates nothing to its source, and therefore he confounds every thing: but he has signified his intention of undertaking at some future opportunity, a comparison between the constitutions of England and France. As he thus renders it a subject of controversy by throwing the gauntlet, I take him up on his own ground. It is in high challenges that high truths have the right of appearing; and I accept it with the more readiness, because it affords me, at the same time, an opportunity of pursuing the subject with respect to governments arising out of society.

But it will be first necessary to define what is meant by a *constitution.* It is not sufficient that we adopt the word; we must fix also a standard signification to it.

A constitution is not a thing in name only, but in fact. It has not an ideal, but a real existence; and wherever it cannot be produced in a visible form, there is none. A constitution is a thing *antecedent* to a government, and a government is only the creature of a constitution. The constitution of a country is not the act of its government, but of the people constituting a government. It is the body of elements, to which you can refer, and quote article by article; and which contains the principles on which the government shall be established, the manner in which it shall be organized, the powers it shall have, the mode of elections, the duration of parliaments, or by what other name such bodies may be called; the powers which the executive part of the government shall have; and, in fine, every thing that relates to the compleat organization of a civil government, and the principles on which it shall act, and by which it shall be bound. A constitution, therefore, is to a government, what the laws made afterwards by that government are to a court of judicature. The court of judicature does not make the laws, neither can it alter them; it only acts in conformity to the laws made; and the government is in like manner governed by the constitution.

Can then Mr. Burke produce the English Constitution? If he cannot, we may fairly conclude, that though it has been so much talked about, no such thing as a constitution exists, or ever did exist, and consequently that the people have yet a constitution to form.

Mr. Burke will not, I presume, deny the position I have already advanced; namely, that governments arise either *out* of the people, or *over* the people. The English government is one of those which arose out of a conquest, and not out of society, and consequently it arose over the people; and though it has been much modified from the opportunity of circumstances since the time of William the Conqueror, the country has never yet regenerated itself, and is therefore without a constitution.

I readily perceive the reason why Mr. Burke declined going into the comparison between the English and French constitutions, because he could not but perceive, when he sat down to the task, that no such thing as a constitution existed on his side the question. His book is certainly bulky enough to have contained all he could say on this subject, and it would have been the best manner in which people could have judged of their separate merits. Why then has he declined the only thing that was worth while to write upon? It was the strongest ground he could take, if the advantages were on his side; but the weakest, if they were not; and his declining to take it, is either a sign that he could not possess it, or could not maintain it.

Mr. Burke has said in a speech last winter in parliament, that when the National Assembly first met in three Orders, (the Tiers Etats, the Clergy, and the Noblesse), that France had then a good constitution. This shews, among numerous other instances, that Mr. Burke does not understand what a constitution is. The persons so met, were not a *constitution,* but a *convention* to make a constitution.

The present National Assembly of France is, strictly speaking, the personal social compact. – The members of it are the delegates of the nation in its *original* character; future assemblies will be the delegates of the nation in its *organized* character. The authority of the present Assembly is different to what the authority of future Assemblies will be. The authority of the present one is to form a constitution: the authority of future Assemblies will be to legislate according to the principles and forms prescribed in that constitution; and if experience should hereafter shew that alterations, amendments, or additions are necessary, the constitution will point out the mode by which such things shall be done, and not leave it to the discretionary power of the future government.

A government on the principles on which constitutional governments arising out of society are established, cannot have the right of altering itself. If it had, it would be arbitrary. It might make itself what it pleased; and wherever such a right is set up, it shews there is no constitution. The act by which the English Parliament empowered itself to sit seven years, shews there is no constitution in England. It might, by the same self-authority,

have sit any greater number of years, or for life. The Bill which the present
Mr. Pitt brought into parliament some years ago, to reform parliament, was
on the same erroneous principle. The right of reform is in the nation in its
original character, and the constitutional method would be by a general
convention elected for the purpose. There is moreover a paradox in the idea
of vitiated bodies reforming themselves.

From these preliminaries I proceed to draw some comparisons. I have
already spoken of the declaration of rights; and as I mean to be as concise
as possible, I shall proceed to other parts of the French constitution.

The constitution of France says, that every man who pays a tax of sixty
sous *per annum,* (2s. and 6d. English), is an elector. – What article will
Mr. Burke place against this? Can any thing be more limited, and at the
same time more capricious, than what the qualifications of electors are
in England? Limited – because not one man in an hundred (I speak much
within compass) is admitted to vote: Capricious – because the lowest character that can be supposed to exist, and who has not so much as the visible
means of an honest livelihood, is an elector in some places; while, in other
places the man who pays very large taxes and with a fair known character,
and the farmer who rents to the amount of three or four hundred pounds a
year, and with a property on that farm to three or four times that amount,
is not admitted to be an elector. Every thing is out of nature, as Mr. Burke
says on another occasion, in this strange chaos, and all sorts of follies are
blended with all sorts of crimes. William the Conqueror and his descendants parcelled out the country in this manner, and bribed one part of it by
what they called Charters, to hold the other parts of it the better subjected
to their will. This is the reason why so many of those Charters abound in
Cornwall. The people were averse to the government established at the
conquest, and the towns were garrisoned and bribed to enslave the country.
All the old Charters are the badges of this conquest, and it is from this
source that the capriciousness of elections arise.

The French constitution says, that the number of representatives for any
place shall be in a ratio to the number of taxable inhabitants or electors.
What article will Mr. Burke place against this? The county of Yorkshire,
which contains near a million of souls, sends two county members; and so
does the county of Rutland, which contains not an hundredth part of that
number. The town of old Sarum, which contains not three houses, sends
two members; and the town of Manchester, which contains upwards of
sixty thousand souls, is not admitted to send any. Is there any principle in
these things? Is there any thing by which you can trace the marks of freedom, or discover those of wisdom? No wonder then Mr. Burke has declined

the comparison, and endeavoured to lead his readers from the point by a wild unsystematical display of paradoxial rhapsodies.

The French constitution says, that the National Assembly shall be elected every two years. – What article will Mr. Burke place against this? Why, that the nation has no right at all in the case: that the government is perfectly arbitrary with respect to this point; and he can quote for his authority, the precedent of a former parliament.

The French constitution says, there shall be no game laws; that the farmer on whose lands wild game shall be found (for it is by the produce of those lands they are fed) shall have a right to what he can take. That there shall be no monopolies of any kind – that all trade shall be free, and every man free to follow any occupation by which he can procure an honest livelihood, and in any place, town or city throughout the nation. – What will Mr. Burke say to this? In England, game is made the property of those at whose expence it is not fed; and with respect to monopolies, the country is cut up into monopolies. Every chartered town is an aristocratical monopoly in itself, and the qualification of electors proceeds out of those chartered monopolies. Is this freedom? Is this what Mr. Burke means by a constitution?

In these chartered monopolies, a man coming from another part of the country, is hunted from them as if he were a foreign enemy. An Englishman is not free of his own country: every one of those places presents a barrier in his way, and tells him he is not a freeman – that he has no rights. Within these monopolies, are other monopolies. A city, such for instance as Bath, which contains between twenty and thirty thousand inhabitants, the right of electing representatives to parliament is monopolised into about thirty-one persons. And within these monopolies are still others. A man even of the same town, whose parents were not in circumstances to give him an occupation, is debarred, in many cases, from the natural right of acquiring one, be his genius or industry what it may.

Are these things examples to hold out to a country regenerating itself from slavery, like France? – Certainly they are not; and certain am I, that when the people of England come to reflect upon them, they will, like France, annihilate those badges of ancient oppression, those traces of a conquered nation. – Had Mr. Burke possessed talents similar to the author "On the Wealth of Nations," he would have comprehended all the parts which enter into, and, by assemblage, form a constitution. He would have reasoned from minutiæ to magnitude. It is not from his prejudices only, but from the disorderly cast of his genius, that he is unfitted for the subject he writes upon. Even his genius is without a constitution. It is a genius at random, and not a genius constituted. But he must say something—He has therefore mounted in the air like a balloon, to draw the eyes of the multitude from the ground they stand upon.

Much is to be learned from the French constitution. Conquest and tyranny transplanted themselves with William the Conqueror from Normandy into England, and the country is yet disfigured with the marks. May then the example of all France contribute to regenerate the freedom which a province of it destroyed!

The French constitution says, That to preserve the national representation from being corrupt, no member of the National Assembly shall be an officer of the government, a place-man, or a pensioner.—What will Mr. Burke place against this? I will whisper his answer: *Loaves* and *fishes*. Ah! this government of loaves and fishes has more mischief in it than people have yet reflected on. The National Assembly has made the discovery, and it holds out the example to the world. Had governments agreed to quarrel on purpose to fleece their countries by taxes, they could not have succeeded better than they have done.

Every thing in the English government appears to me the reverse of what it ought to be, and of what it is said to be. The parliament, imperfectly and capriciously elected as it is, is nevertheless *supposed* to hold the national purse in *trust* for the nation: but in the manner in which an English parliament is constructed, it is like a man being both mortgager and mortgagee; and in the case of misapplication of trust, it is the criminal sitting in judgment upon himself. If those who vote the supplies are the same persons who receive the supplies when voted, and are to account for the expenditure of those supplies to those who voted them, it is *themselves accountable to themselves,* and the Comedy of Errors concludes with the Pantomine of HUSH. Neither the ministerial party, nor the opposition, will touch upon this case. The national purse is the common hack which each mounts upon. It is like what the country people call, "Ride and tie—You ride a little way, and then I[4]."—They order these things better in France.

The French constitution says, that the right of war and peace is in the nation. Where else should it reside, but in those who are to pay the expence?

In England, this right is said to reside in a *metaphor,* shewn at the Tower for sixpence or a shilling a-piece: so are the lions; and it would be a step

4. It is a practice in some parts of the country, when two travellers have but one horse, which like the national purse will not carry double, that the one mounts and rides two or three miles a-head, and then ties the horse to a gate, and walks on. When the second traveller arrives, he takes the horse, rides on, and passes his companion a mile or two, and ties again; and so on——*Ride and tie.*

nearer to reason to say it resided in them, for any inanimate metaphor is no more than a hat or a cap. We can all see the absurdity of worshipping Aaron's molton calf, or Nebuchadnezzar's golden image; but why do men continue to practise in themselves, the absurdities they despise in others?

It may with reason be said, that in the manner the English nation is represented, it signifies not where this right resides, whether in the crown or in the parliament. War is the common harvest of all those who participate in the division and expenditure of public money, in all countries. It is the art of *conquering at home:* the object of it is an increase of revenue; and as revenue cannot be increased without taxes, a pretence must be made for expenditures. In reviewing the history of the English government, its wars and its taxes, a stander-by, not blinded by prejudice, nor warped by interest, would declare, that taxes were not raised to carry on wars, but that wars were raised to carry on taxes.

Mr. Burke, as a Member of the House of Commons, is a part of the English Government; and though he professes himself an enemy to war, he abuses the French Constitution, which seeks to explode it. He holds up the English Government as a model in all its parts, to France; but he should first know the remarks which the French make upon it. They contend, in favour of their own, that the portion of liberty enjoyed in England, is just enough to enslave a country by, more productively than by despotism; and that as the real object of all despotism is revenue, that a government so formed obtains more than it could either by direct despotism, or in a full state of freedom, and is, therefore, on the ground of interest, opposed to both. They account also for the readiness which always appears in such governments for engaging in wars, by remarking on the different motives which produce them. In despotic governments, wars are the effect of pride; but in those governments in which they become the means of taxation, they acquire thereby a more permanent promptitude.

The French Constitution, therefore, to provide against both those evils, have taken away the power of declaring war from kings and ministers, and placed the right where the expence must fall.

When the question on the right of war and peace was agitating in the National Assembly, the people of England appeared to be much interested in the event, and highly to applaud the decision. – As a principle, it applies as much to one country as to another. William the Conqueror, *as a conqueror,* held this power of war and peace in himself, and his descendants have ever since claimed it under him as a right.

Although Mr. Burke has asserted the right of the parliament at the Revolution to bind and controul the nation and posterity for *ever,* he denies, at the same time, that the parliament or the nation had any right to alter what he calls the succession of the crown, in any thing but in part, or by a sort of modification. By his taking this ground, he throws the case back to the *Norman Conquest;* and by thus running a line of succession springing from William the Conqueror to the present day, he makes it necessary to enquire who and what William the Conqueror was, and where he came from; and into the origin, history, and nature of what are called prerogatives. Every thing must have had a beginning, and the fog of time and antiquity should be penetrated to discover it. Let then Mr. Burke bring forward his William of Normandy, for it is to this origin that his argument goes. It also unfortunately happens, in running this line of succession, that another line, parallel thereto, presents itself, which is, that if the succession runs in the line of the conquest, the nation runs in the line of being conquered, and it ought to rescue itself from this reproach.

But it will perhaps be said, that tho' the power of declaring war descends in the heritage of the conquest, it is held in check by the right of the parliament to with-hold the supplies. It will always happen, when a thing is originally wrong, that amendments do not make it right, and it often happens that they do as much mischief one way as good the other: and such is the case here; for if the one rashly declares war as a matter of right, and the other peremptorily with-holds the supplies as a matter of right, the remedy becomes as bad or worse than the disease. The one forces the nation to a combat, and the other ties its hands: But the more probable issue is, that the contrast will end in a collusion between the parties, and be made a screen to both.

On this question of war, three things are to be considered. First, the right of declaring it: Secondly, the expence of supporting it: Thirdly, the mode of conducting it after it is declared. The French constitution places the *right* where the *expence* must fall, and this union can be only in the nation. The mode of conducting it after it is declared, it consigns to the executive department.—Were this the case in all countries, we should hear but little more of wars.

Before I proceed to consider other parts of the French constitution, and by way of relieving the fatigue of argument, I will introduce an anecdote which I had from Dr. Franklin.——

While the Doctor resided in France as minister from America during the war, he had numerous proposals made to him by projectors of every country and of every kind, who wished to go to the land that floweth with milk and honey, America; and among the rest, there was one who offered himself to be King. He introduced his proposal to the Doctor by letter, which is now in the hands of M. Beaumarchais, of Paris – stating, first, that as the Americans had dismissed or sent away[5] their King, that they would want another. Secondly, that himself was a Norman. Thirdly, that he was of a more ancient family than the Dukes of Normandy, and of a more honourable descent, his line having never been bastardized. Fourthly, that there was already a precedent in England, of Kings coming out of Normandy: and on these grounds he rested his offer, *enjoining* that the Doctor would forward it to America. But as the Doctor did not do this, nor yet sent him an answer, the projector wrote a second letter; in which he did not, it is true, threaten to go over and conquer America, but only with great dignity, proposed, that if his offer was not accepted, that an acknowledgment of about £ 30,000 might be made to him for his generosity!——Now, as all arguments respecting succession must necessarily connect that succession with some beginning, Mr. Burke's arguments on this subject go to shew, that there is no English origin of kings, and that they are descendants of the Norman line in right of the Conquest. It may, therefore, be of service to his doctrine to make this story known, and to inform him, that in case of that natural extinction to which all mortality is subject, that kings may again be had from Normandy, on more reasonable terms than William the Conqueror; and consequently that the good people of England, at the Revolution of 1688, might have done much better, had such a generous Norman as *this* known *their* wants, and they had known *his*. The chivalry character which Mr. Burke so much admires, is certainly much easier to make a bargain with than a hard-dealing Dutchman.——But, to return to the matters of the constitution –

The French constitution says, *There shall be no titles;* and of consequence, all that class of equivocal generation, which in some countries is called "*aristocracy,*" and in others "*nobility,*" is done away, and the *peer* is exalted into MAN.

Titles are but nick-names, and every nick-name is a title. The thing is perfectly harmless in itself, but it marks a sort of foppery in the human character which degrades it. It renders man into the diminutive of man in things which are great, and the counterfeit of woman in things which are little. It talks about its fine *blue ribbon* like a girl, and shews its new *garter* like a child. A certain writer of some antiquity, says, "When I was a child, I thought as a child; but when I became a man, I put away childish things."

It is, properly, from the elevated mind of France, that the folly of titles have fallen. It has outgrown the baby-cloaths of *Count* and *Duke,* and

---

5. The word he used was *renvoyé,* dismissed or sent away.

breeched itself in manhood. France has not levelled; it has exalted. It has put down the dwarf, to set up the man. The punyism of a senseless word like *Duke,* or *Count,* or *Earl,* has ceased to please. Even those who possessed them have disowned the gibberish, and, as they outgrew the rickets, have despised the rattle. The genuine mind of man, thirsting for its native home, society, contemns the gewgaws that separate him from it. Titles arc like circles drawn by the magician's wand, to contract the sphere of man's felicity. He lives immured within the Bastille of a word, and surveys at a distance the envied life of man.

Is it then any wonder that titles should fall in France? Is it not a greater wonder they should be kept up any where? What are they? What is their worth, and "what is their amount?" When we think or speak of a *Judge* or a *General,* we associate with it the ideas of office and character; we think of gravity in the one, and bravery in the other; but when we use a word *merely as a title,* no ideas associate with it. Through all the vocabulary of Adam, there is not such an animal as a Duke or a Count; neither can we connect any certain idea to the words. Whether they mean strength or weakness, wisdom or folly, a child or a man, or the rider or the horse, is all equivocal. What respect then can be paid to that which describes nothing, and which means nothing? Imagination has given figure and character to centaurs, satyrs, and down to all the fairy tribe; but titles baffle even the powers of fancy, and are a chimerical non-descript.

But this is not all.—If a whole country is disposed to hold them in contempt, all their value is gone, and none will own them. It is common opinion only that makes them any thing, or nothing, or worse than nothing. There is no occasion to take titles away, for they take themselves away when society concurs to ridicule them. This species of imaginary consequence has visibly declined in every part of Europe, and it hastens to its exit as the world of reason continues to rise. There was a time when the lowest class of what are called nobility was more thought of than the highest is now, and when a man in armour riding throughout Christendom in quest of adventures was more stared at than a modern Duke. The world has seen this folly fall, and it has fallen by being laughed at, and the farce of titles will follow its fate.—The patriots of France have discovered in good time, that rank and dignity in society must take a new ground. The old one has fallen through.—It must now take the substantial ground of character, instead of the chimerical ground of titles; and they have brought their titles to the altar, and made of them a burnt-offering to reason.

If no mischief had annexed itself to the folly of titles, they would not have been worth a serious and formal destruction, such as the National

Assembly have decreed them: and this makes it necessary to enquire further into the nature and character of aristocracy.

That, then, which is called aristocracy in some countries, and nobility in others, arose out of the governments founded upon conquest. It was originally a military order for the purpose of supporting military government, (for such were all governments founded in conquest); and to keep up a succession of this order for the purpose for which it was established, all the younger branches of those families were disinherited, and the law of *primogenitureship* set up.

The nature and character of aristocracy shews itself to us in this law. It is a law against every law of nature, and Nature herself calls for its destruction. Establish family justice, and aristocracy falls. By the aristocratical law of primogenitureship, in a family of six children, five are exposed. Aristocracy has never but *one* child. The rest are begotten to be devoured. They are thrown to the canibal for prey, and the natural parent prepares the unnatural repast.

As every thing which is out of nature in man, affects, more or less, the interest of society, so does this. All the children which the aristocracy disowns (which are all, except the eldest) are, in general, cast like orphans on a parish, to be provided for by the public, but at a greater charge. – Unnecessary offices and places in governments and courts are created at the expence of the public, to maintain them.

With what kind of parental reflections can the father or mother contemplate their younger offspring. By nature they are children, and by marriage they are heirs; but by aristocracy they are bastards and orphans. They are the flesh and blood of their parents in one line, and nothing akin to them in the other. To restore, therefore, parents to their children, and children to their parents – relations to each other, and man to society – and to exterminate the monster Aristocracy, root and branch – the French constitution has destroyed the law of PRIMOGENITURESHIP. Here then lies the monster; and Mr. Burke, if he pleases, may write its epitaph.

Hitherto we have considered aristocracy chiefly in one point of view. We have now to consider it in another. But whether we view it before or behind, or side-ways, or any way else, domestically or publicly, it is still a monster.

In France, aristocracy had one feature less in its countenance than what it has in some other countries. It did not compose a body of hereditary legislators. It was not "*a corporation of aristocracy,*" for such I have heard M. de la Fayette describe an English House of Peers. Let us then examine the grounds upon which the French constitution has resolved against having such an House in France.

Because, in the first place, as is already mentioned, aristocracy is kept up by family tyranny and injustice.

Secondly, Because there is an unnatural unfitness in an aristocracy to be legislators for a nation. Their ideas of *distributive justice* are corrupted at the very source. They begin life by trampling on all their younger brothers and sisters, and relations of every kind, and are taught and educated so to do. With what ideas of justice or honour can that man enter an house of legislation, who absorbs in his own person the inheritance of a whole family of children, or doles out to them some pitiful portion with the insolence of a gift?

Thirdly, Because the idea of hereditary legislators is as inconsistent as that of hereditary judges, or hereditary juries; and as absurd as an hereditary mathematician, or an hereditary wise man; and as ridiculous as an hereditary poet-laureat.

Fourthly, Because a body of men holding themselves accountable to nobody, ought not to be trusted by any body.

Fifthly, Because it is continuing the uncivilized principle of governments founded in conquest, and the base idea of man having property in man, and governing him by personal right.

Sixthly, Because aristocracy has a tendency to degenerate the human species.—By the universal œconomy of nature it is known, and by the instance of the Jews it is proved, that the human species has a tendency to degenerate, in any small number of persons, when separated from the general stock of society, and intermarrying constantly with each other. It defeats even its pretended end, and becomes in time the opposite of what is noble in man. Mr. Burke talks of nobility; let him shew what it is. The greatest characters the world have known, have rose on the democratic floor. Aristocracy has not been able to keep a proportionate pace with democracy. The artificial NOBLE shrinks into a dwarf before the NOBLE of Nature; and in the few instances (for there are some in all countries) in whom nature, as by a miracle, has survived in aristocracy, THOSE MEN DESPISE IT.——But it is time to proceed to a new subject.

The French constitution has reformed the condition of the clergy. It has raised the income of the lower and middle classes, and taken from the higher. None are now less than twelve hundred livres (fifty pounds sterling) nor any higher than about two or three thousand pounds. What will Mr. Burke place against this? Hear what he says.

He says, "that the people of England can see without pain or grudging, an archbishop precede a duke; they can see a bishop of Durham, or a bishop of Winchester, in possession of £.10,000 a-year; and cannot see why it is in worse hands than estates to the like amount in the hands of this earl or that 'squire." And Mr. Burke offers this as an example to France.

As to the first part, whether the archbishop precedes the duke, or the duke the bishop, it is, I believe, to the people in general, somewhat like *Sternhold* and *Hopkins,* or *Hopkins* and *Sternhold;* you may put which you please first: and as I confess that I do not understand the merits of this case, I will not contend it with Mr. Burke.

But with respect to the latter, I have something to say. – Mr. Burke has not put the case right. – The comparison is out of order by being put be-tween the bishop and the earl or the 'squire. It ought to be put between the bishop and the curate, and then it will stand thus: – *The people of England can see without pain or grudging, a bishop of Durham, or a bishop of Winchester, in possession of ten thousand pounds a-year, and a curate on thirty or forty pounds a-year, or less.* – No, Sir, they certainly do not see those things without great pain or grudging. It is a case that applies itself to every man's sense of justice, and is one among many that calls aloud for a constitution.

In France, the cry of *"the church! the church!"* was repeated as often as in Mr. Burke's book, and as loudly as when the dissenters' bill was before the English parliament; but the generality of the French clergy were not to be deceived by this cry any longer. They knew, that whatever the pretence might be, it was themselves who were one of the principal objects of it. It was the cry of the high-beneficed clergy, to prevent any regulation of income taking place between those of ten thousand pounds a-year and the parish priest. They, therefore, joined their case to those of every other op-pressed class of men, and by this union obtained redress.

The French constitution has abolished tythes, that source of perpetual discontent between the tythe-holder and the parishioner. When land is held on tythe, it is in the condition of an estate held between two parties; the one receiving one-tenth, and the other nine-tenths of the produce: and, conse-quently, on principles of equity, if the estate can be improved, and made to produce by that improvement double or treble what it did before, or in any other ratio, the expence of such improvement ought to be borne in like proportion between the parties who are to share the produce. But this is not the case in tythes; the farmer bears the whole expence, and the tythe-holder takes a tenth of the improvement, in addition to the original tenth, and by this means gets the value of two-tenths instead of one. This is another case that calls for a constitution.

The French constitution hath abolished or renounced *Toleration,* and *Intoleration* also, and hath established UNIVERSAL RIGHT OF CONSCIENCE.

Toleration is not the *opposite* of Intoleration, but is the *counterfeit* of it. Both are despotisms. The one assumes to itself the right of with-holding Liberty of Conscience, and the other of granting it. The one is the pope, armed with fire and faggot, and the other is the pope selling or granting indulgences. The former is church and state, and the latter is church and traffic.

But Toleration may be viewed in a much stronger light. Man worships not himself, but his Maker; and the liberty of conscience which he claims, is not for the service of himself, but of his God. In this case, therefore, we must necessarily have the associated idea of two beings; the *mortal* who renders the worship, and the IMMORTAL BEING who is worshipped. Toleration, therefore, places itself, not between man and man, nor between church and church, nor between one denomination of religion and another, but between God and man; between the being who worships, and the BEING who is worshipped; and by the same act of assumed authority by which it tolerates man to pay his worship, it presumptuously and blasphemously sets itself up to tolerate the Almighty to receive it.

Were a Bill brought into any parliament, intitled "AN ACT to tolerate or grant liberty to the Almighty to receive the worship of a Jew or a Turk," or "to prohibit the Almighty from receiving it," all men would startle, and call it blasphemy. There would be an uproar. The presumption of toleration in religious matters would then present itself unmasked: but the presumption is not the less because the name of "Man" only appears to those laws, for the associated idea of the *worshipper* and the *worshipped* cannot be separated. – Who, then, art thou, vain dust and ashes! by whatever name thou art called, whether a King, a Bishop, a Church or a State, a Parliament, or any thing else, that obtrudest thine insignificance between the soul of man and its Maker? Mind thine own concerns. If he believes not as thou believest, it is a proof that thou believest not as he believeth, and there is no earthly power can determine between you.

With respect to what are called denominations of religion, if every one is left to judge of its own religion, there is no such thing as a religion that is wrong: but if they are to judge of each others religion, there is no such thing as a religion that is right; and therefore, all the world are right, or all the world are wrong. But with respect to religion itself, without regard to names, and as directing itself from the universal family of mankind to the Divine object of all adoration, *it is man bringing to his Maker the fruits of his heart;* and though those fruits may differ from each other like the fruits of the earth, the grateful tribute of every one is accepted.

A Bishop of Durham, or a Bishop of Winchester, or the Archbishop who heads the Dukes, will not refuse a tythe-sheaf of wheat, because it is not a cock of hay; nor a cock of hay, because it is not a sheaf of wheat; nor a pig, because it is neither the one nor the other: but these same persons, under the figure of an established church, will not permit their Maker to receive the varied tythes of man's devotion.

One of the continual choruses of Mr. Burke's book is, "Church and State:" he does not mean some one particular church, or some one particular state, but any church and state; and he uses the term as a general figure to hold forth the political doctrine of always uniting the church with the state in every country, and he censures the National Assembly for not having done this in France. – Let us bestow a few thoughts on this subject.

All religions are in their nature mild and benign, and united with principles of morality. They could not have made proselites at first, by professing any thing that was vicious, cruel, persecuting, or immoral. Like every thing else, they had their beginning; and they proceeded by persuasion, exhortation, and example. How then is it that they lose their native mildness, and become morose and intolerant?

It proceeds from the connection which Mr. Burke recommends. By engendering the church with the state, a sort of mule animal, capable only of destroying, and not breeding up, is produced, called *The Church established by Law.* It is a stranger, even from its birth, to any parent mother on which it is begotten, and whom in time it kicks out and destroys.

The inquisition in Spain does not proceed from the religion originally professed, but from this mule-animal, engendered between the church and the state. The burnings in Smithfield proceeded from the same heterogeneous production; and it was the regeneration of this strange animal in England afterwards, that renewed rancour and irreligion among the inhabitants, and that drove the people called Quakers and Dissenters to America. Persecution is not an original feature in *any* religion; but it is always the strongly-marked feature of all law-religions, or religions established by law. Take away the law-establishment, and every religion reassumes its original benignity. In America, a Catholic Priest is a good citizen, a good character, and a good neighbour; an Episcopalian Minister is of the same description: and this proceeds, independent of the men, from there being no law establishment in America.

If also we view this matter in a temporal sense, we shall see the ill effects it has had on the prosperity of nations. The union of church and state has impoverished Spain. The revoking the edict of Nantz drove the silk manufacture from that country into England; and the church and state are now driving the cotton manufacture from England to America and France. Let then Mr. Burke continue to preach his anti-political doctrine of Church and State. It will do some good. The National Assembly will not follow his advice, but will benefit by his folly. It was by observing the ill effects of it in England, that America has been warned against it; and it is by experiencing them in France, that the National Assembly have abolished it, and, like America, has established UNIVERSAL RIGHT OF CONSCIENCE, AND UNIVERSAL RIGHT OF CITIZENSHIP [6].

I will here cease the comparison with respect to the principles of the French constitution, and conclude this part of the subject with a few

6. When in any country we see extraordinary circumstances taking place, they naturally lead any man who has a talent for observation and investigation, to enquire into the causes. The manufactures of Manchester, Birmingham, and Sheffield, are the most principal manufactures in England. From whence did this arise? A little observation will explain the case. The principal, and the generality of the inhabitants of those places, are not of what is called in England, *the church established by law;* and they, or their fathers, (for it is within but a few years), withdrew from the persecution of the chartered towns, where Test-laws more particularly operate, and established a sort of asylum for themselves in those places. It was the only asylum that then offered, for the rest of Europe was worse. – But the case is now changing. France and America receive all comers welcome, and initiate them into all the rights of citizenship. Policy and interest, therefore, will, but perhaps too late, dictate in England, what reason and justice could not. Those manufactures are withdrawing, and are arising in other places. There is now erecting at Passey, three miles from Paris, a large cotton mill, and several are already erected in America. Soon after the rejecting the Bill for repealing the Test-law, one of the richest manufacturers in England said in my hearing, "England, Sir, is not a country for a dissenter to live in – we must go to France." These are truths, and it is doing justice to both parties to tell them. It is chiefly the dissenters that have carried English manufactures to the height they are now at, and the same men have it in their power to carry them away; and though those manufactures will afterwards continue to be made in those places, the foreign market will be lost. There are frequently appearing in the London Gazette, extracts from certain acts to prevent machines, and as far as it can extend to persons, from going out of the country. It appears from these, that the ill effects of the test-laws and church-establishment begin to be much suspected; but the remedy of force can never supply the remedy of reason. In the progress of less than a century, all the unrepresented part of England, of all denominations, which is at least a hundred times the most numerous, may begin to feel the necessity of a constitution, and then all those matters will come regularly before them.

observations on the organization of the formal parts of the French and English governments.

The executive power in each country is in the hands of a person stiled, the King; but the French constitution distinguishes between the King and the Sovereign: It considers the station of King as official, and places Sovereignty in the nation.

The representatives of the nation, which compose the National Assembly, and who are the legislative power, originate in and from the people by election, as an inherent right in the people. – In England it is otherwise; and this arises from the original establishment of what is called its monarchy; for, as by the conquest all the rights of the people or the nation were absorbed into the hands of the Conqueror, and who added the title of King to that of Conqueror, those same matters which in France are now held as rights in the people, or in the nation, are held in England as grants from what is called the Crown. The Parliament in England, in both its branches, were erected by patents from the descendants of the Conqueror. The House of Commons did not originate as a matter of right in the people to delegate or elect, but as a grant or boon.

By the French constitution, the Nation is always named before the King. The third article of the Declaration of rights says, *"The nation is essentially the source* (or fountain) *of all sovereignty."* Mr. Burke argues, that, in England, a King is the fountain – that he is the fountain of all honour. But as this idea is evidently descended from the conquest, I shall make no other remark upon it, than that it is the nature of conquest to turn every thing upside down; and as Mr. Burke will not be refused the privilege of speaking twice, and as there are but two parts in the figure, the *fountain* and the *spout,* he will be right the second time.

The French constitution puts the legislative before the executive; the Law before the King; *La Loi, Le Roi.* This also is in the natural order of things; because laws must have existence, before they can have execution.

A King in France does not, in addressing himself to the National Assembly, say, "My assembly," similar to the phrase used in England of *"my* Parliament["]; neither can he use it consistent with the constitution, nor could it be admitted. There may be propriety in the use of it in England, because, as is before mentioned, both Houses of Parliament originated out of what is called the Crown, by patent or boon – and not out of the inherent rights of the people, as the National Assembly does in France, and whose name designates its origin.

The President of the National Assembly does not ask the King *to grant to the Assembly liberty of speech,* as is the case with the English House of Commons. The constitutional dignity of the National Assembly cannot debase itself. Speech is, in the first place, one of the natural rights of man always retained; and with respect to the National Assembly, the use of it is their *duty*, and the nation is their *authority*. They were elected by the greatest body of men exercising the right of election the European world ever saw. They sprung not from the filth of rotten boroughs, nor are they the vassal representatives of aristocratical ones. Feeling the proper dignity of their character, they support it. Their parliamentary language, whether for or against a question, is free, bold, and manly, and extend to all the parts and circumstances of the case. If any matter or subject respecting the executive department, or the person who presides in it, (the King), comes before them, it is debated on with the spirit of men, and the language of gentlemen; and their answer, or their address, is returned in the same stile. They stand not aloof with the gaping vacuity of vulgar ignorance, nor bend with the cringe of sycophantic insignificance. The graceful pride of truth knows no extremes, and preserves, in every latitude of life, the right-angled character of man.

Let us now look to the other side of the question. – In the addresses of the English Parliaments to their Kings, we see neither the intrepid spirit of the old Parliaments of France, nor the serene dignity of the present National Assembly; neither do we see in them any thing of the stile of English manners, which borders somewhat on bluntness. Since then they are neither of foreign extraction, nor naturally of English production, their origin must be sought for elsewhere, and that origin is the Norman Conquest. They are evidently of the vassalage class of manners, and emphatically mark the prostrate distance that exists in no other condition of men than between the conqueror and the conquered. That this vassalage idea and stile of speaking was not got rid of even at the Revolution of 1688, is evident from the declaration of Parliament to William and Mary, in these words: "We do most humbly and faithfully *submit* ourselves, our heirs and posterities, for ever." Submission is wholly a vassalage term, repugnant to the dignity of Freedom, and an echo of the language used at the Conquest.

As the estimation of all things is by comparison, the Revolution of 1688, however from circumstances it may have been exalted beyond its value, will find its level. It is already on the wane, eclipsed by the enlarging orb of reason, and the luminous revolutions of America and France. In less than another century, it will go, as well as Mr. Burke's labours, "to the family vault of all the Capulets." Mankind will then scarcely believe that a country calling itself free, would send to Holland for a man, and clothe him with power on purpose to put themselves in fear of him, and give him almost a million sterling a-year for leave to *submit* themselves and their posterity, like bond-men and bond-women, for ever.

But there is a truth that ought to be made known: I have had the opportunity of seeing it; which is, *that, notwithstanding appearances, there is not any description of men that despise monarchy so much as courtiers.* But they well know, that if it were seen by others, as it is seen by them, the juggle could not be kept up. They are in the condition of men who get their living by a show, and to whom the folly of that show is so familiar that they ridicule it; but were the audience to be made as wise, in this respect, as themselves, there would be an end to the show and the profits with it. The difference between a republican and a courtier with respect to monarchy is, that the one opposes monarchy believing it to be something, and the other laughs at it knowing it to be nothing.

As I used sometimes to correspond with Mr. Burke, believing him then to be a man of sounder principles than his book shews him to be, I wrote to him last winter from Paris, and gave him an account how prosperously matters were going on. Among other subjects in that letter, I referred to the happy situation the National Assembly were placed in; that they had taken a ground on which their moral duty and their political interest were united. They have not to hold out a language which they do not believe, for the fraudulent purpose of making others believe it. Their station requires no artifice to support it, and can only be maintained by enlightening mankind. It is not their interest to cherish ignorance, but to dispel it. They are not in the case of a ministerial or an opposition party in England, who, though they are opposed, are still united to keep up the common mystery. The National Assembly must throw open a magazine of light. It must shew man the proper character of man; and the nearer it can bring him to that standard, the stronger the National Assembly becomes.

In contemplating the French constitution, we see in it a rational order of things. The principles harmonise with the forms, and both with their origin. It may perhaps be said as an excuse for bad forms, that they are nothing more than forms; but this is a mistake. Forms grow out of principles, and operate to continue the principles they grow from. It is impossible to practise a bad form on any thing but a bad principle. It cannot be ingrafted on a good one; and wherever the forms in any government are bad, it is a certain indication that the principles are bad also.

I will here finally close this subject. I began it by remarking that Mr. Burke had *voluntarily* declined going into a comparison of the English and French constitutions. He apologises (in page 241) for not doing it, by saying that he had not time. Mr. Burke's book was upwards of eight months in hand, and is extended to a volume of three hundred and fifty-six pages. As his omission does injury to his cause, his apology makes it worse; and men on the English side the water will begin to consider, whether there is not some radical defect in what is called the English constitution, that made it necessary in Mr. Burke to suppress the comparison, to avoid bringing it into view.

As Mr. Burke has not written on constitutions, so neither has he written on the French revolution. He gives no account of its commencement or its progress. He only expresses his wonder. "It looks," says he, "to me, as if I were in a great crisis, not of the affairs of France alone, but of all Europe, perhaps of more than Europe. All circumstances taken together, the French revolution is the most astonishing that has hitherto happened in the world."

As wise men are astonished at foolish things, and other people at wise ones, I know not on which ground to account for Mr. Burke's astonishment; but certain it is, that he does not understand the French revolution. It has apparently burst forth like a creation from a chaos, but it is no more than the consequence of a mental revolution priorily existing in France. The mind of the nation had changed beforehand, and the new order of things has naturally followed the new order of thoughts. – I will here, as concisely as I can, trace out the growth of the French revolution, and mark the circumstances that have contributed to produce it.

The despotism of Louis XIV. united with the gaiety of his Court, and the gaudy ostentation of his character, had so humbled, and at the same time so fascinated the mind of France, that the people appeared to have lost all sense of their own dignity in contemplating that of their Grand Monarch: and the whole reign of Louis XV. remarkable only for weakness and effeminacy, made no other alteration than that of spreading a sort of lethargy over the nation, from which it shewed no disposition to rise.

The only signs which appeared of the spirit of Liberty during those periods, are to be found in the writings of the French philosophers. Montesquieu, president of the Parliament of Bourdeaux, went as far as a writer under a despotic government could well proceed; and being obliged to divide himself between principle and prudence, his mind often appears under a veil, and we ought to give him credit for more than he has expressed.

Voltaire, who was both the flatterer and the satirist of despotism, took another line. His forte lay in exposing and ridiculing the superstitions which priest-craft united with state-craft had interwoven with governments. It was not from the purity of his principles, or his love of mankind, (for satire and philanthropy are not naturally concordant), but from his strong capacity of seeing folly in its true shape, and his irresistible propensity to expose it, that he made those attacks. They were however as formidable as if the motives had been virtuous; and he merits the thanks, rather than the esteem of mankind.

On the contrary, we find in the writings of Rousseau, and the Abbé Raynal, a loveliness of sentiment in favour of Liberty, that excites respect, and elevates the human faculties; but having raised this animation, they do not direct its operations and leave the mind in love with an object, without describing the means of possessing it.

The writings of Quisne, Turgot, and the friends of those authors, are of the serious kind; but they laboured under the same disadvantage with Montesquieu: their writings abound with moral maxims of government, but are rather directed to œconomise and reform the administration of the government, than the government itself.

But all those writings and many others had their weight; and by the different manner in which they treated the subject of government, Montesquieu by his judgment and knowledge of laws, Voltaire by his wit, Rousseau and Raynal by their animation, and Quisne and Turgot by their moral maxims and systems of œconomy, readers of every class met with something to their taste, and a spirit of political enquiry began to diffuse itself through the nation at the time the dispute between England and the then colonies of America broke out.

In the war which France afterwards engaged in, it is very well known that the nation appeared to be before hand with the French ministry. Each of them had its view: but those views were directed to different objects; the one sought liberty, and the other retaliation on England. The French officers and soldiers who after this went to America, were eventually placed in the school of Freedom, and learned the practice as well as the principles of it by heart.

As it was impossible to separate the military events which took place in America from the principles of the American revolution, the publication of those events in France necessarily connected themselves with the principles that produced them. Many of the facts were in themselves principles; such as the declaration of American independence, and the treaty of alliance between France and America, which recognised the natural right of man, and justified resistance to oppression.

The then Minister of France, Count Vergennes, was not the friend of America; and it is both justice and gratitude to say, that it was the Queen of France who gave the cause of America a fashion at the French Court. Count

Vergennes was the personal and social friend of Dr. Franklin; and the Doctor had obtained, by his sensible gracefulness, a sort of influence over him; but with respect to principles, Count Vergennes was a despot.

The situation of Dr. Franklin as Minister from America to France, should be taken into the chain of circumstances. The deplomatic character is of itself the narrowest sphere of society that man can act in. It forbids intercourse by a reciprocity of suspicion; and a Deplomatic is a sort of unconnected atom, continually repelling and repelled. But this was not the case with Dr. Franklin. He was not the deplomatic of a Court, but of MAN. His character as a philosopher had been long established, and his circle of society in France was universal.

Count Vergennes resisted for a considerable time the publication of the American constitutions in France, translated into the French language; but even in this he was obliged to give way to public opinion, and a sort of propriety in admitting to appear what he had undertaken to defend. The American constitutions were to liberty, what a grammar is to language: they define its parts of speech, and practically construct them into syntax.

The peculiar situation of the then Marquis de la Fayette is another link in the great chain. He served in America as an American officer under a commission of Congress, and by the universality of his acquaintance, was in close friendship with the civil government of America, as well as with the military line. He spoke the language of the country, entered into the discussions on the principles of government, and was always a welcome friend at any election.

When the war closed, a vast reinforcement to the cause of Liberty spread itself over France, by the return of the French officers and soldiers. A knowledge of the practice was then joined to the theory; and all that was wanting to give it real existence, was opportunity. Man cannot, properly speaking, make circumstances for his purpose, but he always has it in his power to improve them when they occur; and this was the case in France.

M. Neckar was displaced in May 1781; and by the ill management of the finances afterwards, and particularly during the extravagant administration of M. Calonne, the revenue of France, which was nearly twenty-four millions sterling *per* year, was become unequal to the expenditures, not because the revenue had decreased, but because the expences had increased; and this was the circumstance which the nation laid hold of to bring forward a revolution. The English Minister, Mr. Pitt, has frequently alluded to the state of the French finances in his budgets, without understanding the subject. Had the French Parliaments been as ready to register edicts for new taxes, as an English Parliament is to grant them, there had been no derangement in the finances, nor yet any revolution; but this will better explain itself as I proceed.

It will be necessary here to shew how taxes were formerly raised in France. The King, or rather the Court or Ministry acting under the use of that name, framed the edicts for taxes at their own discretion, and sent them to the Parliaments to be registered; for until they were registered by the Parliaments, they were not operative. Disputes had long existed between the Court and the Parliament with respect to the extent of the Parliament's authority on this head. The Court insisted that the authority of Parliament went no further than to remonstrate or shew reasons against the tax, reserving to itself the right of determining whether the reasons were well or ill-founded; and in consequence thereof, either to withdraw the edict as a matter of choice, or to *order* it to be enregistered as a matter of authority. The Parliaments on their part insisted, that they had not only a right to remonstrate, but to reject; and on this ground they were always supported by the nation.

But, to return to the order of my narrative – M. Calonne wanted money; and as he knew the sturdy disposition of the Parliaments with respect to new taxes, he ingeniously sought either to approach them by a more gentle means than that of direct authority, or to get over their heads by a manoeuvre: and, for this purpose, he revived the project of assembling a body of men from the several provinces, under the stile of an "Assembly of the Notables," or Men of Note, who met in 1787, and who were either to recommend taxes to the Parliaments, or to act as a Parliament themselves. An Assembly under this name had been called in 1617.

As we are to view this as the first practical step towards the revolution, it will be proper to enter into some particulars respecting it. The Assembly of the Notables has in some places been mistaken for the States-General, but was wholly a different body; the States-General being always by election. The persons who composed the Assembly of the Notables were all nominated by the King, and consisted of one hundred and forty members. But as M. Calonne could not depend upon a majority of this Assembly in his favour, he very ingeniously arranged them in such a manner as to make forty-four a majority of one hundred and forty: to effect this, he disposed of them into seven separate committees, of twenty members each. Every general question was to be decided, not by a majority of persons, but by a majority of committees; and as eleven votes would make a majority in a committee, and four committees a majority of seven, M. Calonne had good reason to conclude, that as forty-four would determine any general question, he could not be out-voted. But all his plans deceived him, and in the event became his overthrow.

The then Marquis de la Fayette was placed in the second Committee, of which Count D'Artois was president: and as money-matters was the object, it naturally brought into view every circumstance connected with it. M. de la Fayette made a verbal charge against Calonne, for selling crown lands to the amount of two millions of livres, in a manner that appeared to be unknown to the King. The Count D'Artois (as if to intimidate, for the Bastille was then in being) asked the Marquis, if he would render the charge in writing? He replied, that he would. – The Count D'Artois did not demand it, but brought a message from the King to that purport. M. de la Fayette then delivered in his charge in writing, to be given to the King, undertaking to support it. No farther proceedings were had upon this affair; but M. Calonne was soon after dismissed by the King, and set off to England.

As M. de la Fayette, from the experience he had seen in America, was better acquainted with the science of civil government than the generality of the members who composed the Assembly of the Notables could then be, the brunt of the business fell considerably to his share. The plan of those who had a constitution in view, was to contend with the Court on the ground of taxes, and some of them openly professed their object. Disputes frequently arose between Count D'Artois and M. de la Fayette, upon various subjects. With respect to the arrears already incurred, the latter proposed to remedy them, by accommodating the expences to the revenue, instead of the revenue to the expences; and as objects of reform, he proposed to abolish the Bastille, and all the State-prisons throughout the nation, (the keeping of which were attended with great expence), and to suppress *Lettres de Cachet:* But those matters were not then much attended to; and with respect to *Lettres de Cachet, a majority of the Nobles appeared to be in favour of them.*

On the subject of supplying the Treasury by new taxes, the Assembly declined taking the matter on themselves, concurring in the opinion that they had not authority. In a debate on this subject, M. de la Fayette said, that raising money by taxes could only be done by a National Assembly, freely elected by the people, and acting as their representatives. Do you mean, said the Count D'Artois, the *States General?* M. de la Fayette replied, that he did. Will you, said the Count D'Artois, sign what you say, to be given to the King? The other replied, that he not only would do this, but that he would go farther, and say, that the effectual mode would be, for the King to agree to the establishment of a Constitution.

As one of the plans had thus failed, that of getting the Assembly to act as a Parliament, the other came into view, that of recommending. On this subject, the Assembly agreed to recommend two new taxes to be enregistered by the Parliament: the one a stamp-tax, and the other a territorial tax, or sort of land-tax. The two have been estimated at about five millions Sterl. *per ann.* We have now to turn our attention to the Parliaments, on whom the business was again devolving.

The Archbishop of Thoulouse (since Archbishop of Sens, and now a Cardinal) was appointed to the administration of the finances, soon after the dismission of Calonne. He was also made Prime Minister, an office that did not always exist in France. When this office did not exist, the Chief of each of the principal departments transacted business immediately with the King; but when a Prime Minister was appointed, they did business only with him. The Archbishop arrived to more State-authority than any Minister since the Duke de Choiseuil, and the Nation was strongly disposed in his favour; but by a line of conduct scarcely to be accounted for, he perverted every opportunity, turned out a despot, and sunk into disgrace, and a Cardinal.

The Assembly of the Notables having broke up, the new Minister sent the edicts for the two new taxes recommended by the Assembly to the Parliaments, to be enregistered. They of course came first before the Parliament of Paris, who returned for answer, *That with such a revenue as the Nation then supported, the name of taxes ought not to be mentioned, but for the purpose of reducing them;* and threw both the edicts out[7].

On this refusal, the Parliament was ordered to Versailles, where, in the usual form, the King held, what under the old government was called, a Bed of Justice; and the two edicts were enregistered in presence of the Parliament, by an order of State, in the manner mentioned in page [222]. On this, the Parliament immediately returned to Paris, renewed their session in form, and ordered the enregistering to be struck out, declaring that every thing done at Versailles was illegal. All the members of the Parliament were then served with Lettres de Cachet, and exiled to Trois; but as they continued as inflexible in exile as before, and as vengeance did not supply the place of taxes, they were after a short time recalled to Paris.

The edicts were again tendered to them, and the Count D'Artois undertook to act as representative for the King. For this purpose, he came from Versailles to Paris, in a train of procession; and the Parliament were

---

7. When the English Minister, Mr. Pitt, mentions the French finances again in the English Parliament, it would be well that he noticed this as an example.

assembled to receive him. But show and parade had lost their influence in France; and whatever ideas of importance he might set off with, he had to return with those of mortification and disappointment. On alighting from his carriage to ascend the steps of the Parliament House, the crowd (which was numerously collected) threw out trite expressions, saying, "This is Monsieur D'Artois, who wants more of our money to spend." The marked disapprobation which he saw, impressed him with apprehensions; and the word *Aux armes (To arms)* was given out by the officer of the guard who attended him. It was so loudly vociferated, that it echoed through the avenues of the House, and produced a temporary confusion: I was then standing in one of the apartments through which he had to pass, and could not avoid reflecting how wretched was the condition of a disrespected man.

He endeavoured to impress the Parliament by great words, and opened his authority by saying, "The King, our Lord and Master." The Parliament received him very coolly, and with their usual determination not to register the taxes: and in this manner the interview ended.

After this a new subject took place: In the various debates and contests that arose between the Court and the Parliaments on the subject of taxes, the Parliament of Paris at last declared, that although it had been customary for Parliaments to enregister edicts for taxes as a matter of convenience, the right belonged only to the *States-General;* and that, therefore, the Parliament could no longer with propriety continue to debate on what it had not authority to act. The King after this came to Paris, and held a meeting with the Parliament, in which he continued from ten in the morning till about six in the evening; and, in a manner that appeared to proceed from him, as if unconsulted upon with the cabinet or the ministry, gave his word to the Parliament, that the States-General should be convened.

But after this another scene arose, on a ground different from all the former. The minister and the cabinet were averse to calling the States-General: They well knew, that if the States-General were assembled, that themselves must fall; and as the King had not mentioned *any time,* they hit on a project calculated to elude, without appearing to oppose.

For this purpose, the Court set about making a sort of Constitution itself: It was principally the work of M. Lamoignon, Keeper of the Seals, who afterwards shot himself. This new arrangement consisted in establishing a body under the name of a *Cour plénière,* or full Court, in which were invested all the powers that the government might have occasion to make use of. The persons composing this Court were to be nominated by the King; the contended right of taxation was given up on the part of the King, and a new criminal code of laws, and law proceedings, was substituted in room of the former. The thing, in many points, contained better principles than those upon which the government had hitherto been administered: but with respect to the *Cour plénière,* it was no other than a medium through which despotism was to pass, without appearing to act directly from itself.

The Cabinet had high expectations from their new contrivance. The persons who were to compose the *Cour plénière,* were already nominated; and as it was necessary to carry a fair appearance, many of the best characters in the nation were appointed among the number. It was to commence on the 8th of May 1788: But an opposition arose to it, on two grounds – the one as to Principle, the other as to Form.

On the ground of Principle it was contended, That government had not a right to alter itself; and that if the practice was once admitted, it would grow into a principle, and be made a precedent for any future alterations the government might wish to establish: That the right of altering the government was a national right, and not a right of government. – And on the ground of Form, it was contended, That the *Cour plénière* was nothing more than a larger Cabinet.

The then Duke de la Rochefoucault, Luxembourg, De Noailles, and many others, refused to accept the nomination, and strenuously opposed the whole plan. When the edict for establishing this new Court was sent to the Parliaments to be enregistered, and put into execution, they resisted also. The Parliament of Paris not only refused, but denied the authority; and the contest renewed itself between the Parliament and the Cabinet more strongly than ever. While the Parliament were sitting in debate on this subject, the Ministry ordered a regiment of soldiers to surround the House, and form a blockade. The Members sent out for beds and provision, and lived as in a besieged citadel: and as this had no effect, the commanding officer was ordered to enter the Parliament House and seize them, which he did, and some of the principal members were shut up in different prisons. About the same time a deputation of persons arrived from the province of Brittany, to remonstrate against the establishment of the *Cour plénière;* and those the Archbishop sent to the Bastille. But the spirit of the Nation was not to be overcome; and it was so fully sensible of the strong ground it had taken, that of withholding taxes, that it contented itself with keeping up a sort of quiet resistance, which effectually overthrew all the plans at that time formed against it. The project of the *Cour plénière* was at last obliged to be given up, and the Prime Minister not long afterwards followed its fate; and M. Neckar was recalled into office.

The attempt to establish the *Cour plénière* had an effect upon the Nation, which itself did not perceive. It was a sort of new form of government, that insensibly served to put the old one out of sight, and to unhinge it from the superstitious authority of antiquity. It was government dethroning government; and the old one, by attempting to make a new one, made a chasm.

The failure of this scheme renewed the subject of convening the States-General; and this gave rise to a new series of politics. There was no settled form for convening the States-General: all that it positively meant, was a deputation from what was then called the Clergy, the Noblesse, and the Commons; but their numbers, or their proportions, had not been always the same. They had been convened only on extraordinary occasions, the last of which was in 1614; their numbers were then in equal proportions, and they voted by orders.

It could not well escape the sagacity of M. Neckar, that the mode of 1614 would answer neither the purpose of the then government, nor of the nation. As matters were at that time circumstanced, it would have been too contentious to agree upon any thing. The debates would have been endless upon privileges and exemptions, in which neither the wants of the government, nor the wishes of the nation for a constitution, would have been attended to. But as he did not chuse to take the decision upon himself, he summoned again the *Assembly of the Notables,* and referred it to them. This body was in general interested in the decision, being chiefly of the aristocracy and the high paid clergy; and they decided in favour of the mode of 1614. This decision was against the sense of the Nation, and also against the wishes of the Court; for the aristocracy opposed itself to both, and contended for privileges independent of either. The subject was then taken up by the Parliament, who recommended that the number of the Commons should be equal to the other two; and that they should all sit in one house, and vote in one body. The number finally determined on was twelve hundred: six hundred to be chosen by the Commons, (and this was less than their proportion ought to have been when their worth and consequence is considered on a national scale), three hundred by the Clergy, and three hundred by the aristocracy; but with respect to the mode of assembling themselves, whether together or apart, or the manner in which they should vote, those matters were referred[8].

8. Mr. Burke (and I must take the liberty of telling him he is very unacquainted with French affairs), speaking upon this subject, says, "The first thing that struck me in the calling the States-General, was a great departure from the ancient course;"—and he soon after says, "From the moment I read the list, I saw distinctly, and very nearly as it has happened, all that was to follow."–Mr. Burke certainly did

The election that followed, was not a contested election, but an animated one. The candidates were not men, but principles. Societies were formed in Paris, and committees of correspondence and communication established throughout the nation, for the purpose of enlightening the people, and explaining to them the principles of civil government; and so orderly was the election conducted, that it did not give rise even to the rumour of tumult.

The States-General were to meet at Versailles in April 1789, but did not assemble till May. They situated themselves in three separate chambers, or rather the clergy and the aristocracy withdrew each into a separate chamber. The majority of the aristocracy claimed what they called the privilege of voting as a separate body, and of giving their consent or their negative in that manner; and many of the bishops and the high-beneficed clergy claimed the same privilege on the part of their Order.

The *Tiers Etat* (as they were then called) disowned any knowledge of artificial Orders and artificial privileges; and they were not only resolute on this point, but somewhat disdainful. They began to consider aristocracy as a kind of fungus growing out of the corruption of society, that could not be admitted even as a branch of it; and from the disposition the aristocracy had shewn by upholding Lettres de Cachet, and in sundry other instances, it was manifest that no constitution could be formed by admitting men in any other character than as National Men.

After various altercations on this head, the Tiers Etat or Commons (as they were then called) declared themselves (on a motion made for that purpose by the Abbé Sieyes) "THE REPRESENTATIVES OF THE NATION; *and that*

---

not see all that was to follow. I have endeavoured to impress him, as well before as after the States-General met, that there would be a *revolution;* but was not able to make him see it, neither would he believe it. How then he could distinctly see all the parts, when the whole was out of sight, is beyond my comprehension. And with respect to the "departure from the ancient course," besides the natural weakness of the remark, it shews that he is unacquainted with circumstances. The departure was necessary, from the experience had upon it, that the ancient course was a bad one. The States-General of 1614 were called at the commencement of the civil war in the minority of Louis XIII; but by the clash of arranging them by orders, they increased the confusion they were called to compose. The author of *L'Intrigue du Cabinet* (Intrigue of the Cabinet), who wrote before any revolution was thought of in France, speaking of the States-General of 1614, says, "They held the public in suspense five months; and by the questions agitated therein, and the heat with which they were put, it appears that the Great *(les grands)* thought more to satisfy their *particular* passions, than to procure the good of the nation; and the whole time passed away in altercations, ceremonies, and parade." L'Intrigue du Cabinet, vol. i. p. 329.

the two Orders could be considered but as deputies of corporations, and could only have a deliberative voice but when they assembled in a national character with the national representatives." This proceeding extinguished the stile of *Etats Généraux* or States-General, and erected it into the stile it now bears, that of L'Assemble Nationale, or National Assembly.

This motion was not made in a precipitate manner: It was the result of cool deliberation, and concerted between the national representatives and the patriotic members of the two chambers, who saw into the folly, mischief, and injustice of artificial privileged distinctions. It was become evident, that no constitution, worthy of being called by that name, could be established on any thing less than a national ground. The aristocracy had hitherto opposed the despotism of the Court, and affected the language of patriotism; but it opposed it as its rival, (as the English Barons opposed King John); and it now opposed the nation from the same motives.

On carrying this motion, the national representatives, as had been concerted, sent an invitation to the two chambers, to unite with them in a national character, and proceed to business. A majority of the clergy, chiefly of the parish priests, withdrew from the clerical chamber, and joined the nation; and forty-five from the other chamber joined in like manner. There is a sort of secret history belonging to this last circumstance, which is necessary to its explanation: It was not judged prudent that all the patriotic members of the chamber, stiling itself the Nobles, should quit it at once; and in consequence of this arrangement, they drew off by degrees, always leaving some, as well to reason the case, as to watch the suspected. In a little time, the numbers increased from forty-five to eighty, and soon after to a greater number; which, with a majority of the clergy, and the whole of the national representatives, put the mal-contents in a very diminutive condition.

The King, who, very different from the general class called by that name, is a man of a good heart, shewed himself disposed to recommend a union of the three chambers, on the ground the National Assembly had taken; but the mal-contents exerted themselves to prevent it, and began now to have another project in view. Their numbers consisted of a majority of the aristocratical chamber, and a minority of the clerical chamber, chiefly of bishops and high-beneficed clergy; and these men were determined to put every thing to issue, as well by strength as by stratagem. They had no objection to a constitution; but it must be such an one as themselves should dictate, and suited to their own views and particular situations. On the other hand, the Nation disowned knowing any thing of them but as citizens, and

was determined to shut out all such up-start pretensions. The more aristocracy appeared, the more it was despised; there was a visible imbecillity
and want of intellects in the majority, a sort of *je ne sais quoi,* that while
it affected to be more than citizen, was less than man. It lost ground from
contempt more than from hatred; and was rather jeered at as an ass, than
dreaded as a lion. This is the general character of aristocracy, or what are
called Nobles or Nobility, or rather No-ability, in all countries.

The plan of the mal-contents consisted now of two things; either to deliberate and vote by chambers, (or orders), more especially on all questions
respecting a constitution, (by which the aristocratical chamber would have
had a negative on any article of the constitution); or, in case they could not
accomplish this object, to overthrow the National Assembly entirely.

To effect one or other of these objects, they began now to cultivate a
friendship with the despotism they had hitherto attempted to rival, and the
Count D'Artois became their chief. The King (who has since declared himself deceived into their measures) held, according to the old form, *a Bed
of Justice,* in which he accorded to the deliberation and vote *par tete* (by
head) upon several objects; but reserved the deliberation and vote upon all
questions respecting a constitution to the three chambers separately. This
declaration of the King was made against the advice of M. Neckar, who
now began to perceive that he was growing out of fashion at Court, and that
another minister was in contemplation.

As the form of sitting in separate chambers was yet apparently kept up,
though essentially destroyed, the national representatives, immediately after this declaration of the King, resorted to their own chambers, to consult
on a protest against it; and the minority of the chamber (calling itself the
Nobles), who had joined the national cause, retired to a private house, to
consult in like manner. The mal-contents had by this time concerted their
measures with the Court, which Count D'Artois undertook to conduct; and
as they saw from the discontent which the declaration excited, and the opposition making against it, that they could not obtain a controul over the
intended constitution by a separate vote, they prepared themselves for their
final object – that of conspiring against the National Assembly, and overthrowing it.

The next morning, the door of the chamber of the National Assembly
was shut against them, and guarded by troops; and the Members were refused admittance. On this, they withdrew to a tenis-ground in the neighbourhood of Versailles, as the most convenient place they could find, and,
after renewing their session, took an oath never to separate from each other,

under any circumstance whatever, death excepted, until they had established a constitution. As the experiment of shutting up the house had no other effect than that of producing a closer connection in the Members, it was opened again the next day, and the public business recommenced in the usual place.

We now are to have in view the forming of the new Ministry, which was to accomplish the overthrow of the National Assembly. But as force would be necessary, orders were issued to assemble thirty thousand troops, the command of which was given to Broglio, one of the new-intended Ministry, who was recalled from the country for this purpose. But as some management was necessary to keep this plan concealed till the moment it should be ready for execution, it is to this policy that a declaration made by Count D'Artois must be attributed, and which is here proper to be introduced.

It could not but occur, that while the two contents continued to resort to their chambers separate from the National Assembly, that more jealousy would be excited than if they were mixed with it, and that the plot might be suspected. But as they had taken their ground, and now wanted a pretence for quitting it, it was necessary that one should be devised. This was effectually accomplished by a declaration made by Count D'Artois, "*That if they took not a part in the National Assembly, the life of the King would be endangered:*" on which they quitted their chambers, and mixed with the Assembly in one body.

At the time this declaration was made, it was generally treated as a piece of absurdity in Count D'Artois, and calculated merely to relieve the outstanding Members of the two chambers from the diminutive situation they were put in; and if nothing more had followed, this conclusion would have been good. But as things best explain themselves by their events, this apparent union was only a cover to the machinations which were secretly going on; and the declaration accommodated itself to answer that purpose. In a little time the National Assembly found itself surrounded by troops, and thousands daily arriving. On this a very strong declaration was made by the National Assembly to the King, remonstrating on the impropriety of the measure, and demanding the reason. The King, who was not in the secret of this business, as himself afterwards declared, gave substantially for answer, that he had no other object in view than to preserve the public tranquillity, which appeared to be much disturbed.

But in a few days from this time, the plot unravelled itself. M. Neckar and the Ministry were displaced, and a new one formed, of the enemies of the Revolution; and Broglio, with between twenty-five and thirty thousand foreign troops, was arrived to support them. The mask was now thrown off, and matters were come to a crisis. The event was, that in the space of three days, the new Ministry and their abettors found it prudent to fly the nation; the Bastille was taken, and Broglio and his foreign troops dispersed; as is already related in the former part of this work.

There are some curious circumstances in the history of this short-lived ministry, and this short-lived attempt at a counter-revolution. The palace of Versailles, where the Court was sitting, was not more than four hundred yards distant from the hall where the National Assembly was sitting. The two places were at this moment like the separate head-quarters of two combatant armies; yet the Court was as perfectly ignorant of the information which had arrived from Paris to the National Assembly, as if it had resided at an hundred miles distance. The then Marquis de la Fayette, who (as has been already mentioned) was chosen to preside in the National Assembly on this particular occasion, named, by order of the Assembly, three successive deputations to the King, on the day, and up to the evening on which the Bastille was taken, and to inform and confer with him on the state of affairs: but the ministry, who knew not so much as that it was attacked, precluded all communication, and were solacing themselves how dexterously they had succeeded; but in a few hours the accounts arrived so thick and fast, that they had to start from their desks and run. Some set off in one disguise, and some in another, and none in their own character. Their anxiety now was to outride the news lest they should be stopt, which, though it flew fast, flew not so fast as themselves.

It is worth remarking, that the National Assembly neither pursued those fugitive conspirators, nor took any notice of them, nor sought to retaliate in any shape whatever. Occupied with establishing a constitution founded on the Rights of Man and the Authority of the People, the only authority on which government has a right to exist in any country, the National Assembly felt none of those mean passions which mark the character of impertinent governments, founding themselves on their own authority, or on the absurdity of hereditary succession. It is the faculty of the human mind to become what it contemplates, and to act in unison with its object.

The conspiracy being thus dispersed, one of the first works of the National Assembly, instead of vindictive proclamations, as has been the case with other governments, published a Declaration of the Rights of Man, as the basis on which the new constitution was to be built, and which is here subjoined.

DECLARATION OF THE RIGHTS OF MAN AND OF
CITIZENS, BY THE NATIONAL ASSEMBLY OF FRANCE.

"The Representatives of the people of FRANCE formed into a National Assembly, considering that ignorance, neglect, or contempt of human rights, are the sole causes of public misfortunes and corruptions of Government, have resolved to set forth, in a solemn declaration, these natural, imprescriptible, and unalienable rights: that this declaration being constantly present to the minds of the members of the body social, they may be ever kept attentive to their rights and their duties: that the acts of the legislative and executive powers of Government, being capable of being every moment compared with the end of political institutions, may be more respected: and also, that the future claims of the citizens, being directed by simple and incontestible principles, may always tend to the maintenance of the constitution, and the general happiness.

"For these reasons, the NATIONAL ASSEMBLY doth recognize and declare, in the presence of the Supreme Being, and with the hope of his blessing and favour, the following *sacred* rights of men and of citizens:

'I. *Men are born and always continue free, and equal in respect of their rights. Civil distinctions, therefore, can be founded only on public utility.*

'II. *The end of all political associations is the preservation of the natural and imprescriptible rights of man; and these rights are liberty, property, security, and resistance of oppression.*

'III. *The nation is essentially the source of all sovereignty; nor can any* INDIVIDUAL, *or* ANY BODY OF MEN, *be entitled to any authority which is not expressly derived from it.*

'IV. Political Liberty consists in the power of doing whatever does not injure another. The exercise of the natural rights of every man, has no other limits than those which are necessary to secure to every *other* man the free exercise of the same rights; and these limits are determinable only by the law.

'V. The law ought to prohibit only actions hurtful to society. What is not prohibited by the law, should not be hindered; nor should any one be compelled to that which the law does not require.

'VI. The law is an expression of the will of the community. All citizens have a right to concur, either personally, or by their representatives, in its formation. It should be the same to all, whether it protects or punishes; and *all being equal in its sight, are equally eligible to all honours, places, and employments, according to their different abilities, without any other distinction than that created by their virtues and talents.*

'VII. No man should be accused, arrested, or held in confinement, except in cases determined by the law, and according to the forms which it has prescribed. All who promote, solicit, execute, or cause to be executed, arbitrary orders, ought to be punished; and every citizen called upon, or apprehended by virtue of the law, ought immediately to obey, and renders himself culpable by resistance.

'VIII. The law ought to impose no other penalties than such as are absolutely and evidently necessary: and no one ought to be punished, but in virtue of a law promulgated before the offence, and legally applied.

'IX. Every man being presumed innocent till he has been convicted, whenever his detention becomes indispensible, all rigour to him, more than is necessary to secure his person, ought to be provided against by the law.

'X. No man ought to be molested on account of his opinions, not even on account of his *religious* opinions, provided his avowal of them does not disturb the public order established by the law.

'XI. The unrestrained communication of thoughts and opinions being one of the most precious rights of man, every citizen may speak, write, and publish freely, provided he is responsible for the abuse of this liberty in cases determined by the law.

'XII. A public force being necessary to give security to the rights of men and of citizens, that force is instituted for the benefit of the community, and not for the particular benefit of the persons with whom it is entrusted.

'XIII. A common contribution being necessary for the support of the public force, and for defraying the other expences of government, it ought to be divided equally among the members of the community, according to their abilities.

'XIV. Every citizen has a right, either by himself or his representative, to a free voice in determining the necessity of public contributions, the appropriation of them, and their amount, mode of assessment, and duration.

'XV. Every community has a right to demand of all its agents, an account of their conduct.

'XVI. Every community in which a separation of powers and a security of rights is not provided for, wants a constitution.

'XVII. The right to property being inviolable and sacred, no one ought to be deprived of it, except in cases of evident public necessity legally ascertained, and on condition of a previous just indemnity."

OBSERVATIONS ON THE DECLARATION OF RIGHTS.

The three first articles comprehend in general terms, the whole of a Declaration of Rights: All the succeeding articles either originate out of them, or follow as elucidations. The 4th, 5th, and 6th, define more particularly what is only generally expressed in the 1st, 2d, and 3d.

The 7th, 8th, 9th, 10th, and 11th articles, are declaratory of *principles* upon which laws shall be constructed conformable to *rights* already declared. But it is questioned by some very good people in France, as well as in other countries, whether the 10th article sufficiently guarantees the right it is intended to accord with: besides which, it takes off from the divine dignity of religion, and weakens its operative force upon the mind to make it a subject of human laws. It then presents itself to Man, like light intercepted by a cloudy medium, in which the source of it is obscured from his sight, and he sees nothing to reverence in the dusky ray[9].

The remaining articles, beginning with the twelfth, are substantially contained in the principles of the preceding articles; but, in the particular situation which France then was, having to undo what was wrong, as well as to set up what was right, it was proper to be more particular than what in another condition of things would be necessary.

While the Declaration of Rights was before the National Assembly, some of its members remarked, that if a Declaration of Rights was published, it should be accompanied by a Declaration of Duties. The observation discovered a mind that reflected, and it only erred by not reflecting far enough. A Declaration of Rights is, by reciprocity, a Declaration of Duties

---

9. There is a single idea, which, if it strikes rightly upon the mind either in a legal or a religious sense, will prevent any man, or any body of men, or any government, from going wrong on the subject of Religion; which is, that before any human institutions of government were known in the world, there existed, if I may so express it, a compact between God and Man, from the beginning of time; and that as the relation and condition which man in his *individual person* stands in towards his Maker cannot be changed, or any ways altered by any human laws or human authority, that religious devotion, which is a part of this compact, cannot so much as be made a subject of human laws; and that all laws must conform themselves to this prior existing compact, and not assume to make the compact conform to the laws, which, besides being human, are subsequent thereto. The first act of man, when he looked around and saw himself a creature which he did not make, and a world furnished for his reception, must have been devotion; and devotion must ever continue sacred to every individual man, *as it appears right to him;* and governments do mischief by interfering.

also. Whatever is my right as a man, is also the right of another; and it becomes my duty to guarantee, as well as to possess.

The three first articles are the basis of Liberty, as well individual as national; nor can any country be called free, whose government does not take its beginning from the principles they contain, and continue to preserve them pure; and the whole of the Declaration of Rights is of more value to the world, and will do more good, than all the laws and statutes that have yet been promulgated.

In the declaratory exordium which prefaces the Declaration of Rights, we see the solemn and majestic spectacle of a Nation opening its commission, under the auspices of its Creator, to establish a Government; a scene so new, and so transcendently unequalled by any thing in the European world, that the name of a Revolution is diminutive of its character, and it rises into a Regeneration of man. What are the present Governments of Europe, but a scene of iniquity and oppression? What is that of England? Does not its own inhabitants say, It is a market where every man has his price, and where corruption is common traffic, at the expence of a deluded people? No wonder, then, that the French Revolution is traduced. Had it confined itself merely to the destruction of flagrant despotism, perhaps Mr. Burke and some others had been silent. Their cry now is, "It has gone too far:" that is, it has gone too far for them. It stares corruption in the face, and the venal tribe are all alarmed. Their fear discovers itself in their outrage, and they are but publishing the groans of a wounded vice. But from such opposition, the French Revolution, instead of suffering, receives an homage. The more it is struck, the more sparks it will emit; and the fear is, it will not be struck enough. It has nothing to dread from attacks: Truth has given it an establishment; and Time will record it with a name as lasting as his own.

Having now traced the progress of the French Revolution through most of its principal stages, from its commencement to the taking of the Bastille, and its establishment by the Declaration of Rights, I will close the subject with the energetic apostrophe of M. de la Fayette – *May this great monument raised to Liberty, serve as a lesson to the oppressor, and an example to the oppressed!*[10]

---

10. See page [181] of this work. – N. B. Since the taking the Bastille, the occurrences have been published: but the matters recorded in this narrative, are prior to that period; and some of them, as may easily be seen, can be but very little known.

Miscellaneous Chapter.

To prevent interrupting the argument in the preceding part of this work, or the narrative that follows it, I reserved some observations to be thrown together into a Miscellaneous Chapter; by which variety might not be censured for confusion. Mr. Burke's Book is *all* Miscellany. His intention was to make an attack on the French Revolution; but instead of proceeding with an orderly arrangement, he has stormed it with a Mob of ideas, tumbling over and destroying one another.

But this confusion and contradiction in Mr. Burke's Book is easily accounted for. – When a man in a long cause attempts to steer his course by any thing else than some polar truth or principle, he is sure to be lost. It is beyond the compass of his capacity, to keep all the parts of an argument together, and make them unite in one issue, by any other means than having this guide always in view. Neither memory nor invention will supply the want of it. The former fails him, and the latter betrays him.

Notwithstanding the nonsense, for it deserves no better name, that Mr. Burke has asserted about hereditary rights, and hereditary succession, and that a Nation has not a right to form a Government for itself; it happened to fall in his way to give some account of what Government is. "*Government,* says he, *is a contrivance of human wisdom.*"

Admitting that Government is a contrivance of human wisdom, it must necessarily follow, that hereditary succession, and hereditary rights, (as they are called), can make no part of it, because it is impossible to make wisdom hereditary; and on the other hand, *that* cannot be a wise contrivance, which in its operation may commit the government of a nation to the wisdom of an ideot. The ground which Mr. Burke now takes is fatal to every part of his cause. The argument changes from hereditary rights to hereditary wisdom; and the question is, Who is the wisest man? He must now shew that every one in the line of hereditary succession was a Solomon, or his title is not good to be a king. – What a stroke has Mr. Burke now made! To use a sailor's phrase, he has *swabbed the deck,* and scarcely left a name legible in the list of Kings; and he has mowed down and thinned the House of Peers, with a scythe as formidable as Death and Time.

But, Mr. Burke appears to have been aware of this retort, and he has taken care to guard against it, by making government to be not only a *contrivance* of human wisdom, but a *monopoly* of wisdom. He puts the nation as fools on one side, and places his government of wisdom, all wise-men of Gotham, on the other side; and he then proclaims, and says, that "*Men have a* RIGHT *that their* WANTS *should be provided for by this wisdom."* Having thus made proclamation, he next proceeds to explain to them what their *wants* are, and also what their *rights* are[.] In this he has succeeded dextrously, for he makes their wants to be a *want* of wisdom; but as this is but cold comfort, he then informs them, that they have a *right* (not to any of the wisdom) but to be governed by it: and in order to impress them with a solemn reverence for this monopoly-government of wisdom, and of its vast capacity for all purposes, possible or impossible, right or wrong, he proceeds with astrological mysterious importance, to tell to them its powers, in these words – "The Rights of men in government are their advantages; and these are often in balances between differences of good; and in compromises sometimes between *good* and *evil,* and sometimes between *evil* and *evil.* Political reason is a *computing principle;* adding – subtracting – multiplying – and dividing, morally, and not metaphysically or mathematically, true moral demonstrations."

As the wondering audience, whom Mr. Burke supposes himself talking to, may not understand all this learned jargon, I will undertake to be its interpreter. The meaning then, good people, of all this, is, *That government is governed by no principle whatever; that it can make evil good, or good evil, just as it pleases. In short, that government is arbitrary power.*

But there are some things which Mr. Burke has forgotten. *First,* He has not shewn where the wisdom originally came from: and *secondly,* he has not shewn by what authority it first began to act. In the manner he introduces the matter, it is either government stealing wisdom, or wisdom stealing government. It is without an origin, and its powers without authority. In short, it is usurpation.

Whether it be from a sense of shame, or from a consciousness of some radical defect in a government necessary to be kept out of sight, or from both, or from any other cause, I undertake not to determine; but so it is, that a monarchical reasoner never traces government to its source, or from its source. It is one of the *shibboleths* by which he may be known. A thousand years hence, those who shall live in America or in France, will look back with contemplative pride on the origin of their governments, and say, *This was the work of our glorious ancestors!* But what can a monarchical talker say? What has he to exult in? Alas! he has nothing. A certain something forbids him to look back to a beginning, lest some robber or some Robin Hood should rise from the long obscurity of time, and say, *I am the origin.* Hard as Mr. Burke laboured the Regency Bill and hereditary succession two years ago, and much as he dived for precedents, he still had not boldness enough to bring up William of Normandy, and say, *There is the head of the list, there is the fountain of honour,* the son of a prostitute, and the plunderer of the English nation.

The opinions of men with respect to government, are changing fast in all countries. The revolutions of America and France have thrown a beam of light over the world, which reaches into man. The enormous expence of governments have provoked people to think, by making them feel: and when once the veil begins to rend, it admits not of repair. Ignorance [is] of a peculiar nature: once dispelled, and it is impossible to re-establish it. It is not originally a thing of itself, but is only the absence of knowledge; and though man may be *kept* ignorant, he cannot be *made* ignorant. The mind, in discovering truth, acts in the same manner as it acts through the eye in discovering objects; when once any object has been seen, it is impossible to put the mind back to the same condition it was in before it saw it. Those who talk of a counter revolution in France, shew how little they understand of man. There does not exist in the compass of language, an arrangement of words to express so much as the means of effecting a counter revolution. The means must be an obliteration of knowledge; and it has never yet been discovered, how to make man *unknow* his knowledge, or *unthink* his thoughts.

Mr. Burke is labouring in vain to stop the progress of knowledge; and it comes with the worse grace from him, as there is a certain transaction known in the city, which renders him suspected of being a pensioner in a fictitious name. This may account for some strange doctrine he has advanced in his book, which, though he points it at the Revolution Society, is effectually directed against the whole Nation.

"The King of England," says he, "holds *his* Crown (for it does not belong to the Nation, according to Mr. Burke) in *contempt* of the choice of the Revolution Society, who have not a single vote for a King among them either *individually* or *collectively;* and his Majesty's heirs, each in their time and order, will come to the Crown *with the same contempt* of their choice, with which his Majesty has succeeded to that which he now wears."

As to who is king in England or elsewhere, or whether there is any king at all, or whether the people chuse a Cherokee Chief, or a Hessian Hussar for a King, is not a matter that I trouble myself about, be that to themselves; but with respect to the doctrine, so far as it relates to the Rights of Men and Nations, it is as abominable as any thing ever uttered in the most enslaved country under heaven. Whether it sounds worse to my ear, by not being accustomed to hear such despotism, than what it does to the ear of another person, I am not so well a judge of; but of its abominable principle, I am at no loss to judge.

It is not the Revolution Society that Mr. Burke means; it is the Nation, as well in its *original,* as in its *representative* character; and he has taken care to make himself understood, by saying that they have not a vote either *collectively* or *individually.* The Revolution Society is composed of citizens of all denominations, and of members of both the Houses of Parliament; and consequently, if there is not a right to a vote in any of the characters, there can be no right to any either in the nation or in its parliament. This ought to be a caution to every country, how it imports foreign families to be Kings. It is somewhat curious to observe, that although the people of England have been in the habit of talking about Kings, it is always a foreign house of Kings; hating foreigners, yet governed by them. It is now the House of Brunswick, one of the petty tribes of Germany.

It has hitherto been the practice of the English Parliaments, to regulate what was called the succession, (taking it for granted, that the nation then continued to accord to the form of annexing a monarchical branch to its government; for without this, the Parliament could not have had authority to have sent either to Holland or to Hanover, or to impose a King upon the nation against its will.) And this must be the utmost limit to which Parliament can go upon the case; but the right of the nation goes to the *whole* case, because it has the right of changing its *whole* form of government. The right of a Parliament is only a right in trust, a right by delegation, and that but from a very small part of the nation; and one of its Houses has not even this. But the right of the nation is an original right, as universal as taxation. The nation is the paymaster of every thing, and every thing must conform to its general will.

I remember taking notice of a speech in what is called the English House of Peers, by the then Earl of Shelburne, and I think it was at the time he was Minister, which is applicable to this case. I do not directly charge my memory with every particular; but the words and the purport, as nearly as I remember, were these: *That the form of a Government was a matter wholly at the will of a Nation at all times: that if it chose a monarchical form, it had a right to have it so; and if it afterwards chose to be a Republic, it had a right to be a Republic, and to say to a King, we have no longer any occasion for you.*

When Mr. Burke says that "His Majesty's heirs and successors, each in their time and order, will come to the crown with the *same contempt* of their choice with which His Majesty has succeeded to that he wears," it is saying too much even to the humblest individual in the country; part of whose daily labour goes towards making up the million sterling a year, which the country gives the person it stiles a King. Government with insolence, is despotism; but when contempt is added, it becomes worse; and to pay for contempt, is the excess of slavery. This species of Government comes from Germany; and reminds me of what one of the Brunswick soldiers told me, who was taken prisoner by the Americans in the late war: "Ah!" said he, "America is a fine free country, it is worth the people's fighting for; I know the difference by knowing my own; in my country, if the prince say, Eat straw, we eat straw."–God help that country, thought I, be it England or elsewhere, whose liberties are to be protected by German principles of government and princes of Brunswick.

As Mr. Burke sometimes speaks of England, sometimes of France, and sometimes of the world, and of government in general, it is difficult to answer his book without apparently meeting him on the same ground. Although principles of Government are general subjects, it is next to impossible in many cases to separate them from the idea of place and circumstance; and the more so when circumstances are put for arguments, which is frequently the case with Mr. Burke.

In the former part of his Book, addressing himself to the people of France, he says, "No experience has taught us, (meaning the English), that in any other course or method than that of an *hereditary crown,* can our liberties be regularly perpetuated and preserved sacred as our *hereditary right."* I ask Mr. Burke who is to take them away? M. de la Fayette, in speaking to France, says, *"For a Nation to be free, it is sufficient that she wills it."* But Mr. Burke represents England as wanting capacity to take care of itself, and that its liberties must be taken care of by a King, holding it in "contempt." If England is sunk to this, it is preparing itself to eat straw, as in Hanover or in Brunswick. But besides the folly of the declaration, it happens that the facts are all against Mr. Burke. It was by the Government *being hereditary,* that the liberties of the people were endangered. Charles the first, and James the second, are instances of this truth; yet neither of them went so far as to hold the Nation in contempt.

As it is sometimes of advantage to the people of one country, to hear what those of other countries have to say respecting it, it is possible that the people of France may learn something from Mr. Burke's Book, and that the people of England may also learn something from the answers it will occasion. When Nations fall out about freedom, a wide field of debate is opened. The argument commences with the rights of war, without its evils; and as knowledge is the object contended for, the party that sustains the defeat obtains the prize.

Mr. Burke talks about what he calls an hereditary crown, as if it were some production of nature; or as if, like time, it had a power to operate not only independent, but in spite of man; or as if it were a thing or a subject universally consented to. Alas! it has none of those properties, but is the reverse of them all. It is a thing in imagination, the propriety of which is more than doubted, and the legality of which in a few years will be denied.

But, to arrange this matter in a clearer view than what general expressions can convey, it will be necessary to state the distinct heads under which (what is called) an hereditary crown, or, more properly speaking, an hereditary succession to the Government of a Nation, can be considered; which are,

First, The right of a particular family to establish itself.

Secondly, The right of a Nation to establish a particular family.

With respect to the *first* of these heads, that of a family establishing itself with hereditary powers on its own authority, and independent of the consent of a Nation, all men will concur in calling it despotism; and it would be trespassing on their understanding to attempt to prove it.

But the *second* head, that of a Nation establishing a particular family with *hereditary powers,* it does not present itself as despotism on the first reflection; but if men will permit a second reflection to take place, and carry that reflection forward but one remove out of their own persons to that of their offspring, they will then see that hereditary succession becomes in its consequences the same despotism to others, which they reprobated for themselves. It operates to preclude the consent of the succeeding generation, and the preclusion of consent is despotism. When the person who at any time shall be in possession of a Government, or those who stand in succession to him, shall say to a Nation, I hold this power in "contempt" of you, it signifies not on what authority he pretends to say it. It is no relief, but an aggravation to a person in slavery, to reflect that he was sold by his parent; and as that which heightens the criminality of an act cannot be produced to prove the legality of it, hereditary succession cannot be established as a legal thing.

In order to arrive at a more perfect decision on this head, it will be proper to consider the generation which undertakes to establish a family with *hereditary powers,* a-part and separate from the generations which are to follow; and also to consider the character in which the *first* generation acts with respect to succeeding generations.

The generation which first selects a person, and puts him at the head of its Government, either with the title of King, or any other distinction, acts its *own choice,* be it wise or foolish, as a free agent for itself. The person so set up is not hereditary, but selected and appointed; and the generation who sets him up, does not live under an hereditary government, but under a government of its own choice and establishment. Were the generation who sets him up, and the person so set up, to live for ever, it never could become hereditary succession; and of consequence, hereditary succession can only follow on the death of the first parties.

As therefore hereditary succession is out of the question with respect to the *first* generation, we have now to consider the character in which *that* generation acts with respect to the commencing generation, and to all succeeding ones.

It assumes a character, to which it has neither right nor title. It changes itself from a *Legislator* to a *Testator,* and affects to make its Will, which is to have operation after the demise of the makers, to bequeath the Government; and it not only attempts to bequeath, but to establish on the succeeding generation, a new and different form of government under which itself lived. Itself, as is already observed, lived not under an hereditary Government, but under a Government of its own choice and establishment; and it now attempts, by virtue of a will and testament, (and which it has not authority to make), to take from the commencing generation, and all future ones, the rights and free agency by which itself acted.

But, exclusive of the right which any generation has to act collectively as a testator, the objects to which it applies itself in this case, are not within the compass of any law, or of any will or testament.

The rights of men in society, are neither deviseable, nor transferable, nor annihilable, but are descendable only; and it is not in the power of any generation to intercept finally, and cut off the descent. If the present generation, or any other, are disposed to be slaves, it does not lessen the right of the succeeding generation to be free: wrongs cannot have a legal descent. When Mr. Burke attempts to maintain, that the *English Nation did at the Revolution of* 1688, *most solemnly renounce and abdicate their rights for themselves, and for all their posterity for ever;* he speaks a language that merits not reply, and which can only excite contempt for his prostitute principles, or pity for his ignorance.

In whatever light hereditary succession, as growing out of the will and testament of some former generation, presents itself, it is an absurdity. A cannot make a will to take from B the property of B, and give it to C; yet this is the manner in which (what is called) hereditary succession by law operates. A certain former generation made a will to take away the rights of the commencing generation and all future ones, and convey those rights to a third person, who afterwards comes forward, and tells them in

Mr. Burke's language, that they have *no rights,* that their rights are already bequeathed to him, and that he will govern in *contempt* of them. From such principles, and such ignorance, Good Lord deliver the world!

But, after all, what is this metaphor called a crown, or rather what is monarchy? Is it a thing, or is it a name, or is it a fraud? Is it "a contrivance of human wisdom," or of human craft to obtain money from a nation under specious pretences? Is it a thing necessary to a nation? If it is, in what does that necessity consist, what services does it perform, what is its business, and what are its merits? Doth the virtue consist in the metaphor, or in the man? Doth the goldsmith that makes the crown, make the virtue also? Doth it operate like Fortunatus's wishing-cap, or Harlequin's wooden sword? Doth it make a man a conjuror? In fine, what is it? It appears to be a something going much out of fashion, falling into ridicule, and rejected in some countries both as unnecessary and expensive. In America it is considered as an absurdity; and in France it has so far declined, that the goodness of the man, and the respect for his personal character, are the only things that preserve the appearance of its existence.

If Government be what Mr. Burke describes it, "a contrivance of human wisdom," I might ask him, if wisdom was at such a low ebb in England, that it was become necessary to import it from Holland and from Hanover? But I will do the country the justice to say, that was not the case; and even if it was, it mistook the cargo. The wisdom of every country, when properly exerted, is sufficient for all its purposes; and there could exist no more real occasion in England to have sent for a Dutch Stadtholder, or a German Elector, than there was in America to have done a similar thing. If a country does not understand its own affairs, how is a foreigner to understand them, who knows neither its laws, its manners, nor its language? If there existed a man so transcendently wise above all others, that his wisdom was necessary to instruct a nation, some reason might be offered for monarchy; but when we cast our eyes about a country, and observe how every part understands its own affairs; and when we look around the world, and see that of all men in it, the race of kings are the most insignificant in capacity, our reason cannot fail to ask us – What are those men kept for?

If there is any thing in monarchy which we people of America do not understand, I wish Mr. Burke would be so kind as to inform us. I see in America, a government extending over a country ten times as large as England, and conducted with regularity for a fortieth part of the expence which government cost in England. If I ask a man in America, if he wants a King? he retorts, and asks me if I take him for an ideot? How is it that this difference happens? are we more or less wise than others? I see in America, the generality of people living in a stile of plenty unknown in monarchical countries; and I see that the principle of its government, which is that of the *equal Rights of Man,* is making a rapid progress in the world.

If monarchy is a useless thing, why is it kept up anywhere? and if a necessary thing, how can it be dispensed with? That *civil government* is necessary, all civilized nations will agree in; but civil government is republican government. All that part of the government of England which begins with the office of constable, and proceeds through the department of magistrate, quarter-session, and general assize, including trial by jury, is republican government. Nothing of monarchy appears in any part of it, except the name which William the Conqueror imposed upon the English, that of obliging them to call him "Their Sovereign Lord the King."

It is easy to conceive, that a band of interested men, such as place-men, pensioners, Lords of the bed-chamber, Lords of the kitchen, Lords of the necessary-house, and the Lord knows what besides, can find as many reasons for monarchy as their salaries, paid at the expence of the country, amount to, but if I ask the farmer, the manufacturer, the merchant, the tradesman, and down through all the occupations of life to the common labourer, what service monarchy is to him? he can give me no answer. If I ask him what monarchy is, he believes it is something like a sinecure.

Notwithstanding the taxes of England amount to almost seventeen millions a-year, said to be for the expences of Government, it is still evident that the sense of the Nation is left to govern itself, and does govern itself by magistrates and juries, almost at its own charge, on republican principles, exclusive of the expence of taxes. The salaries of the Judges are almost the only charge that is paid out of the revenue. Considering that all the internal government is executed by the people, the taxes of England ought to be the lightest of any nation in Europe; instead of which, they are the contrary. As this cannot be accounted for on the score of civil government, the subject necessarily extends itself to the monarchical part.

When the people of England sent for George the First, (and it would puzzle a wiser man than Mr. Burke to discover for what he could be wanted, or what service he could render), they ought at least to have conditioned for the abandonment of Hanover. Besides the endless German intrigues that must follow from a German Elector being King of England, there is a natural impossibility of uniting in the same person the principles of Freedom and the principles of Despotism, or, as it is usually called in England, Arbitrary Power. A German Elector is in his electorate a despot: How then could it be expected that he should be attached to principles of liberty in one country, while his interest in another was to be supported by despotism?

The union cannot exist; and it might easily have been foreseen, that German Electors would make German Kings, or, in Mr. Burke's words, would assume government with 'contempt.' The English have been in the habit of considering a King of England only in the character in which he appears to them: whereas the same person, while the connection lasts, has a home-seat in another country, the interest of which is different to their own, and the principles of the governments in opposition to each other–To such a person England will appear as a town-residence, and the Electorate as the estate. The English may wish, as I believe they do, success to the principles of Liberty in France, or in Germany; but a German Elector trembles for the fate of despotism in his electorate: and the Duchy of Mecklenburgh, where the present Queen's family governs, is under the same wretched state of arbitrary power, and the people in slavish vassalage.

There never was a time when it became the English to watch continental intrigues more circumspectly than at the present moment, and to distinguish the politics of the Electorate from the politics of the Nation. The revolution of France has entirely changed the ground with respect to England and France, as nations: but the German despots, with Prussia at their head, are combining against Liberty; and the fondness of Mr. Pitt for office, and the interest which all his family-connections have obtained, do not give sufficient security against this intrigue.

As every thing which passes in the world becomes matter for history, I will now quit this subject, and take a concise review of the state of parties and politics in England, as Mr. Burke has done in France.

Whether the present reign commenced with contempt, I leave to Mr. Burke: certain however it is, that it had strongly that appearance. The animosity of the English Nation, it is very well remembered, ran high; and, had the true principles of Liberty been as well understood then as they now promise to be, it is probable the Nation would not have patiently submitted to so much. George the First and Second were sensible of a rival in the remains of the Stuarts; and as they could not but consider themselves as standing on their good behaviour, they had prudence to keep their German principles of Government to themselves; but as the Stuart Family wore away, the prudence became less necessary.

The contest between rights, and what were called prerogatives, continued to heat the Nation till some time after the conclusion of the American War, when all at once it fell a calm–Execration exchanged itself for applause, and Court popularity sprung up like a mushroom in a night.

To account for this sudden transition, it is proper to observe, that there are two distinct species of popularity; the one excited by merit, the other by resentment. As the Nation had formed itself into two parties, and each was extolling the merits of its parliamentary champions for and against prerogative, nothing could operate to give a more general shock than an immediate coalition of the champions themselves. The partisans of each being thus suddenly left in the lurch, and mutually heated with disgust at the measure, felt no other relief than uniting in a common execration against both. A higher stimulus of resentment being thus excited, than what the contest on prerogatives had occasioned, the Nation quitted all former objects of rights and wrongs, and sought only that of gratification. The indignation at the Coalition, so effectually superseded the indignation against the Court, as to extinguish it; and without any change of principles on the part of the Court, the same people who had reprobated its despotism, united with it, to revenge themselves on the Coalition Parliament. The case was not, which they liked best, – but, which they hated most; and the least hated passed for love. The dissolution of the Coalition Parliament, as it afforded the means of gratifying the resentment of the Nation, could not fail to be popular; and from hence arose the popularity of the Court.

Transitions of this kind exhibit a Nation under the government of temper, instead of a fixed and steady principle; and having once committed itself, however rashly, it feels itself urged along to justify by continuance its first proceeding. Measures which at other times it would censure, it now approves, and acts persuasion upon itself to suffocate its judgment.

On the return of a new Parliament, the new Minister, Mr. Pitt, found himself in a secure majority: and the Nation gave him credit, not out of regard to himself, but because it had resolved to do it out of resentment to another. He introduced himself to public notice by a proposed reform of Parliament, which in its operation would have amounted to a public justification of corruption. The Nation was to be at the expence of buying up the rotten boroughs, whereas it ought to punish the persons who deal in the traffic.

Passing over the two bubbles, of the Dutch business, and the million a-year to sink the national debt, the matter which most presents itself, is the affair of the Regency. Never, in the course of my observation, was delusion more successfully acted, nor a nation more completely deceived. – But, to make this appear, it will be necessary to go over the circumstances.

Mr. Fox had stated in the House of Commons, that the Prince of Wales, as heir in succession, had a right in himself to assume the government. This was opposed by Mr. Pitt; and, so far as the opposition was confined to the doctrine, it was just. But the principles which Mr. Pitt maintained on the contrary side, were as bad, or worse in their extent, than those of Mr. Fox;

because they went to establish an aristocracy over the Nation, and over the small representation it has in the House of Commons.

Whether the English form of Government be good or bad, is not in this case the question; but, taking it as it stands, without regard to its merits or demerits, Mr. Pitt was farther from the point than Mr. Fox.

It is supposed to consist of three parts: – while, therefore, the Nation is disposed to continue this form, the parts have a *national standing,* independent of each other, and are not the creatures of each other. Had Mr. Fox passed through Parliament, and said, that the person alluded to claimed on the ground of the Nation, Mr. Pitt must then have contended (what he called) the right of the Parliament, against the right of the Nation.

By the appearance which the contest made, Mr. Fox took the hereditary ground, and Mr. Pitt the parliamentary ground; but the fact is, they both took hereditary ground, and Mr. Pitt took the worst of the two.

What is called the Parliament, is made up of two Houses; one of which is more hereditary, and more beyond the controul of the Nation, than what the Crown (as it is called) is supposed to be. It is an hereditary aristocracy, assuming and asserting indefeasible, irrevocable rights and authority, wholly independent of the Nation. Where then was the merited popularity of exalting this hereditary power over another hereditary power less independent of the Nation than what itself assumed to be, and of absorbing the rights of the Nation into a House over which it has neither election nor controul?

The general impulse of the Nation was right; but it acted without reflection. It approved the opposition made to the right set up by Mr. Fox, without perceiving that Mr. Pitt was supporting another indefeasible right, more remote from the Nation, in opposition to it.

With respect to the House of Commons, it is elected but by a small part of the Nation; but were the election as universal as taxation, which it ought to be, it would still be only the organ of the Nation, and cannot possess inherent rights. – When the National Assembly of France resolves a matter, the resolve is made in right of the Nation; but Mr. Pitt, on all national questions, so far as they refer to the House of Commons, absorbs the rights of the Nation into the organ, and makes the organ into a Nation, and the Nation itself into a cypher.

In a few words, the question on the Regency was a question on a million a-year, which is appropriated to the executive department: and Mr. Pitt could not possess himself of any management of this sum, without setting up the supremacy of Parliament; and when this was accomplished, it was indifferent who should be Regent, as he must be Regent at his own cost. Among the curiosities which this contentious debate afforded, was that of making the Great Seal into a King; the affixing of which to an act, was to be royal authority. If, therefore, Royal Authority is a Great Seal, it consequently is in itself nothing; and a good Constitution would be of infinitely more value to the Nation, than what the three Nominal Powers, as they now stand, are worth.

The continual use of the word *Constitution* in the English Parliament, shews there is none; and that the whole is merely a form of Government without a Constitution, and constituting itself with what powers it pleases. If there were a Constitution, it certainly could be referred to; and the debate on any constitutional point, would terminate by producing the Constitution. One member says, This is Constitution; and another says, That is Constitution – To-day it is one thing; and to-morrow, it is something else – while the maintaining the debate proves there is none. Constitution is now the cant word of Parliament, tuning itself to the ear of the Nation. Formerly it was the *universal supremacy of Parliament* – the *omnipotence of Parliament:* But, since the progress of Liberty in France, those phrases have a despotic harshness in their note; and the English Parliament have catched the fashion from the National Assembly, but without the substance, of speaking of *Constitution.*

As the present generation of people in England did not make the Government, they are not accountable for any of its defects; but that sooner or later it must come into their hands to undergo a constitutional reformation, is as certain as that the same thing has happened in France. If France, with a revenue of nearly twenty-four millions sterling, with an extent of rich and fertile country above four times larger than England, with a population of twenty-four millions of inhabitants to support taxation, with upwards of ninety millions sterling of gold and silver circulating in the nation, and with a debt less than the present debt of England – still found it necessary, from whatever cause, to come to a settlement of its affairs, it solves the problem of funding for both countries.

It is out of the question to say how long, what is called, the English constitution has lasted, and to argue from thence how long it is to last; the question is, how long can the funding system last? It is a thing but of modern invention, and has not yet continued beyond the life of a man; yet in that short space it has so far accumulated, that, together with the current expences, it requires an amount of taxes at least equal to the whole landed rental of the nation in acres to defray the annual expenditures. That a Government could not always have gone on by the same system which has been followed for the last seventy years, must be evident to every man; and for the same reason it cannot always go on.

The funding system is not money; neither is it, properly speaking, credit. It in effect, creates upon paper the sum which it appears to borrow, and lays on a tax to keep the imaginary capital alive by the payment of interest, and sends the annuity to market, to be sold for paper already in circulation. If any credit is given, it is to the disposition of the people to pay the tax, and not to the Government which lays it on. When this disposition expires, what is supposed to be the credit of Government expires with it. The instance of France under the former Government, shews that it is impossible to compel the payment of taxes by force, when a whole nation is determined to take its stand upon that ground.

Mr. Burke, in his review of the finances of France, states the quantity of gold and silver in France, at about eighty-eight millions sterling. In doing this, he has, I presume, divided by the difference of exchange, instead of the standard of twenty-four livres to a pound sterling; for M. Neckar's statement, from which Mr. Burke's is taken, is *two thousand two hundred millions of livres,* which is upwards of ninety-one millions and an half sterling.

M. Neckar in France, and Mr. George Chalmers of the Office of Trade and Plantation in England, of which Lord Hawkesbury is president, published nearly about the same time (1786) an account of the quantity of money in each nation, from the returns of the Mint of each nation. Mr. Chalmers, from the returns of the English Mint at the Tower of London, states the quantity of money in England, including Scotland and Ireland, to be twenty millions sterling[11].

M. Neckar[12] says, that the amount of money in France, recoined from the old coin which was called in, was two thousand five hundred millions of livres, (upwards of one hundred and four millions sterling); and, after deducting for waste, and what may be in the West Indies, and other possible circumstances, states the circulating quantity at home, to be ninety-one millions and an half sterling; but, taking it as Mr. Burke has put it, it is sixty-eight millions more than the national quantity in England.

That the quantity of money in France cannot be under this sum, may at once be seen from the state of the French Revenue, without referring to the

11. See *Estimate of the Comparative Strength of Great Britain,* by G. Chalmers.
12. See Administration of the Finances of France, Vol. III. by M. Neckar.

records of the French Mint for proofs. The revenue of France prior to the Revolution, was nearly twenty-four millions sterling; and as paper had then no existence in France, the whole revenue was collected upon gold and silver; and it would have been impossible to have collected such a quantity of revenue upon a less national quantity than M. Neckar has stated. Before the establishment of paper in England, the revenue was about a fourth part of the national amount of gold and silver, as may be known by referring to the revenue prior to King William, and the quantity of money stated to be in the nation at that time, which was nearly as much as it is now.

It can be of no real service to a Nation, to impose upon itself, or to permit itself to be imposed upon; but the prejudices of some, and the imposition of others, have always represented France as a nation possessing but little money – whereas the quantity is not only more than four times what the quantity is in England, but is considerably greater on a proportion of numbers. To account for this deficiency on the part of England, some reference should be had to the English system of funding. It operates to multiply paper, and to substitute it in the room of money, in various shapes; and the more paper is multiplied, the more opportunities are afforded to export the specie; and it admits of a possibility (by extending it to small notes) of increasing paper, till there is no money left.

I know this is not a pleasant subject to English readers; but the matters I am going to mention, are so important in themselves, as to require the attention of men interested in money-transactions of a public nature. – There is a circumstance stated by M. Neckar, in his treatise on the administration of the finances, which has never been attended to in England, but which forms the only basis whereon to estimate the quantity of money (gold and silver) which ought to be in every nation in Europe, to preserve a relative proportion with other nations.

Lisbon and Cadiz are the two ports into which (money) gold and silver from South America are imported, and which afterwards divides and spreads itself over Europe by means of commerce, and increases the quantity of money in all parts of Europe. If, therefore, the amount of the annual importation into Europe can be known, and the relative proportion of the foreign commerce of the several nations by which it is distributed can be ascertained, they give a rule, sufficiently true, to ascertain the quantity of money which ought to be found in any nation at any given time.

M. Neckar shews from the registers of Lisbon and Cadiz, that the importation of gold and silver into Europe, is five millions sterling annually. He has not taken it on a single year, but on an average of fifteen succeeding years, from 1763 to 1777, both inclusive; in which time, the amount was one thousand eight hundred million livres, which is seventy-five millions sterling[13].

From the commencement of the Hanover succession in 1714, to the time Mr. Chalmers published, is seventy-two years; and the quantity imported into Europe, in that time, would be three hundred and sixty millions sterling.

If the foreign commerce of Great Britain be stated at a sixth part of what the whole foreign commerce of Europe amounts to, (which is probably an inferior estimation to what the gentlemen at the Exchange would allow), the proportion which Britain should draw by commerce of this sum, to keep herself on a proportion with the rest of Europe, would be also a sixth part, which is sixty millions sterling; and if the same allowance for waste and accident be made for England which M. Neckar makes for France, the quantity remaining after these deductions would be fifty-two millions; and this sum ought to have been in the nation (at the time Mr. Chalmers published) in addition to the sum which was in the nation at the commencement of the Hanover succession, and to have made in the whole at least sixty-six millions sterling; instead of which, there were but twenty millions, which is forty-six millions below its proportionate quantity.

As the quantity of gold and silver imported into Lisbon and Cadiz is more exactly ascertained than that of any commodity imported into England; and as the quantity of money coined at the Tower of London is still more positively known; the leading facts do not admit of controversy. Either, therefore, the commerce of England is unproductive of profit, or the gold and silver which it brings in leak continually away by unseen means, at the average rate of about three quarters of a million a-year, which, in the course of seventy-two years, accounts for the deficiency; and its absence is supplied by paper[14].

13. Administration of the Finances of France, Vol. iii.

14. Whether the English commerce does not bring in money, or whether the Government sends it out after it is brought in, is a matter which the parties concerned can best explain; but that the deficiency exists, is not in the power of either to disprove. While Dr. Price, Mr. Eden (now Auckland), Mr. Chalmers, and others, were debating whether the quantity of money in England was greater or less than at the Revolution, the circumstance was not adverted to, that since the Revolution, there cannot have been less than four hundred millions sterling imported into Europe; and therefore, the quantity in England ought at least to have been four times greater than it was at the Revolution, to be on a proportion with Europe. What England is now doing by paper, is what she would have been able to have done by solid money, if gold and silver had come into the nation in the proportion it ought,

The Revolution of France is attended with many novel circumstances, not only in the political sphere, but in the circle of money transactions. Among others, it shews that a Government may be in a state of insolvency, and a Nation rich. So far as the fact is confined to the late Government of France, it was insolvent; because the Nation would no longer support its extravagance, and therefore it could no longer support itself – but with respect to the Nation, all the means existed. A Government may be said to be insolvent, every time it applies to a Nation to discharge its arrears. The insolvency of the late Government of France, and the present Government of England, differed in no other respect than as the disposition of the people differ. The people of France refused their aid to the old Government; and the people of England submit to taxation without enquiry. What is called the Crown in England, has been insolvent several times; the last of which, publicly known, was in May 1777, when it applied to the Nation

---

or had not been sent out; and she is endeavouring to restore by paper, the balance she has lost by money. It is certain, that the gold and silver which arrive annually in the register-ships to Spain and Portugal, do not remain in those countries. Taking the value half in gold and half in silver, it is about four hundred tons annually, and from the number of ships and galloons employed in the trade of bringing those metals from South America to Portugal and Spain, the quantity sufficiently proves itself, without referring to the registers.

In the situation England now is, it is impossible she can increase in money. High taxes not only lessen the property of the individuals, but they lessen also the money-capital of a nation, by inducing smuggling, which can only be carried on by gold and silver. By the politics which the British Government have carried on with the Inland Powers of Germany and the Continent, it has made an enemy of all the Maritime Powers, and is therefore obliged to keep up a large navy; but though the navy is built in England, the naval stores must be purchased from abroad, and that from countries where the greatest part must be paid for in gold and silver. Some fallacious rumours have been set afloat in England to induce a belief of money, and, among others, that of the French refugees bringing great quantities. The idea is ridiculous. The general part of the money in France is silver; and it would take upwards of twenty of the largest broad wheel waggons, with ten horses each, to remove one million sterling of silver. Is it then to be supposed, that a few people fleeing on horse-back, or in post chaises, in a secret manner, and having the French Custom-House to pass, and the sea to cross, could bring even a sufficiency for their own expences?

When millions of money are spoken of, it should be recollected, that such sums can only accumulate in a country by slow degrees, and a long procession of time. The most frugal system that England could now adopt, would not recover in a century the balance she has lost in money since the commencement of the Hanover succession. She is seventy millions behind France, and she must be in some considerable proportion behind every country in Europe, because the returns of the English Mint do not shew an increase of money, while the registers of Lisbon and Cadiz shew a European increase of between three and four hundred millions sterling.

to discharge upwards of £ 600,000, private debts, which otherwise it could not pay.

It was the error of Mr. Pitt, Mr. Burke, and all those who were unacquainted with the affairs of France, to confound the French Nation with the French Government. The French Nation, in effect, endeavoured to render the late Government insolvent, for the purpose of taking government into its own hands; and it reserved its means for the support of the new Government. In a country of such vast extent and population as France, the natural means cannot be wanting; and the political means appear the instant the Nation is disposed to permit them. When Mr. Burke, in a speech last Winter in the British Parliament, *cast his eyes over the map of Europe, and saw a chasm that once was France,* he talked like a dreamer of dreams. The same natural France existed as before, and all the natural means existed with it. The only chasm was that which the extinction of despotism had left, and which was to be filled up with a constitution more formidable in resources than the power which had expired.

Although the French Nation rendered the late Government insolvent, it did not permit the insolvency to act towards the creditors; and the creditors considering the Nation as the real paymaster, and the Government only as the agent, rested themselves on the Nation, in preference to the Government. This appears greatly to disturb Mr. Burke, as the precedent is fatal to the policy by which Governments have supposed themselves secure. They have contracted debts, with a view of attaching what is called the monied interest of a Nation to their support; but the example in France shews, that the permanent security of the creditor is in the Nation, and not in the Government; and that in all possible revolutions that may happen in Governments, the means are always with the Nation, and the Nation always in existence. Mr. Burke argues, that the creditors ought to have abided the fate of the Government which they trusted; but the National Assembly considered them as the creditors of the Nation, and not of the Government – of the master, and not of the steward.

Notwithstanding the late Government could not discharge the current expences, the present Government has paid off a great part of the capital. This has been accomplished by two means; the one by lessening the expences of Government, and the other by the sale of the monastic and ecclesiastical landed estates. The devotees and penitent debauchees, extortioners and misers of former days, to ensure themselves a better world than that which they were about to leave, had bequeathed immense property in trust to the priesthood, for *pious uses;* and the priesthood kept it for themselves.

The National Assembly has ordered it to be sold for the good of the whole Nation, and the priesthood to be decently provided for.

In consequence of the Revolution, the annual interest of the debt of France will be reduced at least six millions sterling, by paying off upwards of one hundred millions of the capital; which, with lessening the former expences of Government at least three millions, will place France in a situation worthy the imitation of Europe.

Upon a whole review of the subject, how vast is the contrast! While Mr. Burke has been talking of a general bankruptcy in France, the National Assembly has been paying off the capital of its debt; and while taxes have increased near a million a-year in England, they have lowered several millions a-year in France. Not a word has either Mr. Burke or Mr. Pitt said about French affairs, or the state of the French finances, in the present Session of Parliament. The subject begins to be too well understood, and imposition serves no longer.

There is a general enigma running through the whole of Mr. Burke's Book. He writes in a rage against the National Assembly; but what is he enraged about? If his assertions were as true as they are groundless, and that France by her Revolution had annihilated her power, and become what he calls a *chasm*, it might excite the grief of a Frenchman, (considering himself as a national man), and provoke his rage against the National Assembly; but why should it excite the rage of Mr. Burke? –Alas! it is not the Nation of France that Mr. Burke means, but the COURT; and every Court in Europe, dreading the same fate, is in mourning. He writes neither in the character of a Frenchman nor an Englishman, but in the fawning character of that creature known in all countries, and a friend to none, a COURT- IER. Whether it be the Court of Versailles, or the Court of St. James or of Carlton-House, or the Court in expectation, signifies not; for the caterpillar principle of all Courts and Courtiers are alike. They form a common policy throughout Europe, detached and separate from the interest of Nations: and while they appear to quarrel, they agree to plunder. Nothing can be more terrible to a Court or a Courtier, than the Revolution of France. That which is a blessing to Nations, is bitterness to them; and as their existence depends on the duplicity of a country, they tremble at the approach of principles, and dread the precedent that threatens their overthrow.

Conclusion.

REASON and Ignorance, the opposites of each other, influence the great bulk of mankind. If either of these can be rendered sufficiently extensive in a country, the machinery of Government goes easily on. Reason obeys itself; and Ignorance submits to whatever is dictated to it.

The two modes of Government which prevail in the world, are, *first,* Government by election and representation: *Secondly,* Government by hereditary succession. The former is generally known by the name of republic; the latter by that of monarchy and aristocracy.

Those two distinct and opposite forms, erect themselves on the two distinct and opposite basis of Reason and Ignorance. – As the exercise of Government requires talents and abilities, and as talents and abilities cannot have hereditary descent, it is evident that hereditary succession requires a belief from man, to which his reason cannot subscribe, and which can only be established upon his ignorance; and the more ignorant any country is, the better it is fitted for this species of Government.

On the contrary, Government in a well constituted republic, requires no belief from man beyond what his reason can give. He sees the *rationale* of the whole system, its origin and its operation; and as it is best supported when best understood, the human faculties act with boldness, and acquire, under this form of Government, a gigantic manliness.

As, therefore, each of those forms acts on a different base, the one moving freely by the aid of reason, the other by ignorance; we have next to consider, what it is that gives motion to that species of Government which is called mixed Government, or, as it is sometimes ludicrously stiled, a Government of *this, that,* and *t'other.*

The moving power in this species of Government, is of necessity, Corruption. However imperfect election and representation may be in mixed Governments, they still give exercise to a greater portion of reason than is convenient to the hereditary Part; and therefore it becomes necessary to buy the reason up. A mixed Government is an imperfect every-thing, cementing and soldering the discordant parts together by corruption, to act as a whole. Mr. Burke appears highly disgusted, that France, since she had resolved on a revolution, did not adopt what he calls *"A British Constitution;"* and the regretful manner in which he expresses himself on this occasion, implies a suspicion, that the British Constitution needed something to keep its defects in countenance.

In mixed Governments there is no responsibility: the parts cover each other till responsibility is lost; and the corruption which moves the machine, contrives at the same time its own escape. When it is laid down as a maxim, that *a King can do no wrong,* it places him in a state of similar security with that of ideots and persons insane, and responsibility is out of the question with respect to himself. It then descends upon the Minister, who shelters himself under a majority in Parliament, which, by places, pensions, and corruption, he can always command; and that majority justifies itself by the same authority with which it protects the Minister. In this rotatory motion, responsibility is thrown off from the parts, and from the whole.

When there is a Part in a Government which can do no wrong, it implies that it does nothing; and is only the machine of another power, by whose advice and direction it acts. What is supposed to be the King in mixed Governments, is the Cabinet; and as the Cabinet is always a part of the Parliament, and the members justifying in one character what they advise and act in another, a mixed Government becomes a continual enigma; entailing upon a country, by the quantity of corruption necessary to solder the parts, the expence of supporting all the forms of Government at once, and finally resolving itself into a Government by Committee; in which the advisers, the actors, the approvers, the justifiers, the persons responsible, and the persons not responsible, are the same persons.

By this pantomimical contrivance, and change of scene and character, the parts help each other out in matters, which, neither of them singly would assume to act. When money is to be obtained, the mass of variety apparently dissolves, and a profusion of parliamentary praises passes between the parts. Each admires with astonishment the wisdom, the liberality, the disinterestedness of the other; and all of them breathe a pitying sigh at the burthens of the Nation.

But in a well-constituted republic, nothing of this soldering, praising, and pitying, can take place; the representation being equal throughout the country, and compleat in itself, however it may be arranged into legislative and executive, they have all one and the same natural source. The parts are not foreigners to each other, like democracy, aristocracy, and monarchy. As there are no discordant distinctions, there is nothing to corrupt by compromise, nor confound by contrivance. Public measures appeal of themselves to the understanding of the Nation, and, resting on their own merits, disown any flattering application to vanity. The continual whine of lamenting the burden of taxes, however successfully it may be practised in mixed Governments, is inconsistent with the sense and spirit of a republic. If taxes are necessary, they are of course advantageous; but if they require an apology, the apology itself implies an impeachment. Why then is man thus imposed upon, or why does he impose upon himself?

When men are spoken of as kings and subjects, or when Government is mentioned under the distinct or combined heads of monarchy, aristocracy, and democracy, what is it that *reasoning* man is to understand by the terms? If there really existed in the world two or more distinct and separate *elements* of human power, we should then see the several origins to which those terms would descriptively apply: but as there is but one species of man, there can be but one element of human power; and that element is man himself. Monarchy, aristocracy, and democracy, are but creatures of imagination; and a thousand such may be contrived, as well as three.

From the Revolutions of America and France, and the symptoms that have appeared in other countries, it is evident that the opinion of the world is changing with respect to systems of Government, and that revolutions are not within the compass of political calculations. The progress of time and circumstances, which men assign to the accomplishment of great changes, is too mechanical to measure the force of the mind, and the rapidity of reflection, by which revolutions are generated: All the old governments have received a shock from those that already appear, and which were once more improbable, and are a greater subject of wonder, than a general revolution in Europe would be now.

When we survey the wretched condition of man under the monarchical and hereditary systems of Government, dragged from his home by one power, or driven by another, and impoverished by taxes more than by enemies, it becomes evident that those systems are bad, and that a general revolution in the principle and construction of Governments is necessary.

What is government more than the management of the affairs of a Nation? It is not, and from its nature cannot be, the property of any particular man or family, but of the whole community, at whose expence it is supported; and though by force or contrivance it has been usurped into an inheritance, the usurpation cannot alter the right of things. Sovereignty, as a matter of right, appertains to the Nation only, and not to any individual; and a Nation has at all times an inherent indefeasible right to abolish any form of Government it finds inconvenient, and establish such as accords with its interest, disposition, and happiness. The romantic and barbarous distinction of men into Kings and subjects, though it may suit the condition of courtiers, cannot that of citizens; and is exploded by the principle upon which Governments are now founded. Every citizen is a member of the Sovereignty, and, as such, can acknowledge no personal subjection; and his obedience can be only to the laws.

When men think of what Government is, they must necessarily suppose it to possess a knowledge of all the objects and matters upon which its authority is to be exercised. In this view of Government, the republican system, as established by America and France, operates to embrace the whole of a Nation; and the knowledge necessary to the interest of all the parts, is to be found in the center, which the parts by representation form: But the old Governments are on a construction that excludes knowledge as well as happiness; Government by Monks, who know nothing of the world beyond the walls of a Convent, is as consistent as government by Kings.

What were formerly called Revolutions, were little more than a change of persons, or an alteration of local circumstances. They rose and fell like things of course, and had nothing in their existence or their fate that could influence beyond the spot that produced them. But what we now see in the world, from the Revolutions of America and France, are a renovation of the natural order of things, a system of principles as universal as truth and the existence of man, and combining moral with political happiness and national prosperity.

'I. *Men are born and always continue free, and equal in respect of their* rights. *Civil distinctions, therefore, can be founded only on public utility.*

'II. *The end of all political associations is the preservation of the natural and imprescriptible rights of man; and these rights are liberty, property, security, and resistance of oppression.*

'III. *The Nation is essentially the source of all Sovereignty; nor can any* INDIVIDUAL, *or* ANY BODY OF MEN, *be entitled to any authority which is not expressly derived from it.*'

In these principles, there is nothing to throw a Nation into confusion by inflaming ambition. They are calculated to call forth wisdom and abilities, and to exercise them for the public good, and not for the emolument or aggrandizement of particular descriptions of men or families. Monarchical sovereignty, the enemy of mankind, and the source of misery, is abolished; and sovereignty itself is restored to its natural and original place, the Nation. Were this the case throughout Europe, the cause of wars would be taken away.

It is attributed to Henry the Fourth of France, a man of an enlarged and benevolent heart, that he proposed, about the year 1610, a plan for abolishing war in Europe. The plan consisted in constituting a European Congress, or as the French Authors stile it, a Pacific Republic; by appointing delegates from the several Nations, who were to act as a Court of arbitration in any disputes that might arise between nation and nation.

Had such a plan been adopted at the time it was proposed, the taxes of England and France, as two of the parties, would have been at least ten millions sterling annually to each Nation less than they were at the commencement of the French Revolution.

To conceive a cause why such a plan has not been adopted, (and that instead of a Congress for the purpose of *preventing* war, it has been called only to *terminate* a war, after a fruitless expence of several years), it will be necessary to consider the interest of Governments as a distinct interest to that of Nations.

Whatever is the cause of taxes to a Nation, becomes also the means of revenue to a Government. Every war terminates with an addition of taxes, and consequently with an addition of revenue; and in any event of war, in the manner they are now commenced and concluded, the power and interest of Governments are increased. War, therefore, from its productiveness, as it easily furnishes the pretence of necessity for taxes and appointments to places and offices, becomes a principal part of the system of old Governments; and to establish any mode to abolish war, however advantageous it might be to Nations, would be to take from such Government the most lucrative of its branches. The frivolous matters upon which war is made, shew the disposition and avidity of Governments to uphold the system of war, and betray the motives upon which they act.

Why are not Republics plunged into war, but because the nature of their Government does not admit of an interest distinct to that of the Nation? Even Holland, though an ill-constructed Republic, and with a commerce extending over the world, existed nearly a century without war: and the instant the form of Government was changed in France, the republican principles of peace and domestic prosperity and œconomy arose with the new Government; and the same consequences would follow the same causes in other Nations.

As war is the system of Government on the old construction, the animosity which Nations reciprocally entertain, is nothing more than what the policy of their Governments excite[s], to keep up the spirit of the system. Each Government accuses the other of perfidy, intrigue, and ambition, as a means of heating the imagination of their respective Nations, and incensing them to hostilities. Man is not the enemy of man, but through the medium of a false system of Government. Instead, therefore, of exclaiming against the ambition of Kings, the exclamation should be directed against the principle of such Governments; and instead of seeking to reform the individual, the wisdom of a Nation should apply itself to reform the system.

Whether the forms and maxims of Governments which are still in practice, were adapted to the condition of the world at the period they were established, is not in this case the question. The older they are, the less correspondence can they have with the present state of things. Time, and change of circumstances and opinions, have the same progressive effect in rendering modes of Government obsolete, as they have upon customs and manners. – Agriculture, commerce, manufactures, and the tranquil arts, by which the prosperity of Nations is best promoted, require a different system of Government, and a different species of knowledge to direct its operations, to what might have been the former condition of the world.

As it is not difficult to perceive, from the enlightened state of mankind, that hereditary Governments are verging to their decline, and that Revolutions on the broad basis of national sovereignty, and Government by representation, are making their way in Europe, it would be an act of wisdom to anticipate their approach, and produce Revolutions by reason and accommodation, rather than commit them to the issue of convulsions.

From what we now see, nothing of reform in the political world ought to be held improbable. It is an age of Revolutions, in which every thing may be looked for. The intrigue of Courts, by which the system of war is kept up, may provoke a confederation of Nations to abolish it: and a European Congress, to patronize the progress of free Government, and promote the civilization of Nations with each other, is an event nearer in probability, than once were the revolutions and alliance of France and America.

FINIS.

RIGHTS OF MAN.

PART

THE SECOND.

COMBINING

PRINCIPLE AND PRACTICE.

BY

THOMAS PAINE,

SECRETARY FOR FOREIGN AFFAIRS TO CONGRESS IN THE
AMERICAN WAR, AND AUTHOR OF THE WORK ENTITLED COMMON
SENSE; AND THE FIRST PART OF THE RIGHTS OF MAN.

To

M. De La Fayette.

AFTER an acquaintance of nearly fifteen years, in difficult situations in
America, and various consultations in Europe, I feel a pleasure in presenting to you this small treatise, in gratitude for your services to my beloved
America, and as a testimony of my esteem for the virtues, public and private, which I know you to possess.

The only point upon which I could ever discover that we differed, was
not as to principles of government, but as to time. For my own part, I think
it equally as injurious to good principles to permit them to linger, as to push

Rights of Man. Part the Second. Combining Principle and Practice (London:
J. S. Jordan, 1792).

them on too fast. That which you suppose accomplishable in fourteen or fifteen years, I may believe practicable in a much shorter period. Mankind, as it appears to me, are always ripe enough to understand their true interest, provided it be presented clearly to their understanding, and that in a manner not to create suspicion by any thing like self-design, nor offend by assuming too much. Where we would wish to reform we must not reproach.

When the American revolution was established, I felt a disposition to sit serenely down and enjoy the calm. It did not appear to me that any object could afterwards arise great enough to make me quit tranquillity, and feel as I had felt before. But when principle, and not place, is the energetic cause of action, a man, I find, is every where the same.

I am now once more in the public world; and as I have not a right to contemplate on so many years of remaining life as you have, I am resolved to labour as fast as I can; and as I am anxious for your aid and your company, I wish you to hasten your principles, and overtake me.

If you make a campaign the ensuing spring, which it is most probable there will be no occasion for, I will come and join you. Should the campaign commence, I hope it will terminate in the extinction of German despotism, and in establishing the freedom of all Germany. When France shall be surrounded with revolutions, she will be in peace and safety, and her taxes, as well as those of Germany, will consequently become less.

Your Sincere,

Affectionate Friend,

THOMAS PAINE.

London, Feb. 9, 1792.

Preface.

WHEN I began the chapter entitled the *"Conclusion"* in the former part of the RIGHTS OF MAN, published last year, it was my intention to have extended it to a greater length; but in casting the whole matter in my mind which I wished to add, I found that I must either make the work too bulky, or contract my plan too much. I therefore brought it to a close as soon as the subject would admit, and reserved what I had further to say to another opportunity.

Several other reasons contributed to produce this determination. I wished to know the manner in which a work, written in a style of thinking and expression different to what had been customary in England, would be received before I proceeded farther. A great field was opening to the view of mankind by means of the French Revolution. Mr. Burke's outrageous opposition thereto brought the controversy into England. He attacked principles which he knew (from information) I would contest with him, because they are principles I believe to be good, and which I have contributed to establish, and conceive myself bound to defend. Had he not urged the controversy, I had most probably been a silent man.

Another reason for deferring the remainder of the work was, that Mr. Burke promised in his first publication to renew the subject at another opportunity, and to make a comparison of what he called the English and French Constitutions. I therefore held myself in reserve for him. He has published two works since, without doing this; which he certainly would not have omitted, had the comparison been in his favour.

In his last work, *"His appeal from the new to the old Whigs,"* he has quoted about ten pages from the *Rights of Man,* and having given himself the trouble of doing this, says, "he shall not attempt in the smallest degree to refute them," meaning the principles therein contained. I am enough acquainted with Mr. Burke to know, that he would if he could. But instead of contesting them, he immediately after consoles himself with saying, that "he has done his part." – He has not done his part. He has not performed his promise of a comparison of constitutions. He started the controversy, he gave the challenge, and has fled from it; and he is now a *case in point* with his own opinion, that, *"the age of chivalry is gone!"*

The title, as well as the substance of his last work, his *"Appeal,"* is his condemnation. Principles must stand on their own merits, and if they are good they certainly will. To put them under the shelter of other men's authority, as Mr. Burke has done, serves to bring them into suspicion. Mr. Burke is not very fond of dividing his honours, but in this case he is artfully dividing the disgrace.

But who are those to whom Mr. Burke has made his appeal? A set of childish thinkers and half-way politicians born in the last century; men who went no farther with any principle than as it suited their purpose as a party; the nation was always left out of the question; and this has been the character of every party from that day to this. The nation sees nothing in such works, or such politics worthy its attention. A little matter will move a party, but it must be something great that moves a nation.

Though I see nothing in Mr. Burke's Appeal worth taking much notice of, there is, however, one expression upon which I shall offer a few remarks. – After quoting largely from the *Rights of Man,* and declining to contest the principles contained in that work, he says, "This will most probably be done *(if such writings shall be thought to deserve any other refutation than that of criminal justice)* by others, who may think with Mr. Burke and with the same zeal."

In the first place, it has not yet been done by any body. Not less, I believe, than eight or ten pamphlets intended as answers to the former part of the "Rights of Man" have been published by different persons, and not one of them, to my knowledge, has extended to a second edition, nor are even the titles of them so much as generally remembered. As I am averse to unnecessarily multiplying publications, I have answered none of them. And as I believe that a man may write himself out of reputation when nobody else can do it, I am careful to avoid that rock.

But as I would decline unnecessary publications on the one hand, so would I avoid every thing that might appear like sullen pride on the other. If Mr. Burke, or any person on his side the question, will produce an answer to the "Rights of Man," that shall extend to an half, or even to a fourth part of the number of copies to which the Rights of Man extended, I will reply to his work. But until this be done, I shall so far take the sense of the public for my guide (and the world knows I am not a flatterer) that what they do not think worth while to read, is not worth mine to answer. I suppose the number of copies to which the first part of the *Rights of Man* extended, taking England, Scotland, and Ireland, is not less than between forty and fifty thousand.

I now come to remark on the remaining part of the quotation I have made from Mr. Burke.

"If," says he, "such writings shall be thought to deserve any other refutation than that of *criminal* justice."

Pardoning the pun, it must be *criminal* justice indeed that should condemn a work as a substitute for not being able to refute it. The greatest condemnation that could be passed upon it would be a refutation. But in proceeding by the method Mr. Burke alludes to, the condemnation would, in the final event, pass upon the criminality of the process and not upon the work, and in this case, I had rather be the author, than be either the judge, or the jury, that should condemn it.

But to come at once to the point. I have differed from some professional gentlemen on the subject of prosecutions, and I since find they are falling into my opinion, which I will here state as fully, but as concisely as I can.

I will first put a case with respect to any law, and then compare it with a government, or with what in England is, or has been, called a constitution.

It would be an act of despotism, or what in England is called arbitrary power, to make a law to prohibit investigating the principles, good or bad, on which such a law, or any other is founded.

If a law be bad, it is one thing to oppose the practice of it, but it is quite a different thing to expose its errors, to reason on its defects, and to shew cause why it should be repealed, or why another ought to be substituted in its place. I have always held it an opinion (making it also my practice) that it is better to obey a bad law, making use at the same time of every argument to shew its errors and procure its repeal, than forcibly to violate it; because the precedent of breaking a bad law might weaken the force, and lead to a discretionary violation, of those which are good.

The case is the same with respect to principles and forms of government, or to what are called constitutions and the parts of which they are composed.

It is for the good of nations, and not for the emolument or aggrandizement of particular individuals, that government ought to be established, and that mankind are at the expence of supporting it. The defects of every government and constitution, both as to principle and form must, on a parity of reasoning, be as open to discussion as the defects of a law, and it is a duty which every man owes to society to point them out. When those defects, and the means of remedying them are generally seen by a nation, that nation will reform its government or its constitution in the one case, as the government repealed or reformed the law in the other. The operation of government is restricted to the making and the administering of laws; but it is to a nation that the right of forming or reforming, generating or regenerating constitutions and governments belong; and consequently those subjects, as subjects of investigation, are always before a country *as a matter of right,* and cannot, without invading the general rights of that country, be made subjects for prosecution. On this ground I will meet Mr. Burke whenever he please. It is better that the whole argument should come out, than to seek to stifle it. It was himself that opened the controversy, and he ought not to desert it.

I do not believe that monarchy and aristocracy will continue seven years longer in any of the enlightened countries in Europe. If better reasons can be shewn for them than against them, they will stand; if the contrary, they will not. Mankind are not now to be told they shall not think, or they shall not read; and publications that go no farther than to investigate principles of government, to invite men to reason and to reflect, and to shew the errors and excellences of different systems, have a right to appear. If they do not excite attention, they are not worth the trouble of a prosecution; and if they do, the prosecution will amount to nothing, since it cannot amount to a prohibition of reading. This would be a sentence on the public, instead of the author, and would also be the most effectual mode of making or hastening revolutions.

On all cases that apply universally to a nation, with respect to systems of government, a jury of *twelve* men is not competent to decide. Where there are no witnesses to be examined, no facts to be proved, and where the whole matter is before the whole public, and the merits or demerits of it resting on their opinion; and where there is nothing to be known in a court, but what every body knows out of it, every twelve men is equally as good a jury as the other, and would most probably reverse each other's verdict; or from the variety of their opinions, not be able to form one. It is one case, whether a nation approve a work, or a plan; but it is quite another case, whether it will commit to any such jury the power of determining whether that nation have a right to, or shall reform its government, or not. I mention those cases, that Mr. Burke may see I have not written on Government without reflecting on what is Law, as well as on what are Rights.—The only effectual jury in such cases would be, a convention of the whole nation fairly elected; for in all such cases the whole nation is the vicinage. If Mr. Burke will propose such a jury, I will wave all privileges of being the citizen of another country, and, defending its principles, abide the issue, provided he will do the same; for my opinion is, that his work and his principles would be condemned instead of mine.

As to the prejudices which men have from education and habit, in favour of any particular form or system of government, those prejudices have yet to stand the test of reason and reflection. In fact, such prejudices are nothing. No man is prejudiced in favour of a thing, knowing it to be wrong. He is attached to it on the belief of its being right; and when he see it is not so, the prejudice will be gone. We have but a defective idea of what prejudice is. It might be said, that until men think for themselves the whole is prejudice, and *not opinion;* for that only is opinion which is the result of reason and reflection. I offer this remark, that Mr. Burke may not confide too much in what has been the customary prejudices of the country.

I do not believe that the people of England have ever been fairly and candidly dealt by. They have been imposed upon by parties, and by men assuming the character of leaders. It is time that the nation should rise above those trifles. It is time to dismiss that inattention which has so long been the encouraging cause of stretching taxation to excess. It is time to dismiss all those songs and toasts which are calculated to enslave, and operate to suffocate reflection. On all such subjects men have but to think, and they will neither act wrong nor be misled. To say that any people are not fit for freedom, is to make poverty their choice, and to say they had rather be loaded with taxes, than not. If such a case could be proved, it would equally prove, that those who govern are not fit to govern them, for they are a part of the same national mass.

But admitting governments to be changed all over Europe; it certainly may be done without convulsion or revenge. It is not worth making changes or revolutions, unless it be for some great national benefit; and when this shall appear to a nation, the danger will be, as in America and France, to those who oppose; and with this reflection I close my Preface.

THOMAS PAINE.

London, Feb. 9, 1792.

Contents.

Rights of Man.
Part II.
Introduction.

WHAT Archimedes said of the mechanical powers, may be applied to Reason and Liberty: *"Had we,"* said he, *"a place to stand upon, we might raise the world."*

The revolution of America presented in politics what was only theory in mechanics. So deeply rooted were all the governments of the old world, and so effectually had the tyranny and the antiquity of habit established itself over the mind, that no beginning could be made in Asia, Africa, or Europe, to reform the political condition of man. Freedom had been hunted round the globe; reason was considered as rebellion; and the slavery of fear had made men afraid to think.

But such is the irresistible nature of truth, that all it asks, and all it wants, is the liberty of appearing. The sun needs no inscription to distinguish him from darkness; and no sooner did the American governments display themselves to the world, than despotism felt a shock, and man began to contemplate redress.

The independence of America, considered merely as a separation from England, would have been a matter but of little importance, had it not been accompanied by a revolution in the principles and practice of governments. She made a stand, not for herself only, but for the world, and looked beyond the advantages herself could receive. Even the Hessian, though hired to fight against her, may live to bless his defeat; and England, condemning the viciousness of its government, rejoice in its miscarriage.

As America was the only spot in the political world, where the principles of universal reformation could begin, so also was it the best in the natural world. An assemblage of circumstances conspired, not only to give birth, but to add gigantic maturity to its principles. The scene which that country presents to the eye of a spectator, has something in it which generates and encourages great ideas. Nature appears to him in magnitude. The mighty objects he beholds, act upon his mind by enlarging it, and he partakes of the greatness he contemplates. – Its first settlers were emigrants from different European nations, and of diversified professions of religion, retiring from the governmental persecutions of the old world, and meeting in the new, not as enemies, but as brothers. The wants which necessarily accompany the cultivation of a wilderness produced among them a state of society, which countries, long harassed by the quarrels and intrigues of governments, had neglected to cherish. In such a situation man becomes what he ought. He sees his species, not with the inhuman idea of a natural enemy, but as kindred; and the example shews to the artificial world, that man must go back to Nature for information.

From the rapid progress which America makes in every species of improvement, it is rational to conclude, that if the governments of Asia, Africa, and Europe, had begun on a principle similar to that of America, or had not been very early corrupted therefrom, that those countries must by this time have been in a far superior condition to what they are. Age after age has passed away, for no other purpose than to behold their wretchedness. – Could we suppose a spectator who knew nothing of the world, and who was put into it merely to make his observations, he would take a great part of the old world to be new, just struggling with the difficulties and hardships of an infant settlement. He could not suppose that the hordes of miserable poor, with which old countries abound, could be any other than those who had not yet had time to provide for themselves. Little would he think they were the consequence of what in such countries is called government.

If, from the more wretched parts of the old world, we look at those which are in an advanced stage of improvement, we still find the greedy hand of government thrusting itself into every corner and crevice of industry, and grasping the spoil of the multitude. Invention is continually exercised, to furnish new pretences for revenue and taxation. It watches prosperity as its prey, and permits none to escape without a tribute.

As revolutions have begun, (and as the probability is always greater against a thing beginning, than of proceeding after it has begun), it is natural to expect that other revolutions will follow. The amazing and still increasing expences with which old governments are conducted, the numerous wars they engage in or provoke, the embarrassments they throw in the way of universal civilization and commerce, and the oppression and usurpation they act at home, have wearied out the patience, and exhausted the property of the world. In such a situation, and with the examples already existing, revolutions are to be looked for. They are become subjects of universal conversation, and may be considered as the *Order of the day*.

If systems of government can be introduced, less expensive, and more productive of general happiness, than those which have existed, all attempts to oppose their progress will in the end be fruitless. Reason, like time, will make its own way, and prejudice will fall in a combat with interest. If universal peace, civilization, and commerce, are ever to be the happy lot of man, it cannot be accomplished but by a revolution in the system of governments. All the monarchical governments are military. War is their trade, plunder and revenue their objects. While such governments continue, peace has not the absolute security of a day. What is the history of all monarchical governments, but a disgustful picture of human wretchedness, and the accidental respite of a few years repose? Wearied with war, and tired with human butchery, they sat down to rest and called it peace. This certainly is not the condition that Heaven intended for man; and if *this be monarchy,* well might monarchy be reckoned among the sins of the Jews.

The revolutions which formerly took place in the world, had nothing in them that interested the bulk of mankind. They extended only to a change of persons and measures but not of principles, and rose or fell among the common transactions of the moment. What we now behold, may not improperly be called a *"counter revolution."* Conquest and tyranny, at some early period, dispossessed man of his rights, and he is now recovering them. And as the tide of all human affairs has its ebb and flow in directions contrary to each other, so also is it in this. Government founded on a *moral theory, on a system of universal peace, on the indefeasible hereditary Rights of Man,* is now revolving from west to east, by a stronger impulse than the government of the sword revolved from east to west. It interests not particular individuals, but nations, in its progress, and promises a new æra to the human race.

The danger to which the success of revolutions is most exposed, is that of attempting them before the principles on which they proceed, and the advantages to result from them, are sufficiently seen and understood. Almost every thing appertaining to the circumstances of a nation, has been absorbed and confounded under the general and mysterious word *government.* Though it avoids taking to its account the errors it commits, and the mischiefs it occasions, it fails not to arrogate to itself whatever has the appearance of prosperity. It robs industry of its honours, by pedanticly making itself the cause of its effects; and purloins from the general character of man, the merits that appertain to him as a social being.

It may therefore be of use, in this day of revolutions, to discriminate between those things which are the effect of government, and those which are not. This will best be done by taking a review of society and civilization, and the consequences resulting therefrom, as things distinct from what are called governments. By beginning with this investigation, we shall be able to assign effects to their proper cause, and analize the mass of common errors.

CHAP. I.

Of Society and Civilization.

GREAT part of that order which reigns among mankind is not the effect of government. It has its origin in the principles of society and the natural constitution of man. It existed prior to government, and would exist if the formality of government was abolished. The mutual dependance and reciprocal interest which man has upon man, and all the parts of a civilized community upon each other, create that great chain of connection which holds it together. The landholder, the farmer, the manufacturer, the merchant, the tradesman, and every occupation, prospers by the aid which each receives from the other, and from the whole. Common interest regulates their concerns, and forms their law; and the laws which common usage ordains, have a greater influence than the laws of government. In fine, society performs for itself almost every thing which is ascribed to government.

To understand the nature and quantity of government proper for man, it is necessary to attend to his character. As Nature created him for social life, she fitted him for the station she intended. In all cases she made his natural wants greater than his individual powers. No one man is capable, without the aid of society, of supplying his own wants; and those wants, acting upon every individual, impel the whole of them into society, as naturally as gravitation acts to a center.

But she has gone further. She has not only forced man into society, by a diversity of wants, which the reciprocal aid of each other can supply, but she has implanted in him a system of social affections, which, though not necessary to his existence, are essential to his happiness. There is no period in life when this love for society ceases to act. It begins and ends with our being.

If we examine, with attention, into the composition and constitution of man, the diversity of his wants, and the diversity of talents in different men for reciprocally accommodating the wants of each other, his propensity to society, and consequently to preserve the advantages resulting from it, we shall easily discover, that a great part of what is called government is mere imposition.

Government is no farther necessary than to supply the few cases to which society and civilization are not conveniently competent; and instances are not wanting to shew, that every thing which government can usefully add thereto, has been performed by the common consent of society, without government.

For upwards of two years from the commencement of the American war, and to a longer period in several of the American States, there were no established forms of government. The old governments had been abolished, and the country was too much occupied in defence, to employ its attention in establishing new governments; yet during this interval, order and harmony were preserved as inviolate as in any country in Europe. There is a natural aptness in man, and more so in society, because it embraces a greater variety of abilities and resource, to accommodate itself to whatever situation it is in. The instant formal government is abolished, society begins to act. A general association takes place, and common interest produces common security.

So far is it from being true, as has been pretended, that the abolition of any formal government is the dissolution of society, that it acts by a contrary impulse, and brings the latter the closer together. All that part of its organization which it had committed to its government, devolves again upon itself, and acts through its medium. When men, as well from natural instinct, as from reciprocal benefits, have habituated themselves to social and civilized life, there is always enough of its principles in practice to carry them through any changes they may find necessary or convenient to make in their government. In short, man is so naturally a creature of society, that it is almost impossible to put him out of it.

Formal government makes but a small part of civilized life; and when even the best that human wisdom can devise is established, it is a thing more in name and idea, than in fact. It is to the great and fundamental principles of society and civilization – to the common usage universally consented to, and mutually and reciprocally maintained – to the unceasing circulation of interest, which, passing through its million channels, invigorates the whole mass of civilized man – it is to these things, infinitely more than to any thing which even the best instituted government can perform, that the safety and prosperity of the individual and of the whole depends.

The more perfect civilization is, the less occasion has it for government, because the more does it regulate its own affairs, and govern itself; but so contrary is the practice of old governments to the reason of the case, that the expences of them increase in the proportion they ought to diminish. It is but few general laws that civilized life requires, and those of such common usefulness, that whether they are enforced by the forms of government or not, the effect will be nearly the same. If we consider what the principles are that first condense men into society, and what the motives that regulate their mutual intercourse afterwards, we shall find, by the time we arrive at what is called government, that nearly the whole of the business is performed by the natural operation of the parts upon each other.

Man, with respect to all those matters, is more a creature of consistency than he is aware, or that governments would wish him to believe. All the great laws of society are laws of nature. Those of trade and commerce, whether with respect to the intercourse of individuals, or of nations, are laws of mutual and reciprocal interest. They are followed and obeyed, because it is the interest of the parties so to do, and not on account of any formal laws their governments may impose or interpose.

But how often is the natural propensity to society disturbed or destroyed by the operations of government! When the latter, instead of being ingrafted on the principles of the former, assumes to exist for itself, and acts by partialities of favour and oppression, it becomes the cause of the mischiefs it ought to prevent.

If we look back to the riots and tumults, which at various times have happened in England, we shall find, that they did not proceed from the want of a government, but that government was itself the generating cause; instead of consolidating society it divided it; it deprived it of its natural cohesion, and engendered discontents and disorders, which otherwise would not have existed. In those associations which men promiscuously form for the purpose of trade, or of any concern, in which government is totally out of the question, and in which they act merely on the principles of society, we see how naturally the various parties unite; and this shews, by comparison, that governments, so far from being always the cause or means of order, are often the destruction of it. The riots of 1780 had no other source than the remains of those prejudices, which the government itself had encouraged. But with respect to England there are also other causes.

Excess and inequality of taxation, however disguised in the means, never fail to appear in their effects. As a great mass of the community are thrown thereby into poverty, and discontent, they are constantly on the brink of commotion; and, deprived, as they unfortunately are, of the means of information, are easily heated to outrage. Whatever the apparent cause of any riots may be, the real one is always want of happiness. It shews that something is wrong in the system of government, that injures the felicity by which society is to be preserved.

But as fact is superior to reasoning, the instance of America presents itself to confirm these observations. – If there is a country in the world, where concord, according to common calculation, would be least expected, it is America. Made up, as it is, of people from different nations[1], accus-

---

1. That part of America which is generally called New-England, including New-Hampshire, Massachusetts, Rhode-Island, and Connecticut, is peopled chiefly by English descendants. In the state of New-York, about half are Dutch, the rest English, Scotch, and Irish. In New-Jersey, a mixture of English and Dutch, with some Scotch and Irish. In Pennsylvania, about one third are English, another Germans, and the remainder Scotch and Irish, with some Swedes. The States to the southward have a greater proportion of English than the middle States, but in all of them there is a mixture; and besides those enumerated, there are a considerable number of French, and some few of all the European nations lying on the coast. The most numerous religious denomination are the Presbyterians; but no one sect is established above another, and all men are equally citizens.

tomed to different forms and habits of government, speaking different languages, and more different in their modes of worship, it would appear that the union of such a people was impracticable; but by the simple operation of constructing government on the principles of society and the rights of man, every difficulty retires, and all the parts are brought into cordial unison. There, the poor are not oppressed, the rich are not privileged. Industry is not mortified by the splendid extravagance of a court rioting at its expence. Their taxes are few, because their government is just; and as there is nothing to render them wretched, there is nothing to engender riots and tumults.

A metaphysical man, like Mr. Burke, would have tortured his invention to discover how such a people could be governed. He would have supposed that some must be managed by fraud, others by force, and all by some contrivance; that genius must be hired to impose upon ignorance, and shew and parade to fascinate the vulgar. Lost in the abundance of his researches, he would have resolved and re-resolved, and finally overlooked the plain and easy road that lay directly before him.

One of the great advantages of the American revolution has been, that it led to a discovery of the principles, and laid open the imposition of governments. All the revolutions till then had been worked within the atmosphere of a court, and never on the great floor of a nation. The parties were always of the class of courtiers; and whatever was their rage for reformation, they carefully preserved the fraud of the profession.

In all cases they took care to represent government as a thing made up of mysteries, which only themselves understood; and they hid from the understanding of the nation, the only thing that was beneficial to know, namely, *That government is nothing more than a national association acting on the principles of society.*

HAVING thus endeavoured to shew, that the social and civilized state of man is capable of performing within itself, almost every thing necessary to its protection and government, it will be proper, on the other hand, to take a review of the present old governments, and examine whether their principles and practice are correspondent thereto.

CHAP. II.

Of the Origin of the Present Old Governments.

IT is impossible that such governments as have hitherto existed in the world, could have commenced by any other means than a total violation of every principle sacred and moral. The obscurity in which the origin of all the present old governments is buried, implies the iniquity and disgrace with which they began. The origin of the present government of America and France will ever be remembered, because it is honourable to record it; but with respect to the rest, even Flattery has consigned them to the tomb of time, without an inscription.

It could have been no difficult thing in the early and solitary ages of the world, while the chief employment of men was that of attending flocks and herds, for a banditti of ruffians to overrun a country, and lay it under contributions. Their power being thus established, the chief of the band contrived to lose the name of Robber in that of Monarch; and hence the origin of Monarchy and Kings.

The origin of the government of England, so far as relates to what is called its line of monarchy, being one of the latest, is perhaps the best recorded. The hatred which the Norman invasion and tyranny begat, must have been deeply rooted in the nation, to have outlived the contrivance to obliterate it. Though not a courtier will talk of the curfeu-bell, not a village in England has forgotten it.

Those bands of robbers having parcelled out the world, and divided it into dominions, began, as is naturally the case, to quarrel with each other. What at first was obtained by violence, was considered by others as lawful to be taken, and a second plunderer succeeded the first. They alternately invaded the dominions which each had assigned to himself, and the brutality with which they treated each other explains the original character of monarchy. It was ruffian torturing ruffian. The conqueror considered the conquered, not as his prisoner, but his property. He led him in triumph rattling in chains, and doomed him, at pleasure, to slavery or death. As time obliterated the history of their beginning, their successors assumed new appearances, to cut off the entail of their disgrace, but their principles and objects remained the same. What at first was plunder, assumed the softer name of revenue; and the power originally usurped, they affected to inherit.

From such beginning of governments, what could be expected, but a continual system of war and extortion? It has established itself into a trade. The vice is not peculiar to one more than to another, but is the common principle of all. There does not exist within such governments, a stamina whereon to ingraft reformation; and the shortest and most effectual remedy is to begin anew.

What scenes of horror, what perfection of iniquity, present themselves in contemplating the character; and reviewing the history of such governments! If we would delineate human nature with a baseness of heart, and hypocrisy of countenance, that reflection would shudder at and humanity disown, it is kings, courts, and cabinets, that must sit for the portrait. Man, naturally as he is, with all his faults about him, is not up to the character.

Can we possibly suppose that if governments had originated in a right principle, and had not an interest in pursuing a wrong one, that the world could have been in the wretched and quarrelsome condition we have seen it? What inducement has the farmer, while following the plough, to lay aside his peaceful pursuits, and go to war with the farmer of another country? or what inducement has the manufacturer? What is dominion to them, or to any class of men in a nation? Does it add an acre to any man's estate, or raise its value? Are not conquest and defeat each of the same price, and taxes the never-failing consequence? – Though this reasoning may be good to a nation, it is not so to a government. War is the Pharo table of governments, and nations the dupes of the game.

If there is any thing to wonder at in this miserable scene of governments, more than might be expected, it is the progress which the peaceful arts of agriculture, manufacture and commerce have made, beneath such a long accumulating load of discouragement and oppression. It serves to shew, that instinct in animals does not act with stronger impulse, than the principles of society and civilization operate in man. Under all discouragements, he pursues his object, and yields to nothing but impossibilities.

CHAP. III.

Of the Old and New Systems
of Government.

NOTHING can appear more contradictory than the principles on which the old governments began, and the condition to which society, civilization, and commerce, are capable of carrying mankind. Government on the old system, is an assumption of power, for the aggrandisement of itself; on the new, a delegation of power, for the common benefit of society. The former supports itself by keeping up a system of war; the latter promotes a system of peace, as the true means of enriching a nation. The one encourages national prejudices; the other promotes universal society, as the means of universal commerce. The one measures its prosperity, by the quantity of revenue it extorts; the other proves its excellence, by the small quantity of taxes it requires.

Mr. Burke has talked of old and new whigs. If he can amuse himself with childish names and distinctions, I shall not interrupt his pleasure. It is not to him, but to the Abbé Sieyes, that I address this chapter. I am already engaged to the latter gentleman, to discuss the subject of monarchical government; and as it naturally occurs in comparing the old and new systems, I make this the opportunity of presenting to him my observations. I shall occasionally take Mr. Burke in my way.

Though it might be proved that the system of government now called the NEW, is the most ancient in principle of all that have existed, being founded on the original inherent Rights of Man: yet, as tyranny and the sword have suspended the exercise of those rights for many centuries past, it serves better the purpose of distinction to call it the *new,* than to claim the right of calling it the old.

The first general distinction between those two systems, is, that the one now called the old is *hereditary,* either in whole or in part; and the new is entirely *representative.* It rejects all hereditary government:

First, As being an imposition on mankind.

Secondly, As inadequate to the purposes for which government is necessary.

With respect to the first of these heads – It cannot be proved by what right hereditary government could begin: neither does there exist within the compass of mortal power, a right to establish it. Man has no authority over posterity in matters of personal right; and therefore, no man, or body of men, had, or can have, a right to set up hereditary government. Were even ourselves to come again into existence, instead of being succeeded by posterity, we have not now the right of taking from ourselves the rights which would then be ours. On what ground, then, do we pretend to take them from others?

All hereditary government is in its nature tyranny. An heritable crown, or an heritable throne, or by what other fanciful name such things may be called, have no other significant explanation than that mankind are heritable property. To inherit a government, is to inherit the people, as if they were flocks and herds.

With respect to the second head, that of being inadequate to the purposes for which government is necessary, we have only to consider what government essentially is, and compare it with the circumstances to which hereditary succession is subject.

Government ought to be a thing always in full maturity. It ought to be so constructed as to be superior to all the accidents to which individual man is subject; and therefore, hereditary succession, by being *subject to them all,* is the most irregular and imperfect of all the systems of government.

We have heard the *Rights of Man* called a *levelling* system; but the only system to which the word *levelling* is truly applicable, is the hereditary monarchical system. It is a system of *mental levelling.* It indiscriminately admits every species of character to the same authority. Vice and virtue, ignorance and wisdom, in short, every quality, good or bad, is put on the same level. Kings succeed each other, not as rationals, but as animals. It signifies not what their mental or moral characters are. Can we then be surprised at the abject state of the human mind in monarchical countries, when the government itself is formed on such an abject levelling system?–It has no fixed character. To day it is one thing; to-morrow it is something else. It changes with the temper of every succeeding individual, and is subject to all the varieties of each. It is government through the medium of passions and accidents. It appears under all the various characters of childhood, decrepitude, dotage, a thing at nurse, in leading-strings, or in crutches. It reverses the wholesome order of nature. It occasionally puts children over men, and the conceits of non-age over wisdom and experience. In short, we cannot conceive a more ridiculous figure of government, than hereditary succession, in all its cases, presents.

Could it be made a decree in nature, or an edict registered in heaven, and man could know it, that virtue and wisdom should invariably appertain to hereditary succession, the objections to it would be removed; but when we see that nature acts as if she disowned and sported with the hereditary system; that the mental characters of successors, in all countries, are below the average of human understanding; that one is a tyrant, another an ideot, a third insane, and some all three together, it is impossible to attach confidence to it, when reason in man has power to act.

It is not to the Abbé Sieyes that I need apply this reasoning; he has already saved me that trouble, by giving his own opinion upon the case. "If it be asked," says he, "what is my opinion with respect to hereditary right, I answer, without hesitation, That, in good theory, an hereditary transmission of any power or office, can never accord with the laws of a true representation. Hereditaryship is, in this sense, as much an attaint upon principle, as an outrage upon society. But let us," continues he, "refer to the history of all elective monarchies and principalities: Is there one in which the elective mode is not worse than the hereditary succession?"

As to debating on which is the worst of the two, is admitting both to be bad; and herein we are agreed. The preference which the Abbé has given, is a condemnation of the thing that he prefers. Such a mode of reasoning on such a subject is inadmissible, because it finally amounts to an accusation upon Providence, as if she had left to man no other choice with respect to government than between two evils, the best of which he admits to be "*an attaint upon principle, and an outrage upon society.*"

Passing over, for the present, all the evils and mischiefs which monarchy has occasioned in the world, nothing can more effectually prove its uselessness in a state of *civil government,* than making it hereditary. Would we make any office hereditary that required wisdom and abilities to fill it? and where wisdom and abilities are not necessary, such an office, whatever it may be, is superfluous or insignificant.

Hereditary succession is a burlesque upon monarchy. It puts it in the most ridiculous light, by presenting it as an office which any child or ideot may fill. It requires some talents to be a common mechanic; but, to be a king, requires only the animal figure of man – a sort of breathing automaton. This sort of superstition may last a few years more, but it cannot long resist the awakened reason and interest of man.

As to Mr. Burke, he is a stickler for monarchy, not altogether as a pensioner, if he is one, which I believe, but as a political man. He has taken up a contemptible opinion of mankind, who, in their turn, are taking up the same of him. He considers them as a herd of beings that must be governed by fraud, effigy and shew; and an idol would be as good a figure of monarchy with him, as a man. I will, however, do him the justice to say, that, with respect to America, he has been very complimentary. He always contended, at least in my hearing, that the people of America were more enlightened than those of England, or of any country in Europe; and that therefore the imposition of shew was not necessary in their governments.

Though the comparison between hereditary and elective monarchy, which the Abbé has made, is unnecessary to the case, because the representative system rejects both; yet, were I to make the comparison, I should decide contrary to what he has done.

The civil wars which have originated from contested hereditary claims, are more numerous, and have been more dreadful, and of longer continuance, than those which have been occasioned by election. All the civil wars in France arose from the hereditary system; they were either produced by hereditary claims, or by the imperfection of the hereditary form, which admits of regencies, or monarchy at nurse. With respect to England, its history is full of the same misfortunes. The contests for succession between the Houses of York and Lancaster, lasted a whole century; and others of a similar nature, have renewed themselves since that period. Those of 1715 and 1745, were of the same kind. The succession war for the crown of Spain, embroiled almost half Europe. The disturbances in Holland are generated from the hereditaryship of the Stadtholder. A government calling itself free, with an hereditary office, is like a thorn in the flesh, that produces a fermentation which endeavours to discharge it.

But I might go further, and place also foreign wars, of whatever kind, to the same cause. It is by adding the evil of hereditary succession to that of monarchy, that a permanent family-interest is created, whose constant objects are dominion and revenue. Poland, though an elective monarchy, has had fewer wars than those which are hereditary; and it is the only government that has made a voluntary essay, though but a small one, to reform the condition of the country.

Having thus glanced at a few of the defects of the old, or hereditary systems of government, let us compare it with the new, or representative system.

The representative system takes society and civilization for its basis; nature, reason, and experience, for its guide.

Experience, in all ages, and in all countries, has demonstrated, that it is impossible to controul Nature in her distribution of mental powers. She gives them as she pleases. Whatever is the rule by which she, apparently to us, scatters them among mankind, that rule remains a secret to man. It would be as ridiculous to attempt to fix the hereditaryship of human beauty, as of wisdom. Whatever wisdom constituently is, it is like a seedless plant; it may be reared when it appears, but it cannot be voluntarily produced. There is always a sufficiency somewhere in the general mass of society for all purposes; but with respect to the parts of society, it is continually changing its place. It rises in one to-day, in another to-morrow, and has most probably visited in rotation every family of the earth, and again withdrawn.

As this is the order of nature, the order of government must necessarily follow it, or government will, as we see it does, degenerate into ignorance. The hereditary system, therefore, is as repugnant to human wisdom, as to human rights; and is as absurd, as it is unjust.

As the republic of letters brings forward the best literary productions, by giving to genius a fair and universal chance; so the representative system of government is calculated to produce the wisest laws, by collecting wisdom from where it can be found. I smile to myself when I contemplate the ridiculous insignificance into which literature and all the sciences would sink, were they made hereditary; and I carry the same idea into governments. An hereditary governor is as inconsistent as an hereditary author. I know not whether Homer or Euclid had sons: but I will venture an opinion, that if they had, and had left their works unfinished, those sons could not have completed them.

Do we need a stronger evidence of the absurdity of hereditary government, than is seen in the descendants of those men, in any line of life, who once were famous? Is there scarcely an instance in which there is not a total reverse of the character? It appears as if the tide of mental faculties flowed as far as it could in certain channels, and then forsook its course, and arose in others. How irrational then is the hereditary system which establishes channels of power, in company with which wisdom refuses to flow! By continuing this absurdity, man is perpetually in contradiction with himself; he accepts, for a king, or a chief magistrate, or a legislator, a person whom he would not elect for a constable.

It appears to general observation, that revolutions create genius and talents; but those events do no more than bring them forward. There is existing in man, a mass of sense lying in a dormant state, and which, unless something excites it to action, will descend with him, in that condition, to the grave. As it is to the advantage of society that the whole of its faculties should be employed, the construction of government ought to be such as to bring forward, by a quiet and regular operation, all that extent of capacity which never fails to appear in revolutions.

This cannot take place in the insipid state of hereditary government, not only because it prevents, but because it operates to benumb. When the mind of a nation is bowed down by any political superstition in its government, such as hereditary succession is, it loses a considerable portion of its powers on all other subjects and objects. Hereditary succession requires the same obedience to ignorance, as to wisdom; and when once the mind can bring itself to pay this indiscriminate reverence, it descends below the stature of mental manhood. It is fit to be great only in little things. It acts a treachery upon itself, and suffocates the sensations that urge to detection.

Though the ancient governments present to us a miserable picture of the condition of man, there is one which above all others exempts itself from the general description. I mean the democracy of the Athenians. We see more to admire, and less to condemn, in that great, extraordinary people, than in any thing which history affords.

Mr. Burke is so little acquainted with constituent principles of government, that he confounds democracy and representation together. Representation was a thing unknown in the ancient democracies. In those the mass of the people met and enacted laws (grammatically speaking) in the first person. Simple democracy was no other than the common-hall of the ancients. It signifies the *form*, as well as the public principle of the government. As these democracies increased in population, and the territory extended, the simple democratical form became unwieldy and impracticable; and as the system of representation was not known, the consequence was, they either degenerated convulsively into monarchies, or became absorbed into such as then existed. Had the system of representation been then understood, as it now is, there is no reason to believe that those forms of government now called monarchical or aristocratical, would ever have taken place. It was the want of some method to consolidate the parts of society, after it became too populous, and too extensive for the simple democratical form, and also the lax and solitary condition of shepherds and herdsmen in other parts of the world, that afforded opportunities to those unnatural modes of government to begin.

As it is necessary to clear away the rubbish of errors, into which the subject of government has been thrown, I shall proceed to remark on some others.

It has always been the political craft of courtiers and court-governments, to abuse something which they called republicanism; but what republicanism was, or is, they never attempt to explain. Let us examine a little into this case.

The only forms of government are, the democratical, the aristocratical, the monarchical, and what is now called the representative.

What is called a *republic*, is not any *particular form* of government. It is wholly characteristical of the purport, matter, or object for which government ought to be instituted, and on which it is to be employed,

RES-PUBLICA, the public affairs, or the public good; or, literally translated, the *public thing*. It is a word of a good original, referring to what ought to be the character and business of government; and in this sense it is naturally opposed to the word *monarchy,* which has a base original signification. It means arbitrary power in an individual person; in the exercise of which, *himself,* and not the *res-publica,* is the object.

Every government that does not act on the principle of a *Republic,* or in other words, that does not make the *res-publica* its whole and sole object, is not a good government. Republican government is no other than government eatablished and conducted for the interest of the public, as well individually as collectively. It is not necessarily connected with any particular form, but it most naturally associates with the representative form, as being best calculated to secure the end for which a nation is at the expence of supporting it.

Various forms of government have affected to style themselves a republic. Poland calls itself a republic, which is an hereditary aristocracy, with what is called an elective monarchy. Holland calls itself a republic, which is chiefly aristocratical, with an hereditary stadtholdership. But the government of America, which is wholly on the system of representation, is the only real republic in character and in practice, that now exists. Its government has no other object than the public business of the nation, and therefore it is properly a republic; and the Americans have taken care that THIS, and no other, shall always be the object of their government, by their rejecting every thing hereditary, and establishing government on the system of representation only.

Those who have said that a republic is not a *form* of government calculated for countries of great extent, mistook, in the first place, the *business* of a government, for *a form* of government; for the *res-publica* equally appertains to every extent of territory and population. And, in the second place, if they meant any thing with respect to *form,* it was the simple democratical form, such as was the mode of government in the ancient democracies, in which there was no representation. The case, therefore, is not, that a republic cannot be extensive, but that it cannot be extensive on the simple democratical form; and the question naturally presents itself, *What is the best form of government for conducting the* RES-PUBLICA, *or the* PUBLIC BUSINESS *of a nation, after it becomes too extensive and populous for the simple democratical form?*

It cannot be monarchy, because monarchy is subject to an objection of the same amount to which the simple democratical form was subject.

It is possible that an individual may lay down a system of principles, on which government shall be constitutionally established to any extent of territory. This is no more than an operation of the mind, acting by its own powers. But the practice upon those principles, as applying to the various and numerous circumstances of a nation, its agriculture, manufacture, trade, commerce, &c. &c. requires a knowledge of a different kind, and which can be had only from the various parts of society. It is an assemblage of practical knowledge, which no one individual can possess; and therefore the monarchical form is as much limited, in useful practice, from the incompetency of knowledge, as was the democratical form, from the multiplicity of population. The one degenerates, by extension, into confusion; the other, into ignorance and incapacity, of which all the great monarchies are an evidence. The monarchical form, therefore, could not be a substitute for the democratical, because it has equal inconveniences.

Much less could it when made hereditary. This is the most effectual of all forms to preclude knowledge. Neither could the high democratical mind have voluntarily yielded itself to be governed by children and idiots, and all the motley insignificance of character, which attends such a mere animal-system, the disgrace and the reproach of reason and of man.

As to the aristocratical form, it has the same vices and defects with the monarchical, except that the chance of abilities is better from the proportion of numbers, but there is still no security for the right use and application of them[2].

Referring, then, to the original simple democracy, it affords the true data from which government on a large scale can begin. It is incapable of extension, not from its principle, but from the inconvenience of its form; and monarchy and aristocracy, from their incapacity. Retaining, then, democracy as the ground, and rejecting the corrupt systems of monarchy and aristocracy, the representative system naturally presents itself; remedying at once the defects of the simple democracy as to form, and the incapacity of the other two with respect to knowledge.

Simple democracy was society governing itself without the aid of secondary means. By ingrafting representation upon democracy, we arrive at a system of government capable of embracing and confederating all the various interests and every extent of territory and population; and that also with advantages as much superior to hereditary government, as the republic of letters is to hereditary literature.

It is on this system that the American government is founded. It is representation ingrafted upon democracy. It has fixed the form by a scale

2. For a character of aristocracy, the reader is referred to *Rights of Man,* Part I. page [210].

parallel in all cases to the extent of the principle. What Athens was in miniature, America will be in magnitude. The one was the wonder of the ancient world; the other is becoming the admiration and model of the present. It is the easiest of all the forms of government to be understood, and the most eligible in practice; and excludes at once the ignorance and insecurity of the hereditary mode, and the inconvenience of the simple democracy.

It is impossible to conceive a system of government capable of acting over such an extent of territory, and such a circle of interests, as is immediately produced by the operation of representation. France, great and populous as it is, is but a spot in the capaciousness of the system. It adapts itself to all possible cases. It is preferable to simple democracy even in small territories. Athens, by representation, would have outrivalled her own democracy.

That which is called government, or rather that which we ought to conceive government to be, is no more than some common center, in which all the parts of society unite. This cannot be accomplished by any method so conducive to the various interests of the community, as by the representative system. It concentrates the knowledge necessary to the interest of the parts, and of the whole. It places government in a state of constant maturity. It is, as has been already observed, never young, never old. It is subject neither to nonage, nor dotage. It is never in the cradle, nor on crutches. It admits not of a separation between knowledge and power, and is superior, as government always ought to be, to all the accidents of individual man, and is therefore superior to what is called monarchy.

A nation is not a body, the figure of which is to be represented by the human body; but is like a body contained within a circle, having a common center, in which every radius meets; and that center is formed by representation. To connect representation with what is called monarchy, is eccentric government. Representation is of itself the delegated monarchy of a nation, and cannot debase itself by dividing it with another.

Mr. Burke has two or three times, in his parliamentary speeches, and in his publications, made use of a jingle of words that convey no ideas. Speaking of government, he says, "It is better to have monarchy for its basis, and republicanism for its corrective, than republicanism for its basis, and monarchy for its corrective." – If he means that it is better to correct folly with wisdom, than wisdom with folly, I will no otherwise contend with him, than that it would be much better to reject the folly entirely.

But what is this thing which Mr. Burke calls monarchy? Will he explain it? All men can understand what representation is; and that it must necesarily include a variety of knowledge and talents. But, what security is there for the same qualities on the part of monarchy? or, when this monarchy is a child, where then is the wisdom? What does it know about government? Who then is the monarch, or where is the monarchy? If it is to be performed by regency, it proves it to be a farce. A regency is a mock species of republic, and the whole of monarchy deserves no better description. It is a thing as various as imagination can paint. It has none of the stable character that government ought to possess. Every succession is a revolution, and every regency a counter-revolution. The whole of it is a scene of perpetual court cabal and intrigue, of which Mr. Burke is himself an instance. To render monarchy consistent with government, the next in succession should not be born a child, but a man at once, and that man a Solomon. It is ridiculous that nations are to wait, and government be interrupted, till boys grow to be men.

Whether I have too little sense to see, or too much to be imposed upon; whether I have too much or too little pride, or of any thing else, I leave out of the question; but certain it is, that what is called monarchy, always appears to me a silly, contemptible thing. I compare it to something kept behind a curtain, about which there is a great deal of bustle and fuss, and a wonderful air of seeming solemnity; but when, by any accident, the curtain happens to be open, and the company see what it is, they burst into laughter.

In the representative system of government, nothing of this can happen. Like the nation itself, it possesses a perpetual stamina, as well of body as of mind, and presents itself on the open theatre of the world in a fair and manly manner. Whatever are its excellences or its defects, they are visible to all. It exists not by fraud and mystery; it deals not in cant and sophistry; but inspires a language, that, passing from heart to heart, is felt and understood.

We must shut our eyes against reason, we must basely degrade our understanding, not to see the folly of what is called monarchy. Nature is orderly in all her works; but this is a mode of government that counteracts nature. It turns the progress of the human faculties upside down. It subjects age to be governed by children, and wisdom by folly.

On the contrary, the representative system is always parallel with the order and immutable laws of nature, and meets the reason of man in every part. For example:

In the American federal government, more power is delegated to the President of the United States, than to any other individual member of congress. He cannot, therefore, be elected to this office under the age of thirty-five years. By this time the judgment of man becomes matured, and he has lived long enough to be acquainted with men and things, and the country with him. – But on the monarchical plan, (exclusive of the numerous chances there are against every man born into the world, of drawing a prize in the lottery of human faculties), the next in succession, whatever he may be, is put at the head of a nation, and of a government, at the age of eighteen years. Does this appear like an act of wisdom? Is it consistent with the proper dignity and the manly character of a nation? Where is the propriety of calling such a lad the father of the people? – In all other cases, a person is a minor until the age of twenty-one years. Before this period, he is not trusted with the management of an acre of land, or with the heritable property of a flock of sheep, or an herd of swine; but, wonderful to tell! he may, at the age of eighteen years, be trusted with a nation.

That monarchy is all a bubble, a mere court artifice to procure money, is evident, (at least to me), in every character in which it can be viewed. It would be impossible, on the rational system of representative government, to make out a bill of expences to such an enormous amount as this deception admits. Government is not of itself a very chargeable institution. The whole expence of the federal government of America, founded, as I have already said, on the system of representation, and extending over a country nearly ten times as large as England, is but six hundred thousand dollars, or one hundred and thirty-five thousand pounds sterling.

I presume, that no man in his sober senses, will compare the character of any of the kings of Europe with that of General Washington. Yet, in France, and also in England, the expence of the civil list only, for the support of one man, is eight times greater than the whole expence of the federal government in America. To assign a reason for this, appears almost impossible. The generality of people in America, especially the poor, are more able to pay taxes, than the generality of people either in France or England.

But the case is, that the representative system diffuses such a body of knowledge throughout a nation, on the subject of government, as to explode ignorance and preclude imposition. The craft of courts cannot be acted on that ground. There is no place for mystery; no where for it to begin. Those who are not in the representation, know as much of the nature of business as those who are. An affectation of mysterious importance would there be scouted. Nations can have no secrets; and the secrets of courts, like those of individuals, are always their defects.

In the representative system, the reason for every thing must publicly appear. Every man is a proprietor in government, and considers it a necessary part of his business to understand. It concerns his interest, because it affects his property. He examines the cost, and compares it with the advantages; and above all, he does not adopt the slavish custom of following what in other governments are called LEADERS.

It can only be by blinding the understanding of man, and making him believe that government is some wonderful mysterious thing, that excessive revenues are obtained. Monarchy is well calculated to ensure this end. It is the popery of government; a thing kept up to amuse the ignorant, and quiet them into taxes.

The government of a free country, properly speaking, is not in the persons, but in the laws. The enacting of those requires no great expence; and when they are administered, the whole of civil government is performed – the rest is all court contrivance.

CHAP. IV.
Of Constitutions.

THAT men mean distinct and separate things when they speak of constitutions and of governments, is evident; or, why are those terms distinctly and separately used? A constitution is not the act of a government, but of a people constituting a government; and government without a constitution, is power without a right.

All power exercised over a nation, must have some beginning. It must be either delegated, or assumed. There are no other sources. All delegated power is trust, and all assumed power is usurpation. Time does not alter the nature and quality of either.

In viewing this subject, the case and circumstances of America present themselves as in the beginning of a world; and our enquiry into the origin of government is shortened, by referring to the facts that have arisen in our own day. We have no occasion to roam for information into the obscure field of antiquity, nor hazard ourselves upon conjecture. We are brought at once to the point of seeing government begin, as if we had lived in the beginning of time. The real volume, not of history, but of facts, is directly before us, unmutilated by contrivance, or the errors of tradition.

I will here concisely state the commencement of the American constitutions; by which the difference between constitutions and governments will sufficiently appear.

It may not be improper to remind the reader, that the United States of America consist of thirteen separate states, each of which established a government for itself, after the declaration of independence, done the fourth of July 1776. Each state acted independently of the rest, in forming its government; but the same general principle pervades the whole. When the several state governments were formed, they proceeded to form the federal government, that acts over the whole in all matters which concern the interest of the whole, or which relate to the intercourse of the several states with each other, or with foreign nations. I will begin with giving an instance from one of the state governments, (that of Pennsylvania), and then proceed to the federal government.

The state of Pennsylvania, though nearly of the same extent of territory as England, was then divided into only twelve counties. Each of those counties had elected a committee at the commencement of the dispute with the English government; and as the city of Philadelphia, which also had its committee, was the most central for intelligence, it became the center of communication to the several county committees. When it became necessary to proceed to the formation of a government, the committee of Philadelphia proposed a conference of all the county committees, to be held in that city, and which met the latter end of July 1776.

Though these committees had been elected by the people, they were not elected expressly for the purpose, nor invested with the authority, of forming a constitution; and as they could not, consistently with the American idea of rights, assume such a power, they could only confer upon the matter, and put it into a train of operation. The conferrees, therefore, did no more than state the case, and recommend to the several counties to elect six representatives for each county, to meet in convention at Philadelphia, with powers to form a constitution, and propose it for public consideration.

This convention, of which Benjamin Franklin was president, having met and deliberated, and agreed upon a constitution, they next ordered it to be published, not as a thing established, but for the consideration of the whole people, their approbation or rejection, and then adjourned to a stated time. When the time of adjournment was expired, the convention re-assembled; and as the general opinion of the people in approbation of it was then known, the constitution was signed, sealed, and proclaimed on the *authority of the people* and the original instrument deposited as a public record. The convention then appointed a day for the general election of the representatives who were to compose the government, and the time it should commence; and having done this, they dissolved, and returned to their several homes and occupations.

In this constitution were laid down, first, a declaration of rights. Then followed the form which the government should have, and the powers it should possess – the authority of the courts of judicature, and of juries – the manner in which elections should be conducted, and the proportion of representatives to the number of electors – the time which each succeeding assembly should continue, which was one year – the mode of levying, and of accounting for the expenditure, of public money – of appointing public officers, &c. &c. &c.

No article of this constitution could be altered or infringed at the discretion of the government that was to ensue. It was to that government a law. But as it would have been unwise to preclude the benefit of experience, and in order also to prevent the accumulation of errors, if any should be found, and to preserve an unison of government with the circumstances of the state at all times, the constitution provided, that, at the expiration of every seven years, a convention should be elected, for the express purpose of revising the constitution, and making alterations, additions, or abolitions therein, if any such should be found necessary.

Here we see a regular process – a government issuing out of a constitution, formed by the people in their original character; and that constitution serving, not only as an authority, but as a law of controul to the government. It was the political bible of the state. Scarcely a family was without it. Every member of the government had a copy; and nothing was more common, when any debate arose on the principle of a bill, or on the extent of any species of authority, than for the members to take the printed constitution out of their pocket, and read the chapter with which such matter in debate was connected.

Having thus given an instance from one of the states, I will shew the proceedings by which the federal constitution of the United States arose and was formed.

Congress, at its two first meetings, in September 1774, and May 1775, was nothing more than a deputation from the legislatures of the several provinces, afterwards states; and had no other authority than what arose from common consent, and the necessity of its acting as a public body. In every thing which related to the internal affairs of America, congress went no further than to issue recommendations to the several provincial assemblies, who at discretion adopted them or not. Nothing on the part of congress was compulsive; yet, in this situation, it was more faithfully and affectionately obeyed, than was any government in Europe. This instance, like that of the national assembly in France, sufficiently shews, that the strength of government does not consist in any thing *within* itself, but in the attachment of a nation, and the interest which the people feel in supporting it. When this is lost, government is but a child in power; and though, like the old government of France, it may harrass individuals for a while, it but facilitates its own fall.

After the declaration of independence, it became consistent with the principle on which representative government is founded, that the authority of congress should be defined and established. Whether that authority should be more or less than congress then discretionarily exercised, was not the question. It was merely the rectitude of the measure.

For this purpose, the act, called the act of confederation, (which was a sort of imperfect federal constitution), was proposed, and, after long deliberation, was concluded in the year 1781. It was not the act of congress, because it is repugnant to the principles of representative government that a body should give power to itself. Congress first informed the several states, of the powers which it conceived were necessary to be invested in the union, to enable it to perform the duties and services required from it; and the states severally agreed with each other, and concenterated in congress those powers.

It may not be improper to observe, that in both those instances, (the one of Pennsylvania, and the other of the United States), there is no such thing as the idea of a compact between the people on one side, and the government on the other. The compact was that of the people with each other, to produce and constitute a government. To suppose that any government can be a party in a compact with the whole people, is to suppose it to have existence before it can have a right to exist. The only instance in which a compact can take place between the people and those who exercise the government, is, that the people shall pay them, while they chuse to employ them.

Government is not a trade which any man or body of men has a right to set up and exercise for his own emolument, but is altogether a trust, in right of those by whom that trust is delegated, and by whom it is always resumeable. It has of itself no rights; they are altogether duties.

Having thus given two instances of the original formation of a constitution, I will shew the manner in which both have been changed since their first establishment.

The powers vested in the governments of the several states, by the state constitutions, were found, upon experience, to be too great; and those vested in the federal government, by the act of confederation, too little. The defect was not in the principle, but in the distribution of power.

Numerous publications, in pamphlets and in the newspapers, appeared, on the propriety and necessity of new modelling the federal government. After some time of public discussion, carried on through the channel of the press, and in conversations, the state of Virginia, experiencing some inconvenience with respect to commerce, proposed holding a continental conference; in consequence of which, a deputation from five or six of the state assemblies met at Anapolis in Maryland, in 1786. This meeting, not conceiving itself sufficiently authorised to go into the business of a reform, did no more than state their general opinions of the propriety of the measure, and recommend that a convention of all the states should be held the year following.

This convention met at Philadelphia in May 1787, of which General Washington was elected president. He was not at that time connected with any of the state governments, or with congress. He delivered up his commission when the war ended, and since then had lived a private citizen.

The convention went deeply into all the subjects; and having, after a variety of debate and investigation, agreed among themselves upon the several parts of a federal constitution, the next question was, the manner of giving it authority and practice.

For this purpose, they did not, like a cabal of courtiers, send for a Dutch Stadtholder, or a German Elector; but they referred the whole matter to the sense and interest of the country.

They first directed, that the proposed constitution should be published. Secondly, that each state should elect a convention, expressly for the purpose of taking it into consideration, and of ratifying or rejecting it; and that as soon as the approbation and ratification of any nine states should be given, that those states should proceed to the election of their proportion of members to the new federal government; and that the operation of it should then begin, and the former federal government cease.

The several states proceeded accordingly to elect their conventions. Some of those conventions ratified the constitution by very large majorities, and two or three unanimously. In others there were much debate and division of opinion. In the Massachusetts convention, which met at Boston, the majority was not above nineteen or twenty, in about three hundred members; but such is the nature of representative government, that it quietly decides all matters by majority. After the debate in the Massachusetts convention was closed, and the vote taken, the objecting members rose, and declared, *"That though they had argued and voted against it, because certain parts appeared to them in a different light to what they appeared to other members; yet, as the vote had decided in favour of the constitution as proposed, they should give it the same practical support as if they had voted for it."*

As soon as nine states had concurred, (and the rest followed in the order their conventions were elected), the old fabric of the federal government was taken down, and the new one erected, of which General Washington is president. – In this place I cannot help remarking, that the character and services of this gentleman are sufficient to put all those men called kings to shame. While they are receiving from the sweat and labours of mankind, a prodigality of pay, to which neither their abilities nor their services can entitle them, he is rendering every service in his power, and refusing every pecuniary reward. He accepted no pay as commander in chief; he accepts none as president of the United States.

After the new federal constitution was established, the state of Pennsylvania, conceiving that some parts of its own constitution required to be altered, elected a convention for that purpose. The proposed alterations were published, and the people concurring therein, they were established.

In forming those constitutions, or in altering them, little or no inconvenience took place. The ordinary course of things was not interrupted, and the advantages have been much. It is always the interest of a far greater number of people in a nation to have things right, than to let them remain wrong; and when public matters are open to debate, and the public judgment free, it will not decide wrong, unless it decides too hastily.

In the two instances of changing the constitutions, the governments then in being were not actors either way. Government has no right to make itself a party in any debate respecting the principles or modes of forming, or of changing, constitutions. It is not for the benefit of those who exercise the powers of government, that constitutions, and the governments issuing from them, are established. In all those matters, the right of judging and acting are in those who pay, and not in those who receive.

A constitution is the property of a nation, and not of those who exercise the government. All the constitutions of America are declared to be established on the authority of the people. In France, the word nation is used instead of the people; but in both cases, a constitution is a thing antecedent to the government, and always distinct therefrom.

In England, it is not difficult to perceive that every thing has a constitution, except the nation. Every society and association that is established, first agreed upon a number of original articles, digested into form, which are its constitution. It then appointed its officers, whose powers and authorities are described in that constitution, and the government of that society then commenced. Those officers, by whatever name they are called, have no authority to add to, alter, or abridge the original articles. It is only to the constituting power that this right belongs.

From the want of understanding the difference between a constitution and a government, Dr. Johnson, and all writers of his description, have always bewildered themselves. They could not but perceive, that there must necessarily be a *controuling* power existing somewhere, and they placed this power in the discretion of the persons exercising the government, instead of placing it in a constitution formed by the nation. When it is in a constitution, it has the nation for its support, and the natural and the political controuling powers are together. The laws which are enacted by governments, controul men only as individuals, but the nation, through its constitution, controuls the whole government, and has a natural ability so to do. The final controuling power, therefore, and the original constituting power, are one and the same power.

Dr. Johnson could not have advanced such a position in any country where there was a constitution; and he is himself an evidence, that no such thing as a constitution exists in England. – But it may be put as a question, not improper to be investigated, That if a constitution does not exist, how came the idea of its existence so generally established?

In order to decide this question, it is necessary to consider a constitution in both its cases: – First, as creating a government and giving it powers. Secondly, as regulating and restraining the powers so given.

If we begin with William of Normandy, we find that the government of England was originally a tyranny, founded on an invasion and conquest of the country. This being admitted, it will then appear, that the exertion of the nation, at different periods, to abate that tyranny, and render it less intolerable, has been credited for a constitution.

Magna Charta, as it was called, (it is now like an almanack of the same date,) was no more than compelling the government to renounce a part of its assumptions. It did not create and give powers to government in the manner a constitution does; but was, as far as it went, of the nature of a re-conquest, and not of a constitution; for could the nation have totally expelled the usurpation, as France has done its despotism, it would then have had a constitution to form.

The history of the Edwards and the Henries, and up to the commencement of the Stuarts, exhibits as many instances of tyranny as could be acted within the limits to which the nation had restricted it. The Stuarts endeavoured to pass those limits, and their fate is well known. In all those instances we see nothing of a constitution, but only of restrictions on assumed power.

After this, another William, descended from the same stock, and claiming from the same origin, gained possession; and of the two evils, *James* and *William,* the nation preferred what it thought the least; since, from circumstances, it must take one. The act, called the Bill of Rights, comes here into view. What is it, but a bargain, which the parts of the government made with each other to divide powers, profits, and privileges? You shall have so much, and I will have the rest; and with respect to the nation, it said, for *your share,* YOU *shall have the right of petitioning.* This being the case, the bill of rights is more properly a bill of wrongs, and of insult. As to what is called the convention parliament, it was a thing that made itself, and then made the authority by which it acted. A few persons got together, and called themselves by that name. Several of them had never been elected, and none of them for the purpose.

From the time of William, a species of government arose, issuing out of this coalition bill of rights; and more so, since the corruption introduced at the Hanover succession, by the agency of Walpole; that can be described by no other name than a despotic legislation. Though the parts may embarrass each other, the whole has no bounds; and the only right it acknowledges out of itself, is the right of petitioning. Where then is the constitution either that gives or that restrains power?

It is not because a part of the government is elective, that makes it less a despotism, if the persons so elected, possess afterwards, as a parliament, unlimited powers. Election, in this case, becomes separated from representation, and the candidates are candidates for despotism.

I cannot believe that any nation, reasoning on its own rights, would have thought of calling those things *a constitution,* if the cry of constitution had not been set up by the government. It has got into circulation like the words *bore* and *quoz,* by being chalked up in the speeches of parliament, as those words were on window shutters and door posts; but whatever the constitution may be in other respects, it has undoubtedly been *the most productive machine of taxation that was ever invented.* The taxes in France, under the new constitution, are not quite thirteen shillings per head[3], and the taxes in England, under what is called its present constitution, are forty-eight shillings and sixpence per head, men, women, and children, amounting to nearly seventeen millions sterling, besides the expence of collection, which is upwards of a million more.

3. The whole amount of the assessed taxes of France, for the present year, is three hundred millions of livres, which is twelve millions and a half sterling; and the incidental taxes are estimated at three millions, making in the whole fifteen millions and a half; which, among twenty-four millions of people, is not quite thirteen shillings per head. France has lessened her taxes since the revolution, nearly nine millions sterling annually. Before the revolution, the city of Paris paid a duty of upwards of thirty per cent. on all articles brought into the city. This tax was collected at the city gates. It was taken off on the first of last May, and the gates taken down.

In a country like England, where the whole of the civil government is executed by the people of every town and county, by means of parish officers, magistrates, quarterly sessions, juries, and assize; without any trouble to what is called the government, or any other expence to the revenue than the salary of the judges, it is astonishing how such a mass of taxes can be employed. Not even the internal defence of the country is paid out of the revenue. On all occasions, whether real or contrived, recourse is continually had to new loans and new taxes. No wonder, then, that a machine of government so advantageous to the advocates of a court, should be so triumphantly extolled! No wonder, that St. James's or St. Stephen's should echo with the continual cry of constitution! No wonder, that the French revolution should be reprobated, and the *res-publica* treated with reproach! The *red book* of England, like the red book of France, will explain the reason[4].

I will now, by way of relaxation, turn a thought or two to Mr. Burke. I ask his pardon for neglecting him so long.

"America," says he, (in his speech on the Canada constitution bill) "never dreamed of such absurd doctrine as the *Rights of Man.*"

Mr. Burke is such a bold presumer, and advances his assertions and his premises with such a deficiency of judgment, that, without troubling ourselves about principles of philosophy or politics, the mere logical conclusions they produce, are ridiculous. For instance,

If governments, as Mr. Burke asserts, are not founded on the Rights of MAN, and are founded on *any rights* at all, they consequently must be founded on the rights of *something* that is *not man.* What then is that something?

Generally speaking, we know of no other creatures that inhabit the earth than man and beast; and in all cases, where only two things offer themselves, and one must be admitted, a negation proved on any one, amounts to an affirmative on the other; and therefore, Mr. Burke, by proving against the Rights of *Man,* proves in behalf of the *beast;* and consequently, proves that government is a beast: and as difficult things sometimes explain each other, we now see the origin of keeping wild beasts in the Tower; for they certainly can be of no other use than to shew the origin of the government. They are in the place of a constitution. O John Bull, what honours thou hast lost by not being a wild beast. Thou mightest, on Mr. Burke's system, have been in the Tower for life.

4. What was called the *livre rouge,* or the red book, in France, was not exactly similar to the court calendar in England; but it sufficiently shewed how a great part of the taxes was lavished.

If Mr. Burke's arguments have not weight enough to keep one serious, the fault is less mine than his; and as I am willing to make an apology to the reader for the liberty I have taken, I hope Mr. Burke will also make his for giving the cause.

Having thus paid Mr. Burke the compliment of remembering him, I return to the subject.

From the want of a constitution in England to restrain and regulate the wild impulse of power, many of the laws are irrational and tyrannical, and the administration of them vague and problematical.

The attention of the government of England, (for I rather chuse to call it by this name, than the English government) appears, since its political connection with Germany, to have been so compleatly engrossed and absorbed by foreign affairs, and the means of raising taxes, that it seems to exist for no other purposes. Domestic concerns are neglected; and, with respect to regular law, there is scarcely such a thing.

Almost every case now must be determined by some precedent, be that precedent good or bad, or whether it properly applies or not; and the practice is become so general, as to suggest a suspicion, that it proceeds from a deeper policy than at first sight appears.

Since the revolution of America, and more so since that of France, this preaching up the doctrine of precedents, drawn from times and circumstances antecedent to those events, has been the studied practice of the English government. The generality of those precedents are founded on principles and opinions, the reverse of what they ought; and the greater distance of time they are drawn from, the more they are to be suspected. But by associating those precedents with a superstitious reverence for ancient things, as monks shew relics and call them holy, the generality of mankind are deceived into the design. Governments now act as if they were afraid to awaken a single reflection in man. They are softly leading him to the sepulchre of precedents, to deaden his faculties and call his attention from the scene of revolutions. They feel that he is arriving at knowledge faster than they wish, and their policy of precedents is the barometer of their fears. This political popery, like the ecclesiastical popery of old, has had its day, and is hastening to its exit. The ragged relic and the antiquated precedent, the monk and the monarch, will moulder together.

Government by precedent, without any regard to the principle of the precedent, is one of the vilest systems that can be set up. In numerous instances, the precedent ought to operate as a warning, and not as an example, and requires to be shunned instead of imitated; but instead of this, precedents are taken in the lump, and put at once for constitution and for law.

Either the doctrine of precedents is policy to keep man in a state of ignorance, or it is a practical consession that wisdom degenerates in governments as governments increase in age, and can only hobble along by the stilts and crutches of precedents. How is it that the same persons who would proudly be thought wiser than their predecessors, appear at the same time only as the ghosts of departed wisdom? How strangely is antiquity treated! To answer some purposes it is spoken of as the times of darkness and ignorance, and to answer others, it is put for the light of the world.

If the doctrine of precedents, is to be followed, the expences of government need not continue the same. Why pay men extravagantly, who have but little to do? If every thing that can happen is already in precedent, legislation is at an end, and precedent, like a dictionary, determines every case. Either, therefore, government has arrived at its dotage, and requires to be renovated, or all the occasions for exercising its wisdom have occured.

We now see all over Europe, and particularly in England, the curious phænomenon of a nation looking one way, and a government the other – the one forward and the other backward. If governments are to go on by precedent, while nations go on by improvement, they must at last come to a final separation; and the sooner, and the more civilly, they determine this point, the better[5].

Having thus spoken of constitutions generally, as things distinct from actual governments, let us proceed to consider the parts of which a constitution is composed.

Opinions differ more on this subject, than with respect to the whole. That a nation ought to have a constitution, as a rule for the conduct of its government, is a simple question in which all men, not directly courtiers, will agree. It is only on the component parts that questions and opinions multiply.

But this difficulty, like every other, will diminish when put into a train of being rightly understood.

The first thing is, that a nation has a right to establish a constitution.

5. In England, the improvements in agriculture, useful arts, manufactures, and commerce, have been made in opposition to the genius of its government, which is that of following precedents. It is from the enterprize and industry of the individuals, and their numerous associations, in which, tritely speaking, government is neither pillow nor bolster, that these improvements have proceeded. No man thought about the government, or who was *in,* or who was *out,* when he was planning or executing those things; and all he had to hope, with respect to government, was, *that it would let him alone.* Three or four very silly ministerial news-papers are continually offending against the spirit of national improvement, by ascribing it to a minister. They may with as much truth ascribe this book to a minister.

Whether it exercises this right in the most judicious manner at first, is quite another case. It exercises it agreeably to the judgment it possesses; and by continuing to do so, all errors will at last be exploded.

When this right is established in a nation, there is no fear that it will be employed to its own injury. A nation can have no interest in being wrong.

Though all the constitutions of America are on one general principle, yet no two of them are exactly alike in their component parts, or in the distribution of the powers which they give to the actual governments. Some are more, and others less complex.

In forming a constitution, it is first necessary to consider what are the ends for which government is necessary? Secondly, what are the best means, and the least expensive, for accomplishing those ends?

Government is nothing more than a national association; and the object of this association is the good of all, as well individually as collectively. Every man wishes to pursue his occupation, and to enjoy the fruits of his labours, and the produce of his property in peace and safety, and with the least possible expence. When these things are accomplished, all the objects for which government ought to be established are answered.

It has been customary to consider government under three distinct general heads. The legislative, the executive, and the judicial.

But if we permit our judgment to act unincumbered by the habit of multiplied terms, we can perceive no more than two divisions of power, of which civil government is composed, namely, that of legislating or enacting laws, and that of executing or administering them. Every thing, therefore, appertaining to civil government, classes itself under one or other of these two divisions.

So far as regards the execution of the laws, that which is called the judicial power, is strictly and properly the executive power of every country. It is that power to which every individual has appeal, and which causes the laws to be executed; neither have we any other clear idea with respect to the official execution of the laws. In England, and also in America and France, this power begins with the magistrate, and proceeds up through all the courts of judicature.

I leave to courtiers to explain what is meant by calling monarchy the executive power. It is merely a name in which acts of government are done; and any other, or none at all, would answer the same purpose. Laws have neither more nor less authority on this account. It must be from the justness of their principles, and the interest which a nation feels therein, that they derive support; if they require any other than this, it is a sign that something in the system of government is imperfect. Laws difficult to be executed cannot be generally good.

With respect to the organization of the *legislative power,* different modes have been adopted in different countries. In America it is generally composed of two houses. In France it consists but of one, but in both countries it is wholly by representation.

The case is, that mankind (from the long tyranny of assumed power) have had so few opportunities of making the necessary trials on modes and principles of government, in order to discover the best, *that government is but now beginning to be known,* and experience is yet wanting to determine many particulars.

The objections against two houses are, first, that there is an inconsistency in any part of a whole legislature, coming to a final determination by vote on any matter, whilst *that matter,* with respect to *that whole,* is yet only in a train of deliberation, and consequently open to new illustrations.

Secondly, That by taking the vote on each, as a separate body, it always admits of the possibility, and is often the case in practice, that the minority governs the majority, and that, in some instances, to a degree of great inconsistency.

Thirdly, That two houses arbitrarily checking or controuling each other is inconsistent; because it cannot be proved, on the principles of just representation, that either should be wiser or better than the other. They may check in the wrong as well as in the right, und therefore, to give the power where we cannot give the wisdom to use it, nor be assured of its being rightly used, renders the hazard at least equal to the precaution[6].

6. With respect to the two houses, of which the English Parliament is composed, they appear to be effectually influenced into one, and, as a legislature, to have no temper of its own. The minister, whoever he at any time may be, touches it as with an opium wand, and it sleeps obedience.

But if we look at the distinct abilities of the two houses, the difference will appear so great, as to shew the inconsistency of placing power where there can be no certainty of the judgment to use it. Wretched as the state of representation is in England, it is manhood compared with what is called the house of Lords; and so little is this nicknamed house regarded, that the people scarcely inquire at any time what it is doing. It appears also to be most under influence, and the furthest removed from the general interest of the nation. In the debate on engaging in the Russian and Turkish war, the majority in the house of peers in favour of it was upwards of ninety, when in the other house, which is more than double its numbers, the majority was sixty-three.

The proceedings, on Mr. Fox's bill, respecting the rights of juries, merits also to be noticed. The persons called the peers were not the objects of that bill. They are already in possession of more privileges than that bill gave to others. They are their own jury, and if any of that house were prosecuted for a libel, he would not suffer,

The objection against a single house is, that it is always in a condition of committing itself too soon. – But it should at the same time be remembered, that when there is a constitution which defines the power, and establishes the principles within which a legislature shall act, there is already a more effectual check provided, and more powerfully operating, than any other check can be. For example,

Were a bill to be brought into any of the American legislatures, similar to that which was passed into an act by the English parliament, at the commencement of George the First, to extend the duration of the assemblies to a longer period than they now sit, the check is in the constitution, which in effect says, *Thus far shalt thou go and no further.*

But in order to remove the objection against a single house, (that of acting with too quick an impulse,) and at the same time to avoid the inconsistencies, in some cases absurdities, arising from two houses, the following method has been proposed as an improvement upon both.

First, To have but one representation.

Secondly, To divide that representation, by lot, into two or three parts.

Thirdly, That every proposed bill, shall be first debated in those parts by succession, that they may become the hearers of each other, but without taking any vote. After which the whole representation to assemble for a general debate and determination by vote.

To this proposed improvement has been added another, for the purpose of keeping the representation in a state of constant renovation; which is, that one-third of the representation of each county, shall go out at the expiration of one year, and the number be replaced by new elections. – Another third at the expiration of the second year replaced in like manner, and every third year to be a general election[7].

But in whatever manner the separate parts of a constitution may be arranged, there is *one* general principle that distinguishes freedom from slavery, which is, that all *hereditary government over a people is to them a species of slavery, and representative government is freedom.*

Considering government in the only light in which it should be considered, that of a NATIONAL ASSOCIATION; it ought to be so constructed

---

even upon conviction, for the first offence. Such inequality in laws ought not to exist in any country. The French constitution says, That *the law is the same to every individual, whether to protect or to punish. All are equal in its sight.*

7. As to the state of representation in England, it is too absurd to be reasoned upon. Almost all the represented parts are decreasing in population, and the unrepresented parts are increasing. A general convention of the nation is necessary to take the whole state of its government into consideration.

as not to be disordered by any accident happening among the parts; and, therefore, no extraordinary power, capable of producing such an effect, should be lodged in the hands of any individual. The death, sickness, absence, or defection, of any one individual in a government, ought to be a matter of no more consequence, with respect to the nation, than if the same circumstance had taken place in a member of the English Parliament, or the French National Assembly.

Scarcely any thing presents a more degrading character of national greatness, than its being thrown into confusion by any thing happening to, or acted by, an individual; and the ridiculousness of the scene is often increased by the natural insignificance of the person by whom it is occasioned. Were a government so constructed, that it could not go on unless a goose or a gander were present in the senate, the difficulties would be just as great and as real on the flight or sickness of the goose, or the gander, as if it were called a King. We laugh at individuals for the silly difficulties they make to themselves, without perceiving, that the greatest of all ridiculous things are acted in governments[8].

All the constitutions of America are on a plan that excludes the childish embarrassments which occur in monarchical countries. No suspension of government can there take place for a moment, from any circumstance whatever. The system of representation provides for every thing, and is the only system in which nations and governments can always appear in their proper character.

As extraordinary power, ought not to be lodged in the hands of any individual, so ought there to be no appropriations of public money to any person, beyond what his services in a state may be worth. It signifies not whether a man be called a president, a king, an emperor, a senator, or by any

8. It is related, that in the canton of Berne, in Swisserland, it had been customary, from time immemorial, to keep a bear at the public expence, and the people had been taught to believe, that if they had not a bear they should all be undone. It happened some years ago, that the bear, then in being, was taken sick and died too suddenly to have his place immediately supplied with another. During this interregnum the people discovered, that the corn grew, and the vintage flourished, and the sun and moon continued to rise and set, and every thing went on the same as before, and, taking courage from these circumstances, they resolved not to keep any more bears; for, said they, "a bear is a very voracious, expensive animal, and we were obliged to pull out his claws, lest he should hurt the citizens."

The story of the bear of Berne was related in some of the French news-papers, at the time of the flight of Louis XVI. and the application of it to monarchy could not be mistaken in France; but it seems, that the aristocracy of Berne applied it to themselves, and have since prohibited the reading of French news-papers.

other name, which propriety or folly may devise, or arrogance assume, it is only a certain service he can perform in the state; and the service of any such individual in the rotine of office, whether such office be called monarchical, presidential, senatorial, or by any other name or title, can never exceed the value of ten thousand pounds a year. All the great services that are done in the world are performed by volunteer characters, who accept nothing for them; but the rotine of office is always regulated to such a general standard of abilities as to be within the compass of numbers in every country to perform, and therefore cannot merit very extraordinary recompence. *Government,* says Swift, *is a plain thing, and fitted to the capacity of many heads.*

It is inhuman to talk of a million sterling a year, paid out of the public taxes of any country, for the support of any individual, whilst thousands who are forced to contribute thereto, are pining with want, and struggling with misery. Government does not consist in a contrast between prisons and palaces, between poverty and pomp; it is not instituted to rob the needy of his mite, and increase the wretchedness of the wretched. – But of this part of the subject I shall speak hereafter, and confine myself at present to political observations.

When extraordinary power and extraordinary pay are allotted to any individual in a government, he becomes the center, round which every kind of corruption generates and forms. Give to any man a million a year, and add thereto the power of creating and disposing of places, at the expence of a country, and the liberties of that country are no longer secure. What is called the splendor of a throne is no other than the corruption of the state. It is made up of a band of parasites, living in luxurious indolence, out of the public taxes.

When once such a vicious system is established it becomes the guard and protection of all inferior abuses. The man who is in the receipt of a million a year is the last person to promote a spirit of reform, lest, in the event, it should reach to himself. It is always his interest to defend inferior abuses, as so many out-works to protect the citadel; and in this species of political fortification, all the parts have such a common dependence that it is never to be expected they will attack each other[9].

---

9. It is scarcely possible to touch on any subject, that will not suggest an allusion to some corruption in governments. The simile of *"fortifications,"* unfortunately involves with it a circumstance, which is directly in point with the matter above alluded to.

Among the numerous instances of abuse which have been acted or protected by governments, ancient or modern, there is not a greater than that of quartering a man and his heirs upon the public, to be maintained at its expence.

Monarchy would not have continued so many ages in the world, had it not been for the abuses it protects. It is the master-fraud, which shelters all others. By admitting a participation of the spoil, it makes itself friends; and when it ceases to do this, it will cease to be the idol of courtiers.

As the principle on which constitutions are now formed rejects all hereditary pretensions to government, it also rejects all that catalogue of assumptions known by the name of prerogatives.

If there is any government where prerogatives might with apparent safety be entrusted to any individual, it is in the fœderal government of America. The President of the United States of America is elected only for four years. He is not only responsible in the general sense of the word, but a particular mode is laid down in the constitution for trying him. He cannot be elected under thirty-five years of age; and he must be a native of the country.

In a comparison of these cases with the government of England, the difference when applied to the latter amounts to an absurdity. In England the person who exercises prerogative is often a foreigner; always half a foreigner, and always married to a foreigner. He is never in full natural or political connection with the country, is not responsible for any thing, and becomes of age at eighteen years; yet such a person is permitted to form foreign alliances, without even the knowledge of the nation, and to make war and peace without its consent.

But this is not all. Though such a person cannot dispose of the government, in the manner of a testator, he dictates the marriage connections, which, in effect, accomplishes a great part of the same end. He cannot directly bequeath half the government to Prussia, but he can form a marriage partnership that will produce almost the same thing. Under such circumstances, it is happy for England that she is not situated on the continent,

---

Humanity dictates a provision for the poor; but by what right, moral or political, does any government assume to say, that the person called the Duke of Richmond, shall be maintained by the public? Yet, if common report is true, not a beggar in London can purchase his wretched pittance of coal, without paying towards the civil list of the Duke of Richmond. Were the whole produce of this imposition but a shilling a year, the iniquitous principle would be still the same; but when it amounts, as it is said to do, to not less than twenty thousand pounds *per ann.* the enormity is too serious to be permitted to remain – This is one of the effects of monarchy and aristocracy.

In stating this case, I am led by no personal dislike. Though I think it mean in any man to live upon the public, the vice originates in the government; and so general is it become, that whether the parties are in the ministry or in the opposition, it makes no difference: they are sure of the guarantee of each other.

or she might, like Holland, fall under the dictatorship of Prussia. Holland, by marriage, is as effectually governed by Prussia, as if the old tyranny of bequeathing the government had been the means.

The presidency in America, (or, as it is sometimes called, the executive,) is the only office from which a foreigner is excluded, and in England it is the only one to which he is admitted. A foreigner cannot be a member of parliament, but he may be what is called a king. If there is any reason for excluding foreigners, it ought to be from those offices where mischief can most be acted, and where, by uniting every bias of interest and attachment, the trust is best secured.

But as nations proceed in the great business of forming constitutions, they will examine with more precision into the nature and business of that department which is called the executive. What the legislative and judicial departments are, every one can see; but with respect to what, in Europe, is called the executive, as distinct from those two, it is either a political superfluity or a chaos of unknown things.

Some kind of official department, to which reports shall be made from the different parts of a nation, or from abroad, to be laid before the national representatives, is all that is necessary; but there is no consistency in calling this the executive; neither can it be considered in any other light than as inferior to the legislative. The sovereign authority in any country is the power of making laws, and every thing else is an official department.

Next to the arrangement of the principles and the organization of the several parts of a constitution, is the provision to be made for the support of the persons to whom the nation shall confide the administration of the constitutional powers.

A nation can have no right to the time and services of any person at his own expence, whom it may chuse to employ or entrust in any department whatever; neither can any reason be given for making provision for the support of any one part of a government and not for the other.

But, admitting that the honour of being entrusted with any part of a government is to be considered a sufficient reward, it ought to be so to every person alike. If the members of the legislature of any country are to serve at their own expence, that which is called the executive, whether monarchical, or by any other name, ought to serve in like manner. It is inconsistent to pay the one, and accept the service of the other gratis.

In America, every department in the government is decently provided for; but no one is extravagantly paid. Every member of Congress, and of the assemblies, is allowed a sufficiency for his expences. Whereas in England, a most prodigal provision is made for the support of one part of the government, and none for the other, the consequence of which is, that the one is furnished with the means of corruption, and the other is put into the condition of being corrupted. Less than a fourth part of such expence, applied as it is in America, would remedy a great part of the corruption.

Another reform in the American constitutions, is the exploding all oaths of personality. The oath of allegiance in America is to the nation only. The putting any individual as a figure for a nation is improper. The happiness of a nation is the superior object, and therefore the intention of an oath of allegiance ought not to be obscured by being figuratively taken, to, or in the name of, any person. The oath, called the civic oath, in France, viz. the "*nation, the law, and the king*," is improper. If taken at all, it ought to be as in America, to the nation only. The law may or may not be good; but, in this place, it can have no other meaning, than as being conducive to the happiness of the nation, and therefore is included in it. The remainder of the oath is improper, on the ground, that all personal oaths ought to be abolished. They are the remains of tyranny on one part, and slavery on the other, and the name of the CREATOR ought not to be introduced to witness the degradation of his creation; or if taken, as is already mentioned, as figurative of the nation, it is in this place redundant. But whatever apology may be made for oaths at the first establishment of a government, they ought not to be permitted afterwards. If a government requires the support of oaths, it is a sign that it is not worth supporting, and ought not to be supported. Make government what it ought to be, and it will support itself.

To conclude this part of the subject: – One of the greatest improvements that has been made for the perpetual security and progress of constitutional liberty, is the provision which the new constitutions make for occasionally revising, altering, and amending them.

The principle upon which Mr. Burke formed his political creed, that "*of binding and controuling posterity to the end of time, and of renouncing and abdicating the rights of all posterity for ever,*" is now become too detestable to be made a subject of debate; and, therefore, I pass it over with no other notice than exposing it.

Government is but now beginning to be known. Hitherto it has been the mere exercise of power, which forbad all effectual enquiry into rights, and grounded itself wholly on possession. While the enemy of liberty was its judge, the progress of its principles must have been small indeed.

The constitutions of America, and also that of France, have either affixed a period for their revision, or laid down the mode by which improvements shall be made. It is perhaps impossible to establish any thing that combines principles with opinions and practice, which the progress of circumstances, through a length of years, will not in some measure derange, or render inconsistent; and, therefore, to prevent inconveniences accumulating, till they discourage reformations or provoke revolutions, it is best to provide the means of regulating them as they occur. The Rights of Man are the rights of all generations of men, and cannot be monopolized by any. That which is worth following, will be followed for the sake of its worth; and it is in this that its security lies, and not in any conditions with which it may be encumbered. When a man leaves property to his heirs, he does not connect it with an obligation that they shall accept it. Why then should we do otherwise with respect to constitutions?

The best constitution that could now be devised, consistent with the condition of the present moment, may be far short of that excellence which a few years may afford. There is a morning of reason rising upon man on the subject of government, that has not appeared before. As the barbarism of the present old governments expires, the moral condition of nations with respect to each other will be changed. Man will not be brought up with the savage idea of considering his species as his enemy, because the accident of birth gave the individuals existence in countries distinguished by different names; and as constitutions have always some relation to external as well as to domestic circumstances, the means of benefiting by every change, foreign or domestic, should be a part of every constitution.

We already see an alteration in the national disposition of England and France towards each other, which, when we look back to only a few years, is itself a revolution. Who could have foreseen, or who would have believed, that a French National Assembly would ever have been a popular toast in England, or that a friendly alliance of the two nations should become the wish of either. It shews, that man, were he not corrupted by governments, is naturally the friend of man, and that human nature is not of itself vicious. That spirit of jealousy and ferocity, which the governments of the two countries inspired, and which they rendered subservient to the purpose of taxation, is now yielding to the dictates of reason, interest, and humanity. The trade of courts is beginning to be understood, and the affectation of mystery, with all the artificial sorcery by which they imposed upon mankind, is on the decline. It has received its death-wound; and though it may linger, it will expire.

Government ought to be as much open to improvement as any thing which appertains to man, instead of which it has been monopolized from age to age, by the most ignorant and vicious of the human race. Need we any other proof of their wretched management, than the excess of debts and taxes with which every nation groans, and the quarrels into which they have precipitated the world?

Just emerging from such a barbarous condition, it is too soon to determine to what extent of improvement government may yet be carried. For what we can foresee, all Europe may form but one great republic, and man be free of the whole.

CHAP. V.

Ways and Means of improving the condition of Europe, interspersed with Miscellaneous Observations.

IN contemplating a subject that embraces with equatorial magnitude the whole region of humanity, it is impossible to confine the pursuit in one single direction. It takes ground on every character and condition that appertains to man, and blends the individual, the nation, and the world.

From a small spark, kindled in America, a flame has arisen, not to be extinguished. Without consuming, like the *Ultima Ratio Regum*, it winds its progress from nation to nation, and conquers by a silent operation. Man finds himself changed, he scarcely perceives how. He acquires a knowledge of his rights by attending justly to his interest, and discovers in the event that the strength and powers of despotism consist wholly in the fear of resisting it, and that, in order *"to be free, it is sufficient that he wills it."*

Having in all the preceding parts of this work endeavoured to establish a system of principles as a basis, on which governments ought to be erected; I shall proceed in this, to the ways and means of rendering them into practice. But in order to introduce this part of the subject with more propriety, and stronger effect, some preliminary observations, deducible from, or connected with, those principles, are necessary.

Whatever the form or constitution of government may be, it ought to have no other object than the *general* happiness. When, instead of this, it operates to create and encrease wretchedness in any of the parts of society, it is on a wrong system, and reformation is necessary.

Customary language has classed the condition of man under the two descriptions of civilized and uncivilized life. To the one it has ascribed felicity and affluence; to the other hardship and want. But, however, our imagination may be impressed by painting and comparison, it is nevertheless true, that a great portion of mankind, in what are called civilized countries, are in a state of poverty and wretchedness, far below the condition of an Indian. I speak not of one country, but of all. It is so in England, it is so all over Europe. Let us enquire into the cause.

It lies not in any natural defect in the principles of civilization, but in preventing those principles having an universal operation; the consequence of which is, a perpetual system of war and expence, that drains the country, and defeats the general felicity of which civilization is capable.

All the European governments (France now excepted) are constructed not on the principle of universal civilization, but on the reverse of it. So far as those governments relate to each other, they are in the same condition as we conceive of savage uncivilized life; they put themselves beyond the law as well of GOD as of man, and are, with respect to principle and reciprocal conduct, like so many individuals in a state of nature.

The inhabitants of every country, under the civilization of laws, easily civilize together, but governments being yet in an uncivilized state, and almost continually at war, they pervert the abundance which civilized life produces to carry on the uncivilized part to a greater extent. By thus engrafting the barbarism of government upon the internal civilization of a country, it draws from the latter, and more especially from the poor, a great portion of those earnings, which should be applied to their own subsistence and comfort.—Apart from all reflections of morality and philosophy, it is a melancholy fact, that more than one-fourth of the labour of mankind is annually consumed by this barbarous system.

What has served to continue this evil, is the pecuniary advantage, which all the governments of Europe have found in keeping up this state of uncivilization. It affords to them pretences for power, and revenue, for which there would be neither occasion nor apology, if the circle of civilization were rendered compleat. Civil government alone, or the government of laws, is not productive of pretences for many taxes; it operates at home, directly under the eye of the country, and precludes the possibility of much imposition. But when the scene is laid in the uncivilized contention of governments, the field of pretences is enlarged, and the country, being no longer a judge, is open to every imposition, which governments please to act.

Not a thirtieth, scarcely a fortieth, part of the taxes which are raised in England are either occasioned by, or applied to, the purposes of civil gov-

ernment. It is not difficult to see, that the whole which the actual government does in this respect, is to enact laws, and that the country administers
and executes them, at its own expence, by means of magistrates, juries, sessions, and assize, over and above the taxes which it pays.

In this view of the case, we have two distinct characters of government;
the one the civil government, or the government of laws, which operates at
home, the other the court or cabinet government, which operates abroad,
on the rude plan of uncivilized life; the one attended with little charge,
the other with boundless extravagance; and so distinct are the two, that
if the latter were to sink, as it were by a sudden opening of the earth, and
totally disappear, the former would not be deranged. It would still proceed,
because it is the common interest of the nation that it should, and all the
means are in practice.

Revolutions, then, have for their object, a change in the moral condition of governments, and with this change the burthen of public taxes will
lessen, and civilization will be left to the enjoyment of that abundance, of
which it is now deprived.

In contemplating the whole of this subject, I extend my views into the
department of commerce. In all my publications, where the matter would
admit, I have been an advocate for commerce, because I am a friend to its
effects. It is a pacific system, operating to cordialize mankind, by rendering
nations, as well as individuals, useful to each other. As to mere theoretical
reformation, I have never preached it up. The most effectual process is that
of improving the condition of man by means of his interest; and it is on this
ground that I take my stand.

If commerce were permitted to act to the universal extent it is capable,
it would extirpate the system of war, and produce a revolution in the uncivilized state of governments. The invention of commerce has arisen since
those governments began, and is the greatest approach towards universal
civilization, that has yet been made by any means not immediately flowing
from moral principles.

Whatever has a tendency to promote the civil intercourse of nations, by
an exchange of benefits, is a subject as worthy of philosophy as of politics.
Commerce is no other than the traffic of two individuals, multiplied on a
scale of numbers; and by the same rule that nature intended the intercourse
of two, she intended that of all. For this purpose she has distributed the
materials of manufactures and commerce, in various and distant parts of a
nation and of the world; and as they cannot be procured by war so cheaply
or so commodiously as by commerce, she has rendered the latter the means
of extirpating the former.

As the two are nearly the opposites of each other, consequently, the uncivilized state of European governments is injurious to commerce. Every kind of destruction or embarrassment serves to lessen the quantity, and it matters but little in what part of the commercial world the reduction begins. Like blood, it cannot be taken from any of the parts, without being taken from the whole mass in circulation, and all partake of the loss. When the ability in any nation to buy is destroyed, it equally involves the seller. Could the government of England destroy the commerce of all other nations, she would most effectually ruin her own.

It is possible that a nation may be the carrier for the world, but she cannot be the merchant. She cannot be the seller and the buyer of her own merchandize. The ability to buy must reside out of herself; and, therefore, the prosperity of any commercial nation is regulated by the prosperity of the rest. If they are poor she cannot be rich, and her condition, be it what it may, is an index of the height of the commercial tide in other nations.

That the principles of commerce, and its universal operation may be understood, without understanding the practice, is a position that reason will not deny; and it is on this ground only that I argue the subject. It is one thing in the counting-house, in the world it is another. With respect to its operation it must necessarily be contemplated as a reciprocal thing; that only one half its powers resides within the nation, and that the whole is as effectually destroyed by destroying the half that resides without, as if the destruction had been committed on that which is within; for neither can act without the other.

When in the last, as well as in former wars, the commerce of England sunk, it was because the general quantity was lessened every where; and it now rises, because commerce is in a rising state in every nation. If England, at this day, imports and exports more than at any former period, the nations with which she trades must necessarily do the same; her imports are their exports, and *vice versa.*

There can be no such thing as a nation flourishing alone in commerce; she can only participate; and the destruction of it in any part must necessarily affect all. When, therefore, governments are at war, the attack is made upon the common stock of commerce, and the consequence is the same as if each had attacked his own.

The present increase of commerce is not to be attributed to ministers, or to any political contrivances, but to its own natural operations in consequence of peace. The regular markets had been destroyed, the channels of trade broken up, the high road of the seas infested with robbers of every nation, and the attention of the world called to other objects. Those interruptions have ceased, and peace has restored the deranged condition of things to their proper order[10].

It is worth remarking, that every nation reckons the balance of trade in its own favour; and therefore something must be irregular in the common ideas upon this subject.

The fact, however, is true, according to what is called a balance; and it is from this cause that commerce is universally supported. Every nation feels the advantage, or it would abandon the practice: but the deception lies in the mode of making up the accounts, and in attributing what are called profits to a wrong cause.

Mr. Pitt has sometimes amused himself, by shewing what he called a balance of trade from the custom-house books. This mode of calculation, not only affords no rule that is true, but one that is false.

In the first place, Every cargo that departs from the custom-house, appears on the books as an export; and, according to the custom-house balance, the losses at sea, and by foreign failures, are all reckoned on the side of profit, because they appear as exports.

Secondly, Because the importation by the smuggling trade does not appear on the custom house books, to arrange against the exports.

No balance, therefore, as applying to superior advantages, can be drawn from those documents; and if we examine the natural operation of commerce, the idea is fallacious; and if true, would soon be injurious. The great support of commerce consists in the balance being a level of benefits among all nations.

Two merchants of different nations trading together, will both become rich, and each makes the balance in his own favour; consequently, they do not get rich out of each other; and it is the same with respect to the nations in which they reside. The case must be, that each nation must get rich out of its own means, and increases that riches by something which it procures from another in exchange.

If a merchant in England sends an article of English manufacture abroad, which costs him a shilling at home, and imports something which sells for two, he makes a balance of one shilling in his own favour: but this is not

10. In America, the increase of commerce is greater in proportion than in England. It is, at this time, at least one half more than at any period prior to the revolution. The greatest number of vessels cleared out of the port of Philadelphia, before the commencement of the war, was between eight and nine hundred. In the year 1788, the number was upwards of twelve hundred. As the state of Pennsylvania is estimated as an eighth part of the United States in population, the whole number of vessels must now be nearly ten thousand.

gained out of the foreign nation or the foreign merchant, for he also does the same by the article he receives, and neither has a balance of advantage upon the other. The original value of the two articles in their proper countries were but two shillings; but by changing their places, they acquire a new idea of value, equal to double what they had at first, and that increased value is equally divided.

There is no otherwise a balance on foreign than on domestic commerce. The merchants of London and Newcastle trade on the same principles, as if they resided in different nations, and make their balances in the same manner: yet London does not get rich out of Newcastle, any more than Newcastle out of London: but coals, the merchandize of Newcastle, have an additional value at London, and London merchandize has the same at Newcastle.

Though the principle of all commerce is the same, the domestic, in a national view, is the part the most beneficial; because the whole of the advantages, on both sides, rests within the nation; whereas, in foreign commerce, it is only a participation of one half.

The most unprofitable of all commerce is that connected with foreign dominion. To a few individuals it may be beneficial, merely because it is commerce; but to the nation it is a loss. The expence of maintaining dominion more than absorbs the profits of any trade. It does not increase the general quantity in the world, but operates to lessen it; and as a greater mass would be afloat by relinquishing dominion, the participation without the expence would be more valuable than a greater quantity with it.

But it is impossible to engross commerce by dominion; and therefore it is still more fallacious. It cannot exist in confined channels, and necessarily breaks out by regular or irregular means, that defeat the attempt; and to succeed would be still worse. France, since the revolution, has been more than indifferent as to foreign possessions; and other nations will become the same, when they investigate the subject with respect to commerce.

To the expence of dominion is to be added that of navies, and when the amount of the two are subtracted from the profits of commerce, it will appear, that what is called the balance of trade, even admitting it to exist, is not enjoyed by the nation, but absorbed by the government.

The idea of having navies for the protection of commerce is delusive. It is putting the means of destruction for the means of protection. Commerce needs no other protection than the reciprocal interest which every nation feels in supporting it—it is common stock—it exists by a balance of advantages to all; and the only interruption it meets, is from the present uncivilized state of governments, and which it is its common interest to reform[11].

Quitting this subject, I now proceed to other matters. – As it is necessary to include England in the prospect of a general reformation, it is proper to enquire into the defects of its government. It is only by each nation reforming its own, that the whole can be improved, and the full benefit of reformation enjoyed. Only partial advantages can flow from partial reforms.

France and England are the only two countries in Europe where a reformation in government could have successfully begun. The one secure by the ocean, and the other by the immensity of its internal strength, could defy the malignancy of foreign despotism. But it is with revolutions as with commerce, the advantages increase by their becoming general, and double to either what each would receive alone.

As a new system is now opening to the view of the world, the European courts are plotting to counteract it. Alliances, contrary to all former systems, are agitating, and a common interest of courts is forming against the common interest of man. This combination draws a line that runs throughout Europe, and presents a cause so entirely new, as to exclude all calculations from former circumstances. While despotism warred with despotism, man had no interest in the contest; but in a cause that unites the soldier with the citizen, and nation with nation, the despotism of courts, though it feels the danger, and meditates revenge, is afraid to strike.

No question has arisen within the records of history that pressed with the importance of the present. It is not whether this or that party shall be in or out, or whig or tory, or high or low shall prevail; but whether man shall inherit his rights, and universal civilization take place? Whether the fruits of his labours shall be enjoyed by himself, or consumed by the profligacy of governments? Whether robbery shall be banished from courts, and wretchedness from countries?

When, in countries that are called civilized, we see age going to the workhouse and youth to the gallows, something must be wrong in the system of government. It would seem, by the exterior appearance of such countries, that all was happiness; but there lies hidden from the eye of common

11. When I saw Mr. Pitt's mode of estimating the balance of trade, in one of his parliamentary speeches, he appeared to me to know nothing of the nature and interest of commerce; and no man has more wantonly tortured it than himself. During a period of peace, it has been havocked with the calamities of war. Three times has it been thrown into stagnation, and the vessels unmanned by impressing, within less than four years of peace.

observation, a mass of wretchedness that has scarcely any other chance, than to expire in poverty or infamy. Its entrance into life is marked with the presage of its fate; and until this is remedied, it is in vain to punish.

Civil government does not consist in executions; but in making that provision for the instruction of youth, and the support of age, as to exclude, as much as possible, profligacy from the one, and despair from the other. Instead of this, the resources of a country are lavished upon kings, upon courts, upon hirelings, imposters, and prostitutes; and even the poor themselves, with all their wants upon them, are compelled to support the fraud that oppresses them.

Why is it, that scarcely any are executed but the poor? The fact is a proof, among other things, of a wretchedness in their condition. Bred up without morals, and cast upon the world without a prospect, they are the exposed sacrifice of vice and legal barbarity. The millions that are superfluously wasted upon governments, are more than sufficient to reform those evils, and to benefit the condition of every man in a nation, not included within the purlieus of a court. This I hope to make appear in the progress of this work.

It is the nature of compassion to associate with misfortune. In taking up this subject I seek no recompence – I fear no consequence. Fortified with that proud integrity, that disdains to triumph or to yield, I will advocate the Rights of Man.

It is to my advantage that I have served an apprenticeship to life. I know the value of moral instruction, and I have seen the danger of the contrary.

At an early period, little more than sixteen years of age, raw and adventurous, and heated with the false heroism of a master[12] who had served in a man of war; I began the carver of my own fortune, and entered on board the Terrible, Privateer, Capt. Death. From this adventure I was happily prevented by the affectionate and moral remonstrance of a good father, who, from his own habits of life, being of the Quaker profession, must begin to look upon me as lost. But the impression, much as it effected at the time, began to wear away, and I entered afterwards in the King of Prussia Privateer, Capt. Mendez, and went with her to sea. Yet, from such a beginning, and with all the inconvenience of early life against me, I am proud to say, that with a perseverance undismayed by difficulties, a disinterestedness that compelled respect, I have not only contributed to raise a new empire in the world, founded on a new system of government, but I have arrived at

12. Rev. William Knowles, master of the grammar school of Thetford, in Norfolk.

an eminence in political literature, the most difficult of all lines to succeed and excel in, which aristocracy, with all its aids, has not been able to reach or to rival.

Knowing my own heart, and feeling myself, as I now do, superior to all the skirmish of party, the inveteracy of interested or mistaken opponents, I answer not to falsehood or abuse, but proceed to the defects of the English government[13].

13. Politics and self-interest have been so uniformly connected, that the world, from being so often deceived, has a right to be suspicious of public characters: but with regard to myself, I am perfectly easy on this head. I did not, at my first setting out in public life, nearly seventeen years ago, turn my thoughts to subjects of government from motives of interest; and my conduct from that moment to this, proves the fact. I saw an opportunity, in which I thought I could do some good, and I followed exactly what my heart dictated. I neither read books, nor studied other people's opinions. I thought for myself. The case was this:

During the suspension of the old governments in America, both prior to, and at the breaking out of hostilities, I was struck with the order and decorum with which every thing was conducted, and impressed with the idea, that a little more than what society naturally performed, was all the government that was necessary; and that monarchy and aristocracy were frauds and impositions upon mankind. On these principles I published the pamphlet Common Sense. The success it met with was beyond any thing since the invention of printing. I gave the copy right up to every state in the union, and the demand ran to not less than one hundred thousand cop ies. I continued the subject in the same manner, under the title of the Crisis, till the complete establishment of the revolution.

After the declaration of Independence, Congress unanimously, and unknown to me, appointed me secretary in the foreign department. This was agreeable to me, because it gave me the opportunity of seeing into the abilities of foreign courts, and their manner of doing business. But a misunderstanding arising between congress and me, respecting one of their commissioners, then in Europe, Mr. Silas Deane, I resigned the office, and declined, at the same time, the pecuniary offers made me by the ministers of France and Spain, M. Gerard and Don Juan Mirralles.

I had by this time so completely gained the ear and confidence of America, and my own independence was become so visible as to give me a range in political writing, beyond, perhaps, what any man ever possessed in any country; and what is more extraordinary, I held it undiminished to the end of the war, and enjoy it in the same manner to the present moment. As my object was not myself, I set out with the determination, and happily with the disposition, of not being moved by praise or censure, friendship or calumny, nor of being drawn from my purpose by any personal altercation; and the man who cannot do this, is not fit for a public character.

When the war ended, I went from Philadelphia to Borden-Town, on the east bank of the Delaware, where I have a small place. Congress was at this time at Prince-Town, fifteen miles distant; and General Washington had taken his headquarters at Rocky-Hill, within the neighbourhood of Congress, for the purpose of resigning up his commission, (the object for which he accepted it being accomplished,) and of

I begin with charters and corporations.

It is a perversion of terms to say, that a charter gives rights. It operates by a contrary effect, that of taking rights away. Rights are inherently in all the inhabitants; but charters, by annulling those rights in the majority, leave the right by exclusion in the hands of a few. If charters were constructed so as to express in direct terms, *"that every inhabitant, who is not a member of*

---

retiring to private life. While he was on this businss, he wrote me the letter which I here subjoin.

Rocky-Hill, Sept. 10, 1783.

I have learned since I have been at this place, that you are at Borden-Town. Whether for the sake of retirement or œconomy, I know not. Be it for either, for both, or whatever it may, if you will come to this place, and partake with me, I shall be exceedingly happy to see you at it.

Your presence may remind Congress of your past services to this country; and if it is in my power to impress them, command my best exertions with freedom, as they will be rendered chearfully by one, who entertains a lively sense of the importance of your works, and who, with much pleasure, subscribes himself,

Your sincere friend,

G. WASHINGTON.

During the war, in the latter end of the year 1780, I formed to myself a design of coming over to England; and communicated it to General Greene, who was then in Philadelphia, on his route to the southward, General Washington being then at too great a distance to communicate with immediately. I was strongly impressed with the idea, that if I could get over to England, without being known, and only remain in safety till I could get out a publication, that I could open the eyes of the country with respect to the madness and stupidity of its government. I saw that the parties in parliament had pitted themselves as far as they could go, and could make no new impressions on each other. General Greene entered fully into my views; but the affair of Arnold and Andrè happening just after, he changed his mind, and, under strong apprehensions for my safety, wrote very pressingly to me from Anapolis, in Maryland, to give up the design, which, with some reluctance, I did. Soon after this I accompanied Col. Lawrens, son of Mr. Lawrens, who was then in the Tower, to France, on business from Congress. We landed at L'Orient; and while I remained there, he being gone forward, a circumstance occurred, that renewed my former design. An English packet from Falmouth to New-York, with the government dispatches on board, was brought into L'Orient. That a packet should be taken, is no extraordinary thing; but that the dispatches should be taken with it, will scarcely be credited, as they are always slung at the cabin window, in a bag loaded with cannon-ball, and ready to be sunk at a moment. The fact, however, is as I have stated it, for the dispatches came into my hands, and I read them. The capture, as I was informed, succeeded by the following stratagem:–The captain of the Madame privateer, who spoke English, on coming up with the packet, passed himself for the captain of an English frigate, and invited the captain of the packet on board, which, when done, he sent some of his own hands back, and secured the mail. But be the circumstance *a corporation, shall not exercise the right of voting,"* such charters would, in the face, be charters, not of rights, but of exclusion. The effect is the same under the form they now stand; and the only persons on whom they operate, are the persons whom they exclude. Those whose rights are guaranteed, by not being taken away, exercise no other rights, than as members of the community they are entitled to without a charter; and, therefore, all charters have no other than an indirect negative operation. They do not give rights to A, but they make a difference in favour of A by taking away the right of B, and consequently are instruments of injustice.

But charters and corporations have a more extensive evil effect, than what relates merely to elections. They are sources of endless contentions in the places where they exist; and they lessen the common rights of national society. A native of England, under the operation of these charters and corporations, cannot be said to be an Englishman in the full sense of the word. He is not free of the nation, in the same manner that a Frenchman is free of France, and an American of America. His rights are circumscribed to the town, and, in some cases, to the parish of his birth; and all other parts, though in his native land, are to him as a foreign country. To acquire a residence in these, he must undergo a local naturalization by purchase, or he is forbidden or expelled the place. This species of feudality is kept up to aggrandize the corporations at the ruin of towns; and the effect is visible.

The generality of corporation towns are in a state of solitary decay, and prevented from further ruin, only by some circumstance in their situation, such as a navigable river, or a plentiful surrounding country. As population is one of the chief sources of wealth, (for without it land itself has no value,) every thing which operates to prevent it must lessen the value of property; and as corporations have not only this tendency, but directly this effect, they cannot but be injurious. If any policy were to be followed, instead of that of general freedom, to every person to settle where he chose,

---

of the capture what it may, I speak with certainty as to the government dispatches. They were sent up to Paris, to Count Vergennes, and when Col. Lawrens and myself returned to America, we took the originals to Congress.

By these dispatches I saw into the stupidity of the English cabinet, far more than I otherwise could have done, and I renewed my former design. But Col. Lawrens was so unwilling to return alone; more especially, as among other matters, we had a charge of upwards of two hundred thousand pounds sterling in money, that I gave into his wishes, and finally gave up my plan. But I am now certain, that if I could have executed it, that it would not have been altogether unsuccessful.

(as in France or America,) it would be more consistent to give encouragement to new comers, than to preclude their admission by exacting premiums from them[14].

The persons most immediately interested in the abolition of corporations, are the inhabitants of the towns where corporations are established. The instances of Manchester, Birmingham, and Sheffield, shew, by contrast, the injury which those Gothic institutions are to property and commerce. A few examples may be found, such as that of London, whose natural and commercial advantage, owing to its situation on the Thames, is capable of bearing up against the political evils of a corporation; but in almost all other cases the fatality is too visible to be doubted or denied.

Though the whole nation is not so directly affected by the depression of property in corporation towns as the inhabitants themselves, it partakes of the consequence. By lessening the value of property, the quantity of national commerce is curtailed. Every man is a customer in proportion to his ability; and as all parts of a nation trade with each other, whatever affects any of the parts, must necessarily communicate to the whole.

As one of the houses of the English parliament is, in a great measure, made up of elections from these corporations; and as it is unnatural that a pure stream should flow from a foul fountain, its vices are but a continuation of the vices of its origin. A man of moral honour and good political principles, cannot submit to the mean drudgery and disgraceful arts, by which such elections are carried. To be a successful candidate, he must be destitute of the qualities that constitute a just legislator: and being thus disciplined to corruption by the mode of entering into parliament, it is not to be expected that the representative should be better than the man.

Mr. Burke, in speaking of the English representation, has advanced as bold a challenge as ever was given in the days of chivalry. "Our representation," says he, "has been found *perfectly adequate to all the purposes* for

14. It is difficult to account for the origin of charter and corporation towns, unless we suppose them to have arisen out of, or been connected with, some species of garrison service, The times in which they began justify this idea. The generality of those towns have been garrisons; and the corporations were charged with the care of the gates of the towns, when no military garrison was present. Their refusing or granting admission to strangers, which has produced the custom of giving, selling, and buying freedom, has more of the nature of garrison authority than civil government. Soldiers are free of all corporations throughout the nation, by the same propriety that every soldier is free of every garrison, and no other persons are. He can follow any employment, with the permission of his officers, in any corporation town throughout the nation.

which a representation of the people can be desired or devised. I defy," continues he, "the enemies of our constitution to shew the contrary."—This declaration from a man, who has been in constant opposition to all the measures of parliament the whole of his political life, a year or two excepted, is most extraordinary; and, comparing him with himself, admits of no other alternative, than that he acted against his judgment as a member, or has declared contrary to it as an author.

But it is not in the representation only that the defects lie, and therefore I proceed in the next place to the aristocracy.

What is called the House of Peers, is constituted on a ground very similar to that, against which there is a law in other cases. It amounts to a combination of persons in one common interest. No reason can be given, why an house of legislation should be composed entirely of men whose occupation consists in letting landed property, than why it should be composed of those who hire, or of brewers, or bakers, or any other separate class of men.

Mr. Burke calls this house, "*the great ground and pillar of security to the landed interest.*" Let us examine this idea.

What pillar of security does the landed interest require more than any other interest in the state, or what right has it to a distinct and separate representation from the general interest of a nation? The only use to be made of this power, (and which it has always made,) is to ward off taxes from itself, and throw the burthen upon such articles of consumption by which itself would be least affected.

That this has been the consequence, (and will always be the consequence of constructing governments on combinations,) is evident with respect to England, from the history of its taxes.

Notwithstanding taxes have encreased and multiplied upon every article of common consumption, the land-tax, which more particularly affects this "pillar," has diminished. In 1788, the amount of the land-tax was 1,950,000£. which is half a million less than it produced almost an hundred years ago[15], notwithstanding the rentals are in many instances doubled since that period.

Before the coming of the Hanoverians, the taxes were divided in nearly equal proportions between the land and articles of consumption, the land bearing rather the largest share: but since that æra, nearly thirteen millions annually of new taxes have been thrown upon consumption. The

15. See Sir John Sinclair's History of the Revenue. The land-tax in 1646 was £ 2,473,499.

consequence of which has been a constant encrease in the number and wretchedness of the poor, and in the amount of the poor-rates. Yet here again the burthen does not fall in equal proportions on the aristocracy with the rest of the community. Their residences, whether in town or country, are not mixed with the habitations of the poor. They live apart from distress, and the expence of relieving it. It is in manufacturing towns and labouring villages that those burthens press the heaviest; in many of which it is one class of poor supporting another.

Several of the most heavy and productive taxes are so contrived, as to give an exemption to this pillar, thus standing in its own defence. The tax upon beer brewed for sale does not affect the aristocracy, who brew their own beer free of this duty. It falls only on those who have not conveniency or ability to brew, and who must purchase it in small quantities. But what will mankind think of the justice of taxation, when they know, that this tax alone, from which the aristocracy are from circumstances exempt, is nearly equal to the whole of the land-tax, being in the year 1788, and it is not less now, 1,666,152£. and with its proportion of the taxes on malt and hops, it exceeds it. – That a single article, thus partially consumed, and that chiefly by the working part, should be subject to a tax, equal to that on the whole rental of a nation, is, perhaps, a fact not to be paralleled in the histories of revenues.

This is one of the consequences resulting from an house of legislation, composed on the ground of a combination of common interest; for whatever their separate politics as to parties may be, in this they are united. Whether a combination acts to raise the price of any article for sale, or the rate of wages; or whether it acts to throw taxes from itself upon another class of the community, the principle and the effect are the same; and if the one be illegal, it will be difficult to shew that the other ought to exist.

It is to no use to say, that taxes are first proposed in the house of commons; for as the other house has always a negative, it can always defend itself; and it would be ridiculous to suppose that its acquiescence in the measures to be proposed were not understood before hand. Besides which, it has obtained so much influence by borough-traffic, and so many of its relations and connections are distributed on both sides of the commons, as to give it, besides an absolute negative in one house, a preponderancy in the other, in all matters of common concern.

It is difficult to discover what is meant by the *landed interest,* if it does not mean a combination of aristocratical land-holders, opposing their own pecuniary interest to that of the farmer, and every branch of trade, commerce, and manufacture. In all other respects it is the only interest that needs no partial protection. It enjoys the general protection of the world.

Every individual, high or low, is interested in the fruits of the earth; men, women, and children, of all ages and degrees, will turn out to assist the farmer, rather than a harvest should not be got in; and they will not act thus by any other property. It is the only one for which the common prayer of mankind is put up, and the only one that can never fail from the want of means. It is the interest, not of the policy, but of the existence of man, and when it ceases he must cease to be.

No other interest in a nation stands on the same united support. Commerce, manufactures, arts, sciences, and every thing else, compared with this, are supported but in parts. Their prosperity or their decay has not the same universal influence. When the vallies laugh and sing, it is not the farmer only, but all creation that rejoices. It is a prosperity that excludes all envy; and this cannot be said of any thing else.

Why then does Mr. Burke talk of his house of peers, as the pillar of the landed interest? Were that pillar to sink into the earth, the same landed property would continue, and the same ploughing, sowing, and reaping would go on. The aristocracy are not the farmers who work the land, and raise the produce, but are the mere consumers of the rent; and when compared with the active world, are the drones, a seraglio of males, who neither collect the honey nor form the hive, but exist only for lazy enjoyment.

Mr. Burke, in his first essay, called aristocracy, "*the Corinthian capital of polished society.*" Towards compleating the figure, he has now added the *pillar*; but still the base is wanting; and whenever a nation chuses to act a Samson, not blind, but bold, down go the temple of Dagon, the Lords and the Philistines.

If a house of legislation is to be composed of men of one class, for the purpose of protecting a distinct interest, all the other interests should have the same. The inequality, as well as the burthen of taxation, arises from admitting it in one case, and not in all. Had there been an house of farmers, there had been no game laws; or an house of merchants and manufacturers, the taxes had neither been so unequal nor so excessive. It is from the power of taxation being in the hands of those who can throw so great a part of it from their own shoulders, that it has raged without a check.

Men of small or moderate estates, are more injured by the taxes being thrown on articles of consumption, than they are eased by warding it from landed property, for the following reasons:

First, They consume more of the productive taxable articles, in proportion to their property, than those of large estates.

Secondly, Their residence is chiefly in towns, and their property in houses; and the encrease of the poor-rates, occasioned by taxes on consumption, is in much greater proportion than the land-tax has been favoured. In Birmingham, the poor-rates are not less than seven shillings in the pound. From this, as is already observed, the aristocracy are in a great measure exempt.

These are but a part of the mischiefs flowing from the wretched scheme of an house of peers.

As a combination, it can always throw a considerable portion of taxes from itself; and as an hereditary house, accountable to nobody, it resembles a rotten borough, whose consent is to be courted by interest. There are but few of its members, who are not in some mode or other participaters, or disposers of the public money. One turns a candle-holder, or a lord in waiting; another a lord of the bed-chamber, a groom of the stole, or any insignificant nominal office, to which a salary is annexed, paid out of the public taxes, and which avoids the direct appearance of corruption. Such situations are derogatory to the character of man; and where they can be submitted to, honour cannot reside.

To all these are to be added the numerous dependants, the long list of younger branches and distant relations, who are to be provided for at the public expence: in short, were an estimation to be made of the charge of aristocracy to a nation, it will be found nearly equal to that of supporting the poor. The Duke of Richmond alone (and there are cases similar to his) takes away as much for himself as would maintain two thousand poor and aged persons. Is it, then, any wonder, that under such a system of government, taxes and rates have multiplied to their present extent?

In stating these matters, I speak an open and disinterested language, dictated by no passion but that of humanity. To me, who have not only refused offers, because I thought them improper, but have declined rewards I might with reputation have accepted, it is no wonder that meanness and imposition appear disgustful. Independence is my happiness, and I view things as they are, without regard to place or person; my country is the world, and my religion is to do good.

Mr. Burke, in speaking of the aristocratical law of primogeniture, says, "it is the standing law of our landed inheritance; and which, without question, has a tendency, and I think," continues he, "a happy tendency, to preserve a character of weight and consequence."

Mr. Burke may call this law what he pleases, but humanity and impartial reflection will denounce it a law of brutal injustice. Were we not accustomed to the daily practice, and did we only hear of it as the law of some distant part of the world, we should conclude that the legislators of such countries had not yet arrived at a state of civilization.

As to its preserving a character of *weight and consequence,* the case appears to me directly the reverse. It is an attaint upon character; a sort of privateering on family property. It may have weight among dependent tenants, but it gives none on a scale of national, and, much less of universal character. Speaking for myself, my parents were not able to give me a shilling, beyond what they gave me in education; and to do this they distressed themselves: yet, I possess more of what is called consequence, in the world, than any one in Mr. Burke's catalogue of aristocrats.

Having thus glanced at some of the defects of the two houses of parliament, I proceed to what is called the crown upon which I shall be very concise.

It signifies a nominal office of a million sterling a year, the business of which consists in receiving the money. Whether the person be wise or foolish, sane or insane, a native or a foreigner, matters not. Every ministry acts upon the same idea that Mr. Burke writes, namely, that the people must be hood-winked, and held in superstitious ignorance by some bugbear or other, and what is called the crown answers this purpose, and therefore it answers all the purposes to be expected from it. This is more than can be said of the other two branches.

The hazard to which this office is exposed in all countries, is not from any thing that can happen to the man, but from what may happen to the nation the danger of its coming to its senses.

It has been customary to call the crown the executive power, and the custom is continued, though the reason has ceased.

It was called the *executive,* because the person whom it signified used, formerly, to sit in the character of a judge, in administering or executing the laws. The tribunals were then a part of the court. The power, therefore, which is now called the judicial, is what was called the executive; and, consequently, one or other of the terms is redundant, and one of the offices useless. When we speak of the crown now, it means nothing; it signifies neither a judge nor a general: besides which it is the laws that govern, and not the man. The old terms are kept up, to give an appearance of consequence to empty forms; and the only effect they have is that of increasing expences.

Before I proceed to the means of rendering governments more conducive to the general happiness of mankind, than they are at present, it will not be improper to take a review of the progress of taxation in England.

It is a general idea, that when taxes are once laid on, they are never taken off. However true this may have been of late, it was not always so. Either, therefore, the people of former times were more watchful over government than those of the present, or government was administered with less extravagance.

It is now seven hundred years since the Norman conquest, and the establishment of what is called the crown. Taking this portion of time in seven separate periods of one hundred years each, the amount of the annual taxes, at each period, will be as follows: –

Annual amount of taxes levied by William the Conqueror,
    beginning in the year 1066, – –   £.400,000
Annual amount of taxes at one hundred years from the
    conquest, (1166) — —   200,000
Annual amount of taxes at two hundred years from the
    conquest, (1266) — —   150,000
Annual amount of taxes at three hundred years from the
    conquest, (1366) — —   130,000
Annual amount of taxes at four hundred years from the
    conquest, (1466) — —   100,000

These statements, and those which follow, are taken from Sir John Sinclair's History of the Revenue; by which it appears, that taxes continued decreasing for four hundred years, at the expiration of which time they were reduced three-fourths, viz. from four hundred thousand pounds to one hundred thousand. The people of England of the present day, have a traditionary and historical idea of the bravery of their ancestors; but whatever their virtues or their vices might have been, they certainly were a people who would not be imposed upon, and who kept government in awe as to taxation, if not as to principle. Though they were not able to expel the monarchical usurpation, they restricted it to a republican œconomy of taxes.

Let us now review the remaining three hundred years.

Annual amount of taxes at five hundred years from the
    conquest, (1566) – –   £.500,000
Annual amount of taxes at six hundred years from the
    conquest, (1666) – –   1,800,000
Annual amount of taxes at the present time, (1791) —   17,000,000

The difference between the first four hundred years and the last three, is so astonishing, as to warrant an opinion, that the national character of the English has changed. It would have been impossible to have dragooned the former English, into the excess of taxation that now exists; and when it is considered that the pay of the army, the navy, and of all the revenue-officers, is the same now as it was above a hundred years ago, when the taxes were not above a tenth part of what they are at present, it appears impossible to account for the enormous increase and expenditure, on any other ground, than extravagance, corruption, and intrigue[16].

With the revolution of 1688, and more so since the Hanover succession, came the destructive system of continental intrigues, and the rage for foreign wars and foreign dominion; systems of such secure mystery that the expences admit of no accounts; a single line stands for millions. To what excess taxation might have extended, had not the French revolution contributed to break up the system, and put an end to pretences, is impossible

16. Several of the court newspapers have of late made frequent mention of Wat Tyler. That his memory should be traduced by court sycophants, and all those who live on the spoil of a public, is not to be wondered at. He was, however the means of checking the rage and injustice of taxation in his time, and the nation owed much to his valour. The history is concisely this: – In the time of Richard the second, a poll-tax was levied, of one shilling per head, upon every person in the nation, of whatever estate or condition, on poor as well as rich, above the age of fifteen years. If any favour was shewn in the law, it was to the rich rather than to the poor; as no person could be charged more than twenty shillings for himself, family, and servants, though ever so numerous; while all other families, under the number of twenty, were charged per head. Poll-taxes had always been odious; but this being also oppressive and unjust, it excited, as it naturally must, universal detestation among the poor and middle classes. The person known by the name of Wat Tyler, whose proper name was Walter, and a tyler by trade, lived at Deptford. The gatherer of the poll-tax, on coming to his house, demanded tax for one of his daughters, whom Tyler declared was under the age of fifteen. The tax-gatherer insisted on satisfying himself, and began an indecent examination of the girl, which enraging the father, he struck him with a hammer, that brought him to the ground, and was the cause of his death.

This circumstance served to bring the discontents to an issue. The inhabitants of the neighbourhood espoused the cause of Tyler, who, in a few days was joined, according to some histories, by upwards of fifty thousand men, and chosen their chief. With this force he marched to London, to demand an abolition of the tax, and a redress of other grievances. The court, finding itself in a forlorn condition, and unable to make resistance, agreed, with Richard at its head, to hold a conference with Tyler in Smithfield, making many fair professions, courtier like, of its dispositions to redress the oppressions. While Richard and Tyler were in conversation on these matters, each being on horseback, Walworth, then mayor of London, and one of the creatures of the court, watched an opportunity, and like a cowardly assassin, stabbed Tyler with a dagger; and two or three others falling upon him, he was instantly sacrificed.

Tyler appears to have been an intrepid disinterested man, with respect to himself. All his proposals made to Richard, were on a more just and public ground, than those which had been made to John by the Barons; and notwithstanding the sycophancy of historians, and men like Mr. Burke, who seek to gloss over a base action of the court by traducing Tyler, his fame will outlive their falsehood. If the Barons merited a monument to be erected in Runnymede, Tyler merits one in Smithfield.

to say. Viewed, as that revolution ought to be, as the fortunate means of lessening the load of taxes of both countries, it is of as much importance to England as to France; and, if properly improved to all the advantages of which it is capable, and to which it leads, deserve as much celebration in one country as the other.

In pursuing this subject, I shall begin with the matter that first presents itself, that of lessening the burthen of taxes; and shall then add such matters and propositions, respecting the three countries of England, France, and America, as, the present prospect of things appears to justify: I mean, an alliance of the three, for the purposes that will be mentioned in their proper place.

What has happened may happen again. By the statement before shewn of the progress of taxation, it is seen, that taxes have been lessened to a fourth part of what they had formerly been. Though the present circumstances do not admit of the same reduction, yet it admits of such a beginning, as may accomplish that end in less time, than in the former case.

The amount of taxes for the year, ending at Michaelmas 1788, was as follows:

Land-tax,	- -	£ 1,950,000
Customs,	- -	3,789,274
Excise, (including old and new malt,)		6,751,727
Stamps,	- -	1,278,214
Miscellaneous taxes and incidents,		1,803,755
		£ 15,572,970

Since the year 1788, upwards of one million, new taxes, have been laid on, besides the produce from the lotteries; and as the taxes have in general been more productive since than before, the amount may be taken, in round numbers, at

£ 17,000,000

N. B. The expence of collection and the drawbacks, which together amount to nearly two millions, are paid out of the gross amount; and the above is the nett sum paid into the exchequer.

This sum of seventeen millions is applied to two different purposes; the one to pay the interest of the national debt, the other to the current expences of each year. About nine millions are appropriated to the former; and the remainder, being nearly eight millions, to the latter. As to the million, said to be applied to the reduction of the debt, it is so much like paying with one hand and taking out with the other, as not to merit much notice.

It happened, fortunately for France, that she possessed national domains for paying off her debt, and thereby lessening her taxes: but as this is not the case in England, her reduction of taxes can only take place by reducing the current expences, which may now be done to the amount of four or five millions annually, as will hereafter appear. When this is accomplished, it will more than counterbalance the enormous charge of the American war; and the saving will be from the same source from whence the evil arose.

As to the national debt, however heavy the interest may be in taxes; yet, as it serves to keep alive a capital, useful to commerce, it balances by its effects a considerable part of its own weight; and as the quantity of gold and silver in England is, by some means or other, short of its proper proportion[17], (being not more than twenty millions, whereas it should be sixty,) it would, besides the injustice, be bad policy to extinguish a capital that serves to supply that defect. But with respect to the current expence, whatever is saved therefrom is gain. The excess may serve to keep corruption alive, but it has no re-action on credit and commerce, like the interest of the debt.

It is now very probable, that the English government (I do not mean the nation) is unfriendly to the French revolution. Whatever serves to expose the intrigue and lessen the influence of courts, by lessening taxation, will be unwelcome to those who feed upon the spoil. Whilst the clamour of French intrigue, arbitrary power, popery, and wooden shoes could be kept up, the nation was easily allured and alarmed into taxes. Those days are now past; deception, it is to be hoped, has reaped its last harvest, and better times are in prospect for both countries, and for the world.

Taking it for granted, that an alliance may be formed between England, France, and America, for the purposes hereafter to be mentioned, the national expences of France and England may consequently be lessened. The same fleets and armies will no longer be necessary to either, and the reduction can be made ship for ship on each side. But to accomplish these objects, the governments must necessarily be fitted to a common and correspondent principle. Confidence can never take place, while an hostile disposition remains in either, or where mystery and secrecy on one side, is opposed to candour and openness on the other.

These matters admitted, the national expences might be put back, *for the sake of a precedent,* to what they were at some period when France and England were not enemies. This, consequently, must be prior to the

---

17. Foreign intrigue, foreign wars, and foreign dominions, will in a great measure account for the deficiency.

Hanover succession, and also to the revolution of 1688[18]. The first instance that presents itself, antecedent to those dates, is in the very wasteful and profligate times of Charles the Second; at which time England and France acted as allies. If I have chosen a period of great extravagancy, it will serve to shew modern extravagance in a still worse light; especially as the pay of the navy, the army, and the revenue officers has not encreased since that time.

The peace establishment was then as follows:–

See Sir John Sinclair's History of the Revenue.

Navy,	-	-	300,000
Army,	-	-	212,000
Ordnance,	-	-	40,000
Civil List	-	-	462,115
			£ 1,014,115

The parliament, however, settled the whole annual peace establishment at 1,200,000[19]. If we go back to the time of Elizabeth, the amount of all the taxes was but half a million, yet the nation sees nothing during that period, that reproaches it with want of consequence.

All circumstances then taken together, arising from the French revolution, from the approaching harmony and reciprocal interest of the two nations, the abolition of court intrigue on both sides, and the progress of knowledge in the science of government, the annual expenditure might be put back to one million and an half, viz.

18. I happened to be in England at the celebration of the centenary of the revolution of 1688. The characters of William and Mary have always appeared to me detestable; the one seeking to destroy his uncle, and the other her father, to get possession of power themselves; yet, as the nation was disposed to think something of that event, I felt hurt at seeing it ascribe the whole reputation of it to a man who had undertaken it as a jobb, and who, besides what he otherwise got, charged six hundred thousand pounds for the expence of the little fleet that brought him from Holland. George the First acted the same close-fisted part as William had done, and bought the Duchy of Bremin with the money he got from England, two hundred and fifty thousand pounds over and above his pay as king; and having thus purchased it at the expence of England, added it to his Hanoverian dominions for his own private profit. In fact, every nation that does not govern itself, is governed as a jobb. England has been the prey of jobbs ever since the revolution.

19. Charles, like his predecessors and successors, finding that war was the harvest of governments, engaged in a war with the Dutch, the expence of which encreased the annual expenditure to £ 1,800,000, as stated under the date of 1666; but the peace establishment was but £ 1,200,000.

Navy,	–	–	500,000
Army,	–	–	500,000
Expences of government,			500,000
			£. 1,500,000

Even this sum is six times greater than the expences of government are in America, yet the civil internal government in England, (I mean that administered by means of quarter sessions, juries, and assize, and which, in fact, is nearly the whole, and performed by the nation,) is less expence upon the revenue, than the same species and portion of government is in America.

It is time that nations should be rational, and not be governed like animals, for the pleasure of their riders. To read the history of kings, a man would be almost inclined to suppose that government consisted in stag-hunting, and that every nation paid a million a year to a huntsman. Man ought to have pride, or shame enough to blush at being thus imposed upon, and when he feel his proper character, he will. Upon all subjects of this nature, there is often passing in the mind, a train of ideas he has not yet accustomed himself to encourage and communicate. Restrained by something that puts on the character of prudence, he acts the hypocrite upon himself as well as to others. It is, however, curious to observe how soon this spell can be dissolved. A single expression, boldly conceived and uttered, will sometimes put a whole company into their proper feelings; and whole nations are acted upon in the same manner.

As to the offices of which any civil government may be composed, it matters but little by what names they are described. In the rotine of business, as before observed, whether a man be stiled a president, a king, an emperor, a senator, or any thing else, it is impossible that any service he can perform, can merit from a nation more than ten thousand pounds a year; and as no man should be paid beyond his services, so every man of a proper heart will not accept more. Public money ought to be touched with the most scrupulous consciousness of honour. It is not the produce of riches only, but of the hard earnings of labour and poverty. It is drawn even from the bitterness of want and misery. Not a beggar passes, or perishes in the streets, whose mite is not in that mass.

Were it possible that the Congress of America, could be so lost to their duty, and to the interest of their constituents, as to offer General Washington, as president of America, a million a year, he would not, and he could not, accept it. His sense of honour is of another kind. It has cost England almost seventy millions sterling, to maintain a family imported from abroad, of very inferior capacity to thousands in the nation; and scarcely a year has passed that has not produced some new mercenary application. Even the physicians bills have been sent to the public to be paid. No wonder that jails are crowded, and taxes and poor-rates encreased. Under such systems, nothing is to be looked for but what has already happened; and as to reformation, whenever it come, it must be from the nation, and not from the government.

To shew that the sum of five hundred thousand pounds is more than sufficient to defray all the expences of government, exclusive of navies and armies, the following estimate is added for any country, of the same extent as England.

In the first place, three hundred representatives, fairly elected, are sufficient for all the purposes to which legislation can apply, and preferable to a larger number. They may be divided into two or three houses, or meet in one, as in France, or in any manner a constitution shall direct.

As representation is always considered, in free countries, as the most honourable of all stations, the allowance made to it is merely to defray the expence which the representatives incur by that service, and not to it as an office.

If an allowance, at the rate of five hundred pounds *per ann.*
be made to every representative, deducting for
non-attendance, the expence, if the whole number
attended for six months, each year, would be } £. 75,000

The official departments cannot reasonably exceed
the following number, with the salaries annexed:

Three offices, at ten thousand pounds each	30,000
Ten ditto, at £. 5000 each	50,000
Twenty ditto, at £. 2000 each	40,000
Forty ditto, at £. 1000 each	40,000
Two hundred ditto, at £. 500 each	100,000
Three hundred ditto, at £. 200 each	60,000
Five hundred ditto, at £. 100 each	50,000
Seven hundred ditto, at £. 75 each	52,500
	£. 497,500

If a nation chuse, it can deduct four *per cent.* from all offices, and make one of twenty thousand *per ann.*

All revenue officers are paid out of the monies they collect, and therefore, are not in this estimation.

The foregoing is not offered as an exact detail of offices, but to shew the number and rate of salaries which five hundred thousand pounds will support; and it will, on experience, be found impracticable to find business sufficient to justify even this expence. As to the manner in which office business is now performed, the Chiefs, in several offices, such as the post-office, and certain offices in the exchequer, &c. do little more than sign their names three or four times a year; and the whole duty is performed by under clerks.

Taking, therefore, one million and an half as a sufficient peace establishment for all the honest purposes of government, which is three hundred thousand pounds more than the peace establishment in the profligate and prodigal times of Charles the Second, (notwithstanding, as has been already observed, the pay and salaries of the army, navy, and revenue officers, continue the same as at that period,) there will remain a surplus of upwards of six millions out of the present current expences. The question then will be, how to dispose of this surplus

Whoever has observed the manner in which trade and taxes twist themselves together, must be sensible of the impossibility of separating them suddenly.

First. Because the articles now on hand are already charged with the duty, and the reduction cannot take place on the present stock.

Secondly. Because, on all those articles on which the duty is charged in the gross, such as per barrel, hogshead, hundred weight, or tun, the abolition of the duty does not admit of being divided down so as fully to relieve the consumer, who purchases by the pint, or the pound. The last duty laid on strong beer and ale, was three shillings per barrel, which, if taken off, would lessen the purchase only half a farthing per pint, and consequently, would not reach to practical relief.

This being the condition of a great part of the taxes, it will be necessary to look for such others as are free from this embarrassment, and where the relief will be direct and visible, and capable of immediate operation.

In the first place, then, the poor-rates are a direct tax which every housekeeper feels, and who knows also, to a farthing, the sum which he pays. The national amount of the whole of the poor rates is not positively known, but can be procured. Sir John Sinclair, in his History of the Revenue, has stated it at £. 2,100,587. A considerable part of which is expended in litigations, in which the poor, instead of being relieved, are tormented. The expence, however, is the same to the parish from whatever cause it arises.

In Birmingham, the amount of the poor-rates is fourteen thousand pounds a year. This, though a large sum, is moderate, compared with the population. Birmingham is said to contain seventy thousand souls, and on a proportion of seventy thousand to fourteen thousand pounds poor-rates, the national amount of poor-rates, taking the population of England at seven millions, would be but one million four hundred thousand pounds. It is, therefore, most probable, that the population of Birmingham is over-rated. Fourteen thousand pounds is the proportion upon fifty thousand souls, taking two millions of poor-rates as the national amount.

Be it, however, what it may, it is no other than the consequence of the excessive burthen of taxes, for, at the time when the taxes were very low, the poor were able to maintain themselves; and there were no poor-rates[20]. In the present state of things, a labouring man, with a wife and two or three children, does not pay less than between seven and eight pounds a year in taxes. He is not sensible of this, because it is disguised to him in the articles which he buys, and he thinks only of their dearness; but as the taxes take from him, at least, a fourth part of his yearly earnings, he is consequently disabled from providing for a family, especially, if himself, or any of them, are afflicted with sickness.

The first step, therefore, of practical relief, would be to abolish the poor-rates entirely, and in lieu thereof, to make a remission of taxes to the poor of double the amount of the present poor-rates, viz. four millions annually out of the surplus taxes. By this measure, the poor would be benefited two millions, and the house-keepers two millions. This alone would be equal to a reduction of one hundred and twenty millions of the national debt, and consequently equal to the whole expence of the American war.

It will then remain to be considered, which is the most effectual mode of distributing this remission of four millions.

It is easily seen, that the poor are generally composed of large families of children, and old people past their labour. If these two classes are provided for, the remedy will so far reach to the full extent of the case, that what remains will be incidental, and, in a great measure, fall within the compass of benefit clubs, which, though of humble invention, merit to be ranked among the best of modern institutions.

Admitting England to contain seven million of souls; if one-fifth thereof are of that class of poor which need support, the number will be one million

---

20. Poor-rates began about the time of Henry the Eighth, when the taxes began to encrease, and they have encreased as the taxes encreased ever since.

four hundred thousand. Of this number, one hundred and forty thousand will be aged poor, as will be hereafter shewn, and for which a distinct provision will be proposed.

There will then remain one million two hundred and sixty thousand, which, at five souls to each family, amount to two hundred and fifty-two thousand families, rendered poor from the expence of children and the weight of taxes.

The number of children under fourteen years of age, in each of those families, will be found to be about five to every two families; some having two, and others three; some one, and others four; some none, and others five; but it rarely happens that more than five are under fourteen years of age, and after this age they are capable of service or of being apprenticed.

Allowing five children (under fourteen years) to every two families,
The number of children will be   -   630,000
The number of parents were they all living,
    would be   -   504,000

It is certain, that if the children are provided for, the parents are relieved of consequence, because it is from the expence of bringing up children that their poverty arises.

Having thus ascertained the greatest number that can be supposed to need support on account of young families, I proceed to the mode of relief or distribution, which is,

To pay as a remission of taxes to every poor family, out of the surplus taxes, and in room of poor-rates, four pounds a year for every child under fourteen years of age; enjoining the parents of such children to send them to school, to learn reading, writing, and common arithmetic; the ministers of every parish, of every denomination, to certify jointly to an office, for that purpose, that this duty is performed.

The amount of this expence will be,
For six hundred and thirty thousand children,
    at four pounds *per ann.* each,   £.2,520,000

By adopting this method, not only the poverty of the parents will be relieved, but ignorance will be banished from the rising generation, and the number of poor will hereafter become less, because their abilities, by the aid of education, will be greater. Many a youth, with good natural genius, who is apprenticed to a mechanical trade, such as a carpenter, joiner, millwright, shipwright, blacksmith, &c. is prevented getting forward the whole of his life, from the want of a little common education when a boy.

I now proceed to the case of the aged.

I divide age into two classes. First, the approach of age beginning at fifty. Secondly, old age commencing at sixty.

At fifty, though the mental faculties of man are in full vigour, and his judgment better than at any preceeding date, the bodily powers for laborious life are on the decline. He cannot bear the same quantity of fatigue as at an earlier period. He begins to earn less, and is less capable of enduring wind and weather; and in those more retired employments where much sight is required, he fails apace, and sees himself, like an old horse, beginning to be turned adrift.

At sixty his labour ought to be over, at least from direct necessity. It is painful to see old age working itself to death, in what are called civilized countries, for daily bread.

To form some judgment of the number of those above fifty years of age, I have several times counted the persons I met in the streets of London, men, women, and children, and have generally found that the average is about one in sixteen or seventeen. If it be said that aged persons do not come much in the streets, so neither do infants; and a great proportion of grown children are in schools, and in work shops as apprentices. Taking then sixteen for a divisor, the whole number of persons, in England, of fifty years and upwards of both sexes, rich and poor, will be four hundred and twenty thousand.

The persons to be provided for out of this gross number will be, husbandmen, common labourers, journeymen of every trade and their wives, sailors, and disbanded soldiers, worn out servants of both sexes, and poor widows.

There will be also a considerable number of middling tradesmen, who having lived decently in the former part of life, begin, as age approaches, to lose their business, and at last fall to decay.

Besides these, there will be constantly thrown off from the revolutions of that wheel, which no man can stop, nor regulate, a number from every class of life connected with commerce and adventure.

To provide for all those accidents, and whatever else may befal, I take the number of persons, who at one time or other of their lives, after fifty years of age, may feel it necessary or comfortable to be better supported, than they can support themselves, and that not as a matter of grace and favour, but of right, at one third of the whole number, which is one hundred and forty thousand, as stated in page [335], and for whom a distinct provision was proposed to be made. If there be more, society, notwithstanding the shew and pomposity of government, is in a deplorable condition in England.

Of this one hundred and forty thousand, I take one half, seventy thousand, to be of the age of fifty and under sixty, and the other half to be sixty years and upwards.—Having thus ascertained the probable proportion of the number of aged persons, I proceed to the mode of rendering their condition comfortable, which is,

To pay to every such person of the age of fifty years, and until he shall arrive at the age of sixty, the sum of six pounds *per ann.* out of the surplus taxes; and ten pounds *per ann.* during life after the age of sixty. The expence of which will be,

Seventy thousand persons at £.6 *per ann.*	420,000
Seventy thousand ditto at £.10 *per ann.*	700,000
	£. 1,120,000

This support, as already remarked, is not of the nature of a charity, but of a right. Every person in England, male and female, pays on an average in taxes, two pounds eight shillings and sixpence *per ann.* from the day of his (or her) birth; and, if the expence of collection be added, he pays two pounds eleven shillings and sixpence; consequently, at the end of fifty years he has paid one hundred and twenty-eight pounds fifteen shillings; and at sixty, one hundred and fifty-four pounds ten shillings. Converting, therefore, his (or her) individual tax into a tontine, the money he shall receive after fifty years, is but little more than the legal interest of the nett money he has paid; the rest is made up from those whose circumstances do not require them to draw such support, and the capital in both cases defrays the expences of government. It is on this ground that I have extended the probable claims to one third of the number of aged persons in the nation,—Is it then better that the lives of one hundred and forty thousand aged persons be rendered comfortable, or that a million a year of public money be expended on any one individual, and him often of the most worthless or insignificant character? Let reason and justice, let honour and humanity, let even hypocrisy, sycophancy and Mr. Burke, let George, let Louis, Leopold, Frederic, Catharine, Cornwallis, or Tippoo Saib, answer the question[21].

21. Reckoning the taxes by families, five to a family, each family pays on an average, 12*l.* 17*s.* 6*d. per ann.* to this sum are to be added the poor-rates. Though all pay taxes in the articles they consume, all do not pay poor-rates. About two millions are exempted, some as not being house-keepers, others as not being able, and the poor themselves who receive the relief. The average, therefore, of poor-rates on the remaining number, is forty shillings for every family of five persons, which makes

The sum thus remitted to the poor will be,

To two hundred and fifty-two thousand poor families,
    containing six hundred and thirty thousand children,   2,520,000
To one hundred and forty thousand aged persons, - -   1,120,000
                                           £ 3,640,000

There will then remain three hundred and sixty thousand pounds out of the four millions, part of which may be applied as follows:

After all the above cases are provided for, there will still be a number of families who, though not properly of the class of poor, yet find it difficult to give education to their children; and such children, under such a case, would be in a worse condition than if their parents were actually poor. A nation under a well regulated government, should permit none to remain uninstructed. It is monarchical and aristocratical government only that requires ignorance for its support.

Suppose then four hundred thousand children to be in this condition, which is a greater number than ought to be supposed, after the provisions already made, the method will be,

To allow for each of those children ten shillings a year for the expence of schooling, for six years each, which will give them six months schooling each year, and half a crown a year for paper and spelling books.

The expence of this will be annually[22] £ 250,000[.]

---

the whole average amount of taxes and rates, 14*l*. 17*s*. 6*d*. For six persons, 17*l*. 17*s*. For seven persons, 20*l*. 16*s*. 6*d*.

The average of taxes in America, under the new or representative system of government, including the interest of the debt contracted in the war, and taking the population at four million of souls, which it now amounts to, and it is daily encreasing, is five shillings per head, men, women, and children. The difference, therefore, between the two governments, is as under,

	England.	America.
	l. s. d.	*l. s. d.*
For a family of five persons	14 17 6	1 5 0
For a family of six persons	17 17 0	1 10 0
For a family of seven persons	20 16 6	1 15 0

22. Public schools do not answer the general purpose of the poor. They are chiefly in corporation towns, from which the country towns and villages are excluded; or if admitted, the distance occasions a great loss of time. Education, to be useful to the poor, should be on the spot; and the best method, I believe, to accomplish this, is to enable the parents to pay the expence themselves. There are always persons of both sexes to be found in every village, especially when growing into years, capable of such an undertaking. Twenty children, at ten shillings each, (and that not

There will then remain one hundred and ten thousand pounds.

Notwithstanding the great modes of relief which the best instituted and best principled government may devise, there will still be a number of smaller cases, which it is good policy as well as beneficence in a nation to consider.

Were twenty shillings to be given to every woman immediately on the birth of a child, who should make the demand, and none will make it beyond whose circumstances do not require it, it might relieve a great deal of instant distress.

There are about two hundred thousand births yearly in England; and if
  claimed, by one fourth,
The amount would be   -   50,000
And twenty shillings to every new-married couple who should
  claim in like manner. This would not exceed the sum of   -   £ 20,000

Also twenty thousand pounds to be appropriated to defray the funeral expences of persons, who, travelling for work, may die at a distance from their friends. By relieving parishes from this charge, the sick stranger will be better treated.

I shall finish this part of the subject with a plan adapted to the particular condition of a metropolis, such as London.

Cases are continually occurring in a metropolis different to those which occur in the country, and for which a different, or rather an additional mode of relief is necessary. In the country, even in large towns, people have a knowledge of each other, and distress never rises to that extreme height it sometimes does in a metropolis. There is no such thing in the country as persons, in the literal sense of the word, starved to death, or dying with cold from the want of a lodging. Yet such cases, and others equally as miserable, happen in London.

Many a youth comes up to London full of expectations, and with little or no money, and unless he gets immediate employment he is already half undone; and boys bred up in London without any means of a livelihood, and as it often happens of dissolute parents, are in a still worse condition; and servants long out of place are not much better off. In short, a world of

---

more than six months each year) would be as much as some livings amount to in the remote parts of England; and there are often distressed clergymen's widows to whom such an income would be acceptable. Whatever is given on this account to children answers two purposes, to them it is education, to those who educate them it is a livelihood.

little cases are continually arising, which busy or affluent life knows not of, to open the first door to distress. Hunger is not among the postponeable wants, and a day, even a few hours, in such a condition, is often the crisis of a life of ruin.

These circumstances, which are the general cause of the little thefts and pilferings that lead to greater, may be prevented. There yet remain twenty thousand pounds out of the four millions of surplus taxes, which, with another fund here-after to be mentioned, amounting to about twenty thousand pounds more, cannot be better applied than to this purpose. The plan then will be,

First, To erect two or more buildings, or take some already erected, capable of containing at least six thousand persons, and to have in each of these places as many kinds of employment as can be contrived, so that every person who shall come may find something which he or she can do.

Secondly, To receive all who shall come, without enquiring who or what they are. The only condition to be, that for so much, or so many hours work, each person shall receive so many meals of wholesome food, and a warm lodging, at least as good as a barrack. That a certain portion of what each person's work shall be worth shall be reserved, and given to him, or her, on their going away; and that each person shall stay as long, or as short time, or come as often as he chuse, on these conditions.

If each person staid three months, it would assist by rotation twenty-four thousand persons annually, though the real number, at all times, would be but six thousand. By establishing an asylum of this kind, such persons to whom temporary distresses occur, would have an opportunity to recruit themselves, and be enabled to look out for better employment.

Allowing that their labour paid but one half the expence of supporting them, after reserving a portion of their earnings for themselves, the sum of forty thousand pounds additional would defray all other charges for even a greater number than six thousand.

The fund very properly convertible to this purpose, in addition to the twenty thousand pounds, remaining of the former fund, will be the produce of the tax upon coals, and so iniquitously and wantonly applied to the support of the Duke of Richmond. It is horrid that any man, more especially at the price coals now are, should live on the distresses of a community; and any government permitting such an abuse, deserves to be dismissed. This fund is said to be about twenty thousand pounds *per annum.*

I shall now conclude this plan with enumerating the several particulars, and then proceed to other matters.

The enumeration is as follows:

First, Abolition of two million poor-rates.

Secondly, Provision for two hundred and fifty-two thousand poor families.

Thirdly, Education for one million and thirty thousand children.

Fourthly, Comfortable provision for one hundred and forty thousand aged persons.

Fifthly, Donation of twenty shillings each for fifty thousand births.

Sixthly, Donation of twenty shillings each for twenty thousand marriages.

Seventhly, Allowance of twenty thousand pounds for the funeral expences of persons travelling for work, and dying at a distance from their friends.

Eighthly, Employment, at all times, for the casual poor in the cities of London and Westminster.

By the operation of this plan, the poor laws, those instruments of civil torture, will be superceded, and the wasteful expence of litigation prevented. The hearts of the humane will not be shocked by ragged and hungry children, and persons of seventy and eighty years of age begging for bread. The dying poor will not be dragged from place to place to breathe their last, as a reprisal of parish upon parish. Widows will have a maintenance for their children, and not be carted away, on the death of their husbands, like culprits and criminals; and children will no longer be considered as encreasing the distresses of their parents. The haunts of the wretched will be known, because it will be to their advantage, and the number of petty crimes, the offspring of distress and poverty, will be lessened. The poor, as well as the rich, will then be interested in the support of government, and the cause and apprehension of riots and tumults will cease. – Ye who sit in ease, and solace yourselves in plenty, and such there are in Turkey and Russia, as well as in England, and who say to yourselves, "Are we not well off," have ye thought of these things? When ye do, ye will cease to speak and feel for yourselves alone.

The plan is easy in practice. It does not embarrass trade by a sudden interruption in the order of taxes, but effects the relief by changing the application of them; and the money necessary for the purpose can be drawn from the excise collections, which are made eight times a year in every market town in England.

Having now arranged and concluded this subject, I proceed to the next.

Taking the present current expences at seven millions and an half, which is the least amount they are now at, there will remain (after the sum of one million and an half be taken for the new current expences, and four millions for the before-mentioned service) the sum of two millions; part of which to be applied as follows:

Though fleets and armies, by an alliance with France, will, in a great measure, become useless, yet the persons who have devoted themselves to those services, and have thereby unfitted themselves for other lines of life, are not to be sufferers by the means that make others happy. They are a different description of men to those who form or hang about a court.

A part of the army will remain at least for some years, and also of the navy, for which a provision is already made in the former part of this plan of one million, which is almost half a million more than the peace establishment of the army and navy in the prodigal times of Charles the Second.

Suppose then fifteen thousand soldiers to be disbanded, and to allow to each of those men three shillings a week during life, clear of all deductions, to be paid in the same manner as the Chelsea College pensioners are paid, and for them to return to their trades and their friends; and also to add fifteen thousand sixpences per week to the pay of the soldiers who shall remain; the annual expence will be,

To the pay of fifteen thousand disbanded soldiers,		
at three shillings per week,	-	£ 117,000
Additional pay to the remaining soldiers,	-	19,500
Carried forward	-	136,500
Brought over	-	136,500
Suppose that the pay to the officers of the		
disbanded corps be of the same amount		
as the sum allowed to the men,	-	117,000
		253,500
To prevent bulky estimations, admit the same		
sum to the disbanded navy as to the		
army, and the same increase of pay, - - -		253,500
Total		507,000

Every year some part of this sum of half a million (I omit the odd seven thousand pounds for the purpose of keeping the account unembarrassed) will fall in, and the whole of it in time, as it is on the ground of life annuities, except the encreased pay of twenty-nine thousand pounds. As it falls in, a part of the taxes may be taken off; for instance, when thirty thousand pounds fall in the duty on hops may be wholly taken off; and as other parts fall in, the duties on candles and soap may be lessened, till at last they will totally cease.

There now remains at least one million and an half of surplus taxes. The tax on houses and windows is one of those direct taxes, which, like the poor-rates, is not confounded with trade; and, when taken off, the relief will be instantly felt. This tax falls heavy on the middling class of people. The amount of this tax by the returns of 1788, was,

			l.	*s.*	*d.*
Houses and windows by the act of 1766,	–	385,459	11	7
Ditto ditto by the act of 1779,	–	130,739	14	5½
		Total	516,199	6	0½

If this tax be struck off, there will then remain about one million of surplus taxes, and as it is always proper to keep a sum in reserve, for incidental matters, it may be best not to extend reductions further, in the first instance, but to consider what may be accomplished by other modes of reform.

Among the taxes most heavily felt is the commutation tax. I shall, therefore, offer a plan for its abolition, by substituting another in its place, which will affect three objects at once:

First, That of removing the burthen to where it can best be borne.

Secondly, Restoring justice among families by a distribution of property.

Thirdly, Extirpating the overgrown influence arising from the unnatural law of primogeniture, and which is one of the principal sources of corruption at elections.

The amount of the commutation tax
    by the returns of 1788, was, – –   £771,657   0   0

When taxes are proposed, the country is amused by the plausible language of taxing luxuries. One thing is called a luxury at one time, and something else at another; but the real luxury does not consist in the article, but in the means of procuring it, and this is always kept out of sight.

I know not why any plant or herb of the field should be a greater luxury in one country than another, but an overgrown estate in either is a luxury at all times, and as such is the proper object of taxation. It is, therefore, right to take those kind tax-making gentlemen up on their own word, and argue on the principle themselves have laid down, that of *taxing luxuries.* If they, or their champion Mr. Burke, who, I fear, is growing out of date like the man in armour, can prove that an estate of twenty, thirty, or forty thousand pounds a year is not a luxury, I will give up the argument.

Admitting that any annual sum, say for instance, one thousand pounds, is necessary or sufficient for the support of a family, consequently the second thousand is of the nature of a luxury, the third still more so, and by proceeding on, we shall at last arrive at a sum that may not improperly be called a prohibitable luxury. It would be impolitic to set bounds to property acquired by industry, and therefore it is right to place the prohibition beyond the probable acquisition to which industry can extend; but there ought to be a limit to property, or the accumulation of it, by bequest. It should pass in some other line. The richest in every nation have poor relations, and those often very near in consanguinity.

The following table of progressive taxation is constructed on the above principles, and as a substitute for the commutation tax. It will reach the point of prohibition by a regular operation, and thereby supercede the aristocratical law of primogeniture.

TABLE I.

A tax on all estates of the clear yearly value of fifty
pounds, after deducting the land tax, and up

		s.	d.	
To £ 500	–	0	3	per pound
From 500 to 1000	–	0	6	per pound
On the second thousand		0	9	per pound
On the third ditto	–	1	0	per pound
On the fourth ditto		1	6	per pound
On the fifth ditto	–	2	0	per pound
On the sixth ditto	–	3	0	per pound
On the seventh ditto		4	0	per pound
On the eighth ditto		5	0	per pound
On the ninth ditto	–	6	0	per pound
On the tenth ditto	–	7	0	per pound
On the eleventh ditto		8	0	per pound
On the twelfth ditto		9	0	per pound
On the thirteenth ditto		10	0	per pound
On the fourteenth ditto		11	0	per pound
On the fifteenth ditto		12	0	per pound
On the sixteenth ditto		13	0	per pound
On the seventeenth ditto		14	0	per pound
On the eighteenth ditto		15	0	per pound
On the nineteenth ditto		16	0	per pound
On the twentieth ditto		17	0	per pound
On the twenty-first ditto		18	0	per pound
On the twenty-second ditto		19	0	per pound
On the twenty-third ditto		20	0	per pound

The foregoing table shews the progression per pound on every progressive thousand. The following table shews the amount of the tax on every thousand separately, and in the last column, the total amount of all the separate sums collected.

TABLE II.

		d.	*l.*	*s.*	*d.*
An estate of £ 50 *per ann.* at 3 per pd. pays		0	12	6	
100	3		1	5	0
200	3		2	10	0
300	3		3	15	0
400	3		5	0	0
500	3		7	5	0

After 500*l.*–the tax of sixpence per pound takes place on the second 500*l.*–consequently an estate of 1000*l. per ann.* pays 21*l.* 15*s.* and so on,

	l.	*s.*	*d.*	*l.*	*s.*	Total amount. *l.*	*s.*
For the 1st	500 at 0	3 per pound		7	5 ⎫	21	15
2d	500 at 0	6		14	10 ⎭		
2d	1000 at 0	9		37	10	59	5
3d	1000 at 1	0		50	0	109	5
4th	1000 at 1	6		75	0	184	5
5th	1000 at 2	0		100	0	284	5
6th	1000 at 3	0		150	0	434	5
7th	1000 at 4	0		200	0	634	5
8th	1000 at 5	0		250	0	880	5
9th	1000 at 6	0		300	0	1180	5
10th	1000 at 7	0		350	0	1530	5
11th	1000 at 8	0		400	0	1930	5
12th	1000 at 9	0		450	0	2380	5
13th	1000 at 10	0		500	0	2880	5
14th	1000 at 11	0		550	0	3430	5
15th	1000 at 12	0		600	0	4030	5
16th	1000 at 13	0		650	0	4680	5
17th	1000 at 14	0		700	0	5380	5
18th	1000 at 15	0		750	0	6130	5
19th	1000 at 16	0		800	0	6930	5
20th	1000 at 17	0		850	0	7780	5

21st	1000 at 18	0	900	0	8680	5
22^{d}	1000 at 19	0	950	0	9630	5
23^{d}	1000 at 20	0	1000	0	10630	5

At the twenty-third thousand the tax becomes twenty shillings in the pound, and consequently every thousand beyond that sum can produce no profit but by dividing the estate. Yet formidable as this tax appears, it will not, I believe, produce so much as the commutation tax; should it produce more, it ought to be lowered to that amount upon estates under two or three thousand a year.

On small and middling estates it is lighter (as it is intended to be) than the commutation tax. It is not till after seven or eight thousand a year that it begins to be heavy. The object is not so much the produce of the tax, as the justice of the measure. The aristocracy has screened itself too much, and this serves to restore a part of the lost equilibrium.

As an instance of its screening itself, it is only necessary to look back to the first establishment of the excise laws, at what is called the Restoration, or the coming of Charles the Second. The aristocratical interest then in power, commuted the feudal services itself was under by laying a tax on beer brewed for *sale;* that is, they compounded with Charles for an exemption from those services for themselves and their heirs, by a tax to be paid by other people. The aristocracy do not purchase beer brewed for sale, but brew their own beer free of the duty, and if any commutation at that time were necessary, it ought to have been at the expence of those for whom the exemptions from those services were intended[23]; instead of which it was thrown on an entire different class of men.

But the chief object of this progressive tax (besides the justice of rendering taxes more equal than they are) is, as already stated, to extirpate the overgrown influence arising from the unnatural law of primogeniture, and which is one of the principal sources of corruption at elections.

It would be attended with no good consequences to enquire how such vast estates as thirty, forty, or fifty thousand a year could commence, and that at a time when commerce and manufactures were not in a state to admit of such acquisitions. Let it be sufficient to remedy the evil by putting them in a condition of descending again to the community, by the quiet means of

23. The tax on beer brewed for sale, from which the aristocracy are exempt, is almost one million more than the present commutation tax, being by the returns of 1788, 1,666,152*l.* and consequently they ought to take on themselves the amount of the commutation tax, as they are already exempted from one which is almost one million greater.

apportioning them among all the heirs and heiresses of those families. This will be the more necessary, because hitherto the aristocracy have quartered their younger children and connections upon the public in useless posts, places, and offices, which when abolished will leave them destitute, unless the law of primogeniture be also abolished or superceded.

A progressive tax will, in a great measure, effect this object, and that as a matter of interest to the parties most immediately concerned, as will be seen by the following table; which shews the nett produce upon every estate, after subtracting the tax. By this it will appear, that after an estate exceeds thirteen or fourteen thousand a year, the remainder produces but little profit to the holder, and consequently will pass either to the younger children, or to other kindred.

TABLE III.

Shewing the nett produce of every estate from one
thousand to twenty-three thousand pounds a year.

No. of thousands per ann.	Total tax subtracted.	Nett produce.
	£.	£.
1000	21	979
2000	59	1941
3000	109	2891
4000	184	3816
5000	284	4716
6000	434	5566
7000	634	6366
8000	880	7120
9000	1180	7820
10,000	1530	8470
11,000	1930	9070
12,000	2380	9620
13,000	2880	10,120
14,000	3430	10,570
15,000	4030	10,970
16,000	4680	11,320
17,000	5380	11,620
18,000	6130	11,870
19,000	6930	12,170
20,000	7780	12,220

21,000	8680	12,320
22,000	9630	12,370
23,000	10,630	12,370

N. B. The odd shillings are dropped in this table.

According to this table, an estate cannot produce more than 12,370*l.* clear of the land tax and the progressive tax, and therefore the dividing such estates will follow as a matter of family interest. An estate of 23,000*l.* a year, divided into five estates of four thousand each and one of three, will be charged only 1129*l.* which is but five *per cent.* but if held by one possessor will be charged 10,630*l.*

Although an enquiry into the origin of those estates be unnecessary, the continuation of them in their present state is another subject. It is a matter of national concern. As hereditary estates, the law has created the evil, and it ought also to provide the remedy. Primogeniture ought to be abolished, not only because it is unnatural and unjust, but because the country suffers by its operation. By cutting off (as before observed) the younger children from their proper portion of inheritance, the public is loaded with the expence of maintaining them; and the freedom of elections violated by the overbearing influence which this unjust monopoly of family property produces. Nor is this all. It occasions a waste of national property. A considerable part of the land of the country is rendered unproductive by the great extent of parks and chases which this law serves to keep up, and this at a time when the annual production of grain is not equal to the national consumption[24]. – In short, the evils of the aristocratical system are so great and numerous, so inconsistent with every thing that is just, wise, natural, and beneficent, that when they are considered, there ought not to be a doubt that many, who are now classed under that description, will wish to see such a system abolished.

What pleasure can they derive from contemplating the exposed condition, and almost certain beggary of their younger offspring? Every aristocratical family has an appendage of family beggars hanging round it, which in a few ages, or a few generations, are shook off, and console themselves with telling their tale in alms-houses, work-houses, and prisons. This is the natural consequence of aristocracy. The peer and the beggar are often of the same family. One extreme produces the other: to make one rich many must be made poor; neither can the system be supported by other means.

There are two classes of people to whom the laws of England are particularly hostile, and those the most helpless; younger children and the

24. See the reports on the corn trade.

poor. Of the former I have just spoken; of the latter I shall mention one instance out of the many that might be produced, and with which I shall close this subject.

Several laws are in existence for regulating and limiting workmen's wages. Why not leave them as free to make their own bargains, as the law-makers are to let their farms and houses? Personal labour is all the property they have. Why is that little, and the little freedom they enjoy to be infringed? But the injustice will appear stronger, if we consider the opera- tion and effect of such laws. When wages are fixed by what is called a law, the legal wages remain stationary, while every thing else is in progression; and as those who make that law, still continue to lay on new taxes by other laws, they encrease the expence of living by one law, and take away the means by another.

But if those gentlemen law-makers and tax-makers thought it right to limit the poor pittance which personal labour can produce, and on which a whole family is to be supported, they certainly must feel themselves hap- pily indulged in a limitation on their own part, of not less than twelve thou- sand a year, and that of property they never acquired, (nor probably any of their ancestors) and of which they have made so ill a use.

Having now finished this subject, I shall bring the several particulars into one view, and then proceed to other matters.

The first EIGHT ARTICLES are brought forward from page [341].

1. Abolition of two million poor-rates.
2. Provision for two hundred and fifty-two thousand poor families, at the rate of four pounds per head for each child under fourteen years of age; which, with the addition of two hundred and fifty thousand pounds, provides also education for one million and thirty thousand children.
3. Annuity of six pounds (per ann.) each for all poor persons, decayed tradesmen, or others (supposed seventy thousand) of the age of fifty years, and until sixty.
4. Annuity of ten pounds each for life for all poor persons, decayed tradesmen, and others (supposed seventy thousand) of the age of sixty years.
5. Donation of twenty shillings each for fifty thousand births.
6. Donation of twenty shillings each for twenty thousand marriages.
7. Allowance of twenty thousand pounds for the funeral expences of persons travelling for work, and dying at a distance from their friends.

8. Employment at all times for the casual poor in the cities of London and Westminster.

SECOND ENUMERATION.

9. Abolition of the tax on houses and windows.

10. Allowance of three shillings per week for life to fifteen thousand disbanded soldiers, and a proportionable allowance to the officers of the disbanded corps.

11. Encrease of pay to the remaining soldiers of 19,500*l.* annually.

12. The same allowance to the disbanded navy, and the same encrease of pay, as to the army.

13. Abolition of the commutation tax.

14. Plan of a progressive tax, operating to extirpate the unjust and unnatural law of primogeniture, and the vicious influence of the aristocratical system[25].

There yet remains, as already stated, one million of surplus taxes. Some part of this will be required for circumstances that do not immediately present themselves, and such part as shall not be wanted, will admit a further reduction of taxes equal to that amount.

Among the claims that justice requires to be made, the condition of the inferior revenue officers will merit attention. It is a reproach to any govern-

---

25. When enquiries are made into the condition of the poor, various degrees of distress will most probably be found, to render a different arrangement preferable to that which is already proposed. Widows with families will be in greater want than where there are husbands living. There is also a difference in the expence of living in different countries; and more so in fuel.

	£.
Suppose then fifty thousand extraordinary cases, at the rate of 10*l.* per family per ann.	– 500,000
100,000 Families, at 8*l.* per family per ann.	- 800,000
100,000 Families, at 7*l.* per family per ann.	- 700,000
104,000 Families, at 5*l.* per family per ann.	- 520,000
And instead of ten shillings per head for the education of other children, to allow fifty shillings per family for that purpose to fifty thousand families	250,000
	2,770,000
140,000 Aged persons as before,	- 1,120,000
	3,890,000

This arrangement amounts to the same sum as stated in page [338], including the 250,000*l.* for education; but it provides (including the aged people) for four hundred and four thousand families, which is almost one third of all the families in England.

ment to waste such an immensity of revenue in sinecures and nominal and unnecessary places and offices, and not allow even a decent livelihood to those on whom the labour falls. The salary of the inferior officers of the revenue has stood at the petty pittance of less than fifty pounds a year for upwards of one hundred years. It ought to be seventy. About one hundred and twenty thousand pounds applied to this purpose, will put all those salaries in a decent condition.

This was proposed to be done almost twenty years ago, but the treasury-board then in being startled at it, as it might lead to similar expectations from the army and navy; and the event was, that the King, or somebody for him, applied to parliament to have his own salary raised an hundred thousand a year, which being done, every thing else was laid aside.

With respect to another class of men, the inferior clergy, I forbear to enlarge on their condition; but all partialities and prejudices for, or against, different modes and forms of religion aside, common justice will determine, whether there ought to be an income of twenty or thirty pounds a year to one man, and of ten thousand to another. I speak on this subject with the more freedom, because I am known not to be a Presbyterian; and therefore the cant cry of court sycophants, about church and meeting, kept up to amuse and bewilder the nation, cannot be raised against me.

Ye simple men, on both sides the question, do ye not see through this courtly craft? If ye can be kept disputing and wrangling about church and meeting, ye just answer the purpose of every courtier, who lives the while on the spoil of the taxes, and laughs at your credulity. Every religion is good that teaches man to be good; and I know of none that instructs him to be bad.

All the before-mentioned calculations, suppose only sixteen millions and an half of taxes paid into the exchequer, after the expence of collection and drawbacks at the custom-house and excise-office are deducted; whereas the sum paid into the exchequer is very nearly, if not quite, seventeen millions. The taxes raised in Scotland and Ireland are expended in those countries, and therefore their savings will come out of their own taxes; but if any part be paid into the English exchequer, it might be remitted. This will not make one hundred thousand pounds a year difference.

There now remains only the national debt to be considered. In the year 1789, the interest, exclusive of the tontine, was 9,150,138*l.* How much the capital has been reduced since that time the minister best knows. But after paying the interest, abolishing the tax on houses and windows, the commutation tax, and the poor rates; and making all the provisions for the poor, for the education of children, the support of the aged, the disbanded part of the army and navy, and encreasing the pay of the remainder, there will be a surplus of one million.

The present scheme of paying off the national debt appears to me, speaking as an indifferent person, to be an ill-concerted, if not a fallacious job. The burthen of the national debt consists not in its being so many millions, or so many hundred millions, but in the quantity of taxes collected every year to pay the interest. If this quantity continue the same, the burthen of the national debt is the same to all intents and purposes, be the capital more or less. The only knowledge which the public can have of the reduction of the debt, must be through the reduction of taxes for paying the interest. The debt, therefore, is not reduced one farthing to the public by all the millions that have been paid; and it would require more money now to purchase up the capital, than when the scheme began.

Digressing for a moment at this point, to which I shall return again, I look back to the appointment of Mr. Pitt, as minister.

I was then in America. The war was over; and though resentment had ceased, memory was still alive.

When the news of the coalition arrived, though it was a matter of no concern to me as a citizen of America, I felt it as a man. It had something in it which shocked, by publicly sporting with decency, if not with principle. It was impudence in Lord North; it was want of firmness in Mr. Fox.

Mr. Pitt was, at that time, what may be called a maiden character in politics. So far from being hackneyed, he appeared not to be initiated into the first mysteries of court intrigue. Every thing was in his favour. Resentment against the coalition served as friendship to him, and his ignorance of vice was credited for virtue. With the return of peace, commerce and prosperity would rise of itself; yet even this encrease was thrown to his account.

When he came to the helm the storm was over, and he had nothing to interrupt his course. It required even ingenuity to be wrong, and he succeeded. A little time shewed him the same sort of man as his predecessors had been. Instead of profiting by those errors which had accumulated a burthen of taxes unparalleled in the world, he sought, I might almost say, he advertised for enemies, and provoked means to encrease taxation. Aiming at something, he knew not what, he ransacked Europe and India for adventures, and abandoning the fair pretensions he began with, became the knight-errant of modern times.

It is unpleasant to see character throw itself away. It is more so to see one's-self deceived. Mr. Pitt had merited nothing, but he promised much. He gave symptoms of a mind superior to the meanness and corruption of courts. His apparent candour encouraged expectations; and the public confidence, stunned, wearied, and confounded by a chaos of parties, revived and attached itself to him. But mistaking, as he has done, the disgust of the nation against the coalition, for merit in himself, he has rushed into measures, which a man less supported would not have presumed to act.

All this seems to shew that change of ministers amounts to nothing. One goes out, another comes in, and still the same measures, vices, and extravagance are pursued. It signifies not who is minister. The defect lies in the system. The foundation and the superstructure of the government is bad. Prop it as you please, it continually sinks into court government and ever will.

I return, as I promised, to the subject of the national debt, that offspring of the Dutch-Anglo revolution, and its handmaid the Hanover succession.

But it is now too late to enquire how it began. Those to whom it is due have advanced the money; and whether it was well or ill spent, or pocketed, is not their crime. It is, however, easy to see, that as the nation proceeds in contemplating the nature and principles of government, and to understand taxes, and make comparisons between those of America, France, and England, it will be next to impossible to keep it in the same torpid state it has hitherto been. Some reform must, from the necessity of the case, soon begin. It is not whether these principles press with little or much force in the present moment. They are out. They are abroad in the world, and no force can stop them. Like a secret told, they are beyond recall; and he must be blind indeed that does not see that a change is already beginning.

Nine millions of dead taxes is a serious thing, and this not only for bad, but in a great measure for foreign government. By putting the power of making war into the hands of foreigners who came for what they could get, little else was to be expected than what has happened.

Reasons are already advanced in this work shewing that whatever the reforms in the taxes may be, they ought to be made in the current expences of government, and not in the part applied to the interest of the national debt. By remitting the taxes of the poor, *they* will be totally relieved, and all discontent on their part will be taken away; and by striking off such of the taxes as are already mentioned, the nation will more than recover the whole expence of the mad American war.

There will then remain only the national debt as a subject of discontent; and in order to remove, or rather to prevent this, it would be good policy in the stock-holders themselves to consider it as property, subject like all other property, to bear some portion of the taxes. It would give to it both popularity and security, and as a great part of its present inconvenience is balanced by the capital which it keeps alive, a measure of this kind would so far add to that balance as to silence objections.

This may be done by such gradual means as to accomplish all that is necessary with the greatest ease and convenience.

Instead of taxing the capital, the best method would be to tax the interest by some progressive ratio, and to lessen the public taxes in the same proportion as the interest diminished.

Suppose the interest was taxed one halfpenny in the pound the first year, a penny more the second, and to proceed by a certain ratio to be determined upon, always less than any other tax upon property. Such a tax would be subtracted from the interest at the time of payment, without any expence of collection.

One halfpenny in the pound would lessen the interest and consequently the taxes, twenty thousand pounds. The tax on waggons amounts to this sum, and this tax might be taken off the first year. The second year the tax on female servants, or some other of the like amount might also be taken off, and by proceeding in this manner, always applying the tax raised from the property of the debt towards its extinction, and not carry it to the current services, it would liberate itself.

The stockholders, notwithstanding this tax, would pay less taxes than they do now. What they would save by the extinction of the poor-rates, and the tax on houses and windows, and the commutation tax, would be considerably greater than what this tax, slow, but certain in its operation, amounts to.

It appears to me to be prudence to look out for measures that may apply under any circumstance that may approach. There is, at this moment, a crisis in the affairs of Europe that requires it. Preparation now is wisdom. If taxation be once let loose, it will be difficult to re-instate it; neither would the relief be so effectual, as to proceed by some certain and gradual reduction.

The fraud, hypocrisy, and imposition of governments, are now beginning to be too well understood to promise them any long career. The farce of monarchy and aristocracy, in all countries, is following that of chivalry, and Mr. Burke is dressing for the funeral. Let it then pass quietly to the tomb of all other follies, and the mourners be comforted.

The time is not very distant when England will laugh at itself for sending to Holland, Hanover, Zell, or Brunswick for men, at the expence of a million a year, who understood neither her laws, her language, nor her interest, and whose capacities would scarcely have fitted them for the office of a parish constable. If government could be trusted to such hands, it must be some easy and simple thing indeed, and materials fit for all the purposes may be found in every town and village in England.

When it shall be said in any country in the world, my poor are happy; neither ignorance nor distress is to be found among them; my jails are empty of prisoners, my streets of beggars; the aged are not in want, the taxes are not oppressive; the rational world is my friend, because I am the friend of its happiness: when these things can be said, then may that country boast its constitution and its government.

Within the space of a few years we have seen two Revolutions, those of America and France. In the former, the contest was long, and the conflict severe; in the latter, the nation acted with such a consolidated impulse, that having no foreign enemy to contend with, the revolution was complete in power the moment it appeared. From both those instances it is evident, that the greatest forces that can be brought into the field of revolutions, are reason and common interest. Where these can have the opportunity of acting, opposition dies with fear, or crumbles away by conviction. It is a great standing which they have now universally obtained; and we may hereafter hope to see revolutions, or changes in governments, produced with the same quiet operation by which any measure, determinable by reason and discussion, is accomplished.

When a nation changes its opinion and habits of thinking, it is no longer to be governed as before; but it would not only be wrong, but bad policy, to attempt by force what ought to be accomplished by reason. Rebellion consists in forcibly opposing the general will of a nation, whether by a party or by a government. There ought, therefore, to be in every nation, a method of occasionally ascertaining the state of public opinion with respect to government. On this point the old government of France was superior to the present government of England, because, on extraordinary occasions, recourse could be had to what was then called the States General. But in England there are no such occasional bodies; and as to those who are now called Representatives, a great part of them are mere machines of the court, placemen, and dependants.

I presume, that though all the people of England pay taxes, not an hundredth part of them are electors, and the members of one of the houses of parliament represent nobody but themselves. There is, therefore, no power but the voluntary will of the people that has a right to act in any matter respecting a general reform; and by the same right that two persons can confer on such a subject, a thousand may. The object in all such preliminary proceedings, is to find out what the general sense of a nation is, and to be governed by it. If it prefer a bad or defective government to a reform, or chuse to pay ten times more taxes than there is occasion for, it has a right so to do; and so long as the majority do not impose conditions on the minority, different to what they impose on themselves, though there may be much error, there is no injustice. Neither will the error continue long. Reason and discussion will soon bring things right, however wrong they may begin. By such a process no tumult is to be apprehended. The poor, in all countries, are naturally both peaceable and grateful in all reforms in which their interest and happiness is included. It is only by neglecting and rejecting them that they become tumultuous.

The objects that now press on the public attention are, the French revolution, and the prospect of a general revolution in governments. Of all nations in Europe, there is none so much interested in the French revolution as England. Enemies for ages, and that at a vast expence, and without any national object, the opportunity now presents itself of amicably closing the scene, and joining their efforts to reform the rest of Europe. By doing this, they will not only prevent the further effusion of blood, and encrease of taxes, but be in a condition of getting rid of a considerable part of their present burthens, as has been already stated. Long experience however has shewn, that reforms of this kind are not those which old governments wish to promote; and therefore it is to nations, and not to such governments, that these matters present themselves.

In the preceding part of this work, I have spoken of an alliance between England, France, and America, for purposes that were to be afterwards mentioned. Though I have no direct authority on the part of America, I have good reason to conclude, that she is disposed to enter into a consideration of such a measure, provided, that the governments with which she might ally, acted as national governments, and not as courts enveloped in intrigue and mystery. That France as a nation, and a national government, would prefer an alliance with England, is a matter of certainty. Nations, like individuals, who have long been enemies, without knowing each other, or knowing why, become the better friends when they discover the errors and impositions under which they had acted.

Admitting, therefore, the probability of such a connection, I will state some matters by which such an alliance, together with that of Holland, might render service, not only to the parties immediately concerned, but to all Europe.

It is, I think, certain, that if the fleets of England, France, and Holland were confederated, they could propose, with effect, a limitation to, and a general dismantling of all the navies in Europe, to a certain proportion to be agreed upon.

First, That no new ship of war shall be built by any power in Europe, themselves included.

Secondly, That all the navies now in existence shall be put back, suppose to one-tenth of their present force. This will save to France and England at least two millions sterling annually to each, and their relative force be in the same proportion as it is now. If men will permit themselves to think, as rational beings ought to think, nothing can appear more ridiculous and absurd, exclusive of all moral reflections, than to be at the expence of building navies, filling them with men; and then hauling them into the ocean, to try which can sink each other fastest. Peace, which costs nothing, is attended with infinitely more advantage, than any victory with all its expence. But this, though it best answers the purpose of nations, does not that of court governments, whose habited policy is pretence for taxation, places, and offices.

It is, I think, also certain, that the above confederated powers, together with that of the United States of America, can propose with effect, to Spain, the independance of South America, and the opening those countries of immense extent and wealth to the general commerce of the world, as North America now is.

With how much more glory, and advantage to itself, does a nation act, when it exerts its powers to rescue the world from bondage, and to create itself friends, than when it employs those powers to encrease ruin, desolation, and misery. The horrid scene that is now acting by the English government in the East-Indies, is fit only to be told of Goths and Vandals, who, destitute of principle, robbed and tortured the world they were incapable of enjoying.

The opening of South America would produce an immense field of commerce, and a ready money market for manufactures, which the eastern world does not. The East is already a country full of manufactures, the importation of which is not only an injury to the manufactures of England, but a drain upon its specie. The balance against England by this trade is regularly upwards of half a million annually sent out in the East-India ships in silver; and this is the reason, together with German intrigue, and German subsidies, there is so little silver in England.

But any war is harvest to such governments, however ruinous it may be to a nation. It serves to keep up deceitful expectations which prevent a people looking into the defects and abuses of government. It is the *lo here!* and the *lo there!* that amuses and cheats the multitude.

Never did so great an opportunity offer itself to England, and to all Europe, as is produced by the two Revolutions of America and France. By the former, freedom has a national champion in the Western world; and by the latter, in Europe. When another nation shall join France, despotism and bad government will scarcely dare to appear. To use a trite expression, the iron is becoming hot all over Europe. The insulted German and the enslaved Spaniard, the Russ and the Pole, are beginning to think. The present age will hereafter merit to be called the Age of reason, and the present generation will appear to the future as the Adam of a new world.

When all the governments of Europe shall be established on the representative system, nations will become acquainted, and the animosities and prejudices fomented by the intrigue and artifice of courts, will cease. The oppressed soldier will become a freeman; and the tortured sailor, no longer dragged along the streets like a felon, will pursue his mercantile voyage in safety. It would be better that nations should continue the pay of their soldiers during their lives, and give them their discharge and restore them to freedom and their friends, and cease recruiting, than retain such multitudes at the same expence, in a condition useless to society and themselves. As soldiers have hitherto been treated in most countries, they might be said to be without a friend. Shunned by the citizen on an apprehension of being enemies to liberty, and too often insulted by those who commanded them, their condition was a double oppression. But where genuine principles of liberty pervade a people, every thing is restored to order; and the soldier civily treated, returns the civility.

In contemplating revolutions, it is easy to perceive that they may arise from two distinct causes; the one, to avoid or get rid of some great calamity; the other, to obtain some great and positive good; and the two may be distinguished by the names of active and passive revolutions. In those which proceed from the former cause, the temper becomes incensed and sowered; and the redress, obtained by danger, is too often sullied by revenge. But in those which proceed from the latter, the heart, rather animated than agitated, enters serenely upon the subject. Reason and discussion, persuasion and conviction, become the weapons in the contest, and it is only when those are attempted to be suppressed that recource is had to violence. When men unite in agreeing that a *thing is good,* could it be obtained, such as relief from a burden of taxes and the extinction of corruption, the object is more than half accomplished. What they approve as the end, they will promote in the means.

Will any man say, in the present excess of taxation, falling so heavily on the poor, that a remission of five pounds annually of taxes to one hundred and four thousand poor families is not a *good thing?* Will he say, that a remission of seven pounds annually to one hundred thousand other poor families – of eight pounds annually to another hundred thousand poor families, and of ten pounds annually to fifty thousand poor and widowed families, are not *good things?* And to proceed a step farther in this climax, will he say, that to provide against the misfortunes to which all human life is subject, by securing six pounds annually for all poor, distressed, and reduced persons of the age of fifty and until sixty, and of ten pounds annually after sixty is not a *good thing?*

Will he say, that an abolition of two million of poor-rates to the housekeepers, and of the whole of the house and window-light tax and of the commutation tax is not a *good thing?* Or will he say, that to abolish corruption is a *bad thing?*

If, therefore, the good to be obtained be worthy of a passive, rational, and costless revolution, it would be bad policy to prefer waiting for a calamity that should force a violent one. I have no idea, considering the reforms which are now passing and spreading throughout Europe, that England will permit herself to be the last; and where the occasion and the opportunity quietly offer, it is better than to wait for a turbulent necessity. It may be considered as an honour to the animal faculties of man to obtain redress by courage and danger, but it is far greater honour to the rational faculties to accomplish the same object by reason, accommodation, and general consent[26].

As reforms, or revolutions, call them which you please, extend themselves among nations, those nations will form connections and conventions, and when a few are thus confederated, the progress will be rapid, till despotism and corrupt government be totally expelled, at least out of two quarters of the world, Europe and America. The Algerine piracy may then be commanded to cease, for it is only by the malicious policy of old governments, against each other, that it exists.

26. I know it is the opinion of many of the most enlightened characters in France (there always will be those who see farther into events than others) not only among the general mass of citizens, but of many of the principal members of the former National Assembly, that the monarchical plan will not continue many years in that country. They have found out, that as wisdom cannot be made hereditary, power ought not; and that, for a man to merit a million stirling a year from a nation, he ought to have a mind capable of comprehending from an atom to a universe; which, if he had, he would be above receiving the pay. But they wished not to appear to lead the nation faster than its own reason and interest dictated. In all the conversations where I have been present upon this subject, the idea always was, that when such a time, from the general opinion of the nation, shall arrive, that the honourable and liberal method would be, to make a handsome present in fee simple to the person whoever he may be, that shall then be in the monarchical office, and for him to retire to the enjoyment of private life, possessing his share of general rights and privileges, and to be no more accountable to the public for his time and his conduct than any other citizen.

Throughout this work, various and numerous as the subjects are, which I have taken up and investigated, there is only a single paragraph upon religion, viz. *"that every religion is good, that teaches man to be good."*

I have carefully avoided to enlarge upon the subject, because I am inclined to believe, that what is called the present ministry wish to see contentions about religion kept up, to prevent the nation turning its attention to subjects of government. It is, as if they were to say, *"Look that way, or any way, but this."*

But as religion is very improperly made a political machine, and the reality of it is thereby destroyed, I will conclude this work with stating in what light religion appears to me.

If we suppose a large family of children, who, on any particular day, or particular circumstance, made it a custom to present to their parent some token of their affection and gratitude, each of them would make a different offering, and most probably in a different manner. Some would pay their congratulations in themes of verse or prose, by some little devices, as their genius dictated, or according to what they thought would please; and, perhaps, the least of all, not able to do any of those things, would ramble into the garden, or the field, and gather what it thought the prettiest flower it could find, though, perhaps, it might be but a simple weed. The parent would be more gratified by such variety, than if the whole of them had acted on a concerted plan, and each had made exactly the same offering. This would have the cold appearance of contrivance, or the harsh one of controul. But of all unwelcome things, nothing could more afflict the parent than to know, that the whole of them had afterwards gotten together by the ears, boys and girls, fighting, scratching, reviling, and abusing each other about which was the best or the worst present.

Why may we not suppose, that the great Father of all is pleased with variety of devotion; and that the greatest offence we can act, is that by which we seek to torment and render each other miserable. For my own part, I am fully satisfied that what I am now doing, with an endeavour to conciliate mankind, to render their condition happy, to unite nations that have hitherto been enemies, and to extirpate the horrid practice of war, and break the chains of slavery and oppression, is acceptable in his sight, and being the best service I can perform, I act it chearfully.

I do not believe that any two men, on what are called doctrinal points, think alike who think at all. It is only those who have not thought that appear to agree. It is in this case as with what is called the British constitution. It has been taken for granted to be good, and encomiums have supplied the place of proof. But when the nation come to examine into its principles and the abuses it admits, it will be found to have more defects than I have pointed out in this work and the former.

As to what are called national religions, we may, with as much propriety, talk of national Gods. It is either political craft or the remains of the Pagan system, when every nation had its separate and particular deity. Among all the writers of the English church clergy, who have treated on the general subject of religion, the present Bishop of Landaff has not been excelled, and it is with much pleasure that I take the opportunity of expressing this token of respect.

I have now gone through the whole of the subject, at least, as far as it appears to me at present. It has been my intention for the five years I have been in Europe, to offer an address to the people of England on the subject of government, if the opportunity presented itself before I returned to America. Mr. Burke has thrown it in my way, and I thank him. On a certain occasion three years ago, I pressed him to propose a national convention to be fairly elected for the purpose of taking the state of the nation into consideration, but I found, that however strongly the parliamentary current was then setting against the party he acted with, their policy was to keep every thing within that field of corruption, and trust to accidents. Long experience had shewn that parliaments would follow any change of ministers, and on this they rested their hopes and their expectations.

Formerly, when divisions arose respecting governments, recourse was had to the sword, and a civil war ensued. That savage custom is exploded by the new system, and reference is had to national conventions. Discussion and the general will arbitrates the question, and to this, private opinion yields with a good grace, and order is preserved uninterrupted.

Some gentlemen have affected to call the principles upon which this work and the former part of *Rights of Man* are founded, "a new fangled doctrine." The question is not whether those principles are new or old, but whether they are right or wrong. Suppose the former, I will shew their effect by a figure easily understood.

It is now towards the middle of February. Were I to take a turn into the country, the trees would present a leafless winterly appearance. As people are apt to pluck twigs as they walk along, I perhaps might do the same, and by chance might observe, that a *single bud* on that twig had begun to swell. I should reason very unnaturally, or rather not reason at all, to suppose *this* was the *only* bud in England which had this appearance. Instead of deciding thus, I should instantly conclude, that the same appearance was beginning, or about to begin, every where; and though the vegetable sleep will continue longer on some trees and plants than on others, and though some of them may not *blossom* for two or three years, all will be in leaf in the summer, except those which are *rotten*. What pace the political summer may keep with the natural no human foresight can determine. It is, however, not difficult to perceive that the spring is begun. – Thus wishing, as I sincerely do, freedom and happiness to all nations, I close the

SECOND PART.

Appendix.

AS the publication of this work has been delayed beyond the time intended, I think it not improper, all circumstances considered, to state the causes that have occasioned the delay.

The reader will probably observe, that some parts in the plan contained in this work for reducing the taxes, and certain parts in Mr. Pitt's speech at the opening of the present session, Tuesday, January 31, are so much alike, as to induce a belief, that either the Author had taken the hint from Mr. Pitt, or Mr. Pitt from the Author. – I will first point out the parts that are similar, and then state such circumstances as I am acquainted with, leaving the reader to make his own conclusion.

Considering it almost an unprecedented case, that taxes should be proposed to be taken off, it is equally as extraordinary that such a measure should occur to two persons at the same time; and still more so, (considering the vast variety and multiplicity of taxes) that they should hit on the same specific taxes. Mr. Pitt has mentioned, in his speech, the tax on *Carts* and *Waggons* – that on *Female Servants* – the lowering the tax on *Candles,* and the taking off the tax of three shillings on *Houses* having under seven windows.

Every one of those specific taxes are a part of the plan contained in this work, and proposed also to be taken off. Mr. Pitt's plan, it is true, goes no farther than to a reduction of three hundred and twenty thousand pounds; and the reduction proposed in this work to nearly six millions. I have made my calculations on only sixteen millions and an half of revenue, still asserting that it was "very nearly, if not quite, seventeen millions." Mr. Pitt states it at 16,690,000. I know enough of the matter to say, that he has not *over*stated it. Having thus given the particulars, which correspond in this work and his speech, I will state a chain of circumstances that may lead to some explanation.

The first hint for lessening the taxes, and that as a consequence flowing from the French revolution, is to be found in the ADDRESS and DECLARATION of the Gentlemen who met at the Thatched-House Tavern, August 20, 1791. Among many other particulars stated in that Address is the following, put as an interrogation to the government opposers of the French Revolution. *"Are they sorry that the pretence for new oppressive taxes, and the occasion for continuing many old taxes will be at an end?*["]

It is well known, that the persons who chiefly frequent the Thatched-House Tavern, are men of court connections, and so much did they take this Address and Declaration respecting the French revolution and the reduction of taxes in disgust, that the Landlord was under the necessity of informing the Gentlemen, who composed the meeting of the twentieth of August, and who proposed holding another meeting, that he could not receive them[27].

What was only hinted at in the Address and Declaration, respecting taxes and principles of government, will be found reduced to a regular system in this work. But as Mr. Pitt's speech contains some of the same things respecting taxes, I now come to give the circumstances before alluded to.

The case is: This work was intended to be published just before the meeting of Parliament, and for that purpose a considerable part of the copy was put into the printer's hands in September, and all the remaining copy, as far as page [354], which contains the parts to which Mr. Pitt's speech is similar, was given to him full six weeks before the meeting of parliament, and he was informed of the time at which it was to appear. He had composed nearly the whole about a fortnight before the time of Parliament meeting, and had printed as far as page [327], and had given me a proof of

---

27. The gentleman who signed the address and declaration as chairman of the meeting, M. Horne Tooke, being generally supposed to be the person who drew it up, and having spoken much in commendation of it, has been jocularly accused of praising his own work. To free him from this embarrassment, and to save him the repeated trouble of mentioning the author, as he has not failed to do, I make no hesitation in saying, that as the opportunity of benefiting by the French Revolution easily occurred to me, I drew up the publication in question, and shewed it to him and some other gentlemen; who, fully approving it, held a meeting for the purpose of making it public, and subscribed to the amount of fifty guineas to defray the expence of advertising. I believe there are at this time, in England, a greater number of men acting on disinterested principles, and determined to look into the nature and practices of government themselves, and not blindly trust, as has hitherto been the case, either to government generally, or to parliaments, or to parliamentary opposition, than at any former period. Had this been done a century ago, corruption and taxation had not arrived to the height they are now at.

the next sheet, up to page [336]. It was then in sufficient forwardness to be out at the time proposed, as two other sheets were ready for striking off. I had before told him, that if he thought he should be straightened for time, I would get part of the work done at another press, which he desired me not to do. In this manner the work stood on the Tuesday fortnight preceding the meeting of Parliament, when all at once, without any previous intimation, though I had been with him the evening before, he sent me, by one of his workmen, all the remaining copy, from page [327], declining to go on with the work *on any consideration.*

To account for this extraordinary conduct I was totally at a loss, as he stopped at the part where the arguments on systems and principles of government closed, and where the plan for the reduction of taxes, the education of children, and the support of the poor and the aged begins; and still more especially, as he had, at the time of his beginning to print, and before he had seen the whole copy, offered a thousand pounds for the copy-right, together with the future copy-right of the former part of the Rights of Man. I told the person who brought me this offer that I should not accept it, and wished it not to be renewed, giving him as my reason, that though I believed the printer to be an honest man, I would never put it in the power of any printer or publisher to suppress or alter a work of mine, by making him master of the copy, or give to him the right of selling it to any minister or to any other person, or to treat as a mere matter of traffic, that which I intended should operate as a principle.

His refusal to complete the work (which he could not purchase) obliged me to seek for another printer, and this of consequence would throw the publication back till after the meeting of Parliament, otherways it would have appeared that Mr. Pitt had only taken up a part of the plan which I had more fully stated.

Whether that gentleman, or any other, had seen the work, or any part of it, is more than I have authority to say. But the manner in which the work was returned, and the particular time at which this was done, and that after the offers he had made, are suspicious circumstances. I know what the opinion of booksellers and publishers is upon such a case, but as to my own opinion, I chuse to make no declaration. There are many ways by which proof sheets may be procured by other persons before a work publicly appear[s]; to which I shall add a certain circumstance, which is,

A ministerial bookseller in Piccadilly who has been employed, as common report says, by a clerk of one of the boards closely connected with the ministry (the board of trade and plantation of which Hawksbury is president) to publish what he calls my Life (I wish his own life and that those of the cabinet were as good) used to have his books printed at the same printing-office that I employed; but when the former part of *Rights of Man* came out, he took his work away in dudgeon; and about a week or ten days before the printer returned my copy, he came to make him an offer of his work again, which was accepted. This would consequently give him admission into the printing-office where the sheets of this work were then lying; and as booksellers and printers are free with each other, he would have the opportunity of seeing what was going on. – Be the case however as it may, Mr. Pitt's plan, little and diminutive as it is, would have had a very awkward appearance, had this work appeared at the time the printer had engaged to finish it.

I have now stated the particulars which occasioned the delay, from the proposal to purchase, to the refusal to print. If all the Gentlemen are innocent, it is very unfortunate for them that such a variety of suspicious circumstances should, without any design, arrange themselves together.

Having now finished this part, I will conclude with stating another circumstance.

About a fortnight or three weeks before the meeting of Parliament, a small addition, amounting to about twelve shillings and six pence a year, was made to the pay of the soldiers, or rather, their pay was docked so much less. Some Gentlemen who knew, in part, that this work would contain a plan of reforms respecting the oppressed condition of soldiers wished me to add a note to the work, signifying, that the part upon that subject had been in the printer's hands some weeks before that addition of pay was proposed. I declined doing this, lest it should be interpreted into an air of vanity, or an endeavour to excite suspicion (for which, perhaps, there might be no grounds) that some of the government gentlemen, had, by some means or other, made out what this work would contain: and had not the printing been interrupted so as to occasion a delay beyond the time fixed for publication, nothing contained in this appendix would have appeared.

– THOMAS PAINE.

REASONS

FOR

WISHING TO PRESERVE

THE

LIFE

OF

LOUIS CAPET.

AS DELIVERED TO THE

NATIONAL CONVENTION.

By THOMAS PAINE.

MEMBER OF THE NATIONAL CONVENTION, AND AUTHOR OF
COMMON SENSE, A LETTER TO THE ABBE RAYNAL, &C. &C. &C.

REASONS, &c.

Citizen President,

MY hatred and abhorrence of monarchy are sufficiently known; they originate in principles of Reason and Conviction, nor, except with life, can they ever be extirpated; but my compassion for the unfortunate, whether friend or enemy, is equally lively and sincere.

I voted that Louis should be tried, because it was necessary to afford proofs to the world of the perfidy, corruption and abomination of the monarchical system. The infinity of evidence that has been produced, exposes them in the most glaring and hideous colours. Thence it results, that monarchy, whatever form it may assume, arbitrary or otherwise, becomes neces-

"Reasons for Wishing to Preserve the Life of Louis Capet. As Delivered to the National Convention" (London: James Ridgway, 1793).

sarily a centre, round which are united every species of corruption, and that the *kingly trade* is no less destructive of all morality in the human breast, than the trade of an executioner is destructive of its sensibility.

I remember, during my residence in another country, that I was exceedingly struck with a sentence of M. Autheine, at the Jacobines, which corresponds exactly with my own idea, "Make me a king to-day," said he, "and I shall be a robber to-morrow."

Nevertheless, I am inclined to believe, that if Louis Capet had been born in an obscure condition, had he lived within the circle of an amiable and respectable neighbourhood, at liberty to practice the duties of domestic life, had he been thus situated, I cannot believe that he would have shewn himself destitute of social virtues; we are in a moment of fermentation like this, naturally little indulgent to his vices, or rather to those of monarchical governments, we regard them with additional horror and indignation; not that they are more heinous than those of his predecessors, but because our eyes are now open, and the veil of delusion at length withdrawn, yet the lamentable, degraded state to which he is actually reduced, is surely far less imputable to him, than to the Constituent Assembly, which, of its own authority, without consent or advice of the people, restored him to the throne.

I was in Paris at the time of the flight, or abdication of Louis XVI, and when he was taken and brought back. The proposal of restoring to him the supreme power struck me with amazement; and although at that time, I was not a French Citizen, yet as a Citizen of the World, I employed all the efforts that depended on me to prevent it.

A small society, composed only of five persons, two of whom are now members of the Convention, took, at that time, the name of the Republican Club, (Societé Republicaine). This society opposed the restoration of Louis, not so much on account of his own personal offences, as in order to overthrow the monarchy, and to erect on its ruins the Republican System, and an equal representation.

With this design, I traced out in the English language certain propositions, which were translated, with some trifling alterations, and signed by Achilles Duchetclet, actually Lieutenant-General in the army of the French Republic, and at that time one of the five members which composed our little party; the law requiring the signature of a citizen at bottom of each printed paper.

The paper was indignantly torn by Malonet and brought forth in this very room as an article of accusation against the Person who had signed it, the Author, and their adherents, but such is the revolution of events, that this paper is now revived, and brought forth for a very opposite purpose; – To remind the Nation of the error of that unfortunate day, that fatal error of having not then banished Louis XVI. from its bosom, and to plead this day in favour of his Exile, preferably to his death.

The paper in question was conceived in the following terms:

"Brethren and Fellow Citizens,

The serene tranquillity, the mutual confidence which prevailed amongst us during the time of the late King's escape, the indifference with which we beheld him return, are unequivocal proofs that the absence of a King is more desirable than his presence, and that he is not only a Political superfluity, but a grievous burthen pressing hard on the whole Nation.

Let us not be imposed on by sophisms: All that concerns this man, is reduced to four points.

He has abdicated the Throne in having fled from his post. Abdication and desertion are not characterized by the length of absence; but by the single act of flight. In the present instance, the act is every thing, and the time nothing.

The Nation can never give back its confidence to a Man who false to his trust, perjured to his oath, conspires a clandestine flight, obtains a fraudulent Passport, conceals a King of France under the disguise of a Valet, directs his course towards a frontier covered with traitors and deserters, and evidently meditates a return into our country, with a force capable of imposing his own despotic Laws.

Whether his flight ought to be considered as his own act, or the act of those who fled with him. Was it a spontaneous resolution of his own, or was it inspired into him by others? The alternative is immaterial: Whether Fool or Hypocrite, Idiot or Traitor, he has proved himself equally unworthy of the vast important functions that had been delegated to him.

In every sense that the question can be considered, the reciprocal obligation which subsisted between us is dissolved. He holds no longer authority: We owe him no longer obedience; We see in him now no more than an indifferent Person; we can regard him only as Louis Capet.

The history of France presents little else than a long series of public calamity, which takes its source from the vices of her Kings; We have been the wretched victims that have never ceased to suffer either for them or by them. The Catalogue of their oppressions was complete, but to complete the sum of their crimes, treason yet was wanting: Now, the only vacancy is filled up, the dreadful list is full; The system is exhausted; There are no remaining errors for them to commit, their reign is consequently at an end.

What kind of office must that be in a Government which requires neither experience nor ability to execute? that may be abandoned to the desperate chance of birth, that may be filled by an Idiot, a Madman, a Tyrant, with equal effect, as by the good, the virtuous and the wise. An office of this nature is a mere nonentity; It is a place of Shew, not of Use. Let France then, arrived at the age of Reason, no longer be deluded by the sound of words, and let her deliberately examine, if a King, however insignificant and contemptible in himself, may not at the same time be extremely dangerous.

The thirty millions which it costs to support a King in the eclat of stupid brutal Luxury, present us with an easy method of reducing taxes, which reduction would at once release the people, and stop the progress of political corruption. The grandeur of nations consists not, as Kings pretend in the splendor of Thrones, but in a conscious sense of their own dignity, and in a Just disdain of those barbarous follies, and crimes, which under the sanction of Royalty, have hitherto desolated Europe.

As to the Personal Safety of Mr. Louis Capet, it is so much the more confirmed as France will not stop to degrade herself by a spirit of Revenge against a Wretch, who has dishonoured himself. In defending a just and glorious cause, it is not possible to degrade it, and the universal tranquillity which prevails, is an undeniable proof that a free People know how to respect themselves."

Having thus explained the principles and exertions of the Republicans at that fatal period when Louis was reinstated in full Possession of the executive Power which by his flight had been suspended, I return to the subject, and to the deplorable condition in which the Man is now actually involved.

What was neglected at the time of which I have been speaking, has been since brought about by the force of necessity; The wilful treacherous defects in the former constitution have been brought to light, the continual alarm of Treason and Conspiracy rouzed the Nation and produced eventually a second revolution. The People have beat down Royalty, never, never to rise again; They have brought Louis Capet to the bar, and demonstrated in the face of the whole World, the Intrigues, the Cabals, the falsehood, corruption, and rooted depravity, the inevitable effects of monarchical Governments. There remains then only one question to be considered, what is to be done with this Man?

For myself, I freely confess that when I reflect on the unaccountable folly, that restored the executive Power to his hands, all covered as he was with Perjuries and Treason, I am far more ready to condemn the Constituent Assembly than the unfortunate Prisoner Louis Capet.

But abstracted from every other consideration, there is one circumstance in his Life which ought to cover, or at least to palliate, a great number of his transgressions, and this very circumstance affords the French Nation a blessed occasion of extricating itself from the yoke of Kings, without defiling itself in the impurities of their blood.

It is to France alone I know, that the United States of America owe that support which enabled them to shake off the unjust and tyrannical yoke of *****.[1] The ardour and zeal which she displayed to provide both men and money, were the natural consequences of a thirst for Liberty. But as the Nation at that time, restrained by the shackles of her own Government, could only act by means of a Monarchical organ, this organ – whatever in other respects the object might be – certainly performed a good, a great action. Let then these United States be the safeguard and asylum of Louis Capet. There, hereafter, far removed from the miseries and crimes of Royalty, he may learn, from the constant aspect of Public prosperity, that the true system of Government consists, not in Kings, but in fair, equal and honourable Representation.

In relating this circumstance, and in submitting this proposition, I consider myself as a citizen of both countries. I submit it as a citizen of America, who feels the debt of gratitude which he owes to every Frenchman. I submit it also as a Man, who, although the enemy of Kings, cannot forget that they are subject to human frailties. I support my proposition as a Citizen of the French Republic, because it appears to me the best, the most politic measure, that can be adopted.

As far as my experience in public life extends, I have ever observed, that the great mass of the People are invariably just, both in their intentions, and in their object; but the true method of accomplishing that effect, does not always shew itself in the first instance.

For example, the English Nation had groaned under the despotism of the Stuarts. Hence Charles the First lost his life; yet Charles the Second was restored to all the plenitude of power, which his father had lost.

Forty years had not expired, when the same family strove to re-establish their ancient oppressions; so the nation then banished from its territories the whole race. The remedy was effectual. The Stuart family sunk into obscurity, confounded itself with the multitude, and is at length extinct.

The French Nation, more enlightened than England was at that time, has carried her measures of Government to a greater length. France is not satisfied with exposing the guilt of the Monarch, she has penetrated into the vices and horrors of the Monarchy. She has shewn them clear as daylight, and for ever crushed that infernal system; and he, whoever he may be, that

1. [Editors' note:] Britain.

should ever dare to reclaim those rights, he would be regarded not as a Pretender, but punished as a Traitor.

Two brothers of Louis Capet have banished themselves from the Country; but they are obliged to comply with the spirit and etiquette of the Courts where they reside. They can advance no pretensions on their own account, so long as Louis shall live.

The history of Monarchy, in France, was a system pregnant with crimes and murders, cancelling all natural ties, even those by which brothers are united. We know how often they have assassinated each other, to pave a way to Power. As those hopes which the Emigrants had reposed in Louis XVI. are fled; the last which remains rests upon his death; and their situation inclines them to desire this catastrophe, that they may once again rally round a more active chief, and try one further effort under the fortune of the Ci-devant Monsieur and d'Artois.

That such an enterprise would precipitate them into a new abyss of calamity and disgrace, it is not difficult to foresee; but yet it might be attended with mutual loss, and it is our duty as Legislators, not to spill a drop of blood, when our purpose may be effectually accomplished without it.

It has been already proposed to abolish the punishment of death; and it is with infinite satisfaction, that I recollect the humane and excellent oration pronounced by Robespierre, on that subject, in the Constituent Assembly. This cause must find its advocates in every corner, where enlightened Politicians, and lovers of Humanity exist; and it ought, above all, to find them in this Assembly.

Monarchical Governments have trained the Human race, and inured it to the sanguinary arts and refinements of punishment; and it is exactly the same punishment, which has so long shocked the sight and tormented the patience of the People, that now, in their turn, they practise in revenge on their oppressors. But it becomes us to be strictly on our guard against the abomination and perversity of Monarchical examples: as France has been the first of European Nations to abolish Royalty, let her also be the first to abolish the Punishment of Death, and to find out a milder and more effectual substitute.

In the particular case now under consideration, I submit the following propositions:—1st. That the National Convention shall pronounce sentence of Banishment on Louis and his Family. 2. That Louis Capet shall be detained in prison till the end of the War; and at that epoch for the sentence of banishment to be executed.

THE

AGE

OF

REASON,

BEING

AN INVESTIGATION OF TRUE AND FABULOUS THEOLOGY,

BY THOMAS PAINE.

SECRETARY FOR FOREIGN AFFAIRS TO CONGRESS IN THE
AMERICAN WAR, AND AUTHOR OF THE WORKS ENTITLED
COMMON SENSE AND RIGHTS OF MAN, &C.

IT has been my intention, for several years past, to publish my thoughts upon religion. I am well aware of the difficulties that attend the subject; and from that consideration, had reserved it to a more advanced period of life. I intended it to be the last offering I should make to my fellow-citizens of all nations; and that at a time, when the purity of the motive that induced me to it, could not admit of a question, even by those who might disapprove the work.

The circumstance that has now taken place in France, of the total abolition of the whole national order of priesthood, and of every thing appertaining to compulsive systems of religion, and compulsive articles of faith, has not only precipitated my intention, but rendered a work of this kind exceed-

The Age of Reason: Being an Investigation of True and of Fabulous Theology (Paris: Barrois, 1794).

ingly necessary; left, in the general wreck of superstition, of false systems of government, and false theology, we lose sight of morality, of humanity, and of the theology that is true.

As several of my colleagues, and others of my fellow-citizens of France, have given me the example of making their voluntary and individual profession of faith, I also will make mine; and I do this with all that sincerity and frankness with which the mind of man communicates with itself.

I believe in one God, and no more; and I hope for happiness beyond this life.

I believe the equality of man, and I believe that religious duties consist in doing justice, loving mercy, and endeavouring to make our fellow-creatures happy.

But lest it should be supposed that I believe many other things in addition to these, I shall, in the progress of this work, declare the things I do not believe, and my reasons for not believing them.

I do not believe in the creed professed by the Jewish church, by the Roman church, by the Greek church, by the Turkish church, by the Protestant church, nor by any church that I know of. My own mind is my own church.

All national institutions of churches, whether Jewish, Christian, or Turkish, appear to me no other than human inventions set up to terrify and enslave mankind, and monopolize power and profit.

I do not mean by this declaration to condemn those who believe otherwise. They have the same right to their belief as I have to mine. But it is necessary to the happiness of man, that he be mentally faithful to himself. Infidelity does not consist in believing, or in disbelieving: it consists in professing to believe what he does not believe.

It is impossible to calculate the moral mischief, if I may so express it, that mental lying has produced in society. When a man has so far corrupted and prostituted the chastity of his mind, as to subscribe his professional belief to things he does not believe, he has prepared himself for the commission of every other crime. He takes up the trade of a priest for the sake of gain, and in order to *qualify* himself for that trade, he begins with a perjury. Can we conceive any thing more destructive to morality than this?

Soon after I had published the pamphlet, COMMON-SENSE, in America, I saw the exceeding probability that a Revolution in the System of Government, would be followed by a revolution in the system of religion. The adulterous connection of church and state, wherever it had taken place, whether Jewish, Christian, or Turkish, had so effectually prohibited, by pains and penalties, every discussion upon established creeds, and upon first principles of religion, that until the system of government should be changed, those subjects could not be brought fairly and openly before the world: but that whenever this should be done, a revolution in the system of religion would follow. Human inventions and priest-craft would be detected; and man would return to the pure, unmixed, and unadulterated belief of one God, and no more.

Every national church or religion has established itself by pretending some special mission from God communicated to certain individuals. The Jews have their Moses; the Christians their Jesus Christ, their apostles and saints; and the Turks their Mahomet; as if the way to God was not open to every man alike.

Each of those churches show certain books which they call *revelation,* or the word of God. The Jews say that their word of God was given by God to Moses face to face; the Christians say, that their word of God came by divine inspiration; and the Turks say, that their word of God (the Koran) was brought by an angel from heaven. Each of those churches accuses the other of unbelief; and, for my own part, I disbelieve them all.

As it is necessary to affix right ideas to words, I will, before I proceed further into the subject, offer some observations on the word *revelation.* Revelation, when applied to religion, means something communicated *immediately* from God to man.

No one will deny or dispute the power of the Almighty to make such a communication if he pleases. But admitting, for the sake of a case, that something has been revealed to a certain person, and not revealed to any other person, it is revelation to that person only. When he tells it to a second person, a second to a third, a third to a fourth, and so on, it ceases to be a revelation to all those persons. It is revelation to the first person only, and *hearsay* to every other; and consequently, they are not obliged to believe it.

It is a contradiction in terms and ideas to call any thing a revelation that comes to us at second hand, either verbally or in writing. Revelation is necessarily limited to the first communication. After this, it is only an account of something which that person says was a revelation made to him; and though he may find himself obliged to believe it, it cannot be incumbent on me to believe it in the same manner, for it was not a revelation made to *me,* and I have only his word for it that it was made to *him.*

When Moses told the children of Israel that he received the two tables of the commandments from the hand of God, they were not obliged to believe him, because they had no other authority for it than his telling them so; and I have no other authority for it than some historian telling me so. The commandments carrying no internal evidence of divinity with them. They contain some good moral precepts, such as any man qualified to be a law-giver or a legislator could produce himself, without having recourse to supernatural intervention.[1]

When I am told that the Koran was written in heaven, and brought to Mahomet by an angel, the account comes to near the same kind of hearsay evidence, and second hand authority, as the former. I did not see the angel myself, and therefore I have a right not to believe it.

When also I am told that a woman, called the Virgin Mary, said, or gave out, that she was with child without any cohabitation with a man, and that her betrothed husband, Joseph, said, that an angel told him so, I have a right to believe them or not: such a circumstance required a much stronger evidence than their bare word for it: but we have not even this; for neither Joseph nor Mary wrote any such matter themselves. It is only reported by others that *they said so*. It is hearsay upon hearsay, and I do not chuse to rest my belief upon such evidence.

It is, however, not difficult to account for the credit that was given to the story of Jesus Christ being the Son of God. He was born when the heathen mythology had still some fashion and repute in the world, and that mythology had prepared the people for the belief of such a story. Almost all the extraordinary men that lived under the heathen mythology were reputed to be the sons of some of their gods. It was not a new thing at that time to believe a man to have been celestially begotten: the intercourse of gods with women was then a matter of familiar opinion. Their Jupiter, according to their accounts, had cohabited with hundreds: the story, therefore, had nothing in it either new, wonderful, or obscene: it was conformable to the opinions that then prevailed among the people called Gentiles, or mythologists, and it was those people only that believed it. The Jews who had kept strictly to the belief of one God, and no more, and who had always rejected the heathen mythology, never credited the story.

It is curious to observe how the theory of what is called the Christian church, sprung out of the tail of the heathen mythology. A direct incorporation took place in the first instance, by making the reputed founder to be celestially begotten. The trinity of gods that then followed was no other than a reduction of the former plurality, which was about twenty or

1. This is, however, necessary to except the declaration, which says, that God *visits the sins of the fathers upon the children.* It is contrary to every principle of moral justice.

thirty thousand. The statue of Mary succeeded the statue of Diana of Ephesus. The deification of heroes, changed into the cannonization of saints. The mythologists had gods for every thing; the Christian mythologists had saints for every thing. The church became as crouded with the one, as the pantheon had been with the other; and Rome was the place of both. The Christian theory is little else than the idolatry of the ancient mythologists, accommodated to the purposes of power and revenue; and it yet remains to reason and philosophy to abolish the amphibious fraud.

Nothing that is here said can apply, even with the most distant disrespect, to the *real* character of Jesus Christ. He was a virtuous and an amiable man. The morality that he preached and practised was of the most benevolent kind; and though similar systems of morality had been preached by Confucius, and by some of the Greek philosophers, many years before; by the quakers since; and by many good men in all ages; it has not been exceeded by any.

Jesus Christ wrote no account of himself, of his birth, parentage, or any thing else. Not a line of what is called the New Testament is of his writing. The history of him is altogether the work of other people; and as to the account given of his resurrection and ascension, it was the necessary counterpart to the story of his birth. His historians, having brought him into the world in a supernatural manner, were obliged to take him out again in the same manner, or the first part of the story must have fallen to the ground.

The wretched contrivance with which this latter part is told, exceeds every thing that went before it. The first part, that of the miraculous conception, was not a thing that admitted of publicity; and therefore the tellers of this part of the story, had this advantage, that though they might not be credited, they could not be detected. They could not be expected to prove it, because it was not one of those things that admitted of proof, and it was impossible that the person of whom it was told could prove it himself.

But the resurrection of a dead person from the grave, and his ascension through the air, is a thing very different as to the evidence it admits of, to the invisible conception of a child in the womb. The resurrection and ascension, supposing them to have taken place, admitted of public and occular demonstration, like that of the ascension of a balloon, or the sun at noon day, to all Jerusalem at least. A thing which every body is required to believe, requires that the proof and evidence of it should be equal to all, and universal; and as the public visibility of this last related act was the only evidence that could give sanction to the former part, the whole of it falls to the ground, because that evidence never was given. Instead of this, a small number of persons, not more than eight or nine, are introduced as proxies for the whole world, to say, they *saw it,* and all the rest of the world are called upon to believe it. But it appears that Thomas did not believe the resurrection; and, as they say, would not believe, without having occular and manual demonstration himself. *So neither will I;* and the reason is equally as good for me and for every other person, as for Thomas.

It is in vain to attempt to palliate or disguise this matter. The story, so far as relates to the supernatural part, has every mark of fraud and imposition stamped upon the face of it. Who were the authors of it is as impossible for us now to know, as it is for us to be assured, that the books in which the account is related, were written by the persons whose names they bear. The best surviving evidence we now have respecting this affair is the Jews. They are regularly descended from the people who lived in the times this resurrection and ascension is said to have happened, and they say, *it is not true.* It has long appeared to me a strange inconsistency to cite the Jews as a proof of the truth of the story. It is just the same as if a man were to say, I will prove the truth of what I have told you, by producing the people who say it is false.

That such a person as Jesus Christ existed, and that he was crucified, which was the mode of execution at that day, are historical relations strictly within the limits of probability. He preached most excellent morality, and the equality of man; but he preached also against the corruptions and avarice of the Jewish priests; and this brought upon him the hatred and vengeance of the whole order of priest-hood. The accusation which those priests brought against him, was that of sedition and conspiracy against the Roman government, to which the Jews were then subject and tributary; and it is not improbable that the Roman government might have some secret apprehension of the effects of his doctrine as well as the Jewish priests; neither is it improbable that Jesus Christ had in contemplation the delivery of the Jewish nation from the bondage of the Romans. Between the two, however, this virtuous reformer and revolutionist lost his life.

It is upon this plain narrative of facts, together with another case I am going to mention, that the Christian mythologists, calling themselves the Christian church, have erected their fable, which for absurdity and extravagance is not exceeded by any thing that is to be found in the mythology of the ancients.

The ancient mythologists tell that the race of Giants made war against Jupiter, and that one of them threw an hundred rocks against him at one throw; that Jupiter defeated him with thunder, and confined him afterwards under Mount Etna; and that every time the Giant turns himself, Mount Etna belches fire. It is here easy to see that the circumstance of the mountain, that of its being a volcano, suggested the idea of the fable; and that the fable is made to fit and wind itself up with that circumstance.

The Christian mythologists tell that their Satan made war against the Almighty, who defeated him, and confined him afterwards, not under a mountain, but in a pit. It is here easy to see that the first fable suggested the idea of the second; for the fable of Jupiter and the Giants was told many hundred years before that of Satan.

Thus far the ancient and the Christian mythologists differ very little from each other. But the latter have contrived to carry the matter much farther. They have contrived to connect the fabulous part of the story of Jesus Christ, with the fable originating from Mount Etna: and in order to make all the parts of the story tye together, they have taken to their aid the traditions of the Jews; for the Christian mythology is made up partly from the ancient mythology, and partly from the Jewish traditions.

The Christian mythologists, after having confined Satan in a pit, were obliged to let him out again, to bring on the sequel of the fable. He is then introduced into the garden of Eden in the shape of a snake, or a serpent, and in that shape he enters into familiar conversation with Eve, who is no ways surprised to hear a snake talk; and the issue of this tête-à-tête is, that he persuades her to eat an apple, and the eating of that apple, damns all mankind.

After giving Satan this triumph over the whole creation, one would have supposed that the church mythologists would have been kind enough to send him back again to the pit; or, if they had not done this, that they would have put a mountain upon him, (for they say that their faith can remove a mountain) or have put him *under* a mountain, as the former mythologists had done, to prevent his getting again among the women, and doing more mischief. But instead of this, they leave him at large without even obliging him to give his parole. The secret of which is, that they could not do without him; and after being at the trouble of making him, they bribed him to stay. They promised him ALL the Jews, ALL the Turks by anticipation, nine-tenths of the world beside, and Mahomet into the bargain. After this, who can doubt the bountifulness of the Christian mythology?

Having thus made an insurrection and a battle in heaven, in which none of the combatants could be either killed or wounded – put Satan into the pit – let him out again – given him a triumph over the whole creation – damned all mankind by the eating of an apple, these Christian mythologists bring the two ends of their fable together. They represent this virtuous and amiable man, Jesus Christ, to be at once both God and man, and also the Son of God, celestially begotten on purpose to be sacrificed, because, they say, that Eve in her longing had eaten an apple.

Putting aside every thing that might excite laughter by its absurdity, or detestation by its prophaneness, and confining ourselves merely to an examination of the parts, it is impossible to conceive a story more derogatory to the Almighty, more inconsistent with his wisdom, more contradictory to his power, than this story is.

In order to make for it a foundation to rise upon, the inventors were under the necessity of giving to the being, whom they call Satan, a power equally as great, if not greater, than they attribute to the Almighty. They have not only given him the power of liberating himself from the pit, after what they call his fall, but they have made that power increase afterwards to infinity. Before this fall, they represent him only as an angel of limited existence, as they represent the rest. After his fall, he becomes, by their account, omnipresent. He exists every where, and at the same time. He occupies the whole immensity of space.

Not content with this deification of Satan, they represent him as defeating by stratagem, in the shape of an animal of the creation, all the power and wisdom of the Almighty. They represent him as having compelled the Almighty to the *direct necessity* either of surrendering the whole of the creation to the government and sovereignty of this Satan, or of capitulating for its redemption by coming down upon earth, and exhibiting himself upon a cross in the shape of a man.

Had the inventors of this story told it the contrary way, that is, had they represented the Almighty as compelling Satan to exhibit *himself* on a cross in the shape of a snake, as a punishment for his new transgression, the story would have been less absurd, less contradictory. But instead of this, they make the transgressor triumph, and the Almighty fall.

That many good men have believed this strange fable and lived very good lives under that belief (for credulity is not a crime) is what I have no doubt of. In the first place, they were educated to believe it, and they would have believed any thing else in the same manner. There are also many who have been so enthusiastically enraptured by what they conceived to be the infinite love of God to man, in making a sacrifice of himself, that the vehemence of the idea has forbidden and deterred them from examining into the absurdity and profaneness of the story. The more unnatural any thing is, the more is it capable of becoming the object of dismal admiration.

But if objects for gratitude and admiration are our desire, do they not present themselves every hour to our eyes? Do we not see a fair creation prepared to receive us the instant we were born—a world furnished to our hands that cost us nothing? Is it we that light up the sun; that pour down the rain; and fill the earth with abundance? Whether we sleep or wake, the vast machinery of the universe still goes on. Are these things, and the blessings they indicate in future, nothing to us? Can our gross feelings be excited by no other subjects than tragedy and suicide? Or is the gloomy pride of man become so intolerable, that nothing can flatter it but a sacrifice of the Creator?

I know that this bold investigation will alarm many, but it would be paying too great a compliment to their credulity to forbear it upon that account. The times and the subject demand it to be done. The suspicion that the theory of what is called the Christian church is fabulous, is becoming very extensive in all countries; and it will be a consolation to men staggering under that suspicion, and doubting what to believe and what to disbelieve, to see the subject freely investigated. I therefore pass on to an examination of the books called the Old and the New Testament.

These books, beginning with Genesis and ending with Revelations (which by the bye is a book of riddles that requires a Revelation to explain it) are, we are told, the word of God. It is therefore proper for us to know who told us so, that we may know what credit to give to the report. The answer to this question is, that nobody can tell, except that we tell one another so. The case, however, historically appears to be as follows:

When the church mythologists established their system, they collected all the writings they could find, and managed them as they pleased. It is a matter altogether of uncertainty to us whether such of the writings as now appear, under the name of the Old and the New Testament, are in the same state in which those collectors say they found them; or whether they added, altered, abridged, or dressed them up.

Be this as it may, they decided by *vote* which of the books out of the collection they had made, should be the WORD OF GOD, and which should not. They rejected several; they voted others to be doubtful, such as the books called the Apocraphy; and those books which had a majority of votes, were voted to be the word of God. Had they voted otherwise, all the people, since calling themselves christians, had believed otherwise; for the belief of the one comes from the vote of the other. Who the people were that did all this, we know nothing of; they called themselves by the general name of the church; and this is all we know of the matter.

As we have no other external evidence or authority for believing those books to be the word of God, than what I have mentioned, which is no evidence or authority at all, I come, in the next place, to examine the internal evidence contained in the books themselves.

In the former part of this essay, I have spoken of revelation. I now proceed further with that subject, for the purpose of applying it to the books in question.

Revelation is a communication of something, which the person, to whom that thing is revealed, did not know before. For if I have done a thing, or seen it done, it needs no revelation to tell me I have done it, or seen it, nor to enable me to tell it, or to write it.

Revelation, therefore, cannot be applied to any thing done upon earth of which man is himself the actor or the witness; and consequently all the historical and anecdotal part of the Bible, which is almost the whole of it, is not within the meaning and compass of the word revelation, and therefore is not the word of God.

When Samson ran off with the gate-posts of Gaza, if he ever did so (and whether he did or not is nothing to us) or when he visited his Delilah, or caught his foxes, or did any thing else, what has revelation to do with these things? If they were facts, he could tell them himself; or his secretary, if he kept one, could write them, if they were worth either telling or writing; and if they were fictions, revelation could not make them true; and whether true or not, we are neither the better nor the wiser for knowing them.—When we contemplate the immensity of that Being, who directs and governs the incomprehensible WHOLE, of which the utmost ken of human sight can discover but a part, we ought to feel shame at calling such paltry stories the word of God.

As to the account of the creation, with which the book of Genesis opens, it has all the appearance of being a tradition which the Israelites had among them before they came into Egypt; and after their departure from that country, they put it at the head of their history, without telling, as it is most probable that they did not know, how they came by it. The manner in which the account opens, shews it to be traditionary. It begins abruptly. It is nobody that speaks. It is nobody that hears. It is addressed to nobody. It has neither first, second, nor third person. It has every criterion of being a tradition. It has no voucher. Moses does not take it upon himself by introducing it with the formality that he uses on other occasions, such as that of saying, "*The Lord spake unto Moses, saying.*"

Why it has been called the Mosaic account of the creation, I am at a loss to conceive. Moses, I believe, was too good a judge of such subjects to put his name to that account. He had been educated among the Egyptians, who were a people as well skilled in science, and particularly in astronomy, as any people of their day; and the silence and caution that Moses observes, in not authenticating the account, is a good negative evidence that he neither told it, nor believed it. – The case is, that every nation of people has been world-makers, and the Israelites had as much right to set up the trade of world-making as any of the rest; and as Moses was not an Israelite, he might not chuse to contradict the tradition. The account, however, is harmless; and this is more than can be said for many other parts of the Bible.

Whenever we read the obscene stories, the voluptuous debaucheries, the cruel and torturous executions, the unrelenting vindictiveness, with which more than half the Bible is filled, it would be more consistent that we called it the word of a demon, than the word of God. It is a history of wickedness, that has served to corrupt and brutalize mankind; and, for my own part, I sincerely detest it, as I detest every thing that is cruel.

We scarcely meet with any thing, a few phrases excepted, but what deserves either our abhorrence, or our contempt, till we come to the miscellaneous parts of the Bible. In the anonymous publications, the Psalms and the book of Job, more particularly in the latter, we find a great deal of elevated sentiment reverentially expressed of the power and benignity of the Almighty; but they stand on no higher rank than many other compositions on similar subjects, as well before that time as since.

The proverbs, which are said to be Solomon's, though most probably a collection (because they discover a knowledge of life, which his situation excluded him from knowing) are an instructive table of ethics. They are inferior in keenness to the proverbs of the Spaniards, and not more wise and œconomical than those of the American Franklin.

All the remaining parts of the Bible, generally known by the name of the prophets, are the works of the Jewish poets and itinerant preachers, who mixed poetry, anecdote, and devotion together; and those works still retain the air and stile of poetry, though in translation.[2]

There is not, throughout the whole book, called the Bible, any word that describes to us what we call a poet, nor any word that describes what we call poetry. The case is, that the word *prophet,* to which later times have

2. As there are many readers who do not see that a composition is poetry unless it be in rhyme, it is for their information that I add this note.

Poetry consists principally in two things: Imagery and composition. The composition of poetry differs from that of prose in the manner of mixing long and short syllables together. Take a long syllable out of a line of poetry, and put a short one in the room of it, or put a long syllable where a short one should be, and that line will lose its poetical harmony. It will have an effect upon the line like that of misplacing a note in a song.

The imagery in those books, called the prophets, appertains altogether to poetry. It is fictitious and often extravagant, and not admissible in any other kind of writing than poetry.

affixed a new idea, was the Bible word for poet, and the word *prophesying* meant the art of making poetry. It also meant the art of playing poetry to a tune upon any instrument of music.

We read of prophesying with pipes, tabrets, and horns. Of prophesying with harps, with psalteries, with cymbals, and with every other instrument of music then in fashion. Were we now to speak of prophesying with a fiddle, or with a pipe and tabor, the expression would have no meaning, or would appear ridiculous, and to some people contemptuous, because we have changed the meaning of the word.

We are told of Saul being among the *prophets,* and also that he prophesied; but we are not told what *they prophesied,* nor what *he prophesied.* The case is, there was nothing to tell; for these prophets were a company of musicians and poets; and Saul joined in the concert; and this was called *prophesying.*

The account given of this affair in the book called Samuel, is, that Saul met a *company* of prophets; a whole company of them! coming down with a psaltery, a tabret, a pipe, and a harp, and that they prophesied, and that he prophesied with them. But it appears afterwards, that Saul prophesied badly, that is, he performed his part badly; for it is said, that "an *evil spirit from God*[3] came upon Saul, and he prophesied."

Now were there no other passage in the book, called the Bible, than this, to demonstrate to us that we have lost the original meaning of the word

---

To shew that these writings are composed in poetical numbers, I will take ten syllables as they stand in the book, and make a line of the same number of syllables (heroic measure) that shall rhyme with the last word. It will then be seen, that the composition of those books is poetical measure. The instance I shall first produce is from Isaiah.

"*Hear, O ye heavens, and give ear, O earth.*"
'Tis God himself that calls attention forth.

Another instance I shall quote is from the mournful Jeremiah, to which I shall add two other lines, for the purpose of carrying out the figure, and shewing the intention of the poet.

"*O! that mine head were waters, and mine eyes*"
Were fountains, flowing like the liquid skies;
Then would I give the mighty flood release,
And weep a deluge for the human race.

3. As those men, who call themselves divines and commentators, are very fond of puzzling one another, I leave them to contest the meaning of the first part of the phrase, that of, *an evil spirit of God.* I keep to my text. I keep to the meaning of the word prophesy.

prophesy, and substituted another meaning in its place, this alone would be sufficient; for it is impossible to use and apply the word *prophesy* in the place it is here used and applied, if we give to it the sense which later times have affixed to it. The manner in which it is here used strips it of all religious meaning, and shews that a man might then be a *prophet,* or might *prophesy,* as he may now be a poet, or a musician, without any regard to the morality or the immorality of his character. The word was originally a term of science, promiscuously applied to poetry and to music, and not restricted to any subject upon which poetry and music might be exercised.

Deborah and Barak are called prophets, not because they predicated any thing, but because they composed the poem or song that bears their name in celebration of an act already done: David is ranked among the prophets, for he was a musician; and was also reputed to be (though perhaps very erroneously) the author of the psalms. But Abraham, Isaac, and Jacob, are not called prophets. It does not appear from any accounts we have that they could either sing, play music, or make poetry.

We are told of the greater and the lesser prophets. They might as well tell us of the greater and the lesser God; for there cannot be degrees in prophesying consistently with its modern sense. But there are degrees in poetry, and therefore the phrase is reconcilable to the case, when we understand by it the greater and the lesser poets.

It is altogether unnecessary, after this, to offer any observations upon what those men, stiled prophets, have written. The axe goes at once to the root, by shewing that the original meaning of the word has been mistaken, and consequently all the inferences that have been drawn from those books, the devotional respect that has been paid to them, and the laboured commentaries that have been written upon them, under that mistaken meaning, are not worth disputing about. – In many things, however, the writings of the Jewish poets, deserve a better fate than that of being bound up, as they now are, with the trash that accompanies them, under the abused name of the word of God.

If we permit ourselves to conceive right ideas of things, we must necessarily affix the idea, not only of unchangeableness, but of the utter impossibility of any change taking place, by any means or accident whatever, in that which we would honour with the name of the word of God; and therefore the word of God cannot exist in any written or human language.

The continually progressive change to which the meaning of words is subject, the want of an universal language which renders translations necessary, the errors to which translations are again subject, the mistakes of copyists and printers, together with the possibility of wilful alteration, are of themselves evidences, that human language, whether in speech or in print, cannot be the vehicle of the word of God.—The word of God exists in something else.

Did the book, called the Bible, excel in purity of ideas and expression, all the books that are now extant in the world, I would not take it for my rule of faith, as being the word of God; because the possibility would nevertheless exist of my being imposed upon. But when I see throughout the greatest part of this book, scarcely any thing but a history of the grossest vices, and a collection of the most paltry and contemptible tales, I cannot dishonour my Creator by calling it by his name.

Thus much for the Bible. I now go on to the book called the New Testament. The *new* Testament! that is, the *new* Will, as if there could be two wills of the Creator.

Had it been the object or the intention of Jesus Christ to establish a new religion, he would undoubtedly have written the system himself, or *procured it to be written* in his life time. But there is no publication extant authenticated with his name. All the books called the New Testament were written after his death. He was a Jew by birth and by profession; and he was the son of God in like manner that every other person is; for the Creator is the Father of All.

The first four books, called Matthew, Mark, Luke, and John, do not give a history of the life of Jesus Christ, but only detached anecdotes of him. It appears from these books, that the whole time of his being a preacher was not more than eighteen months; and it was only during this short time, that those men became acquainted with him. They make mention of him, at the age of twelve years, sitting, they say, among the Jewish doctors, asking and answering them questions. As this was several years before their acquaintance with him began, it is most probable they had this anecdote from his parents. From this time there is no account of him for about sixteen years. Where he lived, or how he employed himself during this interval, is not known. Most probably he was working at his father's trade, which was that of a carpenter. It does not appear that he had any school education, and the probability is that he could not write, for his parents were extremely poor, as appears from their not being able to pay for a bed when he was born.

It is somewhat curious that the three persons, whose names are the most universally recorded, were of very obscure parentage. Moses was a foundling, Jesus Christ was born in a stable, and Mahomet was a mule-driver. The first and the last of these men, were founders of different systems of religion; but Jesus Christ founded no new system. He called men to the practice of moral virtues, and the belief of one God. The great trait in his character is philanthropy.

The manner in which he was apprehended, shews that he was not much known at that time; and it shews also that the meetings he then held with his followers were in secret; and that he had given over, or suspended, preaching publicly. Judas could no otherways betray him than by giving information where he was, and pointing him out to the officers that went to arrest him; and the reason for employing and paying Judas to do this, could arise only from the causes already mentioned, that of his not being much known, and living concealed.

The idea of his concealment not only agrees very ill with his reputed divinity, but associates with it something of pusillanimity; and his being betrayed, or in other words, his being apprehended, on the information of one of his followers, shews that he did not intend to be apprehended, and consequently that he did not intend to be crucified.

The Christian mythologists tell us, that Christ died for the sins of the world, and that he came on *purpose to die*. Would it not then have been the same if he had died of a fever, or of the small pox, of old age, or of any thing else?

The declaratory sentence which, they say, was passed upon Adam in case he ate of the apple, was not, that *thou shalt surely be crucified, but thou shalt surely die*. The sentence was death, and not the *manner of dying*. Crucifixion, therefore, or any other particular manner of dying, made no part of the sentence that Adam was to suffer, and consequently, even upon their own tactic, it could make no part of the sentence that Christ was to suffer in the room of Adam. A fever would have done as well as a cross, if there was any occasion for either.

This sentence of death which, they tell us, was thus passed upon Adam, must either have meant dying naturally, that is, ceasing to live, or, have meant what these mythologists call damnation: and consequently, the act of dying on the part of Jesus Christ, must, according to their system, apply as a prevention to one or other of these two *things* happening to Adam and to us.

That it does not prevent our dying is evident, because we all die; and if their accounts of longevity be true, men die faster since the crucifixion than before: and with respect to the second explanation, (including with it the *natural death* of Jesus Christ as a substitute for the *eternal death or damnation* of all mankind) it is impertinently representing the Creator as coming off, or revoking the sentence, by a pun or a quibble upon the word *death*. That manufacturer of quibbles, St. Paul, if he wrote the books that bear his name, has helped this quibble on, by making another quibble upon the word *Adam.* He makes there to be two Adams; the one who sins in fact, and suffers by proxy; the other who sins by proxy and suffers in fact. A religion thus interlarded with quibble, subterfuge and pun, has a tendency to instruct its professors in the practice of these arts. They acquire the habit without being aware of the cause.

If Jesus Christ was the Being which those mythologists tell us he was, and that he came into this world to *suffer,* which is a word they sometimes use instead of *to die,* the only real suffering he could have endured would have been *to live.* His existence here was a state of exilement or transportation from heaven, and the way back to his original country was to die. – In fine, every thing in this strange system is the reverse of what it pretends to be. It is the reverse of truth, and I become so tired with examining into its inconsistencies and absurdities, that I hasten to the conclusion of it, in order to proceed to something better.

How much, or what parts of the books called the New Testament, were written by the persons whose names they bear, is what we can know nothing of, neither are we certain in what language they were originally written. The matters they now contain may be classed under two heads: anecdote, and epistolary correspondence.

The four books already mentioned, Matthew, Mark, Luke, and John, are altogether anecdotal. They relate events after they had taken place. They tell what Jesus Christ did and said, and what others did and said to him; and in several instances they relate the same event differently. Revelation is necessarily out of the question with respect to those books; not only because of the disagreement of the writers, but because revelation cannot be applied to the relating of facts by the persons who saw them done, nor to the relating or recording of any discourse or conversation by those who heard it. The book, called the Acts of the Apostles, an anonymous work, belongs also to the anecdotal part.

All the other parts of the New Testament, except the book of enigmas, called the Revelations, are a collection of letters under the name of Epistles; and the forgery of letters has been such a common practice in the world, that the probability is, at least, equal, whether they are genuine or forged. One thing, however, is much less equivocal, which is, that out of the matters contained in those books, together with the assistance of some old stories, the church has set up a system of religion very contradictory to the character of the person whose name it bears. It has set up a religion of pomp and of revenue in pretended imitation of a person whose life was humility and poverty.

The invention of a purgatory, and of the releasing of souls therefrom, by prayers, bought of the church with money; the selling of pardons, dispensations, and indulgences, are revenue laws, without bearing that name or carrying that appearance. But the case nevertheless is, that those things derive their origin from the proxysm of the crucifixion, and the theory deduced therefrom, which was, that one person could stand in the place of another, and could perform meritorious services for him. The probability therefore is, that the whole theory or doctrine of what is called the redemption (which is said to have been accomplished by the act of one person in the room of another) was originally fabricated on purpose to bring forward and build all those secondary and pecuniary redemptions upon; and that the passages in the books upon which the idea or theory of redemption is built, have been manufactured and fabricated for that purpose. Why are we to give this church credit, when she tells us that those books are genuine in every part, any more than we give her credit for every thing else she has told us; or for the miracles she says she has performed. That she *could* fabricate writings is certain, because she could write; and the composition of the writings in question, is of that kind that any body might do it; and that she *did* fabricate them is not more inconsistent with probability, than that she should tell us, as she has done, that she could and did work miracles.

Since then no external evidence can, at this long distance of time, be produced to prove whether the church fabricated the doctrine called redemption or not (for such evidence, whether for or against, would be subject to the same suspicion of being fabricated) the case can only be referred to the internal evidence which the thing carries of itself; and this affords a very strong presumption of its being a fabrication. For the internal evidence is, that the theory or doctrine of redemption has for its basis, an idea of pecuniary justice, and not that of moral justice.

If I owe a person money and cannot pay him, and he threatens to put me in prison, another person can take the debt upon himself, and pay it for me. But if I have committed a crime, every circumstance of the case is changed. Moral justice cannot take the innocent for the guilty, even if the innocent would offer itself. To suppose justice to do this, is to destroy the principle of its existence, which is the thing itself. It is then no longer justice. It is indiscriminate revenge.

This single reflection will shew that the doctrine of redemption is founded on a mere pecuniary idea corresponding to that of a debt which another person might pay; and as this pecuniary idea corresponds again with the system of second redemptions obtained through the means of money given to the church, for pardons, the probability is, that the same persons fabricated both the one and the other of those theories; and that, in truth, there is no such thing as redemption; that it is fabulous; and that man stands in the same relative condition with his Maker he ever did stand since man existed; and that it is his greatest consolation to think so.

Let him believe this, and he will live more consistently and morally than by any other system. It is by his being taught to contemplate himself as an out-law, as an out-cast, as a beggar, as a mumper, as one thrown, as it were, on a dunghill, at an immense distance from his Creator, and who must make his approaches by creeping and cringing to intermediate beings, that he conceives either a contemptuous disregard for every thing under the name of religion, or becomes indifferent, or turns, what he calls, devout. In the latter case, he consumes his life in grief, or the affectation of it. His prayers are reproaches. His humility is ingratitude. He calls himself a worm, and the fertile earth a dunghill; and all the blessings of life by the thankless name of vanities. He despises the choicest gift of God to man, the GIFT OF REASON; and having endeavoured to force upon himself the belief of a system against which reason revolts, he ungratefully calls it *human reason;* as if man could give reason to himself.

Yet with all this strange appearance of humility, and this contempt for human reason, he ventures into the boldest presumptions. He finds fault with every thing. His selfishness is never satisfied; his ingratitude is never at an end. He takes on himself to direct the Almighty what to do, even in the government of the universe. He prays dictatorially. When it is sun-shine, he prays for rain, and when it is rain, he prays for sun-shine. He follows the same idea in every thing that he prays for; for what is the amount of all his prayers, but an attempt to make the Almighty change his mind, and act otherwise than he does. It is as if he were to say – thou knowest not so well as I.

But some perhaps will say, Are we to have no word of God – No revelation? I answer yes. There is a word of God; there is a revelation.

THE WORD OF GOD IS THE CREATION WE BEHOLD: And it is in *this word,* which no human invention can counterfeit or alter, that God speaketh universally to man.

Human language is local and changeable, and is therefore incapable of being used as the means of unchangeable and universal information. The idea that God sent Jesus Christ to publish, as they say, the glad tidings to all nations, from one end of the earth unto the other, is consistent only with the ignorance of those who know nothing of the extent of the world, and who believed, as those world-saviours believed, and continued to believe, for several centuries (and that in contradiction to the discoveries of philosophers, and the experience of navigators) that the earth was flat like a trencher; and that a man might walk to the end of it.

But how was Jesus Christ to make any thing known to all nations? He could speak but one language, which was Hebrew; and there are in the world several hundred languages. Scarcely any two nations speak the same language, or understand each other; and as to translations, every man who knows any thing of languages, knows that it is impossible to translate from one language into another not only without losing a great part of the original, but frequently of mistaking the sense: and besides all this, the art of printing was wholly unknown at the time Christ lived.

It is always necessary that the means that are to accomplish any end, be equal to the accomplishment of that end, or the end cannot be accomplished. It is in this, that the difference between finite and infinite power and wisdom discovers itself. Man frequently fails in accomplishing his end, from a natural inability of the power to the purpose; and frequently from the want of wisdom to apply power properly. But it is impossible for infinite power and wisdom to fail as man faileth. The means it useth are always equal to the end: but human language, more especially as there is not an universal language, is incapable of being used as an universal means of unchangeable and uniform information; and therefore it is not the means that God useth in manifesting himself universally to man.

It is only in the CREATION that all our ideas and conceptions of a *word of God* can unite. The creation speaketh an universal language, independently of human speech or human language, multiplied and various as they be. It is an ever existing original, which every man can read. It cannot be forged; it cannot be counterfeited; it cannot be lost; it cannot be altered; it cannot be suppressed. It does not depend upon the will of man whether it shall be published or not; it publishes itself from one end of the earth to the other. It preaches to all nations and to all worlds; and this *word of God* reveals to man all that is necessary for man to know of God.

Do we want to contemplate his power? We see it in the immensity of the creation. Do we want to contemplate his wisdom? We see it in the unchangeable order by which the incomprehensible Whole is governed. Do we want to contemplate his munificence? We see it in the abundance with which he fills the earth. Do we want to contemplate his mercy? We see it in his not withholding that abundance even from the unthankful. In fine, do we want to know what God is? Search not the book called the scripture, which any human hand might make, but the scripture called the Creation.

The only idea man can affix to the name of God, is, that of a *first cause,* the cause of all things. And incomprehensibly difficult as it is for man to conceive what a first cause is, he arrives at the belief of it, from the ten-fold greater difficulty of disbelieving it. It is difficult beyond description to conceive that space can have no end; but it is more difficult to conceive an end. It is difficult beyond the power of man to conceive an eternal duration of what we call time; but it is more impossible to conceive a time when there shall be no time. In like manner of reasoning, every thing we behold carries in itself the internal evidence that it did not make itself. Every man is an evidence to himself, that he did not make himself; neither could his father make himself, nor his grandfather, nor any of his race; neither could any tree, plant, or animal, make itself: and it is the conviction arising from this evidence, that carries us on, as it were, by necessity, to the belief of a first cause eternally existing, of a nature totally different to any material existence we know of, and by the power of which all things exist, and this first cause man calls God.

It is only by the exercise of reason, that man can discover God. Take away that reason, and he would be incapable of understanding any thing; and, in this case, it would be just as consistent to read even the book called the Bible, to a horse as to a man. How then is it that those people pretend to reject reason?

Almost the only parts in the book, called the Bible, that convey to us any idea of God, are some chapters in Job, and the 19th psalm. I recollect no other. Those parts are true *deistical* compositions; for they treat of the *Deity* through his works. They take the book of Creation as the word of God; they refer to no other book; and all the inferences they make are drawn from that volume.

I insert, in this place, the 19th psalm, as paraphrased into English verse, by Addison. I recollect not the prose, and where I write this I have not the opportunity of seeing it.

> The spacious firmament on high,
> With all the blue etherial sky,
> And spangled heavens, a shining frame,
> Their great original proclaim.
> The unwearied sun, from day to day,
> Does his Creator's power display,
> And publishes to every land,
> The work of an Almighty hand.
> Soon as the evening shades prevail,
> The moon takes up the wond'rous tale,
> And nightly to the list'ning earth

Repeats the story of her birth.
Whilst all the stars that round her burn,
And all the planets in their turn,
Confirm the tidings as they roll,
And spread the truth from pole to pole.
What tho' in solemn silence, all
Move round this dark terrestrial ball,
What tho' no real voice, nor sound,
Amidst their radiant orbs be found,
In reason's ear they all rejoice,
And utter forth a glorious voice;
For ever singing as they shine,
THE HAND THAT MADE US IS DIVINE.

What more does man want to know than that the hand, or power, that made these things is divine, is omnipotent. Let him believe this, with the force it is impossible to repel if he permits his reason to act, and his rule of moral life will follow of course.

The allusions in Job have all of them the same tendency with this psalm; that of deducing or proving a truth, that would be otherwise unknown, from truths already known.

I recollect not enough of the passages in Job to insert them correctly: but there is one that occurs to me that is applicable to the subject I am speaking upon. "Canst thou by searching find out God; canst thou find out the Almighty to perfection."

I know not how the printers have pointed this passage, for I keep no Bible: but it contains two distinct questions that admits of distinct answers.

First, Canst thou by *searching* find out God? Yes. Because, in the first place, I know I did not make myself, and yet I have existence; and by *searching* into the nature of other things, I find that no other thing could make itself; and yet millions of other things exist; therefore it is, that I know, by positive conclusion resulting from this search, that there is a power superior to all those things, and that power is God.

Secondly, Canst thou find out the Almighty to *perfection*? No. Not only because the power and wisdom he has manifested in the structure of the creation that I behold, is to me incomprehensible; but because even this manifestation, great as it is, is probably but a small display of that immensity of power and wisdom, by which millions of other worlds, to me invisible by their distance, were created and continue to exist.

It is evident that both these questions were put to the reason of the person to whom they are supposed to have been addressed; and it is only by admitting the first question to be answered affirmatively, that the second could follow. It would have been unnecessary, and even absurd, to have put a second question more difficult than the first, if the first question had been answered negatively. The two questions have different objects, the first refers to the existence of God, the second to his attributes. Reason can discover the one, but it falls infinitely short in discovering the whole of the other.

I recollect not a single passage in all the writings ascribed to the men, called apostles, that convey any idea of what God is. Those writings are chiefly controversial; and the gloominess of the subject they dwell upon, that of a man dying in agony on a cross, is better suited to the gloomy genius of a monk in a cell, by whom it is not impossible they were written, than to any man breathing the open air of the creation. The only passage that occurs to me, that has any reference to the works of God, by which only his power and wisdom can be known, is related to have been spoken by Jesus Christ, as a remedy against distrustful care. "Behold the lilies of the field, they toil not, neither do they spin." This, however, is far inferior to the allusions in Job, and in the nineteenth psalm; but it is similar in idea, and the modesty of the imagery is correspondent to the modesty of the man.

As to the christian system of faith, it appears to me as a species of atheism; a sort of religious denial of God. It professes to believe in a man rather than in God. It is a compound made up chiefly of manism with but little deism, and is as near to atheism as twilight is to darkness. It introduces between man and his Maker an opaque body which it calls a redeemer; as the moon introduces her opaque self between the earth and the sun, and it produces by this means a religious or an irreligious eclipse of light. It has put the whole orbit of reason into shade.

The effect of this obscurity has been that of turning every thing upside down, and representing it in reverse; and among the revolutions it has thus magically produced, it has made a revolution in Theology.

That which is now called natural philosophy, embracing the whole circle of science, of which astronomy occupies the chief place, is the study of the works of God and of the power and wisdom of God in his works, and is the true theology.

As to the theology that is now studied in its place, it is the study of human opinions and of human fancies concerning God. It is not the study of

God himself in the works that he has made, but in the works or writings that man has made; and it is not among the least of the mischiefs that the christian system has done to the world, that it has abandoned the original and beautiful system of theology, like a beautiful innocent to distress and reproach, to make room for the hag of superstition.

The book of Job, and the 19th psalm, which even the church admits to be more ancient than the chronological order in which they stand in the book called the Bible, are theological orations conformable to the original system of theology. The internal evidence of those orations proves to a demonstration, that the study and contemplation of the works of creation, and of the power and wisdom of God revealed and manifested in those works, made a great part of the religious devotion of the times in which they were written; and it was this devotional study and contemplation that led to the discovery of the principles upon which, what are now called Sciences, are established; and it is to the discovery of these principles that almost all the Arts that contribute to the convenience of human life, owe their existence. Every principal art has some science for its parent, though the person who mechanically performs the work does not always, and but very seldom, perceive the connection.

It is a fraud of the christian system to call the sciences *human inventions;* it is only the application of them that is human. Every science has for its basis a system of principles as fixed and unalterable as those by which the universe is regulated and governed. Man cannot make principles; he can only discover them:

For example. Every person who looks at an almanack sees an account when an eclipse will take place, and he sees also that it never fails to take place according to the account there given. This shews that man is acquainted with the laws by which the heavenly bodies move. But it would be something worse than ignorance, were any church on earth to say, that those laws are an human invention.

It would also be ignorance, or something worse, to say, that the scientific principles, by the aid of which man is enabled to calculate and foreknow when an eclipse will take place, are an human invention. Man cannot invent any thing that is eternal and immutable; and the scientific principles he employs for this purpose, must, and are, of necessity, as eternal and immutable as the laws by which the heavenly bodies move, or they could not be used as they are, to ascertain the time when, and the manner how, an eclipse will take place.

The scientific principles that man employs to obtain the fore-knowledge of an eclipse, or of any thing else relating to the motion of the heavenly

bodies, are contained chiefly in that part of science that is called trigonom-
etry, or the properties of a triangle, which, when applied to the study of the
heavenly bodies, is called astronomy; when applied to direct the course of
a ship on the ocean, it is called navigation; when applied to the construction
of figures drawn by a rule and compass, it is called geometry; when applied to the construction of plans of edifices, it is called architecture; when
applied to the measurement of any portion of the surface of the earth, it is
called land-surveying. In fine, it is the soul of science. It is an eternal truth:
it contains the *mathematical demonstration* of which man speaks, and the
extent of its uses are unknown.

It may be said, that man can make or draw a triangle, and therefore a
triangle is an human invention.

But the triangle, when drawn, is no other than the image of the principle: it is a delineation to the eye, and from thence to the mind, of a principle that would otherwise be imperceptible. The triangle does not make
the principle, any more than a candle taken into a room that was dark,
makes the chairs and tables that before were invisible. All the properties of
a triangle exist independently of the figure, and existed before any triangle
was drawn or thought of by man. Man had no more to do in the formation
of those properties, or principles, than he had to do in making the laws by
which the heavenly bodies move; and therefore the one must have the same
divine origin as the other.

In the same manner as it may be said, that man can make a triangle,
so also may it be said, he can make the mechanical instrument, called a
lever. But the principle by which the lever acts, is a thing distinct from the
instrument, and would exist if the instrument did not: it attaches itself to the
instrument after it is made; the instrument therefore can act no otherwise
than it does act; neither can all the effort of human invention make it act
otherwise. That which, in all such cases, man calls the *effect*, is no other
than the principle itself rendered perceptible to the senses.

Since then man cannot make principles, from whence did he gain a
knowledge of them, so as to be able to apply them, not only to things on
earth, but to ascertain the motion of bodies so immensely distant from him
as all the heavenly bodies are? From whence, I ask, *could* he gain that
knowledge, but from the study of the true theology?

It is the structure of the universe that has taught this knowledge to man.
That structure is an ever existing exhibition of every principle upon which
every part of mathematical science is founded. The offspring of this science is mechanics; for mechanics is no other than the principles of science
applied practically. The man who proportions the several parts of a mill,

uses the same scientific principles, as if he had the power of constructing an universe: but as he cannot give to matter that invisible agency, by which all the component parts of the immense machine of the universe have influence upon each other, and act in motional unison together without any apparent contact, and to which man has given the name of attraction, gravitation, and repulsion, he supplies the place of that agency by the humble imitation of teeth and cogs. All the parts of man's microcosm must visibly touch. But could he gain a knowledge of that agency, so as to be able to apply it in practice, we might then say, that another *canonical book* of the word of God had been discovered.

If man could alter the properties of the lever, so also could he alter the properties of the triangle: for a lever (taking that sort of lever, which is called a steel-yard for the sake of explanation) forms, when in motion, a triangle. The line it descends from, (one point of that line being in the fulcrum) the line it descends to, and the chord of the arc, which the end of the lever describes in the air, are the three sides of a triangle. The other arm of the lever describes also a triangle; and the corresponding sides of those two triangles, calculated scientifically or measured geometrically; and also the sines, tangents, and secants generated from the angles, and geometrically measured, have the same proportions to each other, as the different weights have that will balance each other on the lever, leaving the weight of the lever out of the case.

It may also be said that man can make a wheel and axis, that he can put wheels of different magnitudes together, and produce a mill. Still the case comes back to the same point, which is, that he did not make the principle that gives the wheels those powers. That principle is as unalterable as in the former cases, or rather it is the same principle under a different appearance to the eye.

The power that two wheels, of different magnitudes, have upon each other, is in the same proportion as if the semi-diameter of the two wheels were joined together and made into that kind of lever I have described, suspended at the part where the semi-diameters join; for the two wheels, scientifically considered, are no other than the two circles generated by the motion of the compound lever.

It is from the study of the true theology that all our knowledge of science is derived, and it is from that knowledge that all the arts have originated.

The Almighty lecturer, by displaying the principles of science in the structure of the universe, has invited man to study and to imitation. It is as if he had said to the inhabitants of this globe that we call ours, "I have made an earth for man to dwell upon, and I have rendered the starry heavens visible, to teach him science and the arts. He can now provide for his own comfort, AND LEARN FROM MY MUNIFICENCE TO ALL, TO BE KIND TO EACH OTHER."

Of what use is it, unless it be to teach man something, that his eye is endowed with the power of beholding, to an incomprehensible distance, an immensity of worlds revolving in the ocean of space? Or of what use is it that this immensity of worlds is visible to man? What has man to do with the Pleiades, with Orion, with Sirius, with the star he calls the north star, with the moving orbs he has named Saturn, Jupiter, Mars, Venus, and Mercury, if no uses are to follow from their being visible? A less power of vision would have been sufficient for man, if the immensity he now possesses were given only to waste itself, as it were, on an immense desert of space glittering with shows.

It is only by contemplating what he calls the starry heavens, as the book and school of science, that he discovers any use in their being visible to him, or any advantage resulting from his immensity of vision. But when he contemplates the subject in this light, he sees an additional motive for saying that *nothing was made in vain;* for in vain would be this power of vision if it taught man nothing.

As the christian system of faith has made a revolution in theology, so also has it made a revolution in the state of learning. That which is now called learning was not learning originally. Learning does not consist, as the schools now make it consist, in the knowledge of languages, but in the knowledge of things to which language gives names.

The Greeks were a learned people; but learning with them, did not consist in speaking Greek, any more than in a Roman's speaking Latin, or a Frenchman's speaking French, or an Englishman's speaking English. From what we know of the Greeks, it does not appear that they knew or studied any language but their own; and this was one cause of their becoming so learned; it afforded them more time to apply themselves to better studies. The schools of the Greeks were schools of science and philosophy, and not of languages: and it is in the knowledge of the things that science and philosophy teach, that learning consists.

Almost all the scientific learning that now exists, came to us from the Greeks, or the people who spoke the Greek language. It therefore became necessary to the people of other nations, who spoke a different language, that some among them should learn the Greek language, in order that the learning the Greeks had, might be made known in those nations, by translating the Greek books of science and philosophy into the mother tongue of each nation.

The study therefore of the Greek language, (and in the same manner for the Latin) was no other than the drudgery business of a linguist; and the language thus obtained, was no other than the means, or as it were, the tools, employed to obtain the learning the Greeks had. It made no part of the learning itself; and was so distinct from it, as to make it exceeding probable, that the persons who had studied Greek sufficiently to translate those works, such, for instance, as Euclid's Elements, did not understand any of the learning the works contained.

As there is now nothing new to be learned from the dead languages, all the useful books being already translated, the languages are become useless, and the time expended in teaching and in learning them is wasted. So far as the study of languages may contribute to the progress and communication of knowledge (for it has nothing to do with the *creation* of knowledge) it is only in the living languages that new knowledge is to be found: and certain it is, that, in general, a youth will learn more of a living language in one year, than of a dead language in seven; and it is but seldem that the teacher knows much of it himself. The difficulty of learning the dead languages does not arise from any superior abstruseness in the languages themselves, but in their *being dead,* and the pronunciation entirely lost. It would be the same thing with any other language when it becomes dead. The best Greek linguist, that now exists, does not understand Greek so well as a Grecian plowman did, or a Grecian milkmaid; and the same for the Latin, compared with a plowman or a milkmaid of the Romans; and with respect to pronunciation, and idiom, not so well as the cows that she milked. It would therefore be advantageous to the state of learning, to abolish the study of the dead languages, and to make learning consist, as it originally did, in scientific knowledge.

The apology that is sometimes made for continuing to teach the dead languages is, that they are taught at a time when a child is not capable of exerting any other mental faculty than that of memory. But this is altogether erroneous. The human mind has a natural disposition to scientific knowledge, and to the things connected with it. The first and favourite amusement of a child, even before it begins to play, is that of imitating the works of man. It builds houses with cards or sticks; it navigates the little ocean of a bowl of water with a paper boat; or dams the stream of a gutter, and contrives something which it calls a mill; and it interests itself in the fate of its works with a care that resembles affection. It afterwards goes to school, where its genius is killed by the barren study of a dead language, and the philosopher is lost in the linguist.

But the apology that is now made for continuing to teach the dead languages, could not be the cause at first of cutting down learning to the narrow and humble sphere of linguistry; the cause, therefore, must be sought for elsewhere. In all researches of this kind, the best evidence that can be produced, is the internal evidence the thing carries with itself, and the evidence of circumstances that unites with it, both of which, in this case, are not difficult to be discovered.

Putting then aside, as matter of distinct consideration, the outrage offered to the moral justice of God, by supposing him to make the innocent suffer for the guilty, and also the loose morality and low contrivance of supposing him to change himself into the shape of a man, in order to make an excuse to himself for not executing his supposed sentence upon Adam; putting, I say, those things aside, as matter of distinct consideration, it is certain, that what is called the christian system of faith, including in it the whimsical account of the creation; the strange story of Eve, the snake, and the apple; the amphibious idea of a man-god; the corporeal idea of the death of a god, the mythological idea of a family of gods; and the christian system of arithmetic, that three are one, and one is three, are all irreconcileable, not only to the divine gift of reason that God has given to man, but to the knowledge that man gains of the power and wisdom of God, by the aid of the sciences, and by studying the structure of the universe that God has made.

The setters up, therefore, and the advocates of the christian system of faith, could not but foresee that the continually progressive knowledge that man would gain by the aid of science, of the power and wisdom of God, manifested in the structure of the universe, and in all the works of creation, would militate against, and call into question, the truth of their system of faith; and therefore it became necessary to their purpose to cut learning down to a size less dangerous to their project, and this they effected by restricting the idea of learning to the dead study of dead languages.

They not only rejected the study of science out of the christian schools, but they persecuted it; and it is only within about the last two centuries that the study has been revived. So late as 1610 Galileo, a Florentine, discovered and introduced the use of telescopes, and by applying them to observe the motions and appearances of the heavenly bodies, afforded additional means for ascertaining the true structure of the universe. Instead of being esteemed for these discoveries, he was sentenced to renounce them, or the opinions resulting from them, as a damnable heresy. And prior to that time Vigilius was condemned to be burned for asserting the antipodes, or in other words, that the earth was a globe, and habitable in every part where there was land; yet the truth of this is now too well known even to be told.

If the belief of errors not morally bad did no mischief, it would make no part of the moral duty of man to oppose and remove them. There was no moral ill in believing the earth was flat like a trencher, any more than there was moral virtue in believing it was round like a globe; neither was there any moral ill in believing that the Creator made no other world than this, any more than there was moral virtue in believing that he made millions, and that the infinity of space is filled with worlds. But when a system of religion is made to grow out of a supposed system of creation that is not true, and to unite itself therewith in a manner almost inseparable therefrom, the case assumes an entirely different ground. It is then that errors, not morally bad, become fraught with the same mischiefs as if they were. It is then that the truth, though otherwise indifferent itself, becomes an essential, by becoming the criterion, that either confirms by corresponding evidence, or denies by contradictory evidence, the reality of the religion itself. In this view of the case it is the moral duty of man to obtain every possible evidence, that the structure of the heathens, or any other part of creation affords, with respect to systems of religion. But this, the supporters or partizans of the christian system, as if dreading the result, incessantly opposed, and not only rejected the sciences, but persecuted the professors. Had Newton or Descartes lived three or four hundred years ago, and pursued their studies as they did, it is most probable they would not have lived to finish them; and had Franklin drawn lightning from the clouds at the same time, it would have been at the hazard of expiring for it in flames.

Latter times have laid all the blame upon the Goths and Vandals, but, however unwilling the partizans of the Christian system may be to believe or to acknowledge it, it is nevertheless true, that the age of ignorance commenced with the Christian system. There was more knowledge in the world before that period than for many centuries afterwards; and as to religious knowledge, the Christian system, as already said, was only another species of mythology; and the mythology to which it succeeded, was a corruption of an ancient system of theism.[4]

4. It is impossible for us now to know at what time the heathen mythology began; but it is certain, from the internal evidence that it carries, that it did not begin in the same state or condition in which it ended. All the gods of that mythology, except Saturn, were of modern invention. The supposed reign of Saturn was prior to that which is called the heathen mythology, and was so far a species of theism that it admitted the belief of only one God. Saturn is supposed to have abdicated the government in favour of his three sons and one daughter, Jupiter, Pluto, Neptune and

It is owing to this long interregnum of science, *and to no other cause,* that we have now to look back through a vast chasm of many hundred years to the respectable characters we call the ancients. Had the progression of knowledge gone on proportionably with the stock that before existed, that chasm would have been filled up with characters rising superior in knowledge to each other; and those ancients, we now so much admire, would have appeared respectably in the back ground of the scene. But the christian system laid all waste; and if we take our stand about the beginning of the sixteenth century, we look back through that long chasm, to the times of the ancients, as over a vast sandy desart, in which not a shrub appears to intercept the vision to the fertile hills beyond.

It is an inconsistency, scarcely possible to be credited, that any thing should exist under the name of a *religion,* that held it to be *irreligious* to study and contemplate the structure of the universe that God had made. But the fact is too well established to be denied. The event that served more than any other, to break the first link in this long chain of despotic ignorance, is that known by the name of the reformation by Luther. From that time, though it does not appear to have made any part of the intention of Luther, or of those who are called reformers, the Sciences began to revive, and Liberality, their natural associate, began to appear. This was the only public good the reformation did; for with respect to religious good, it might as well not have taken place. The mythology still continued the same; and a multiplicity of national popes grew out of the downfal of the Pope of Christendom.

Having thus shewn, from the internal evidence of things, the cause that produced a change in the state of learning, and the motive for substituting

---

Juno: after this, thousands of other gods and demi-gods were imaginarily created, and the calendar of gods increased as fast as the calendar of saints, and the calendar of courts have increased since.

All the corruptions that have taken place in theology, and in religion, have been produced by admitting of what man calls *revealed religion.* The mythologists pretended to more revealed religion than the christians do. They had their oracles and their priests, who were supposed to receive and deliver the word of God verbally on almost all occasions.

Since then all corruptions, down from Moloch to modern predestinarianism, and the human sacrifices of the heathens to the christian sacrifice of the Creator, have been produced by admitting what is called *revealed religion,* the most effectual means to prevent all such evils and impositions, and is not to admit of any other revelation than that which is manifested in the book of Creation; and to contemplate the Creation, as the only true and real word of God that ever did or ever will exist, and that every thing else, called the word of God is fable and imposition.

the study of the dead languages in the place of the Sciences, I proceed, in addition to the several observations already made in the former part of this work, to compare, or rather to confront, the evidence that the structure of the universe affords, with the christian system of religion. But as I cannot begin this part better than by referring to the ideas that occurred to me at an early part of life, and which I doubt not have occurred in some degree to almost every other person at one time or other, I shall state what those ideas were, and add thereto such other matter as shall arise out of the subject, giving to the whole, by way of preface, a short introduction.

My father being of the quaker profession, it was my good fortune to have an exceedingly good moral education, and a tolerable stock of useful learning. Though I went to the grammar school,[5] I did not learn Latin, not only because I had no inclination to learn languages, but because of the objection the quakers have against the books in which the language is taught. But this did not prevent me from being acquainted with the subjects of all the Latin books used in the school.

The natural bent of my mind was to science. I had some turn, and I believe some talent for poetry; but this I rather repressed than encouraged, as leading too much into the field of imagination. As soon as I was able I purchased a pair of globes, and attended the philosophical lectures of Martin and Ferguson, and became afterwards acquainted with Dr. Bevis, of the society, called the Royal Society, then living in the Temple, and an excellent astronomer.

I had no disposition for what was called politics. It presented to my mind no other idea than is contained in the word Jockeyship. When, therefore, I turned my thoughts towards matters of government, I had to form a system for myself, that accorded with the moral and philosophic principles in which I had been educated. I saw, or at least I thought I saw, a vast scene opening itself to the world in the affairs of America; and it appeared to me, that unless the Americans changed the plan they were then pursuing, with respect to the government of England, and declare themselves independent, they would not only involve themselves in a multiplicity of new difficulties, but shut out the prospect that was then offering itself to mankind through their means. It was from these motives that I published the work known by the name of *Common Sense,* which is the first work I ever did publish: and so far as I can judge of myself, I believe I never should have been known in the world as an author on any subject whatever, had it not been for the

5. The same school, Thetford in Norfolk, that the present counsellor Mingay went to, and under the same master.

affairs of America. I wrote *Common Sense* the latter end of the year 1775, and published it the first of January 1776. Independence was declared the fourth of July following.

Any person who has made observations on the state and progress of the human mind, by observing his own, cannot but have observed, that there are two distinct classes of what are called Thoughts: those that we produce in ourselves by reflection and the act of thinking, and those that bolt into the mind of their own accord. I have always made it a rule to treat those voluntary visitors with civility, taking care to examine, as well as I was able, if they were worth entertaining; and it is from them I have acquired almost all the knowledge that I have. As to the learning that any person gains from school education, it serves only, like a small capital, to put him in the way of beginning learning for himself afterwards. Every person of learning is finally his own teacher; the reason of which is, that principles, being of a distinct quality to circumstances, cannot be impressed upon the memory. Their place of mental residence is the understanding, and they are never so lasting as when they begin by conception. Thus much for the introductory part.

From the time I was capable of conceiving an idea, and acting upon it by reflection, I either doubted the truth of the christian system, or thought it to be a strange affair; I scarcely new which it was: but I well remember, when about seven or eight years of age, hearing a sermon read by a relation of mine, who was a great devotee of the church, upon the subject of what is called *Redemption by the death of the Son of God.* After the sermon was ended I went into the garden, and as I was going down the garden steps (for I perfectly recollect the spot) I revolted at the recollection of what I had heard, and thought to myself that it was making God Almighty act like a passionate man that killed his son when he could not revenge himself any other way; and as I was sure a man would be hanged that did such a thing, I could not see for what purpose they preached such sermons. This was not one of those kind of thoughts that had any thing in it of childish levity; it was to me a serious reflection arising from the idea I had, that God was too good to do such an action, and also too almighty to be under any necessity of doing it. I believe in the same manner to this moment; and I moreover believe, that any system of religion that has any thing in it that shocks the mind of a child, cannot be a true system.

It seems as if parents of the christian profession were ashamed to tell their children any thing about the principles of their religion. They sometimes instruct them in morals, and talk to them of the goodness of what they call Providence; for the christian mythology has five deities: there is God the Father, God the Son, God the Holy Ghost, the God Providence, and the Goddess Nature. But the christian story of God the Father putting his son to death, or employing people to do it (for that is the plain language of the story) cannot be told by a parent to a child; and to tell him that it was done to make mankind happier and better is making the story still worse, as if mankind could be improved by the example of murder; and to tell him that all this is a mystery, is only making an excuse for the incredibility of it.

How different is this to the pure and simple profession of Deism! The true deist has but one Deity; and his religion consists in contemplating the power, wisdom, and benignity of the Deity in his works, and in endeavouring to imitate him in every thing moral, scientifical, and mechanical.

The religion that approaches the nearest of all others to true deism, in the moral and benign part thereof, is that professed by the quakers, but they have contracted themselves too much by leaving the works of God out of their system. Though I reverence their philanthropy, I cannot help smiling at the conceit, that if the taste of a quaker could have been consulted at the creation, what a silent and drab-coloured creation it would have been! Not a flower would have blossomed its gaities, nor a bird been permitted to sing.

Quitting these reflections, I proceed to other matters. After I had made myself master of the use of the globes and of the orrery,[6] and conceived an idea of the infinity of space, and of the eternal divisibility of matter, and obtained, at least, a general knowledge of what is called natural philosophy, I began to compare, or, as I have before said, to confront, the internal evidence those things afford with the christian system of faith.

Though it is not a direct article of the christian system that this world that we inhabit is the whole of the habitable creation, yet it is so worked up therewith, from what is called the Mosaic account of the creation, the story of Eve and the apple, and the counterpart of that story, the death of the Son of God, that to believe otherwise, that is, to believe that God created a plurality of worlds, at least as numerous as what we call stars, renders the

6. As this book may fall into the hands of persons who do not know what an orrery is, it is for their information I add this note, as the name gives no idea of the uses of the thing. The orrery has its name from the person who invented it. It is a machinery of clock-work representing the universe in miniature: and in which the revolution of the earth round itself and round the sun, the revolution of the moon round the earth, the revolution of the planets round the sun, their relative distances from the sun, as the center of the whole system, their relative distances from each other, and their different magnitudes, are represented as they really exist in what we call the heavens.

christian system of faith at once little and ridiculous; and scatters it in the mind like feathers in the air. The two beliefs cannot be held together in the same mind; and he who thinks that he believes both, has thought but little of either.

Though the belief of a plurality of worlds was familiar to the ancients, it is only within the last three centuries that the extent and dimensions of this globe that we inhabit, have been ascertained. Several vessels, following the tract of the ocean, have sailed entirely round the world, as a man may march in a circle, and come round by the contrary side of the circle to the spot he set out from. The circular dimensions of our world in the widest part, as a man would measure the widest round of an apple or a ball, is only twenty five thousand and twenty English miles, reckoning sixty nine miles and an half to an equatorial degree, and may be sailed round in the space of about three years.[7]

A world of this extent may, at first thought, appear to us to be great; but if we compare it with the immensity of space in which it is suspended, like a bubble or a balloon in the air, it is infinitely less in proportion than the smallest grain of sand is to the size of the world, or the finest particle of dew to the whole ocean; and is therefore but small; and, as will be hereafter shewn, is only *one* of a system of worlds, of which the universal creation is composed.

It is not difficult to gain some faint idea of the immensity of space in which this and all the other worlds are suspended, if we follow a progression of ideas. When we think of the size or dimensions of a room, our ideas limit themselves to the walls, and there they stop. But when our eye, or our imagination, darts into space, that is, when it looks upward into what we call the open air, we cannot conceive any walls or boundaries it can have; and if for the sake of resting our ideas, we suppose a boundary, the question immediately renews itself, and asks, what is beyond that boundary? and in the same manner, what is beyond the next boundary? and so on, till the fatigued imagination returns and says, *there is no end.* Certainly, then, the Creator was not pent for room when he made this world no larger than it is; and we have to seek the reason in something else.

If we take a survey of our own world, or rather of this, of which the Creator has given us the use, as our portion in the immense system of creation,

---

7. Allowing a ship to sail, on an average, three miles in an hour, she would sail entirely round the world in less than one year, if she could sail in a direct circle; but she is obliged to follow the course of the ocean.

we find every part of it, the earth, the waters, and the air that surround it, filled, and, as it were, crouded with life, down from the largest animals that we know of, to the smallest insects the naked eye can behold, and from thence to others still smaller, and totally invisible without the assistance of the microscope. Every tree, every plant, every leaf, serves not only as an habitation, but as a world to some numerous race, till animal existence becomes so exceedingly refined, that the effluvia of a blade of grass would be food for thousands.

Since then no part of our earth is left unoccupied, why is it to be supposed, that the immensity of space is a naked void, lying in eternal waste. There is room for millions of worlds as large or larger than ours, and each of them millions of miles apart from each other.

Having now arrived at this point, if we carry our ideas only one thought further, we shall see, perhaps, the true reason, at least a very good reason for our happiness, why the Creator, instead of making one immense world, extending over an immense quantity of space, has preferred dividing that quantity of matter into several distinct and separate worlds, which we call planets, of which our earth is one. But before I explain my ideas upon this subject, it is necessary (not for the sake of those that already know, but for those who do not) to shew what the system of the universe is.

That part of the universe, that is called the solar system (meaning the system of worlds to which our earth belongs, and of which Sol, or in English language the Sun, is the center) consists, besides the Sun, or six distinct orbs, or planets, or worlds, besides the secondary bodies, called the satellites, or moons, of which our earth has one that attends her in her annual revolution round the sun, in like manner as the other satellites, or moons, attend the planets, or worlds, to which they severally belong, as may be seen by the assistance of the telescope.

The Sun is the center, round which those six worlds, or planets, revolve at different distances therefrom, and in circles concentric to each other. Each world keeps constantly in nearly the same tract round the Sun, and continues, at the same time, turning round itself, in nearly an upright position, as a top turns round itself when it is spinning on the ground, and leans a little sideways.

It is this leaning of the earth, (23½ degrees) that occasions summer and winter, and the different length of days and nights. If the earth turned round itself in a position perpendicular to the plane or level of the circle it moves in round the Sun, as a top turns round when it stands erect on the ground, the days and nights would be always of the same length, twelve hours day, and twelve hours night, and the season would be uniformly the same throughout the year.

Every time that a planet (our earth for example) turns round itself, it makes what we call day and night; and every time it goes entirely round the Sun, it makes what we call a year, consequently our world turns three hundred and sixty-five times round itself, in going once round the Sun.[8]

The names that the ancients gave to those six worlds, and which are still called by the same names, are Mercury, Venus, this world that we call ours, Mars, Jupiter, and Saturn. They appear larger to the eye than the stars, being many million miles nearer to our earth than any of the stars are. The planet Venus is that which is called the evening star, and sometimes the morning star, as she happens to set after, or rise before the Sun, which, in either case, is never more than three hours.

The Sun, as before said, being the center, the planet, or world, nearest the Sun, is Mercury; his distance from the Sun is thirty-four million miles, and he moves round in a circle always at that distance from the Sun, as a top may be supposed to spin round in the tract in which a horse goes in a mill. The second world is Venus; she is fifty-seven million miles distant from the Sun, and consequently moves round in a circle much greater than that of Mercury. The third world is this that we inhabit, and which is eighty-eight million miles distant from the Sun, and consequently moves round in a circle greater than that of Venus. The fourth world is Mars; he is distant from the Sun one hundred and thirty-four million miles, and consequently moves round in a circle greater than that of our earth. The fifth is Jupiter; he is distant from the Sun five hundred and fifty-seven million miles, and consequently moves round in a circle greater than that of Mars. The sixth world is Saturn; he is distant from the Sun seven hundred and sixty-three million miles, and consequently moves round in a circle that surrounds the circles or orbits of all the other worlds or planets.

The space, therefore, in the air, or in the immensity of space, that our solar system takes up for the several worlds to perform their revolutions in round the sun, is of the extent in a strait line of the whole diameter of the orbit or circle, in which Saturn moves round the Sun, which being double his distance from the Sun, is fifteen hundred and twenty-six million miles; and its circular extent is nearly five thousand million, and its

---

8. Those who supposed that the Sun went round the earth every twenty-four hours, made the same mistake in idea, that a cook would do in fact, that should make the fire go round the meat, instead of the meat turning round itself towards the fire.

globical content is almost three thousand five hundred million times three thousand five hundred million square miles.[9]

But this, immense as it is, is only one system of worlds. Beyond this, at a vast distance into space, far beyond all power of calculation, are the stars called the fixed stars. They are called fixed, because they have no revolutionary motion as the six worlds or planets have that I have been describing. Those fixed stars continue always at the same distance from each other, and always in the same place, as the Sun does in the center of our system. The probability therefore is, that each of those fixed stars is also a Sun, round which another system of worlds or planets, though too remote for us to discover, performs its revolutions, as our system of worlds does round our central Sun.

By this easy progression of ideas, the immensity of space will appear to us to be filled with systems of worlds; and that no part of space lies at waste, any more than any part of our globe of earth and water is left unoccupied.

Having thus endeavoured to convey, in a familiar and easy manner, some idea of the structure of the universe, I return to explain what I before alluded to, namely, the great benefits arising to man in consequence of the Creator having made a *plurality* of worlds, such as our system is, consisting of a central sun and six worlds, besides satellites, in preference to that of creating one world only of a vast extent.

It is an idea I have never lost sight of, that all our knowledge of science is derived from the revolutions (exhibited to our eye, and from thence to our understanding) which those several planets, or worlds, of which our system is composed, make in their circuit round the Sun.

Had then the quantity of matter which these six worlds contain been blended into one solitary globe, the consequence to us would have been,

---

9. If it should be asked, how can man know these things? I have one plain answer to give, which is, that man knows how to calculate an eclipse, and also how to calculate, to a minute of time, when the planet Venus, in making her revolutions round the Sun, will come in a strait line between our earth, and the Sun, and will appear to us about the size of a large pea passing across the face of the Sun. This happens but twice in about an hundred years, at the distance of about eight years from each other, and has happened twice in our time, both of which were foreknown by calculation. It can also be known when they will happen again for a thousand years to come, or to any other portion of time. As, therefore, man could not be able to do those things if he did not understand the solar system, and the manner in which the revolutions of the several planets or worlds are performed, the fact of calculating an eclipse or a transit of Venus, is a proof in point that the knowledge exists; and as to a few thousand, or even a few million miles more or less, it makes scarcely any sensible difference in such immense distances.

that either no revolutionary motion would have existed, or not a sufficiency of it, to give us the ideas and the knowledge of science we now have; and it is from the sciences that all the mechanical arts that contribute so much to our earthly felicity and comfort are derived.

As therefore the Creator made nothing in vain, so also must it be believed that he organized the structure of the universe in the most advantageous manner for the benefit of man; and as we see, and from experience feel, the benefits we derive from the structure of the universe, formed as it is, which benefits we should not have had the opportunity of enjoying, if the structure, so far as relates to our system, had been a solitary globe, we can discover, at least, one reason why a *plurality* of worlds has been made, and that reason calls forth the devotional gratitude of man, as well as his admiration.

But it is not to us, the inhabitants of this globe, only, that the benefits arising from a plurality of worlds are limited. The inhabitants of each of the worlds, of which our system is composed, enjoy the same opportunities of knowledge as we do. They behold the revolutionary motions of our earth, as we behold theirs. All the planets revolve in sight of each other; and therefore the same universal school of science presents itself to all.

Neither does the knowledge stop here. The system of worlds, next to us, exhibits in its revolutions, the same principles and school of science, to the inhabitants of their system, as our system does to us, and in like manner throughout the immensity of space.

Our ideas, not only of the almightiness of the Creator, but of his wisdom and his beneficence, become enlarged in proportion as we contemplate the extent and the structure of the universe. The solitary idea of a solitary world rolling, or at rest, in the immense ocean of space, gives place to the cheerful idea of a society of worlds, so happily contrived, as to administer, even by their motion, instruction to man. We see our own earth filled with abundance; but we forget to consider how much of that abundance is owing to the scientific knowledge the vast machinery of the universe has unfolded.

But, in the midst of those reflections, what are we to think of the christian system of faith that forms itself upon the idea of only one world, and that of no greater extent, as is before shewn, than twenty five thousand miles. An extent, which a man walking at the rate of three miles an hour, for twelve hours in the day, could he keep on in a circular direction, would walk entirely round in less than two years. Alas! what is this to the mighty ocean of space, and the almighty power of the Creator!

From whence then could arise the solitary and strange conceit that the Almighty, who had millions of worlds equally dependent on his protection, should quit the care of all the rest, and come to die in our world, because, they say, one man and one woman had eaten an apple. And, on the other hand, are we to suppose that every world, in the boundless creation, had an Eve, an apple, a serpent, and a redeemer. In this case, the person who is irreverently called the Son of God, and sometimes God himself, would have nothing else to do than to travel from world to world, in an endless succession of death, with scarcely a momentary interval of life.

It has been, by rejecting the evidence, that the word, or works of God in the creation, affords to our senses, and the action of our reason upon that evidence, that so many wild and whimsical systems of faith, and of religion, have been fabricated and set up. There may be many systems of religion, that so far from being morally bad, are in many respects morally good: but there can be but ONE that is true; and that one, necessarily must, as it ever will, be in all things consistent with the ever existing word of God that we behold in his works. But such is the strange construction of the Christian system of faith, that every evidence the heavens affords to man, either directly contradicts it, or renders it absurd.

It is possible to believe, and I always feel pleasure in encouraging myself to believe it, that there have been men in the world who persuaded themselves that, what is called *a pious fraud,* might, at least under particular circumstances, be productive of some good. But the fraud being once established, could not afterwards be explained; for it is with a pious fraud, as with a bad action, it begets a calamitous necessity of going on.

The persons who first preached the Christian system of faith, and in some measure combined with it the morality preached by Jesus Christ, might persuade themselves that it was better than the heathen mythology that then prevailed. From the first preachers, the fraud went on to the second, and to the third, till the idea of its being a pious fraud became lost in the belief of its being true; and that belief came again encouraged by the interest of those who made a livelihood by preaching it.

But though such a belief might, by such means, be rendered almost general among the laity, it is next to impossible to account for the continual persecution carried on by the church, for several hundred years, against the sciences and against the professors of science, if the church had not some record or some tradition, that it was originally no other than a pious fraud, or did not foresee, that it could not be maintained against the evidence that the structure of the universe afforded.

Having thus shewn the irreconcileable inconsistencies between the real word of God existing in the universe, and that which is called, *the word of God,* as shewn to us in a printed book, that any man might make, I proceed to speak of the three principal means that have been employed in all ages, and perhaps in all countries, to impose upon mankind.

Those three means are, Mystery, Miracle, and Prophecy. The two first are incompatible with true religion, and the third ought always to be suspected.

With respect to mystery, every thing we behold is, in one sense a mystery, to us. Our own existence is a mystery: the whole vegetable world is a mystery. We cannot account how it is that an acorn, when put into the ground, is made to develop itself, and become an oak. We know not how it is that the seed we sow unfolds and multiplies itself, and returns to us such an abundant interest for so small a capital.

The fact, however, as distinct from the operating cause, is not a mystery because we see it; and we know also the means we are to use, which is no other than putting the seed in the ground. We know therefore as much as is necessary for us to know; and that part of the operation that we do not know, and which if we did, we could not perform, the Creator takes upon himself and performs it for us. We are therefore better off than if we had been let into the secret, and left to do it for ourselves.

But though every created thing is in this sense a mystery, the word mystery cannot be applied to *moral truth,* any more than obscurity can be applied to light. The God in whom we believe is a God of moral truth, and not a God of mystery or obscurity. Mystery is the antagonist of truth. It is a fog of human invention, that obscures truth and represents it in distortion. Truth never invelops *itself* in mystery; and the mystery in which it is at any time enveloped, is the work of its antagonist, and never of itself.

Religion, therefore, being the belief of a God, and the practice of moral truth, cannot have connection with mystery. The belief of a God, so far from having any thing of mystery in it, is of all beliefs the most easy, because it arises to us, as is before observed, out of necessity. And the practice of moral truth, or in other words, a practical imitation of the moral goodness of God, is no other than our acting towards each other, as he acts benignly towards all. We cannot *serve* God in the manner we serve those who cannot do without such service; and, therefore, the only idea we can have of serving God, is that of contributing to the happiness of the living creation that God has made. This cannot be done by retiring ourselves from the society of the world, and spending a recluse life in selfish devotion.

The very nature and design of religion, if I may so express it, prove even to demonstration, that it must be free from every thing of mystery, and unincumbered with every thing that is mysterious. Religion, considered as a duty, is incumbent upon every living soul alike, and therefore must be on a level to the understanding and comprehension of all. Man does not learn religion as he learns the secrets and mysteries of a trade. He learns the theory of religion by reflection. It arises out of the action of his own mind upon the things which he sees, or upon what he may happen to hear or to read, and the practice joins itself thereto.

When men, whether from policy or pious fraud, set up systems of religion incompatible with the word or works of God in the creation, and not only above but repugnant to human comprehension, they were under the necessity of inventing, or adopting, a word that should serve as a bar to all questions, inquiries, and speculations. The word *mystery* answered this purpose; and thus it has happened, that religion, which, in itself, is without mystery, has been corrupted into a fog of mysteries.

As *mystery* answered all general purposes, *miracle* followed as an occasional auxiliary. The former served to bewilder the mind, the latter to puzzle the senses. The one was the lingo; the other the legerdemain.

But before going further into this subject, it will be proper to inquire what is to be understood by a miracle.

In the same sense that every thing may be said to be a mystery, so also may it be said, that every thing is a miracle, and that no one thing is a greater miracle than another. The elephant, though larger, is not a greater miracle than a mite; nor a mountain a greater miracle than an atom. To an almighty power, it is no more difficult to make the one than the other, and no more difficult to make a million of worlds, than to make one. Every thing therefore is a miracle in one sense, whilst, in the other sense, there is no such thing as a miracle. It is a miracle when compared to our power, and to our comprehension. It is not a miracle compared to the power that performs it. But as nothing in this description conveys the idea that is affixed to the word miracle, it is necessary to carry the inquiry further.

Mankind have conceived to themselves certain laws by which, what they call, nature, is supposed to act; and that a miracle is something contrary to the operation and effect of those laws. But unless we know the whole extent of those laws, and of what are commonly called, the powers of nature, we are not able to judge whether any thing that may appear to us wonderful, or miraculous, be within, or be beyond, or be contrary to, her natural power of acting.

The ascension of a man several miles high into the air, would have every thing in it that constitutes the idea of a miracle, if it were not known that a species of air can be generated several times lighter than the common atmospheric air, and yet possess elasticity enough to prevent the balloon, in which that light air is inclosed, from being compressed into as many times less bulk, by the common air that surrounds it. In like manner, extracting flashes or sparks of fire from the human body as visibly as from a steel struck with a flint, and causing iron or steel to move without any visible agent, would also give the idea of a miracle, if we were not acquainted with electricity and magnetism: so also would many other experiments in natural philosophy, to those who are not acquainted with the subject. The restoring persons to life, who are to appearance dead, as is practised upon drowned persons, would also be a miracle, if it were not known that animation is capable of being suspended without being extinct.

Besides these, there are performances by slight of hand, and by persons acting in concert, that have a miraculous appearance, which, when known, are thought nothing of. And besides these, there are mechanical and optical deceptions. There is now an exhibition in Paris of ghosts or spectres, which, though it is not imposed upon the spectators as a fact, has an astonishing appearance. As therefore we know not the extent to which either nature or art can go, there is no positive criterion to determine what a miracle is; and mankind, in giving credit to appearances, under the idea of their being miracles, are subject to be continually imposed upon.

Since then appearances are so capable of deceiving, and things not real have a strong resemblance to things that are, nothing can be more inconsistent, than to suppose, that the Almighty would make use of means, such as are called miracles, that would subject the person who performed them to the suspicion of being an impostor, and the person who related them to be suspected of lying, and the doctrine intended to be supported thereby, to be suspected as a fabulous invention.

Of all the modes of evidence that ever were invented to obtain belief to any system or opinion, to which the name of religion has been given, that of *miracle*, however successful the imposition may have been, is the most inconsistent. For, in the first place, whenever recourse is had to show, for the purpose of procuring that belief (for a miracle, under any idea of the word, is a show) it implies a lameness or weakness in the doctrine that is preached. And, in the second place, it is degrading the Almighty into the character of a show-man, playing tricks to amuse and make the people stare and wonder. It is also the most equivocal sort of evidence that can be set up; for the belief is not to depend upon the thing called a miracle, but upon the credit of the reporter, who says that he saw it; and therefore the thing, were it true, would have no better chance of being believed than if it were a lie.

Suppose, I were to say, that when I sat down to write this book, a hand presented itself in the air, took up the pen, and wrote every word that is herein written; would any body believe me? certainly they would not. Would they believe me a whit the more if the thing had been a fact? certainly they would not. Since then, a real miracle, were it to happen, would be subject to the same fate as the falshood, the inconsistency becomes the greater, of supposing the Almighty would make use of means that would not answer the purpose for which they were intended, even if they were real.

If we are to suppose a miracle to be something so entirely out of the course of what is called nature, that she must go out of that course to accomplish it; and we see an account given of such miracle by the person who said he saw it, it raises a question in the mind very easily decided, which is, Is it more probable that nature should go out of her course, or that a man should tell a lie? We have never seen, in our time, nature go out of her course, but we have good reason to believe that millions of lies have been told in the same time; it is therefore at least millions to one, that the reporter of a miracle tells a lie.

The story of the whale swallowing Jonah, though a whale is large enough to do it, borders greatly on the marvellous; but it would have approached nearer to the idea of a miracle, if Jonah had swallowed the whale. In this, which may serve for all cases of miracles, the matter would decide itself as before stated, namely, Is it more probable that a man should have swallowed a whale, or told a lie?

But supposing that Jonah had really swallowed the whale, and gone with it in his belly to Nineveh, and to convince the people that it was true, have cast it up in their sight of the full length and size of a whale, would they not have believed him to have been the devil instead of a prophet? or, if the whale had carried Jonah to Nineveh, and cast him up in the same public manner, would they not have believed the whale to have been the devil, and Jonah one of his imps?

The most extraordinary of all the things called miracles, related in the New Testament, is that of the devil flying away with Jesus Christ, and carrying him to the top of a high mountain; and to the top of the highest pinnacle of the temple, and showing him, and promising to him *all the kingdoms of the world.* How happened it that he did not discover America? or is it only with *kingdoms* that his sooty highness has any interest?

I have too much respect for the moral character of Christ, to believe that he told this whale of a miracle himself; neither is it easy to account for what purpose it could have been fabricated, unless it were to impose upon the connoisseurs of miracles, as is sometimes practised upon the connoisseurs of Queen Anne's farthings, and collectors of relics and antiquities; or to render the belief of miracles ridiculous, by outdoing miracle, as Don

Quixote outdid chivalry; or to embarrass the belief of miracles by making it doubtful by what power, whether of God, or of the devil, any thing called a miracle was performed. It requires, however, a great deal of faith in the devil to believe this miracle.

In every point of view, in which those things called miracles can be placed and considered, the reality of them is improbable, and their existence unnecessary. They would not, as before observed, answer any useful purpose, even if they were true; for it is more difficult to obtain belief to a miracle, than to a principle evidently moral, without any miracle. Moral principle speaks universally for itself. Miracle could be but a thing of the moment, and seen but by a few; after this, it requires a transfer of faith, from God to man, to believe a miracle upon man's report. Instead therefore of admitting the recitals of miracles, as evidence of any system of religion being true, they ought to be considered as symptoms of its being fabulous. It is necessary to the full and upright character of truth, that it rejects the crutch; and it is consistent with the character of fable, to seek the aid that truth rejects. Thus much for mystery and miracle.

As mystery and miracle took charge of the past and the present, prophecy took charge of the future, and rounded the tenses of faith. It was not sufficient to know what had been done, but what would be done. The supposed prophet was the supposed historian of times to come; and if he happened, in shooting with a long bow of a thousand years, to strike within a thousand miles of a mark, the ingenuity of posterity could make it point-blank; and if he happened to be directly wrong, it was only to suppose, as in the case of Jonah and Nineveh, that God had repented himself, and changed his mind. What a fool do fabulous systems make of man!

It has been shewn in a former part of this work, that the original meaning of the words *prophet* and *prophesying* has been changed, and that a prophet, in the sense the word is now used, is a creature of modern invention; and it is owing to this change in the meaning of the words, that the flights and metaphors of the Jewish poets, and phrases and expressions now rendered obscure by our not being acquainted with the local circumstances to which they applied at the time they were used, have been erected into prophecies, and made to bend to explanations at the will and whimsical conceits of sectaries, expounders, and commentators. Every thing unintelligible was prophetical, and every thing insignificant was typical. A blunder would have served for a prophecy; and a dish-clout for a type.

If by a prophet we are to suppose a man, to whom the Almighty communicated some event that would take place in future, either there were such men, or there were not. If there were, it is consistent to believe that the event, so communicated, would be told in terms that could be understood; and not related in such a loose and obscure manner as to be out of the comprehension of those that heard it, and so equivocal as to fit almost any circumstance that might happen afterwards. It is conceiving very irreverently of the Almighty to suppose he would deal in this jesting manner with mankind: yet all the things called prophecies, in the book called the Bible, come under this description.

But it is with prophecy, as it is with miracle. It could not answer the purpose even if it were real. Those to whom a prophecy should be told, could not tell whether the man prophesied or lied, or whether it had been revealed to him, or whether he conceited it: and if the thing that he prophesied, or pretended to prophesy, should happen, or something like it among the multitude of things that are daily happening, nobody could again know whether he foreknew it, or guessed at it, or whether it was accidental. A prophet, therefore, is a character useless and unnecessary; and the safe side of the case is, to guard against being imposed upon by not giving credit to such relations.

Upon the whole, mystery, miracle, and prophecy, are appendages that belong to fabulous and not to true religion. They are the means by which so many *Lo heres!* and *Lo theres!* have been spread about the world, and religion been made into a trade. The success of one impostor gave encouragement to another, and the quieting salvo of doing *some good* by keeping up a *pious fraud,* protected them from remorse.

Having now extended the subject to a greater length than I first intended, I shall bring it to a close by abstracting a summary from the whole.

First, That the idea or belief of a word of God existing in print, or in writing, or in speech, is inconsistent in itself for the reasons already assigned. These reasons, among many others, are the want of an universal language; the mutability of language; the errors to which translations are subject; the possibility of totally suppressing such a word; the probability of altering it, or of fabricating the whole, and imposing it upon the world.

Secondly, That the creation we behold is the real and ever existing word of God, in which we cannot be deceived. It proclaimeth his power, it demonstrates his wisdom, it manifests his goodness and beneficence.

Thirdly, That the moral duty of man consists in imitating the moral goodness and beneficence of God manifested in the creation towards all his creatures. That seeing, as we daily do, the goodness of God to all men, it is an example calling upon all men to practise the same towards each other, and consequently that every thing of persecution and revenge between man and man, and every thing of cruelty to animals is a violation of moral duty.

I trouble not myself about the manner of future existence. I content myself with believing, even to positive conviction, that the power that gave me existence is able to continue it, in any form and manner he pleases, either with or without this body; and it appears more probable to me that I shall continue to exist hereafter, than that I should have had existence, as I now have, before that existence began.

It is certain that, in one point, all nations of the earth, and all religions agree. All believe in a God. The things in which they disagree, are the redundancies annexed to that belief; and therefore, if ever an universal religion should prevail, it will not be believing any thing new, but in getting rid of redundancies, and believing as man believed at first. Adam, if ever there was such a man, was created a Deist; but in the mean time let every man follow, as he has a right to do, the religion and the worship he prefers.

THE END.

THE

AGE OF REASON.
PART THE SECOND.

BEING

AN INVESTIGATION

OF

TRUE AND OF FABULOUS THEOLOGY.

BY THOMAS PAINE,

Author of the Works intituled,

COMMON SENSE – RIGHTS OF MAN, PART FIRST AND
SECOND – AND DISSERTATIONS ON FIRST PRINCIPLES
OF GOVERNMENT.

Preface.

I HAVE mentioned in the former part of *The Age of Reason,* that it had long
been my intention to publish my thoughts upon Religion; but that I had
originally reserved it to a later period in life, intending it to be the last work
I should undertake. The circumstances, however, which existed in France
in the latter end of the year 1790, determined me to delay it no longer. The

*The Age of Reason. Part the Second. Being an Investigation of True and of Fabu-
lous Theology* (London: H. D. Symonds, 1795).

just and humane principles of the Revolution, which Philosophy had first diffused, had been departed from. The Idea, always dangerous to Society as it is derogatory to the Almighty – that priests could forgive sins – though it seemed to exist no longer, had blunted the feelings of humanity, and callously prepared men for the commission of all manner of crimes. The intolerant spirit of religious persecution had transferred itself into politics; the tribunals, styled Revolutionary, supplied the place of the Inquisition; and the Guillotine of the State out did the Fire and Faggot of the Church. I saw many of my most intimate friends destroyed; others daily carried to prison; and I had reason to believe, and had also intimations given me, that the same danger was approaching myself.

Under these disadvantages, I began the former part of the Age of Reason; I had, besides, neither Bible nor Testament to refer to, though I was writing against both; nor could I procure any; notwithstanding which, I have produced a work that no Bible Believer, though writing at his ease, and with a Library of Church Books about him, can refute. Towards the latter end of December of that year, a motion was made and carried, to exclude foreigners from the Convention. There were but two in it, Anacharsis Clootz and myself, and I saw I was particularly pointed at by Bourdon de l'Oise, in his speech on that motion.

Conceiving, after this, that I had but a few days of liberty, I sat down, and brought the work to a close as speedily as possible; and I had not finished it more than six hours, in the state it has since appeared, before a guard came, about three in the morning, with an order, signed by the two Committees of Public Safety and Surety General, for putting me in arrestation as a foreigner, and conveying me to the prison of the Luxembourg. I contrived, in my way there, to call on Joel Barlow, and I put the Manuscript of the work into his hands, as more safe than in my possession in prison: and not knowing what might be the fate in France, either of the writer or the work, I addressed it to the protection of the citizens of the United States.

It is with justice that I say, that the guard who executed this order, and the interpreter of the Committee of General Surety, who accompanied them to examine my papers, treated me not only with civility, but with respect. The keeper of the Luxembourg, Benoit, a man of a good heart, shewed to me every friendship in his power, as did also all his family, while he continued in that station. He was removed from it, put into arrestation, and carried before the tribunal upon a malignant accusation, but acquitted.

After I had been in the Luxembourg about three weeks, the Americans, then in Paris, went in a body to the Convention, to reclaim me as their countryman and friend; but were answered by the President, Vadier, who was also President of the Committee of Surety General, and had signed the order for my arrestation, that I was born in England. I heard no more after this, from any person out of the walls of the Prison, till the fall of Robespierre, on the 9th of Thermidor.

About two months before this event, I was seized with a fever, that in its progress had every symptom of becoming mortal. It was then that I remembered with renewed satisfaction, and congratulated myself most sincerely, on having written the former part of "The Age of Reason." I had then but little expectation of surviving, and those about me had less. I know therefore, by experience, the conscientious trial of my own principles.

I was then with three chamber comrades: Joseph Vanhuele of Bruges, Charles Bastini, and Michael Robyns of Louvain. The unceasing and anxious attention of these three friends to me, by night and day, I remember with gratitude, and mention with pleasure. It happened that a physician (Dr. Graham) and a surgeon (Mr. Bond) part of the suite of General O'Hara, were then in the Luxembourg: I ask not myself, whether it be convenient to them, as men under the English Government, that I express to them my thanks; but I should reproach myself if I did not; and also to the physician of the Luxembourg, Dr. Marhashi.

I have some reason to believe, because I cannot discover any other cause, that this illness preserved me in existence. Among the papers of Robespierre, that were examined and reported upon to the Convention by a Committee of Deputies, is a note in the hand-writing of Robespierre, in the following words:

Demander que Thomas Paine soit decreté d'accusation, pour l'interêt de l'Amerique autant que de la France.	Demand that Thomas Paine be decreed of accusation, for the interest of America as well as of France.

From what cause it was that the intention was not put in execution, I know not, and cannot inform myself; and I ascribe it to impossibility, on account of that illness.

The Convention, to repair as much as lay in their power the injustice I had sustained, invited me publicly and unanimously to return into the Convention, and which I accepted, to shew I could bear an injury without permitting it to injure my principles, or my disposition. It is not because right principles have been violated, that they are to be abandoned.

I have seen, since I have been at liberty, several publications written, some in America, and some in England, as answers to the former part of

"The Age of Reason." If these authors can amuse themselves by so doing, I shall not interrupt them. They may write against the work, and against me, as much as they please; they do me more service than they intend, and I can have no objection that they write on. They will find, however, by this Second Part, without its being written as an answer to them, that they must return to their work, and spin their cobweb over again. The first is brushed away by accident.

They will now find that I have furnished myself with a Bible and Testament; and I can say also, that I have found them to be much worse books than I had conceived. If I have erred in any thing, in the former part of the Age of Reason, it has been by speaking better of some parts of those Books than they deserved.

I observe, that all my opponents resort, more or less, to what they call Scripture-Evidence and Bible Authority, to help them out. They are so little masters of the subject, as to confound a dispute about authenticity with a dispute about doctrines; I will however put them right, that if they should be disposed to write any more, they may know how to begin.

– THOMAS PAINE

The
Age of Reason.
Part the Second.

IT has often been said that any thing may be proved from the Bible; but before any thing can be admitted as proved by Bible, the Bible itself must be proved to be true; for if the Bible be not true, or the truth of it be doubtful, it ceases to have authority, and cannot be admitted as proof of any thing.

It has been the practice of all Christian commentators on the Bible, and of all Christian priests and preachers, to impose the Bible on the world as a mass of truth, and as the word of God; they have disputed and wrangled, and have anathematized each other about the supposeable meaning of particular parts and passages therein; one has said and insisted that such a passage meant such a thing; another, that it meant directly the contrary; and a third, that it meant neither one nor the other, but something different from both; and this they have called *understanding* the Bible.

It has happened, that all the answers which I have seen to the former part of the *Age of Reason* have been written by priests; and these pious men, like their predecessors, contend and wrangle, and pretend to *understand* the Bible; each understands it differently, but each understands it best; and they have agreed in nothing, but in telling their readers, that Thomas Paine understands it not.

Now, instead of wasting their time, and heating themselves in fractious disputations about doctrinal points drawn from the Bible, these men *ought to know,* and if they do not, it is civility to inform them, that the first thing to be understood is, whether there is sufficient authority for believing the Bible to be the word of God, or whether there is not?

There are matters in that book, said to be done by *the express command* of God, that are as shocking to humanity, and to every idea we have of moral justice, as any thing done by Robespierre, by Carrier, by Joseph le Bon, in France; by the English government, in the East-Indies; or by any other assassin in modern times. When we read in the books ascribed to Moses, Joshua, &c. that they (the Israelites) came by stealth upon whole nations of people, who, as the history itself shews, had given them no offence; *that they put all those nations to the sword; that they spared neither age nor infancy; that they utterly destroyed men, women, and children; that they left not a soul to breathe;* expressions that are repeated over and over again in those books, and that too with exulting ferocity: are we sure these things are facts? are we sure that the Creator of man commissioned these things to be done? are we sure that the books that tell us so, were written by his authority?

It is not the antiquity of a tale, that is any evidence of [its] truth; on the contrary, it is a symptom of [its] being fabulous; for the more ancient any history pretends to be, the more it has the resemblance of a fable. The origin of every nation is buried in fabulous tradition, and that of the Jews is as much to be suspected as any other. To charge the commission of acts upon the Almighty, which in their own nature, and by every rule of moral justice, are crimes, as all assassination is, and more especially the assassination of infants, is [a] matter of serious concern. The Bible tells us, that those assassinations were done by the *express command of God.* To believe therefore the Bible to be true, we must *unbelieve* all our belief in the moral justice of God; for wherein could crying or smiling infants offend? And to read the Bible without horror, we must undo every thing that is tender, sympathising, and benevolent in the heart of man. Speaking for myself, if I had no other evidence that the Bible is fabulous, than the sacrifice I must make to believe it to be true, that alone would be sufficient to determine my choice.

But in addition to all the moral evidence against the Bible, I will, in the progress of this work, produce such other evidence, as even a priest cannot deny; and shew from that evidence, that the Bible is not entitled to credit, as being the word of God.

But before I proceed to this examination, I will shew wherein the Bible differs from all other ancient writings with respect to the nature of the evidence necessary to establish [its] authenticity; and this is the more proper to be done, because the advocates of the Bible, in their answers to the former part of the *Age of Reason,* undertake to say, and they put some stress thereon, that the authenticity of the Bible is as well established, as that of any other ancient book: as if our belief of the one could become any rule for our belief of the other.

I know, however, but of one ancient book that authoritatively challenges universal consent and belief; and that is *Euclid's Elements of Geometry;*[1] and the reason is, because it is a book of self-evident demonstration, entirely independent of [its] author, and of every thing relating to time, place, and circumstance. The matters contained in that book, would have the same authority they now have, had they been written by any other person, or had the work been anonymous, or had the author never been known; for the identical certainty of who was the author, makes no part of our belief of the matters contained in the book. But it is quite otherwise with respect to the books ascribed to Moses, to Joshua, to Samuel, &c.: those are books of *testimony,* and they testify of things naturally incredible; and therefore the whole of our belief, as to the authenticity of those books, rests, in the first place, upon the *certainty* that they were written by Moses, Joshua, and Samuel; secondly, upon the credit we give to their testimony. We may believe the first, that is, may believe the certainty of the authorship, and yet not the testimony; in the same manner that we may believe that a certain person gave evidence upon a case, and yet not believe the evidence that he gave. But if it should be found, that the books ascribed to Moses, Joshua, and Samuel, were not written by Moses, Joshua, and Samuel, every part of the authority and authenticity of those books is gone at once; for there can be no such thing as forged or invented testimony; neither can there be anonymous testimony, more especially as to things naturally incredible; such as that of talking with God face to face, or that of the sun and moon standing still at the command of a man.

The greatest part of the other ancient books are works of genius; of which kind are those ascribed to Homer, to Plato, to Aristotle, to Demosthenes, to Cicero, &c. Here again the author is not an essential in the credit

1. Euclid, according to chronological history, lived three hundred years before Christ, and about one hundred before Archimedes; he was of the city of Alexandria.

we give to any of those works; for as works of genius, they would have the same merit they have now, were they anonymous. Nobody believes the Trojan story, as related by Homer, to be true; for it is the poet only that is admired; and the merit of the poet will remain, though the story be fabulous. But if we disbelieve the matters related by the Bible authors, (Moses for instance,) as we disbelieve the things related by Homer, there remains nothing of Moses in our estimation, but an impostor. As to the ancient historians, from Herodotus to Tacitus, we credit them as far as they relate things probable and credible, and no further; for if we do, we must believe the two miracles which Tacitus relates were performed by Vespasian, that of curing a lame man, and a blind man, in just the same manner as the same things are told of Jesus Christ by his historians. We must also believe the miracle cited by Josephus, that of the sea of Pamphilia opening to let Alexander and his army pass, as is related of the Red Sea in Exodus. These miracles are quite as well authenticated as the Bible miracles, and yet we do not believe them; consequently the degree of evidence necessary to establish our belief of things naturally incredible, whether in the Bible or elsewhere, is far greater than that which obtains our belief to natural and probable things; and therefore the advocates for the Bible have no claim to our belief of the Bible, because that we believe things stated in other ancient writings; since we believe the things stated in those writings no further than they are probable and credible, or because they are self-evident, like Euclid; or admire them because they are elegant, like Homer; or approve them because they are sedate, like Plato; or judicious, like Aristotle.

Having premised those things, I proceed to examine the authenticity of the Bible; and I begin with what are called the five books of Moses, *Genesis, Exodus, Leviticus, Numbers,* and *Deuteronomy.* My intention is to shew, that those books are spurious, and that Moses is not the author of them; and still further, that they were not written in the time of Moses, nor till several hundred years afterwards; that they are no other than an attempted history of the life of Moses, and of the times in which he is said to have lived, and also of the times prior thereto, written by some very ignorant and stupid pretenders to authorship, several hundred years after the death of Moses; as men now write histories of things that happened, or are supposed to have happened, several hundred, or several thousand years ago.

The evidence that I shall produce in this case is from the books themselves; and I will confine myself to this evidence only. Were I to refer for proofs to any of the ancient authors, whom the advocates of the Bible call prophane authors, they would controvert that authority, as I controvert their's: I will therefore meet them on their own ground, and oppose them with their own weapon, the Bible.

In the first place, there is no affirmative evidence that Moses is the author of those books; and that he is the author, is altogether an unfounded opinion got abroad, nobody knows how. The style and manner in which those books are written, give no room to believe, or even to suppose, they were written by Moses; for it is altogether the style and manner of another person speaking of Moses. In Exodus, Leviticus, and Numbers, (for every thing in Genesis is prior to the times of Moses, and not the least allusion is made to him therein,) the whole, I say, of these books is in the third person; it is always, *the Lord said unto Moses, or Moses said unto the Lord; or Moses said unto the people, or the people said unto Moses;* and this is the style and manner that historians use, in speaking of the persons whose lives and actions they are writing. It may be said, that a man may speak of himself in the third person, and therefore it may be supposed that Moses did; but supposition proves nothing; and if the advocates for the belief that Moses wrote those books himself, have nothing better to advance than supposition, they may as well be silent.

But granting the grammatical right, that Moses might speak of himself in the third person, because any man might speak of himself in that manner, it cannot be admitted as a fact in those books, that it is Moses who speaks, without rendering Moses truly ridiculous and absurd:—for example, Numbers, chap. xii. ver. 3, *"Now the man Moses was very meek above all the men which were on the face of the earth."* If Moses said this of himself, instead of being the meekest of men, he was one of the most vain and arrogant of coxcombs; and the advocates for those books may now take which side they please, for both sides are against them: if Moses was not the author, the books are without authority; and if he was the author, the author is without credit, because, to boast of *meekness,* is the reverse of meekness, and is *a lie in sentiment.*

In Deuteronomy, the style and manner of writing marks more evidently than in the former books, that Moses is not the writer. The manner here used is dramatical; the writer opens the subject by a short introductory discourse, and then introduces Moses as in the act of speaking, and when he has made Moses finish his harangue, he (the writer) resumes his own part, and speaks till he brings Moses forward again, and at last closes the scene with an account of the death, funeral, and character of Moses.

This interchange of speakers occurs four times in this book: from the first verse of the first chapter, to the end of the fifth verse, it is the writer who speaks; he then introduces Moses as in the act of making his harangue, and this continues to the end of the 40th verse of the fourth chapter; here the writer drops Moses, and speaks historically of what was done in consequence of what Moses, when living, is supposed to have said, and which the writer has dramatically rehearsed.

The writer opens the subject again in the first verse of the fifth chapter, though it is only by saying, that Moses called the people of Israel together; he then introduces Moses as before, and continues him, as in the act of speaking, to the end of the 26th chapter. He does the same thing at the beginning of the 27th chapter, and continues Moses, as in the act of speaking, to the end of the 28th chapter. At the 29th chapter the writer speaks again through the whole of the first verse, and the first line of the second verse, where he introduces Moses for the last time, and continues him, as in the act of speaking, to the end of the 33d chapter.

The writer having now finished the rehearsal on the part of Moses, comes forward, and speaks through the whole of the last chapter: he begins by telling the reader, that Moses went up to the top of Pisgah, that he saw from thence the land which (the writer says) had been promised to Abraham, Isaac, and Jacob; that *he,* Moses, died there, in the land of Moab, but that no man knoweth of his sepulchre unto this day, that is, unto the time in which the writer lived, who wrote the book of Deuteronomy. The writer then tells us, that Moses was one hundred and ten years of age when he died – that his eye was not dim, nor his natural force abated; and he concludes, by saying, that there arose not a prophet *since* in Israel like unto Moses, whom, says this anonymous writer, the Lord knew face to face.

Having thus shewn, as far as grammatical evidence applies, that Moses was not the writer of those books, I will, after making a few observations on the inconsistencies of the writer of the book of Deuteronomy, proceed to shew, from the historical and chonological evidence contained in those books, that Moses *was not,* because *he could not be,* the writer of them; and consequently, that there is no authority for believing, that the inhuman and horrid butcheries of men, women, and children, told of in those books, were done, as those books say they were, at the command of God. It is a duty incumbent on every true deist, that he vindicates the moral justice of God, against the calumnies of the Bible.

The writer of the book of Deuteronomy, whoever he was, for it is an anonymous work, is obscure, and also in contradiction with himself in the account he has given of Moses.

After telling that Moses went to the top of Pisgah, (and it does not appear from any account that he ever came down again,) he tells us, that

Moses died *there* in the land of Moab, and that *he* buried him in a valley in the land of Moab; but as there is no antecedent to the pronoun *he,* there is no knowing who the *he* was, that did bury him. If the writer meant that *he* (God) buried him, how should *he* (the writer) know it? or why should we (the readers) believe him? since we know not who the writer was that tells us so, for certainly Moses could not himself tell where he was buried.

The writer also tells us, that no man knoweth where the sepulchre of Moses is *unto this day,* meaning the time in which this writer lived; how then should he know that Moses was buried in a valley in the land of Moab? for as the writer lived long after the time of Moses, as is evident from his using the expression, *unto this day,* meaning a great length of time after the death of Moses, he certainly was not at his funeral; and, on the other hand, it is impossible that Moses himself could say, that *no man knoweth where the sepulchre is unto this day.* To make Moses the speaker, would be an improvement on the play of a child that hides itself, and cries, *nobody can find me;* nobody can find Moses.

This writer has no where told us how he came by the speeches which he has put into the mouth of Moses to speak, and therefore we have a right to conclude, that he either composed them himself, or wrote them from oral tradition. One or other of these is the more probable, since he has given, in the fifth chapter, a table of commandments, in which that called the fourth commandment is different from the fourth commandment in the twentieth chapter of Exodus In that of Exodus, the reason given for keeping the seventh day is, because (says the commandment) God made the heavens and the earth in six days, and rested on the seventh; but in that of Deuteronomy, the reason given is, that it was the day on which the children of Israel came out of Egypt, and *therefore,* says this commandment, *the Lord thy God commanded thee to keep the sabbath-day. This* makes no mention of the creation, nor *that* of the coming out of Egypt. There are also many things given as laws of Moses in this book, that are not to be found in any of the other books, among which is that inhuman and brutal law, chap. xxi. ver. 18, 19, 20, 21, which authorizes parents, the father and the mother, to bring their own children to have them stoned to death, for what it is pleased to call stubbornness. But priests have always been fond of preaching up Deuteronomy, for Deuteronomy preaches up tythes: and it is from this book, chap. xxv. ver. 4, they have taken the phrase and applied it to tything, that *thou shalt not muzzle the ox when he treadeth out the corn:* and that this might not escape observation, they have noted it in the table of contents, at the head of the chapter, though it is only a single verse of less than two lines.

O priests! priests! ye are willing to be compared to an ox, for the sake of tythes. Though it is impossible for us to know *identically* who the writer of Deuteronomy was, it is not difficult to discover him *professionally,* that he was some Jewish priest, who lived, as I shall shew in the course of this work, at least three hundred and fifty years after the time of Moses.

I come now to speak of the historical and chronological evidence. The chronology that I shall use is the Bible chronology; for I mean not to go out of the Bible for evidence of any thing, but to make the Bible itself prove historically and chronologically that Moses is not the author of the books ascribed to him. It is therefore proper that I inform the reader, (such an one, at least, as may not have the opportunity of knowing it,) that in the larger Bibles, and also in some smaller ones, there is a series of chronology printed in the margin of every page, for the purpose of shewing how long the historical matters stated in each page happened, or are supposed to have happened, before Christ, and consequently the distance of time between one historical circumstance and another.

I begin with the book of Genesis. In the 14th chapter of Genesis, the writer gives an account of Lot being taken prisoner in a battle between the four kings against five, and carried off; and that when the account of Lot being taken, came to Abraham, he armed all his household, and marched to rescue Lot from the captors; and that he pursued them unto Dan (ver. 14).

To shew in what manner this expression of *pursuing them unto Dan* applies to the case in question, I will refer to two circumstances, the one in America, the other in France. The city now called New York, in America, was originally New Amsterdam; and the town in France, lately called Havre-Marat, was before called Havre-de-Grace. New Amsterdam was changed to New York in the year 1664; Havre-de-Grace to Havre-Marat in the year 1793. Should, therefore, any writing be found, though without date, in which the name of New York should be mentioned, it would be certain evidence that such a writing could not have been written before, and must have been written after New Amsterdam was changed to New York, and consequently not till after the year 1664, or at least during the course of that year. And in like manner, any dateless writing, with the name of Havre-Marat, would be certain evidence that such a writing must have been written after Havre-de-Grace became Havre-Marat, and consequently not till after the year 1793, or at least during the course of that year.

I now come to the application of those cases, and to shew that there was no such place as *Dan,* till many years after the death of Moses; and consequently that Moses could not be the writer of the book of Genesis, where this account of pursuing them unto *Dan* is given.

The place that is called Dan in the Bible, was originally a town of the Gentiles, called Laish; and when the tribe of Dan seized upon this town, they changed [its] name to Dan, in commemoration of Dan, who was the father of that tribe, and the great grandson of Abraham.

To establish this in proof, it is necessary to refer from Genesis to the 18th chapter of the book called the book of Judges. It is there said, (ver. 27,) that *they* (the Danites) *came unto Laish to a people that were quiet and secure, and they smote them with the edge of the sword,* (the Bible is filled with murder,) *and burned the city with fire; and they built a city,* (ver. 28,) and dwelt therein, *and they called the name of the city Dan, after the name of Dan their father: howbeit the name of the city was Laish at the first.*

This account of the Danites taking possession of Laish, and changing it to Dan, is placed in the book of Judges immediately after the death of Samson. The death of Samson is said to have happened 1120 years before Christ, and that of Moses 1451 before Christ; and therefore, according to the historical arrangement, the place was not called Dan till 331 years after the death of Moses.

There is a striking confusion between the historical and the chronological arrangement in the book of Judges. The five last chapters, as they stand in the book, 17, 18, 19, 20, 21, are put chronologically before all the preceding chapters; they are made to be 28 years before the 16th chapter, 266 before the 15th, 245 before the 13th, 195 before the 9th, 90 before the 4th, and 15 years before the 1st chapter. This shews the uncertain and fabulous state of the Bible. According to the chronological arrangement, the taking of Laish, and giving it the name of Dan, is made to be twenty years after the death of Joshua, who was the successor of Moses: and by the historical order, as it stands in the book, it is made to be 306 years after the death of Joshua, and 331 after that of Moses; but they both exclude Moses from being the writer of Genesis, because, according to either of the statements, no such a place as Dan existed in the time of Moses; and therefore the writer of Genesis must have been some person who lived after the town of Laish had the name of Dan; and who that person was nobody knows, and consequently the book of Genesis is anonymous, and without authority.

I proceed now to state another point of historical and chronological evidence, and to shew therefrom, as in the preceding case, that Moses is not the author of the book of Genesis.

In the 36th chapter of Genesis there is given a genealogy of the sons and descendants of Esau, who are called Edomites, and also a list, by name, of the kings of Edom; in enumerating of which, it is said, verse 31, "*And these are the kings that reigned in Edom, before there reigned any king over the children of Israel."*

Now, were any dateless writing to be found, in which, speaking of any past events, the writer should say, those things happened before there was any congress in America, or before there was any convention in France, it would be evidence that such writing could not have been written before, and could only be written after there was a congress in America, or a convention in France, as the case might be; and consequently that it could not be written by any person who died before there was a congress in the one country, or a convention in the other.

Nothing is more frequent, as well in history as in conversation, than to refer to a fact in the room of a date; it is most natural so to do, first, because a fact fixes itself in the memory better than a date; secondly, because the fact includes the date, and serves to excite two ideas at once; and this manner of speaking by circumstances, implies as positively, that the fact alluded to *is past,* as if it was so expressed. When a person, in speaking upon any matter, says, it was before I was married, or before my son was born, or before I went to America, or before I went to France, it is absolutely understood, and intended to be understood, that he has been married, that he has had a son, that he has been in America, or been in France. Language does not admit of using this mode of expression in any other sense; and whenever such an expression is found any where, it can only be understood in the sense in which only it could have been used.

The passage, therefore, that I have quoted,—"that these are the kings that reigned in Edom, before there reigned *any* king over the children of Israel," could only have been written after the first king began to reign over them; and consequently that the book of Genesis, so far from having been written by Moses, could not have been written till the time of Saul at least. This is the positive sense of the passage: but the expression, *any* king, implies more kings than one; at least, it implies two; and this will carry it to the time of David; and if taken in a general sense, it carries itself through all times of the Jewish monarchy.

Had we met with this verse in any part of the Bible that *professed* to have been written after kings began to reign in Israel, it would have been impossible not to have seen the application of it. It happens then that this is the case; the two books of Chronicles, which give a history of *all* the kings of Israel, are *professedly,* as well as in fact, written after the Jewish monarchy began; and this verse that I have quoted, and all the remaining verses of the 36th chapter of Genesis, are, word for word, in the 1st chapter of Chronicles, beginning at the 43d verse.

It was with consistency that the writer of the Chronicles could say, as he has said, 1st Chron. chap. i. verse 43, *These are the kings that reigned in Edom, before there reigned any king over the children of Israel,* because he was going to give, and has given, a list of the kings that had reigned in Israel; but as it is impossible that the same expression could have been used before that period, it is as certain as any thing can be proved from historical language, that this part of Genesis is taken from Chronicles, and that Genesis is not so old as Chronicles, and probably not so old as the book of Homer, or as Æsop's Fables; admitting Homer to have been, as the tables of chronology state, contemporary with David or Solomon, and Æsop to have lived about the end of the Jewish monarchy.

Take away from Genesis the belief that Moses was the author, on which only the strange belief that it is the word of God has stood, and there remains nothing of Genesis, but an anonymous book of stories, fables, and traditionary or invented absurdities, or of downright lies. The story of Eve and the serpent, and of Noah and his ark, drops to a level with the Arabian Tales, without the merit of being entertaining; and the account of men living to eight and nine hundred years, becomes as fabulous as the immortality of the giants of the Mythology.

Besides, the character of Moses, as stated in the Bible, is the most horrid that can be imagined. If those accounts be true, he was the wretch that first began and carried on wars on the score, or on the pretence of religion; and under that mask, or that infatuation, committed the most unexampled atrocities that are to be found in the history of any nation, of which I will state only one instance.

When the Jewish army returned from one of their plundering and murdering excursions, the account goes on as follows, Numbers, chap. xxxi. ver. 13.

"And Moses, and Eleazar the priest, and all the princes of the congregation, went forth to meet them without the camp; and Moses was wroth with the officers of the host, with the captains over thousands, and captains over hundreds, which came from the battle; and Moses said unto them, *Have ye saved all the women alive?* behold, these caused the children of Israel, through the counsel of Balaam, to commit trespass against the Lord in the matter of Peor, and there was a plague among the congregation of the Lord. Now, therefore, *kill every male among the little ones, and kill every woman that hath known a man by lying with him; but all the women-children that have not known a man by lying with him, keep alive for yourselves.*"

Among the detestable villains that in any period of the world have disgraced the name of man, it is impossible to find a greater than Moses, if this account be true. Here is an order to butcher the boys, to massacre the mothers, and debauch the daughters.

Let any mother put herself in the situation of those mothers; one child murdered, another destined to violation, and herself in the hands of an executioner: let any daughter put herself in the situation of those daughters, destined as prey to the murderers of a mother and a brother, and what will be their feelings? It is in vain that we attempt to impose upon nature, for nature will have her course, and the religion that tortures all her social ties is a false religion.

After this detestable order, follows an account of the plunder taken, and the manner of dividing it; and here it is that the profaneness of priestly hypocrisy increases the catalogues of crimes. Verse 37, *"And the Lord's tribute* of the sheep was six hundred and threescore and fifteen; and the beeves were thirty and six thousand, of which the *Lord's tribute* was threescore and twelve; and the asses were thirty thousand, of which the Lord's tribute was threescore and one; and the persons were thirty thousand, of which the Lord's tribute was thirty and two." In short, the matters contained in this chapter, as well as in many other parts of the Bible, are too horrid for humanity to read, or for decency to hear; for it appears from the 35th verse of this chapter, that the number of women-children consigned to debauchery by the order of Moses was thirty-two thousand.

People in general know not what wickedness there is in this pretended word of God. Brought up in habits of superstition, they take it for granted, that the Bible is true, and that it is good; they permit themselves not to doubt of it; and they carry the ideas they form of the benevolence of the Almighty to the book which they have been taught to believe was written by his authority. Good heavens! it is quite another thing! it is a book of lies, wickedness, and blasphemy; for what can be greater blasphemy than to ascribe the wickedness of man to the orders of the Almighty?

But to return to my subject, that of shewing that Moses is not the author of the books ascribed to him, and that the Bible is spurious. The two instances I have already given would be sufficient, without any additional evidence, to invalidate the authenticity of any book that pretended to be four or five hundred years more ancient than the matters it speaks of, or refers to, as facts; for in the case *of pursuing them unto Dan,* and of the *kings that reigned over the children of Israel,* not even the flimsy pretence of prophecy can be pleaded. The expressions are in the preter tense, and it would be downright idiotism to say that a man could prophesy in the preter tense.

But there are many other passages scattered throughout those books, that unite in the same point of evidence. It is said in Exodus (another of the books ascribed to Moses), chap. xvi. ver. 34, "And the children of Israel did eat manna *until they came to a land inhabited;* they did eat manna *until they came unto the borders of the land of Canaan.*"

Whether the children of Israel ate manna or not, or what manna was, or whether it was any thing more than a kind of fungus, or small mushroom, or other vegetable substance, common to that part of the country, makes nothing to my argument; all that I mean to shew is, that it is not Moses that could write this account, because the account extends itself beyond the life and time of Moses. Moses, according to the Bible, (but it is such a book of lies and contradictions, there is no knowing which part to believe, or whether any,) died in the wilderness, and never came upon the borders of the land of Canaan; and consequently it could not be he, that said what the children of Israel did, or what they ate when they came there. This account of eating manna, which they tell us was written by Moses, extends itself to the time of Joshua, the successor of Moses; as appears by the account given in the book of Joshua, after the children of Israel had passed the river Jordan, and came unto the borders of the land of Canaan. Joshua, chap. v. ver. 12, "*And the manna ceased on the morrow, after they had eaten of the old corn of the land; neither had the children of Israel manna any more, but they did eat of the fruit of the land of Canaan that year.*"

But a more remarkable instance than this occurs in Deuteronomy; which, while it shews that Moses could not be the writer of that book, shews also the fabulous notions that prevailed at that time about giants. In the third chapter of Deuteronomy, among the conquests said to be made by Moses, is an account of the taking of Og, king of Bashan, verse 11. "For only Og, king of Bashan, remained of the race of giants; behold, his bedstead was a bedstead of iron, is it not in *Rabbath* of the children of Ammom? nine cubits was the length thereof, and four cubits the breadth of it, after the cubit of a man." A cubit is 1 foot $9^{888}/_{1000}$ inches. The length, therefore, of the bed was 10 feet 4 inches, and the breadth 7 feet 4 inches: thus much for this giant's bed. Now for the historical part, which, though the evidence is not so direct and positive as in the former cases, is nevertheless very presumable and corroborating evidence, and is better than the *best* evidence on the contrary side.

The writer, by way of proving the existence of this giant, refers to his bed, as to an *ancient relick,* and says, is it not in Rabbath (or Rabbah) of the children of Ammon? meaning, that it is; for such is frequently the

Bible method of affirming a thing. But it could not be Moses that said this, because Moses could know nothing about Rabbah, nor of what was in it. Rabbah was not a city belonging to this giant king, nor was it one of the cities that Moses took. The knowledge, therefore, that this bed was at Rabbah, and of the particulars of [its] dimensions, must be referred to the time when Rabbah was taken, and this was not till four hundred years after the death of Moses, for which see 2 Sam. chap. xii. ver. 26. "And Joab (David's general) fought against *Rabbah of the children of Ammon,* and took the royal city."

As I am not undertaking to point out all the contradictions in time, place, and circumstance, that abound in the book ascribed to Moses, and which prove to a demonstration, that those books could not be written by Moses, nor in the time of Moses; I proceed to the book of Joshua, and to shew that Joshua is not the author of that book, and that it is anonymous, and without authority. The evidence I shall produce is contained in the book itself: I will not go out of the Bible for proof against the supposed authenticity of the Bible. False testimony is always good against itself.

Joshua, according to the first chapter of Joshua, was the immediate successor of Moses; he was moreover a military man, which Moses was not; and he continued as chief of the people of Israel twenty-five years; that is, from the time that Moses died, which, according to the Bible chronology, was 1451 years before Christ, until 1426 years before Christ, when, according to the same chronology, Joshua died. If therefore we find in this book, said to have been written by Joshua, references to *facts done* after the death of Joshua, it is evidence that Joshua could not be the author; and also that the book could not have been written till after the time of the latest fact which it records. As to the character of the book, it is horrid; it is a military history of rapine and murder; as savage and brutal, as those recorded of his predecessor in villainy and hypocrisy, Moses; and the blasphemy consists, as in the former books, in ascribing those deeds to the orders of the Almighty.

In the first place, the book of Joshua, as is the case in the preceding books, is written in the third person; it is the historian of Joshua that speaks, for it would have been absurd and vain-glorious, that Joshua should say of himself, as is said of him in the last verse of the sixth chapter, that "*his fame was noised throughout all the country.*" I now come more immediately to the proof.

In the 24th chapter, ver. 31, it is said, "And Israel served the Lord all the days of Joshua, and *all the days of the elders that over-lived Joshua.*" Now in the name of common sense, can it be Joshua that relates what people had done after he was dead? This account must not only have been written by some historian that lived after Joshua, but that lived also after the elders that had out-lived Joshua.

There are several passages of a general meaning with respect to time, scattered throughout the book of Joshua, that carries the time in which the book was written to a distance from the time of Joshua, but without marking by exclusion any particular time, as in the passage above quoted. In that passage the time that intervened between the death of Joshua, and the death of the elders, is excluded descriptively and absolutely, and the evidence substantiates that the book could not have been written till after the death of the last.

But though the passages to which I allude, and which I am going to quote, do not designate any particular time by exclusion, they imply a time far more distant from the days of Joshua, than is contained between the death of Joshua and the death of the elders. Such is the passage, chap. x. ver. 14; where, after giving an account that the sun stood still upon Gibeon, and the moon in the valley of Ajalon, at the command of Joshua, (a tale fit only to amuse children,) the passage says – "And there was no day like that, before it, nor *after it,* that the Lord harkened to the voice of a man."

This tale of the sun standing still upon mount Gibeon, and the moon in the valley of Ajalon, is one of those fables that detects itself Such a circumstance could not have happened without being known all over the world. One half would have wondered why the sun did not rise, and the other why it did not set; and the tradition of it would be universal; whereas there is not a nation in the world that knows any thing about it. But why must the moon stand still? What occasion could there be for moon-light in the day-time, and that too while the sun shined? As a poetical figure, the whole is well enough; it is akin to that in the song of Deborah and Baruk, *The stars in their courses fought against Sisera;* but it is inferior to the figurative declaration of Mahomet, to the persons who came to expostulate with him on his goings on; *Wert thou,* said he, *to come to me with the sun in thy right hand, and the moon in thy left, it should not alter my career.* For Joshua to have exceeded Mahomet, he should have put the sun and moon one in each pocket, and carried them as Guy Faux carried his dark lanthorn, and taken them out to shine as he might happen to want them. The sublime and the ridiculous are often so nearly related, that it is difficult to class them separately. One step above the sublime, makes the ridiculous; and one step above the ridiculous, makes the sublime again; the account, however, abstracted from the poetical fancy, shews the ignorance of Joshua, for he should have commanded the earth to have stood still.

The time implied by the expression *after it,* that is, after that day, being put in comparison with all the time that passed *before it,* must, in order to give any expressive signification to the passage, mean a *great length of time:*–for example, it would have been ridiculous to have said so the next day, or the next week, or the next month, or the next year; to give therefore meaning to the passage, comparative with the wonder it relates, and the prior time it alludes to, it must mean centuries of years; less however than one, would be trifling; and less than two, would be barely admissible.

A distant but general time is also expressed in the 8th chapter, where, after giving an account of the taking the city of Ai, it is said, ver. 28, "And Joshua burned Ai, and made it an heap for ever, a desolation *unto this day;*" and again, ver. 29, where speaking of the king of Ai, whom Joshua had hanged, and buried at the entering of the gate, it is said, "And he raised thereon a great heap of stones, which remaineth *unto this day,*" that is, unto the day or time in which the writer of the book of Joshua lived. And again, in the 10th chapter, where, after speaking of the five kings, whom Joshua had hanged on five trees, and then thrown in a cave, it is said, "And he laid great stones on the cave's mouth, which remain *unto this very day.*"

In enumerating the several exploits of Joshua, and of the tribes, and of the places which they conquered or attempted, it is said, chap. xv. ver. 63, "As for the Jebusites, the inhabitants of Jerusalem, the children of Judah could not drive them out; but the Jebusites dwell with the children of Judah *at Jerusalem unto this day.*" The question upon this passage is, At what time did the Jebusites and the children of Judah dwell together at Jerusalem? As this matter occurs again in the first chapter of Judges, I shall reserve my observations till I come to that part.

Having thus shewn from the book of Joshua itself, without any auxiliary evidence whatever, that Joshua is not the author of that book, and that it is anonymous, and consequently without authority, I proceed, as before-mentioned, to the book of Judges.

The book of Judges is anonymous on the face of it; and therefore, even the pretence is wanting to call it the word of God; it has not so much as a nominal voucher; it is altogether fatherless.

This book begins with the same expression as the book of Joshua. That of Joshua begins, chap. i. ver. 1, *Now after the death of Moses,* &c. and this of Judges begins, *Now after the death of Joshua,* &c. This, and the similarity of style between the two books, indicate that they are the work of the same author; but who he was, is altogether unknown; the only point that the book proves is, that the author lived long after the time of Joshua; for though it begins as if it followed immediately after his death, the second chapter is an epitome or abstract of the whole book, which, according to the Bible chronology, extends [its] history through a space of 306 years; that is, from the death of Joshua, 1426 years before Christ, to the death of Samson, 1120 years before Christ, and only 25 years before Saul went *to seek his father's asses, and was made king.* But there is good reason to believe, that it was not written till the time of David at least, and that the book of Joshua was not written before the same time.

In the first chapter of Judges, the writer, after announcing the death of Joshua, proceeds to tell what happened between the children of Judah and the native inhabitants of the land of Canaan. In this statement, the writer, having abruptly mentioned Jerusalem in the 7th verse, says immediately after, in the 8th verse, by way of explanation, "Now the children of Judah *had* fought against Jerusalem, and *taken* it;" consequently, this book could not have been written before Jerusalem had been taken. The readers will recollect the quotation I have just before made from the 15th chapter of Joshua, ver. 63, where it is said, that *the Jebusites dwell with the children of Judah at Jerusalem at this day;* meaning the time when the book of Joshua was written.

The evidence I have already produced, to prove that the books I have hitherto treated of, were not written by the persons to whom they are ascribed, nor till many years after their death, if such persons ever lived, is already so abundant, that I can afford to admit this passage with less weight than I am entitled to draw from it. For the case is, that so far as the Bible can be credited as an history, the city of Jerusalem was not taken till the time of David; and consequently, that the book of Joshua, and of Judges, were not written till after the commencement of the reign of David, which was 370 years after the death of Joshua.

The name of the city that was afterwards called Jerusalem, was originally Jebus, or Jebusi, and was the capital of the Jebusites. The account of David's taking this city is given in 2 Samuel, chap. v. ver. 4, &c.; also in 1 Chron. chap. xiv. ver. 4, &c. There is no mention in any part of the Bible that it was ever taken before, nor any account that favours such an opinion. It is not said, either in Samuel or in Chronicles, that they *utterly destroyed men, women, and children; that they left not a soul to breathe,* as is said of their other conquests; and the silence here observed, implies that it was taken by capitulation, and that the Jebusites, the native inhabitants, continued to live in the place after it was taken. The account, therefore, given in Joshua, that *the Jebusites dwell with the children of Judah* at Jerusalem at this day, corresponds to no other time than after the taking of the city by David.

Having now shewn, that every book in the Bible, from Genesis to Judges, is without authenticity, I come to the book of Ruth, an idle, bungling story, foolishly told, nobody knows by whom, about a strolling country girl creeping slily to bed to her cousin Boaz. Pretty stuff indeed to be called the word of God! It is, however, one of the best books in the Bible, for it is free from murder and rapine.

I come next to the two books of Samuel, and to shew that those books were not written by Samuel, nor till a great length of time after the death of Samuel; and that they are, like all the former books, anonymous, and without authority.

To be convinced that these books have been written much later than the time of Samuel, and consequently not by him, it is only necessary to read the account which the writer gives of Saul going to seek his father's asses, and of his interview with Samuel, of whom Saul went to inquire about those lost asses, as foolish people now-a-days go to a conjurer to inquire after lost things.

The writer, in relating this story of Saul, Samuel, and the asses, does not tell it as a thing that had just then happened, but as a *story* ancient *in the time this writer lived:* for he tells it in the language or terms used at the time that *Samuel* lived, which obliges the writer to explain the story in the terms or language used in the time the *writer* lived.

Samuel, in the account given of him in the first of those books, chap. ix. is called *the seer;* and it is by this term that Saul inquires after him, ver. 11, "And as they (Saul and his servant) went up the hill to the city, they found young maidens going out to draw water; and they said unto them, *Is the seer here?*" Saul then went according to the direction of these maidens, and met Samuel without knowing him, and said to him, ver. 18, "Tell me, I pray thee, where the *seer's house is?* and Samuel answered Saul, and said, *I am the seer.*"

As the writer of the book of Samuel relates these questions and answers, in the language or manner of speaking used in the time they are said to have been spoken; and as that manner of speaking was out of use when this author wrote, he found it necessary, in order to make the story understood, to explain the terms in which these questions and answers are spoken; and he does this in the other verse, where he says, "*Before-time* in Israel, when a man went to inquire of God, thus he spake, Come let us go to the seer; for he that is now called a prophet, was *before-time* called a seer." This proves, as I have before said, that this story of Saul, Samuel, and the asses, was an ancient story at the time the book of Samuel was written, and consequently that Samuel did not write it, and that that book is without authenticity.

But if we go further into those books, the evidence is still more positive that Samuel is not the writer of them; for they relate things that did not happen till several years after the death of Samuel. Samuel died before Saul; for the 1st of Samuel, chap. xxviii. tells, that Saul and the witch of Endor conjured Samuel up after he was dead; yet the history of matters contained in those books, is extended through the remaining part of Saul's life, and to the latter end of the life of David, who succeeded Saul. The account of the death and burial of Samuel (a thing which he could not write himself) is related in the 25th chapter of the first book of Samuel; and the chronology affixed to this chapter makes this to be 1060 years before Christ; yet the history of this *first* book is brought down to 1056 years before Christ, that is, to the death of Saul, which was not four years after the death of Samuel.

The second book of Samuel begins with an account of things that did not happen till four years after Samuel was dead; for it begins with the reign of David, who succeeded Saul, and it goes on to the end of David's reign, which was forty-three years after the death of Samuel; and therefore the books are in themselves positive evidence that they were not written by Samuel.

I have now gone through all the books in the first part of the Bible, to which the names of persons are affixed, as being the authors of those books, and which the church, stiling itself the Christian church, have imposed upon the world as the writings of Moses, Joshua, and Samuel; and I have detected and proved the falshood of this imposition. And now, ye priests, of every description, who have preached and written against the former part of the *Age of Reason,* what have ye to say? Will ye, with all this mass of evidence against you, and staring you in the face, still have the assurance to march into your pulpits, and continue to impose these books on your congregations, as the works of *inspired penmen,* and the word of God? when it is as evident as demonstration can make truth appear, that the persons who, ye say, are the authors, are *not* the authors, and that ye know not who the authors are. What shadow of pretence have ye now to produce, for continuing the blasphemous fraud? What have ye still to offer against the pure and moral religion of deism, in support of your system of falshood, idolatry, and pretended revelation? Had the cruel and murdering orders, with which the Bible is filled, and the numberless torturing executions of men, women, and children, in consequence of those orders, been ascribed to some friend, whose memory you revered, you would have

glowed with satisfaction at detecting the falshood of the charge, and gloried in defending his injured fame. It is because ye are sunk in the cruelty of
superstition, or feel no interest in the honour of your Creator, that ye listen
to the horrid tales of the Bible, or hear them with callous indifference. The
evidence I have produced, and shall still produce in the course of this work,
to prove that the Bible is without authority, will, whilst it wounds the stubbornness of a priest, relieve and tranquillize the minds of millions: it will
free them from all those hard thoughts of the Almighty, which priest-craft
and the Bible had infused into their minds, and which stood in everlasting
opposition to all their ideas of his moral justice and benevolence.

I come now to the two books of Kings, and the two books of Chronicles.
Those books are altogether historical, and are chiefly confined to lives and
actions of the Jewish kings, who in general were a parcel of rascals: but
these are matters with which we have no more concern, than we have with
the Roman emperors, or Homer's account of the Trojan war. Besides which,
as those books are anonymous, and as we know nothing of the writer, or of
his character, it is impossible for us to know what degree of credit to give
to the matters related therein. Like all other ancient histories, they appear to
be a jumble of fable and of fact, and of probable and of improbable things,
but which distance of time and place, and change of circumstances in the
world, have rendered obsolete and uninteresting.

The chief use I shall make of those books, will be that of comparing
them with each other, and with other parts of the Bible, to shew the confusion, contradiction, and cruelty, in this pretended word of God.

The first book of Kings begins with the reign of Solomon, which, according to the Bible chronology, was 1015 years before Christ; and the
second book ends 588 years before Christ, being a little after the reign of
Zedekiah, whom Nebuchadnezzar, after taking Jerusalem, and conquering
the Jews, carried captive to Babylon. The two books include a space of four
hundred and twenty-seven years.

The two books of Chronicles are an history of the same times, and in
general of the same persons, by another author; for it would be absurd to
suppose that the same author wrote the history twice over. The first book
of Chronicles (after giving the genealogy from Adam to Saul, which takes
up the first nine chapters) begins with the reign of David; and the last book
ends, as in the last book of Kings, soon after the reign of Zedekiah, about
588 years before Christ. The two last verses of the last chapter bring the
history fifty-two years more forward, that is, to 536. But these verses do
not belong to the book, as I shall shew, when I come to speak of the book
of Ezra.

The two books of Kings, besides the history of Saul, David, and Solomon, who reigned over *all* Israel, contain an abstract of the lives of seventeen kings and one queen, who are stiled kings of Judah; and of nineteen, who are stiled kings of Israel; for the Jewish nation, immediately on the death of Solomon, split into two parties, who chose separate kings, and who carried on most rancorous wars against each other.

Those two books are little more than a history of assassinations, treachery, and wars. The cruelty that the Jews had accustomed themselves to practise on the Canaanites, whose country they had savagely invaded, under a pretended gift from God, they afterwards practised as furiously on each other. Scarcely half their kings died a natural death, and in some instances, whole families were destroyed to secure possession to the successor, who, after a few years, and sometimes only a few months, or less, shared the same fate. In the tenth chapter of the second book of Kings, an account is given of two baskets full of children's heads, 70 in number, being exposed at the entrance of the city; they were the children of Ahab, and were murdered by the orders of Jehu, whom Elisha, the pretended man of God, had anointed to be king over Israel, on purpose to commit this bloody deed, and assassinate his predecessor. And in the account of the reign of Manaham, one of the kings of Israel, who had murdered Shallum, who had reigned but one month, it is said, 2 Kings, chap. xv. ver. 16, that Manaham smote the city of Tiphsah, because they opened not the city to him, *and all the women therein that were with child be ripped up.*

Could we permit ourselves to suppose that the Almighty would distinguish any nation of people by the name of *his chosen people,* we must suppose that people to have been an example to all the rest of the world of the purest piety and humanity, and not such a nation of ruffians and cutthroats as the ancient Jews were; a people, who, corrupted by, and copying after such monsters and impostors as Moses and Aaron, Joshua, Samuel, and David, had distinguished themselves above all others, on the face of the known earth, for barbarity and wickedness. If we will not stubbornly shut our eyes, and steel our hearts, it is impossible not to see, in spite of all that long-established superstition imposes upon the mind, that the flattering appellation of *his chosen people* is no other than a *lie,* which the priests and leaders of the Jews had invented, to cover the baseness of their own characters; and which Christian priests, sometimes as corrupt, and often as cruel, have professed to believe.

The two books of Chronicles are a repetition of the same crimes; but the history is broken in several places, by the author leaving out the reign of some of their kings; and in this, as well as in that of Kings, there is such a frequent transition of kings of Judah, to kings of Israel, and from kings of Israel, to kings of Judah, that the narrative is obscure in the reading. In the same book the history sometimes contradicts itself; for example, in the second book of Kings, chap. i. ver. 8, we are told, but in rather ambiguous terms, that after the death of Ahaziah, king of Israel, Jehoram, or Joram, (who was of the house of Ahab,) reigned in his stead in the *second year* of Jehoram, or Joram, son of Jehoshaphat, king of Judah; – and in chap. viii. ver. 16, of the same book, it is said, and in the *fifth year* of Joram, the son of Ahab, king of Israel, Jehoshaphat being then king of Judah, Jehoram, the son of Jehoshaphat, king of Judah, began to reign; that is, one chapter says, that Joram of Judah, began to reign in the *second year* of Joram of Israel; and the other chapter says, that Joram of Israel began to reign in the *fifth year* of Joram of Judah.

Several of the most extraordinary matters related in one history, as having happened during the reign of such and such of their kings, are not to be found in the other in relating the reign of the same king: for example, the two first rival kings, after the death of Solomon, were Rehoboam and Jeroboam; and in 1 Kings, chap. xii. and xiii. an account is given of Jeroboam making an offering of burnt incense, and that a man, who is there called a man of God, cried out against the altar, chap. xiii. ver. 2, "O altar, altar! thus saith the Lord: Behold, a child shall be born unto the house of David, Josiah by name, and upon thee shall he offer the priests of the high places, that burn incense upon thee, and men's bones shall be burnt upon thee." – Ver. 3, "And it came to pass, when king Jeroboam heard the saying of the man of God, which had cried against the altar in Bethel, that he put forth his hand from the altar, saying, *Lay hold on him;* and his hand which he put out against him, *dried up, so that he could not pull it in again to him.*"

One would think that such an extraordinary case as this, (which is spoken of as a judgment,) happening to the chief of one of the parties, and at the first moment of the separation of the Israelites into two nations, would, if it had been true, been recorded in both histories. But though men in late times have believed *all that the prophets have said unto them,* it does not appear, that those prophets, or historians, believed each other: they knew each other too well.

A long account also is given in Kings about Elijah. It runs through several chapters, and concludes with telling, 2 Kings, chap. ii. ver. 11, "And it came to pass, as they (Elijah and Elisha) still went on, and talked, that behold there appeared *a chariot of fire, and horses of fire,* and parted both asunder, and Elijah *went up by a whirlwind to heaven.*" Hum! this the author of Chronicles, miraculous as the story is, makes no mention of, though he mentions Elijah by name; neither does he say any thing of the story related in the second chapter of the same book of Kings, of a parcel of children calling Elisha *bald head, bald head;* that this *man of God,* ver. 24, "turned back, and looked upon them, and *cursed them in the name of the Lord;* and there came forth two she-bears out of the wood, and tore forty and two children of them." He also passes over in silence the story told, 2 Kings, chap. xiii. that when they were burying a man in the sepulchre, where Elisha had been buried, it happened that the dead man, as they were letting him down, (ver. 21,) "touched the bones of Elisha, and he (the dead man) *revived, and stood up on his feet.*" The story does not tell us whether they buried the man, notwithstanding he revived and stood up on his feet, or drew him up again. Upon all these stories, the writer of Chronicles is as silent, as any writer of the present day, who did not chuse to be accused of *lying,* or at least of *romancing,* would be about stories of the same kind.

But, however these two historians may differ from each other, with respect to the tales related by either, they are silent alike with respect to those men stiled prophets, whose writings fill up the latter part of the Bible. Isaiah, who lived in the time of Hezekiah, is mentioned in Kings, and again in Chronicles, when these historians are speaking of that reign; but, except in one or two instances at most, and those very slightly, none of the rest are so much as spoken of, or even their existence hinted at; though, according to the Bible chronology, they lived within the time those histories were written; some of them long before. If those prophets, as they are called, were men of importance in their day, as the compilers of the Bible, and priests, and commentators, have since represented them to be, how can it be accounted for, that only one of these histories should say any thing about them?

The history in the books of Kings and of Chronicles is brought forward, as I have already said, to the year 885[2] before Christ: it will therefore be proper to examine, which of these prophets lived before that period.

Here follows a table of all the prophets, with the times in which they lived before Christ, according to the chronology affixed to the first chapter of each of the books of the prophets; and also of the number of years they lived before the books of Kings and Chronicles were written.

2. [Editors' note:] This year should be 588.

TABLE.

Names.	Years before Christ.	Years bef. Kings and Chron.	Observations.
Isaiah –	760	172	mentioned.
Jeremiah –	629	41	{ mentioned only in the last chap. of Chron.
Ezekiel –	595	7	not mentioned.
Daniel –	607	19	not mentioned.
Hosea –	785	97	not mentioned.
Joel –	800	212	not mentioned.
Amos –	789	199	not mentioned.
Obadiah –	789	199	not mentioned
Jonah –	862	274	see the note.[3]
Micah –	750	162	not mentioned.
Nahum –	713	125	not mentioned.
Habakuk –	626	38	not mentioned.
Zephaniah –	630	42	not mentioned.
Haggai Zechariah Malachi }	after the year 588.		

This table is either not very honourable for the Bible historians, or not very honourable for the Bible prophets; and I leave to priests, and commentators, who are very learned in little things, to settle the point of *etiquette* between the two; and to assign a reason, why the authors of Kings and Chronicles have treated those prophets, whom, in the former part of the *Age of Reason,* I have considered as poets, with as much degrading silence as any historian of the present day would treat Peter Pindar.

I have one observation more to make on the book of Chronicles; after which, I shall pass on to review the remaining books of the Bible.

In my observations on the book of Genesis, I have quoted a passage from the 36th chapter, ver. 31, which evidently refers to a time, *after* that kings began to reign over the children of Israel; and I have shewn, that as

3. In Kings, chap. xiv. ver. 25, the name of Jonah is mentioned, on account of the restoration of a tract of land by Jeroboam; but nothing further of him is said, nor is any allusion made to the book of Jonah, nor to his expedition to Nineveh, nor to his encounter with the whale.

this verse is verbatim the same as in Chronicles, chap. i. ver. 43, where it stands consistently with the order of history, which in Genesis it does not, the verse in Genesis, and a great part of the 36th chapter, have been taken from Chronicles; and that the book of Genesis, though it is placed first in the Bible, and ascribed to Moses, has been manufactured by some unknown person, after the book of Chronicles was written, which was not until at least eight hundred and sixty years after the time of Moses.

The evidence I proceed by, to substantiate this, is regular, and has in it but two stages. First, I have already stated, that the passage in Genesis refers itself for *time* to Chronicles; secondly, that the book of Chronicles, to which this passage refers itself, was not *begun* to be written until at least eight hundred and sixty years after the time of Moses. To prove this, we have only to look into the thirteenth verse of the third chapter of the first book of Chronicles, where the writer, in giving the genealogy of the descendants of David, mentions *Zedekiah:* and it was in the time of *Zedekiah* that Nebuchadnezzar conquered Jerusalem, 588 years before Christ, and consequently more than 860 years after Moses. Those who have superstitiously boasted of the antiquity of the Bible, and particularly of the books ascribed to Moses, have done it without examination, and without any other authority than that of one credulous man telling it to another; for, so far as historical and chronological evidence applies, the very first book in the Bible is not so ancient as the book of Homer, by more than three hundred years, and is about the same age with Æsop's Fables.

I am not contending for the morality of Homer; on the contrary, I think it a book of false glory, tending to inspire immoral and mischievous notions of honour; and with respect to Æsop, though the moral is in general just, the fable is often cruel; and the cruelty of the fable does more injury to the heart, especially in a child, than the moral does good to the judgment.

Having now dismissed Kings and Chronicles, I come to the next in course, the book of Ezra.

As one proof, among others I shall produce, to shew the disorder in which this pretended word of God, the Bible, has been put together, and the uncertainty of who the authors were, we have only to look at the three first verses in Ezra, and the two last in Chronicles; for by what kind of cutting and shuffling has it been, that the three first verses in Ezra should be the two last verses in Chronicles, or that the two last in Chronicles should be the three first in Ezra? Either the authors did not know their own works, or the compilers did not know the authors.

Two last Verses of Chronicles.

Ver. 22. Now in the first year of Cyrus, king of Persia, that the word of the Lord, spoken by the mouth of Jeremiah, might be accomplished, the Lord stirred up the spirit of Cyrus, king of Persia, that he made a proclamation throughout all his kingdom, and put it also in writing, saying,

23. Thus saith Cyrus, king of Persia, All the kingdoms of the earth hath the Lord God of heaven given me; and he hath charged me to build him an house in Jerusalem, which is in Judah. Who is there among you of all his people? the Lord his God be with him, and let him go up.

Three first Verses of Ezra.

Ver. 1. Now in the first year of Cyrus, king of Persia, that the word of the Lord, by the mouth of Jeremiah, might be fulfilled, the Lord stirred up the spirit of Cyrus, king of Persia, that he made a proclamation throughout all his kingdom, and put it also in writing, saying,

2. Thus saith Cyrus, king of Persia, The Lord God of heaven hath given me all the kingdoms of the earth; and he hath charged me to build him an house at Jerusalem, which is in Judah.

3. Who is there among you of all his people? his God be with him, and let him go up *to Jerusalem, which is in Judah, and build the house of the Lord God of Israel (he is the God) which is in Jerusalem.*

The last verse in Chronicles is broken abruptly, and ends in the middle of a phrase with the word *up,* without signifying to what place. This abrupt break, and the appearance of the same verses in different books, shew, as I have already said, the disorder and ignorance in which the Bible has been put together, and that the compilers of it had no authority for what they were doing, nor we any authority for believing what they have done.[4]

4. I observed, as I passed along, several broken and senseless passages in the Bible, without thinking them of consequence enough to be introduced in the body of the work; such as that, 1 Samuel, chap. xiii. ver. 1, where it is said, "Saul reigned *one year;* and when he had reigned *two* years over Israel, Saul chose him three thousand men, &c." The first part of the verse, that Saul reigned *one year,* has no sense, since it does not tell us what Saul did, nor say any thing of what happened at the end of *that one year;* and it is, besides, mere absurdity to say he reigned *one*

The only thing that has any appearance of certainty in the book of Ezra, is the time in which it was written, which was immediately after the return of the Jews from the Babylonian captivity, about 536 years before Christ. Ezra (who, according to the Jewish commentators, is the same person as is called Esdras in the Apocrypha) was one of the persons who returned, and who, it is probable, wrote the account of that affair. Nehemiah, whose book follows next to Ezra, was another of the returned persons; and who, it is also probable, wrote the account of the same affair, in the book that bears his name. But those accounts are nothing to us, nor to any other persons, unless it be to the Jews, as a part of the history of their nation: and there is just as much of the word of God in those books, as there is in any of the histories of France, or Rapin's History of England, or the history of any other country.

But even in matters of historical record, neither of those writers are to be depended upon. In the second chapter of Ezra, the writer gives a list of the tribes and families, and of the precise number of souls of each that returned from Babylon to Jerusalem; and this enrollment of the persons so returned,

---

year, when the very next phrase says he had reigned two; for if he had reigned two, it was impossible not to have reigned one.

Another instance occurs in Joshua, chap. v. where the writer tells us a story of an angel (for such the table of contents, at the head of the chapter, calls him) appearing unto Joshua; and the story ends abruptly, and without any conclusion. The story is as follows:–Verse 13, "And it came to pass, when Joshua was by Jericho, that he lifted up his eyes and looked, and behold there stood a man over-against him with his sword drawn in his hand; and Joshua went up to him, and said unto him, Art thou for us, or for our adversaries?" Verse 14, "And he said, Nay; but as captain of the hosts of the Lord am I now come. And Joshua fell on his face to the earth, and did worship, and said unto him, *What saith my Lord unto his servant?*" Verse 15, "And the captain of the Lord's host said unto Joshua, Loose thy shoe from off thy foot; for the place whereon thou standest is holy. And Joshua did so."–And what then? nothing: for here the story ends, and the chapter too.

Either this story is broken off in the middle, or it is a story told by some Jewish humourist, in ridicule of Joshua's pretended mission from God; and the compilers of the Bible, not perceiving the design of the story, have told it as a serious matter. As a story of humour and ridicule, it has a great deal of point; for it pompously introduces an angel in the figure of a man, with a drawn sword in his hand, before whom Joshua *falls on his face to the earth, and worships* (which is contrary to their second commandment); and then, this most important embassy from heaven ends, in telling Joshua *to pull off his shoe.* It might as well have told him to pull up his breeches.

It is certain, however, that the Jews did not credit every thing their leaders told them, as appears from the cavalier manner in which they speak of Moses, when he was gone into the mount. "As for *this* Moses, say they, *we know not what is become of him."* Exod. chap. xxxii. ver 1.

appears to have been one of the principal objects for writing the book; but in this there is an error that destroys the intention of the undertaking.

The writer begins his enrollment in the following manner: Chap. ii. ver. 3, "The children of Parosh, two thousand one hundred seventy and two." Verse 4, "The children of Shephatiah, three hundred seventy and two." And in this manner he proceeds through all the families; and in the 64th verse, he makes a total, and says, the whole congregation together was *forty and two thousand three hundred and threescore.*

But whoever will take the trouble of casting up the several particulars, will find that the total is but 29,818; so that the error is 12,542.[5] What certainty then can there be in the Bible for any thing?

Nehemiah, in like manner, gives a list of the returned families, and of the number of each family. He begins as in Ezra, by saying, chap. vii. ver. 8, "The children of Parosh, two thousand three hundred and seventy-two;" and so on through all the families. This list differs in several of the particulars from that of Ezra. In the 66th verse, Nehemiah makes a total, and says, as Ezra had said, "The whole congregation together was forty and two thousand three hundred and threescore." But the particulars of this list make a total but of 31,089, so that the error here is 11,271. These writers may do well enough for Bible makers, but not for any thing where truth and exactness are necessary.

The next book in course is the book of Esther. If Madam Esther thought it any honour to offer herself as a kept mistress to Ahasuerus, or as a rival to queen Vashti, who had refused to come to a drunken king, in the midst of a drunken company, to be made a shew of, (for the account says, they

5. Particulars of the families from the second chapter of Ezra.

Chap. ii.		Bt. over 11,577		Bt. over 15,783		Bt. over 19,444	
Ver. 3	2172	Ver. 13	666	Ver. 23	128	Ver. 33	125
4	372	14	2056	24	42	34	345
5	775	15	454	25	143	35	3630
6	2812	16	98	26	621	36	973
7	1254	17	323	27	122	37	1052
8	945	18	112	28	223	38	1247
9	760	19	223	29	52	39	1017
10	642	20	95	30	156	40	74
11	623	21	123	31	1254	41	128
12	1222	22	56	32	320	42	139
						58	392
						60	652
	11,577		15,783		19,444	Total	29,818

had been drinking seven days, and were merry,) let Esther and Mordecai look to that, it is no business of our's, at least it is none of mine; besides which, the story has a great deal the appearance of being fabulous, and is also anonymous. I pass on to the book of Job.

The book of Job differs in character from all the books we have hitherto passed over. Treachery and murder make no part of this book; it is full of the meditations of a mind strongly impressed with the vicissitudes of human life; and by turns sinking under, and struggling against the pressure. It is a highly wrought composition, between willing submission and involuntary discontent; and shews man, as he sometimes is, more disposed to be resigned than he is capable of being. Patience has but a small share in the character of the person of whom the book treats; on the contrary, his grief is often impetuous; but he still endeavours to keep a guard upon it, and seems determined, in the midst of accumulating ills, to impose upon himself the hard duty of contentment.

I have spoken in a respectful manner of the book of Job in the former part of the *Age of Reason,* but without knowing at that time what I have learned since; which is, that from all the evidence that can be collected, the book of Job does not belong to the Bible.

I have seen the opinion of two Hebrew commentators, Abenezra and Spinosa, upon this subject; they both say that the book of Job carries no internal evidence of being an Hebrew book; that the genius of the composition, and the drama of the piece, are not Hebrew, that it has been translated from another language into Hebrew, and that the author of the book was a Gentile; that the character represented under the name of Satan (which is the first and only time this name is mentioned in the Bible) does not correspond to any Hebrew idea; and that the two convocations which the Deity is supposed to have made of those, whom the poem calls sons of God, and the familiarity which this supposed Satan is stated to have with the Deity, are in the same case.

It may also be observed, that the book shews itself to be the production of a mind cultivated in science, which the Jews, so far from being famous for, were very ignorant of. The allusions to objects of natural philosophy are frequent and strong, and are of a different cast to any thing in the books known to be Hebrew. The astronomical names Pleïades, Orion, and Arcturus, are Greek, and not Hebrew names; and as it does not appear from any thing that is to be found in the Bible, that the Jews knew any thing of astronomy, or that they studied it, they had no translation for those names into their own language, but adopted the names as they found them in the poem.

That the Jews did translate the literary productions of the Gentile nations into the Hebrew language, and mix them with their own, is not a matter of doubt; the first chapter of Proverbs is an evidence of this: it is there said, ver. 1, *The words of king Lemuel, the prophecy which his mother taught him.* This verse stands as a preface to the proverbs that follow, and which are not the proverbs of Solomon, but of Lemuel; and this Lemuel was not one of the kings of Israel, nor of Judah, but of some other country, and consequently a Gentile. The Jews, however, have adopted his proverbs; and as they cannot give any account who the author of the book of Job was, nor how they came by the book; and as it differs in character from the Hebrew writings, and stands totally unconnected with every other book and chapter in the Bible before it, and after it, it has all the circumstantial evidence of being originally a book of the Gentiles.[6]

The Bible-makers, and those regulators of time, the Bible chronologists, appear to have been at a loss where to place, and how to dispose of the book of Job; for it contains no one historical circumstance, nor allusion to any, that might serve to determine [its] place in the Bible. But it would not have answered the purpose of these men to have informed the world of their ignorance; and therefore they have affixed to it the æra of 1520 years before Christ, which is during the time the Israelites were in Egypt, and for which they have just as much authority as I should have for saying it was a thousand years before that period. The probability, however, is, that it is older than any book in the Bible; and it is the only one that can be read without indignation or disgust.

We know nothing of what the ancient gentile world (as it is called) was before the time of the Jews, whose practice has been to calumniate

6. The prayer known by the name of *Agur's prayer,* in the 30th chapter of Proverbs, immediately preceding the proverbs of Lemuel, and which is the only sensible, well-conceived, and well-expressed prayer in the Bible, has much the appearance of being a prayer taken from the Gentiles. The name of Agur occurs on no other occasion than this; and he is introduced, together with the prayer ascribed to him, in the same manner, and nearly in the same words, that Lemuel and his proverbs are introduced in the chapter that follows. The first verse of the 30th chapter says, "The words of Agur, the son of Jakeh, even the prophecy:" here the word prophecy is used with the same application it has in the following chapter of Lemuel, unconnected with any thing of prediction. The prayer of Agur is in the 8th and 9th verse, *"Remove far from me vanity and lies; give me neither riches nor poverty, but feed me with food convenient for me: lest I be full and deny thee, and say, Who is the Lord? or lest I be poor and steal, and take the name of my God in vain."* This has not any of the marks of being a Jewish prayer; for the Jews never prayed but when they were in trouble, and never for any thing but victory, vengeance, or riches.

and blacken the character of all other nations; and it is from the Jewish accounts that we have learned to call them heathens. But as far as we know to the contrary, they were a just and a moral people, and not addicted, like the Jews, to cruelty and revenge, but of whose profession of faith we are unacquainted. It appears to have been their custom to personify both virtue and vice, by statues and images, as is done now-a-days both by statuary and by painting; but it does not follow from this, that they worshipped them any more than we do. I pass on to the book of *Psalms,* of which it is not necessary to make much observation. Some of them are moral, and others are very revengeful, and the greater part relates to certain local circumstances of the Jewish nation at the time they were written, with which we have nothing to do. It is, however, an error, or an imposition, to call them the Psalms of David; they are a collection, as song-books are now-a-days, from different song-writers, who lived at different times. The 137th Psalm could not have been written till more than four hundred years after the time of David, because it is written in commemoration of an event, the captivity of the Jews in Babylon, which did not happen till that distance of time. *"By the rivers of Babylon we sat down; yea, we wept when we remembered Zion. We hanged our harps upon the willows, in the midst thereof; for there they that carried us away captive, required of us a song, saying, Sing us one of the songs of Zion."* As a man would say to an American, or to a Frenchman, or to an Englishman, Sing us one of your American songs, or your French songs, or your English songs. This remark, with respect to the time this psalm was written, is of no other use than to shew (among others already mentioned) the general imposition the world has been under, with respect to the authors of the Bible. No regard has been paid to time, place, and circumstance; and the names of persons have been affixed to the several books, which it was as impossible they should write, as that a man should walk in procession at his own funeral.

The book of Proverbs. These, like the Psalms, are a collection, and that from authors belonging to other nations than those of the Jewish nation, as I have shewn in the observations upon the book of Job: besides which, some of the proverbs ascribed to Solomon, did not appear till two hundred and fifty years after the death of Solomon; for it is said in the first verse of the 25th chapter, *"These are also proverbs of Solomon, which the men of Hezekiah king of Judah copied out."* It was two hundred and fifty years from the time of Solomon to the time of Hezekiah. When a man is famous, and his name is abroad, he is made the putative father of things he never said or did; and this most probably has been the fashion of that day, to make proverbs, as it is now to make jest-books, and father them upon those who never saw them.

The book of *Ecclesiastes,* or the *Preacher,* is also ascribed to Solomon, and that with much reason, if not with truth. It is written as the solitary reflections of a worn-out debauchee, such as Solomon was, who looking back on scenes he can no longer enjoy, cries out, *All is vanity!* A great deal of the metaphor and of the sentiment is obscure, most probably by translation; but enough is left to shew they were strongly pointed in the original.[7]

From what is transmitted to us of the character of Solomon, he was witty, ostentatious, dissolute, and at last melancholy: he lived fast, and died, tired of the world, at the age of fifty-eight years.

Seven hundred wives, and three hundred concubines, are worse than none; and however it may carry with it the appearance of heightened enjoyment, it defeats all the felicity of affection, by leaving it no point to fix upon; divided love is never happy. This was the case with Solomon; and if he could not, with all his pretensions to wisdom, discover it beforehand, he merited, unpitied, the mortification he afterwards endured. In this point of view, his preaching is unnecessary, because, to know the consequences, it is only necessary to know the case. Seven hundred wives, and three hundred concubines, would have stood in place of the whole book. It was needless after this to say, that all was vanity and vexation of spirit; for it is impossible to derive happiness from the company of those whom we deprive of happiness.

To be happy in old age, it is necessary that we accustom ourselves to objects that can accompany the mind all the way through life, and that we take the rest as good in their day. The mere man of pleasure is miserable in old age; and the mere drudge in business is but little better: whereas, natural philosophy, mathematical and mechanical sciences, are a continual source of tranquil pleasure, and in spite of the gloomy dogma of priests, and of superstition, the study of those things is the study of the true theology; it teaches man to know and to admire the Creator, for the principles of science are in the creation, are unchangeable, and of divine origin.

Those who knew Benjamin Franklin, will recollect, that his mind was ever young; his temper ever serene; science, that never grows grey, was always his mistress. Without an object, we become like an invalid in an hospital waiting for death.

---

7. *Those that look out of the window shall be darkened,* is an obscure figure translation for loss of sight.

Solomon's Songs are amorous and foolish enough, but which wrinkled fanaticism has called divine. The compilers of the Bible have placed these songs after the book of Ecclesiastes; and the chronologists have affixed to them the æra of 1014 years before Christ, at which time Solomon, according to the same chronology, was nineteen years of age, and was then forming his seraglio of wives and concubines. The Bible-makers and the chronologists should have managed this matter a little better, and either have said nothing about the time, or chosen a time less inconsistent with the supposed divinity of those songs; for Solomon was then in the honeymoon of one thousand debaucheries.

It should also have occurred to them, that as he wrote, if he did write, the book of Ecclesiastes, long after these songs, and in which he exclaims, that all is vanity and vexation of spirit; that he included those songs in that description. This is the more probable, because he says, or somebody for him, Ecclesiastes, chap. ii. ver. 8, "*I got me men-singers and women-singers,* (most probably to sing those songs) *and musical instruments of all sorts;* and behold (ver. 11) all was vanity and vexation of spirit." The compilers, however, have done their work but by halves; for as they have given us the songs, they should have given us the tunes, that we might sing them.

Those books, called the books of the Prophets, fill up all the remaining part of the Bible; they are sixteen in number, beginning with Isaiah, and ending with Malachi, of which I have given a list, in the observations upon Chronicles. Of these sixteen prophets, all of whom, except the three last, lived within the time the books of Kings and Chronicles were written; two only, Isaiah and Jeremiah, are mentioned in the history of those books. I shall leave the character of the men called prophets, to another part of the work.

Whoever will take the trouble of reading the book ascribed to Isaiah, will find it one of the most wild and disorderly compositions ever put together; it has neither beginning, middle, nor end; and except a short historical part, and a few sketches of history in two or three of the first chapters, is one continued, incoherent, bombastical rant, full of extravagant metaphor, without application, and destitute of meaning; a school-boy would scarcely have been excuseable for writing such stuff; it is (at least in translation) that kind of composition and false taste, that is properly called prose run mad.

The historical part begins at the 36th chapter, and is continued to the end of the 39th chapter. It relates some matters that are said to have passed during the reign of Hezekiah, king of Judah, at which time Isaiah lived. This fragment of history begins and ends abruptly; it has not the least connection with the chapter that precedes it, nor with that which follows it, nor with any other in the book. It is probable, that Isaiah wrote this fragment himself, because he was an actor in the circumstances it treats of; but except this part, there are scarcely two chapters that have any connection with each other; one is entitled, at the beginning of the first verse, the burden of Babylon; another, the burden of Babylon; another, the burden of Moab; another, the burden of Damascus; another, the burden of Egypt; another, the burden of the Desart of the Sea; another, the burden of the Valley of Vision; as you would say, the story of the knight, of the burning mountain, the story of Cinderilla, or the Wood, &c. &c.

I have already shewn in the instance of the two last verses of Chronicles, and the three first in Ezra, that the compilers of the Bible mixed and confounded the writings of different authors with each other; which alone, were there no other cause, is sufficient to destroy the authenticity of any compilation, because it is more than presumptive evidence, that the compilers are ignorant who the authors were. A very glaring instance of this occurs in the book ascribed to Isaiah: the latter part of the 44th chapter, and the beginning of the 45th, so far from having been written by Isaiah, could only have been written by some person, who lived at least an hundred and fifty years after Isaiah was dead.

These chapters are a compliment to *Cyrus,* who permitted the Jews to return to Jerusalem from the Babylonian captivity, to rebuild Jerusalem and the temple, as is stated in Ezra. The last verse of the 44th chapter, and the beginning of the 45th, are in the following words: *"That saith of Cyrus, he is my shepherd, and shall perform all my pleasure; even saying to Jerusalem, thou shalt be built; and to the temple, thy foundations shall be laid; thus saith the Lord to his anointed, to Cyrus, whose right-hand I have holden to subdue nations before him, and I will loose the loins of kings to open before him the two-leaved gates, and the gates shall not be shut; I will go before thee, &c."*

What audacity of church, and priestly ignorance, it is to impose this book upon the world, as the writing of Isaiah! when Isaiah, according to their own chronology, died soon after the death of Hezekiah, which was six hundred and ninety-eight years before Christ; and the decree of Cyrus, in favour of the Jews returning to Jerusalem, was, according to the same chronology, 536 years before Christ; which is a distance of time, between the two, of one hundred and sixty-two years. I do not suppose, that the compilers of the Bible made these books; but rather that they picked up some loose, anonymous essays, and put them together, under the names of such authors, as best suited their purpose. They have encouraged the imposition, which is next to inventing it; for it was impossible but they must have observed it.

When we see the studied craft of the scripture-makers, in making every part of this romantic book of school-boy's eloquence, bend to the monstrous idea of a Son of God, begotten by a ghost on the body of a virgin, there is no imposition; we are not justified in suspecting them of it. Every phrase and circumstance are marked with the barbarous hand of superstitious torture, and forced into meanings, it was impossible they could have. The head of every chapter, and the top of every page, are blazoned with the names of Christ and the church; that the unwary reader might suck in the error before he began to read.

Behold a virgin shall conceive, and bear a son, Isaiah, chap. vii. ver. 14, has been interpreted to mean the person, called Jesus Christ, and his mother Mary, and has been echoed through christendom for more than a thousand years; and such has been the rage of this opinion, that scarcely a spot in it, but has been stained with blood, and marked with desolation, in consequence of it. Though it is not my intention to enter into controversy on subjects of this kind, but to confine myself to shew that the Bible is spurious; and thus, by taking away the foundation, to overthrow at once the whole structure of superstition raised thereon; I will, however, stop a moment to expose the fallacious application of this passage.

Whether Isaiah was playing a trick with Ahaz, king of Judah, to whom this passage is spoken, is no business of mine; I mean only to shew the misapplication of the passage, and that it has no more reference to Christ and his mother, than it has to me and my mother. The story is simply this:

The king of Syria and the king of Israel (I have already mentioned, that the Jews were split into two nations, one of which was called Judah, the capital of which was Jerusalem, and the other Israel) made war jointly against Ahaz, king of Judah, and marched their armies towards Jerusalem. Ahaz and his people became alarmed, and the account says, ver. 2, *"Their hearts were moved, as the trees of wood are moved with the wind."*

In this situation of things, Isaiah addresses himself to Ahaz, and assures him in the *name of the Lord,* (the cant phrase of all the prophets,) that these two kings should not succeed against him; and to satisfy Ahaz that this should be the case, tells him to ask a sign. This, the account says, Ahaz declined doing, giving as a reason, that he would not tempt the Lord; upon which, Isaiah, who is the speaker, says, ver. 14, "Therefore the Lord himself shall give you a sign; *behold, a virgin shall conceive and bear a son;"* and the 16th verse says, *"And before this child shall know to refuse the evil, and choose the good, the land* which thou abhorrest or dreadest (meaning

Syria and the kingdom of Israel) shall be forsaken of both her kings." Here then was the sign, and the time limited for the completion of the assurance or promise; namely, before this child should know to refuse the evil, and choose the good.

Isaiah having committed himself thus far, it became necessary to him, in order to avoid the imputation of being a false prophet, and the consequence thereof, to take measures to make this sign appear. It certainly was not a difficult thing, in any time of the world, to find a girl with child, or to make her so; and perhaps Isaiah knew of one before-hand; for I do not suppose that the prophets of that day were any more to be trusted, than the priests of this: be that however as it may, he says in the next chapter, ver. 2, "And I took unto me faithful witnesses to record, Uriah the priest, and Zechariah the son of Jeberechiah, and *I went unto the prophetess, and she conceived and bore a son.*"

Here then is the whole story, foolish as it is, of this child and this virgin; and it is upon the barefaced perversion of this story, that the book of Matthew, and the impudence, and sordid interest of priests in later times, have founded a theory, which they call the gospel; and have applied this story to signify the person they call Jesus Christ; begotten, they say, by a ghost, whom they call holy, on the body of a woman, engaged in marriage, and afterwards married, whom they call a virgin seven hundred years after this foolish story was told; a theory, which, speaking for myself, I hesitate not to believe, and to say, is as fabulous, and as false as God is true[8].

But to shew the imposition and falshood of Isaiah, we have only to attend to the sequel of this story; which, though it is passed over in silence in the book of Isaiah, is related in the 28th chapter of 2 Chronicles; and which is, that instead of these two kings failing in their attempt against Ahaz, king of Judah, as Isaiah had pretended to foretel in the name of the Lord, they *succeeded;* Ahaz was defeated and destroyed; an hundred and twenty thousand of his people were slaughtered; Jerusalem was plundered; and two hundred thousand women, and sons, and daughters, carried into captivity. Thus much for this lying prophet and impostor Isaiah, and the book of falsehoods, that bears his name. I pass on to the book of

Jeremiah. This prophet, as he is called, lived in the time that Nebuchadnezzar besieged Jerusalem, in the reign of Zedekiah, the last king of Judah;

---

8. In the 14th verse of the chapter, it is said, that the child should be called Immanuel; but this name was not given to either of the children, otherwise than as a character, which the word signifies. That of the prophet was called Maher-shalal-hash-baz, and that of Mary was called Jesus.

and the suspicion was strong against him, that he was a traitor in the interest of Nebuchadnezzar. Every thing relating to Jeremiah shews him to have been a man of an equivocal character; in his metaphor of the potter and the clay, chap. xviii. he guards his prognostications in such a crafty manner, as always to leave himself a door to escape by, in case the event should be contrary to what he had predicted.

In the 7th and 8th verses of that chapter, he makes the Almighty to say, "At what instant I shall speak concerning a nation, and concerning a kingdom, to pluck up, and to pull down, and destroy it, if that nation, against whom I have pronounced, turn from their evil, I will repent me of the evil that I thought to do unto them." Here was a proviso against one side of the case: now for the other side.

Verses 9 and 10, "At what instant I shall speak concerning a nation and concerning a kingdom, to build and to plant it, if it do evil in my sight, that it obey not my voice; then *I will repent me of the good wherewith I said I would benefit them.*" Here is a proviso against the other side, and according to this plan of prophesying, a prophet could never be wrong, however mistaken the Almighty might be. This sort of absurd subterfuge, and this manner of speaking of the Almighty, as one would speak of a man, is consistent with nothing but the stupidity of the Bible.

As to the authenticity of the book, it is only necessary to read it in order to decide positively, that, though some passages recorded therein may have been spoken by Jeremiah, he is not the author of the book. The historical parts, if they can be called by that name, are in the most confused condition; the same events are several times repeated, and that in a manner different, and sometimes in contradiction to each other; and this disorder runs even to the last chapter, where the history, upon which the greater part of the book has been employed, begins a-new, and ends abruptly. The book has all the appearance of being a medley of unconnected anecdotes, respecting persons and things of that time, collected together in the same rude manner, as if the various and contradictory accounts, that are to be found in a bundle of news-papers, respecting persons and things of the present day, were put together without date, order, or explanation. I will give two or three examples of this kind.

It appears from the account of the 37th chapter, that the army of Nebuchadnezzar, which is called the army of the Chaldeans, had besieged Jerusalem some time; and on their hearing, that the army of Pharaoh, of Egypt, was marching against them, they raised the siege, and retreated for a time. It may here be proper to mention, in order to understand this confused history, that Nebuchadnezzar had besieged and taken Jerusalem during the reign of Jehoiakim, the predecessor of Zedekiah; and that it was Nebu-chadnezzar who had made Zedekiah king, or rather vice-roy; and that this second siege, of which the book of Jeremiah treats, was in consequence of the revolt of Zedekiah against Nebuchadnezzar. This will, in some mea-sure, account for the suspicion that affixes itself to Jeremiah, of being a traitor, and in the interest of Nebuchadnezzar; whom Jeremiah calls in the 43d chapter, ver. 10, the servant of God.

The 11th verse of this chapter (the 37th) says, "And it came to pass, that, when the army of the Chaldeans was broken up from Jerusalem, for fear of Pharaoh's army, then Jeremiah went forth out of Jerusalem, to go (as this account states) into the land of Benjamin, to separate himself thence in the midst of the people: and when he was in the gate of Benjamin, a captain of the ward was there, whose name was Irijah; and he took Jeremiah the prophet, saying, *Thou fallest away to the Chaldeans:* then Jeremiah said, *It is false; I fall not away to the Chaldeans.* Jeremiah being thus stopt and accused, was, after being examined, committed to prison, on suspicion of being a traitor; where he remained, as is stated in the last verse of this chapter.

But the next chapter gives an account of the imprisonment of Jeremiah, which has no connection with *this* account; but ascribes his imprisonment to another circumstance, and for which we must go back to the 21st chapter. It is there stated, verse 1, that Zedekiah sent Pashur, the son of Malchiah, and Zephaniah, the son of Maaseiah the priest, to Jeremiah, to inquire of him concerning Nebuchadnezzar, whose army was then before Jerusalem: and Jeremiah said to them, verse 8, "Thus saith the Lord, Behold, I set be-fore you the way of life, and the way of death: he that abideth in this city, shall die by the sword and by the famine, and by the pestilence; *but he that goeth out and falleth to the Chaldeans that besiege you, he shall live, and his life shall be unto him for a prey.*"

This interview and conference breaks off abruptly at the end of the 10th verse of the 21st chapter; and such is the disorder of this book, that we have to pass over sixteen chapters upon various subjects, in order to come at the continuation and event of this conference; and this brings us to the 1st verse of the 38th chapter, as I have just mentioned.

The 38th chapter opens with saying, "Then Shaphatiah, the son of Mat-tan; and Gedaliah, the son of Pashur; and Jucal, the son of Shelemiah; and Pashur, the son of Malchiah; (here are more persons mentioned, than in the 21st chapter) heard the words that Jeremiah spoke unto the people, saying, *Thus saith the Lord, He that remaineth in this city, shall die by the sword, by the famine, and by the pestilence; but he that goeth forth to the*

Chaldeans, shall live; for he shall have his life for a prey, and shall live; (which are the words of the conference,) therefore, (say they to Zedekiah,) We beseech thee, let this man be put to death; *for thus he weakeneth the hands of the men of war that remain in this city, and the hands of all the people in speaking such words unto them; for this man seeketh not the welfare of the people, but the hurt:*" and at the 6th verse, it is said, "Then they took Jeremiah, and put him into a dungeon of Malchiah."

These two accounts are different and contradictory. The one ascribes his imprisonment to his attempt to *escape out of the city;* the other, to his *preaching and prophesying in the city:* the one, to his being seized by the guard at the gate; the other, to his being accused before Zedekiah, by the conferees.[9]

In the next chapter (the 39th) we have another instance of the disordered state of this book; for, notwithstanding the siege of the city, by Nebuchadnezzar, has been the subject of several of the preceding chapters, particularly the 37th and 38th, the 39th chapter begins as if not a word had been

9. I observed two chapters, 16th and 17th, in the first book of Samuel, that contradict each other with respect to David, and the manner he became acquainted with Saul, as the 37th and 38th chapters of the book of Jeremiah contradict each other with respect to the cause of Jeremiah's imprisonment.

In the 16th chapter of Samuel, it is said, that an evil spirit from God troubled Saul, and that his servants advised him (as a remedy) "to seek out a man, who was a cunning player upon the harp:" and Saul said, verse 17, "Provide now a man that can play well, and bring him unto me. Then answered one of the servants, and said, Behold I have seen a son of Jesse, the Bethlehemite, that is cunning in playing, and a mighty man, and a man o' war, and prudent in matters, and a comely person, and the Lord is with him: wherefore Saul sent messengers unto Jesse, and said, Send me David thy son. And (verse 21) David came to Saul, and stood before him, and he loved him greatly; and he became his armour-bearer: and when the evil spirit from God was upon Saul, (verse 23) David took his harp, and played with his hand, and Saul was refreshed, and was well."

But the next chapter (17th) gives an account, all different to this, of the manner that Saul and David became acquainted. Here it is ascribed to David's encounter with Goliath, when David was sent by his father to carry provision to his brethren in the camp. In the 55th verse of this chapter, it is said, "And when Saul saw David go forth against the Philistine (Goliah), he said to Abner, the captain of the host, Abner, whose son is this youth? And Abner said, As thy soul liveth, O king, I cannot tell. And the king said, Inquire thou whose son the stripling is. And as David returned from the slaughter of the Philistine, Abner took him, and brought him before Saul, with the head of the Philistine in his hand; and Saul said unto him, Whose son art thou, thou young man? And David answered, I am the son of thy servant Jesse, the Bethlehemite." These two accounts belie each other, because each of them supposes Saul and David not to have known each other before. This book, the Bible, is too ridiculous even for criticism.

said upon the subject; and as if the reader was still to be informed of every particular respecting it; for it begins with saying, verse 1st, *"In the ninth year of Zedekiah, king of Judah, in the tenth month, came Nebuchadnezzar, king of Babylon, and all his army against Jerusalem, and besieged it, &c. &c."*

But the instance in the last chapter (the 52d) is still more glaring; for, though the story has been told over and over again, this chapter still supposes the reader not to know any thing of it; for it begins by saying, verse 1st, *"Zedekiah was one and twenty years old, when he began to reign, and he reigned eleven years in Jerusalem; and his mother's name was Hamutal, the daughter of Jeremiah of Libnah. (Ver. 4,) And it came to pass, in the ninth year of his reign, in the tenth month, that Nebuchadnezzar, king of Babylon, came, he and all his army, against Jerusalem, and pitched against it, &c. &c."*

It is not possible that any one man, and more particularly Jeremiah, could have been the writer of this book. The errors are such, as could not have been committed by any person sitting down to compose a work. Were I, or any other man, to write in such a disordered manner, no body would read what was written; and every body would suppose, that the writer was in a state of insanity. The only way therefore to account for the disorder is, that the book is a medley of detached unauthenticated anecdotes, put together by some stupid book-maker, under the name of Jeremiah; because many of them refer to him, and to the circumstances of the times he lived in.

Of the duplicity, and of the false prediction of Jeremiah, I shall mention two instances; and then proceed to review the remainder of the Bible.

It appears from the 38th chapter, that when Jeremiah was in prison, Zedekiah sent for him; and at this interview, which was private, Jeremiah pressed it strongly on Zedekiah to surrender himself to the enemy. *"If, says he, verse 17, thou wilt assuredly go forth unto the king of Babylon's princes, then thy soul shall live, &c."* Zedekiah was apprehensive, that what passed at this conference should be known; and he said to Jeremiah, verse 25, "If the princes (meaning those of Judah) hear, that I have talked with thee; and they come unto thee, and say unto thee, Declare unto us now, what thou hast said unto the king; hide it not from us, and we will not put thee to death; and also what the king said unto thee: then thou shalt say unto them, I presented my supplication before the king, that he would not cause me to return to Jonathan's house, to die there. Then came all the princes unto Jeremiah, and asked him; and *he told them according to all the words the king had commanded."* Thus, this man of God, as he is called, could tell a lie, or very strongly prevaricate, when he supposed it would answer his purpose:

for certainly he did not go to Zedekiah, to make his supplication; neither did he make it: he went, because he was sent for; and he employed that opportunity, to advise Zedekiah to surrender himself to Nebuchadnezzar.

In the 34th chapter is a prophecy of Jeremiah to Zedekiah in these words, ver. 2, "Thus saith the Lord, Behold I will give this city into the hands of the king of Babylon, and will burn it with fire; and thou shalt not escape out of his hand, but thou shalt surely be taken, and delivered into his hand; and thine eyes shall behold the eyes of the king of Babylon, and he shall speak with thee mouth to mouth, and thou shalt go to Babylon. *Yet hear the word of the Lord; O Zedekiah, king of Judah, thus saith the Lord, Thou shalt not die by the sword, but thou shalt die in peace; and with the burnings of thy fathers, the former kings that were before thee, so shall they burn odours for thee, and will lament thee, saying, Ah, lord! for I have pronounced the word, saith the Lord.*"

Now, instead of Zedekiah beholding the eyes of the king of Babylon, and speaking with him mouth to mouth, and dying in peace, and with the burning of odours, as at the funeral of his fathers (as Jeremiah had declared, the Lord himself had pronounced), the reverse, according to the 52d chapter, was the case: it is there said, ver. 10, "That the king of Babylon slew the sons of Zedekiah before his eyes; then he put out the eyes of Zedekiah, and bound him in chains, and carried him to Babylon, and put him in prison till the day of his death." What then can we say of these prophets, but that they are impostors and liars?

As for Jeremiah, he pronounced none of those evils. He was taken into favour by Nebuchadnezzar, who gave him in charge to the captain of the guard, chap. xxxix. ver. 12, "Take him (said he), and look well to him, and do him no harm; but do unto him even as he shall say unto thee." Jeremiah joined himself afterwards to Nebuchadnezzar, and went about prophesying for him against the Egyptians, who had marched to the relief of Jerusalem while it was besieged. Thus much for another of the lying prophets, and the book that bears his name.

I have been the more particular in treating of the books ascribed to Isaiah and Jeremiah, because those two are spoken of in the books of Kings and Chronicles, whilst the others are not. The remainder of the books ascribed to the men called prophets, I shall not trouble myself much about, but take them collectively into the observations I shall offer on the character of the men called prophets.

In the former part of the *Age of Reason,* I have said that the word prophet was the Bible-word for poet, and that the flights and metaphors of the Jewish poets have been foolishly erected into what are now called prophecies. I am sufficiently justified in this opinion, not only because the books called the prophecies are written in poetical language, but because there is no word in the Bible, except it be the word prophet, that describes what we mean by poet. I have also said, that the word signified a performer upon musical instruments, of which I have given some instances; such as that of a company of prophets, prophesying with psalteries, with tabrets, with pipes, with harps, &c. and Saul prophesied with them, 1 Sam. chap. x. ver. 5. It appears from this passage, and from other parts in the book of Samuel, that the word prophet was confined to signify poetry and music; for the person, who was supposed to have a visionary insight into things concealed, was not a prophet, but a *seer*,[10] 1 Sam. chap. ix. ver. 9; and it was not till after the word *seer* went out of use, (which was, most probably, when Saul banished those he called wizards,) that the profession of the seer, or the art of seeing, became incorporated into the word prophet.

According to the *modern* meaning of the word prophet and prophesying, it signifies foretelling events to a great distance of time; and it became necessary to the inventors of the gospel to give it this latitude of meaning, in order to apply, or to stretch what they call the prophecies of the Old Testament, to the times of the New. But according to the Old Testament, the prophesying of the seer, and afterwards of the prophet, so far as the meaning of the word seer was incorporated into that of prophet, had reference only to things of the time then passing, or very closely connected with it; such as the event of a battle they were going to engage in, or of a journey, or of an enterprize they were going to undertake, or of any circumstance then pending, or of any difficulty they were then in; all of which had immediate reference to themselves, (as in the case already mentioned of Ahaz and Isaiah with respect to the expression, *Behold a virgin shall conceive, and bear a son,*) and not to any distant future time. It was that kind of prophesying, that corresponds to what we call fortune-telling; such as casting nativities, predicting riches, fortunate or unfortunate marriages, conjuring for lost goods, &c. and it is the fraud of the Christian church, not that of the Jews, and the ignorance and the superstition of modern, not that of ancient times, that elevated those poetical–musical–conjuring–dreaming–strolling gentry, into the rank they have since had.

But besides this general character of all the prophets, they had a particular character. They were in parties, and they prophesied for, or against, according to the party they were with, as the poetical and political writers

10. I know not what is the Hebrew word that corresponds to the word seer in English: but I observe it is translated into French by *Le Voyant,* from the verb *voir* to *see,* and which means the person who *sees,* or the seer.

of the present day write in defence of the party they associate with, against the other.

After the Jews were divided into two nations, that of Judah and that of Israel, each party had [its] prophets, who abused and accused each other of being false prophets, lying prophets, impostors, &c.

The prophets of the party of Judah prophesied against the prophets of the party of Israel; and those of the party of Israel against those of Judah. This party prophesying shewed itself immediately on the separation of the first two rival kings, Rehoboam and Jeroboam. The prophet that cursed, or prophesied against the altar, that Jeroboam had built in Bethel, was of the party of Judah, where Rehoboam was king; and he was waylaid on his return home by a prophet of the party of Israel, who said unto him, (1 Kings, chap. xiii.) "*Art thou the man of God that came from Judah?* and *he said, I am.*" Then the prophet of the party of Israel said to him, "*I am a prophet also as thou art,* (signifying of Judah,) *and an angel spake unto me by the word of the Lord, saying, Bring him back with thee unto thine house, that he may eat bread and drink water: but,* says the 18th verse, *he lied unto him.*" The event, however, according to the story, is, the prophet of Judah never got back to Judah; for he was found dead on the road by the contrivance of the prophet of Israel, who no doubt was called a true prophet by his own party, and the prophet of Judah a lying prophet.

In the third chapter of the second of Kings, a story is related of prophesying, or conjuring, that shews, in several particulars, the character of a prophet. Jehoshaphat, king of Judah, and Joram, king of Israel, had for a while ceased their party animosity, and entered into an alliance; and those two, together with the king of Edom, engaged in a war against the king of Moab. After uniting, and marching their armies, the story says, they were in great distress for water, upon which Jehoshaphat said, "*Is there not here a prophet of the Lord, that we may inquire of the Lord by him? and one of the servants of the king of Israel said, Here is Elisha.* (Elisha was of the party of Judah.) *And Jehoshaphat the king of Judah said, The word of the Lord is with him.*" The story then says, that these three kings went down to Elisha; and when Elisha (who, as I have said, was a Judahmite prophet) saw the king of Israel, he said unto him, "*What have I to do with thee, get thee to the prophets of thy father, and the prophets of thy mother. Nay, but said the king of Israel, the Lord hath called these three kings together, to deliver them into the hand of the king of Moab*" (meaning, because of the distress they were in for water); upon which Elisha said, "*As the Lord of hosts liveth, before whom I stand, surely, were it not that I regard the presence of Jehoshaphat, king of Judah, I would not look towards thee, nor see thee.*" Here is all the venom and vulgarity of a party prophet. We have now to see the performance or manner of prophesying.

Ver. 15, "*Bring me,* said Elisha, *a minstrel; and it came to pass, when the minstrel played, that the hand of the Lord came upon him.*" Here is the farce of the conjurer. Now for the prophecy: "*And Elisha said,* (singing, most probably, to the tune he was playing,) *Thus saith the Lord, Make this valley full of ditches;*" which was just telling them what every countryman might have told them, without either fiddle or farce, that the way to get water was to dig for it.

But as every conjurer is not famous alike for the same thing, so neither were those prophets; for though all of them, at least those I have spoken of, were famous for lying, some of them excelled in cursing. Elisha, whom I have just mentioned, was a chief in this branch of prophesying: it was he that cursed the forty-two children in the name of the Lord, whom the two she-bears came and devoured. We are to suppose that those children were of the party of Israel; but as those who will curse will lie, there is just as much credit to be given to this story of Elisha's two she-bears, as there is to that of the dragon of Wantley, of whom it is said,

Poor children three devoured he,
That could not with him grapple;
And at one sup he eat them up,
As a man would eat an apple.

There was another description of men, called prophets, that amused themselves with dreams and visions; but whether by night or by day, we know not. These, if they were not quite harmless, were but little mischievous. Of this class are

Ezekiel and Daniel; and the first question upon those books, as upon all the others, is, Are they genuine? that is, were they written by Ezekiel and Daniel?

Of this there is no proof; but so far as my own opinion goes, I am more inclined to believe they were, than that they were not. My reasons for this opinion are as follow: First, Because those books do not contain internal evidence, to prove they were not written by Ezekiel and Daniel, as the books ascribed to Moses, Joshua, Samuel, &c. &c.

Secondly, Because they were not written till after the Babylonish captivity began; and there is good reason to believe, that not any book in the Bible was written before that period: at least it is proveable, from the books themselves, as I have already shewn, that they were not written till after the commencement of the Jewish monarchy.

Thirdly, Because the manner in which the books ascribed to Ezekiel and Daniel are written, agrees with the condition these men were in at the time of writing them.

Had the numerous commentators and priests, who have foolishly employed or wasted their time in pretending to expound and unriddle those books, been carried into captivity, as Ezekiel and Daniel were, it would greatly have improved their intellects, in comprehending the reason for this mode of writing, and have saved them the trouble of racking their invention, as they have done to no purpose; for they would have found, that themselves would be obliged to write whatever they had to write, respecting their own affairs, or those of their friends, or of their country, in a concealed manner, as those men have done.

These two books differ from all the rest; for it is only these that are filled with accounts of dreams and visions; and this difference arose from the situation the writers were in, as prisoners of war, or prisoners of state, in a foreign country, which obliged them to convey even the most trifling information to each other, and all their political projects or opinions, in obscure and metaphorical terms. They pretended to have dreamed dreams, and seen visions, because it was unsafe for them to speak facts or plain language. We ought, however, to suppose, that the persons to whom they wrote understood what they meant, and that it was not intended any body else should. But these busy commentators and priests have been puzzling their wits to find out what it was not intended they should know, and with which they have nothing to do.

Ezekiel and Daniel were carried prisoners to Babylon, under the first captivity, in the time of Jehoiakim, nine years before the second captivity in the time of Zedekiah. The Jews were then still numerous, and had considerable force at Jerusalem; and it is natural to suppose, that men, in the situation of Ezekiel and Daniel, would be meditating the recovery of their country, and their own deliverance. It is reasonable to suppose, that the accounts of dreams and visions, with which these books are filled, are no other than a disguised mode of correspondence, to facilitate those objects: it served them as a cypher, or secret alphabet. If they are not this, they are tales, reveries, and nonsense; or at least a fanciful way of wearing off the wearisomeness of captivity: but the presumption is, they are the former.

Ezekiel begins his book, by speaking of a vision of *cherubims,* and of a vision of a *wheel within a wheel,* which he says he saw by the river Chebar, in the land of his captivity. Is it not reasonable to suppose, that by the cherubims he meant the temple at Jerusalem, where they had figures of cherubims? and by a wheel within a wheel, (which, as a figure, has always been understood to signify political contrivance,) the project, or means of recovering Jerusalem? In the latter part of his book, he supposes himself transported to Jerusalem, and into the temple; and he refers back to the vision on the river Chebar, and says, chap. xliii. ver. 3, that this last vision was like the vision on the river Chebar; which indicates, that those pretended dreams and visions had for their object the recovery of Jerusalem, and nothing further.

As to the romantic interpretations and applications, wild as the dreams and visions they undertake to explain, which commentators and priests have made of these books, that of converting into things, which they call prophecies, and making them bend to times and circumstances, as far remote even as the present day, it shews the fraud, or the extreme folly, to which credulity or priestcraft can go.

Scarcely any thing can be more absurd, than to suppose, that men situated as Ezekiel and Daniel were, whose country was over-run, and in the possession of the enemy, all their friends and relations in captivity abroad, or in slavery at home, or massacred, or in continual danger of it; scarcely any thing, I say, can be more absurd, than to suppose, that such men should find nothing to do, but that of employing their time and their thoughts about what was to happen to other nations a thousand or two thousand years after they should be dead; at the same time, nothing more natural than that they should meditate the recovery of Jerusalem, and their own deliverance; and that this was the sole object of all the obscure and apparently frantic writing contained in those books.

In this sense, the mode of writing used in those two books being forced by necessity, and not adopted by choice, is not irrational; but if we are to view the books as prophecies, they are false. In the 29th chapter of Ezekiel, speaking of Egypt, it is said, ver. 11, "*No foot of man shall pass through it, nor foot of beast shall pass through it; neither shall it be inhabited for forty years.*" This is what never came to pass, and consequently it is false, as all the books I have already reviewed are. I here close this part of the subject.

In the former part of the *Age of Reason,* I have spoken of Jonah, and of the story of him and the whale. A fit story for ridicule, if it was written to be believed; or of laughter, if it was intended to try what credulity could swallow; for if it could swallow Jonah and the whale, it can swallow any thing.

But, as is already shewn in the observations on the book of Job, and of Proverbs, it is not always certain which of the books in the Bible are originally Hebrew, or only translations from books of the Gentiles into Hebrew; and as the book of Jonah, so far from treating of the affairs of the Jews, says nothing upon that subject, but treats altogether of the Gentiles, it is more probable that it is a book of the Gentiles, than of the Jews; and that it has been written as a fable, to expose the nonsense, and satirize the vicious and malignant character of a Bible prophet, or a predicting priest.

Jonah is represented, first, as a disobedient prophet, running away from his mission, and taking shelter on board a vessel of the Gentiles, bound from Joppa to Tarshish; as if he ignorantly supposed, by such a paltry contrivance, he could hide himself, where God could not find him. The vessel is overtaken by a storm at sea; and the mariners, all of whom are Gentiles, believing it to be a judgment, on account of some one on board who had committed a crime, agreed to cast lots, to discover the offender; and the lot fell upon Jonah. But before this, they had cast all their wares and merchandize over-board, to lighten the vessel, while Jonah, like a stupid fellow, was fast asleep in the hold.

After the lot had designated Jonah to be the offender, they questioned him to know who, and what he was? and he told them *he was an Hebrew;* and the story implies, that he confessed himself to be guilty. But these Gentiles, instead of sacrificing him at once, without pity or mercy, as a company of Bible-prophets, or priests, would have done by a Gentile in the same case; and as it is related, Samuel had done by Agag, and Moses by the women and children; they endeavoured to save him, though at the risk of their own lives: for the account says, "*Nevertheless* (that is, though Jonah was a Jew and a foreigner, and the cause of all their misfortunes, and the loss of their cargo,) *the men rowed hard to bring the boat to land, but they could not, for the sea wrought, and was tempestuous against them.*" Still, however, they were unwilling to put the fate of lot into execution, and they cried, says the account, unto the Lord, saying, "*We beseech thee, O Lord, let us not perish for this man's life, and lay not upon us innocent blood; for thou, O Lord, hast done as it pleased thee.*" Meaning thereby, that they did not presume to judge Jonah guilty, since he might be innocent; but that they considered the lot, that had fallen upon him, as a decree of God, or as it *pleased God.* The address of this prayer shews that the Gentiles worshipped *one Supreme Being,* and that they were not idolators, as the Jews represented them to be. But the storm still continuing, and the danger increasing, they put the fate of the lot into execution, and cast Jonah into the sea; where, according to the story, a great fish swallowed him up whole and alive.

We have now to consider Jonah securely housed from the storm in the fish's belly. Here we are told that he prayed; but the prayer is a made-up prayer, taken from various parts of the Psalms, without connection or

468   The Age of Reason. Part the Second

consistency, and adapted to the distress, but not at all to the condition, that Jonah was in. It is such a prayer as a Gentile, who might know something of the Psalms, could copy out for him. This circumstance alone, were there no other, is sufficient to indicate that the whole is a made-up story. The prayer, however, is supposed to have answered the purpose, and the story goes on, (taking up, at the same time, the cant language of a Bible-prophet,) saying, *"The Lord spake unto the fish,* and it vomited out Jonah upon the dry land."

Jonah then receives a second mission to Nineveh, with which he sets out; and we have now to consider him as a preacher. The distress he is represented to have suffered, the remembrance of his own disobedience as the cause of it, and miraculous escape he is supposed to have had, were sufficient, one would conceive, to have impressed him with sympathy and benevolence in the execution of his mission; but, instead of this, he enters the city with denunciation and malediction in his mouth, crying, *"Yet forty days, and Nineveh shall be overthrewn."*

We have now to consider this supposed missionary in the last act of his mission; and here it is that the malevolent spirit of a Bible-prophet, or of a predicting priest, appears in all that blackness of character, that men ascribe to the being they call the devil.

Having published his prediction, he withdrew, says the story, to the east side of the city. – But for what? not to contemplate in retirement the mercy of his Creator to himself, or to others, but wait, with malignant impatience, the destruction of Nineveh. It came to pass, however, as the story relates, that the Ninevites reformed, and that God, according to the Bible phrase, repented him of the evil he had said he would do unto them, and did it not. This, saith the first verse of the last chapter, *displeased Jonah exceedingly, and he was very angry.* His obdurate heart would rather that all Nineveh should be destroyed, and every soul, young and old, perish in [its] ruins, than that his prediction should not be fulfilled. To expose the character of a prophet still more, a gourd is made to grow up in the night, that promises him an agreeable shelter from the heat of the sun, in the place to which he is retired; and the next morning it dies.

Here the rage of the prophet becomes excessive, and he is ready to destroy himself. *"It is better,* said he, *for me to die than to live."* This brings on a supposed expostulation between the Almighty and the prophet; in which the former says, *"Doest thou well to be angry for the gourd? And Jonah said, I do well to be angry, even unto death. Then said the Lord, Thou hast had pity on the gourd, for which thou hast not laboured, neither madest it to grow, which came up in a night; and should not I spare Nineveh, that great city, in which are more than threescore thousand persons, that cannot discern between their right hand and their left?"*

Here is both the winding up of the satire, and the moral of the fable. As a satire, it strikes against the character of all the Bible prophets, and against all the indiscriminate judgments upon men, women, and children, with which this lying book, the Bible, is crowded; such as Noah's flood, the destruction of the cities of Sodom and Gomorrah, the extirpation of the Canaanites, even to sucking infants, and women with child; because the same reflection, *that there are more than threescore thousand persons that cannot discern between their right hand and their left,* meaning young children, applies to all their cases. It satirizes also the supposed partiality of the Creator for one nation, more than for another.

As a moral, it preaches against the malevolent spirit of prediction; for as certainly as a man predicts ill, he becomes inclined to wish it. The pride of having his judgment right, hardens his heart, till at last he beholds with satisfaction, or sees with disappointment, the accomplishment or the failure of his predictions.——This book ends with the same kind of strong and well-directed point against prophets, prophecies, and indiscriminate judgments, as the chapter, that Benjamin Franklin made for the Bible, about Abraham and the stranger, ending against the intolerant spirit of religious persecution. Thus much for the book of Jonah.

Of the poetical parts of the Bible, that are called prophecies, I have spoken in the former part of the *Age of Reason,* and already in this; where I have said that the word *prophet* is the Bible-word for *poet;* and that the flights and metaphors of those poets, many of which are become obscure by the lapse of time and the change of circumstance, have been ridiculously erected into things, called prophecies, and applied to purposes the writers never thought of. When a priest quotes any of those passages, he unriddles it agreeably to his own views, and imposes that explanation upon his congregation as the meaning of the writer. The *whore of Babylon* has been the common whore of all the priests, and each has accused the other of keeping the strumpet: so well do they agree in their explanations.

Here now remain only a few books, which they call the books of the lesser prophets; and as I have already shewn that the greater are impostors, it would be cowardice to disturb the repose of the little ones. Let them sleep then, in the arms of their nurses, the priests, and both be forgotten together.

I have now gone through the Bible, as a man would go through a wood with an axe on his shoulder, and fell trees. Here they lie; and the priests, if they can, may replant them. They may, perhaps, stick them in the ground, but they will never make them grow.———I pass on to the books of the New Testament.

THE NEW TESTAMENT.

The New Testament, they tell us, is founded upon the prophecies of the Old; if so, it must follow the fate of [its] foundation.

As it is nothing extraordinary that a woman should be with child before she was married, and that the son she might bring forth should be executed, even unjustly; I see no reason for not believing that such a woman as Mary, and such a man as Joseph, and Jesus, existed; their mere existence is a matter of indifference, about which there is no ground, either to believe, or to disbelieve, and which comes under the common head of, *It may be so; and what then?* The probability, however, is, that there were such persons, or at least such as resembled them in part of the circumstances, because almost all romantic stories have been suggested by some actual circumstance; as the adventures of Robinson Crusoe, not a word of which is true, were suggested by the case of Alexander Selkirk.

It is not then the existence, or non-existence, of the persons that I trouble myself about; it is the fable of Jesus Christ, as is told in the New Testament, and the wild and visionary doctrine raised thereon, against which I contend. The story, taking it as it is told, is blasphemously obscene. It gives an account of a young woman engaged to be married, and while under this engagement, she is, to speak plain language, debauched by a ghost, under the impious pretence (Luke, chap. i. ver. 35,) that *"the Holy Ghost shall come upon thee, and the power of the Highest shall overshadow thee."* Notwithstanding which, Joseph afterwards marries her as his wife, and in his turn rivals the ghost. This is putting the story into intelligible language, and when told in this manner, there is not a priest but must be ashamed to own it.[11]

Obscenity in matters of faith, however wrapped up, is always a token of fable and imposture; for it is necessary to our serious belief in God, that we do not connect it with stories that run, as this does, into ludicrous interpretations. This story is, upon the face of it, the same kind of story as that of Jupiter and Leda, or Jupiter and Europa, or any of the amorous adventures of Jupiter; and shews, as is already stated in the former part of the *Age of Reason,* that the Christian faith is built upon the heathen mythology.

11. Mary, the supposed virgin mother of Jesus, had several other children, sons and daughters. See Matt. Chap. xiii. ver. 55, 56.

As the historical parts of the New Testament, so far as concerns Jesus Christ, are confined to a very short space of time, less than two years, and all within the same country, and nearly to the same spot, the discordance of time, place, and circumstance, which detects the fallacy of the books of the Old Testament, and proves them to be impositions, cannot be expected to be found here in the same abundance. The New Testament, compared with the Old, is like a farce of one act, in which there is not room for very numerous violations of the unities. There are, however, some glaring contradictions, which, exclusive of the fallacy of the pretended prophecies, are sufficient to shew the story of Jesus Christ to be false.

I lay it down as a position which cannot be controverted, first, that the *agreement* of all the parts of a story does not prove that story to be true, because the parts may agree, and the whole may be false; secondly, that the *disagreement* of the parts of a story proves the *whole cannot be true*. The agreement does not prove truth, but the disagreement proves falshood positively.

The history of Jesus Christ is contained in the four books ascribed to Matthew, Mark, Luke, and John. The first chapter of Matthew begins with giving a genealogy of Jesus Christ; and in the third chapter of Luke, there is also given a genealogy of Jesus Christ. Did these two agree, it would not prove the genealogy to be true, because it might, nevertheless, be a fabrication; but if they contradict each other in every particular, it proves falshood absolutely. If Matthew speak truth, Luke speaks falshood; and if Luke speak truth, Matthew speaks falshood: and as there is no authority for believing one more than the other, there is no authority for believing either; and if they cannot be believed, even in the very first thing they say, and set out to prove, they are not entitled to be believed in any thing they say afterwards. Truth is an uniform thing; and as to inspiration and revelation, were we to admit it, it is impossible to suppose it can be contradictory. Either then the men called apostles were impostors, or the books ascribed to them have been written by other persons, and fathered upon them, as is the case in the Old Testament.

The book of Matthew gives, chap. i. ver. 6, a genealogy by name from David, up, through Joseph, the husband of Mary, to Christ; and makes there to be *twenty-eight* generations. The book of Luke gives also a genealogy by name from Christ, through Joseph, the husband of Mary, down to David, and makes there to be *forty-three* generations; besides which, there are only the two names of David and Joseph that are alike in the two lists. I here insert both genealogical lists, and for the sake of perspicuity and comparison, have placed them both in the same direction, that is, from Joseph down to David.

Genealogy, according to Matthew.	Genealogy, according to Luke.
Christ.	Christ.
2 Joseph.	2 Joseph.
3 Jacob.	3 Heli.
4 Matthan.	4 Matthat.
5 Eleazar.	5 Levi.
6 Eliud.	6 Melchi.
7 Achim.	7 Janna.
8 Sadoc.	8 Joseph.
9 Azor.	9 Mattathias.
10 Eliakim.	10 Amos.
11 Abiud.	11 Naum.
12 Zorobabel.	12 Esli.
13 Salathiel.	13 Nagge.
14 Jechonias.	14 Maath.
15 Josias.	15 Mattathias.
16 Amon.	16 Semei.
17 Manasses.	17 Joseph.
18 Ezekias.	18 Juda.
19 Achaz.	19 Joanna.
20 Joatham.	20 Rhesa.
21 Ozias.	21 Zorobabel.
22 Joram.	22 Salathiel.
23 Josaphat.	23 Neri.
24 Asa.	24 Melchi.
25 Abia.	25 Addi.
26 Roboam.	26 Cosam.
27 Solomon.	27 Elmodam.
28 David.	28 Er.
	29 Jose.
	30 Eliezer.
	31 Jorim.
	32 Matthat.
	33 Levi.
	34 Simeon.
	35 Juda.
	36 Joseph.
	37 Jonan.
	38 Eliakim.
	39 Melea.

40 Menan.
41 Mattatha.
42 Nathan.
43 David.

From the birth of David to the birth of Christ is upwards of 1080 years; and as the life-time of Christ is not included, there are but 27 full generations. To find therefore the average age of each person mentioned in the first list, at the time his first son was born, it is only necessary to divide 1080 by 27, which gives 40 years for each person. As the life-time of man was then but of the same extent it is now, it is an absurdity to suppose, that 27 following generations should all be old bachelors, before they married; and the more so, when we are told, that Solomon, the next in succession to David, had a house full of wives and mistresses, before he was twenty-one years of age. So far from this genealogy being a solemn truth, it is not even a reasonable lie. The list of Luke gives about twenty-six years for the average age, and this is too much.

Now, if these men, Matthew and Luke, set out with a falshood between them (as these two accounts shew they do) in the very commencement of their history of Jesus Christ, and of who, and of what he was, what authority (as I have before asked) is there left for believing the strange things they tell us afterwards? If they cannot be believed in their account of his natural genealogy, how are we to believe them, when they tell us, he was the son of God, begotten by a ghost; and that an angel announced this in secret to his mother? If they lied in one genealogy, why are we to believe them in the other? If his natural genealogy be manufactured, which it certainly is, why are we not to suppose, that his celestial genealogy is manufactured also; and that the whole is fabulous? Can any man of serious reflection hazard his future happiness upon the belief of a story naturally impossible; repugnant to every idea of decency; and related by persons already detected of falshood? Is it not more safe, that we stop ourselves at the plain, pure, and unmixed belief of one God, which is deism, than that we commit ourselves on an ocean of improbable, irrational, indecent, and contradictory tales?

The first question, however, upon the books of the New Testament, as upon those of the Old, is, Are they genuine? were they written by the persons to whom they are ascribed? for it is upon this ground only, that the strange things related therein, have been credited. Upon this point, there is no *direct proof for, or against;* and all that this state of a case proves, is *doubtfulness;* and doubtfulness is the opposite of belief. The state, therefore, that the books are in, proves against themselves as far as this kind of proof can go.

But, exclusive of this, the presumption is, that the books called the Evangelists, and ascribed to Matthew, Mark, Luke, and John, were not written by Matthew, Mark, Luke, and John; and that they are impositions. The disordered state of the history in these four books, the silence of one book upon matters related in the other, and the disagreement that is to be found among them, implies, that they are the productions of some unconnected individuals, many years after the things they pretend to relate, each of whom made his own legend; and not the writings of men living intimately together, as the men called apostles are supposed to have done: in fine, that they have been manufactured, as the books of the Old Testament have been, by other persons, than those, whose names they bear.

The story of the angel, announcing, what the church calls, the *immaculate conception,* is not so much as mentioned in the books ascribed to Mark, and John; and is differently related in Matthew, and Luke. The former says, the angel appeared to Joseph; the latter says, it was to Mary; but either Joseph or Mary was the worst evidence that could be thought of; for it was others that should have testified *for them,* and not they for themselves. Were any girl that is now with child to say, and even to swear it, that she was gotten with child by a ghost, and that an angel told her so, would she be believed? Certainly she would not. Why then are we to believe the same thing of another whom we never saw, told by nobody knows who, nor when, nor where? How strange and inconsistent is it, that the same circumstances that would weaken the belief even of a probable story, should be given as a motive for believing this one that has, upon the face of it, every token of absolute impossibility, and imposture.

The story of Herod destroying all the children under two years old, belongs altogether to the writer of the book of Matthew; and not one of the rest mentions any thing about it. Had such a circumstance been true, the universality of it must have made it known to all the writers; and the thing would have been too striking, to have been omitted by any. The writer tells us, that Jesus escaped this slaughter, because Joseph and Mary were warned by an angel, to flee with him into Egypt; but he forgot to make provision for John, who was then under two years of age. John, however, who staid behind, fared as well as Jesus, who fled; and therefore the story circumstantially belies itself.

Not any two of these writers agree in reciting, *exactly in the same words,* the written inscription, short as it is, which they tell us, was put over Christ when he was crucified: and besides this, Mark says, He was crucified at the third hour (nine in the morning); and John says, it was the sixth hour (twelve at noon).[12]

The inscription is thus stated in those books.

Matthew——This is Jesus the king of the Jews.

Mark——The king of the Jews.

Luke——This is the king of the Jews.

John——Jesus of Nazareth the king of the Jews.

We may infer from these circumstances, trivial as they are, that those writers, whoever they were, and in whatever time they lived, were not present at the scene. The only one of the men, called apostles, who appears to have been near the spot, was Peter; and when he was accused of being one of Jesus's followers, it is said (Matthew, chap. xxvi. ver. 74,) *"Then Peter began to curse and swear, saying, I know not the man:"* yet we are now called upon to believe this same Peter, convicted, by their own account, of perjury. For what reason, or on what authority, should we do this?

The accounts that are given of the circumstances, that they tell us attended the crucifixion, are differently related in those four books.

The book ascribed to Matthew says, *"There was darkness over all the land, from the sixth hour unto the ninth hour – that the veil of the temple was rent in twain from the top to the bottom – that there was an earthquake – that the rocks rent – that the graves opened – that the bodies of many of the saints that slept, arose, and came out of their graves after the resurrection, and went into the holy city, and appeared unto many."* Such is the account which this dashing writer of the book of Matthew gives; but in which he is not supported by the writers of the other books.

The writer of the book ascribed to Mark, in detailing the circumstances of the crucifixion, makes no mention of any earthquake, nor of the rocks rending, nor of the graves opening, nor of the dead men walking out. The writer of the book of Luke is silent also upon the same points. And as to the writer of the book of John, though he details all the circumstances of the crucifixion down to the burial of Christ, he says nothing about either the darkness – the veil of the temple – the earthquake – the rocks – the graves – nor the dead men.

Now if it had been true, that those things had happened; and if the writers of those books had lived at the time they did happen, and had been the

12. According to John, the sentence was not passed till about the sixth hour (noon), and consequently, the execution could not be till the afternoon: but Mark says expressly, that he was crucified at the third hour, (nine in the morning,) chap. xv. ver. 25. John, chap. xix. ver. 14.

persons they are said to be, namely, the four men called apostles, Matthew, Mark, Luke, and John, it was not possible for them, as true historians, even without the aid of inspiration, not to have recorded them. The things, supposing them to have been facts, were of too much notoriety not to have been known, and of too much importance not to have been told. All these supposed apostles must have been witnesses of the earthquake, if there had been any; for it was not possible for them to have been absent from it; the opening of the graves, and the resurrection of the dead men, and their walking about the city, is of still greater importance than the earthquake. An earthquake is always possible, and natural, and proves nothing; but this opening of the graves is supernatural, and in point to their doctrine, their cause, and their apostleship. Had it been true, it would have filled up whole chapters of those books, and been the chosen theme, and general chorus of all the writers; but instead of this, little and trivial things, and mere prat-tling conversations of, *he said this,* and *she said that,* are often tediously detailed, while this most important of all, had it been true, is passed off in a slovenly manner, by a single dash of the pen, and that by one writer only, and not so much as hinted at by the rest.

It is an easy thing to tell a lie, but it is difficult to support the lie after it is told. The writer of the book of Matthew should have told us who the saints were that came to life again, and went into the city, and what became of them afterwards, and who it was that saw them; for he is not hardy enough to say that he saw them himself; – whether they came out naked, and all in natural buff, he-saints and she-saints; or whether they came full dressed, and where they got their dresses; whether they went to their former habita-tions, and reclaimed their wives, their husbands, and their property, and how they were received; whether they entered ejectments for the recovery of their possessions, or brought actions of *crim. con.* against the rival inter-lopers; whether they remained on earth, and followed their former occupa-tions of preaching or working; or whether they died again, or went back to their graves alive, and buried themselves.

Strange indeed, that an army of saints should return to life, and nobody know who they were, nor who it was that saw them, and that not a word more should be said upon the subject, nor these saints have any thing to tell us! Had it been the prophets who (as we are told) had formerly prophesied of these things, *they* must have had a great deal to say. They could have told us every thing, and we should have had posthumous prophecies, with notes and commentaries upon the first, a little better at least than we have now. Had it been Moses, and Aaron, and Joshua, and Samuel, and David, not an unconverted Jew had remained in all Jerusalem. Had it been John the Baptist, and the saints of the times then present, every body would have known them, and they would have out-preached and out-famed all the other apostles. But instead of this, these saints are made to pop up, like Jonah's gourd in the night, for no purpose at all, but to wither in the morning. Thus much for this part of the story.

The tale of the resurrection follows that of the crucifixion; and in this, as well as in that, the writers, whoever they were, disagree so much, as to make it evident that none of them were there.

The book of Matthew states, that when Christ was put in the sepulchre, the Jews applied to Pilate for a watch or a guard to be placed over the sepulchre, to prevent the body being stolen by the disciples; and that in consequence of this request, the sepulchre *was made sure, sealing the stone* that covered the mouth, and setting a watch. But the other books say nothing about this application, nor about the sealing, nor the guard, nor the watch; and according to their accounts, there were none. Matthew, however, follows up this part of the story of the guard or the watch with a second part, that I shall notice in the conclusion, as it serves to detect the fallacy of those books.

The book of Matthew continues [its] account, and says, (chap. xxviii. ver. 1,) that at the end of the sabbath as it began to *dawn*, towards the first day of the week, came *Mary Magdalene* and the *other Mary*, to see the sepulchre. Mark says it was sun-rising, and John says it was dark. Luke says it was Mary Magdalene, and *Joanna*, and *Mary the mother* of James, and *other women*, that came to the sepulchre; and John states, that Mary Magdalene came alone. So well do they agree about their first evidence! they all, however, appear to have known most about Mary Magdalene; she was a woman of a large acquaintance, and it was not an ill conjecture that she might be upon the stroll.

The book of Matthew goes on to say, (ver. 2,) "And behold there was a great earthquake, for the angel of the Lord descended from heaven, and came and rolled back the stone from the door, and *sat upon it.*" But the other books say nothing about any earthquake, nor about the angel rolling back the stone, and *sitting upon it;* and according to their accounts, there was no angel *sitting there.* Mark says, the angel *was within the sepulchre, sitting* on the right side. Luke says there were two, and they were both standing up; and John says, they were both sitting down, one at the head, and the other at the feet.

Matthew says, that the angel that was sitting upon the stone on the outside of the sepulchre, told the two Marys, that Christ was risen, and that the women went *away* quickly. Mark says, that the women, upon seeing the stone rolled away, and wondering at it, went *into* the sepulchre, and that it was the angel that was *sitting* within on the right side, that told them so. Luke says, it was the two angels that were standing up; and John says, it was Jesus Christ himself that told it to Mary Magdalene; and that she did not go into the sepulchre, but only stooped down and looked in.

Now if the writers of these four books had gone into any court of justice, to prove an *alibi,* (for it is of the nature of an alibi that is here attempted to be proved, namely, the absence of a dead body, by supernatural means,) and had given their evidence in the same contradictory manner as it is here given, they would have been in danger of having their ears cropt for perjury, and would have justly deserved it. Yet this is the evidence, and these are the books, that have been imposed upon the world, as being given by divine inspiration, and as the unchangeable word of God.

The writer of the book of Matthew, after giving this account, relates a story that is not to be found in any of the other books, and which is the same I have just before alluded to.

"Now, says he, (that is, after the conversation the women had had with the angel sitting upon the stone,) behold some of the watch (meaning the watch that he had said had been placed over the sepulchre) came into the city, and shewed unto the chief priests all the things that were done; and when they were assembled with the elders, and had taken counsel, they gave large money unto the soldiers, saying, Say ye, that his disciples came by night, and stole him away while we *slept;* and if this come to the governor's ears, we will persuade him, and secure you. So they took the money, and did as they were taught; and this saying (that his disciples stole him away) is commonly reported among the Jews *until this day.*"

The expression, *until this day,* is an evidence that the book ascribed to Matthew was not written by Matthew, and that it has been manufactured long after the times and things of which it pretends to treat; for the expression implies a great length of intervening time. It would be inconsistent in us to speak in this manner of any thing happening in our own time. To give, therefore, intelligible meaning to the expression, we must suppose a lapse of some generations at least, for this manner of speaking carries the mind back to ancient time.

The absurdity also of the story is worth noticing; for it shews the writer of the book of Matthew to have been an exceeding weak and foolish man. He tells a story, that contradicts itself in point of possibility; for though the guard, if there were any, might be made to say that the body was taken away while they were *asleep,* that same sleep must also have prevented their knowing how, and by whom it was done; and yet they are made to say, that it was the disciples who did it. Were a man to tender his evidence of something that he should say was done, and of the manner of doing it, and of the persons who did it, while he was asleep, and could know nothing of the matter, such evidence could not be received: it will do well enough for Testament evidence, but not for any thing where truth is concerned.

I come now to that part of the evidence in those books, that respects the pretended appearance of Christ after this pretended resurrection.

The writer of the book of Matthew relates, that the angel that was sitting on the stone at the mouth of the sepulchre, said to the two Marys, chap. xxviii. ver. 7, *"Behold Christ is gone before you into Galilee, there shall ye see him; lo, I have told you."* And the same writer, at the two next verses, (8, 9,) makes Christ himself to speak to the same purpose to these women, immediately after the angel had told it to them, and that they ran quickly to tell it to the disciples; and at the 16th verse it is said, *"Then the eleven disciples went away into Galilee,* into a mountain where Jesus had appointed them; and when they saw him, they worshipped him."

But the writer of the book of John tells a story very different to this; for he says, chap. xx. ver. 19, *"Then the same day at evening, being the first day of the week,* (that is, the same day that Christ is said to have risen,) *when the doors were shut, where the disciples were assembled, for fear of the Jews, came Jesus and stood in the midst of them."*

According to Matthew, the eleven were marching to Galilee, to meet Jesus in a mountain, by his own appointment, at the very time when, according to John, they were assembled in another place, and that not by appointment, but in secret, for fear of the Jews.

The writer of the book of Luke contradicts that of Matthew more pointedly than John does; for he says expressly, that the meeting was in *Jerusalem* the evening of the same day that he (Christ) rose, and that the *eleven* were *there.* See Luke, chap. xxiv. ver. 13, 33.

Now it is not possible, unless we admit these supposed disciples the right of wilful lying, that the writers of those books could be any of the eleven persons called disciples; for if, according to Matthew, the eleven went into Galilee to meet Jesus in a mountain, by his own appointment, on the same day that he is said to have risen, Luke and John must have been two of that eleven; yet the writer of Luke says expressly, and John implies as much, that the meeting was that same day, in a house in Jerusalem; and on the other hand, if, according to Luke and John, the *eleven* were assembled in a house in Jerusalem, Matthew must have been one of that eleven; yet Matthew says, the meeting was in a mountain in Galilee, and consequently the evidence given in those books destroys each other.

The writer of the book of Mark says nothing about any meeting in Galilee; but he says, chap. xvi. ver. 12, that Christ, after his resurrection, appeared in *another form* to two of them, as they walked into the country, and that these two told it to the residue, who would not believe them. Luke also tells a story, in which he keeps Christ employed the whole of the day of this pretended resurrection, until the evening, and which totally invalidates the account of going to the mountain in Galilee. He says, that two of them, without saying which two, went that *same day* to a village called Emmaus, threescore furlongs (seven miles and an half) from Jerusalem, and that Christ in disguise went with them, and staid with them unto the evening, and supped with them, and then vanished out of their sight, and re-appeared that same evening, at the meeting of the eleven in Jerusalem.

This is the contradictory manner in which the evidence of this pretended re-appearance of Christ is stated; the only point in which the writers agree, is the skulking privacy of that re-appearance; for whether it was in the recess of a mountain in Galilee, or in a shut-up house in Jerusalem, it was still skulking. To what cause then are we to assign this skulking? On the one hand, it is directly repugnant to the supposed or pretended end, that of convincing the world that Christ was risen; and on the other hand, to have asserted the publicity of it, would have exposed the writers of those books to public detection; and therefore they have been under the necessity of making it a private affair.

As to the account of Christ being seen by more than five hundred at once, it is Paul only who says it, and not the five hundred who say it for themselves. It is therefore the testimony but of one man, and that too of a man, who did not, according to the same account, believe a word of the matter himself, at the time it is said to have happened. His evidence, supposing him to have been the writer of the 15th chapter of Corinthians, where this account is given, is like that of a man, who comes into a court of justice to swear, that what he had sworn before is false. A man may often see reason, and he has too always the right of changing his opinion; but this liberty does not extend to matters of fact.

I now come to the last scene, that of the ascension into heaven. Here all fear of the Jews, and of every thing else, must necessarily have been out of the question; it was that which, if true, was to seal the whole; and upon which the reality of the future mission of the disciples was to rest for proof. Words, whether declarations, or promises that passed in private, either in the recess of a mountain in Galilee, or in a shut-up house in Jerusalem, even supposing them to have been spoken, could not be evidence in public: it was therefore necessary that this last scene should preclude the possibility of denial and dispute; and that it should be, as I have stated in the former part of the *Age of Reason,* as public and as visible, as the sun at noon-day; at least, it ought to have been as public as the crucifixion is reported to have been. But to come to the point.—

In the first place, the writer of the book of Matthew does not say a syllable about it; neither does the writer of the book of John. This being the case, is it possible to suppose, that those writers, who affect to be even minute in other matters, would have been silent upon this, had it been true? The writer of the book of Mark passes it off in a careless, slovenly manner, with a single dash of the pen; as if he was tired of romancing, or ashamed of the story. So also does the writer of Luke. And even between these two, there is not an apparent agreement, as to the place where this final parting is said to have been.

The book of Mark says, that Christ appeared to the eleven, as they sat at meat; alluding to the meeting of the eleven at Jerusalem: he then states the conversation, that he says passed at that meeting; and immediately after says, (as a school-boy would finish a dull story,) "*So then,* after the Lord had spoken unto them, he was received up into heaven, and sat on the right hand of God." But the writer of Luke says, that the ascension was from Bethany; that *he* (Christ) *led them out as far as Bethany, and was parted from them there, and was carried up into heaven.* So also was Mahomet: and as to Moses, the *apostle* Jude says, ver 9, *That Michael and the devil disputed about his body.* While we believe such fables as these, or either of them, we believe unworthily of the Almighty.

I have now gone through the examination of the four books ascribed to Matthew, Mark, Luke, and John; and when it is considered that the whole space of time, from the crucifixion to what is called the ascension, is but a few days, apparently not more than three or four, and that all the circumstances are reported to have happened nearly about the same spot, Jerusalem, it is, I believe, impossible to find, in any story upon record, so many, and such glaring absurdities, contradictions, and falshoods, as are in those books. They are more numerous and striking, than I had any expectation of finding when I began this examination, and far more so than I had any idea of, when I wrote the former part of the *Age of Reason.* I had then neither Bible nor Testament to refer to, nor could I procure any. My own situation, even as to existence, was becoming every day more precarious; and as I was willing to leave something behind me upon the subject, I was obliged to be quick and concise. The quotations I then made, were from memory only, but they are correct; and the opinions I have advanced in that work, are the effect of the most clear and long established conviction, – that the Bible and Testament are impositions upon the world; – that the fall of man, the account of Jesus Christ being the Son of God, and of his dying to appease the wrath of God, and of salvation by that strange means, are all fabulous inventions, dishonourable to the wisdom and power of the Almighty; – that the only true religion is deism, by which I then meant and now mean the belief of one God, and an imitation of his moral character, or the practice of what are called moral virtues; – and that it was upon this only (so far as religion is concerned) that I rested all my hopes of happiness hereafter. So say I now – and so help me God.

But to return to the subject. – Though it is impossible, at this distance of time, to ascertain as a fact, who were the writers of those four books (and this alone is sufficient to hold them in doubt, and where we doubt, we do not believe,) it is not difficult to ascertain negatively, that they were not written by the persons to whom they are ascribed. The contradictions in those books demonstrate two things.

First, that the writers cannot have been eye-witnesses and ear-witnesses of the matters they relate, or they would have related them without those contradictions; and consequently that the books have not been written by the persons called apostles, who are supposed to have been witnesses of this kind.

Secondly, that the writers, whoever they were, have not acted in concerted imposition; but each writer, separately, and individually for himself, and without the knowledge of the other.

The same evidence that applies to prove the one, applies equally to prove both these cases; that is, that the books were not written by the men called apostles, and also that they are not a concerted imposition. As to inspiration, it is altogether out of the question; we may as well attempt to unite truth and falshood, as inspiration and contradiction.

If four men are eye-witnesses and ear-witnesses to a scene, they will, without any concert among them, agree as to the time and place, when and where that scene happened. Their individual knowledge of the *thing,* each one knowing it for himself, renders concert totally unnecessary; the one will not say it was in a mountain in the country, and the other at a house in town; the one will not say it was at sun-rise, and the other that it was dark. For in whatever place it was, and at whatever time it was, they know it equally alike.

And on the other hand, if four men concert a story, they will make their separate relations of that story agree and corroborate each other to support the whole. *That* concert supplies the want of fact in the one case, as the knowledge of the fact supersedes, in the other case, the necessity of concert. The same contradictions, therefore, that prove there has been no concert, prove also, that the reporters had no knowledge of the fact, (or rather of that which they relate as a fact,) and detect also the falshood of their reports. Those books, therefore, have neither been written by the men called apostles, nor by impostors in concert. How then have they been written?

I am not one of those who are fond of believing there is much of that which is called wilful lying, or lying originally, except in the case of men setting up to be prophets, as in the Old Testament; for prophesying is lying professionally. In almost all other cases, it is not difficult to discover the progress, by which even simple supposition, with the aid of credulity, will in time grow into a lie, and at last be told as a fact; and whenever we can find a charitable reason for a thing of this kind, we ought not to indulge a severe one.

The story of Jesus Christ appearing after he was dead, is the story of an apparition; such as timid imagination can always create in vision, and credulity believe. Stories of this kind had been told of the assassination of Julius Cæsar not many years before, and they generally have their origin in violent deaths, or in execution of innocent persons. In cases of this kind, compassion lends [its] aid, and benevolently stretches the story. It goes on a little and a little farther, till it becomes a *most certain truth* Once start a ghost, and credulity fills up the history of [its] life, and assigns the cause of [its] appearance; one tells it one way, another another way, till there are as many stories about the ghost, and about the proprietor of the ghost, as there are about Jesus Christ in these four books.

The story of the appearance of Jesus Christ is told with that strange mixture of the natural and the impossible, that distinguishes a legendary tale from fact. He is represented as suddenly coming in, and going out, when the doors are shut, and of vanishing out of sight, and appearing again, as one would conceive of an unsubstantial vision; then again he is hungry, sits down to meat, and eats his supper. But as those who tell stories of this kind, never provide for all the cases, so it is here: they have told us, that when he arose, he left his grave cloaths behind him; but they have forgotten to provide other cloaths for him to appear in afterwards, or to tell us what he did with them, when he ascended; whether he stripped all off, or went up, cloaths and all. In the case of Elijah, they have been careful enough to make him throw down his mantle; how it happened not to be burnt in the chariot of fire, *they* also have not told us. But as imagination supplies all deficiencies of this kind, we may suppose, if we please, that it was made of salamander's wool.

Those who are not much acquainted with ecclesiastical history may suppose, that the book called the New Testament has existed ever since the time of Jesus Christ, as they suppose that the books ascribed to Moses, have existed ever since the time of Moses. But the fact is historically otherwise; there was no such book as the New Testament, till more than three hundred years after the time that Christ is said to have lived.

At what time the books ascribed to Matthew, Mark, Luke, and John, began to appear, is altogether a matter of uncertainty. There is not the least shadow of evidence of who the persons were that wrote them; and they might as well have been called by the names of any of the other supposed apostles, as by the names they are now called. The originals are not in the possession of any christian church existing, any more than the two tables of stones written on, as they pretend, by the finger of God, upon mount Sinai, and given to Moses, are in the possession of the Jews. And even if they were, there is no possibility of proving the hand-writing in either case. At the time those four books were written, there was no printing, and consequently there could be no publication, otherwise than by written copies, which any man might make, or alter at pleasure, and call them originals. Can we suppose it is consistent with the wisdom of the Almighty, to commit himself and his will to man upon such precarious means as these; or that it is consistent we should pin our faith upon such uncertainty? We cannot make, nor alter, nor even imitate so much as a blade of grass, that he has made, and yet we can make or alter *words of God,* as easily as words of man.[13]

About three hundred and fifty years after the time that Christ is said to have lived, several writings of the kind I am speaking of, were scattered in the hands of divers individuals; and as the church had begun to form itself into a hierarchy, or church government with temporal powers, it set itself about collecting them into a code, as we now see them, called *The New Testament.* They decided by vote, as I have before said in the former part of

---

13. The former part of the *Age of Reason* has not been published two years, and there is already an expression in it that is not mine. The expression is, *The book of Luke was carried by a majority of one vote only.* It may be true, but it is not I that have said it. Some person, who might know of that circumstance, has added it in a note at the bottom of the page of some of the editions, printed either in England, or in America; and the printers, after that, have erected it into the body of the work, and made me the author of it. If this has happened within such a short space of time notwithstanding the aid of printing, which prevents the alteration of copies individually; what may not have happened in a much greater length of time, when there was no printing, and when any man who could write, could make a written copy, and call it an original, by Matthew, Mark, Luke, or John?

the *Age of Reason,* which of those writings, out of the collection they had made, should be the *word of God,* and which should not. The Rabbins of the Jews had decided, by vote, upon the books of the Bible before.

As the object of the church was, as is the case in all national establishments of churches, power and revenue, and terror the means it used; it is consistent to suppose, that the most miraculous and wonderful of the writings they had collected, stood the best chance of being voted. And as to the authenticity of the books, the *vote stands in the place of it;* for it can be traced no higher.

Disputes, however, ran high among the people then calling themselves Christians; not only as to points of doctrine, but as to the authenticity of the books. In the contest between the persons called Saint Augustine, and Fauste, about the year 400, the latter says, "The books, called the Evangelists, have been composed long after the times of the apostles, by some obscure men, who fearing that the world would not give credit to their relation of matters, of which they could not be informed, have published them under the names of the apostles; and which are so full of sottishness and discordant relations, that there is neither agreement, nor connection between them."

And in another place, addressing himself to the advocates of those books, as being the word of God, he says, "It is thus that your predecessors have inserted, in the scriptures of our Lord, many things, which, though they carry his name, agree not with his doctrine. This is not surprising, *since that we have often proved,* that these things have not been written by himself, nor by his apostles, but that for the greatest part they are founded upon *tales,* upon *vague reports,* and put together by I know not what, half-Jews, with but little agreement between them; and which they have nevertheless published under the names of the apostles of our Lord, and have thus attributed to them their own *errors and their lies.*"[14]

The reader will see by these extracts that the authenticity of the books of the New Testament was denied, and the books treated as tales, forgeries, and lies, at the time they were voted to be the word of God. But the interest of the church, with the assistance of the faggot, bore down the opposition, and at last oppressed all investigation. Miracles followed upon miracles, if we will believe them, and men were taught to say they believed, whether they believed or not. But (by way of throwing in a thought) the French

---

14. I have taken these two extracts from Boulanger's Life of Paul, written in French. Boulanger has quoted them from the writings of Augustine against Fauste, to which he refers.

revolution has excommunicated the church from the power of working miracles; she has not been able, with the assistance of all her saints, to work *one* miracle since the revolution began; and as she never stood in greater need than now, we may, without the aid of divination, conclude, that all her former miracles are tricks and lies.[15]

When we consider the lapse of more than three hundred years intervening between the time that Christ is said to have lived, and the time the New Testament was formed into a book, we must see, even without the assistance of historical evidence, the exceeding uncertainty there is of [its] authenticity. The authenticity of the book of Homer, so far as regards the authorship, is much better established than that of the New Testament, though Homer is a thousand years the more ancient. It was only an exceeding good poet that could have written the book of Homer, and therefore few men only could have attempted it; and a man capable of doing it, would not have thrown away his own fame, by giving it to another. In like manner, there were but few that could have composed Euclid's Elements, because none but an exceeding good geometrician could have been the author of that work.

But with respect to the books of the New Testament, particularly such parts as tell us of the resurrection and ascension of Christ, any person who could tell a story of an apparition, or of a *man's walking,* could have made

15. Boulanger, in his Life of St. Paul, has collected from the ecclesiastical histories, and the writings of the fathers, as they are called, several matters, which shew the opinions that prevailed among the different sects of Christians, at the time the Testament, as we now see it, was voted to be the word of God. The following extracts are from the second chapter of that work.

"The Marcionists (a Christian sect) assured that the evangelists were filled with falsities. The Manichtions, who formed a very numerous sect at the commencement of Christianity, *rejected as false all the New Testament;* and shewed other writings quite different, that they gave for authentic. The Corinthians, like the Marcionists, admitted not the Acts of the Apostles. The Eucratics and the Sevenians adopted neither the Acts, nor the Epistles of Paul. Chrysostome, in a homily, which he made upon the Acts of the Apostles, says, that in his time, about the year 400, many people knew nothing either of the author, or of the book. St. Irene, who lived before that time, reports that the Valentinians, like several other sects of the Christians, accused the scriptures of being filled with errors, imperfections, and contradictions. The Ebionists, or Nazarenes, who were the first Christians, rejected all the Epistles of Paul, and regarded him as an impostor. They report, among other things, that he was originally a Pagan, that he came to Jerusalem, where he lived some time; and that having a mind to marry the daughter of the high-priest, he caused himself to be circumcised; but that not being able to obtain her, he quarrelled with the Jews, and wrote against circumcision, and against the observation of the sabbath, and against all the legal ordinances."

such books; for the story is most wretchedly told. The chance, therefore, of forgery in the Testament, is millions to one greater than in the case of Homer or Euclid. Of the numerous priests or parsons of the present day, bishops and all, every one of them can make a sermon, or translate a scrap of Latin, especially if it has been translated a thousand times before: but is there any amongst them that can write poetry like Homer, or science like Euclid? The sum total of a parson's learning, with very few exceptions, is, a b, ab, and hic, hæc, hoc; and their knowledge of science is, three times one is three; and this is more than sufficient to have enabled them, had they lived at the time, to have written all the books of the New Testament.

As the opportunities of forgery were greater, so also was the inducement. A man could gain no advantage by writing under the name of Homer or Euclid; if he could write equal to them, it would be better that he wrote under his own name; if inferior, he could not succeed. Pride would prevent the former, and impossibility the latter. But with respect to such books as compose the New Testament, all the inducements were on the side of forgery. The best imagined history that could have been made at the distance of two or three hundred years after the time, could not have passed for an original under the name of the real writer; the whole chance of success lay in forgery; for the church wanted pretence for [its] new doctrine, and truth and talents were out of the question.

But as it is not uncommon (as before observed) to relate stories of persons *walking* after they are dead, and of ghosts and apparitions of such as have fallen by some violent or extraordinary means, and as the people of that day were in the habit of believing such things, and of the appearance of angels, and also of devils, and of their getting into people's insides, and shaking them like a fit of an ague, and of their being cast out again as if by an emetic; (Mary Magdalene, the book of Mark tells us, had brought up, or been brought to bed of, seven devils;) it was nothing extraordinary that some story of this kind should get abroad of the person called Jesus Christ, and afterwards become the foundation of the four books ascribed to Matthew, Mark, Luke, and John. Each writer told the tale as he heard it, or thereabout, and gave to his book the name of the saint, or the apostle, whom tradition had given as the eye-witness. It is only upon this ground that the contradictions in those books can be accounted for; and if this be not the case, they are downright impositions, lies, and forgeries, without even the apology of credulity.

That they have been written by a sort of half Jews, as the foregoing quotations mention, is discernible enough. The frequent references made to that chief assassin and impostor Moses, and to the men called prophets, establishes this point; and on the other hand, the church has complimented the fraud, by admitting the Bible and the Testament to reply to each other. Between the Christian-Jew, and the Christian-Gentile, the thing called a prophecy, and the thing prophesied of; the type, and the thing typified; the sign, and the thing signified; have been industriously rumaged up, and fitted together like old locks and picklock-keys. The story, foolishly enough told, of Eve and the serpent, and naturally enough as to the enmity between men and serpents; (for the serpent always bites about the *heel,* because it cannot reach higher; and the man always knocks the serpent about the *head,* as the most effectual way to prevent [its] biting;[16]) this foolish story, I say, has been made into a prophecy, a type, and a promise to begin with: and the lying imposition of Isaiah to Ahaz, *That a virgin should conceive and bear a son,* as a sign that Ahaz should conquer, when the event was, that he was defeated, (as already noticed in the observations on the book of Isaiah,) has been perverted, and made to serve as a winder up.

Jonah and the whale are also made into signs and types. Jonah is Jesus, and the whale is the grave; for it is said, (and they have made Christ to say it of himself,) Matt. chap. xii. ver. 40, "For as Jonah was *three days* and *three nights* in the whale's belly, so shall the Son of man be *three days* and *three nights* in the heart of the earth." But it happens aukwardly enough that Christ, according to their own account, was but two nights and one day in the grave; about 36 hours, instead of 72; that is, the Friday night, the Saturday, and the Saturday night; for he was up, on the Sunday morning, by sun-rise or before. But as this fits quite as well as the *bite* and the *kick* in Genesis, and the *virgin* and her *son* in Isaiah, it will pass in the lump of *orthodox* things. Thus much for the historical part of the Testament, and [its] evidences.

THE EPISTLES OF PAUL.

The epistles ascribed to Paul, being fourteen in number, almost fill up the remaining part of the Testament. Whether those epistles were written by the person to whom they are ascribed, is a matter of no great importance, since that the writer, whoever he was, attempts to prove his doctrine by argument. He does not pretend to have been witness to any of the scenes told of the resurrection and the ascension, and he declares that he had not believed them.

16. "It shall bruise thy *head,* and thou shalt bruise his *heel,*" Genesis, chap. iii. ver. 15.

The story of his being struck to the ground as he was journeying to Damascus, has nothing in it miraculous or extraordinary; he escaped with life, and that is more than many others have done who have been struck with lightning; and that he should lose his sight for three days, and be unable to eat or drink during that time, is nothing more than is common in such conditions. His companions that were with him appear not to have suffered in the same manner, for they were well enough to lead him the remainder of the journey; neither did they pretend to have seen any vision.

The character of the person called Paul, according to the accounts given of him, has in it a great deal of violence and fanaticism; he had persecuted with as much heat as he preached afterwards; the stroke he had received had changed his thinking, without altering his constitution; and either as a Jew or a Christian he was the same zealot. Such men are never good moral evidences of any doctrine they preach. They are always in extremes, as well of action as of belief.

The doctrine he sets out to prove by argument, is the resurrection of the same body, and he advances this as an evidence of immortality. But so much will men differ in their manner of thinking, and in the conclusions they draw from the same premises, that this doctrine of the resurrection of the same body, so far from being an evidence of immortality, appears to me to furnish an evidence against it: for, if I have already died in this body, and am raised again in the same body in which I have died, it is presumptive evidence that I shall die again. That resurrection no more secures me against the repetition of dying, than an ague fit, when past, secures me against another. To believe therefore in immortality, I must have a more elevated idea, than is contained in the gloomy doctrine of the resurrection.

Besides, as a matter of choice, as well as of hope, I had rather have a better body and a more convenient form, than the present. Every animal in the creation excels us in something. The winged insects, without mentioning doves or eagles, can pass over more space, and with greater ease, in a few minutes, than man can in an hour. The glide of the smallest fish, in proportion to [its] bulk, exceeds us in motion, almost beyond comparison, and without weariness. Even the sluggish snail can ascend from the bottom of a dungeon, where man, by the want of that ability, would perish; and a spider can launch itself from the top, as playful amusement. The personal powers of man are so limited, and his heavy frame so little constructed to extensive enjoyment, that there is nothing to induce us to wish the opinion of Paul to be true. It is too little for the magnitude of the scene; too mean for the sublimity of the subject.

But all other arguments apart, the *consciousness of existence* is the only conceivable idea we can have of another life; and the continuance of that consciousness is immortality. The consciousness of existence, or the knowing that we exist, is not necessarily confined to the same form, nor to the same matter, even in this life.

We have not in all cases the same form, nor in any case the same matter that composed our bodies twenty or thirty years ago; and yet we are conscious of being the same persons. Even legs and arms, which make up almost half the human frame, are not necessary to the consciousness of existence. They may be lost, or taken away, and the full consciousness of existence remain; and were their place supplied by wings, or other appendages, we cannot conceive that it could alter our consciousness of existence. In short, we know not how much, or rather how little, of our composition it is, and how exquisitely fine that little is, that creates in us this consciousness of existence; and all beyond that is like the pulp of a peach, distinct and separate from the vegetative speck in the kernel.

Who can say what exceeding fine action of fine matter it is, that produces a thought in what we call the mind? And yet that thought, when produced, as I now produce the thought I am writing, is capable of becoming immortal, and is the only production of man that has that capacity.

Statues of brass or marble will perish; and statues made in imitation of them are not the same statues, nor the same workmanship, any more than a copy of a picture is the same picture. But print and reprint a thought a thousand times over, and with materials of any kind, carve it in wood, or engrave it on stone, the thought is eternally and identically the same thought in every case. It has a capacity of unimpaired existence, unaffected by change of matter, and is essentially distinct, and of a nature different from every thing else that we know of, or can conceive. If then the thing produced has in itself a capacity of being immortal, it is more than a token that the power that produced it, which is the self-same thing as consciousness of existence, can be immortal also; and that independently of the matter it was first connected with, as the thought is of the printing, or writing, it first appeared in. The one idea is not more difficult to believe than the other; and we can see that one is true.

That the consciousness of existence is not dependent on the same form or the same matter, is demonstrated to our senses in the works of the creation, so far as our senses are capable of receiving that demonstration. A very numerous part of the animal creation preaches to us, far better than Paul, the belief of a life hereafter. Their little life resembles an earth and a heaven, a present and a future state; and comprises, if it may be so expressed, immortality in miniature.

The most beautiful parts of the creation, to our eyes, are the winged insects; and they are not so originally. They acquire that form and that inimitable brilliancy by progressive changes. The slow and creeping caterpillar-worm of to-day, passes in a few days to a torpid figure and a state resembling death; and in the next change comes forth in all the miniature magnificence of life, a splendid butterfly. No resemblance of the former creature remains; every thing is changed; all his powers are new, and life is to him another thing. We cannot conceive, that the consciousness of existence is not the same in this state of the animal as before: why then must I believe that the resurrection of the same body is necessary to continue to me the consciousness of existence hereafter?

In the former part of the *Age of Reason* I have called the creation the true and only real word of God; and this instance, or this text, in the book of creation, not only shews to us that this thing may be so, but that it is so; and that the belief of a future state is *a rational belief,* founded upon facts visible on the creation: for it is not more difficult to believe that we shall exist hereafter in a better state and form than at present, than that a worm should become a butterfly, and quit the dunghill for the atmosphere, if we did not know it as a fact.

As to the doubtful jargon ascribed to Paul in the 15th chapter of 1 Corinthians, which makes part of the burial-service of some Christians, it is as destitute of meaning as the tolling of the bell at the funeral. It explains nothing to the understanding; it illustrates nothing to the imagination; but leaves the reader to find any meaning if he can.

"All flesh," says he, "is not the same flesh. There is one flesh of men, another of fishes, and another of birds." And what then? nothing. A cook could have said as much. "There are also," says he, "bodies celestial, and bodies terrestrial; the glory of the celestial is *one,* and the glory of the terrestrial is *another.*" And what then? a thing. And what is the difference? nothing that he has told. "There is," says he, "one glory of the sun, and another glory of the moon, and another glory of the stars." And what then? nothing; except that he says that *one star differeth from another star in glory,* instead of distance; and he might as well have told us, that the moon did not shine as bright as the sun. All this is nothing better than the jargon of a conjuror, who picks up phrases he does not understand, to confound the credulous people who come to have their fortune told. Priests and conjurors are of the same trade.

Sometimes Paul affects to be a naturalist, and to prove his system of resurrection from the principles of vegetation. *"Thou fool,"* says he, *"that which thou sowest is not quickened, except it die."* To which one might reply in his own language, and say, Thou fool, Paul, that which thou sowest is not quickened, except it die *not;* for the grain that dies in the ground, never does, nor can vegetate. The living grains only produce the next crop. But the metaphor, in point of view, is no simile. It is succession and resurrection.

The progress of an animal, from one state of being to another, as from a worm to a butterfly, applies to the case; but this of the grain does not; and shews Paul to have been, what he says of others, *a fool.*

Whether the fourteen epistles ascribed to Paul were written by him or not, is a matter of indifference; they are either argumentative or dogmatical; and as the argument is defective, and the dogmatical part is merely presumptive, it signifies not who wrote them. And the same may be said for the remaining parts of the Testament. It is not upon the Epistles, but upon what is called the Gospel, contained in the four books ascribed to Matthew, Mark, Luke, and John, and upon the pretended prophecies, that the theory of the church, calling itself the Christian church, is founded. The epistles are dependent upon those, and must follow their fate; for if the story of Jesus Christ be fabulous, all reasoning founded upon it, as a supposed truth, must fall with it.

We know, from history, that one of the principal leaders of this church, Athanasius, lived at the time the New Testament was formed; and we know also, from the absurd jargon he has left us, under the name of a creed, the character of the men who formed the New Testament;[17] and we know also from the same history, that the authenticity of the books, of which it is composed, was denied at the time. It is upon the vote of such as Athanasius, that the Testament was decreed to be the word of God; and nothing can present to us a more strange idea, than that of decreeing the word of God by vote. Those who rest their faith upon such authority, put man in the place of God, and have no true foundation for future happiness. Credulity, however, is not a crime; but it becomes criminal by resisting conviction. It is strangling in the womb of the conscience the efforts it makes to ascertain truth. We should never force belief upon ourselves in any thing.

I here close the subject on the Old Testament, and the New. The evidence I have produced, to prove them forgeries, is extracted from the books themselves, and acts, like a two-edged sword, either way. If the evidence be denied, the authenticity of the scriptures is denied with it; for it

17. Athanasius died, according to the church chronology, in the year 371.

is scripture-evidence; and if the evidence be admitted, the authenticity of the books is disproved. The contradictory impossibilities contained in the Old Testament, and the New, put them in the case of a man who swears *for* and *against*. Either evidence convicts him of perjury, and equally destroys reputation.

Should the Bible and Testament hereafter fall, it is not I that have been the occasion. I have done no more, than extract the evidence from the confused mass of matters with which it is mixed, and arrange that evidence in a point of light to be clearly seen, and easily comprehended: and having done this, I leave the reader to judge for himself, as I have judged for myself.

Conclusion.

In the former part of the *Age of Reason*, I have spoken of the three frauds, *mystery, miracle,* and *prophecy:* and as I have seen nothing in any of the answers to that work, that in the least affects what I have there said upon those subjects, I shall not encumber this second part with additions, that are not necessary.

I have spoken also in the same work upon what is called *revelation*, and have shewn the absurd misapplication of that term to the books of the Old Testament, and the New; for certainly revelation is out of the question in reciting any thing of which man has been the actor, or the witness. That which a man has done or seen needs no revelation to tell him he has done it, or seen it, for he knows it already; nor to enable him to tell it, or to write it. It is ignorance, or imposition, to apply the term revelation in such cases; yet the Bible and Testament are classed under this fraudulent description of being all *revelation.*

Revelation then, so far as the term has relation between God and man, can only be applied to something which God reveals of his *will* to man; but though the power of the Almighty, to make such a communication, is necessarily admitted, because to that power all things are possible, yet, the thing so revealed (if any thing ever was revealed, and which, by the bye, it is impossible to prove) is revelation to the person *only to whom it is made.* His account of it to another is not revelation; and whoever puts faith in that account, puts it in the man from whom the account comes; and that man may have been deceived, or may have dreamed it; or he may be an impostor, and may lie. There is no possible criterion whereby to judge of the truth of what he tells; for even the morality of it would be no proof of revelation.

In all such cases, the proper answer would be, *"When it is revealed to me, I will believe it to be revelation; but it is not, and cannot be incumbent upon me to believe it to be revelation before; neither is it proper that I should take the word of man as the word of God, and put man in the place of God."* This is the manner in which I have spoken of revelation in the former part of the *Age of Reason;* and which, whilst it reverentially admits revelation as a possible thing, because, as before said, to the Almighty all things are possible, it prevents the imposition of one man upon another, and precludes the wicked use of pretended revelation.

But though, speaking for myself, I thus admit the possibility of revelation; I totally disbelieve, that the Almighty ever did communicate any thing to man, by any mode of speech, in any language, or by any kind of vision, or appearance, or by any means which our senses are capable of receiving, otherwise than by the universal display of himself in the works of the creation, and by that repugnance we feel in ourselves to bad actions, and disposition to good ones.

The most detestable wickedness, the most horrid cruelties, and the greatest miseries, that have afflicted the human race, have had their origin in this thing called revelation, or revealed religion. It has been the most dishonourable belief against the character of the Divinity, the most destructive to morality, and the peace and happiness of man, that ever was propagated since man began to exist. It is better, far better, that we admitted, if it were possible, a thousand devils to roam at large, and to preach publicly the doctrine of devils, if there were any such, than that we permitted one such impostor or monster as Moses, Joshua, Samuel, and the Bible-prophets, to come with the pretended word of God in his mouth, and have credit among us.

Whence arose all the horrid assassinations of whole nations, of men, women, and infants, with which the Bible is filled, and the bloody persecutions, and tortures unto death, and religious wars, that since that time have laid Europe in blood and ashes; whence arose they, but from this impious thing called revealed religion, and this monstrous belief, that God has spoken to man? The lies of the Bible have been the cause of the one, and the lies of the Testament the other.

Some Christians pretend, that Christianity was not established by the sword; but of what period of time do they speak? It was impossible that *twelve* men could *begin* with the sword; they had not the power; but no sooner were the professors of Christianity sufficiently powerful to employ the sword, than they did so, and the stake and the faggot too; and Mahomet could not do it sooner. By the same spirit that Peter cut off the ear of the high priest's servant, (if the story be true,) he would cut off his head, and the head of his master, had he been able. Besides this, Christianity grounds itself originally upon the Bible, and the Bible was established altogether by the sword, and that in the worst use of it; not to terrify, but to extirpate. The Jews made no converts; butchered all. The Bible is the fire of the Testament, and both are called the *word of God*. The Christians read both books; the ministers preach from both books; and this thing called Christianity is made up of both. It is then false to say, that Christianity was not established by the sword.

The only sect that has not persecuted are the Quakers; and the only reason that can be given for it, is, that they are rather Deists than Christians. They do not believe much about Jesus Christ, and they call the scriptures a dead letter. Had they called them by a worse name, they had been nearer the truth.

It is incumbent on every man who reverences the character of the Creator, and who wishes to lessen the catalogue of artificial miseries, and remove the cause that has sown persecutions thick among mankind, to expel all ideas of revealed religion as a dangerous heresy, and an impious fraud. What is it that we have learned from this pretended thing called revealed religion? – nothing that is useful to man, and every thing that is dishonourable to his Maker. What is it the Bible teaches us? – rapine, cruelty, and murder. What is it the Testament teaches us? – to believe that the Almighty committed debauchery with a woman, engaged to be married; and the belief of this debauchery is called faith.

As to the fragments of morality that are irregularly and thinly scattered in those books, they make no part of this pretended thing, revealed religion. They are the natural dictates of conscience, and the bonds by which society is held together, and without which, it cannot exist; and are nearly the same in all religions, and in all societies. The Testament teaches nothing new upon this subject; and where it attempts to exceed, it becomes mean, and ridiculous. The doctrine of not retaliating injuries is much better expressed in Proverbs, which is a collection as well from the Gentiles, as the Jews, than it is in the Testament. It is there said, Proverbs xxv. ver. 21, *"If thine enemy be hungry, give him bread to eat; and if he be thirsty, give him water to drink:"*[18] but when it is said, as in the Testament, *"If a man smite thee on*

18. According to what is called Christ's sermon on the mount in the book of Matthew, where, among some good things, a great deal of this feigned morality is introduced, it is there expressly said, that the doctrine of forbearance, or of not retaliating injuries, *was not any part of the doctrine of the Jews;* and as this doctrine is found in Proverbs, it must, according to that statement, have been copied from

the right cheek, turn to him the other also;" it is assassinating the dignity of forbearance, and sinking man into a *spaniel.*

Loving enemies is another dogma of feigned morality, and has besides no meaning. It is incumbent on man, as a moralist, that he does not revenge an injury; and it is equally as good in a political sense, for there is no end to retaliation; each retaliates on the other, and calls it justice: but to love in proportion to the injury, if it could be done, would be to offer a premium for a crime. Besides, the word *enemies* is too vague and general to be used in a moral maxim, which ought always to be clear and defined, like a proverb. If a man be the enemy of another from mistake and prejudice, as in the case of religious opinions, and sometimes in politics, that man is different to an enemy at heart with a criminal intention; and it is incumbent upon us, and it contributes also to our own tranquillity, that we put the best construction upon a thing that it will bear. But even this erroneous motive in him makes no motive for love on the other part; and to say that we can love voluntarily, and without a motive, is morally and physically impossible.

Morality is injured by prescribing to it duties, that, in the first place, are impossible to be performed; and, if they could be, would be productive of evil; or, as before said, be premiums for crime. The maxim *of doing as we would be done unto* does not include this strange doctrine of loving enemies; for no man expects to be loved himself for his crime, or for his enmity.

Those who preach this doctrine of loving their enemies, are in general the greatest persecutors, and they act consistently by so doing; for the doctrine is hypocritical; and it is natural that hypocrisy should act the reverse of what it preaches. For my own part, I disown the doctrine, and consider it as a feigned or fabulous morality; yet the man does not exist that can say, I have persecuted him, or any man, or any set of men, either in the American revolution, or in the French revolution; or that I have, in any case, returned evil for evil. But it is not incumbent on man to reward a bad action with a good one, or to return good for evil; and wherever it is done, it is a voluntary act, and not a duty. It is also absurd to suppose, that such doctrine

---

the Gentiles, from whom Christ learned it. Those men, whom Jewish and Christian idolaters have abusively called heathens, had much better and clearer ideas of justice and morality than are to be found in the Old Testament, so far as it is Jewish; or in the New. The answer of Solon on the question, "Which is the most perfect popular government," has never been exceeded by any man since his time, as containing a maxim of political morality. *"That,* says he, *where the least injury done to the meanest individual, is considered as an insult on the whole constitution."* Solon lived above 500 years before Christ.

can make any part of a revealed religion. We imitate the moral character of the Creator by forbearing with each other, for he forbears with all: but this doctrine would imply that he loved man, not in proportion as he was good, but as he was bad.

If we consider the nature of our condition here, we must see there is no occasion for such a thing as *revealed religion*. What is it we want to know? Does not the creation, the universe we behold, preach to us the existence of an Almighty power, that governs and regulates the whole? And is not the evidence that this creation holds out to our senses infinitely stronger than any thing we can read in a book, that any impostor might make, and call the word of God? As for morality, the knowledge of it exists in every man's conscience.

Here we are. The existence of an Almighty power is sufficiently demonstrated to us, though we cannot conceive, as it is impossible we should, the nature and manner of [its] existence. We cannot conceive how we came here ourselves, and yet we know for a fact that we are here. We must know also, that the power that called us into being can, if he please, and when he pleases, call us to account for the manner in which we have lived here; and therefore, without seeking any other motive for the belief, it is rational to believe that he will, for we know beforehand that he can. The probability, or even possibility of the thing is all that we ought to know; for if we knew it as a fact, we should be the mere slaves of terror, our belief would have no merit, and our best actions no virtue.

Deism then teaches us, without the possibility of being deceived, all that is necessary or proper to be known. The creation is the Bible of the deist. He there reads, in the hand-writing of the Creator himself, the certainty of his existence; and all other Bibles and Testaments are to him forgeries. The probability that we may be called to account hereafter, will, to a reflecting mind, have the influence of belief; for it is not our belief, or our disbelief, that can make or unmake the fact. As this is the state we are in, and which it is proper we should be in, as free agents, it is the fool only, and not the philosopher, or even the prudent man, that will live as if there were no God.

But the belief of a God is so weakened by being mixed with the strange fable of the Christian creed, and with the wild adventures related in the Bible, and the obscurity and obscene nonsense of the Testament, that the mind of man is bewildered as in a fog. Viewing all these things in a confused mass, he confounds fact with fable; and as he cannot believe all, he feels a disposition to reject all. But the belief of a God, is a belief distinct from all other things, and ought not to be confounded with any. The notion of a Trinity of Gods has enfeebled the belief of *one* God. A multiplication of beliefs acts as a division of belief; and in proportion as any thing is divided, it is weakened.

Religion, by such means, becomes a thing of form, instead of fact; of notion, instead of principle; morality is banished to make room for an imaginary thing, called faith, and this faith has [its] origin in a supposed debauchery; a man is preached instead of God; an execution as an object for gratitude; the preachers daub themselves with the blood, like a troop of assassins, and pretend to admire the brilliancy it gives them; they preach a humdrum sermon on the merits of the execution; then praise Jesus Christ for being executed, and condemn the Jews for doing it.

A man, by hearing all their nonsense lumped and preached together, confounds the God of the creation with the imagined God of the Christians, and lives as if there were none.

Of all the systems of religion that ever were invented, there is none more derogatory to the Almighty, more unedifying to man, more repugnant to reason, and more contradictory in itself, than this thing called Christianity. Too absurd for belief, too impossible to convince, and too inconsistent for practice, it renders the heart torpid, or produces only atheists and fanatics. As an engine of power, it serves the purpose of despotism; and as a means of wealth, the avarice of priests; but so far as respects the good of man in general, it leads to nothing here, or hereafter.

The only religion that has not been invented, and that has in it every evidence of divine originality, is pure and simple deism. It must have been the first, and will probably be the last that man believes. But pure and simple deism does not answer the purpose of despotic governments. They cannot lay hold of religion as an engine, but by mixing it with human inventions, and making their own authority a part; neither does it answer the avarice of priests, but by incorporating themselves and their functions with it, and becoming, like the government, a party in the system. It is this that forms the otherwise mysterious connection of church and state; the church humane, and the state tyrannic.

Were a man impressed as fully and as strongly as he ought to be, with the belief of a God, his moral life would be regulated by the force of this belief: he would stand in awe of God, and of himself, and would not do the thing that could not be concealed from either. To give this belief the full opportunity of force, it is necessary that it acts alone. This is deism.

But when, according to the Christian Trinitarian scheme, one part of God is represented by a dying man, and another part, called the Holy

Ghost, by a flying pigeon, it is impossible that belief can attach itself to such wild conceits.[19]

It has been the scheme of the Christian church, and of all the other invented systems of religion, to hold man in ignorance of the Creator, as it is of government to hold him in ignorance of his rights. The systems of the one are as false as those of the other, and are calculated for mutual support. The study of theology, as it stands in Christian churches, is the study of nothing; it is founded on nothing; it rests on no principles; it proceeds by no authorities; it has no data; it can demonstrate nothing; and admits of no conclusion. Not any thing can be studied as a science, without our being in possession of the principles upon which it is founded; and as this is not the case with Christian theology, it is therefore the study of nothing.

Instead then of studying theology, as is now done, out of the Bible and Testament, the meanings of which books are always controverted, and the authenticity of which is disproved, it is necessary that we refer to the Bible of the creation. The principles we discover there, are eternal, and of divine origin: they are the foundation of all the science that exists in the world, and must be the foundation of theology.

We can know God only through his works. We cannot have a conception of any one attribute, but by following some principle that leads to it. We have only a confused idea of his power, if we have not the means of comprehending something of [its] immensity. We can have no idea of his wisdom, but by knowing the order and manner in which it acts. The principles of science lead to this knowledge; for the Creator of man is the Creator of science, and it is through that medium that man can see God, as it were, face to face.

Could a man be placed in a situation, and endowed with power of vision, to behold at one view, and to contemplate deliberately, the structure of the universe, to mark the movements of the several planets, the cause of their varying appearances, the unerring order in which they revolve, even to the remotest comet, their connection and dependance on each other, and to know the system of laws, established by the Creator, that governs and regulates the whole; he would then conceive, far beyond what any

19. The book called the book of Matthew, says, chap. iii. ver. 16, that *the Holy Christ descended in the shape of a dove.* It might as well have said a goose; the creatures are equally harmless, and the one is as much a nonsensical lie as the other. The second of Acts, ver. 2, 3, says, that it descended in a mighty *rushing wind,* in the shape of *cloven tongues;* perhaps it was cloven feet. Such absurd stuff is fit only for tales of witches and wizards.

church-theology can teach him, the power, the wisdom, the vastness, the munificence of the Creator: he would then see, that all the knowledge man has of science, and that all the mechanical arts, by which he renders his situation comfortable here, are derived from that source: his mind, exalted by the scene, and convinced by the fact, would increase in gratitude, as it increased in knowledge: his religion or his worship would become united with his improvement as a man: any employment he followed, that had connection with the principles of the creation, as every thing of agriculture, of science, and of the mechanical arts has, would teach him more of God, and of the gratitude he owes to him, than any theological Christian sermon he now hears. Great objects inspire great thoughts; great munificence excites great gratitude; but the groveling tales and doctrines of the Bible and the Testament are fit only to excite contempt.

Though man cannot arrive, at least in this life, at the actual scene I have described, he can demonstrate it; because he has knowledge of the principles upon which the creation is constructed. We know that the greatest works can be represented in model, and that the universe can be represented by the same means. The same principles by which we measure an inch, or an acre of ground, will measure to millions in extent. A circle of an inch diameter has the same geometrical properties as a circle that would circumscribe the universe. The same properties of a triangle, that will demonstrate upon paper the course of a ship, will do it on the ocean; and when applied to what are called the heavenly bodies, will ascertain, to a minute, the time of an eclipse, though those bodies are millions of miles distant from us. This knowledge is of divine origin; and it is from the Bible of the creation that man has learned it, and not from the stupid Bible of the church, that teaches man nothing.[20]

20. The Bible-makers have undertaken to give us, in the first chapter of Genesis, an account of the creation; and in doing this, they have demonstrated nothing but their ignorance. They make there to have been three days and three nights, evenings and mornings, before there was any sun; when it is the presence or absence of the sun that is the cause of day and night, and his rising and setting that of morning and evening. Besides, it is a puerile and pitiful idea, to suppose the Almighty to say, *Let there be light.* It is the imperative manner of speaking that a conjurer uses, when he says to his cups and balls, *Presto, be gone.* Longinus calls this expression the *sublime;* and by the same rule, the conjurer is sublime too, for the manner of speaking is expressively and grammatically the same. When authors and critics talk of the sublime, they see not how nearly it borders on the ridiculous. The sublime of the critics, like some parts of Edmund Burke's *sublime* and *beautiful,* is like a wind-mill just visible in a fog, which imagination might distort into a flying mountain, or an archangel, or a flock of wild geese.

All the knowledge man has of science and of machinery, by the aid of which his existence is rendered comfortable upon earth, and without which he would be scarcely distinguishable in appearance and condition from a common animal, comes from the great machine and structure of the universe. The constant and unwearied observations of our ancestors, upon the movements and revolutions of the heavenly bodies, in what are supposed to have been the early ages of the world, have brought this knowledge upon earth. It is not Moses and the prophets, nor Jesus Christ, nor his apostles, that have done it. The Almighty is the great mechanic of the creation, the first philosopher, and original teacher of all science. Let us then learn to reverence our master, and let us not forget the labours of our ancestors.

Had we at this day no knowledge of machinery, and were it possible that man could have a view, as I have before described, of the structure and machinery of the universe, he would soon conceive the idea of constructing some at least of the mechanical works we now have; and the idea so conceived, would progressively advance in practice. Or could a model of the universe, such as is called an orrery, be presented before him, and put in motion, his mind would arrive at the same idea. Such an object, and such a subject, would, whilst it improved him in knowledge useful to himself as a man and a member of society, as well as entertaining, afford far better matter for impressing him with a knowledge of, and a belief in the Creator, and of the reverence and gratitude that man owes to him, than the stupid texts of the Bible and the Testament, from which, be the talents of the preacher what they may, only stupid sermons can be preached. If man must preach, let him preach something that is edifying, and from texts that are known to be true.

The Bible of the creation is inexhaustible in texts. Every part of science, whether connected with the geometry of the universe, with the systems of animal and vegetable life, or with the properties of inanimate matter, is a text as well for devotion as for philosophy; for gratitude, as for human improvement. It will, perhaps, be said, that if such a revolution in the system of religion take place, every preacher ought to be a philosopher. *Most certainly,* and every house of devotion a school of science.

It has been by wandering from the immutable laws of science, and the right use of reason, and setting up an invented thing called revealed religion, that so many wild and blasphemous conceits have been formed of the Almighty. The Jews have made him the assassin of the human species, to make room for the religion of the Jews. The Christians have made him the murderer of himself, and the founder of a new religion to supersede and expel the Jewish religion. And to find pretence and admission for these things, they must have supposed his power or his wisdom imperfect, or his will changeable; and the changeableness of the will is the imperfection of the judgment. The philosopher knows that the laws of the Creator have never changed, with respect either to the principles of science, or the properties of matter. Why then is it to be supposed they have changed with respect to men?

I here close the subject. I have shewn, in all the foregoing part of this work, that the Bible and Testament are impositions and forgeries; and I leave the evidence I have produced in proof of it, to be refuted, if any one can do it; and I leave the ideas that are suggested in the conclusion of the work, to rest on the mind of the reader; certain as I am, that when opinions are free, either in matters of government or religion, truth will finally and powerfully prevail.

END OF THE SECOND PART OF THE AGE OF REASON.

DISSERTATION

ON

FIRST-PRINCIPLES

OF

GOVERNMENT.

BY THOMAS PAINE,

AUTHOR OF COMMON SENSE; RIGHTS OF MAN; AGE OF REASON, &c.

THERE is no subject more interesting to every man than the subject of government. His security, be he rich or poor, and, in a great measure, his prosperity is connected therewith; it is therefore his interest as well as his duty to make himself acquainted with its principles, and what the practice ought to be.

Every art and science, however imperfectly known at first, has been studied, improved, and brought to what we call perfection by the progressive labours of succeeding generations; but the science of government has stood still. No improvement has been made in the principle and scarcely any in the practice till the American revolution began. In all the countries of Europe (except in France) the same forms and systems that were erected in the remote ages of ignorance still continue, and their antiquity is put in the place of principle; it is forbidden to investigate their origin or by what right they exist; if it be asked how has this happened, the answer is easy; they are established on a principle that is false, and they employ their power to prevent detection.

Dissertation on First-Principles of Government (Paris: English Press, 1795).

Notwithstanding the mystery with which the science of government has been enveloped, for the purpose of enslaving, plundering, and imposing upon mankind, it is of all things the least mysterious and the most easy to be understood. The meanest capacity cannot be at a loss, if it begins its enquiries at the right point. Every art and science has some point, or alphabet, at which the study of that art or science begins, and by the assistance of which the progress is facilitated. The same method ought to be observed with respect to the science of government.

Instead then of embarrassing the subject in the outset with the numerous subdivisions, under which different forms of government have been classed, such as aristocracy, democracy, oligarchy, monarchy, &c. the better method will be to begin with what may be called primary divisions, or those under which all the several subdivisions will be comprehended.

The primary divisions are but two.

First, government by election and representation.

Secondly, government by hereditary succession.

All the several forms and systems of government, however numerous or diversified, class themselves under one or other of those primary divisions; for either they are on the system of representation, or on that of hereditary succession. As to that equivocal thing called mixed government, such as the late government of Holland and the present government of England, it does not make an exception to the general rule, because the parts separately considered are either representative or hereditary.

Beginning then our enquiries at this point, we have first to examine into the nature of those two primary divisions. If they are equally right in principle, it is mere matter of opinion which we prefer. If the one be demonstratively better than the other, that difference should direct our choice; but if one of them be so absolutely false as not to have a right to existence, the matter settles itself at once; because a negative proved on one thing, where two only are offered, and one must be accepted, amounts to an affirmative on the other.

The revolutions that are now spreading themselves in the world have their origin in this state of the case, and the present war is a conflict between the representative system founded on the rights of the people and the hereditary system founded in usurpation. As to what are called Monarchy, Royalty, and Aristocracy, they do not, either as things or as terms, sufficiently describe the hereditary system; they are but secondary things or signs of the hereditary system, and which fall of themselves if that system has not a right to exist. Were there no such terms as Monarchy, Royalty and Aristocracy, or were other terms substituted in their place, the hereditary system, if it continued, would not be altered thereby. It would be the same system under any other titulary name as it is now.

The character therefore of the revolutions of the present day distinguishes itself most definitively by grounding itself on the system of representative government in opposition to the hereditary. No other distinction reaches the whole of the principle.

Having thus opened the case generally, I proceed, in the first place, to examine the hereditary system, because it has the priority in point of time. The representative system is the invention of the modern world; and that no doubt may arise as to my own opinion, I declare it before hand, which is, *that there is not a problem in Euclid more mathematically true than that hereditary government has not a right to exist. When therefore we take from any man the exercise of hereditary power, we take away that which he never had the right to possess, and which no law or custom could, or ever can, give him a title to.*

The arguments that have hitherto been employed against the hereditary system have been chiefly founded upon the absurdity of it, and its incompetency to the purpose of good government. Nothing can present to our judgement, or to our imagination, a figure of greater absurdity, than that of seeing the government of a nation fall, as it frequently does, into the hands of a lad necessarily destitute of experience and often little better than a fool. It is an insult to every man of years, of character, and of talent, in a country. The moment we begin to reason upon the hereditary system it falls into derision; let but a single idea begin and a thousand will soon follow. Insignificance, imbecility, childhood, dotage, want of moral character; in fine, every defect serious or laughable unite to hold up the hereditary system as a figure of ridicule. Leaving however the ridiculousness of the thing to the reflections of the reader, I proceed to the more important part of the question, namely, whether such a system has a right to exist?

To be satisfied of the right of a thing to exist, we must be satisfied that it had a right to begin. If it had not a right to begin, it has not a right to continue. By what right then did the hereditary system begin? Let a man but ask himself this question, and he will find that he cannot satisfy himself with an answer.

The right which any man, or any family had to set itself up at first to govern a nation, and to establish itself hereditarily, was no other than the right which Robespierre had to do the same thing in France. If he had none, they had none. If they had any, he had as much, for it is impossible to discover superiority of right in any family, by virtue of which hereditary government could begin. The Capets, the Guelphs, the Robespierres, the

Marats, are all on the same standing as to the question of right. It belongs exclusively to none.

It is one step towards liberty, to perceive that hereditary government could not begin as an exclusive right in any family. The next point will be, whether, having once began, it could grow into a right by the influence of time?

This would be supposing an absurdity; for either it is putting time in the place of principle, or making it superior to principle; whereas time has no more connection with, or influence upon principle, than principle has upon time. The wrong which began a thousand years ago, is as much a wrong, as if it began to day; and the right which originates to day, is as much a right as if it had the sanction of a thousand years. Time with respect to principles is an eternal NOW: it has no operation upon them: it changes nothing of their nature and qualities. But what have we to do with a thousand years. Our life time is but a short portion of that period, and if we find the wrong in existence as soon as we begin to live, that is the point of time at which it begins to us; and our right to resist it, is the same as if it had never existed before.

As hereditary government could not begin as a natural right in any family, nor derive after its commencement any right from time, we have only to examine whether there exist in a nation a right to set it up and establish it by what is called law, as has been done in England. I answer NO; and that any law or any constitution made for that purpose is an act of treason against the rights of every minor in the nation, at the time it is made, and against the rights of all succeeding generations. I shall speak upon each of those cases. First, of the minor at the time such law is made. Secondly, of the generations that are to follow.

A nation in a collective sense, comprehends all the individuals of whatever age, from just born to just dying. Of these, one part will be minors, the other aged. The average of life is not exactly the same in every climate and country, but in general the minority in years are the majority in numbers, that is, the number of persons under twenty one years, is greater than the number of persons above that age. This difference in number is not necessary to the establishment of the principle I mean to lay down, but it serves to shew the justice of it more strongly. The principle would be equally good, if the majority in years were also the majority in numbers.

The rights of minors are as sacred as the rights of the aged. The difference is altogether in the different age of the two parties and nothing in the nature of the rights; the rights are the same rights; and are to be preserved inviolate for the inheritance of the minors when they shall come of age. During the minority of minors, their rights are under the sacred guardianship of the aged. The minor, cannot surrender them; the guardian cannot dispossess him; consequently, the aged part of a nation who are the lawmakers for the *time being,* and who, in the march of life, are but a few years a head of those who are yet minors, and to whom they must shortly give place, have not and cannot have the right to make a law to set up and establish hereditary government, or, to speak more distinctly, *an hereditary succession of governors;* because it is an attempt to deprive every minor in the nation, at the time such a law is made, of his inheritance of rights, when he shall come of age, and to subjugate him to a system of government to which, during his minority, he could neither consent nor object.

If a person, who is a minor at the time such a law is proposed, had happened to have been born a few years sooner, so as to be of the age of twenty one years at the time of proposing it, his right to have objected against it, to have exposed the injustice and tyrannical principles of it, and to have voted against it, will be admitted on all sides, If, therefore, the law operates to prevent his exercising the same rights after he comes of age as he would have had a right to exercise had he been of age at the time, it is, undeniably, a law to take away and annul the rights of every person in the nation who shall be a minor at the time of making such a law, and consequently the right to make it cannot exist.

I come now to speak of government by hereditary succession as it applies to succeeding generations; and to shew that in this case, as in the case of minors, there does not exist in a nation a right to set it up.

A nation, though continually existing, is continually in a state of renewal and succession. It is never stationary. Every day produces new births, carries minors forward to maturity, and old persons from the stage. In this ever running flood of generations there is no part superior in authority to another. Could we conceive an idea of superiority in any, at what point of time, or in what century of the world, are we to fix it? To what cause are we to ascribe it? By what evidence are we to prove it? By what criterion are we to know it? A single reflection will teach us that our ancestors, like ourselves, were but tenants for life in the great freehold of rights. The fee-absolute was not in them, it is not in us, it belongs to the whole family of man, thro' all ages. If we think otherwise than this, we think either as slaves or as tyrants. As slaves, if we think that any former generation had a right to bind us; as tyrants, if we think that we have authority to bind the generations that are to follow.

It may not be inapplicable to the subject, to endeavour to define what is to be understood by a generation in the sense the word is here used.

As a natural term its meaning is sufficiently clear. The father, the son, the grandson are so many distinct generations. But when we speak of a generation as describing the persons in whom legal authority resides, as distinct from another generation of the same description who are to succeed them, it comprehends all those who are above the age of twenty one years, at the time we count from; and a generation of this kind will continue in authority between fourteen and twenty one years, that is, until the number of minors, who shall have arrived at age, shall be greater than the number of persons remaining of the former stock.

For example, if France at this or any other moment, contain twenty four millions of souls, twelve millions will be males, and twelve females. Of the twelve millions of males, six millions will be of the age of twenty one years, and six will be under, and the authority to govern will reside in the first six. But every day will make some alteration, and in twenty one years every one of those minors who survive will have arrived at age, and the greater part of the former stock will be gone: the majority of persons then living, in whom the legal authority resides, will be composed of those who, twenty one years before, had no legal existence. Those will be fathers and grand fathers in their turn, and in the next twenty one years, (or less) another race of minors, arrived at age, will succeed them, and so on.

As this is ever the case, and as every generation is equal in rights to another, it consequently follows, that there cannot be a right in any to establish government by hereditary succession, because it would be supposing itself possessed of a right superior to the rest, namely, that of commanding by its own authority how the world shall be hereafter governed, and who shall govern it. Every age and generation is and must be (as a matter of right) as free to act for itself in all cases, as the age and generation that preceded it. The vanity and presumption of governing beyond the grave is the most ridiculous and insolent of all tyrannies. Man has no property in man, neither has one generation a property in the generations that are to follow.

In the first part of *Rights of Man* I have spoken of government by hereditary succession; and I will here close the subject with an extract from that work, which states it under the two following heads.

"First, of the right of any family to establish itself with hereditary power.

"Secondly, of the right of a nation to establish a particular family.

"With respect to the first of those heads, that of a family establishing itself with hereditary powers on its own authority independent of the nation, all men will concur in calling it despotism, and it would be trespassing on their understanding to attempt to prove it.

"But the second head, that of a nation, that is, of a generation for the time being, establishing a particular family with hereditary powers, it does not present itself as despotism on the first reflection; but if men will permit a second reflection to take place, and carry that reflection forward, even but one remove out of their own persons to that of their offspring, they will then see, that hereditary succession becomes the same despotism to others, which the first persons reprobated for themselves. It operates to preclude the consent of the succeeding generation, and the preclusion of consent is despotism.

"In order to see this matter more clearly, let us consider the generation which undertakes to establish a family with hereditary powers, separately from the generations which are to follow.

"The generation which first selects a person and puts him at the head of its government, either with the title of king, or any other nominal distinction, acts its own choice, as a free agent for itself, be that choice wise or foolish. The person so set up, is *not hereditary*, but selected and appointed; and the generation which sets him up does not live under an hereditary government, but under a government of its own choice. Were the person so set up, and the generation who sets him up, to live for ever, it never could become hereditary succession, and of consequence, hereditary succession can only follow on the death of the first parties.

"As therefore hereditary succession is out of the question, with respect to the first generation, we have next to consider the character in which that generation acts towards the commencing generation and to all succeeding ones.

"It assumes a character to which it has neither right nor title; for it changes itself from a legislator to a testator, and affects to make a will and testament, which is to have operation, after the demise of the makers, to bequeath the government; and it not only attempts to bequeath, but to establish on the succeeding generation a new and different form of government under which itself lived. Itself, as already observed, lived not under an hereditary government, but under a government of its own choice; and it now attempts, by virtue of a will and testament, which it has not authority to make, to take from the commencing generation, and from all future ones, the right and free agency by which itself acted.

"In whatever light hereditary succession, as growing out of the will and testament of some former generation, presents itself, it is both criminal and absurd. A cannot make a will to take from B the property of B and give it to C; yet this is the manner in which, what is called hereditary succession by law, operates. A certain generation makes a will, under the form of a law to take away the rights of the commencing generation, and of all future generations, and convey those rights to a third person who afterwards comes forward and assumes the government in consequence of that illicit conveyance."

The history of the English parliament furnishes an example of this kind; and which merits to be recorded as being the greatest instance of legislative ignorance and want of principle that is to be found in the history of any country. The case is as follows:

The English parliament of 1688, imported a man and his wife from Holland, *William* and *Mary*, and made them king and queen of England. Having done this, the said parliament made a law to convey the government of the country to the heirs of William and Mary in the following words, "We, the lords-spiritual and temporal, and commons, do in the name of the people of England, most humbly and faithfully submit *ourselves, our heirs, and posterities,* to William and Mary, *their heirs and posterities* for ever." And in a subsequent law, as quoted by Edmund Burke, the said parliament, in the name of the people of England then living, *binds the said people, their heirs and posterities, to William and Mary, their heirs and posterities, to the end of time.*

It is not sufficient that we laugh at the ignorance of such law makers; it is necessary that we reprobate their want of principle. The constituent assembly of France 1789 fell into the same vice as the parliament of England had done, and assumed to establish an hereditary succession in the family of the Capets, as an act of the constitution of that year. That every nation, *for the time being,* has a right to govern itself as it pleases, must always be admitted; but government by hereditary succession, is government for another race of people and not for itself; and as those on whom it is to operate, are not yet in existence or are minors, so neither is the right in existence to set it up for them, and to assume such a right is treason against the right of posterity.

I here close the arguments on the first head, that of government by hereditary succession; and proceed to the second, that of government by election and representation; or as it may be concisely expressed, *representative government* in contra-distinction to *hereditary government.*

Reasoning by exclusion, if *hereditary government* has not a right to exist, and that it has not is proveable, *representative government* is admitted of course.

In contemplating government by election and representation, we amuse not ourselves in enquiring when or how, or by what right it began. Its origin is ever in view. Man is himself the origin and the evidence of the right. It appertains to him in right of his existence, and his person is the title deed.

The true and only true basis of representative government is equality of Rights. Every man has a right to one vote and no more in the choice of representatives. The rich have no more right to exclude the poor from the right of voting, or of electing and being elected, than the poor have to exclude the rich; and wherever it is attempted, or proposed, on either side, it is a question of force and not of right. Who is he that would exclude another? That other has the same right to exclude him.

That which is now called aristocracy implies an inequality of rights, but who are the persons that have a right to establish this inequality? Will the rich exclude themselves? No. Will the poor exclude themselves! No. By what right then can any be excluded? It would be a question, if any man or class of men have a right to exclude themselves; but, be this as it may, they cannot have the right to exclude another. The poor will not delegate such a right to the rich, nor the rich to the poor, and to assume it, is not only to assume arbitrary power, but to assume a right to commit robbery. Personal rights, of which the right of voting for representatives is one, are a species of property of the most sacred kind: and he that would employ his pecuniary property, or presume upon the influence it gives him, to dispossess or rob another of his property of rights, uses that pecuniary property, as he would use fire arms, and merits to have it taken from him.

Inequality of rights is created by a combination in one part of the community to exclude another part from its rights. Whenever it be made an article of a constitution, or a law, that the right of voting, or of electing and being elected, shall appertain exclusively to persons possessing a certain quantity of property, be it little or much, it is a combination of the persons possessing that quantity, to exclude those who do not possess the same quantity. It is investing themselves with powers as a self-created part of society, to the exclusion of the rest.

It is always to be taken for granted, that those who oppose an equality of rights, never mean the exclusion should take place on themselves; and in this view of the case, pardoning the vanity of the thing, aristocracy is a subject of laughter. This self-soothing vanity is encouraged by another idea not less selfish, which is, that the opposers conceive they are playing a safe game, in which there is a chance to gain and none to lose; that at any rate the doctrine of equality includes *them,* and that if they cannot get more rights than those whom they oppose and would exclude, they shall not have less. This opinion has already been fatal to thousands who, not contented with *equal rights,* have sought more till they lost all, and experienced in themselves the degrading *inequality* they endeavoured to fix upon others.

In any view of the case it is dangerous and impolitic, sometimes ridiculous, and always unjust, to make property the criterion of the right of voting. If the sum, or value of the property upon which the right is to take place be considerable, it will exclude a majority of the people, and unite them in a common interest against the government and against those who support it, and as the power is always with the majority, they can overturn such a government and its supporters whenever they please.

If, in order to avoid this danger, a small quantity of property be fixed, as the criterion of the right, it exhibits liberty in disgrace, by putting it in competition with accident and insignificance. When a brood-mare shall fortunately produce a foal or a mule, that by being worth the sum in question, shall convey to its owner the right of voting, or by its death take it from him, in whom does the origin of such a right exist? Is it in the man, or in the mule? When we consider how many ways property may be acquired without merit, and lost without a crime, we ought to spurn the idea of making it a criterion of rights.

But the offensive part of the case is, that this exclusion from the right of voting implies a stigma on the moral character of the persons excluded; and this is what no part of the community has a right to pronounce upon another part. No external circumstance can justify it; wealth is no proof of moral character; nor poverty of the want of it. On the contrary, wealth is often the presumptive evidence of dishonesty; and poverty the negative evidence of innocence. If therefore property, whether little or much, be made a criterion, the means by which that property has been acquired, ought to be made a criterion also.

The only ground upon which exclusion from the right of voting is consistent with justice, would be to inflict it as a punishment for a certain time upon those who should propose to take away that right from others. The right of voting for representatives is the primary right by which other rights are protected. To take away this right is to reduce a man to a state of slavery, for slavery consists in being subject to the will of another, and he that has not a vote in the election of representatives, is in this case. The proposal therefore to disfranchise any class of men is as criminal as the proposal to take away property. When we speak of right, we ought always to unite with it the idea of duties: right becomes duties by reciprocity. The right which I enjoy becomes my duty to guarantee it to another, and he to me; and those who violate the duty justly incur a forfeiture of the right.

In a political view of the case, the strength and permanent security of government is in proportion to the number of people interested in supporting it. The true policy therefore is to interest the whole by an equality of rights, for the danger arises from exclusions. It is possible to exclude men from the right of voting, but it is impossible to exclude them from the right of rebelling against that exclusion; and when all other rights are taken away, the right of rebellion is made perfect.

While men could be persuaded they had no rights, or that rights appertained only to a certain class of men, or that government was a thing existing in right of itself, it was not difficult to govern them authoritatively. The ignorance in which they were held, and the superstition in which they were instructed, furnished the means of doing it; but when the ignorance is gone, and the superstition with it; when they perceive the imposition that has been acted upon them; when they reflect that the cultivator and the manufacturer are the primary means of all the wealth that exists in the world, beyond what nature spontaneously produces; when they begin to feel their consequence by their usefulness, and their right as members of society, it is then no longer possible to govern them as before. The fraud once detected cannot be re-acted. To attempt it is to provoke derision, or invite destruction.

That property w[i]ll ever be unequal is certain. Industry, superiority of talents, dexterity of management, extreme frugality, fortunate opportunities, or the opposite, or the mean of those things, will ever produce that effect without having recourse to the harsh ill sounding names of avarice, and oppression; and beside this, there are some men who, though they do not despise wealth, will not stoop to the drudgery or the means of acquiring it, nor will be troubled with the care of it, beyond their wants or their independence; whilst in others, there is an avidity to obtain it by every means not punishable; it makes the sole business of their lives, and they follow it as a religion. All that is required with respect to property is to obtain it honestly, and not employ it criminally; but it is always criminally employed, when it is made a criterion for exclusive rights.

In institutions that are purely pecuniary, such as that of a bank or a commercial company, the rights of the members composing that company are wholly created by the property they invest therein; and no other rights are represented in the government of that company, than what arise out of that property; neither has that government cognizance of *any thing but property*.

But the case is totally different with respect to the institution of civil government, organized on the system of representation. Such a government has cognizance of *every thing* and of *every man* as a member of the national society, whether he has property or not; and therefore the principle requires that *every man* and *every kind of right* be represented, of which the right to acquire and to hold property is but one, and that not of the most essential kind. The protection of a man's person is more sacred than the protection of property; and besides this, the faculty of performing any kind of work or service by which he acquires a livelihood, or maintains his family, is of the nature of property. It is property to him; he has acquired it; and it is as much the object of his protection, as exterior property, possessed without that faculty, can be the object of protection to another person.

I have always believed that the best security for property, be it much or little, is to remove from every part of the community, as far as can possibly be done, every cause of complaint, and every motive to violence; and this can only be done by an equality of rights. When rights are secure, property is secure in consequence. But when property is made a pretence for unequal or exclusive rights, it weakens the right to hold the property, and provokes indignation and tumult; for it is unnatural to believe that property can be secure under the guarantee of a society injured in its rights by the influence of that property.

Next to the injustice and ill-policy of making property a pretence for exclusive rights, is the unaccountable absurdity of giving to mere *sound* the idea of property, and annexing to it certain rights; for what else is a *title* but sound. Nature is often giving to the world some extraordinary men who arrive at fame by merit and universal consent, such as Aristotle, Socrates, Plato, &c. These were truly great or noble. But when government sets up a manufactory of nobles, it is as absurd, as if she undertook to manufacture wise men. Her nobles are all counterfeits.

This wax-work order has assumed the name of aristocracy; and the disgrace of it would be lessened if it could be considered only as childish imbecility. We pardon foppery because of its insignificance, and on the same ground we might pardon the foppery of Titles. But the origin of aristocracy was worse than foppery. It was robbery. The first aristocrats in all countries were brigands. Those of latter times, sycophants.

It is very well known that in England, (and the same will be found in other countries) the great landed estates now held in descent were plundered from the quiet inhabitants at the conquest. The possibility did not exist of acquiring such estates honestly. If it be asked how they could have been acquired, no answer but that of robbery can be given. That they were not acquired by trade, by commerce, by manufactures, by agriculture, or by any reputable employment is certain. How then were they acquired? Blush aristocracy to hear your origin, for your progenitors were Thieves. They were the Robespierres and the Jacobins of that day. When they had committed the robbery, they endeavoured to lose the disgrace of it, by sinking their real names under fictitious ones, which they called Titles. It is ever the practice of Felons to act in this manner. They never pass by their real names.

As property honestly obtained, is best secured by an equality of rights, so ill-gotten property depends for protection on a monopoly of rights. He who has robbed another of his property will next endeavour to disarm him of his rights, to secure that property; for when the robber becomes the legislator, he believes himself secure. That part of the government of England that is called the house of lords, was originally composed of persons who had committed the robberies of which I have been speaking. It was an association for the protection of the property they had stolen.

But besides the criminality of the origin of aristocracy, it has an injurious effect on the moral and physical character of man. Like slavery it debilitates the human faculties; for as the mind bowed down by slavery loses in silence its elastic powers, so, in the contrary extreme, when it is buoyed up by folly it becomes incapable of exerting them, and dwindles into imbecility. It is impossible that a mind employed upon ribbands and titles can ever be great. The childishness of the objects consumes the man.

It is at all times necessary, and more particularly so, during the progress of a revolution, and until right ideas confirm themselves by habit, that we frequently refresh our patriotism by reference to first principles. It is by tracing things to their origin that we learn to understand them; and it is by keeping that line and that origin always in view, that we never forget them.

An enquiry into the origin of Rights will demonstrate to us that *rights* are not *gifts* from one man to another, nor from one class of men to another; for who is he who could be the first giver, or by what principle, or on what authority, could he possess the right of giving? A declaration of rights is not a creation of them, nor a donation of them. It is a manifest of the principle by which they exist, followed by a detail of what the rights are; for every civil right has a natural right for its foundation, and it includes the principle of a reciprocal guarantee of those rights from man to man. As therefore it is impossible to discover any origin of rights otherwise than in the origin of man, it consequently follows, that rights appertain to man in right of his existence only, and must therefore be equal to every man. The principle of an *equality of rights* is clear and simple. Every man can understand it, and it is by understanding his rights that he learns his duties; for where the rights of men are equal, every man must finally see the necessity of protecting the rights of others as the most effectual security for his own. But if in the formation of a constitution, we depart from the principle of equal rights, or attempt any modification of it, we plunge into a labyrinth of difficulties from which there is no way out, but by retreating. Where are we to stop? Or by what principle are we to find out the point to stop at, that shall discriminate between men of the same country, part of whom shall be free, and the rest not? If property is to be made the criterion, it is a total departure from every moral principle of liberty, because it is attaching rights to mere matter, and making man the agent of that matter. It is moreover holding up property as an apple of discord, and not only exciting but justifying war against it; for I maintain the principle, that when property is used as an instrument to take away the rights of those who may happen not to possess property, it is used to an unlawful purpose, as fire-arms would be in a similar case.

In a state of nature stands[1] are equal in rights, but they are not equal in power; the weak cannot protect himself against the strong. This being the case, the institution of civil society is for the purpose of making an equalization of powers that shall be parallel to, and a guarantee of the equality of rights. The laws of a country when properly constructed apply to this purpose. Every man takes the arm of the law for his protection as more effectual than his own; and therefore every man has an equal right in the formation of the government and of the laws by which he is to be governed and judged. In extensive countries and societies, such as America and France, this right, in the individual, can only be exercised by delegation, that is, by election and representation; and hence it is that the institution of representative government arises.

Hitherto I have confined myself to matters of principle only. First, that hereditary government has not a right to exist; that it cannot be established on any principle of right; and that it is a violation of all principle. Secondly, that government by election and representation has its origin in the natural and eternal rights of man; for whether a man be his own law-giver, as he would be in a state of nature; or whether he exercises his portion of legislative sovereignty in his own person, as might be the case in small democra[c]ies where all could assemble for the formation of the laws by which they were to be governed; or whether he exercises it in the choice of persons to represent him in a national assembly of representatives, the origin of the right is the same in all cases. The first, as is before observed, is defective in power; the second, is practicable only in democracies of

---

1. [Editors' note:] In later editions, this word was changed to "all men."

small extent; the third is the greatest scale upon which human government can be instituted.

Next to matters of *principle,* are matters of *opinion,* and it is necessary to distinguish between the two. Whether the rights of men shall be equal is not a matter of opinion but of right, and consequently of principle; for men do not hold their rights as grants from each other, but each one in right of himself. Society is the guardian but not the giver. And as in extensive societies, such as America and France, the right of the individual, in matters of government, cannot be exercised but by election and representation; it consequently follows, that the only system of government, consistent with principle, where simple democracy is impracticable, is the representative system. But as to the organical part, or the manner in which the several parts of government shall be arranged and composed, it is altogether *matter of opinion.* It is necessary that all the parts be conformable with the *principle of equal rights;* and so long as this principle be religiously adhered to, no very material error can take place, neither can any error continue long, in that part that falls within the province of opinion.

In all matters of opinion, the social compact, or the principle by which society is held together, requires that the majority of opinions becomes the rule for the whole, and that the minority yields practical obedience thereto. This is perfectly conformable to the principle of equal rights. For, in the first place, every man has a *right to give an opinion,* but no man has a right that his opinion should *govern the rest.* In the second place, it is not supposed to be known before hand on which side of any question, whether for or against, any man's opinion will fall. He may happen to be in a majority upon some questions, and in a minority upon others; and by the same rule that he expects obedience in the one case, he must yield it in the other.——All the disorders that have arisen in France during the progress of the revolution have had their origin, not in the *principle of equal rights,* but in the violation of that principle. The principle of equal rights has been repeatedly violated, and that not by the majority but by the minority, and *that minority has been composed of men possessing property as well as of men without property; property therefore, even upon the experience already had, is no more a criterion of character than it is of rights.* It will sometimes happen that the minority are right, and the majority are wrong, but as soon as experience proves this to be the case, the minority will increase to a majority, and the error will reform itself by the tranquil operation of freedom of opinion and equality of rights. Nothing therefore can justify an insurrection, neither can it ever be necessary, where rights are equal and opinions free.

Taking then the principle of equal rights as the foundation of the revolution, and consequently of the constitution, the organical part, or the manner in which the several parts of the government shall be arranged in the constitution, will, as is already said, fall within the province of opinion.

Various methods will present themselves upon a question of this kind, and tho' experience is yet wanting to determine which is the best, it has, I think, sufficiently decided which is the worst. That is the worst, which in its deliberations and decisions is subject to the precipitancy and passion of an individual; and when the whole legislature is crouded into one body, it is an individual in mass. In all cases of deliberation it is necessary to have a corps of reserve, and it would be better to divide the representation by lot into two parts, and let them revise and correct each other, than that the whole should sit together and debate at once.

Representative government is not necessarily confined to any one particular form. The principle is the same in all the forms under which it can be arranged. The equal rights of the people is the root from which the whole springs, and the branches may be arranged as present opinion or future experience shall best direct. As to that *hospital of incurables* (as Chesterfield calls it) the British house of peers, it is an excressence growing out of corruption; and there is no more affinity or resemblance between any of the branches of a legislative body originating from the rights of the people, and the aforesaid house of peers, than between a regular member of the human body and an ulcerated wen.

As to that part of government that is called the *executive,* it is necessary in the first place to fix a precise meaning to the word.

There are but two divisions into which power can be arranged. First, that of willing or decreeing the laws; secondly, that of executing or putting them in practice. The former, corresponds to the intellectual faculties of the human mind, which reasons and determines what shall be done; the second, to the mechanical powers of the human body that puts that determination into practice. If the former decides, and the latter does not perform, it is a state of imbecility; and if the latter acts without the predetermination of the former, it is a state of lunacy. The executive department therefore is official, and is subordinate to the legislative, as the body is to the mind in a state of health; for, it is impossible to conceive the idea of two sovereignties, a sovereignty to *will,* and a sovereignty to *act.* The executive is not invested with the power of deliberating whether it shall act or not; it has no discretionary authority in the case; for it can *act no other thing* tha[n] what the laws decree, and it is *obliged* to act conformably thereto; and in this view of the case, the executive is made up of all the official departments that execute the laws, of which, that which is called the judiciary is the chief.

But mankind have conceived an idea that *some kind of authority* is necessary to *superintend* the execution of the laws, and to see that they are faithfully performed; and it is by confounding this superintending authority with the official execution that we get embarrassed about the term *executive power.* –All the parts in the governments of the united states of America that are called THE EXECUTIVE, are no other than authorities to superintend the execution of the laws; and they are so far independent of the legislative, that they know the legislative only thro' the laws, and cannot be controuled or directed by it, through any other medium.

In what manner this superintending authority shall be appointed or composed, is a matter that falls within the province of opinion. Some may prefer one method and some another; and in all cases, where opinion only and not principle is concerned, the majority of opinions forms the rule for all. There are however some things deducible from reason, and evidenced by experience, that serve to guide our decision upon the case. The one is, never to invest any individual with extraordinary power; for besides his being tempted to misuse it, it will excite contention and commotion in the nation for the office. Secondly, never to invest power long in the hands of any number of individuals. The inconveniences that may be supposed to accompany frequent changes, are less to be feared than the danger that arises from long continuance.

I shall conclude this discourse with offering some observations on the means of *preserving liberty;* for it is not only necessary that we establish it, but that we preserve it.

It is, in the first place, necessary that we distinguish between the means made use of to overthrow despotism, in order to prepare the way for the establishment of liberty, and the means to be used after the despotism is overthrown.

The means made use of in the first case are justified by necessity. Those means are in general insurrections; for whilst the established government of despotism continues in any country it is scarcely possible that any other means can be used. It is also certain that in the commencement of a revolution, the revolutionary party permit to themselves a *discretionary exercise of power* regulated more by circumstances than by principle, which were the practice to continue, liberty would never be established, or if established would soon be overthrown. It is never to be expected in a revolution that every man is to change his opinion at the same moment. There never yet was any truth or any principle so irresistibly obvious, that all men believed it at once. Time and reason must co-operate with each other to the final establishment of any principle; and therefore those who may happen to be first convinced have not a right to persecute others, on whom conviction operates more slowly. The moral principle of revolutions is to instruct; not to destroy.

Had a constitution been established two years ago (as ought to have been done) the violences that have since desolated France, and injured the character of the revolution, would, in my opinion, have been prevented. The nation would then have had a bond of union, and every individual would have known the line of conduct he was to follow. But instead of this, a revolutionary government, a thing without either principle or authority, was substituted in its place; virtue and crime depended upon accident; and that which was patriotism one day became treason the next. All these things have followed from the want of a constitution; for it is the nature and intention of a constitution to *prevent governing by party,* by establishing a common principle that shall limit and controul the power and impulse of party, and that says to all parties, THUS FAR SHALT THOU GO AND NO FURTHER. But in the absence of a constitution men look entirely to party; and instead of principle governing party, party governs principle.

An avidity to punish is always dangerous to liberty. It leads men to stretch, to misinterpret, and to misapply even the best of laws. He that would make his own liberty secure, must guard even his enemy from oppression; for if he violates this duty, he establishes a precedent that will reach to himself.

– THOMAS PAINE.

LETTER

TO

GEORGE WASHINGTON,

PRESIDENT OF THE UNITED STATES OF AMERICA.

ON

AFFAIRS PUBLIC AND PRIVATE.

BY THOMAS PAINE,
AUTHOR OF THE WORKS ENTITLED, COMMON SENSE, RIGHTS OF MAN,
AGE OF REASON, &c.

Thomas Paine,
to
George Washington,

Paris, July 30th, 1796,

AS censure is but awkwardly softened by apology, I shall offer you no apology for this letter. The eventful crisis to which your double politics have conducted the affairs of your country requires an investigation un-cramped by ceremony.

There was a time when the fame of America, moral and political, stood fair and high in the world. The lustre of her revolution extended itself to every individual; and to be a citizen of America gave a title to respect in Europe. Neither meanness nor ingratitude had then mingled itself into the

Letter to George Washington, President of the United States of America. On Affairs Public and Private (Philadelphia: Benjamin Franklin Bache, 1796).

composition of her character. Her resistance to the attempted tyranny of England left her unsuspected of the one, and her open acknowledgment of the aid she received from France precluded all suspicion of the other. The Washington of politics had not then appeared.

At the time I left America (April 1787) the continental convention that formed the federal constitution was on the point of meeting. Since that time new schemes of politics and new distinctions of parties, have arisen. The term *Antifederalist* has been applied to all those who combated the defects of that constitution, or opposed the measures of your administration. It was only to the absolute necessity of establishing some federal authority, extending equally over all the States, that an instrument, so inconsistent as the present federal constitution is, obtained a suffrage. I would have voted for it myself, had I been in America, or even for a worse rather than have had none; provided it contained the means of remedying its defects by the same appeal to the people by which it was to be established. It is always better policy to leave removeable errors to expose themselves, than to hazard too much in contending against them theoretically.

I have introduced those observations, not only to mark the general difference between antifederalist and anti-constitutionalist, but to preclude the effect and even the application, of the former of those terms to myself. I declare myself opposed to several matters in the constitution, particularly to the manner in which, what is called the Executive, is formed, and to the long duration of the Senate; and if I live to return to America I will use all my endeavours to have them altered.[1] I also declare myself opposed to almost the whole of your administration; for I know it to have been deceitful, if not even perfidious, as I shall shew in the course of this letter. But as to the point of consolidating the States into a federal government, it so happens, that the proposition for that purpose came originally from myself. I proposed it in a letter to Chancellor Livingston in the spring of the year 1782, whilst that gentleman was minister for foreign affairs. The five per cent. duty recommended by Congress had then fallen through, having been adopted by some of the States, altered by others, rejected by Rhode Island, and repealed by Virginia after it had been consented to. The proposal in the letter I allude to was to get over the whole difficulty at once, by annexing a continental legislative body to Congress; for, in order to have any law of

---

1. I have always been opposed to the mode of refining Government up to an individual, or what is called a single Executive. Such a man will always be the chief of a party. A plurality is far better: It combines the mass of a nation better together: And besides this, it is necessary to the manly mind of a republic, that it loses the debasing idea of obeying an individual.

the Union uniform, the case could only be, that either Congress, as it then stood, must frame the law, and the States severally adopt it without alteration, or, the States must elect a Continental Legislature for the purpose. Chancellor Livingston, Robert Morris, Governeur Morris and myself had a meeting at the house of Robert Morris on the subject of that letter. There was no diversity of opinion on the proposition for a Continental Legislature. The only difficulty was on the manner of bringing the proposition forward. For my own part, as I considered it as a remedy in reserve, that could be applied at any time, *when the States saw themselves wrong enough to be put right* (which did not appear to me to be the case at that time) I did not see the propriety of urging it precipitately, and declined being the publisher of it myself. After this account of a fact, the leaders of your party will scarcely have the hardiness to apply to me the term of antifederalist. But I can go to a date and to a fact beyond this; for the proposition for electing a Continental Convention to form the Continental Government is one of the subjects treated of in the pamphlet *Common Sense.*

Having thus cleared away a little of the rubbish that might otherwise have lain in my way, I return to the point of time at which the present Federal Constitution and your administration began. It was very well said by an anonymous writer in Philadelphia, about a year before that period, that *"thirteen staves and ne'er a hoop will not make a barrel,"* and as any kind of hooping the barrel, however defectively executed, would be better than none, it was scarcely possible but that considerable advantages must arise from the federal hooping of the States. It was with pleasure that every sincere friend to America beheld, as the natural effect of union, her rising prosperity; and it was with grief they saw that prosperity mixed, even in the blossom, with the germ of corruption. Monopolies of every kind marked your administration almost in the moment of its commencement. The lands obtained by the revolution were lavished upon partizans; the interest of the disbanded soldier was sold to the speculator; injustice was acted under the pretence of faith; and the chief of the army became the patron of the fraud. From such a beginning what could be expected, but what has happened? A mean and servile submission to the insults of one nation, treachery and ingratitude to another.

Some vices make their approach with such a splendid appearance, that we scarcely know to what class of moral distinctions they belong. They are rather virtues corrupted, than vices originally. But meanness and ingratitude have nothing equivocal in their character. There is not a trait in them that renders them doubtful. They are so originally vice, that they are generated in the dung of other vices, and crawl into existence with the filth upon their back. The fugitives have found protection in you, and the levee-room is their place of rendezvous.

As the Federal Constitution is a copy, not quite so base as the original, of the form of the British government, an imitation of its vices was naturally to be expected. So intimate is the connection between *form* and *practice,* that to adopt the one is to invite the other. Imitation is naturally progressive, and is rapidly so in matters that are vicious.

Soon after the Federal Constitution arrived in England, I received a letter from a female literary correspondent (a native of New York) very well mixed with friendship, sentiment and politics. In my answer to that letter I permitted myself to ramble into the wilderness of imagination, and to anticipate what might hereafter be the condition of America. I had no idea that the picture I then drew was realizing so fast, and still less that, Mr. Washington was hurrying it on. As the extract I allude to is congenial with the subject I am upon, I here transcribe it.

"You touch me on a very tender point when you say, *that my friends on your side the water can not be reconciled to the idea of my abandoning America, even for my native England.* They are right. I had rather see my horse Button eating the grass of Bordentown or Morrisenia, than see all the pomp and shew of Europe.

"A thousand years hence, for I must indulge a few thoughts, perhaps in less, America may be what England now is. The innocence of her character, that won the hearts of all nations in her favour, may sound like a romance, and her inimitable virtue as if it had never been. The ruins of that liberty, which thousands bled to obtain, may just furnish materials for a village tale, or extort a sigh from rustic sensibility; whilst the fashionable of that day, enveloped in dissipation, shall deride the principle and deny the fact.

"When we contemplate the fall of empires & the extinction of the nations of the ancient world, we see but little more to excite our regret than the mouldering ruins of pompous palaces, magnificent monuments, lofty pyramids, and walls and towers of the most costly workmanship: But when the empire of America shall fall, the subject for contemplative sorrow will be infinitely greater than crumbling brass or marble can inspire. It will not then be said, here stood a temple of vast antiquity, here rose a babel of invisible height, or there a palace of sumptuous extravagance; but here, ah painful thought! the noblest work of human wisdom, the grandest scene of human glory, the fair cause of freedom rose and fell. Read this, and then ask, if I forget America?"

Impressed, as I was, with apprehensions of this kind, I had America constantly in mind in all the publications I afterwards made. The first, and still more, the second part of Rights of Man bear evident marks of this watchfulness; and the Dissertation on First Principles of Government goes more directly to the point than either of the former. I now pass on to other subjects.

It will be supposed by those into whose hands this letter may fall, that I have some personal resentment against you; I will therefore settle this point before I proceed farther.

If I have any resentment, you must acknowledge that I have not been hasty in declaring it; neither would it be now declared (for what are private resentments to the public) if the cause of it did not unite itself as well with your public as your private character, and with the motives of your political conduct.

The part I acted in the American revolution is well known; I shall not here repeat it. I know also that had it not been for the aid received from France in men, money and ships, that your cold and unmilitary conduct (as I shall shew in the course of this letter) would, in all probability, have lost America; at least she would not have been the independent nation she now is. You slept away your time in the field till the finances of the country were completely exhausted, and you have but little share in the glory of the final event. It is time, sir, to speak the undisguised language of historical truth.

Elevated to the chair of the Presidency you assumed the merit of every thing to yourself, and the natural ingratitude of your constitution began to appear. You commenced your Presidential career by encouraging and swallowing the grossest adulation, and you travelled America from one end-to the other, to put yourself in the way of receiving it. You have as many addresses in your chest as James the II. As to what were your views, for if you are not great enough to have ambition you are little enough to have vanity, they cannot be directly inferred from expressions of your own; but the partizans of your politics have divulged the secret.

John Adams has said (and John, it is known, was always a speller after places and offices, and never thought his little services were highly enough paid) John has said, that as Mr. Washington had no child, that the Presidency should be made hereditary in the family of Lund Washington. John might then have counted upon some sine-cure for himself and a provision for his descendants. He did not go so far as to say also, that the Vice Presidency should be hereditary in the family of John Adams. He prudently left that to stand upon the ground, that one good turn deserves another.[2]

---

2. Two persons to whom John Adams said this, told me of it. The secretary of Mr. Jay was present when it was told to me.

John Adams is one of those men who never contemplated the origin of government, or comprehended any thing of first principles. If he had, he must have seen that the right to set up and establish hereditary government never did, and never can, exist in any generation, at any time whatever; that it is of the nature of treason; because it is an attempt to take away the rights of all the minors living at that time, and of all succeeding generations. It is of a degree beyond common treason. It is a sin against nature. The equal right of generations is a right fixed in the nature of things. It belongs to the son when of age, as it belonged to the father before him. John Adams would himself deny the right that any former deceased generation could have to decree authoritatively a succession of Governors over him, or over his children; and yet he assumes the pretended right, treasonable as it is, of acting it himself. His ignorance is his best excuse.

John Jay has said (and this John was always the sycophant of every thing in power, from Mr. Girard in America to Grenville in England) John Jay has said, that the Senate should have been appointed for life. He would then have been sure of never wanting a lucrative appointment for himself, nor have had any fears about impeachments. These are the disguised traitors that call themselves federalists.[3]

Could I have known to what degree of corruption & perfidy the administrative part of the government in America had descended, I could have been at no loss to have understood the reservedness of Mr. Washington towards me, during my imprisonment in the Luxembourg. There are cases in which silence is a loud language.

I will here explain the cause of my imprisonment, and return to Mr. Washington afterwards.

In the course of that rage, terror and suspicion, which the brutal letter of the Duke of Brunswick first started into existence in France, it happened, that almost every man who was opposed to violence, or who was not violent himself, became suspected. I had constantly been opposed to every thing which was of the nature, or of the appearance, of violence; but as I had always done it in a manner that shewed it to be a principle founded in my heart, and not a political manœuvre, it precluded the pretence of accusing me. I was reached, however, under another pretence.

A decree was passed to imprison all persons born in England; but as I was a member of the Convention, and had been complimented with the

---

3. If Mr. Jay desires to know on what authority I say this, I will give that authority publicly when he chuses to call for it.

honorary stile of Citizen of France, as Mr. Washington and some other Americans had been, this decree fell short of reaching me. A motion was afterwards made and carried, supported chiefly by Bourdon de l'Oise, for expelling foreigners from the Convention. My expulsion being thus effected, the two committees of Public Safety and of General Surety, of which Robespierre was the dictator, put me in arrestation under the former decree for imprisoning persons born in England. Having thus shewn under what pretence the imprisonment was effected, I come to speak of such parts of the case as apply between me and Mr. Washington, either as President or as an individual.

I have always considered that a foreigner, such as I was in fact with respect to France, might be a member of a Convention for forming a constitution, without affecting his right of citizenship in the country to which he belongs, but not a member of a government after a constitution is formed; and I have uniformly acted upon this distinction. To be a member of a government requires that a person be in allegiance to that government and to the country locally. But a constitution being a thing of principle and not of action, and which, after it be formed, is to be referred to the people for their approbation or rejection, does not require allegiance in the persons forming and proposing it; and besides this, it is only to the thing after it be formed and established, and to the country after its governmental character is fixed by the adoption of a constitution, that allegiance can be given. No oath of allegiance or of citizenship was required of the members who composed the Convention, there was nothing existing in form to swear allegiance to. If any such condition had been required I could not, as Citizen of America in fact, though Citizen of France by compliment, have accepted a seat in the Convention.

As my citizenship in America was not altered or diminished, by any thing I had done in Europe (on the contrary it ought to have been considered as strengthened, for it was the American principle of government that I was endeavouring to spread in Europe) and as it is the duty of every government to charge itself with the care of any of its citizens who may happen to fall under an arbitrary persecution abroad, and is also one of the reasons for which Ambassadors or Ministers are appointed, – it was the duty of the executive department in America to have made (at least) some enquiries about me, as soon as it heard of my imprisonment. But if this had not been the case, that government owed it to me on every ground and principle of honor and gratitude. Mr. Washington owed it to me on every score of private acquaintance, I will not now say, friendship; for it has for some time been known, by those who know him, that he has no friendships; that he is incapable of forming any; he can serve or desert a man or a cause with constitutional indifference; and it is this cold hermophrodite faculty that imposed itself upon the world, and was credited for a while by enemies as by friends, for prudence, moderation and impartiality.

Soon after that I was put in arrestation and imprisoned in the Luxembourg, the Americans who were then in Paris went in a body to the bar of the Convention to reclaim me. They were answered by the, then, President, Vadier, who has since absconded, that *I was born in England,* and it was signified to them by some of the Committee of Surety General, to whom they were referred (I have been told it was Billaud Varrennes) that their reclamation of me was only the act of individuals without any authority from the American government.

A few days after this, all communication from persons imprisoned to any person without the prison was cut off by an order of the Police. I neither saw, nor heard from, any body for six months; and the only hope that remained to me was, that a new minister would arrive from America to supercede Morris, and that he would be authorised to enquire into the cause of my imprisonment. But even this hope, in the state to which matters were daily arriving, was too remote to have any consolatory effect, and I contented myself with the thought, that I might be remembered when it would be too late. There is perhaps no condition from which a man conscious of his own uprightness cannot derive consolation; for it is in itself a consolation for him to find that he can bear that condition with calmness and fortitude.

From about the middle of March (1794) to the fall of Robespierre, 29th July, (9th of Thermidor) the state of things in the prison was a continued scene of horror. No man could count upon life for twenty hours. To such a pitch of rage and suspicion was Robespierre and his committee arrived, that it seemed as if they feared to leave a man to live. Scarcely a night passed but in which ten, twenty, thirty, forty, fifty or more were taken out of the prison, carried before a pretended tribunal in the morning, and guillotined before night. One hundred and sixty nine were taken out of the Luxembourg in one night in the month of July and one hundred and sixty of them guillotined. A list of two hundred more, according to the report in the prison, was preparing a few days before Robespierre fell. In this last list I have good reason to believe I was included. A memorandum, in the hand writing of Robespierre, was afterwards produced in the Convention, by the committee to whom the papers of Robespierre were referred, in these words:

"Dcmander que Thomas Paine soit
decreté d'accusation, pour l'interet de
l'Amerique autant que de la France."

Demand that Thomas Paine be
decreed of accusation, for the
interest of America as well as
of France.

I had then been imprisoned seven months, and the silence of the executive government of America, Mr. Washington, upon the case and upon
every thing respecting me, was explanation enough to Robespierre that he
might proceed to extremities.

A violent fever which had nearly terminated my existence, was, I believe, the circumstance that preserved it. I was not in a condition to be
removed, or to know of what was passing, or of what had passed for more
than a month. It makes a blank in my remembrance of life. The first thing I
was informed of was the fall of Robespierre.

About a week after this Mr. Monroe arrived to supercede Gouverneur
Morris, and as soon as I was able to write a note legible enough to be read,
I found a way to convey one to him, by means of the man who lighted the
lamps in the prison; and whose unabated friendship to me, from whom he
had never reccived any service, and with difficulty accepted any recompence, puts the character of Mr. Washington to shame.

In a few days I received a message from Mr. Monroe, conveyed to me in
a note from an intermediate person, with assurance of his friendship, and
expressing a desire that I would rest the case in his hands. After a fortnight
or more had passed and hearing nothing further, I wrote to a friend who
was then in Paris, a citizen of Philadelphia, requesting him to inform me
what was the true situation of things with respect to me. I was sure that
something was the matter. I began to have hard thoughts of Mr. Washington; but I was unwilling to encourage them.

In about ten days I received an answer to my letter in which the writer
says: "Mr. Monroe has told me that he has no orders (meaning from the
President, Mr. Washington) respecting you, but that he (Mr. Monroe) will
do every thing in his power to liberate you; but from what I learn from the
Americans lately arrived in Paris, you are not considered, either by the
American government or by the individuals, as an American citizen."

I was now at no loss to understand Mr. Washington and his new fangled
faction, and that their policy was silently to leave me to fall in France. They
were rushing as fast as they could venture, without awakening the jealousy
of America, into all the vices and corruptions of the British government;
and it was no more consistent with the policy of Mr. Washington, and those
who immediately surrounded him, than it was with that of Robespierre or

of Pitt, that I should survive. They have however, missed the mark and the reaction is upon themselves.

Upon the receipt of the letter just alluded to, I sent a memorial to Mr. Monroe which the reader will find in the appendix, and I received from him the following answer. It is dated the 18th of September, but did not come to hand till about the 10th of October. I was then falling into a relapse, the weather was becoming damp and cold, fuel was not to be had, and the abscess in my side, the consequence of these things, and of the want of air and exercise, was beginning to form and which has continued immoveable ever since. Here follows Mr. Monroe's letter.

–Paris, Sept. 18, 1794.

DEAR SIR,

I was favoured soon after my arrival here with several letters from you and more latterly with one in the character of memorial, upon the subject of your confinement; and should have answered them at the times they were respectively written had I not concluded you would have calculated with certainty upon the deep interest I take in your welfare and the pleasure with which I shall embrace every opportunity in my power to serve you. I should still pursue the same course, and for reasons which must obviously occur, if I did not find that you are disquieted with apprehensions upon interesting points, & which justice to you and our country equally forbid you should entertain. You mention that you have been informed you are not considered as an American citizen by the Americans, and that you have likewise heard that I had no instructions respecting you by the government. I doubt not the person who gave you the information meant well, but I suspect he did not even convey accurately his own ideas on the first point; for I presume the most he could say is that you had likewise become a French citizen and which by no means deprived you of being an American one. Even this however may be doubted, I mean the acquisition of citizenship in France, and I confess you have said much to shew that it has not been made. I really suspect that this was all that the gentleman who wrote you, and those Americans he heard speak upon the subject, meant. It becomes my duty however to declare to you, that I consider you as an American citizen, and that you are considered universally in that character by the people of America. As such you are entitled to my attention; and so far as it can be given consistently with those obligations which are mutual between every government and even a transient passenger you shall receive it.

The Congress have never decided upon the subject of citizenship in a manner to regard the present case. By being with us through the revolution you are of our country as absolutely as if you had been born there, and you are no more of England than every native American is. This is the true doctrine in the present case, so far as it becomes complicated with any other consideration. I have mentioned it to make you easy upon the only point which could give you any disquietude.

Is it necessary for me to tell you how much all your countrymen, I speak of the great mass of the people, are interested in your welfare? They have not forgotten the history of their own revolution and the difficult scenes through which they passed; nor do they review its several stages without reviving in their bosoms a due sensibility of the merits of those who served them in that great and arduous conflict. The crime of ingratitude has not yet stained, and I trust never will stain, our national character. You are considered by them as not only having rendered important services in our own revolution, but as being, on a more extensive scale, the friend of human rights, and a distinguished, an able, advocate in favour of public liberty. To the welfare of Thomas Paine the Americans are not, nor can they be, indifferent.

Of the sense which the President has always entertained of your merits and of his friendly disposition towards you, you are too well assured to require any declaration of it from me. That I forward his wishes in seeking your safety is what I well know, and this will form an additional obligation on me to perform what I should otherwise consider as a duty.

You are, in my opinion, at present, menaced by no kind of danger. To liberate you will be the object of my endeavours, and as soon as possible. But you must, until that event shall be accomplished, bear your situation with patience and fortitude. You will likewise have the justice to recollect, that I am placed here upon a difficult theatre,[4] many important objects to attend to, with few to consult. It becomes me in pursuit of those to regulate my conduct in respect to each, as to the manner and the time, as will, in my judgment, be best calculated to accomplish the whole. With great esteem and respect consider me personally your friend.

– JAMES MONROE.

The part in Mr. Monroe's letter in which he speaks of the President (Mr. Washington) is put in soft language. Mr. Monroe knew what Mr. Washington had said formerly, and he was willing to keep that in view. But the

4. This I presume alludes to the embarrassments which the strange conduct of Gouv. Morris had occasioned, and which, I well know, had created suspicions upon the sincerity of Mr. Washington.

fact is, not only that Mr. Washington had given no orders to Mr. Monroe, as the letter stated; but he did not so much as say to him, enquire if Mr. Paine be dead or alive, in prison or out, or see if there is any assistance we can given him.

While these matters were passing the liberations from the prisons were numerous; from twenty to forty in the course of almost every twenty four hours. The continuance of my imprisonment, after a new minister had arrived immediately from America, which was now more than two months, was a matter so obviously strange, that I found the character of the American government spoken of in very unqualified terms of reproach; not only by those who still remained in prison, but by those who were liberated, and by persons who had access to the prison from without. Under these circumstances I wrote again to Mr. Monroe, and found occasion, among other things to say: "It will not add to the popularity of Mr. Washington to have it believed in America, as it is believed here, that he connives at my imprisonment."

The case, so far as it respected Mr. Monroe was, that having to get over the difficulties which the strange conduct of Gouverneur Morris had thrown in the way of a successor, and having no authority from the American government to speak officially upon any thing relating to me, he found himself obliged to proceed by unofficial means with individual members; for though Robespierre was overthrown, the Robesp[i]errian members of the Committee of Public Safety still remained in considerable force, and had they found out that Mr. Monroe had no official authority upon the case, they would have paid little or no regard to his reclamation of me. In the mean time my health was suffering exceedingly, the dreary prospect of winter was coming on, and imprisonment was still a thing of danger.

After the Robespierrian members of the Committee were removed by the expiration of their time of serving, Mr. Monroe reclaimed me, and I was liberated the 4th of November. Mr. Monroe arrived in Paris the beginning of August before. All that period of my imprisonment, at least, I owe not to Robespierre, but to his colleague in projects, George Washington. Immediately upon my liberation Mr. Monroe invited me to his house, where I remained more than a year and an half; and I speak of his aid and his friendship, as an open hearted man will always do in such a case, with respect and gratitude.

Soon after my liberation the Convention passed an unanimous vote to invite me to return to my seat among them. The times were still unsettled and dangerous, as well from without as from within, for the coalition was unbroken, and the constitution not settled. I chose, however, to accept the invitation; for as I undertake nothing but what I believe to be right, I abandon nothing that I undertake; and I was willing also to shew, that, as I was not of a cast of mind to be deterred by prospects or retro-prospects of danger, so neither were my principles to be weakened by misfortune, or perverted by disgust.

Being now once more abroad in the world I began to find that I was not the only one who had conceived an unfavourable opinion of Mr. Washington. It was evident that his character was on the decline as well among Americans as among foreigners of different nations. From being the chief of a government, he had made himself the chief of a party; and his integrity was questioned, for his politics had a doubtful appearance. The mission of Mr. Jay to London, notwithstanding there was an American minister there already, had then taken place, and was beginning to be talked of. It appeared to others, as it did to me, to be enveloped in mystery, which every day served either to encrease or to explain into matter of suspicion.

In the year 1790, or about that time, Mr. Washington as President had sent Gouverneur Morris to London as his secret agent to have some communication with the British ministry. To cover the agency of Morris it was given out, I know not by whom, that he went as an agent from Robert Morris to borrow money in Europe, and the report was permitted to pass uncontradicted. The event of Morris's negociation was, that Mr. Hammond was sent minister from England to America, and Pinckney from America to England, and himself minister to France. It while Morris was minister in France he was not an emissary of the British ministry and the coalesced powers, he gave strong reasons to suspect him of it. No one who saw his conduct, and heard his conversation, could doubt his being in their interest; and had he not got off at the time he did, after his recall, he would have been in arrestation. Some letters of his had fallen into the hands of the Committee of Public Safety, and enquiry was making after him.

A great bustle has been made by Mr. Washington about the conduct of Genet in America; while that of his own minister, Morris, in France was infinitely more reproachable. If Genet was imprudent or rash, he was not treacherous; but Morris was all three. He was the enemy of the French revolution in every stage of it. But, notwithstanding this conduct on the part of Morris, and the known profligacy of his character, Mr. Washington, in a letter he wrote to him at the time of recalling him on the complaint and request of the Committee of Public Safety, assures him, that though he had complied with that request, he still retained the same esteem and friendship for him as before. This letter Morris was foolish enough to tell of; and, as his own character and conduct were notorious, the telling of it could have but one effect, which was that of implicating the character of the writer.

Morris still loiters in Europe, chiefly in England; and Mr. Washington is still in correspondence with him; Mr. Washington ought therefore to expect, especially since his conduct in the affair of Jay's treaty, that France must consider Morris and Washington as men of the same description. The chief difference, however, between the two is (for in politics there is none) that the one is profligate enough to profess an indifference about *moral* principles, and the other is prudent enough to conceal the want of them.

About three months after I was at liberty, the official note of Jay to Grenville on the subject of the capture of American vessels by British cruisers appeared in the American papers that arrived at Paris. Every thing was of a-piece. Every thing was mean. The same kind of character went to all circumstances public or private. Disgusted at this national degradation, as well as at the particular conduct of Mr. Washington to me, I wrote to him (Mr. Washington) on the 22d of February (1795) under cover to the then Secretary of State (Mr. Randolph) and entrusted the letter to Mr. Letombe, who was appointed French consul to Philadelphia, and was on the point of taking his departure. When I supposed Mr. Letombe had failed, I mentioned the letter to Mr. Monroe, and as I was then in his house, I shewed it to him. He expressed a wish that I would recall it, which he supposed might be done, as he had learned that Mr. Letombe had not then failed. I agreed to do so, and it was returned by Mr. Letombe under cover to Mr. Monroe.

The letter, however, will now reach Mr. Washington publicly, in the course of this work.

About the month of September following, I had a severe relapse, which gave occasion to the report of my death. I had felt it coming on a considerable time before, which occasioned me to hasten the work I had then in hand, the *Second part of the Age of Reason.* When I had finished that work, I bestowed another letter on Mr. Washington, which I sent under cover to Mr. Benj. Franklin Bache of Philadelphia. The letter is as follows.

To George Washington, President of the United States.

Paris, Sept. 20th, 1795.

Sir,

I had written you a letter by Mr. Letombe, French consul, but at the request of Mr. Monroe I withdrew it, and the letter is still by me. I was the more easily prevailed upon to do this, as it was then my intention to have returned to America the latter end of the present year, 1795; but the illness I now suffer prevents me. In case I had come, I should have applied to you for such parts of your official letters (and of your private ones, if you had chosen to give them) as contained any instructions or directions either to Mr. Monroe, or to Mr. Morris, or to any other person respecting me; for, after you were informed of my imprisonment in France, it was incumbent on you to have made some enquiry into the cause, as you might very well conclude, that I had not the opportunity of informing you of it. I cannot understand your silence upon this subject upon any other ground, than as connivance at my imprisonment; and this is the manner it is understood here, and will be understood in America, unless you can give me authority for contradicting it. I therefore write you this letter, to propose to you to send me copies of any letters you have written, that may remove that suspicion. In the preface to the second part of the Age of Reason, I have given a memorandum from the hand writing of Robespierre, in which he proposed a decree of accusation against me, "*for the interest of America as well as of France.*" He could have no cause for putting America into the case, but by interpreting the silence of the American government into connivance and consent. I was imprisoned on the ground of being born in England; and your silence in not enquiring into the cause of that imprisonment and reclaiming me against it, was tacitly giving me up. I ought not to have suspected you of treachery; but whether I recover from the illness I now suffer or not, I shall continue to think you treacherous, till you give me cause to think otherwise. I am sure you would have found yourself more at your ease had you acted by me as you ought; for, whether your desertion of me was intended to gratify the English government, or to let me fall into destruction in France, that you might exclaim the louder against the French revolution, or whether you hoped by my extinction to meet with less opposition in mounting up the American government, – either of these will involve you in reproach you will not easily shake off.

– THOMAS PAINE.

Here follows the letter above alluded to, which I had stopped in complaisance to Mr. Monroe.

To GEORGE WASHINGTON, PRESIDENT of the UNITED STATES.

Paris, Feb. 22d, 1795.

SIR,

As it is always painful to reproach those one would wish to respect, it is not without some difficulty that I have taken the resolution to write to you.

The dangers to which I have been exposed cannot have been unknown to you, and the guarded silence you have observed upon that circumstance is what I ought not to have expected from you, either as a friend or as President of the United States.

You know enough of my character to be assured, that I could not have deserved imprisonment in France, and without knowing any thing more than this, you had sufficient ground to have taken some interest for my safety. Every motive arising from recollection of times past, ought to have suggested to you the propriety of such a measure. But I cannot find that you have so much as directed any enquiry to be made, whether I was in prison or at liberty, dead or alive; what the cause of that imprisonment was, or whether there was any service or assistance you could render. Is this what I ought to have expected from America after the part I have acted towards her, or will it redound to her honour or to yours, that I tell the story. I do not hesitate to say, that you have not served America with more disinterestedness or greater zeal, or more fidelity, than myself, and I know not if with better effect. After the revolution of America was established I ventured into new scenes of difficulties to extend the principles which that revolution had produced, and you rested at home to partake of the advantages. In the progress of events you beheld yourself a President in America and me a prisoner in France. You folded your arms, forgot your friend, and became silent.

As every thing I have been doing in Europe was connected with my wishes for the prosperity of America, I ought to be the more surprised at this conduct on the part of her government. It leaves me but one mode of explanation, which is, *that every thing is not as it ought to be amongst you,* and that the presence of a man who might disapprove, and who had credit enough with the Country to be heard and believed, was not wished for. This was the operating motive with the despotic faction that imprisoned me in France (tho' the pretence was, that I was a foreigner) and those that have been silent and inactive towards me in America, appear to me to have acted from the same motive, of wishing me out of the way. It is impossible for me to discover any other.

Considering the part I have acted in the revolution of America it is natural that I feel interested in whatever relates to her character and prosperity. Though I am not on the spot, to see what is immediately acting there, I see some part of what she is acting in Europe. For your own sake, as well as for that of America, I was both surprised and concerned at the appointment of Gouverneur Morris to be minister to France. His conduct has proved that the opinion I had formed of that appointment was well founded. I wrote that opinion to Mr. Jefferson at the time, and I was frank enough to say the same thing to Morris – *that it was an unfortunate appointment.* His prating, insignificant pomposity, rendered him at once offensive, suspected, and ridiculous; and his total neglect of all business had so disgusted the Americans, that they proposed entering a protest against him. He carried this neglect to such an extreme, that it was necessary to inform him of it, and I asked him one day if he did not feel himself ashamed to take the money of the country and do nothing for it. But Morris is so fond of profit and voluptuousness that he cares nothing about character. Had he not been removed at the time he was, I think his conduct would have precipitated the two countries into a rupture; and in this case, hated *systematically,* as America is and ever will be by the British government, and suspected by France, the commerce of America would have fallen a prey to both countries.

If the inconsistent conduct of Morris exposed the interest of America to some hazard in France, the pusillanimous conduct of Mr. Jay in England has rendered the character of the American government contemptible in Europe. Is it possible that any man who has contributed to the independence of America, and to free her from the tyranny and injustice of the British government, can read, without shame and indignation, the note of Jay to Grenville. It is a satire upon the declaration of Independence, and an encouragement to the British government to treat America with contempt. At the time this minister of petitions was acting this miserable part, he had every means in his hands to enable him to have done his business as he ought. The success or failure of his mission depended upon the success or failure of the French arms. Had France failed, Mr. Jay might have put his humble petition in his pocket and gone home. The case happened to be otherwise, and he has sacrificed the honour and perhaps all the advantages of it, by turning petitioner. I take it for granted, that he was sent to demand indemnification for the captured property; and in this case, if he thought he wanted a preamble to his demand, he might have said: "That tho' the government of England might suppose itself under the necessity of seizing American property bound to France, yet that supposed necessity could not preclude indemnification to the proprietors, who, acting under the authority of their own government, were not accountable to any other." – But Mr. Jay sets out with an implied recognition of the right of the British government to seize and condemn; for he enters his complaint against the *irregularity* of the seizures and the condemnation, as if they were reprehensible only by not being *conformable* to the *terms* of the proclamation under which they were seized. Instead of being the Envoy of a government he goes over like a lawyer to demand a new trial. I can hardly help believing, that Grenville wrote the note himself and Jay signed it, for the stile of it is domestic and not diplomatic. The term, *His* Majesty, used without any descriptive epithet, always signifies the king whom the Minister that speaks represents. If this sinking of the demand into a petition was a juggle between Grenville and Jay, to cover the indemnification, I think it will end in another juggle, that of never paying the money, and be made use of afterwards to preclude the right of demanding it; for Mr. Jay has virtually disowned the right, *by appealing to the magnanimity of his Majesty against the capturers.* He has appointed this magnanimous Majesty to be umpire in the case, and the government of the United States must abide by the decision. If, Sir, I turn some part of this affair into ridicule, it is to avoid the unpleasant sensation of serious indignation.

Among other things, which I confess I do not understand, is the proclamation of neutrality. This has always appeared to me as an assumption on the part of the executive not warranted by the constitution. But passing this over, as a disputable case, and considering it only as political, the consequence has been that of sustaining the losses of war without the balance of reprisals. When the profession of neutrality on the part of America was answered by hostilities on the part of Britain, the object and intention of that neutrality existed no longer, and to maintain it after this was not only to encourage further insults and depredations, but was an informal breach of neutrality towards France, by passively contributing to the aid of her enemy. That the government of England considered the American government as pusillanimous is evident from the encreasing insolence of the former towards the latter, till the affair of General Wayne. She then saw it might be possible to kick a government into some degree of spirit. So far as the proclamation of neutrality was intended to prevent a dissolute spirit of privateering in America under foreign colours, it was undoubtedly laudable; but to continue it as a government neutrality, after the commerce of the country was made war upon, was submission and not neutrality. I have heard so much about this thing called neutrality, that I know not if the ungenerous and dishonorable silence (for I must call it such) that has been observed by your part of the government towards me, during my imprisonment, has not in some measure arisen from that policy.

Tho' I have written you this letter, you ought not to suppose it has been an agreeable undertaking to me. On the contrary, I assure you, it has cost me some disquietude. I am sorry you have given me cause to do it; for as I have always remembered your former friendship with pleasure, I suffer a loss by your depriving me of that sentiment.

– THOMAS PAINE.

That this letter was not written in very good temper is very evident; but it was just such a letter as his conduct appeared to me to merit, and every thing on his part since has served to confirm that opinion. Had I wanted a commentary on his silence with respect to my imprisonment in France, some of his faction has furnished me with it. What I here allude to is a publication in a Philadelphia paper, copied afterwards into a New York paper, both under the patronage of the Washington faction, in which the writer, still supposing me in prison in France, wonders at my lengthy respite from the scaffold; and he marks his politics still further by saying: "It appears moreover, that the people of England did not relish his (Thomas Paine's) opinions quite so well as he expected, and that for one of his last pieces, as destructive to the peace and happiness of their country, (meaning, I suppose, the *Rights of Man*) they threatened our knight-errant with such serious vengeance, that, to avoid a trip to Botany-bay, he fled over to France, as a less dangerous voyage."

I am not refuting or contradicting the falshood of this publication, for it is sufficiently notorious; neither am I censuring the writer; on the contrary I thank him for the explanation he has incautiously given of the principles of the Washington faction. Insignificant, however, as the piece is, it was capable of having had some ill effect, had it arrived in France during my imprisonment and in the time of Robespierre; and I am not uncharitable in supposing that this was the intention of the writer.[5]

I have now done with Mr. Washington on the score of private affairs. It would have been far more agreeable to me, had his conduct been such as not to have merited these reproaches. Errors or caprices of the temper can be pardoned and forgotten; but a cold deliberate crime of the heart, such as Mr. Washington is capable of acting, is not to be washed away. I now proceed to other matter.

After Jay's note to Grenville arrived in Paris from America, the character of every thing that was to follow might be easily foreseen; and it was upon this anticipation that my letter of February 22d was founded. The event has proved, that I was not mistaken, except that it has been much worse than I expected.

It would naturally occur to Mr. Washington, that the secrecy of Jay's mission to England, where there was already an American minister, could not but create some suspicion in the French government; especially as the

---

5. I know not who the writer of the piece is; but some late Americans say it is Phineas Bond, an American refugee, and now a British Consul; and that he writes under the signature of Peter Skunk, or Peter Porcupine, or some such signature.

conduct of Morris had been notorious, and the intimacy of Mr. Washington with Morris was known.

The character which Mr. Washington has attempted to act in the world, is a sort of non-describable, cameleon-coloured thing, called *prudence*. It is, in many cases, a substitute for principle, and is so nearly allied to hypocrisy, that it easily slides into it. His genius for prudence furnished him in this instance with an expedient, that served, as is the natural and general character of all expedients, to diminish the embarrassments of the moment and multiply them afterwards; for he authorised it to be made known to the French government, as a confidential matter (Mr. Washington should recollect that I was a member of the Convention, & had the means of knowing what I here state) he authorized it, I say, to be made known, and that for the purpose of preventing any uneasiness to France on the score of Mr. Jay's mission to England, that the object of that mission, and of Mr. Jay's authority, was restricted to that of demanding the surrender of the western posts and indemnification for the cargoes captured in American vessels. Mr. Washington knows that this was untrue; and knowing this, he had good reason to himself for refusing to furnish the House of Representatives with copies of the instructions given to Jay; as he might suspect, among other things, that he should also be called upon for copies of instructions given to other ministers, and that in the contradiction of instructions his want of integrity would be detected. Mr. Washington may now, perhaps, learn, when it is too late, to be of any use to him, that a man will pass better through the world with a thousand open errors upon his back, than in being detected in ONE sly falshood. When one is detected, a thousand are suspected.

The first account that arrived in Paris of a treaty being negociated by Mr. Jay (for nobody suspected any) came in an English newspaper, which announced that a treaty *offensive* and *defensive* had been concluded between the United States of America and England. This was immediately denied by every American in Paris, as an impossible thing; and though it was disbelieved by the French, it imprinted a suspicion that some underhand business was going forward.[6] At length the treaty itself arrived, and every well-affected American blushed with shame.

6. It was the embarrassment into which the affairs and credit of America were thrown at this instant by the report above alluded to, that made it necessary to contradict it, and that by every means arising from opinion or founded upon authority. The Committee of Public Safety, existing at that time, had agreed to the full execution, on their part, of the treaty between America and France, notwithstanding some equivocal conduct on the part of the American government, not very consistent with the good faith of an ally; but they were not in a disposition to be imposed upon by a

It is curious to observe how the appearances of character will change, whilst the root that produces them remains the same. The Washington administration having waded through the slough of negociation, and whilst it amused France with professions of friendship contrived to injure her, immediately throws off the hypocrite, and assumes the swaggering air of a bravado. The party papers of that imbecile administration were on this occasion filled with paragraphs about *Sovereignty*. A paltroon may boast of his sovereign right to let another kick him, and this is the only kind of sovereignty shewn in the treaty with England. But these dashing paragraphs, as Timothy Pickering well knows, were intended for France; without whose assistance in men, money and ships, Mr. Washington would have cut but a poor figure in the American war. But of his military talents I shall speak hereafter.

I mean not to enter into any discussion of any article of Jay's treaty: I shall speak only upon the whole of it. It is attempted to be justified on the ground of its not being a violation of any article or articles of the treaty pre-existing with France. But the sovereign right of explanation does not lie with George Washington and his man Timothy; France, on her part, has, at least, an equal right; and when nations dispute, it is not so much about words as about things.

A man, such as the world calls, a sharper, and versed, as Jay must be supposed to be, in the quibbles of the law, may find a way to enter into engagements, and make bargains in such a manner as to cheat some other party, without that party being able, as the phrase is, *to take the law of him*. This often happens in the cabalistical circle of what is called law. But when this is attempted to be acted on the national scale of treaties, it is too despicable to be defended, or to be permitted to exist. Yet this is the trick upon which Jay's treaty is founded, so far as it has relation to the treaty pre-existing with France. It is a counter-treaty to that treaty, and perverts all the

---

counter-treaty. That Jay had no instructions beyond the points above stated, or none that could possibly be construed to extend to the length the British treaty goes, was a matter believed in America, in England and in France; and without going to any other source it followed naturally from the message of the President to Congress, when he nominated Jay upon that mission. The secretary of Mr. Jay came to Paris soon after the treaty with England had been concluded, and brought with him a copy of Mr. Jay's instructions, which he offered to shew to me as a *justification of Jay*. I advised him, as a friend, not to shew them to any body, and did not permit him to shew them to me. Who is it, said I to him, that you intend to implicate as censureable by shewing those instructions? Perhaps that implication may fall upon your own government. Though I did not see the instructions, I could not be at a loss to understand, that the American administration had been playing a double game.

great articles of that treaty to the injury of France, and makes them operate as a bounty to England with whom France is at war.

The Washington administration shews great desire, that the treaty between France and the United States be preserved. Nobody can doubt their sincerity upon this matter. There is not a British minister, a British merchant, or a British agent or sailor in America, that does not anxiously wish the same thing. The treaty with France serves now as a passport to supply England with naval stores and other articles of American produce, whilst the same articles, when coming to France, are made contraband or seizable by Jay's treaty with England. The treaty with France says, that neutral ships make neutral property, and thereby gives protection to English property on board American ships; and Jay's treaty delivers up French property on board American ships to be seized by the English. It is too paltry to talk of faith, of national honour, and of the preservation of treaties, whilst such a bare-faced treachery as this stares the world in the face.

The Washington administration may save itself the trouble of proving to the French government its *most faithful* intentions of preserving the treaty with France; for France has now no desire that it should be preserved. She had nominated an Envoy extraordinary to America, to make Mr. Washington and his government a present of the treaty, and to have no more to do with *that* or with *him*. It was, at the same time, officially declared to the American minister at Paris, *that the French Republic had rather have the American government for an open enemy than a treacherous friend.* This, sir, together with the internal distractions caused in America, and the loss of character in the world, is the *eventful crisis,* alluded to in the beginning of this letter, to which your double politics have brought the affairs of your country. It is time that the eyes of America be opened upon you.

How France would have conducted herself towards America and American commerce after all treaty stipulations had ceased, and under the sense of services rendered and injuries received, I know not. It is, however, an unpleasant reflection, that in all national quarrels, the innocent, and even the friendly, part of the community, become involved with the culpable and the unfriendly; and as the accounts that arrived from America continued to manifest an invariable attachment in the general mass of the people to their original ally, in opposition to the new-fangled Washington faction, – the resolutions that had been taken were suspended. It happened also fortunately enough, that Gouverneur Morris was not minister at this time.

There is, however, one point that yet remains in embryo, and which, among other things, serves to shew the ignorance of the Washington treaty-makers, and their inattention to pre-existing treaties when they were employing themselves in framing or ratifying the new treaty with England.

The second article of the treaty of commerce between the United States and France says: "The most christian king and the United States engage mutually, not to grant any particular favour to other nations in respect of commerce and navigation that shall not immediately become common to the other party, who shall enjoy the same favour freely, if the concession was freely made, or on allowing the same compensation if the concession was conditional."

All the concessions therefore made to England by Jay's treaty are, through the medium of this second article in the pre-existing treaty, made to France, and become engrafted into the treaty with France, and can be exercised by her as a matter of right, the same as by England.

Jay's treaty makes a concession to England, and that unconditionally, of seizing naval stores in American ships and condemning them as contraband. It makes also a concession to England to seize provisions and *other articles* in American ships. *Other articles* are *all other articles,* and none but an ignoramus, or something worse, would have put such a phrase into a treaty. The condition annexed to this case is, that the provisions and other articles so seized are to be paid for at a price to be agreed upon. Mr. Washington, as President, ratified this treaty after he knew the British government had recommenced an indiscriminate seizure of provisions and of all other articles in American ships; and it is now known that those seizures were made to fit out the expedition going to Quiberon Bay, and it was known, before hand that they would be made. The evidence goes, also, a good way to prove that Jay and Grenville understood each other upon that subject. Mr. Pinckney, when he passed through France on his way to Spain, spoke of the recommencement of the seizures as a thing that would take place. The French government had by some means received information from London to the same purpose, with the addition, that the recommencement of the seizures would cause no misunderstanding between the British and American governments. Grenville, in defending himself against the opposition in Parliament on account of the scarcity of corn, said (see his speech at the opening of the Parliament that met Oct. 29th 1795) that *the supplies for the Quiberon expedition were furnished out of the American ships;* and all the accounts received at that time from England stated, that those seizures were made under the treaty. After the supplies for the Quiberon expedition had been procured and the expected success had failed, the seizures were counter-manded; and, had the French seized provision vessels going to England, it is probable that the Quiberon expedition could not have been attempted.

In one point of view, the treaty with England operates as a loan to the English government. It gives permission to that government to take American property at sea to any amount and pay for it when it suits her; and besides this, the treaty is in every point of view a surrender of the rights of American commerce and navigation, and a refusal to France of the rights of neutrality. The American flag is not now a neutral flag to France: Jay's treaty of surrender gives a monopoly of it to England.

On the contrary, the treaty of commerce between America and France was formed on the most liberal principles, and calculated to give the greatest encouragement to the infant commerce of America. France was neither a carrier nor an exporter of naval stores or of provisions. Those articles belonged wholly to America, and they had all the protection in that treaty which a treaty could give. But so much has that treaty been perverted, that the liberality of it, on the part of France, has served to encourage Jay to form a counter-treaty with England; for he must have supposed the hands of France tied up by her treaty with America, when he was making such large concessions in favour of England. The injury which Mr. Washington's administration has done to the character as well as to the commerce of America is too great to be repaired by him. Foreign nations will be shy of making treaties with a government that has given the faithless example of perverting the liberality of a former treaty to the injury of the party with whom it was made.

In what a fraudulent light must Mr. Washington's character appear in the world, when his declarations and his conduct are compared together! Here follows the letter he wrote to the Committee of Public Safety whilst Jay was negociating in profound secrecy this treacherous treaty.

"George Washington, President of the United States of America, to the Representatives of the French people, members of the Committee of Public Safety of the *French Republic, the great and good friend and ally of the United States.*

"On the intimation of the wish of the French Republic, that a new minister should be sent from the United States, I resolved to manifest my sense of the readiness with which *my* request was fulfilled [that of recalling Genet] by immediately fulfilling the request of your government [that of recalling Morris.]

"It was some time before a character could be obtained, worthy of the high office of expressing the attachment of the United States to the happiness of our allies, *and drawing closer the bonds of our friendship.* I have now made choice of James Monroe, one of our distinguished citizens, to reside near the French republic, in quality of minister plenipotentiary of the United States of America. He is instructed to bear to you our *sincere solicitude for your welfare, and to cultivate with zeal the cordiality so happily subsisting between us.* From a knowledge of his fidelity, probity and good conduct, I have entire confidence that he will render himself acceptable to you, and give effect to our desire of preserving and *advancing, on all occasions, the interest and connection of the two nations.* I beseech you therefore to give full credence to whatever he shall say to you on the part of the United States, and, *most of all, when he shall assure you that your prosperity is an object of our affection,* and I pray God to have the French republic in his holy keeping.

— G°. WASHINGTON."

Was it by entering into a treaty with England, to surrender French property on board American ships to be seized by the English, whilst English property on board American ships was declared by the French treaty not to be seizable, *that the bonds of friendship between America and France were to be drawn the closer?* Was it by declaring naval stores contraband when coming to France, when by the French treaty they were not contraband when going to England, that the *connection between France and America was to be advanced?* Was it by opening the American ports to the British navy in the present war, from which ports that same navy had been expelled by the aid solicited from France in the American war (and that aid gratuitously given) that the gratitude of America was to be shewn, and the *solicitude* spoken of in the letter demonstrated?

As the letter was addressed to the Committee of Public Safety, Mr Washington did not expect it would get abroad in the world, or be seen by any other eye than that of Robespierre, or be heard by any other ear than that of the Committee; that it would pass as a whisper across the Atlantic, from one dark chamber to the other, and there terminate. It was calculated to remove from the mind of the Committee all suspicion upon Jay's mission to England, and, in this point of view, it was suited to the circumstances of the moment then passing; but as the event of that mission has proved the letter to be hypocritical, it serves no other purpose of the present moment than to shew that the writer is not to be credited. Two circumstances served to make the reading of the letter necessary in the Convention. The one was, that those who succeeded on the fall of Robespierre, found it most proper to act with publicity; the other, to extinguish the suspicions which the strange conduct of Morris had occasioned in France.

When the British treaty, and the ratification of it by Mr. Washington, was known in France, all further declarations from him of his good disposition, as an ally and a friend, passed for so many cyphers; but still it appeared necessary to him to keep up the farce of declarations. It is stipulated in the British treaty, that commissioners are to report at the end of two years on the case of *neutral ships making neutral property.* In the mean time neutral ships do *not* make neutral property, according to the British treaty, and they *do,* according to the French treaty. The preservation, therefore, of the French treaty became of great importance to England, as by that means she can employ American ships as carriers, whilst the same advantage is denied to France. Whether the French treaty could exist as a matter of right after this clandestine perversion of it, could not but give some apprehensions to the partizans of the British treaty, and it became necessary to them to make up, by fine words, what was wanting in good actions.

An opportunity offered to that purpose. The Convention, on the public reception of Mr. Monroe, ordered the American flag and the French flag to be displayed unitedly in the hall of the Convention. Mr. Monroe made a present of an American flag for the purpose. The Convention returned this compliment by sending a French flag to America, to be presented by their minister, Mr. Adet, to the American government. This resolution passed long before Jay's treaty was known or suspected; it passed in the days of confidence; but the flag was not presented by Mr. Adet till several months after the treaty had been ratified. Mr. Washington made this the occasion of saying some fine things to the French Minister, and the better to get himself into tune to do this, he began by saying the finest things of himself.

"Born, sir (said he) in a land of liberty; *having* early learned its value; *having* engaged in a perilous conflict to defend it; *having,* in a word, devoted the best years of my life to secure its permanent establishment in my own country; *my* anxious recollections, *my* sympathetic feelings, and *my* best wishes are irresistibly excited, whenever, in any country, I see an oppressed people unfurl the banners of freedom."

Mr. Washington having expended so many fine phrases upon himself, was obliged to invent a new one for the French, and he calls them "wonderful people!" The coalesced powers acknowledge as much.

It is laughable to hear Mr. Washington talk of his *sympathetic feelings,* who has always been remarked, even among his friends, for not having any. He has, however, given no proof of any to me. As to the pompous encomiums he so liberally pays to himself, on the score of the American revolution, the reality of them may be questioned; and since he has forced them so much into notice, it is fair to examine his pretensions.

A stranger might be led to suppose from the egotism with which Mr. Washington speaks, that himself, and himself only, had generated, conducted, compleated, and established the revolution: In fine, that it was all his own doing.

In the first place, as to the political part, he had no share in it; and therefore the whole of *that* is out of the question with respect to him. There remains then only the military part, and it would have been prudent in Mr. Washington not to have awakened enquiry upon that subject. Fame then was cheap; he enjoyed it cheaply; and nobody was disposed to take away the laurels, that, whether they were *acquired* or not, had been *given.*

Mr. Washington's merit consisted in constancy. But constancy was the common virtue of the revolution. Who was there that was inconstant? I know of but one military defection, that of Arnold; and I know of no political defection, among those who made themselves eminent, when the revolution was formed by the declaration of independence. Even Silas Deane, though he attempted to defraud, did not betray.

But when we speak of military character, something more is to be understood than constancy; and something more *ought* to be understood than the Fabian system of *doing nothing.* The *nothing* part can be done by any body. Old Mrs. Thompson, the house-keeper of head-quarters (who threatened to make the sun and the *wind* shine through Rivington of New York) could have done it as well as Mr. Washington. Deborah would have been as good as Barak.

Mr. Washington had the nominal rank of Commander in Chief; but he was not so in fact. He had in reality only a separate command. He had no controul over, or direction of, the army to the northward, under Gates, that captured Burgoyne; nor of that to the south, under Green, that recovered the southern States. The nominal rank, however, of Commander in chief, served to throw upon him the lustre of those actions, and to make him appear as the soul and centre of all the military operations in America.

He commenced his command June 1775, during the time the Massachusetts army lay before Boston, and after the affair of Bunker-hill. The commencement of his command was the commencement of inactivity. Nothing was afterwards done, or attempted to be done, during the nine months he remained before Boston. If we may judge from the resistance made at Concord and afterwards at Bunker-hill, there was a spirit of enterprise at that time, which the presence of Mr. Washington chilled into cold defence.

By the advantage of a good exterior, he attracts respect, which his habitual silence tends to preserve; but he has not the talent of inspiring ardour in an army. The enemy removed from Boston in March 1776, to wait for reinforcements from Europe, and to take a more advantageous position at New York.

The inactivity of the campaign of 1775 on the part of General Washington, when the enemy had a less force than in any future period of the war, and the injudicious choice of positions taken by him in the campaign of 1776, when the enemy had its greatest force, necessarily produced the losses and misfortunes that marked that gloomy campaign. The positions taken were either islands or necks of land. In the former, the enemy, by the aid of their ships could bring their whole force against a part of Gen. Washington's, as in the affair of Long-Island, and in the latter he might be shut up as in the bottom of a bag. This had nearly been the case at New York, and it was so in part; it was actually the case at Fort Washington; and would have been the case at Fort Lee if Gen. Greene had not moved precipitately off, leaving every thing behind, and by gaining Hackinsach bridge, got out of the bag of Bergen neck. How far Mr. Washington, as a General, is blameable for these matters, I am not undertaking to determine, but they are evidently defects in military geography. The successful skirmishes at the close of that campaign (matters they would scarcely be noticed in a better state of things) make the brilliant exploits of Gen. Washington's seven campaigns.—No wonder we see so much pusillanimity in the *President* when we see so little enterprise in the *General.*

The campaign of 1777 became famous, not by any thing on the part of Gen. Washington, but by the capture of Gen. Burgoyne and the army under his command, by the Northern army at Saratoga under Gen. Gates. So totally distinct and unconnected were the two armies of Washington and Gates, and so independent was the latter of the authority of the nominal Commander in Chief, that the two Generals did not so much as correspond, and it was only by a letter of Gen. (since Governor) Clinton, that General Washington was informed of that event. The British took possession of Philadelphia this year, which they evacuated the next, just time enough to save their heavy baggage and fleet of transports from capture by the French Admiral d'Estaing, who arrived at the mouth of the Delaware soon after.

The capture of Burgoyne gave an eclat in Europe to the American arms, and facilitated the alliance with France. The eclat, however, was not kept up by any thing on the part of Gen. Washington. The same unfortunate langour that marked his entrance into the field continued always. Discontents began to prevail strongly against him, and a party was formed in Congress, whilst sitting at York-Town, in Pennsylvania, for removing him from the command of the army. The hope, however, of better times, the news of the alliance with France, and the unwillingness of shewing discontent, dissipated the matter.

Nothing was done in the campaigns of 1778, 1779, 1780, in the part where Gen. Washington commanded, except the taking Stony Point by Gen. Wayne. The Southern States in the mean time were over-run by the enemy. They were afterwards recovered by Gen. Greene, who had in a very great measure created the army that accomplished that recovery. In all this Gen. Washington had no share. The Fabian system of war, followed by him, began now to unfold itself with all its evils, for what is Fabian war without Fabian means to support it.

The finances of Congress, depending wholly on emissions of paper money, were exhausted. Its credit was gone. The continental treasury was not able to pay the expence of a brigade of waggons to transport the necessary stores to the army, and yet the sole object, the establishment of the revolution, was a thing of remote distance. The time I am now speaking of is the latter end of the year 1780.

In this situation of things it was found not only expedient but absolutely necessary for Congress to state the whole case to its ally. I knew more of this matter (before it came into Congress or was known to General Washington) of its progress, and its issue, than I chuse to state in this letter. Col. John Laurens was sent to France as Envoy Extraordinary on this occasion, and by a private agreement between him and me I accompanied him. We sailed from Boston in the Alliance frigate, Feb. 11th, 1781. France had already done much in accepting and paying bills drawn by Congress. She was now called upon to do more. The event of Col. Laurens's mission, with the aid of the venerable minister, Franklin, was, that France gave in money, as a present, six millions of livres and ten millions more as a loan, and agreed to send a fleet of not less than thirty sail of the line, at her own expence, as an aid to America. Col. Laurens and myself returned from Brest the 1st of June following, taking with us two millions and an half of livres (upwards of one hundred thousand pounds sterling) of the money given, and convoying two ships with stores.

We arrived at Boston the 25th August following. De Grasse arrived with the French fleet in the Chesapeak at the same time, and was afterwards joined by that of Barras, making 31 sail of the line. The money was transported in waggons from Boston to the Bank at Philadelphia, of which Mr. Thomas Willing, who has since put himself at the head of the list of petitioners in favour of the British treaty, was then President, and it was by the aid of this money, and of this fleet, and of Rochambeau's army, that Cornwallis was taken; the lawrels of which have been unjustly given to Mr. Washington. His merit in that affair was no more than that of any other American officer.

I have had, and still have, as much pride in the American revolution as any man, or as Mr. Washington has a right to have; but that pride has never made me forgetful from whence the great aid came that compleated the business. Foreign aid (that of France) was calculated upon at the commencement of the revolution. It is one of the subjects treated of in the pamphlet *Common Sense,* but as a matter that could not be hoped for, unless Independence was declared.

It is as well the ingratitude as the pusillanimity of Mr. Washington and the Washington faction, that has brought upon America the loss of character she now suffers in the world, and the numerous evils her commerce has undergone, and to which it is yet exposed. The British ministry soon found out what sort of men they had to deal with, and they dealt with them accordingly; and if further explanation was wanting, it has been fully given since in the snivelling address of the New-York Chamber of Commerce to the President, and in that of sundry merchants of Philadelphia, which was not much better.

When the revolution of America was finally established by the termination of the war, the world gave her credit for great character; and she had nothing to do but to stand firm upon that ground. The British ministry had their hands too full of trouble to have provoked unnecessarily a rupture with her, had she shewn a proper resolution to defend her rights. But encouraged as they were by the submissive character of her executive administration, they proceeded from insult to insult till none more were left to be offered. The proposals made by Sweden and Denmark to the American administration were disregarded. I know not if so much as an answer has been returned to them. The minister *penitentiary* (as some of the British prints called him) Mr. Jay, was sent on a pilgrimage to London, to make all up by penance and petition. In the mean time the lengthy and drowsy writer of the pieces signed *Camillus* held himself in reserve to vindicate every thing; and to sound, in America, the tocsin of terror upon the inexhaustible resources of England. Her resources, says he, are greater than those of all the other powers. This man is so intoxicated with fear and finance that he knows not the difference between *plus* and *minus* – between an hundred pounds in hand, and an hundred pounds worse than nothing.

The commerce of America, so far as it had been established by all the treaties that had been formed prior to that by Jay, was free, and the principles upon which it was established were good. That ground ought never to have been departed from. It was the justifiable ground of right, and no temporary difficulties ought to have induced an abandonment of it. The case now is otherwise. The ground, the scene, the pretensions, the every thing, are changed. The commerce of America is, by Jay's treaty, put under foreign dominion. The sea is not free for her. Her right to navigate it is reduced to the right of escaping; that is, until some ship of England or France, stops her vessels and carries them into port. Every article of American produce, whether from the sea or the land, fish, flesh, vegetable, or manufacture, is, by Jay's treaty, made either contraband or seizable. Nothing is exempt. In all other treaties of commerce the article which enumerates the contraband articles, such as fire arms, gun powder, &c. is followed by another article which enumerates the articles not contraband: but it is not so in Jay's treaty. There is no exempting article. Its place is supplied by the article for seizing and carrying into port; and the sweeping phrase of "provisions and *other articles,*" includes every thing. There never was such a base and servile treaty of surrender since treaties began to exist.

This is the ground upon which America now stands. All her rights of commerce and navigation have to commence anew, and that with loss of character to begin with. If there is sense enough left in the heart to call a blush into the cheek, the Washington administration must be ashamed to appear.——And as to you, sir, treacherous in private friendship (for so you have been to me, and that in the day of danger) and a hypocrite in public life, the world will be puzzled to decide, whether you are an apostate or an impostor; whether you have abandoned good principles, or whether you ever had any?

– THOMAS PAINE.

AGRARIAN JUSTICE,

OPPOSED TO

AGRARIAN LAW,

AND TO

AGRARIAN MONOPOLY.

BEING A PLAN FOR

MELIORATING THE CONDITION
OF MAN,

By Creating in every Nation a

NATIONAL FUND,

To Pay to every Person, when arrived at the Age of *Twenty-one Years,* the Sum of *Fifteen Pounds* Sterling, to enable *him* or *her* to begin the World;

AND ALSO,

Ten Pounds Sterling per Annum during life to every Person now living of the Age of *Fifty Years,* and to all others when they shall arrive at that Age, to enable them to live in Old Age without Wretchedness, and go decently out of the World.

BY THOMAS PAINE,

AUTHOR OF COMMON SENSE, RIGHTS OF MAN, AGE OF REASON, &c. &c.

Agrarian Justice, Opposed to Agrarian Law, and to Agrarian Monopoly. (London: J. Adlard and J. Parsons, 1797).

Preface.

THE following little Piece was written in the winter of 1795 and 96; and, as I had not determined whether to publish it during the present war, or to wait till the commencement of a peace, it has lain by me, without alteration or addition, from the time it was written.

What has determined me to publish it now is, a Sermon, preached by WATSON, *Bishop of Landaff.* Some of my Readers will recollect, that this Bishop wrote a Book, entitled *An Apology for the Bible,* in answer to my *Second Part of the Age of Reason.* I procured a copy of his book, and he may depend upon hearing from me on that subject.

At the end of the Bishop's book is a List of the Works he has written, among which is the Sermon alluded to; it is entitled,

"THE WISDOM AND GOODNESS OF GOD, IN HAVING MADE BOTH RICH AND POOR; with an Appendix, containing REFLECTIONS ON THE PRESENT STATE OF ENGLAND AND FRANCE."

The error contained in the title of this Sermon, determined me to publish my AGRARIAN JUSTICE. It is wrong to say that God made *Rich* and *Poor;* he made only *Male* and *Female;* and he gave them the earth for their inheritance,   *   *   *

      *   *   *   *   *

      *   *   *   *   *

      *   *   *   *   *

      *   *   *   *   *

      *   *   *   *   *

      *   *   *   *   *

      *   *   *   *   *

Instead of preaching to encourage one part of mankind in insolence   *

      *   *   *   *   *

      *   *   *   *   *

      *   *   *   *   *

      *   *   *   it would be better

that Priests employed their time to render the general condition of man less miserable than it is. Practical religion consists in doing good; and the only way of serving God is, that of endeavouring to make his creation happy. All preaching that has not this for its object is nonsense and hypocrisy.

– THOMAS PAINE.

Agrarian Justice,
opposed to
Agrarian Law,
And to Agrarian Monopoly,
being a plan for
Meliorating the Condition of Man, &c.

TO preserve the benefits of what is called civilized life, and to remedy, at the same time, the evils it has produced, ought to be considered as one of the first objects of reformed legislation.

Whether that state that is proudly, perhaps erroneously, called civilization, has most promoted or most injured the general happiness of man, is a question that may be strongly contested. – On one side, the spectator is dazzled by splendid appearances; on the other he is shocked by extremes of wretchedness; both of which he has erected. The most affluent and the most miserable of the human race are to be found in the countries that are called civilized.

To understand what the state of society ought to be, it is necessary to have some idea of the natural and primitive state of man; such as it is at this day among the Indians of North America. There is not, in that state, any of those spectacles of human misery which poverty and want present to our eyes, in all the towns and streets of Europe. Poverty, therefore, is a thing created by that which is called civilized life. It exists not in the natural state. On the other hand, the natural state is without those advantages which flow from Agriculture, Arts, Science, and Manufactures.

The life of an Indian is a continual holiday, compared with the poor of Europe; and, on the other hand, it appears to be abject when compared to the rich. Civilization, therefore, or that which is so called, has operated, two ways, to make one part of society more affluent, and the other part more wretched, than would have been the lot of either in a natural state.

It is always possible to go from the natural to the civilized state, but it is never possible to go from the civilized to the natural state. The reason is, that man, in a natural state, subsisting by hunting, requires ten times the quantity of land to range over, to procure himself sustenance, than would support him in a civilized state, where the earth is cultivated. When therefore a country becomes populous by the additional aids of cultivation, arts, and science, there is a necessity of preserving things in that state; because, without it, there cannot be sustenance for more, perhaps, than a tenth part of its inhabitants. The thing therefore now to be done, is, to remedy the evils, and preserve the benefits, that have arisen to society, by passing from the natural to that which is called the civilized state.

Taking then the matter up on this ground, the first principle of civilization ought to have been, and ought still to be, that the condition of every person born into the world, after a state of civilization commences, ought not to be worse than if he had been born before that period. But the fact is, that the condition of millions, in every country in Europe, is far worse than if they had been born before civilization began, or had been born among the Indians of North America of the present day. I will shew how this fact has happened.

It is a position not to be controverted, that the earth, in its natural uncultivated state, was, and ever would have continued to be, the COMMON PROPERTY OF THE HUMAN RACE. In that state every man would have been born to property. He would have been a joint life-proprietor with the rest in the property of the soil, and in all its natural productions, vegetable and animal.

But the earth, in its natural state, as before said, is capable of supporting but a small number of inhabitants compared with what it is capable of doing in a cultivated state. And as it is impossible to separate the improvement made by cultivation, from the earth itself, upon which that improvement is made, the idea of landed property arose from that inseparable connection; but it is nevertheless true, that it is the value of the improvement only, and not the earth itself, that is individual property. Every proprietor therefore of cultivated land, owes to the community a *ground-rent;* for I know no better term to express the idea by, for the land which he holds: and it is from this ground-rent that the fund proposed in this plan is to issue.

It is deducible, as well from the nature of the thing, as from all the histories transmitted to us, that the idea of landed property commenced with cultivation, and that there was no such thing as landed property before that time. It could not exist in the first state of man, that of hunters. It did not exist in the second state, that of shepherds: Neither Abraham, Isaac, Jacob, or Job, so far as the history of the Bible may be credited in probable things, were owners of land. Their property consisted, as is always enumerated, in flocks and herds, and they travelled with them from place to place. The frequent contentions at that time about the use of a well in the dry country of Arabia, where those people lived, shew also there was no landed property. It was not admitted that land could be located as property.

There could be no such thing as landed property originally. Man did not make the earth, and, though he had a natural right to *occupy* it, he had no right to *locate* as *his property* in perpetuity any part of it: neither did the Creator of the earth open a land-office, from whence the first title-deeds should issue. From whence then arose the idea of landed property? I answer as before, that when cultivation began, the idea of landed property began with it, from the impossibility of separating the improvement made by cultivation from the earth itself upon which that improvement was made. The value of the improvement so far exceeded the value of the natural earth, at that time, as to absorb it; till, in the end, the common right of all became confounded into the cultivated right of the individual. But they are nevertheless distinct species of rights, and will continue to be so as long as the earth endures.

It is only by tracing things to their origin, that we can gain rightful ideas of them, and it is by gaining such ideas that we discover the boundary that divides right from wrong, and which teaches every man to know his own. I have entitled this tract *Agrarian Justice,* to distinguish it from *Agrarian Law.* Nothing could be more unjust than Agrarian Law in a country improved by cultivation; for though every man, as an inhabitant of the earth, is a joint proprietor of it in its natural state, it does not follow that he is a joint proprietor of cultivated earth. The additional value made by cultivation, after the system was admitted, became the property of those who did it, or who inherited it from them, or who purchased it. It had originally an owner. Whilst, therefore, I advocate the right, and interest myself in the hard case of all those who have been thrown out of their natural inheritance by the introduction of the system of landed property, I equally defend the right of the possessor to the part which is his.

Cultivation is, at least, one of the greatest natural improvements ever made by human invention. It has given to created earth a ten-fold value. But the landed monopoly, that began with it, has produced the greatest evil. It has dispossessed more than half the inhabitants of every nation of their natural inheritance, without providing for them, as ought to have been done, as an indemnification for that loss, and has thereby created a species of poverty and wretchedness that did not exist before.

In advocating the case of the persons thus dispossessed, it is a right and not a charity that I am pleading for. But it is that kind of right which, being neglected at first, could not be brought forward afterwards, till heaven had opened the way by a revolution in the system of government. Let us then do honour to revolutions by justice, and give currency to their principles by blessings.

Having thus, in a few words, opened the merits of the case, I proceed to the plan I have to propose, which is,

To create a National Fund, out of which there shall be paid to every person, when arrived at the age of twenty-one years, the sum of Fifteen Pounds sterling, *as a compensation in part for the loss of his or her natural inheritance by the introduction of the system of landed property.*
AND ALSO,
The sum of Ten Pounds *per annum, during life, to every person now living of the age of fifty years, and to all others as they shall arrive at that age.*

MEANS BY WHICH THE FUND IS TO BE CREATED.

I have already established the principle, namely, that the earth, in its natural uncultivated state, was, and ever would have continued to be, the COMMON PROPERTY OF THE HUMAN RACE that in that state every person would have been born to property – and that the system of landed property, by its inseparable connection with cultivation, and with what is called civilized life, has absorbed the property of all those whom it dispossessed, without providing, as ought to have been done, an indemnification for that loss.

The fault, however, is not in the present possessors. No complaint is intended, or ought to be alledged against them, unless they adopt the crime by opposing justice. The fault is in the system, and it has stolen imperceptibly upon the world, aided afterwards by the Agrarian law of the sword. But the fault can be made to reform itself by successive generations, without diminishing or deranging the property of any of the present possessors, and yet the operation of the fund can commence, and be in full activity the first year of its establishment, or soon after, as I shall shew.

It is proposed that the payments, as already stated, be made to every person, rich or poor. It is best to make it so, to prevent invidious distinctions. It is also right it should be so, because it is in lieu of the natural inheritance, which, as a right, belongs to every man, over and above the property he may have created or inherited from those who did. Such persons as do not chuse to receive it, can throw it into the common fund.

Taking it then for granted, that no person ought to be in a worse condition when born under what is called a state of civilization, than he would have been, had he been born in a state of nature, and that civilization ought to have made, and ought still to make, provision for that purpose, it can only be done by subtracting from property a portion equal in value to the natural inheritance it has absorbed.

Various methods may be proposed for this purpose, but that which appears to be the best, not only because it will operate without deranging any present possessors, or without interfering with the collection of taxes, or emprunts necessary for the purpose of government and the revolution, but because it will be the least troublesome and the most effectual, and also because the subtraction will be made at a time that best admits it, which is, at the moment that property is passing by the death of one person to the possession of another. In this case, the bequeather gives nothing; the receiver pays nothing. The only matter to him is, that the monopoly of natural inheritance, to which there never was a right, begins to cease in his person. A generous man would not wish it to continue, and a just man will rejoice to see it abolished.

My state of health prevents my making sufficient enquiries with respect to the doctrine of probabilities, whereon to found calculations with such degrees of certainty as they are capable of. What, therefore, I offer on this head is more the result of observation and reflection, than of received information; but I believe it will be found to agree sufficiently enough with fact.

In the first place, taking twenty-one years as the epoch of maturity, all the property of a nation, real and personal, is always in the possession of persons above that age. It is then necessary to know as a datum of calculation, the average of years which persons above that age will live. I take this average to be about thirty years, for though many persons will live forty, fifty, or sixty years after the age of twenty-one years, others will die much sooner, and some in every year of that time.

Taking then thirty years as the average of time, it will give, without any material variation, one way or other, the average of time in which the whole property or capital of a nation, or a sum equal thereto, will have passed through one entire revolution in descent, that is, will have gone by deaths to new possessors; for though, in many instances, some parts of this capital will remain forty, fifty, or sixty years in the possession of one person, other parts will have revolved two or three times before that thirty years expire, which will bring it to that average; for were one half the capital of a nation to revolve twice in thirty years, it would produce the same fund as if the whole revolved once.

Taking then thirty years as the average of time in which the whole capital of a nation, or a sum equal thereto, will revolve once, the thirtieth part thereof will be the sum that will revolve every year, that is, will go by deaths to new possessors; and this last sum being thus known, and the ratio per cent. to be subtracted from it being determined, will give the annual amount or income of the proposed fund, to be applied as already mentioned.

In looking over the discourse of the English Minister, Pitt, in his opening of what is called in England the budget, (the scheme of finance for the year 1796,) I find an estimate of the national capital of that country. As this estimate of a national capital is prepared ready to my hand, I take it as a datum to act upon. When a calculation is made upon the known capital of any nation, combined with its population, it will serve as a scale for any other nation, in proportion as its capital and population be more or less. I am the more disposed to take this estimate of Mr. Pitt, for the purpose of shewing to that Minister, upon his own calculation, how much better money may be employed, than in wasting it, as he has done, on the wild project of setting up Bourbon kings. What, in the name of Heaven, are Bourbon kings to the people of England? It is better that the people have bread.

Mr. Pitt states the national capital of England, real and personal, to be one thousand three hundred millions sterling, which is about one-fourth part of the national capital of France, including Belgia. The event of the last harvest in each country proves that the soil of France is more productive than that of England, and that it can better support twenty-four or twenty-five millions of inhabitants than that of England can seven, or seven and an half.

The 30th part of this capital of £.1,300,000,000 is £.43,333,333, which is the part that will revolve every year by deaths in that country to new possessors; and the sum that will annually revolve in France in the proportion of four to one, will be about one hundred and seventy-three millions sterling. From this sum of £.43,333,333 annually revolving, is to be subtracted the value of the natural inheritance absorbed in it, which perhaps, in fair justice, cannot be taken at less, and ought not to be taken at more, than a tenth part.

It will always happen, that of the property thus revolving by deaths every year, part will descend in a direct line to sons and daughters, and the other part collaterally, and the proportion will be found to be about three to one; that is, about 30 millions of the above sum will descend to direct heirs, and the remaining sum of £.13,333,333 to more distant relations, and part to strangers.

Considering then that man is always related to society, that relationship will become comparatively greater in proportion as the next of kin is more distant. It is therefore consistent with civilization to say that where there are no direct heirs, society shall be heir to a part over and above the tenth part *due* to society. If this additional part be from five to ten or twelve per cent. in proportion as the next of kin be nearer or more remote, so as to average with the escheats that may fall, which ought always to go to society and not to the government, an addition of ten per cent. more, the produce from the annual sum of £.43,333,333 will be,

From 30,000,000 – at ten per cent   3,000,000

From 13,333,333 at 10 per cent. with ⎫

    the addition of 10   ⎬   2,666,666

    per cent. more   ⎭   _____

£.43,333333 ·   £.5,666,666

Having thus arrived at the annual amount of the proposed fund, I come, in the next place, to speak of the population proportioned to this fund, and to compare it with uses to which the fund is to be applied.

The population (I mean that of England) does not exceed seven millions and a half, and the number of persons above the age of fifty will in that case be about four hundred thousand. There would not however be more than that number that would accept the proposed ten pounds sterling per annum, though they would be entitled to it. I have no idea it would be accepted by many persons who had a yearly income of two or three hundred pounds sterling. But as we often see instances of rich people falling into sudden poverty, even at the age of sixty, they would always have the right of drawing all the arrears due to them. – Four millions, therefore, of the above annual sum of £.5,666,666, will be required for four hundred thousand aged persons, at ten pounds sterling each.

I come now to speak of the persons annually arriving at twenty-one years of age. If all the persons who died were above the age of twenty-one years, the number of persons annually arriving at that age, must be equal to the annual number of deaths to keep the population stationary. But the greater part die under the age of twenty-one, and therefore the number of persons annually arriving at twenty-one, will be less than half the number of deaths. The whole number of deaths upon a population of seven millions and a half, will be about 220,000 annually. The number arriving at 21 years of age will be about 100,000. The whole number of these will not receive the proposed fifteen pounds, for the reasons already mentioned, though, as in the former case, they would be intitled to it. Admitting then that a tenth part declined receiving it, the amount would stand thus:

Fund annually . . . . £.5,666,666

To 400,000 aged persons

    at £. 10 each . . . . £.4,000,000

To . . 90,000 persons of 21
years, £. 15 sterling each   1,850,000 ⎤
                                              ⎬   5,350,000
                         remains ⎦   £.316,666

There are in every country a number of blind and lame persons, totally incapable of earning a livelihood. But as it will always happen that the greater number of blind persons will be among those who are above the age of fifty years, they will be provided for in that class. The remaining sum of £.316,666, will provide for the lame and blind under that age, at the same rate of £.10 annually for each person.

Having now gone through all the necessary calculations, and stated the particulars of the plan, I shall conclude with some observations.

It is not charity but a right—not bounty but justice, that I am pleading for The present state of what is called civilization, is   *   *   *   *   It is the reverse of what it ought to be, and   *   *   *   *

The contrast of affluence and wretchedness continually meeting and offending the eye, is like dead and living bodies chained together. Though I care as little about riches as any man, I am a friend to riches because they are capable of good. I care not how affluent some may be, provided that none be miserable in consequence of it. But it is impossible to enjoy affluence with the felicity it is capable of being enjoyed, whilst so much misery is mingled in the scene. The sight of the misery, and the unpleasant sensations it suggests, which though they may be suffocated cannot be extinguished, are a greater draw-back upon the felicity of affluence than the proposed 10 per cent. upon property is worth. He that would not give the one to get rid of the other, has no charity, even for himself.

There are in every country some magnificent charities established by individuals. It is however but little that any individual can do when the whole extent of the misery to be relieved be considered. He may satisfy his conscience, but not his heart. He may give all that he has, and that all will relieve but little. It is only by organizing civilization upon such principles as to act like a system of pullies, that the whole weight of misery can be removed.

The plan here proposed will reach the whole. It will immediately relieve and take out of view three classes of wretchedness. The blind, the lame, and the aged poor; and it will furnish the rising generation with means to prevent their becoming poor; and it will do this, without deranging or interfering with any national measures. To shew that this will be the case, it is sufficient to observe, that the operation and effect of the plan will, in all cases, be the same, as if every individual were *voluntarily* to make his will, and dispose of his property, in the manner here proposed.

But it is justice and not charity, that is the principle of the plan. In all great cases it is necessary to have a principle more universally active than charity; and with respect to justice, it ought not to be left to the choice of detached individuals, whether they will do justice or not. Considering then the plan on the ground of justice, it ought to be the act of the whole, growing spontaneously out of the principles of the revolution, and the reputation of it to be national and not individual.

A plan upon this principle would benefit the revolution by the energy that springs from the consciousness of justice. It would multiply also the national resources; for property, like vegetation, encreases by off-sets. When a young couple begins the world, the difference is exceedingly great whether they begin with nothing or with fifteen pounds apiece. With this aid they could buy a cow, and implements to cultivate a few acres of land; and instead of becoming burthens upon society, which is always the case, where children are produced faster than they can be fed, would be put in the way of becoming useful and profitable citizens. The national domains also would sell the better, if pecuniary aids were provided to cultivate them in small lots.

It is the practice of what has unjustly obtained the name of civilization (and the practice merits not to be called either charity or policy) to make some provision for persons becoming poor and wretched, only at the time they become so. – Would it not, even as a matter of economy, be far better, to devise means to prevent their becoming poor. This can best be done by making every person, when arrived at the age of twenty-one years, an inheritor of something to begin with. The rugged face of society, chequered with the extremes of affluence and of want, proves that some extraordinary violence has been committed upon it, and calls on justice for redress. The great mass of the poor, in all countries, are become an hereditary race, and it is next to impossible for them to get out of that state of themselves. It ought also to be observed, that this mass increases in all the countries that are called civilized. More persons fall annually into it, than get out of it.

Though in a plan, in which justice and humanity are the foundation-principles, interest ought not to be admitted into the calculation, yet it is always of advantage to the establishment of any plan, to shew that it is beneficial as a matter of interest. The success of any proposed plan, submitted to public consideration, must finally depend on the numbers interested in supporting it, united with the justice of its principles.

The plan here proposed will benefit all, without injuring any. It will consolidate the interest of the republic with that of the individual. To the numerous class dispossessed of their natural inheritance by the system of landed property, it will be an act of national justice. To persons dying possessed of moderate fortunes, it will operate as a tontine to their children, more beneficial than the sum of money paid into the fund: and it will give to the accumulation of riches a degree of security that none of the old governments of Europe, now tottering on their foundations, can give.

I do not suppose that more than one family in ten, in any of the countries of Europe, has, when the head of the family dies, a clear property left of five hundred pounds sterling. To all such the plan is advantageous. That property would pay fifty pounds into the fund, and if there were only two children under age, they would receive fifteen pounds each (thirty pounds) on coming of age, and be entitled to ten pounds a year after fifty. It is from the overgrown acquisition of property that the fund will support itself; and I know that the possessors of such property in England, though they would eventually be benefited by the protection of nine tenths of it, will exclaim against the plan. But, without entering into any enquiry how they came by that property, let them recollect, that they have been the advocates of this war, and that Mr. Pitt has already laid on more new taxes to be raised annually upon the people of England, and that for supporting the despotism of Austria and the Bourbons, against the liberties of France, than would annually pay all the sums proposed in this plan.

I have made the calculations, stated in this plan, upon what is called personal, as well as upon landed property. The reason for making it upon land is already explained; and the reason for taking personal property into the calculation, is equally well founded, though on a different principle. Land, as before said, is the free gift of the Creator in common to the human race. Personal property is the *effect of Society;* and it is as impossible for an individual to acquire personal property without the aid of Society, as it is for him to make land originally. Separate an individual from society, and give him an island or a continent to possess, and he cannot acquire personal property. He cannot become rich. So inseparably are the means connected with the end, in all cases, that where the former do not exist, the latter cannot be obtained. All accumulation therefore of personal property, beyond what a man's own hands produce, is derived to him by living in society; and he owes, on every principle of justice, of gratitude, and of civilization, a part of that accumulation back again to society from whence the whole came. This is putting the matter on a general principle, and perhaps it is best to do so; for if we examine the case minutely, it will be found, that the accumulation of personal property is, in many instances, the effect of paying too little for the labour that produced it; the consequence of which is, that the working hand perishes in old age, and the employer abounds in affluence. It is perhaps impossible to proportion exactly the price of labour to the profits it produces; and it will also be said, as an apology for injustice, that were a workman to receive an increase of wages daily, he would not save it against old age nor be much the better for it in the interim. Make then Society the treasurer to guard it for him in a common fund, for it is no reason that because he might not make a good use of it for himself that another shall take it.

The state of civilization that has prevailed throughout Europe, is as unjust in its principle, as it is horrid in its effects; and it is the consciousness of this, and the apprehension that such a state cannot continue when once investigation begins in any country, that makes the possessors of property dread every idea of a revolution. It is the *hazard* and not the principles of a revolution that retards their progress. This being the case, it is necessary, as well for the protection of property, as for the sake of justice and humanity, to form a system, that whilst it preserves one part of society from wretchedness, shall secure the other from depredation.

The superstitious awe, the enslaving reverence, that formerly surrounded affluence, is passing away in all countries, and leaving the possessor of property to the convulsion of accidents. When wealth and splendour, instead of fascinating the multitude, excite emotions of disgust; when, instead of drawing forth admiration, it is beheld as an insult upon wretchedness: when the ostentatious appearance it makes serves to call the right of it in question, the case of property becomes critical, and it is only in a system of justice that the possessor can contemplate security.

To remove the danger, it is necessary to remove the antipathies, and this can only be done by making property productive of a national blessing, extending to every individual. When the riches of one man above another shall increase the national fund in the same proportion; when it shall be seen that the prosperity of that fund depends on the prosperity of individuals; when the more riches a man acquires, the better it shall be for the general mass; it is then that antipathies will cease, and property be placed on the permanent basis of national interest and protection.

I have no property in France to become subject to the plan I propose. What I have, which is not much, is in the United States of America. But I will pay one hundred pounds sterling towards this fund in France, the instant it shall be established; and I will pay the same sum in England, whenever a similar establishment shall take place in that country.

A revolution in the state of civilization, is the necessary companion of revolutions in the system of government. If a revolution in any country be from bad to good, or from good to bad, the state of what is called civilization in that country, must be made conformable thereto, to give that revolution effects. Despotic government supports itself by abject civilization, in which debasement of the human mind, and wretchedness in the mass of the people, are the chief criterians. Such governments consider man merely as an animal; that the exercise of intellectual faculty is not his privilege; *that he has nothing to do with the laws, but to obey them;*[1] and they politically depend more upon breaking the spirit of the people by poverty, than they fear enraging it by desperation.

It is a revolution in the state of civilization, that will give perfection to the revolution of France. Already the conviction that government, by representation, is the true system of government, is spreading itself fast in the world. The reasonableness of it can be seen by all. The justness of it makes itself felt even by its opposers. But when a system of civilization, growing out of that system of government, shall be so organized, that not a man or woman born in the republic, but shall inherit some means of beginning the world, and see before them the certainty of escaping the miseries, that under other governments accompany old age, the revolution of France will have an advocate and an ally in the heart of all nations.

An army of principles will penetrate where an army of soldiers cannot – It will succeed where diplomatic management would fail – It is neither the Rhine, the Channel, nor the Ocean, that can arrest its progress – It will march on the horizon of the world, and it will conquer.

– *THOMAS PAINE.*

MEANS FOR CARRYING THE PROPOSED PLAN INTO EXECUTION, AND TO RENDER IT AT THE SAME TIME CONDUCIVE TO THE PUBLIC INTEREST.

I.

Each canton shall elect in its primary assemblies, three persons, as commissioners for that canton, who shall take cognizance, and keep a register

1. Expression of Horsley, an English Bishop, in the English parliament.

of all matters happening in that canton, conformable to the charter that shall be established by law, for carrying this plan into execution.

II.

The law shall fix the manner in which the property of deceased persons shall be ascertained.

III.

When the amount of the property of any deceased person shall be ascertained, the principal heir to that property, or the eldest of the co-heirs, if of lawful age, or if under age, the person authorized by the will of the deceased to represent him, or them, shall give bond to the commissioners of the canton, to pay the said tenth part thereof, within the space of one year, in four equal quarterly payments, or sooner, at the choice of the payers. One half of the whole property shall remain as security until the bond be paid off.

IV.

The bonds shall be registered in the office of the commissioners of the canton, and the original bonds shall be deposited in the national bank at Paris. The bank shall publish every quarter of a year the amount of the bonds in its possession, and also the bonds that shall have been paid off, or what parts thereof, since the last quarterly publication.

V.

The national bank shall issue bank notes upon the security of the bonds in its possession. The notes so issued, shall be applied to pay the pensions of aged persons, and the compensations to persons arriving at twenty-one years of age. – It is both reasonable and generous to suppose, that persons not under immediate necessity, will suspend their right of drawing on the fund, until it acquire, as it will do, a greater degree of ability. In this case, it is proposed, that an honorary register be kept in each canton, of the names of the persons thus suspending that right, at least during the present war.

VI.

As the inheritors of property must always take up their bonds in four quarterly payments, or sooner if they chuse, there will always be numeraire arriving at the bank after the expiration of the first quarter, to exchange for the bank notes that shall be brought in.

VII.

The bank notes being thus got into circulation, upon the best of all possible security, that of actual property to more than four times the amount of the bonds upon which the notes are issued, and with numeraire continually arriving at the bank to exchange or pay them off whenever they shall be presented for that purpose, they will acquire a permanent value in all parts of the republic. They can therefore be received in payment of taxes or emprunts, equal to numeraire, because the government can always receive numeraire for them at the bank.

VIII.

It will be necessary that the payments of the ten *per cent.* be made in numeraire for the first year, from the establishment of the plan. But after the expiration of the first year, the inheritors of property may pay the ten *per cent.* either in bank notes issued upon the fund, or in numeraire. If the payments be in numeraire, it will lie as a deposit at the bank, to be exchanged for a quantity of notes equal to that amount; and if in notes issued upon the fund, it will cause a demand upon the fund equal thereto; and thus the operation of the plan will create means to carry itself into execution.

Finis.

OF THE

RELIGION OF DEISM COMPARED

WITH THE

CHRISTIAN RELIGION,

and the superiority of the former over the latter.

Every person of whatever religious denomination he may be is a DEIST in the first article of his Creed. Deism from the latin word DEUS, God, is the belief of a God, and this belief is the first article of every man's creed.

It is on this article, universally consented to by all mankind, that the Deist builds his church, and here he rests. Whenever we step aside from this article, by mixing it with articles of human invention, we wander into a labyrinth of uncertainty and fable, and become exposed to every kind of imposition by pretenders to revelation. The Persian shews the *Zendavista* of Zoroaster the law-giver of Persia, and calls it the *divine law;* the Bremen shews the *shaster,* revealed, he says by God to Bruma, and given to him out of a cloud; the Jew shews what he calls the law of Moses, given, he says, by God on the Mount Sinai; the Christian shews a collection of books and epistles written by nobody knows who, and called the New Testament, and the Mahometan shews the Koran, given, he says, by God to Mahomet; each of these calls itself *revealed religion,* and the *only* true word of God, and this the followers of each profess to believe from the habit of education, and each believes the others are imposed upon.

But when the divine gift of reason begins to expand itself in the mind and calls man to reflection, he then reads and contemplates God in his works and not in books pretending to be revelation. The Creation is the bible of a true believer in God. Every thing in this vast volume inspires him

"Of the Religion of Deism Compared with the Christian Religion, and the Superiority of the Former over the Latter," in *The Prospect, or View of the Moral World,* June 30, 1804, pp. 235–239; July 7, 1804, pp. 243–247.

with sublime ideas of the Creator. The little and paltry, and often obscene, tales of the bible sink into wretchedness when put in comparison with this mighty work. The Deist needs none of those tricks and shows called miracles to confirm his faith, for what can be a greater miracle than the creation itself and his own existence.

There is a happiness in Deism, when rightly understood, that is not to be found in any other system of religion. All other systems have something in them that either shock our reason or are repugnant to it, and man, if he thinks at all, must stifle his reason in order to force himself to believe them. But in Deism our reason and our belief become happily united. The wonderful structure of the universe and every thing we behold in the system of creation prove to us, far better than books can do, the existence of a God, and at the same time proclaim his attributes. It is by the exercise of our reason that we are enabled to contemplate God in his works and imitate him in his ways. When we see his care and goodness extended over all his creatures, it teaches us our duty towards each other, while it calls forth our gratitude to him. It is by forgetting God in his works, and running after books of pretended revelation that man has wandered from the strait path of duty and happiness, and become by turns the victim of doubt and the dupe of delusion.

Except in the first article in the Christian creed, that of believing in God, there is not an article in it but fills the mind with doubt as to the truth of it the instant man begins to think. Now every article in a creed that is necessary to the happiness and salvation of man ought to be as evident to the reason and comprehension of man as the first article is, for God has not given us reason for the purpose of confounding us, but that we should use it for our own happiness and his glory.

The truth of the first article is proved by God himself and is universal, for *the creation is of itself demonstration of the existence of a Creator.* But the second article, that of God's begetting a son, is not proved in like manner, and stands on no other authority than that of tale. Certain books in what is called the New Testament tell us that Joseph dreamed an angel told him so. (Matthew chap. 1, v. 20.) "And behold the angel of the Lord appeared unto Joseph in a dream, saying, Joseph thou son of David, fear not to take unto thee Mary thy wife, for that which is conceived in her is of the holy ghost." The evidence upon this article bears no comparison with the evidence upon the first article, and therefore is not entitled to the same credit, and ought not to be made an article in a creed, because the evidence of it is defective, and what evidence there is, is doubtful and suspicious. We do not believe the first article on the authority of books, whether called Bibles or Korans, nor yet on the visionary authority of dreams, but on the authority of God's own visible works in the creation. The nations who never heard of such books, nor of such people as Jews, Christians, or Mahometans, believe the existence of a God as fully as we do, because it is self-evident. The work of man's hands is a proof of the existence of man as fully as his personal appearance would be. When we see a watch we have as positive evidence of the existence of a watch-maker as if we saw him; and in like manner the creation is evidence to our reason and our senses of the existence of a Creator. But there is nothing in the works of God that is evidence that he begat a son, nor any thing in the system of creation that corroborates such an idea, and therefore we are not authorised in believing it. What truth there may be in the story that Mary, before she was married to Joseph, was kept by one of the Roman soldiers, and was with child by him, I leave to be settled between the Jews and the Christians. The story however has probability on its side, for her husband Joseph suspected and was jealous of her, and was going to put her away. "Joseph her husband being a just man, and not willing to make her a public example, was going to put her away privately." (Matthew chap. 1, v. 19).

I have already said that "whenever we step aside from the first article (that of believing in God) we wander into a labyrinth of uncertainty," and here is evidence of the justness of the remark, for it is impossible for us to decide who was Jesus Christ's father. But presumption can assume any thing, and therefore it makes Joseph's dream to be of equal authority with the existence of God, and to help it on it calls it revelation. It is impossible for the mind of man in its serious moments, however it may have been entangled by education, or beset by priest craft, not to stand still and doubt upon the truth of this article and of its creed. But this is not all.

The second article of the Christian creed having brought the son of Mary into the world (and this Mary according to the Chronological tables was a girl of only fifteen years of age when this son was born) the next article goes on to account for his being begotten, which was, that when he grew a man he should be put to death to expiate, they say, the sin that Adam brought into the world by eating an apple or some kind of forbidden fruit.

But though this is the creed of the church of Rome, from whence the Protestants borrowed it, it is a creed, which that church has manufactured of itself, for it is not contained in, nor derived from, the book called the New Testament. The four books called the Evangelists, Matthew, Mark, Luke, and John, which give, or pretend to give, the birth, sayings, life, preaching, and death of Jesus Christ, make no mention of what is called the fall of man, nor is the name of Adam to be found in any of those books, which it certainly would be if the writers of them believed that Jesus was begotten, born, and died for the purpose of redeeming mankind from the sin which Adam had brought into the world. Jesus never speaks of Adam himself, of the Garden of Eden, nor of what is called the fall of man. Neither did the early Christians believe the story of the fall of man to be fact, but held it to be allegory. The person called St. Augustine[,] says in his City of God, that the adventure of Eve and the serpent and the account of Paradise, were generally considered in his time as allegory, and he treats them as such himself without attempting to give any explanation of them, but thinks a better might be given than had been offered.

Origen, another of the ancient fathers of the Church, treats the account of the creation in Genesis, and the story of the Garden of Eden and the fall of man, as fable or fiction.

What man of good sense, says he, can ever persuade himself that there was a first, a second, and a third day, and that each of those days had a night, when there was yet neither sun, moon, nor stars! (N. B. According to the account in Genesis, chap. 1, the sun and moon was not made until the fourth day)—What man, continues he, can be stupid enough to believe that God acting the part of a gardener had planted a garden in the east; that the tree of life was a real tree, and that the fruit of it had the virtue of making those who eat of it live forever.

The Jews did not believe the first chapters of Genisis to be fact. Muimonides, one of the most learned and celebrated of the Jewish authors who lived in the eleventh century, says, in his book MORE NEBACHIM. We ought not to understand nor take according to the letter that which is written in the book of the creation, (the book of Genesis.) Taken, says he, according to the letter, especially with respect to the work of four days, it gives the most absurd and extravagant ideas of God.

But the church of Rome having set up its new religion which it called Christianity, and invented the creed which it named the apostles creed, in which it calls Jesus the *only son of God, conceived by the Holy Ghost, and born of the Virgin Mary,* things of which it is impossible that man or woman can have any idea, and consequently no belief but in words, and for which there is no authority but the idle story of Joseph's dream in the first chapter of Matthew, which any designing impostor or foolish fanatic might make, it then manufactured the allegories in the book of Genesis into fact, and the allegorical tree of life and tree of knowledge into real trees, contrary to the belief of the first christians, and for which there is not the least authority in any of the books of the New Testament, for in none of them is there any mention made of such place as the Garden of Eden, nor of any thing that is said to have happened there.

But the church of Rome could not erect the person called Jesus into a Saviour of the World without making the allegories in the book of Genesis into fact, though the New Testament, as before observed, gives no authority for it. All at once the allegorical tree of knowledge became, according to the church, a real tree, the fruit of it real fruit, and the eating of it sinful. As priest-craft was always the enemy of knowledge, because priest craft supports itself by keeping people in delusion and ignorance, it was consistent with its policy to make the acquisition of knowledge a real sin.

The church of Rome having done this, it then brings forward Jesus the son of Mary as suffering death to redeem mankind from sin, which Adam, it says, had brought into the world by eating the fruit of the tree of knowledge. But as it is impossible for reason to believe such a story because it can see no reason for it, nor have any evidence of it, the church then tells us we must not regard our reason, but must *believe,* as it were, and that through thick and thin, as if God had given man reason like a play-thing, or a rattle, on purpose to make fun of him. Reason is the forbidden tree of priest-craft, and may serve to explain the allegory of the forbidden tree of knowledge, for we may reasonably suppose the allegory had some meaning and application at the time it was invented. It was the practice of the eastern nations to convey their meaning by allegory, and relate it in the manner of fact. Jesus followed the same method, yet nobody ever supposed the allegory or parable of the Rich Man and Lazarus, the Prodigal Son, the Ten Virgins, &c. were facts. Why then should the tree of knowledge, which is far more romantic in idea than the parable in the New Testament are, be supposed to be a real tree.[1] The answer to this is, because the church could not make its new-fangled system, which it called Christianity, hold together without it. To have made Christ to die on account of an allegorical tree would have been too bare-faced a fable.

But the account, as it is given of Jesus in the New Testament even visionary as it is, does not support the creed of the church that he died for the redemption of the world. According to that account he was crucified and buried on the Friday and rose again in good health on the Sunday

---

1. The remark of Emperor Julien, on the story of the Tree of Knowledge is worth observing. "If," said he, "there ever had been, or could be, a Tree of Knowledge, instead of God forbidding man to eat thereof, it would be that of which he would order him to eat the most."

morning, for we do not hear that he was sick. This cannot be called dying, and is rather making fun of death than suffering it. There are thousands of men and women also, who, if they could know they should come back again in good health in about thirty-six hours, would prefer such kind of death for the sake of the experiment, and to know what the other side of the grave was. Why then should that which would be only a voyage of curious amusement to us be magnified into merit and sufferings in him? If a God he could not suffer death, for immortality cannot die, and as a man his death could be no more than the death of any other person.

The belief of the redemption of Jesus Christ is altogether an invention of the church of Rome and not the doctrine of the New Testament. What the writers of the New Testament attempt to prove by the story of Jesus is, the *resurrection of the same body from the grave,* which was the belief of the Pharisees, in opposition to the Sadducees (a sect of Jews) who denied it. Paul, who was brought up a Pharisee, labours hard at this point for it was the creed of his own Pharisaical church. The XV chap. 1 of Corinthians is full of supposed cases and assertions about the resurrection of the same body, but there is not a word in it about redemption. This chapter makes part of the funeral service of the Episcopal church. The dogma of the redemption is the fable of priest-craft invented since the time the New Testament was compiled, and the agreeable delusion of it suited with the depravity of immoral livers. When men are taught to ascribe all their crimes and vices to the temptations of the Devil, and to believe that Jesus, by his death, rubs all off and pays their passage to heaven gratis, they become as careless in morals as a spendthrift would be of money, were he told that his father had engaged to pay off all his scores. It is a doctrine, not only dangerous to morals in this world, but to our happiness in the next world, because it holds out such a cheap, easy, and lazy way of getting to heaven as has a tendency to induce men to hug the delusion of it to their own injury.

But there are times when men have serious thoughts, and it is at such times when they begin to think, that they begin to doubt the truth of the Christian Religion, and well they may, for it is too fanciful and too full of conjecture, inconsistency, improbability, and irrationality, to afford consolation to the thoughtful man. His reason revolts against his creed. He sees that none of its articles are proved, or can be proved. He may believe that such a person as is called Jesus (for Christ was not his name) was born and grew to be a man, because it is no more than a natural and probable case. But who is to prove he is the son of God, that he was begotten by the Holy Ghost? Of these things there can be no proof, and that which admits not of proof, and is against the laws of probability and the order of nature, which God himself has established, is not an object for belief. God has not given man reason to embarrass him, but to prevent his being imposed upon.

He may believe that Jesus was crucified, because many others were crucified, but who is to prove he was crucified *for the sins of the world?* This article has no evidence not even in the New Testament; and if it had, where is the proof that the New Testament, in relating things neither probable nor proveable, is to be believed as true? When an article in a creed does not admit of proof nor of probability the salvo is to call it revelation; But this is only putting one difficulty in the place of another, for it is as impossible to prove a thing to be revelation as it is to prove that Mary was gotten with child by the Holy Ghost.

Here it is that the religion of Deism is superior to the Christian religion. It is free from all those invented and torturing articles that shock our reason or injure our humanity, and with which the Christian religion abounds. Its creed is pure and sublimely simple. It believes in God and there it rests. It honours reason as the choicest gift of God to man, and the faculty by which he is enabled to contemplate the power, wisdom, and goodness of the Creator displayed in the creation; and reposing itself on his protection, both here and hereafter, it avoids all presumptuous beliefs, and rejects, as the fabulous inventions of men, all books pretending to revelation.

– T. P.

OF THE TERM
"LIBERTY OF THE PRESS"

The writer of this remembers a remark made to him by Mr. Jefferson concerning the English Newspapers which at that time, 1787, while Mr. Jefferson was Minister at Paris, were most vulgarly abusive. The remark applies with equal force to the federal papers of America. The remark was, that "the licentiousness of the press produces the same effect as the reverse of the press was intended to do if the restraint, he said, was to prevent things being told, and the licentiousness of the press prevents things being believed when they are told." We have in this state an evidence of the truth of this remark. The number of federal papers in the city and state of New-York are more than five to one to the number of republican papers, yet the majority of the elections go always against the federal papers, which is demonstrative evidence that the licentiousness of those papers are destitute of credit.

Whoever has made observations on the characters of nations will find it generally true, that the manners of a nation, or of a party, can be better ascertained from the character of its press than from any other public circumstance. If its press is licentious, its manners are not good. Nobody believes a common liar, or a common defamer.

Nothing is more common with Printers, especially of Newspapers, than the continual cry of the *liberty of the press,* as if, because they are Printers they are to have more privileges than other people. As the term *"liberty of the press"* is adopted in this country without being understood, I will state the origin of it and shew what it means. The term comes from England and the case was as follows.

Prior to what is called in England *the revolution,* which was in 1688, no work could be published in that country without first obtaining the permission of an officer appointed by the government for inspecting works intended for publication. The same was the case in France, except that in France there were forty who were called *censors,* and in England there was but one called Impremateur.

"Of the Term 'Liberty of the Press,'" in *The American Citizen,* October 20, 1806.

At the revolution the office of Impremateur was abolished and as works could then be published without first obtaining the permission of the government officer, the press was, in consequence of that abolition, said to be free, and it was from this circumstance that the term *liberty of the press* arose. The press, which is a tongue in the eye, was then put exactly in the case of the human tongue. A man does not ask liberty before hand to say something he has a mind to say, but he becomes answerable afterwards for the atrocities he may utter. In like manner, if a man makes the press utter atrocious things he becomes as answerable for them as if he had uttered them by word of mouth. Mr. Jefferson has said in his inaugural speech, that *"error of opinion might be tolerated when reason was left free to combat it."* This is sound philosophy in cases of error. But there is a difference between error and licentiousness.

Some lawyers in defending their clients (for the generality of lawyers like Swiss soldiers will fight on either side) have often given their opinion of what they defined the liberty of the press to be. One said it was this; another said it was that, and so on, according to the case they were pleading. Now these men ought to have known that the term, *liberty of the press,* arose from a FACT, the abolition of the office of Imprimateur, and that opinion has nothing to do with the case. The term refers to the fact of Printing *free from prior restraint,* and not at all to the matter Printed whether good or bad. The public at large, or in case of prosecution, a jury of the country will be the judges of the matter.

– COMMON SENSE.

Essays

Thomas Paine

The English Dimension

J. C. D. CLARK

More than almost any other author in the canon of the history of political thought, the "usable Paine" devised mainly by twentieth-century academics has obscured the "historic Paine," the real-life actor in the eighteenth-century public realm. Paine was not alone in this: significantly unhistoric "usable" versions were created of political theorists from John Locke to Edmund Burke and of literary figures from Daniel Defoe to Samuel Johnson; but Paine was the most closely integrated into subsequent political purposes.

This occlusion made Paine a blank canvas onto which later commentators projected their evolving priorities: Paine was widely celebrated as providing blueprints of later society. Even so, Paine scholarship is far from equally distributed. Despite his significance for the American Revolution, the French Revolution, and Britain's *révolution manquée* (the "failed revolution," a revolution that some claim Britain ought to have had but did not), there is some academic attention to Paine in France and Britain,[1] but a major Paine industry in the United States. The explanation is clear: in the United States Paine was swept up into the republic's "myth of origins." There, many academics still implicitly treat him as an American whose primary significance is for that society's present-day "civil religion."[2] Much Paine scholarship is therefore both proleptic and normative. Prolepsis is the methodological error of assuming that some future idea or phenomenon already existed in past time; it links with the normative celebration of past actors as champions of modern values. Both are problematic for academic history, whose role is not to praise or to blame but to understand.

This essay will set out what Paine was *not*, by reviewing some of the successive presentist interpretations imposed on him in previous English-language editions of his works. It will then outline a case for what Paine *was*. It will argue that Paine was not a draughtsman who foresaw a democratic, modernizing future, but a man whose mind was formed in England in the 1740s and 1750s; not a modern atheist but a premodern deist whose belief in a God working through general laws rather than through revelation, Christ, or the agency of the Church was similarly of the early eighteenth century; a man whose deism explains his drastically simplifying view of politics and science alike; a principled optimist about human nature, whatever atrocities he witnessed.

Since the idea of "the Enlightenment" was absent in Paine's lifetime, his society's reforming causes were not united under any overarching ideology: many campaigns or crusades were therefore missing from the historic Paine's commitments that later commentators expected to find there. The historic Paine favored a wide electorate but never quite grasped the English doctrine (new from the 1770s) of universal manhood suffrage based on personality; nor did women's rights or anti-slavery figure largely in his thought (as they did not in the England of the 1750s). Paine was against monarchy and aristocracy for older reasons, because he rejected their underpinning, the hereditary principle, on the theological grounds of humanity's original equality by creation;[3] not because he anticipated the class-based politics of the nineteenth century. Even his program of social security chiefly extended the practice of English poor relief in his youth, and hardly anticipated those later ideologies "socialism" and "radicalism." Paine remained a culturally bound Englishman in exile, not a citizen of the world at home everywhere and drawing on all cultures eclectically.

Paine is widely understood by reference to two momentous episodes that are conventionally but misleadingly seen as forward-looking: the American and French Revolutions. Yet those vast and complex phenomena were driven by long-existing causes particular to those societies, not by general principles later triumphant. This makes it plausible that Paine failed to foresee either; that he understood less about those two episodes than his recent enthusiasts suppose; that his contribution to them was smaller; that he learned little from them; and that his mind-set, values, and frame of reference remained largely those of an English freethinker of the reign of George II, confidently repeating his religious teaching and its political consequences in the new situations into which he blundered. Paine was widely read in his day, but a politically aware mass reading public was the creation of the Reformation and the 1640s, not of the late eighteenth century: Paine's reception and subsequent influence need to be more carefully specified than they conventionally are.

The "historic Paine" reveals, by contrast, the successive misinterpretations perpetuated by previous editions of his works. These older interpretations are particularly vulnerable to recent historiographical developments, which have recast the context for Paine as well as for many of the social and political movements of his day. What, then, were these older misinterpretations? They have much to do with the evolving priorities of the hege-monic "civil religion," myth of origins, or self-image of the United States.

One once-plausible convention was to relate Paine to the materialist vision in which the United States was pictured as the best poor man's country. In 1922 Paine was "the Ragged Philosopher of his age. . . . For the Anglo-Saxon proletariat . . . he is still the classic textbook of radical thought . . . he means most to Americans."[4] In 1945, Philip S. Foner, a his-torian of the American labor movement, hailed Paine as "a working man," a "spokesman for the city artisans and mechanics," inspired by "the poverty and suffering of the masses" to "improve the status of the laboring classes"; this was part of "the struggle for democracy in America," evidenced by the Pennsylvania constitution of 1776, containing universal white male suf-frage, which was "drawn up by Paine and Franklin." In that spirit, claimed Foner, Paine wrote against negro slavery as early as the spring of 1775.[5] Paine was depicted as a person repeatedly offended by the injustices he witnessed and continually drawn to crusade against them: "Thomas Paine was one of those great humanitarian spirits. . . . Paine, throughout life, was revolted by human suffering. . . . Paine . . . was perpetually brought face to face with misery and poverty."[6] Henry Collins, a British historian of a related conception, the "British working class movement," echoed Foner in 1969: Paine's writings on the American Revolution were of "staggering modernity"; Paine's "sympathies were with the poor"; his message "has relevance today." Common Sense "anticipated the doctrine of the Jacobins"; Paine reached "the threshold of socialism."[7] As late as 2011, Claire Grogan endorsed E. P. Thompson's view, published in 1963, that Rights of Man was "a foundation text of the English working-class movement"; Grogan judged that it "is central to the Labour Party."[8]

This explanation largely disappeared in Britain, but not in America, where it evolved. In 1984 Penguin Classics reissued Henry Collins's edi-tion of 1969, with a new introduction by the American Eric Foner. There, the nephew of Philip Foner hailed Paine's Common Sense as an account of "the world significance of the American Revolution," and his Rights of Man as "a classic statement of the egalitarian, democratic faith of the Age of Revolution." Paine, "an artisan himself . . . forged a special relationship with the radical artisan community of Pennsylvania," the social constitu-ency that proved most receptive to "the democratic, egalitarian emphasis of Paine's republicanism." Paine, therefore, "often spoke for the artisans of the cities"; by his so doing, "English radicalism was transformed"[9] (into, by implication, an American egalitarianism). "In Paine's artisanal roots we find a primitive mold of his class perspective on society and politics"; the "pivotal influence on Thomas Paine was his perception of America during the year prior to writing and publishing *Common Sense*."[10] As late as 2010, the Harvard edition of Paine's *Common Sense* depicted a Paine "frustrated by his experiences with the class hierarchy of Britain."[11]

Paine was thereby fused with then-hegemonic understandings of the American founding as having been built around timeless, universally applicable, and secular natural or human rights; this shaded, from the mid-twentieth century, into an identification of Paine with "the Enlightenment." The trend began with the religious freethinker Moncure Conway's important edition of 1894–1896, saluting Paine's writings as having been "the founders of republican liberty in America and Europe."[12] From the 1940s, one organizing category became dominant. Paine's ideas "are those of The Enlightenment, focused upon contemporary tyrannies."[13] In the 1960s, Paine was regarded as "a typical figure of the Enlightenment."[14]

This identification partly depended on the dominant role then assigned to John Locke. In 1976 Isaac Kramnick, an American, similarly hailed Paine as "instinctively progressive"; he had written, claimed Kramnick, against slavery and, in *The Pennsylvania Magazine,* for women's rights. *Common Sense* began from "Lockean liberalism" in public affairs, "the basic liberal vision"; that pamphlet also articulated "the rage of English radicalism," expressed not so much by "the workers" as by "the bourgeoisie."[15] Kramnick was seconded in 1989 by another American, Bruce Kuklick: he identified Paine as "a bourgeois revolutionary" who gave focus to "anger about the English class system of the eighteenth century." Inconsistently, Paine was "something of an outsider" in America, since "the colonial uprising was mainly middle-class, 'bourgeois,' in its orientation." Paine's religious views were an "obvious extension" of his interests in Newtonian physics and "the American Enlightenment," and went with "the philosophy of natural rights."[16] Alan Taylor too wrote of "Paine's radicalism"; somehow simultaneously, "Paine favored the classical liberalism of John Locke and Adam Smith."[17]

Thus was a novel intellectual cocktail mixed for present-day consumption. Paine's *Rights of Man* was "resolutely modern for its discussions of popular sovereignty, constitutions, hereditary rule, and much else"; the work was "bent on exporting the egalitarian principles of the American Revolution, the new rights of the new world, to Europe." It "offers the most prominent defense of the idea of universal natural rights, or as we today mostly say, human rights, of any book originally written in English. . . . Playing midwife to this conception of the individual's relation to state and community, where rights are basic to rather than merely incidental to gov-

ernment, is thus Paine's most enduring accomplishment." Consequently,
"Paine's principles, especially in the United States, have also virtually become the political second nature of modernity."[18] Paine's ideas "embody
to an uncommonly pure degree the letter and the spirit of Enlightenment
liberalism."[19]

In *Rights of Man* Paine "presents an impassioned defense of the Enlightenment principles of freedom and equality"; it was "the only comprehensive account he gave of his understanding of Enlightenment humanism."[20]
A Paine who was "[a]lways ahead of his time" was the Paine who "made
America 'the cause of all mankind' and used its example to show how to
make good on the Enlightenment promise."[21] Paine's *The Age of Reason*
"reflects the basic principles of the Enlightenment worldview."[22] Paine was
to be explained as "a leading voice of what we might call the Revolutionary
Enlightenment"; for him, American independence in 1783 meant "the Enlightenment vindicated"; "*The Rights of Man* [sic] . . . defended the French
Revolution along with the key premise of the Revolutionary Enlightenment: that the earth belonged to the living, who could alter or abolish their
inheritance to suit their needs and rights." "Together, the works of Paine
and [Mary] Wollstonecraft in the early 1790s signal the high-water mark of
the Revolutionary Enlightenment."[23]

As long as the United States sustained the international hegemony of
its civil religion, this vision was influential beyond its borders. In 1995, a
Briton, Mark Philp, depicted Paine as "the world's first international revolutionary . . . a man of multiple citizenships. . . . In abandoning his native
country in 1774, he left behind all particular attachments." *Common Sense*,
for example, "proclaims universal values"; Paine's political views were not
obviously indebted to other political theorists, but Paine was "insisting on
the radicalism" of the American Revolution as a transformative influence
on Europe.[24] Such endorsements from abroad flattered more numerous
domestic American celebrations. To the American Gordon Wood in 2003,
Paine was "the political pamphleteer whose impassioned democratic voice
played a pivotal role in the struggle for American independence and in
the egalitarian revolution that swept the Western world in the late eighteenth century." Paine was "particularly influenced by the work of two
leading figures of the Enlightenment, Isaac Newton and John Locke." By
the time he returned to Europe in 1787, Paine "had come to see himself as
the intellectual progenitor of revolutions." *Rights of Man* "sums up what
he [Paine] had learned about constitutionalism and political theory during
his years in America."[25] More recently, American commentators have become preoccupied by what is conventionally termed British "imperialism"

or "colonialism." In 2004 the American Edward Larkin hailed *Common Sense* as a pamphlet that had "directly contested the authority of British colonialism in America." It was a "major American manifesto" because Paine "takes some of the ideas that were circulating in the colonies at the time and refashions them to promote his ideal vision of democracy to a popular audience."[26]

These misinterpretations were characteristically American. Since the framing of these models, many British perspectives have significantly changed. Despite Paine's role in the French Revolution, nineteenth- and twentieth-century French historians seldom sustained such proleptic historical myths about Paine's significance for the France of their day or for the meaning of its Revolution of 1789.[27] All these interpretations once seemed self-evident, yet all now call for reexamination.

With the progressive weakening of the politics of class in recent decades, historians increasingly appreciate that class had only ever been a language of politics, not a structural feature automatically generated in industrializing societies, and a language that was devised only after Paine's lifetime. Consequently, he did not conceive of "the working class" or any synonym for it, and did not defend such a reification. He did not picture the existence of a "middle class" or "bourgeoisie," but nor did his contemporaries in the English-speaking world. Poverty was not central to his political thought. His antipathy to the power of kings and aristocrats came from an older order. Although he had worked as an artisan, he never attributed to artisans, even urban artisans, any special political character or role. There is no evidence that Paine took with him to America in 1774 any resentment at what was only later identified as the English class system, and when back in England and France after 1787 he moved in the circles of the nobility without recording any sense that class divides were being crossed.

Paine was the child of a small country town, Thetford, but although he lived in London, Philadelphia, and Paris, he nowhere commented on any process of urbanization or thought that the great city heralded a new form of civilization built around manufacturing industry. Paine's very English ambition, on the contrary, was to become a small freeholder, an independent yeoman, and although he proved a failure as a farmer in America, he looked to individual industriousness to solve the problem of poverty once the injustice of man's ancestral expulsion from the land had been rectified by modest cash transfer payments. Paine's economics thus had nothing to do with the new doctrine of "socialism," which emerged only in the 1820s.

The key term for Paine was not class "fraternity" but individual "freedom," and this he sought to spread; freedom itself would, he argued, create a setting in which employment, consumption, and trade would operate for the good of rich and poor alike. Given freedom, "Let the rich man enjoy his riches, and the poor man comfort himself in his poverty."[28] Paine's aims were not those of early socialists: "I defend the cause of the poor, of the manufacturers, of the tradesmen, of the farmers, and of all those on whom the real burden of taxes falls – but above all, I defend the cause of humanity."[29] Paine defended humanity, not the working class, in a world in which most income was still derived from agriculture, not manufacturing or services: as he wrote in 1780, "Lands are the real riches of the habitable world, and the natural funds of America."[30] Accordingly, from Adam Smith's *Wealth of Nations* Paine responded most to Smith's condemnation of the enormous debts that the monarchies of the old world had amassed by their engagement in repeated wars.[31] Although Paine protested against the cruelty and misconduct of governments, especially in their colonies, he never systematized these critiques to protest against "imperialism" or "colonialism," concepts only derived from the economic theory of the late nineteenth century.[32] The revolution of 1776 was theoretically articulate but was not normally defined against a notion of a "British Empire"; that concept was strikingly absent from the Declaration of Independence and from writings of the period, *Common Sense* included.

Rights of Man. Part the Second famously contained the outlines of a system of social security; yet this was not as novel as it appears. While an exciseman in Lewes, Sussex, in 1768–1774, Paine had been a member of the vestry of St. Michael's parish, and was involved in the regular payments to the poor, for many purposes, that were administered at parish level.[33] Even during the French Revolution, *Rights of Man. Part the Second* did not propose social security payments as an engine of social revolution, still less advocate them for America or France. Neither revolution led to any such result. Even Paine's *Agrarian Justice* (1797) went little further.

The twentieth-century tendency retrospectively to group approved causes under the umbrellas of "the working-class movement" or "the Enlightenment" has been problematized in Paine's case by the discovery that the anonymous essays of 1775 in the Philadelphia press on slavery and women are wrongly attributed to him. Although he disapproved of slavery, it never achieved prominence in his writings; despite knowing and sharing a publisher with Mary Wollstonecraft, he made only a few asides on women's rights, and published no sustained consideration of the issue.

Paine failed to defend the rights of Native Americans, another gorilla in the corner of the room in 1776. This problematization has continued with the contention that in English discourse "the Enlightenment" was a term of historical art coined in the late nineteenth century, popularized from the mid-twentieth, and projected back onto the eighteenth in order to promote a range of present-day campaigns:[34] Paine could not have been part of a movement that did not yet exist in the minds of his contemporaries.

In Paine's lifetime there was, similarly, no such ideology as "liberalism" for him to adopt or reject. It was once conventional retrospectively to recruit John Locke (1632–1704) as a founding father of "the Enlightenment" and to identify his doctrine as "Lockeian liberalism." Yet Locke, although an influential figure in eighteenth-century epistemology, sanctioned practices (for example: slavery; capital punishment for crimes against property; what he called the "subjection" of wives to their husbands) in many ways inimical to practices later termed "enlightened." Paine specifically denied having read Locke; in English discourse "liberalism" was newly coined in England in the 1810s, and even then only weakly reified.[35] Although Locke gave a central place in his political writings to natural law and to rights derived from it, Paine's *Common Sense* argued from Scripture more than from natural law. Despite their titles, Paine's *Rights of Man* and *Rights of Man. Part the Second* contained no worked-out theory of natural rights; *The Age of Reason* said nothing to show that its age was essentially reasonable.

Was Paine a democrat? True, he always favored a wide franchise, but on older premises he generally held that "men" (ignoring women) were entitled to vote as taxpayers or property owners rather than as individuals. He did not participate in the formulation, by heterodox English Dissenters like Richard Price and Joseph Priestley, of the new ideology of universal manhood suffrage based on personality.[36] In October 1776, the Englishman John Cartwright set out a coherent program combining universal manhood suffrage, annual elections, the secret ballot, salaries for MPs, and equal electoral districts.[37] Paine never adopted this formula, and it is not clear that he ever read Cartwright. Paine was out of the country and was still abroad when this ideology was placed on the agenda of parliamentary politics in the Westminster election of 1780. It has now been established that Paine had no hand in drafting the Pennsylvania constitution of 1776, whose extensive franchise is still sometimes taken as demonstrating his views.[38] The American Revolution, like the French, was a war of ideas, triggered by principled disputes; but the pursuit of universal manhood suffrage was not among them, and Paine did not hail either revolution as essentially democratic in present-day terms. Even in *Rights of Man,* Paine argued that the franchise for elections to the House of Commons should be "as universal as taxation";[39] his most famous work still expressed the older mind-set.

Paine's sense of the ideal extent of the franchise steadily widened, but he never adopted the slogan "annual parliaments and universal suffrage" used as a mantra by Cartwright and the London-based Society for Constitutional Information. Although Paine had contacts with the SCI and the London Corresponding Society while in England in the 1790s, his role in subsequent English reforming or quasi-revolutionary politics (for example, antislavery; Chartism; franchise extension in 1867 and 1884; the suffragette movement) was often small or nonexistent. Only in the history of English freethinking did Paine enjoy a posthumous prominence; but freethinking was to lead via agnosticism to atheism, positions that the deist Paine had repudiated. Paine consistently championed the representative system, "representation ingrafted upon democracy" rather than "simple democracy,"[40] but the most famous and successful example of the representative system, the Westminster Parliament, was already operative in the Britain that Paine rejected with hatred. For the future development of democracy, what was most influential was the actual practice of Britain's constitutional monarchy and the United States' constitutional presidency, not Paine's theories.

Similarly, Paine did not advocate "radicalism." This was the proper name for a new ideology, coined in England in the 1820s to signify a fusion of universal suffrage, militant atheism, and Ricardian economics.[41] Paine came close to the first of these components, but never on the principled grounds that its supporters took as fundamental. He indignantly repudiated atheism and remained an outspoken theist. David Ricardo (1772–1823) was best known for his *Principles of Political Economy and Taxation* (London, 1817) with its clear division of interests between social blocs and its indictment of the landowner; but Paine (d. 1809) had taken a quite different view, objecting to landowners on grounds of an ancient wrong, not a present structural function. Historians' discussions of "radicalism" in Britain or America during Paine's lifetime are therefore at best without meaning, at worst, distorting: the American Revolution was socially transformative, but not because it was caused by, or implemented, "radicalism." Both Paine and Marx were foes of inequality, but Paine traced inequality to the hereditary principle, while Marx traced it to the inner dynamics of capitalism. For Paine, "the distinctions of rich, and poor, may, in a great measure be accounted for, and that without having recourse to the harsh ill sounding names of oppression and avarice."[42] Paine's antipathy to the hereditary system was premised on theology (kingship was "the most prosperous invention the Devil ever set on foot for the promotion of idolatry");[43] Marx's antipathy to capitalism was premised on economics.

Paine emigrated to Pennsylvania in 1774 with no sense that a revolution was impending. He had written nothing in condemnation of British "colonialism" or "imperialism"; indeed he had been an enthusiastic combatant in the war of 1756–1763, in which Britain's overseas possessions had been massively extended. Paine famously announced to American colonists in *Common Sense* that "We have it in our power to begin the world over again."[44] In a secular sense, this was impossible, and his pamphlet demands interpretation not as a prophetic emancipation but as a product of Paine's English religious experience, mobilized in a new context. Paine's use of Scripture in *Common Sense* was not that of a deist; but there is evidence that he there employed Scripture tactically rather than as a believer in revelation, and prudently concealed his deist beliefs until, expecting execution in the Terror, there was no longer a reason for concealment. What Paine wrote in *Common Sense* was more a bitter negation of his homeland and its essential features (as he perceived them) than an inspired blueprint for a future American society.

Common Sense has been given, in retrospect, a legendary role, ubiquitous, transformative, and unifying; but this needs qualification. In April 1776 Paine boasted (without knowledge) a circulation of 120,000, which in 1779 he raised to 150,000; by 1945 this had been inflated by one historian: "shortly after its publication almost half a million copies were sold."[45] The true total was far less; mass distribution in winter was nearly impossible; it was reprinted in only seven of the thirteen colonies; many leading colonists at first resisted its extremist recommendations.[46] In 1776 Paine's pamphlet intruded into a transatlantic legal and constitutional debate that had been conducted with great sophistication since the Stamp Act controversy of 1765 or earlier, but *Common Sense* said nothing on that debate. Appropriately, Paine does not feature in the latest survey of the subject.[47] There is no evidence that Paine knew much about the controversy: *Common Sense* mentioned no American public figure and no American publication. The first half of Paine's pamphlet concerned England, and was possibly drafted by him there; the second half contained little that was specific about the colonies. When he published *Common Sense,* Paine had not set foot outside Philadelphia; he was no Tocqueville, who assiduously toured the new republic before writing *Democracy in America.* The denominational dynamics of the colonies made the American Revolution in part a war of religion,[48] but of these conflicts Paine initially knew little and in retrospect wrote nothing. *Common Sense* was a heartfelt negation of Paine's native England, but hardly a blueprint for a new state.

Far from seeing himself as an intellectual progenitor of revolutions, Paine left the United States for Europe in 1787 with no sense that the American Revolution would trigger others. In 1782 he had replied to the Frenchman Guillaume Raynal's justified scepticism about Americans having defended "the happiness of mankind" in their rebellion by asserting the opposite: "we saw not a temporary good for the present race only, but a continued good to all posterity."[49] But this was a brief contradiction, highly generalized and without specific application, and a claim that Paine did not follow up or develop until his *Rights of Man. Part the Second* (1792). It was the English Nonconformist minister Richard Price who in 1789 famously wrote of a revolution "after setting AMERICA free, reflected to FRANCE, and there kindled into a blaze that lays despotism in ashes, and warms and illuminates EUROPE!"[50] Paine adopted this vision only later. Indeed, the American Revolution hardly had such a domino effect: France's involvement in the American war led to her fiscal collapse in the late 1780s, but French society was driven by its own principled commitments and inner conflicts more than by any copying of the example of a distant and foreign population. In Britain, where the most direct catalytic effects of the American Revolution might have been expected, they were initially very limited.

It was too easy, in the twentieth century, to depict Paine as a "modern." But in his own day the "moderns" were merely those who had succeeded the "ancients," the inhabitants of ancient Greece and Rome. His era lacked the idea, coined only in the late nineteenth century, of "modernity" as a state of being, brought about by a "process" termed "modernization," which forced people to be for "modernity" or against it. Without that idea, it is meaningless to label Paine a "progressive," enjoying a vision of "modernity" that his opponents lacked.

Paine's self-image as a citizen of the world equally demands qualification. The phrase had been familiar in English culture since the late sixteenth century or earlier, and was not an invention of the American colonies in the late eighteenth. Paine explicitly claimed to be "a man who considers the world as his home . . . I have long banished the contracted ideas, I was, like other people, brought up in."[51] Yet he had not escaped his cultural inheritance; his boast was a default position, created by his exile from his homeland, not the result of a worked-out theory of human brotherhood and international solidarity, still less of familiarity with other cultures. From 1776 Paine did his best to claim American citizenship, not to abjure all national allegiance. The two republics in whose birth he had a role, the United

States and France, soon abandoned any principled pursuit of *fraternité*, adopting instead legal definitions of citizenship as formal as those of the kingdoms of prerevolutionary Europe.

It might be argued that Paine failed in a project of universal citizenship; more probably, he never clearly framed such a project. More than has been appreciated, Paine moved in a cultural cocoon; it was certainly not airtight, but it had a significant limiting effect on his thought. He wrote nothing to show that he recognized anything essentially different about American popular culture. Despite his residence in France from 1792 to 1802, he never learned to speak French. There Paine moved mainly in the circles of British and American expatriates or of Frenchmen who spoke English; only by the end of his stay was he able to read a newspaper in French. Since French was still the most widely used language in Europe, this argued no great cosmopolitanism. Of other modern languages he knew nothing.

In assessing Paine's cultural indebtedness, one problem is his success-fully propagated public image – that he reasoned from first principles. In 1792, he claimed:

> I did not, at my first setting out in public life . . . turn my thoughts to subjects of government from motives of interest. . . . I saw an opportu-nity, in which I thought I could do some good, and I followed exactly what my heart dictated. I neither read books, nor studied other people's opinions. I thought for myself.[52]

Undoubtedly, Paine did think for himself. Yet he also talked to other people, developed his early ideas in the intellectual settings in which he found himself, and read many books. All these things happened first in En-gland. He developed English ideas, he responded to English circumstances, and he read English books.[53] Indeed, almost all his reading was in En-glish sources, or works recently published in English translation. Even the idea of making the world new could only derive from the idea of the "new birth" stressed in English religious revivalism, especially the Methodism with which the young Paine evidently had two brief associations; there is no evidence that it derived from anything that he found in Philadelphia in 1775.

Paine carried with him to the New World some very old and very En-glish intellectual baggage. Although his ideas did in a few ways develop over time, the evidence for any extensive development is surprisingly scanty. Moreover, Paine was English, not British: Scotland and Ireland hardly appeared in his thinking, and even after Irish revolutionaries called on him in Paris in the 1790s, enlisting his backing for a rising in their homeland, Ireland still featured little in his writings. This was remarkable, since Ireland was the place in the British Isles with the greatest potential for revolution, realized in 1798.

Most of the scant evidence for Paine's early intellectual formation concerns his eager imbibing of popular Newtonianism in London in the 1750s, yet this did not explain his commitment to English deism: mid-century Newtonians were generally Trinitarian Christians. Nor was deism the only English commitment that Paine absorbed. While in Philadelphia, Paine's employer Robert Aitken was one of the colonial booksellers who reprinted the English weekly paper *The Crisis,* a slashing and visceral assault on monarchy that preceded *Common Sense.* When Paine borrowed the title for his own series of pamphlets, *The American Crisis,* what was remarkable was the moderation of his language compared with the English originals he echoed, like John Wilkes's *The North Briton,* Junius's *Letters,* and *The Crisis.* English models like these provided Paine with almost all that he needed for *Common Sense.* While in France, he published his religious opinions in *The Age of Reason* and *The Age of Reason. Part the Second,* but there too his sources prove to be almost wholly English: there is no evidence that Paine learned anything significant from the religious views of American or French freethinkers.

Paine expressed a series of generalized objections to monarchy from *Common Sense* onward, but the origin of that doctrine in Paine's mind is problematic: Newtonianism did not entail it. The question is answered by evidence that throughout his writings Paine rehearsed (as well as a theological case) a series of specific objections to monarchy, drawn from English history. Paine's mind was formed in the decades before 1760, years in which the legitimacy of monarchy was framed almost wholly as a dynastic alternative between the houses of Hanover and Stuart, not between monarchy as such and republicanism.

Paine's zeal against the hereditary principle has seemed so self-evident a truth in the United States that the origin of that commitment was obscured. The politics of dynasticism offers a clue. Paine was, throughout, an anti-Jacobite, but the long persistence of the Jacobite threat gave urgency to Jacobite ideology, and its hostility to William III and the Georges was echoed by the English opposition (often a strange alliance of Tory-Jacobites and opposition Whigs). Paine was unusual in carrying this hostility to the extreme of antipathy to monarchy in general. His comments on the house of Stuart were adverse; but his comments on the houses of Orange and Hanover were far more negative. Those houses caused England's involvement in foreign wars:

With the revolution of 1688, and more so since the Hanover succession [in 1714], came the destructive system of continental intrigues, and the rage for foreign wars and foreign dominion; systems of such secure mystery that the expences admit of no accounts; a single line stands for millions. . . . I happened to be in England at the celebration of the centenary of the revolution of 1688. The characters of William and Mary have always appeared to me detestable; the one seeking to destroy his uncle, and the other her father, to get possession of power themselves. . . . George the First acted the same close-fisted part as William had done, and bought the Duchy of Bremin with the money he got from England, two hundred and fifty thousand pounds over and above his pay as king; and having thus purchased it at the expence of England, added it to his Hanoverian dominions for his own private profit. In fact, every nation that does not govern itself, is governed as a jobb [i.e., as a corrupt arrangement]. England has been the prey of jobbs ever since the revolution [of 1688].[54]

Poverty, for Paine, was caused primarily by the burden of taxation, and taxes were caused primarily by wars: "So much has the weight and oppression of taxes increased since the Revolution, and especially since the year 1714," that is, the Hanoverian accession. "It has cost England almost seventy millions sterling, to maintain a family imported from abroad, of very inferior capacity to thousands in the nation; and scarcely a year has passed that has not produced some new mercenary application."[55]

Whigs like Edmund Burke looked on the Revolution of 1688 as the foundation of English liberties, but for Paine, William of Orange was only the lesser of two evils. "As to what is called the convention parliament [of 1689, which recognized William and Mary as sovereigns], it was a thing that made itself, and then made the authority by which it acted." An illegal regime was only made worse by "the corruption introduced at the Hanover succession, by the agency of Walpole."[56] At the trial of Paine for *Rights of Man. Part the Second* in 1792, the prosecution cited paragraphs that, Paine thought, "relate chiefly to certain facts, such as the Revolution of 1688, and the coming of George the First, commonly called the House of Hanover, or the House of Brunswick, or some such house." The indictment cited too the Bill of Rights of 1689, condemned by Paine for declaring that the Lords and Commons *"submit themselves, their heirs, and posterity for ever"* to William and Mary. This was merely the contrivance of courtiers, Paine had written, "for the purpose of keeping up an expensive and enormous Civil

List. . . . Let such men cry up the House of Orange, or the House of Brunswick, if they please. They would cry up any other house if it suited their purpose, and give as good reasons for it."[57]

Paine demonstrated how the House of Hanover survived from Tobias Smollett's *History of England,* describing the Hanoverian Duke of Cumberland's savagery in laying waste parts of Scotland after the battle of Culloden in 1746. America would have experienced the same treatment, argued Paine, had Britain won the Revolutionary War.[58] Why did George III obstinately persist in that conflict? If he were defeated, "Is he afraid they will send him to Hanover, or what does he fear?"[59] Things were worse under George III, for the existence of a Stuart option had restrained the abuses of George I and George II.[60] As late as 1797, Paine argued that European wars in the eighteenth century had been caused by "the mischievous compound of an elector of the Germanic body and a king of England . . . Let the elector retire to his electorate, and the world will have peace."[61] By 1797, this was a remarkably outdated analysis.

Once recognized, Paine's vehemently anti-Williamite and anti-Hanoverian comments on recent British history leap from his pages. They also emphasize how many other English idioms of political discourse were absent in his works. Paine did not speak the language of the religious sectaries of the 1640s. Apart from one quotation from Milton, he did not echo the "Commonwealthmen," those intellectuals who, after the 1660s, looked back for inspiration to the republican experiments of the Interregnum.[62] In the 1660s arose the separated denominations of Nonconformists (especially Presbyterians, Congregationalists, and Baptists), each with a sense of its own history and pertinacious grievances against the established Church of England; Paine did not participate in these arguments (not even that between Quakers and the Church), although they continued long after his death. He did not praise the Revolution of 1688 or hail it as securing a mixed and balanced constitution: in *Common Sense* he called that notion "farcical."[63] Paine explicitly stated that he had never read the works of John Locke, and no evidence contradicts him. None of these languages of politics did Paine speak. He was locked instead into a specific and detailed English polemic of the early eighteenth century. Paine's commitments were previously obscured by outstanding scholarship on the "Commonwealth" tradition, scholarship preoccupied with the long-term legacy of the 1640s (which now seems modest)[64] rather than with the long-term legacy of 1688 (now revealed as much larger); the recent change in focus toward 1688 brings Paine's politics more clearly into view.

Anti-Hanoverianism was, moreover, largely a British phenomenon. Before the 1760s American colonists were almost always noisily loyal to the house of Hanover, since the Stuart alternative was anathema to them.[65] Republicanism hardly featured in the American colonies before 1776, while England saw embittered anti-Hanoverian rhetoric and ideological conflict that went far beyond any of the transatlantic controversies of the 1760s. What attuned Paine with the colonial American population was his use of English religious imagery and argument in *Common Sense;* what lost him the esteem of citizens of the new American republic was the publication of Paine's advanced English deistic views in *The Age of Reason.* By contrast, neither traditional Biblical argument nor English deism gave Paine any significant traction in the French Revolution: where, to later writers, it seemed that deism might have created common ground with Robespierre, in reality Robespierre almost brought Paine to the guillotine.

Paine, like Burke, was less of a visionary than recent readers have supposed, but a better exemplar of the culture of his own day.[66] The catalytic role of *Common Sense* has been exaggerated: Paine did not cause the American Revolution, and in France in 1789 his role was smaller still. Recent American authors have typically credited Paine with a leading role in the French Revolution; this hero worship contrasts strongly with the great French historians of that revolution, who in multivolume works were seldom or never drawn even to mention Paine. Still less are their colleagues who write on nineteenth-century French political thought.[67]

Indeed Paine was out of his depth in the French Revolution, a vast and chaotic juggernaut that English and American opinion found almost impossible to explain, still less to influence. If the first half of *Common Sense* spoke to English conflicts and may have been written in England, both *Rights of Man* and *Rights of Man. Part the Second* were certainly composed in London, not Paris. The first had little to say about the French situation beyond a short narrative of high-political events that Paine cannot have observed, an account that was awkwardly inserted in *Rights of Man* in a way that repeated some of the ground already covered: it was a narrative, in a different prose style, that Paine may have derived from a French source, probably the Marquis de Lafayette, whose role it celebrated.[68] If so, it is evidence not for Paine's own understanding of the French Revolution, but for the Frenchman's self-serving interpretation of it that his English client unknowingly swallowed. *Rights of Man. Part the Second* shied away from a deeper exploration of the French Revolution and showed instead the possible influence of the London-based Society for Constitutional Information. Neither part of *Rights of Man* offered an adequate history or analysis of the outbreak of the French Revolution.

Paine is still regarded as an important author by virtue of giving present-day readers easy access to the American and French Revolutions, in prose of revealing simplicity. Yet although Paine often recorded his wish to compose histories of both episodes, he failed to do so. In the American case, he was precommitted to a view that responsibility for the American war lay wholly with the British government but lacked the high-political evidence that would explain British statesmen's conduct; he therefore ignored the evidence all around him for what had happened in the colonies. In the French case, Paine, without command of the language, was unable to see below the surface of political events in Paris and was precommitted to a theory that ignored the significance of revolutionary violence. He failed therefore to explain why a promising revolution (as he now it) had been so catastrophically blown off course.

In the appendix to the third edition of *Common Sense* (1776), Paine had expressed the closing aspiration that colonists would rise above the (English) identities of Whig and Tory, joining in a shared patriotism; yet once back in the new United States after 1802, Paine persisted in a lurid binary view of American party politics, a view still indebted to the English polarity that dated from the Exclusion Crisis of the 1680s. Two revolutions had made little difference to his core beliefs; although he extrapolated those beliefs in a few areas, he seldom did so logically or systematically. Paine was a member of "the world of expatriate radicals, fighting British battles on American soil,"[69] and, one might add, on French soil also.

Paine's thought did change in some ways over the course of his career, but seldom primarily from international experience. He came to give acknowledgement to the importance of commerce and its nexus,[70] although comment on the salience of commercial society in England was as old as the age of Daniel Defoe and had no special relation to the American or French Revolutions. Paine came to stress the need for conventions to meet to establish constitutions, bypassing existing corrupt assemblies; but this idea echoed England's "Convention Parliament" of 1689 before there were American Revolutionary examples. He modified his earlier confidence that social virtues would ensure the rectitude of unicameral legislatures and became open to the idea of bicameral assemblies, although this again echoed the Westminster model rather than the new American states. He came to acknowledge, at least in occasional phrases, the equal right of females to social security payments, although this too was the long-established practice of English poor relief and had not brought the wider equality of women; it did not reflect gender relations in America or France. In the 1790s Paine advocated an extended system of national social security, although not inferring from this any newly corporatist conception of the nature of government: no such system emerged in the early American or French republics. In *Agrarian Justice* he formulated a new distinction between artificial property (the result of human improvement) and natural property ("such as earth, air, water"[71]) in order to justify redistributive taxes on the former, but this argument rested on the much older English idea (based on an account of revelation in Genesis that the deist Paine had rejected in *The Age of Reason*) that God, at the Creation, had given the world to mankind in common. Few of these changes, in an English context, were wholly new; but that was one reason why Paine was able to appeal so effectively to his audience.

Paine had an astonishing career, but his celebrity in his lifetime is more difficult to explain than it seemed when the "age of revolutions" was understood as the appropriate application of self-evident general principles. He was a remarkable writer; he could express what many people had thought with less cogency; but these qualities did not make him a prophet. It was a shared and long-established Anglo-American cultural sphere of reference that made it possible for him to be an effective participant in the colonial events of 1776, since there was little, and perhaps nothing, that was specifically and uniquely American about the origins of the "American" Revolution (there was, of course, much that was specifically American about its consequences; but of the very different society that developed after 1776, Paine understood little).[72]

Consequently, with the exception of atheists arguing against theists,[73] Paine's ideas are seldom now employed functionally to solve present-day problems but, instead, are invoked only rhetorically. His significance for the present-day reader is not in granting privileged access to any exceptionalist American civic culture or "founding principles," still less to the civic culture of the other great republic born during Paine's lifetime, but rather in revealing how that era was retrospectively reinterpreted for English-speaking readers in terms significantly different from the historic ones. For any political writer, lasting fame is chiefly a matter of being put to a succession of new uses, changing subtly over time. Historical research can reveal such changes and shifts of perspective. "Great writers" often seem to later readers to transcend their contexts; in reality, none can do so, for all are historically grounded. This has an important consequence: societies that fail to understand their histories are condemned to believe their political rhetoric. That is why Paine should be studied, not celebrated.

NOTES

1. French scholarship on Paine deserves its own study; reasons of space preclude this here.

2. The recent use of the concept is owed to Robert N. Bellah, "Civil Religion in America," *Daedalus* 96 (1967), pp. 1–21; for Paine's alleged congruence with it, see p. 15.

3. Thomas Paine, "Of Monarchy and Hereditary Succession," in *Common Sense* (1776).

4. *Selections from the Writings of Thomas Paine*, ed. Carl Van Doren (New York: Modern Library, [1922]), intro., pp. vii–viii.

5. *The Complete Writings of Thomas Paine*, ed. Philip S. Fonei, 2 vols. (New York: Citadel Press, 1945) (hereafter cited as *CW*), vol. 1, intro., pp. x–xii, xv, xix.

6. Thomas Paine, *Common Sense and other Political Writings,* ed. Nelson F. Adkins (New York: Liberal Arts Press, 1953), intro., pp xi, xvii

7. Thomas Paine, *Rights of Man,* ed. Henry Collins (Harmondsworth, UK: Penguin, 1969), intro., pp. 10–11, 13, 15–16, 18, 43.

8. Thomas Paine, *Rights of Man,* ed. Claire Grogan (Peterborough, Ontario: Broadview Press, 2011), intro., pp. 9, 16, quoting E. P. Thompson, *The Making of the English Working Class* (Harmondsworth, UK: Penguin, 1963), p. 99

9. Thomas Paine, *Rights of Man,* intro. by Eric Foner (Harmondsworth, UK: Penguin, 1984), intro., pp. 7, 9, 12, 16.

10. Thomas Paine, *Common Sense and Related Writings,* ed. Thomas P. Slaughter (Boston: Bedford/St. Martin's, 2001), intro., p. vii.

11. Thomas Paine, *Common Sense,* ed. Alan Taylor (Cambridge, MA: Belknap Press, 2010), intro., pp. ix, xx–xxi.

12. *The Writings of Thomas Paine,* ed. Moncure Daniel Conway, 4 vols. (New York: G. P. Putnam's Sons, 1894–1896), vol. 1, intro., p. v. Conway was a pioneering Paine scholar, but he misled succeeding generations by including many anonymous essays from the Philadelphia press of 1775 and attributing them, without evidence, to Paine. Even recent scholars sometimes rely on these misattributions.

13. Thomas Paine, *Representative Selections,* ed. Harry Hayden Clark (New York: American Book Company, 1944), intro., p. v.

14. Thomas Paine, *Common Sense, The Rights of Man, and other Essential Writings,* ed. Sidney Hook (New York: Meridian, 1969), intro., pp. xii, xx.

15. Thomas Paine, *Common Sense,* ed. Isaac Kramnick (Harmondsworth, UK: Penguin, 1976), intro., pp. 28, 38–41; on "bourgeois radicalism," pp. 46–55. For Paine's "political liberalism" or "bourgeois liberalism," and for "English

radicalism" from the 1760s and "Paine's radicalism," see also *Thomas Paine Reader,* eds. Michael Foot and Isaac Kramnick (Harmondsworth, UK: Penguin, 1987), intro., pp. 13, 22, 28.

16. Thomas Paine, *Political Writings,* ed. Bruce Kuklick (Cambridge: Cambridge University Press, 1989), intro., pp. vii, ix–x, xiii (an edition that misprints the titles of Paine's greatest works, pp. 49, 145, 205).

17. Paine, *Common Sense,* ed. Taylor, intro., p. xxi.

18. Thomas Paine, *Rights of Man,* ed. Gregory Claeys (Indianapolis: Hackett, 1992), intro., pp. vii–viii, xxiv.

19. Thomas Paine, *Common Sense,* intro. by Gregory Tietjen (New York: Barnes & Noble, 1995), intro., pp. xviii, xxii.

20. Thomas Paine, *Rights of Man,* ed. David Taffel (New York: Barnes & Noble, 2004), intro., p. vii.

21. Thomas Paine, *Common Sense and Other Writings,* ed. Joyce Appleby (New York: Barnes & Noble, 2005), intro., pp. xxii, xxxiii, xxxv.

22. Thomas Paine, *The Age of Reason,* ed. Kerry Walters (Peterborough, Ontario: Broadview Press, 2011), intro., pp. 10–15, 30.

23. Thomas Paine, *Common Sense and Other Writings,* ed. J. M. Opal (New York: W. W. Norton, 2012), intro., pp. viii, xxvii.

24. Thomas Paine, *Rights of Man, Common Sense, and Other Political Writings,* ed. Mark Philp (Oxford: Oxford University Press, 1995), intro., pp. vii, ix, xxiv.

25. Thomas Paine, *Common Sense and Other Writings,* ed. Gordon S. Wood (New York: Modern Library, 2003), intro., pp. v, xvi, xxi.

26. Thomas Paine, *Common Sense,* ed. Edward Larkin (Peterborough, Ontario: Broadview Press, 2004), intro., pp. 7, 9–10, 15.

27. See, for example, Paine's complete absence from François Furet, *Revolutionary France 1770–1880,* trans. Antonia Nevill (1988; Oxford: Blackwell, 1992).

28. Paine, "A Serious Address to the People of Pennsylvania on the Present Situation of Their Affairs," *Pennsylvania Packet,* 1, 5, 10, 12 December 1778, in *CW,* vol. 2, pp. 278, 282–283, 286.

29. Paine, *Prospects on the Rubicon* (1787), in *CW,* vol. 2, p. 632.

30. Paine, *Public Good* (Philadelphia, 1780), in *CW,* vol. 2, p. 329.

31. Paine, *The Decline and Fall of the English System of Finance* (London and Paris, 1796), in *CW,* vol. 2, pp. 652, 654–656.

32. That "imperialism" and "colonialism" are present-day American preoccupations in Paine scholarship is suggested by an edition prepared by a campaigner for Indian independence and former professor at the University of Calcutta, in

which the concepts are strikingly absent: Thomas Paine, *Selected Writings,* ed. N. Gangulee (London: Nicholson & Watson, 1947).

33. Audrey Williamson, *Thomas Paine: His Life, Work and Times* (London: Allen and Unwin, 1973), pp. 37–38.

34. For an anticipation of a monograph on this theme, see J. C. D. Clark, *"The Enlightenment:* Catégories, traductions, et objets sociaux," in "Les Lumières dans leur siècle," eds. Gérard Laudin and Didier Masseau, special issue of *Lumières* 17–18 (2011), pp. 19–39. German and French discourse developed on different chronologies.

35. For liberalism: J. C. D. Clark, *English Society 1660–1832: Religion, Ideology and Politics During the Ancien Regime,* 2nd ed. (Cambridge: Cambridge University Press, 2000), pp. 6–8. For Paine's denial that he read Locke, pp. 139–140; for Paine's political thought, pp. 385–396; for its setting, pp. 126–164.

36. For the theological origins of universal suffrage see Clark, *English Society 1660–1832,* pp. 382–384, 396–397.

37. John Cartwright, *Take Your Choice!* (London: J. Almon, 1776).

38. Foner's correction: *CW,* vol. 2, pp. 269–270.

39. Paine, *Rights of Man* (1791), this volume, p. 248.

40. Paine, *Rights of Man. Part the Second* (1792), this volume, p. 285; echoing Paine, *Common Sense,* this volume, p. 9.

41. J. C. D. Clark, "How Ideologies are Born: The Case of Radicalism," in Clark, *Our Shadowed Present: Modernism, Postmodernism and History* (Stanford: Stanford University Press, 2004), pp. 110–145.

42. Paine, *Common Sense,* this volume, p. 12.

43. Ibid., pp. 13, 16.

44. Ibid., p. 46.

45. Foner, in *CW,* vol. 1, intro., p. xiv.

46. Trish Loughran, "Disseminating *Common Sense:* Thomas Paine and the Problem of the Early National Bestseller," *American Literature* 78 (2006), pp. 1–28.

47. Jack P. Greene, *The Constitutional Origins of the American Revolution* (Cambridge: Cambridge University Press, 2011).

48. J. C. D. Clark, *The Language of Liberty 1660–1832: Political Discourse and Social Dynamics in the Anglo-American World* (Cambridge: Cambridge University Press, 1994).

49. Paine, *Letter to the Abbé Raynal* (1782), in *CW,* vol. 2, p. 238.

50. Richard Price, *A Discourse on the Love of our Country* (London: T. Cadell, 1789), p. 50.

51. Paine to Lansdowne, September 21, 1787, in *CW,* vol. 2, p. 1265.

52. Paine, *Rights of Man. Part the Second,* this volume, p. 317, fn13.

53. Mark Philp – in Paine, *Rights of Man,* ed. Philp – provides excellent notes to Paine's English sources but does not infer from them the interpretation advanced here.

54. Paine, *Rights of Man. Part the Second,* this volume, pp. 327, 330, fn18.

55. Paine to Henry Dundas, Secretary of State, June 6, 1792, *CW,* vol. 2, p. 453. Paine, *Rights of Man. Part the Second,* this volume, pp. 331–332.

56. Paine, *Rights of Man. Part the Second,* this volume, p. 296.

57. Paine, *Letter Addressed to the Addressers on the Late Proclamation* (1792), in *CW,* vol. 2, pp. 495–496.

58. Paine cited T. Smollett, *A Complete History of England, from the Descent of Julius Caesar, to the Treaty of Aix la Chapelle, 1748,* 3rd ed., 11 vols. (London: Richard Baldwin, 1760), vol. 11, pp. 239–240.

59. Paine, *The American Crisis,* X (5 March 1781), in *CW,* vol. I, pp. 191, 195–196.

60. Paine, *Rights of Man,* this volume, p. 246.

61. Paine, *To the People of France and the French Armies* (1797), in *CW,* vol. 2, pp. 607–608.

62. Caroline Robbins, *The Eighteenth-Century Commonwealthman* (Cambridge, MA: Harvard University Press, 1959).

63. Paine, *Common Sense,* this volume, p. 11.

64. In Bernard Bailyn's classic *The Ideological Origins of the American Revolution* (Cambridge, MA: Belknap Press, 1967), which adopted Caroline Robbins's Commonwealth model, Paine plays remarkably little part except when *Common Sense* became a target for the criticism of certain colonial Americans: pp. 285–291.

65. Benjamin Lewis Price, *Nursing Fathers: American Colonists' Conception of English Protestant Kingship, 1688–1776* (Lanham, MD: Lexington Books, 1999); Brendan McConville, *The King's Three Faces: The Rise and Fall of Royal America, 1688–1776* (Chapel Hill: University of North Carolina Press, 2006).

66. Edmund Burke, *Reflections on the Revolution in France,* ed. J. C. D. Clark (Stanford, CA: Stanford University Press, 2001), pp. 23–111, at p. 80.

67. Jeremy Jennings, *Revolution and the Republic: A History of Political Thought in France since the Eighteenth Century* (Oxford: Oxford University Press, 2011) records only Paine's quick rejection in France as *fraternité* gave way to xenophobia (p. 203), but nothing of Paine's subsequent intellectual influence in that society.

68. What I suggest is the interpolated passage is Paine, *Rights of Man,* this volume, pp. 219–232.

69. Michael Durey, *Transatlantic Radicals and the Early American Republic* (Lawrence: University Press of Kansas, 1997), pp. ix, 49, 242–244. Durey's term is, strictly, inaccurate: in the 1790s an English "radical," short for "radical reformer," meant a believer in parliamentary reform on the principle of universal manhood suffrage. Paine never quite adopted this new ideology.

70. See especially Gregory Claeys, *Thomas Paine: Social and Political Thought* (London: Unwin Hyman, 1989).

71. Foner, *CW*, vol. 1, p. 606.

72. It has been argued that the interpretations of the American Revolution dominant within the United States have not greatly changed since the 1970s (Greene, *Constitutional Origins*, p. xx). The present essay on Paine reflects the author's contrasting model: that the "American" Revolution was a transatlantic episode explicable only in relation to its British dimension; and secondly, that that revolution was not a secular episode, so that its explanation demands the integration of the themes of religion and law.

73. A. J. Ayer, *Thomas Paine* (London: Secker & Warburg, 1988); Christopher Hitchens, *Thomas Paine's Rights of Man: A Biography* (London: Atlantic, 2006); idem., *God Is Not Great: The Case against Religion* (London: Atlantic, 2007).

Thomas Paine, Quakerism, and the Limits of Religious Liberty during the American Revolution

JANE E. CALVERT

Thomas Paine has long been considered a champion of rights and liberty on both sides of the Atlantic. With his impassioned writings, he played a large role in leading America to independence and inspired a budding democratic experiment in Pennsylvania. Later, he became an advocate of what some have considered the forerunner of the welfare state by calling for aid and equity for the least fortunate members of society.[1] Always a self-proclaimed friend to religious liberty, Paine aimed to free men from superstition and bondage to unreason through his writings on deism.

Scholarly fashion has attributed much of Paine's humanitarian zeal and penchant for reform to his Quaker upbringing. Indeed, some biographers go so far as to call him a Quaker.[2] More realistic assessments have tempered this claim, finding no formal affiliation with the Religious Society of Friends but still extensive Quakerly influence on Paine's sociopolitical thought and action.[3] Indeed, many of the causes Paine championed were historically dear to Quakers, especially religious liberty, a broad political franchise, and aid to the poor. Paine himself noted his Quaker education and referred with approval to their principles.[4] More than this even, a plausible argument might be made that it was not just the Quakers' causes that Paine adopted but also their reformist enthusiasm. By Paine's day, members of the Society of Friends were much subdued compared to their radical seventeenth-century forebears, but they still led the way in causes such as abolitionism.[5] Paine's desire to provoke the complacent or the closed-minded and anger them into change is reminiscent of earlier Friends who, to publicize their message, preached on street corners, shouted down establishment ministers in their own churches, ran naked through the streets, and smashed tea services in public.[6]

But while we persist in emphasizing Paine's affinities with Quakerism, we miss a crucial historical moment, one that sheds light not just on Paine's thought and action in particular but also on a troubling moment at the founding of America. Examining Paine's attitude toward Quakers closely, we find that it was much more complicated than at first glance, especially during the early years of the American Revolution. Far from sympathizing or identifying with Pennsylvania Friends, Paine was their ruthless opponent and an instigator of their persecution–persecution such as they had not experienced since the seventeenth century under Anglican and Puritan establishments in England and Massachusetts. If we are to understand Paine's role in the American Revolution fully, we cannot ignore the means he used to achieve his ends. Paine biographer John Keane argues that he was "the first great critic of the dark side of modern revolutions."[7] True though this may be, he also actively encouraged one of the darkest moments of the American Revolution.[8] His actions press us to reexamine a perennial American problem–how we manage religious and political dissent and preserve civil liberties in times of war.

The following pages first explore briefly the background and principles of Pennsylvania Quakers, in order to set the scene for Paine's entrée into that world. Next, using Paine's and the Quakers' writings, we follow events as the colonies moved toward independence and during the first years of the Revolutionary War. We see how Paine, in a rare moment of skillful coalition-building, used the volatile political tensions, and particularly anti-Quaker sentiment, that already existed in Pennsylvania to garner support for the revolutionary cause. In doing so, he abandoned a key principle he professed to share with Quakers, religious liberty. We are left to wonder whether Paine's successful campaign against the Quakers actually helped or hurt the cause he was championing.

When Paine arrived in Pennsylvania in late 1774, he entered a province that was struggling not just against Britain but also against itself.[9] It was this internal strife, as much as any British policy or action, that animated the people of Pennsylvania during the revolutionary era. The immediacy of provincial struggles often overshadowed larger, national ones. Paine, an avid observer of political cultures, with a proclivity for detecting discontent, quickly became conversant in the debate and exploited long-standing animosities and prejudices in the name of the American cause. In doing so, he contributed to a very specific strain of what Robert G. Parkinson calls the "common cause" rhetoric, in which, to excite patriotism and build support for revolution, American leaders vilified anyone who appeared to disagree with them.[10] In this case, the villains were Quakers.

According to the Quakers' critics, including many historians, Friends' refusal to support the Revolution was obvious–they were Tories or Loyalists.[11]

But this is a simplistic and inaccurate assessment of the situation in Pennsylvania. This assumption takes the revolutionary rhetoric at face value and ignores the history of provincial Pennsylvania and the real position and concerns of the Society of Friends. The tensions between Quaker leaders and non-Quaker inhabitants in Pennsylvania actually reached back decades. Moreover, the conflict between Quakers and Revolutionaries was, as far as Quakers were concerned, less about loyalty to one regime or another and more about the protection of religious liberty.[12] This is a crucial point to acknowledge if we are to understand the Quaker position during the Revolution, as well as the significance of Paine's and others' attacks against them.

Liberty of conscience was a fundamental theological tenet of Quakerism, which Friends made the cornerstone of the Pennsylvania constitution, the 1701 Charter of Privileges. Not only did the charter allow freedom of worship for all the inhabitants, it enabled Quakers to engage fully in the polity because it freed them from the requirement to swear oaths, their objection to which would normally have kept them out of public office, off juries, and out of witness boxes. It also allowed them to abstain from engaging in war, which, as the charter noted, would have been "contrary to their religious Persuasion."[13]

Despite Friends' seemingly "liberal" policies, which included no official religious establishment, Quaker rule was overbearing to some. Pennsylvania was a de facto theocracy, with Philadelphia Yearly Meeting (PYM; the Quaker church) controlling the Pennsylvania Assembly.[14] Since the founding of the colony, Quakers had been accused by non-Quakers of preferring their own members as legislators and imposing distinctly Quaker laws and norms on the populace, and this despite being a minority in the colony.[15] They were charged with trying to "Quakerize" Pennsylvania. In 1764, tensions simmering below the surface erupted into overt hostilities over the matter of the protection of frontier settlers from Indian attacks.[16] Quakers, being friends to the Indians as well as pacifists, resisted raising a militia for the purpose. The frontiersmen, who were militant Scotch-Irish Presbyterians, took matters into their own hands, massacred a number of friendly Indians, and marched on Philadelphia. Known as the Paxton Riot, the planned attack was averted, but the anger and resentment that prompted it remained. The Scotch-Irish were convinced that the Quakers, by manipulating the voting process, were disproportionately represented in the assembly and that they would continue to impose their agenda on unwilling or unsuspecting non-Quakers. Adding to the tension was that Quakers controlled the colony not just politically, but economically. They were among the wealthiest merchants in the colonies, which only increased the gulf between them and their backcountry Calvinist constituents. Placing them at greater odds with many Americans, Quakers were abolitionists, and slaves were widely seen as allies of the British during the Revolution.[17]

The crux of the matter in the case of the Paxton Riot was the Quakers' Peace Testimony and the suitability of a pacifist denomination controlling civil government. The Quakers' pacifism was also at issue throughout the conflict with Britain, during which the controversy expanded beyond just an isolated matter of provincial policy to, as we might see it, a test of the strength of American ideals of liberty and justice in a moment of crisis.

On the eve of the Revolution, Quakers were in an extraordinarily difficult position. In the first place, their pacifism meant that they did not believe that revolution – the overthrow of the government by violent means – was a legitimate option for alleviating oppression. It is important to recognize, however, that *pacifism* for Quakers historically did not mean *passivity*. Vigorous protest was allowed, as long as it did not turn violent or encourage violence in others. Their earliest treatises as a society emphasized their refusal to engage in plots to overthrow the government, yet openly declared that they would resist encroachments on their rights. Their approach was novel.[18] During their days of severe religious persecution in England and Massachusetts, they pioneered the theory and practice of civil disobedience and contributed to the peaceful abolition of laws against dissenters. Likewise, as leaders of Pennsylvania, they had a long history of resisting nonviolently any perceived attacks on their liberties and privileges by the crown or the proprietors. As recently as 1765, Quakers had been among the leaders of the resistance to Britain; their refusal to obey the Stamp Act, although nonviolent, was seen by some colonists as extreme, even rebellious.[19] But by the passage of the Townshend Acts in 1767, the Quaker leadership had begun to have reservations about resistance. Although many believed that Britain had a "mistaken policy," they ceased their protest because they knew that most Americans had no commitment to peace, and matters would quickly get out of hand, leading to violence or, worse, revolution.[20]

The second and closely related difficulty concerned preserving their religious liberty. Were Quakers to choose a side in the conflict, regardless of which one, this right would be threatened. If the British won, their charter would certainly be abolished and an Anglican establishment imposed. The best they could hope for in this scenario would be toleration of their dissenting ways. The "Centinel" letters in 1768 warned against precisely this danger after a group of Anglicans appealed to Parliament for the establishment of an American episcopate. It was *"To the Honour of the Friends"* that *"the* Charter of Privileges *from* William Penn *to the People establishes* unalterably *an entire Liberty in religious Matters."* But "[h]ow long we shall enjoy the Happiness of this Constitution, if Establishments can be imposed on us without our consent, is very uncertain."[21] Yet the risk to religious liberty was perhaps greater if America became independent. Without the protection of the British constitution, there was at least equal certainty that the Quakers' inveterate enemies, the Presbyterians, would take control of Pennsylvania and exact retribution for the perceived wrongs of the Quaker colonial leaders. Both groups—reformed Calvinists and Anglicans—had a history of persecuting Quakers. But Pennsylvania Quakers knew that the Presbyterians were angry, volatile, and vengeful, whereas Anglicans had not molested them for years.[22] They therefore surveyed the political landscape, assessed the safety of their religious liberty, and in 1775 officially began restricting their activities to humanitarian causes.[23] In 1776, they admonished their members to "decline from having any Share in the Authority & Powers of Government, & to circumscribe themselves within plain & narrow bounds."[24] Accordingly, most Quakers became neutral. Of those who did not, most—about one-fifth of the male Quaker population—joined the American cause, calling themselves "Free Quakers." A much smaller number sided with the British. Most who participated in war were disowned by PYM.[25]

Pacifism and neutrality are not, however, the same things. Although the Society of Friends had always been pacifist, it had never been neutral. In fact, William Penn himself derided neutrality as cowardice and hypocrisy when injustices were witnessed.[26] And through their entire history, Friends had never sat on the sidelines. The question was: what would the Quakers stand for now—the ill-defined liberties of a disparate group of colonies, or the constitutionally protected religious liberty on which their existence depended? There is thus a sense in which the Quakers were indeed loyalists—but their loyalty was not to the British constitution or Crown. Rather, their loyalty was to their core theological principles and their own uniquely Quaker constitution in Pennsylvania. For the majority of Quakers who objected to revolution, the fealty they expressed toward Britain was a means to an end—the preservation of the Pennsylvania constitution and their unique religious liberties.

Thomas Paine also claimed to value religious liberty. Scholars have accepted his portrayal of himself as one of the greatest advocates of it, which, indeed, after the American Revolution, he became. To determine one's own religion, he argued in *Rights of Man,* is a "natural right," and he inveighed against anything that stood in the way, including mere religious toleration, which he called a "despotism."[27] He demanded the "universal right of conscience" for all, as the French had proclaimed. But even the French *Declaration of the Rights of Man and of the Citizen* (1789) was not free enough for Paine. Article X said that "No man ought to be molested on account of his opinions, not even on account of his *religious* opinions, provided his avowal of them does not disturb the public order established by the law." Paine objected that the last clause was too restrictive, arguing that "it takes off from the divine dignity of religion, and weakens its operative force upon the mind to make it a subject of human laws."[28] But, when pressed by politics, Paine's actions said something quite different from his words.

With his Quaker background, Paine was undoubtedly aware of the Quakers' historic concern for religious liberty and thus the reasons for their difficult position during the American Revolution. But Quakers' liberty was not Paine's primary concern. His concern was effecting revolution. To Paine, the Quaker position went against best policy and practice. But more than simple disagreement and frustration with the tenets of Quakerism or anger at the Quakers who would not be convinced to abandon their pacifism, when the American cause seemed to be in jeopardy, Paine's writings against Quakers took on another purpose. The Quakers became a convenient foil and the means for rallying the non-Quaker Pennsylvanians against Britain. Paine had learned quickly under the tutelage of Benjamin Franklin and other Pennsylvania insiders that the Presbyterians were less interested in overthrowing British rule than deposing the Quakers, their more-immediate adversaries. If he could paint the Quakers and the British as one and the same, he could move the sometimes sluggish and self-interested masses in Pennsylvania to revolution. He thus seized on the complicated matter of Quaker pacifism to vilify Friends and willfully misrepresent the majority of Quakers as something they were not—Tories and traitors.

Paine's writings against Quakers spanned a relatively short but critical period, from a year before independence in 1775 to the spring of 1777. Over this time, we see a noticeable evolution in his approach, from simply disagreeing with their pacific stance to recommending imprisonment of their leaders. Throughout, Paine's frustration and increasing anger at Quakers is clear. Equally clear is that in his efforts to nullify the Quaker influence in Pennsylvania, he was willing to disregard not just one of the core principles of Quakerism, but also the Quakers' religious right to hold it.

Paine began his campaign innocuously enough. In July of 1775, shortly after hostilities became open, he published "Thoughts on Defensive War." His tack was to portray himself as sympathetic to the Quaker cause of peace but ultimately to deride it as foolish and futile. Writing as "A Lover of Peace," he proclaimed himself "a Quaker" in that he too wished for the end of all war. "Could the peaceable principle of the Quakers be universally established," he says, "arms and the art of war would be wholly extirpated. But we live not in a world of angels."[29] Worse than this, even, he paints a picture of the continued "reign of Satan" and a world with an "unprincipled enemy," stained with the blood of their own children, who can only be subdued by arms. Pacifists, according to Paine, are either too "superstitiously religious, or too cowardly" to fight for the protection of even their own property. Yet he is careful here neither to appear entirely hostile to Quaker interests, nor to alienate them completely. The second half of the essay argues for religious liberty. "[T]ill spiritual freedom was made manifest," writes Paine, "political liberty did not exist"; and "spiritual freedom is the root of political liberty."[30] Although this sounds sympathetic to Friends' interests, Paine's formulation of the problem and the solution excludes the possibility that pacifism is compatible with either religious or political liberty. These, in Paine's world, are liberties that require violence to preserve.

By October 1775, as reconciliation efforts with Britain were clearly failing and militia units mustered, Pennsylvanians bristled at the Quakers' pacifism. Several petitions arrived in the assembly from groups protesting their exemptions from military service and contributions. Friends in turn mounted a protest, which they based on their charter rights. The petitions, they argued in a lengthy memorial, were "so manifestly repugnant to the Laws and Charter of this Province, and which, if enforced, must subvert that most essential of all Privileges, *Liberty of Conscience*" and "occasion the grievous Suffering of many conscientious People of divers religious Denominations."[31] The entire memorial was to remind the assembly of what was in the Pennsylvania constitution and to specify that pacifism was a seminal component of religious liberty for Quakers. The liberty-of-conscience clause in the charter "hath ever been understood," they said, "to be the fundamental Part of the Constitution of this Province from its first settlement." Furthermore, liberty of conscience "was not limited to the Acts of public Worship only." Those who believed it was, they asserted, were not considering the clause fully and were misinterpreting it.[32]

Countermemorials disputed the Quakers' interpretation of the charter and accused them of adhering to "the antiquated and absurd Doctrine of *passive Obedience*," traditionally the Tory response to oppression.[33] Whether intentional or not, this was a misrepresentation of the Quaker position. Friends' memorial had explained that though we believe it our Duty to submit to the Powers, which in the Course of divine Providence are set over us, where there hath been, or is any Oppression, or Cause of Suffering, we are engaged with Christian Meekness and Firmness to petition and remonstrate against them, and to endeavor by just Reasoning and Arguments to assert our Rights and Privileges, in order to obtain relief.[34]

Thus they described a mode of protest that was neither passive nor necessarily obedient. One could submit to the government, they believed, without necessarily submitting to an unjust law. But the Quakers refrained from describing their whole program of dissent. Retreating from their own history, they omitted that they had also engaged in civil disobedience, that is, breaking unjust laws peacefully and publicly to encourage constitutional reform.[35] This was clearly not a technique they wished to employ or publicize at this time. Still, there was no argument for the less-direct Tory approach of passive obedience.

The debate reached a new pitch in the winter and spring of 1776. In January, Paine published *Common Sense,* his influential call for independence from Britain. Here he does not mention Quakers explicitly but only describes advocates of reconciliation as "[i]nterested men, who are not to be trusted; weak men, who *cannot* see; [and] prejudiced men, who *will not see.*" He explains that "[e]very quiet method for peace hath been ineffectual."[36] Understanding now that the would-be Revolutionaries were much more of a threat than British Anglicans, Quakers believed that *Common Sense* demanded their response. Within days, they published their *Ancient Testimony,* addressed to the people of America. Under the signature of John Pemberton, clerk of PYM, it implored Americans to follow "principles dictated by the Spirit of Christ" as "the most certain and effectual means of preventing the extreme misery and desolation of wars and bloodshed." They reminded their readers that in the history of Pennsylvania, "while the principles of justice and mercy continued to preside, [Pennsylvanians] were preserved in tranquility and peace, free from the desolating calamities of war." In essence, they asked Americans to live godly lives and to respect the government. This would have been provocative enough, but they made one serious misstep. They portrayed themselves as always having been not just pacifist, but neutral and apolitical, not having been "busy bodies" in government. Coming from a group that had dominated one of the largest American colonies for almost a century and had been active in others, this claim was patently false. Moreover, they ended with a plea that could be interpreted as not just Loyalist but also self-interested: that the colonists maintain their "just and necessary subordination to the king, and those who are lawfully placed in authority under him"[37] – in other words, the Pennsylvania Assembly, which Quakers and their supporters still controlled.

Paine could not let the *Testimony* stand unchallenged. In a third edition of *Common Sense,* published in April, he wrote directly to the Quakers in a searing attack. His purpose was to quell any potential influence the *Testimony* might have by discrediting the authors as not only unrepresentative of the Society of Friends but not real Quakers at all. In doing so, Paine put forth some dubious arguments of his own. While claiming he "never dishonors religion either by ridiculing, or cavilling at any denomination whatsoever" and that he too loved peace, he called Quakers "hypocritical" and bigots. His attack was warranted, he argued, "for [John Pemberton et al.] are not to be considered as the whole body of the Quakers but only as a factional and fractional part thereof." Although it is true that the conflict had caused dissension among Friends, including the establishment of a new group of "fighting Quakers," members of the Society of Friends were largely unified in this case, and, moreover, they had always allowed themselves to be represented by the clerk of the meeting, the highest administrative position in a society that did not have a formal hierarchy of spiritual leaders. For Paine, Pemberton and other leading Friends were simply easy targets – visible, powerful, wealthy, and already resented by many. Paine's charge that Pemberton represented the Society of Friends "without a proper authority for so doing" is false.[38]

Paine's quite legitimate criticism centered on the Quakers' claim of neutrality and apoliticism. Here his Quaker education served him well. He knew that Quakers had never shrunk from confronting injustice, regardless of the rank of their opponent. To disprove their current claim of neutrality, he quoted the Quakers' only theologian, Robert Barclay. The passage, extracted from *Apology for the True Christian Divinity* (1676), a book second only to the Bible in importance for Quakers, is one in which Barclay upbraids King Charles II for his sins and for listening to his corrupt ministers rather than to God. Later, Paine would reiterate, "never did the conduct of men oppose their own doctrine more notoriously than the present race of Quakers. They have artfully changed themselves into a different sort of people to what they used to be, and yet have the address to persuade each other they are not altered."[39]

Beyond highlighting this change in policy, Paine's task was easy. He merely had to point out that the "inconsistency is too glaring" when a group claiming to be apolitical by publishing a political pamphlet. "[W]hat occasion," he demanded, "is there for your *political testimony* if you fully believe what it contains? And the very publishing it proves, that either, ye do not believe what ye profess, or have not virtue enough to practise what ye believe." His advice to Quakers was probably sound: "Wherefore, as ye refuse to be the means on one side, ye ought not to be meddlers on the other; but to wait the issue in silence."[40] William Penn would have agreed with Paine, to a point. He wrote, "A wise Neuter joins with neither"; he "only has room to be a *Peace-maker.*" "But," Penn added significantly, he "*uses* both, as his honest Interest leads him."[41] Paine's words must have resonated, because Friends took his advice. It was at this point that they turned toward real neutrality—no more engagement in any political behavior. Accordingly, the *Testimony* was the last time PYM addressed the American people. But, in keeping with Penn's words, they did not give up pressing the authorities for their "honest interest"—religious liberty.

The debate turned subtly on the definition of a Quaker and how a Quaker should or should not engage in the political world. Although peaceful protest had defined Quakerism for more than one hundred years, Quakers split on the matter, with one part abandoning the pacifism and the other abandoning the protest. This was essentially a doctrinal dispute within Quakerism; but it was complicated by the fact that they controlled the government and wielded significant socioeconomic influence. Paine was an Englishman, newly arrived in America, and no member of the Society of Friends, yet he nonetheless assumed authority to define what a Pennsylvania Quaker should be. "[W]e do not complain against you because ye are *Quakers,*" he inveighed, "but because ye pretend to *be* and are NOT Quakers."[42] A question the dispute raised is whether a religious group has a right to define or redefine itself. Neutrality may have been a new position for Quakers, but the Revolutionaries were fond of saying that self-preservation was a natural right. If, then, the Quakers believed that their self-preservation was best achieved by becoming neutral, was this not likewise their right? The answer from the radicals was an ever-louder "no." As though with foreknowledge of events to come, Paine sent a warning to Friends that must have sounded very much like a threat: "Say not that ye are persecuted, neither endeavor to make us the authors of that reproach, which, ye are bringing upon yourselves."[43]

By the end of April, sentiment for revolution was rising, yet the Pennsylvania Assembly, still dominated by Quakers and their allies, stood in the way. The revolutionary leadership pinned their hopes on a new election on May 1, which they thought "will give a finishing Blow to the Quaker Interest in this City."[44] But they were disappointed; Quakers maintained their ascendancy. Then, once again, Paine stepped in, dedicating his fourth and

final "Forester" letter to the problem. The first three of these letters were
written to refute the Loyalist author "Cato"; his aim in the last was finally
to discredit the Quakers, the Pennsylvania Assembly, and their constitution.
The Quakers, he explained, suffered from "unanswerable ignorance" and
were at the "summit of inconsistency." Stoking the old provincial animosities, he reminded Pennsylvanians of the Paxtons' grievances in 1763. "We
can trace the iniquity in this province to the fountain head," he wrote, "and
see by what delusions it has imposed on others. The guilt centres in a few,
and flows from the same source, that a few years ago avariciously suffered
the frontiers of this province to be deluged in blood." Paine threatened,
"[A]nd though the vengeance of Heaven hath slept since, it may awake
too soon for [the Quakers'] repose." Encouraging a provincial rebellion
in Pennsylvania, he denied the legitimacy of the government and constitution by equating them with those of England. "The House of Assembly in
its present form is disqualified for such business," he argued, "because it
is a branch from that power against whom we are contending."[45] This, of
course, was untrue, as Pennsylvania, although it had received its original
charter from the Crown, had never been a royal government and had often
itself been at odds with the Crown. Furthermore, he dissembled, "in Pennsylvania, as well as in England, there is *no constitution,* but only a *temporary form of government.*"[46] Equally untrue was this statement; no one in
the colony, even those who did not value the seventy-five-year-old charter
highly, believed it was temporary.[47] Yet this equation was a first step in a
new campaign – turning Quakers into Tories in the public mind.

Paine warned the Quakers again, "You have done your utmost and must
abide the consequences."[48] The consequences were swift. On May 10, two
days after the publication of the final "Forester" letter and with British
warships closing in on Philadelphia, John Adams proposed in Congress to
replace colonial governments where there was "no government sufficient
to the exigencies of their affairs."[49] Though he did not specify Pennsylvania in particular, this was the government he had foremost in mind.[50] The
radicals, with Thomas Paine among them, then met to strategize the demise
of the Quaker-controlled assembly.[51] A larger public meeting that followed
on May 20 was essentially "a polite death sentence" for the assembly, a
relatively orderly coup of a legally established and elected government,
one legitimated by the people of Pennsylvania.[52] Echoing Paine's arguments, Pennsylvanians declared that the "House of the Assembly is a part
of that power from which we are trying to break away."[53] The assembly
continued to meet for a few weeks, but with no more power to legislate or
resist independence.

At this point, however, it is important to note, there remained in Philadelphia some genuine desire to preserve liberty of conscience and a respect for religious differences. When Congress recommended a fast for May 17 to bolster the American cause, the Committee of Philadelphia issued an order on the 16th that inhabitants "forbear from any kind of insult to [Quakers], or any others who may, from conscientious scruples, or from a regard to their religious professions, refuse to keep the said Fast."[54] This liberal attitude, however, was evaporating quickly.

Now freed from the burden of a "Quaker junto," America declared independence and the Pennsylvania radicals set about writing a new constitution.[55] Although Paine did not have a hand in it, scholars concur that the authors were inspired by the republican ideals set forth in *Common Sense* and that Paine approved of the result.[56] By contrast, the moderates of Pennsylvania were appalled. Aside from the basic problem that the unelected radicals had not actually been authorized by the people to write a new constitution, these men, many with no legal training or political experience, crafted a document that, as the moderates saw it, violated historical constitutional principles and put the civil liberties of Pennsylvanians in danger. Among the flaws they found were that "the Christian religion is not treated with proper respect."[57] Another was that citizens of Pennsylvania were prescribed tests of loyalty to a new government that many believed was illegitimate.[58] The new constitution was imposed on the people without their approval, on September 28.

For moderates, the autumn of 1776 was a time of discontent, protest, and resistance. Many, even some who supported independence, refused to swear loyalty to an illegitimate government and a faulty and, for all practical purposes, unamendable constitution forced upon them.[59] In an epistle dated December 20, which would become the center of the dispute, Quakers wrote to "all who make religious profession with us" and declared their disapproval of and resistance to the new Pennsylvania constitution on religious grounds. "[W]e may with Christian firmness and fortitude," they stated, "withstand and refuse to submit to the arbitrary injunctions and ordinances of men, who assume to themselves the power of compelling others." They objected to being forced "to join in carrying on war." They also objected to precisely what Paine had been doing in his publications against them, "prescribing modes of determining our religious principles." The way the radicals were now doing this was "by imposing tests not warranted by the precepts of Christ, or the laws of the happy constitution, under which we and others, long enjoyed tranquility and peace."[60] As always, their main concern was that the old Pennsylvania charter had prohibited religious discrimination and any new one ought to as well. Ultimately, they admonished their brethren to "[l]et not the fear of suffering, either in person or property, prevail on any to join with or promote any work or preparation for war." Although a clear and straightforward statement of Quaker principles for religious liberty, according to the Pennsylvania constitution, this epistle would haunt them very soon.

Though the epistle was addressed to members of the Society of Friends, it provoked a memorial from "a reputable number" of Philadelphia residents to the Pennsylvania Council of Safety. After the requisite disclaimers that they "hold pure the doctrine of universal liberty of conscience" and they "persecute no man, neither will we abet in the persecution of any man for religion's sake," they proceeded to denounce the epistle and the Quakers. Perhaps counting on few people having read it, the memorialists described it in terms that bore little resemblance to the epistle's actual tone or content. "[T]he anger and political virulence with which their instructions are given, and the abuse with which they stigmatize all ranks of men" proved Quakers' ill intent, which was to weaken American defenses and welcome the British into the city. Citing the Quakers' reference to the "happy constitution"–by which Quakers meant the *Pennsylvania* constitution–the memorialists intentionally misconstrued the words to mean the *British* constitution and concluded, "If this be not treason, we know not what may properly be called by that name." Their recommendation to the council was to "commit the signer [John Pemberton], together with such other persons as they can discover were concerned therein, into custody, until such time as some mode of trial shall ascertain the full degree of their guilt and punishment."[61] For the time being, however, the council, occupied with bigger problems, did nothing. Thomas Paine, however, read the memorial and took note.

The year 1776 did not end well for Pennsylvania. The war was going badly, and the new state government was in collapse. Moderates in the government, disappointed in their calls to reform the constitution, had walked out of the assembly, effectively paralyzing it. Desertions from the militia had begun as early as the summer of 1776, and now, with the British threatening to march on Philadelphia, Congress stepped in and declared martial law. Paine saw the urgency of the cause and began his famous series of letters, *The Crisis,* by admonishing the "summer soldier and the sunshine patriot" for their lack of commitment.[62] Anxious to reinvigorate the patriot cause, Paine needed a rallying point. In the second *Crisis,* he turned to the Quakers and their December 20 epistle in what would be the beginning of a sustained and damaging attack.

Twenty years later, in the heat of the French Revolution, Paine would advocate moderation and tolerance for dissenters. He explained,

> It is never to be expected in a revolution that every man is to change his opinion at the same moment. There never yet was any truth or any principle so irresistibly obvious, that all men believed it at once. Time and reason must co-operate with each other to the final establishment of any principle; and therefore those who may happen to be first convinced have not a right to persecute others, on whom conviction operates more slowly. The moral principle of revolutions is to instruct; not to destroy.[63]

This calm and reasonable expression was the opposite of the approach Paine took to the Quakers during the American Revolution. Now, in these soul-trying times, he opted for destruction. Continuing the tack he began the previous spring to encourage the overthrow of the Pennsylvania government, he again painted them as allies of the British. He twisted the December 20 epistle for his purposes. Here they allegedly "declar[e]" their attachment to the British government."[64] Characterizing it as "a publication evidently intended to promote sedition and treason, and encourage the enemy, who were then within a day's march of this city, to proceed on and possess it," Paine misrepresented the content.[65] "[T]he Quakers forgot their own principles [of pacifism]," he said, "when in their late testimony they called *this connection* with these military and miserable appendages hanging to it, '*The happy constitution.*'"[66] But Paine and the revolutionary leadership likely knew that the Quakers were not referring to the British constitution but the Pennsylvania 1701 constitution. There was no question about this when the sides had debated the interpretation of the Pennsylvania constitution in their competing memorials to the assembly in October of 1775. But now, it was in the interest of the cause to have a clear enemy close at hand.

Though Paine would assert in *Rights of Man. Part the Second* that "religion is very improperly made a political machine," he apparently had no qualms about using it as such in the American Revolution.[67] He thus transitioned from criticizing Quakers' neutrality to levying charges of Toryism and treason. He defined his terms in *The Crisis:*

> *He that is not a supporter of the independent states of America, in the same degree that his religious and political principles would suffer him to support the government of any other country, of which he called himself a subject, is, in the American sense of the word,* A TORY; *and the*

instant that he endeavors to bring his toryism into practice, he becomes
A TRAITOR.[68]

To be clear, here a Tory is someone who is more supportive of Britain
than America. By this definition, most Americans at one time or another
would have been Tories.[69] But not only were Quakers unwilling to defend
their country, according to Paine, they would not defend even their own
virtue. They were corrupt and debauched. They were actually in bed with
the king of England and cheerfully allowing themselves to be ravished,
literally and figuratively. After making clear that the prostitutes of New
York were Tories, Paine transitioned to Quakers. "[T]he present king of
England," he explained, "who seduced and took into keeping a sister of
their society, is reverenced and supported with repeated testimonies, while
the friendly noodle from whom she was taken (and who is now in this city)
continues a drudge in the service of his rival, as if proud of being cuckolded
by a creature called a king."[70] How could anyone not have contempt for a
Quaker?

By Paine's definition, one becomes a traitor through activity. But the
"practice" part of his definition was the problem for those going after
Quakers. The only flimsy evidence that Paine or anyone could dredge up
as proof that Quakers were traitors was the December 20 epistle. Paine
followed the lead of the memorialists, and when the words did not fit, he
forced them, twisting the language to say something it did not. Furthermore, the Quakers' alleged crime was not just nonsupport of the American
cause or even allegiance to Britain; it was the betrayal of their own principles. He wrote, "The common phrase with these people is, '*Our principles are peace.*' To which may be replied, *and your practices are the
reverse;* for never did the conduct of men oppose their own doctrine more
notoriously than the present race of the Quakers." Paine acknowledged that
"this apostasy of the Quakers from themselves" was not ordinarily the public's business but, he insisted, the "design and consequences were pointed
against" America. "Oh ye fallen, cringing priest and Pemberton-ridden
people!" he exclaimed. "[W]hat more can we say of ye than that a religious
Quaker is a valuable character, and a political Quaker a real Jesuit." To call
someone a "Jesuit" was to assign him the ultimate traitor status, someone
who was against all the fundamental principles of society, akin to "witch"
in the 1690s, "communist" in the 1950s, and "Muslim" and "socialist" in
the 2000s. For some Americans in the Revolution, the word "Quaker" took
on this meaning as well. The December 20 epistle thus became "a matter
of criminality" that should be punished by the state.[71]

Now Paine was no longer satisfied with smears and threats. He urged action. Lamenting in his third *Crisis* that the memorial calling for the arrest of Pemberton and others "was suffered to pass away unnoticed, to the encouragement of new acts of treason, the general danger of the cause, and the disgrace of the state," Paine reproduced it in its entirety for the benefit of the public. And he had a few other suggestions. Tories, including Quakers, should be banned from office, because "[i]t is unnatural and impolitic to admit men who would root up our independence to have any share in our legislation, either as electors or representatives."[72] Further, because "[Quakers] have voluntarily read themselves out of the continental meeting, and cannot hope to be restored to it again, but by payment and penitence," they should also be disenfranchised and subjected to fines, tests, and other punishments.[73] "Men," he reasoned, "whose political principles are founded on avarice, are beyond the reach of reason, and the only cure of toryism of this cast, is to tax it."[74] Refusing to acknowledge the Quakers' increasingly pressing concern for religious liberty, Paine oversimplified the situation, again blaming them for the harassment they suffered. "Had the Quakers minded their religion and their business," he said, "they might have lived through this dispute in enviable ease, and none would have molested them."[75] But the words and actions of the Revolutionaries make this speculation ring hollow. After all, refusing to engage in war *was* their religion, and, moreover, when Friends wanted to "mind their religion" by attending their Yearly Meeting, there were suggestions by military leaders to shoot them and "leave their bodies lying in the road."[76] They were imprisoned for not affirming allegiance to a persecuting government, and their property was distrained in the thousands of pounds.[77] As for their businesses, when they tried, as their fellow Pennsylvanians once recommended, "following their respective occupations as on any other day," instead of observing fasts and lighting windows, they received accusations of greed and avarice, and the destruction of their property.[78] Congressman Edward Rutledge wanted to "make a point of hanging" Quaker merchants who would not accept the risky and devalued Continental currency.[79]

The radicals were receptive to Paine's suggestions for how to solve the Quaker problem, and in the second year of independence began a concerted campaign against them. Violence erupted on July 4, 1777, against Quakers who refused to light their windows in celebration of independence. Radicals broke windows and damaged property. After a Quaker merchant complained to Congressman Henry Laurens that the windows of his shop had been smashed, Laurens responded in what can only be understood as a further threat of violence and bodily harm: he told the Quaker that he "might depend upon this as a type of broken bones to that Glass unless they soon reformed or removed out of the Country."[80]

With anti-Quakerism at a high pitch and General Howe again approaching Philadelphia, Congress and the Pennsylvania government were now prepared to act on Paine's advice in *The Crisis*. But without evidence of treason – the December epistle was clearly not enough – the governments could do little. Their solution: fabricate evidence. Accordingly, on August 25, General John Sullivan sent Congress a set of forged papers from a fictitious Quaker meeting in Spanktown, New Jersey, allegedly giving the enemy intelligence about American positions. Congress ordered the Pennsylvania Executive Council to arrest eleven Quakers. After warrantless searches of their houses, on August 31, it arrested forty-one men, Quakers and non-Quakers, and ultimately held twenty-six of them, mostly Quakers. These, including John Pemberton, were exiled to Virginia, where they were held for eight months, habeas corpus denied. Two of them died in custody, many became ill, and some had their livelihoods destroyed.[81] In truth, there was no crime, no treason, and not even a formal charge. It was rather merely, as Richard Henry Lee revealed, the "universal ill fame of some capital persons, [which] has occasioned the arrest of old Pemberton and several others." It was a preemptive measure "to prevent their mischievous interposition in favor of the enemy at this critical moment when the enemies army is on its way here, with professed design to give this City up to the pillage of the soldiery."[82]

In an uncertain time, Congress had allowed itself to succumb to paranoia and prejudice, or "hysteria and vindictiveness," as one historian put it.[83] It was convinced of the Quakers' guilt, not by real evidence or judicial process, but by mob actions and inflammatory rhetoric such as Paine's. Where the delegates used to differentiate, speaking of "Quakers & Tories," they now referred to "Tory quakers."[84] Though no plots could be discovered, Quakers were seen as "the most dangerous Enemies in the World," with "a uniform, fixed enmity to American measures."[85] John Adams, who disliked Quakers as much as anyone, knew that they were no real threat. In March of 1777 he had proclaimed that they were "as dull as Beetles. From these neither good is to be expected nor Evil to be apprehended. They are a kind of neutral Tribe, or the Race of the insipids."[86] But now, only a few months later and swept up with the anti-Quaker fervor, Adams changed his tune. Indeed, he was on the committee that recommended their arrest. He said,

> We have been obliged to attempt to humble the Pride of some Jesuits who call themselves Quakers, but who love Money and Land better than

Liberty or Religion. The Hypocrites are endeavouring to raise the Cry of Persecution, and to give this Matter a religious Turn, but they cant succeed. The World knows them and their Communications.[87]

Yet the actions of Congress suggest they were not so confident that the public would automatically assume the Quakers' guilt. To minimize the effect of Quaker petitions, Congress ordered all of them published together in one issue of a newspaper.[88] Furthermore, revealing doubts about the legitimacy of the entire operation, a New Hampshire delegate confessed, "I fear we shall fail of that proof that is Expected."[89]

In October, Congressman Elbridge Gerry revealed that the arrests had done little good. Indeed, the arrests were so generally unpopular that they may have undermined the credibility of Congress and the Pennsylvania government.[90] "[T]here is not such a Collection of disaffected people on the Continent," he said, "as of the quakers inhabiting [eastern] Pennsylvania." But more importantly, he acknowledged that the disaffection was not about Loyalism at all. It was, as it had been all along, about the defects in the Pennsylvania constitution. "The Disputes about the Constitution of this State," he continued, "have produced such a Division & Torpor thro out the same, as renders it at present an inactive, lifeless, unwieldy, Mass."[91] But the suspicions died hard, and delegates continued to blame Friends for all the troubles in the state. "The sly broad Brims who do not take Arms against us in great Numbers are assiduous in the Task of undermining our Resources," complained Gouverneur Morris.[92]

By 1778, however, sentiments were turning in favor of the Quakers—or at least against the flagrant injustices against them. The radicals, who had maintained their ascendance with the help of Congress, were criticized by those who disapproved of the treatment of Quakers and other religious and political dissenters. And these critics identified the spiritual leader of the radicals. "Is it possible," wrote "Hampden" in the *Pennsylvania Ledger,* "that all the false conclusions, drawn forth from airy nothings by Mr. Payne, can convince you that your present situation is an eligible one? . . . Reflection on the fate of a . . . Pemberton, appalls the most intrepid." His conclusion portended ill for the entire revolutionary endeavor: "Thus doth America stand another melancholy instance where that little word Liberty, bawled forth from the mouths of artful and designing men, hath seduced the freest people on the face of the globe, to the arms of the most abject slavery."[93] But this warning did not mean the end of the civil rage.

In March of 1778, an act of attainder was passed in the Pennsylvania Assembly. Legally very problematic, acts of attainder allowed individuals to be condemned of treason in absentia, their civil rights abolished, and a death sentence pronounced. That year, 396 people were conditionally attainted. Of these, approximately 130 turned themselves in, including two Quakers in July.[94] As they awaited trial, the body of Friends continued to press for the restoration of their charter privileges and remind their fellow Pennsylvanians of their common history. In August, prominent Friend Nicholas Waln offered an appeal to the Pennsylvania Assembly: "We fervently desire," he wrote, "you may consider the generous and liberal foundation of the charter and laws agreed upon in England between our first worthy Proprietor William Penn and our ancestors whereby they apprehended religious and civil liberty would be secured inviolate to themselves and their posterity." As two brethren sat in jail, Waln asserted, "We believe every attempt to abridge us of that liberty will be a departure from the true spirit of government which ought to influence all well regulated legislatures."[95] Those in Congress were not favorably impressed. Indeed, vitriol seemed to be growing. "These Quakers," exclaimed Samuel Adams, "are in general a sly artful People." His hatred seems to have been grounded on little more than distaste for their corporate exclusivity, hardly a crime. "They carefully educate their Children in their own contracted Opinions and Manners," he complained, "and I dare say they have in their Heads as perfect a System of Uniformity of Worship in their Way, and are busily employd about spiritual Domination as ever Laud himself was."[96] Animosity toward Quakers was less about patriotism than it was about xenophobia.

In Paine's more mature thinking about revolutions twenty years later, he wrote, "in the commencement of a revolution, the revolutionary party permit to themselves a *discretionary exercise of power* regulated more by circumstances than by principle, which were the practice to continue, liberty would never be established, or if established would soon be overthrown."[97] Joseph Reed, assistant to the Pennsylvania attorney general and soon-to-be president of the state, seemed intent on exercising this "discretionary" power to its fullest. "The Designs of a Tory, Proprietary Quaker Party," he said in October, "are too obvious; & if not crushed in the Bud will produce a plentiful Crop of Mixing & Dissension thro this State."[98] Despite the best efforts of the defendants' attorney, James Wilson, Reed enforced the execution of the two Quaker Loyalists on November 4, 1778. Of the 396 persons conditionally attainted that year, the Quakers were the only persons executed.[99]

By then, it seems, the "discretionary" phase in Pennsylvania was beginning to wane. The public outcry for clemency for the two Quakers had been loud, coming from all points along the political spectrum, including from patriot Thomas McKean, the chief justice of the Supreme Court.[100] And into the next year, the tumult in Pennsylvania and the injustices committed by the revolutionary government gained notoriety. John Adams, rediscovering his distaste for Paine-style democracy, lamented the situation: "The people of Pennsylvania in two years," he wrote to Benjamin Rush in 1779, "will be glad to petition the crown of Britain for reconciliation in order to be delivered from the tyranny of their Constitution."[101] Pennsylvanians did not apply to England, but in 1782, they did elect to the presidency the former leader of the resistance to independence, leading opponent of the 1776 constitution, and Quaker "fellow traveler" John Dickinson to restore moderation to the state.[102]

Quakers were not the only inhabitants of Pennsylvania who felt the effects of the radicals' policies, but they were targeted like no others. Neither was Paine the sole cause of their persecution. But he heightened and manipulated anti-Quaker sentiment more skillfully than any other polemicist of the day. Through his pen, sentiments murmured in taverns or expressed in personal letters between congressmen were brought out into the streets and into the State House chambers. Emboldened, the public and policy makers acted. And as to whether any of the actions against the Quakers furthered the war effort, as Paine maintained they would: there is no evidence to suggest that they did. On the contrary, the denial of civil rights for this particular religious group had lasting repercussions. The legacy of his attacks survived well after the Revolution, hindering the Quakers' effectiveness in reform movements such as abolition.[103]

In an ironic twist, Paine had a unique opportunity to reflect on his role in Pennsylvania politics and the treatment of the Quakers. Years later in France, as that Revolution turned to the dark side, Paine found himself in the shadows, no longer leader but victim. His cries of excess and injustice are strikingly familiar:

> The intolerant spirit of religious persecution had transferred itself into politics; the tribunals, styled Revolutionary, supplied the place of the Inquisition; and the Guillotine of the State out did the Fire and Faggot of the Church. I saw many of my most intimate friends destroyed; others daily carried to prison; and I had reason to believe, and had also intimations given me, that the same danger was approaching myself.[104]

Certainly the excesses of the American Revolution were minimal compared to those of the French, unless of course, you were one of the Quakers who was harassed, imprisoned, robbed, bankrupted, or executed by the Revolutionaries. But we must wonder if Paine had any sense of the irony or a glimmering of recognition as he experienced these things and wrote these words. If he did, there is no record.

After the American Revolution, Paine did not devote much more time or energy to Quakerism. The only other mention we find of Quakerism in his writings after 1777 is in the second part of *The Age of Reason,* where he pays them what could, from the Quaker perspective, only be considered a backhanded compliment. "The only sect that has not persecuted," he offers, "are the Quakers; and the only reason that can be given for it, is, that they are rather Deists than Christians. They do not believe much about Jesus Christ, and they call the scriptures a dead letter."[105] Surely Paine knew better. Eighteenth-century Quakerism was very much based on the teachings of Christ, and Scripture was a foundational source for Friends. He may have been catering to what he knew to be the fanciful prejudices of the French about Quakers. Many of the *philosophes* held Quakerism up as an ideal civil religion, believing that it was entirely rationalistic and noncoercive.[106] Quakers disagreed vehemently with the former characterization, as Miers Fisher's rebuttal to *The Age of Reason* shows, and their theocracy in Pennsylvania disproves the latter.[107]

Ultimately the relationship between Paine and Quakers ended the way it seems always to have been – a tense and uncomfortable intimacy. Quakers despised Paine's religious views, and many despised Paine himself. But when he lay suffering on his deathbed, they came to comfort him.[108] Seeking the solace of the closest thing he had to a spiritual home, in his will he wrote, "I know not if the society of people, called Quakers, admit a person to be buried in their burying ground, who does not belong to their society, but if they do, or will admit me, I would prefer being buried there."[109] When he made his request, he even offered to pay the cost of the burial himself. Always pushing the Quakers to conform to his idea of them rather than accepting them for what they were, when Paine was denied, he wept and called the decision "foolish."[110]

Raised with Quakerism, Thomas Paine had a better sense of the faith than many, and he admired Friends in his own way. But it seems he never really understood them deeply, and it is clear that he neither understood nor respected Pennsylvania Quakers; or if he did, his sympathy for their religious priorities was subordinate to his political aims. His campaign against them only hindered the laudable aims of the Revolution and, at best, serves as a lesson of how not to treat dissenters.

NOTES

The author would like to thank the following people for reading and commenting on drafts: the attenders of the Kentucky Early American Studies Seminar, Mark Summers, Ian Shapiro, Jonathan Clark, Eileen Hunt Botting, Richard B. Bernstein, David Armitage, Rogers Smith, and, as always, Eric Kiltinen.

1. See, among many, John W. Seaman, "Thomas Paine: Ransom, Civil Peace, and the Natural Right to Welfare," *Political Theory* 16, no. 1 (1988): pp. 120–142; Jack Fruchtman, Jr., *The Political Philosophy of Thomas Paine* (Baltimore: Johns Hopkins University Press, 2009), pp. 119–133. Paine's originality on this point is debatable, since there was already a social welfare system in England, on which he drew.

2. Many scholars have followed Moncure D. Conway, *The Life of Thomas Paine: With a History of his Literary, Political, and Religious Career in America, France, and England,* 2 vols. (New York: G. P. Putnam's Sons, 1893), vol. 2: p. 201; and Moncure D. Conway, ed., *The Writings of Thomas Paine,* 4 vols. (New York: G. P. Putnam's Sons, 1894–1892), vol. 2: p. 262. See, as corrective, Robert P. Falk, "Thomas Paine: Deist or Quaker?" *The Pennsylvania Magazine of History and Biography* [hereafter *PMHB*] 62, no. 1 (1938): pp. 52–63.

3. Mary Agnes Best, *Thomas Paine: Prophet and Martyr of Democracy* (New York: Harcourt, Brace, 1927), pp. 8, 10, 31, 40, 175, 307, 406; Audrey Williamson, *Thomas Paine: His Life, Work and Times* (New York: St. Martin's Press, 1973), pp. 24–26; John Keane, *Tom Paine: A Political Life* (New York: Grove Press, 1995), pp. 18, 20–25, 27–28, 41; Craig Nelson, *Thomas Paine* (New York: Penguin, 2006), pp. 16–17, 18, 40, 261; Gregory Claeys, *Thomas Paine: Social and Political Thought* (Boston: Unwin Hyman, 1989), passim, esp. pp. 101–104.

4. On his education, see Thomas Paine [hereafter TP], *The Age of Reason,* this volume, p. 402. On his approval, see *Age of Reason,* this volume, pp. 494, 495; TP to Camille Jordan, 1797, in Conway, *Writings of Paine,* pp. 250, 252, 253; TP to Samuel Adams, January 1, 1803, in Conway, *Writings of Paine,* p. 204.

5. Paine, it should be noted, did not actively take up abolitionism. See James V. Lynch, "The Limits of Revolutionary Radicalism: Tom Paine and Slavery," *PMHB* 123, no. 3 (1999): pp. 177–199.

6. On Quakers' radical beginnings, see Hugh Barbour, *The Quakers in Puritan England* (New Haven: Yale University Press, 1964).

7. Keane, *Tom Paine,* p. 103.

8. For a brief account of this episode with different conclusions from those offered here, see Robert P. Falk, "Thomas Paine and the Attitude of the Quakers to the American Revolution," *PMHB* 63, no. 3 (1939): pp. 302–310.

9. For detailed examinations of this period, see Robert L. Brunhouse, *The Counter-Revolution in Pennsylvania* (Harrisburg: Pennsylvania Historical and Museum Commission, 1971); J. Paul Selsam, *The Pennsylvania Constitution of 1776: A Study in Revolutionary Democracy* (New York: Da Capo Press, 1971); Richard Ryerson, *The Revolution Is Now Begun: The Radical Committees of Philadelphia, 1765–1776* (Philadelphia: University of Pennsylvania Press, 1978); Anne M. Ousterhout, *A State Divided: Opposition in Pennsylvania to the American Revolution* (New York: Greenwood Press, 1987); Steven Rosswurm, *Arms, Country, and Class: The Philadelphia Militia and the "Lower Sort" during the American Revolution, 1775–1783* (New Brunswick, NJ: Rutgers University Press, 1987).

10. Robert G. Parkinson, "'Manifest Signs of Passion': The First Federal Congress, Anti-Slavery, and Legacies of the Revolutionary War," in *Contesting Slavery: The Politics of Bondage and Freedom in the New American Nation,* ed. John Craig Hammond and Matthew Mason (Charlottesville: University Press of Virginia, 2011), pp. 49–68.

11. Most discussions of Paine's response to the Quakers assume they were Loyalists and thus do not question the justice of Paine's attacks. An exception is Samuel Edwards, who writes, "Paine's charges against Quakers were as unfair as they were ridiculous"; *Rebel! A Biography of Thomas Paine* (New York: Praeger Publishing, 1974), p. 50.

12. Even the following discussion is much simplified. For treatment that presents a more-complicated picture of Quakers during the Revolution, see Richard Bauman, *For the Reputation of Truth: Politics, Religion, and Conflict among the Pennsylvania Quakers, 1750–1800* (Baltimore: Johns Hopkins University Press, 1971). See also Isaac Sharpless, *The Quakers in the Revolution* (1902; repr., Honolulu: University Press of the Pacific, 2002); Arthur J. Mekeel, *The Relation of the Quakers to the American Revolution* (Washington, DC: University Press of America, 1979).

13. "The Charter of Privileges," in *The Papers of William Penn,* ed. Richard Dunn and Mary Maples Dunn, 5 vols. (Philadelphia: University of Pennsylvania Press, 1981–1987), 4: pp. 105–109.

14. On Quaker Pennsylvania, see Alan Tully, *Forming American Politics: Ideals, Interests, and Institutions in Colonial New York and Pennsylvania* (Baltimore: Johns Hopkins University Press, 1994), pp. 275–309; Jane E. Calvert, *Quaker Constitutionalism and the Political Thought of John Dickinson* (New York: Cambridge University Press, 2009), esp. pp. 136–176.

15. During this era, PYM had approximately 30,000 members. According to the first U.S. census in 1790, the population of Pennsylvania was 434,373.

Edwin S. Gaustad, Philip L. Barlow, Richard W. Dishno, *New Historical Atlas of Religion in America* (New York: Oxford University Press, 2000), pp. 42–45.

16. See Kevin Kenny, *Peaceable Kingdom Lost: The Paxton Boys and the Destruction of William Penn's Holy Experiment* (New York: Oxford University Press, 2009).

17. Parkinson, "'Manifest Signs of Passion,'" passim.

18. On the Quaker theory of resistance, see Calvert, *Quaker Constitutionalism*, esp. pp. 25–99.

19. "A Letter from the Committee of Correspondence in Barbados, to their Agent in London," in John Dickinson, *An Address to the Committee of Correspondence in Barbados* (Philadelphia: William Bradford, 1766), pp. ii–iv.

20. James Pemberton to Samuel Fothergill, May 5, 1775, in Sharpless, *Quakers in the Revolution*, p. 121.

21. John Dickinson, "Centinel No. VIII," *Pennsylvania Journal*, May 12, 1768.

22. See Nathan Kozuskanich, "'Falling under the Domination Totally of Presbyterians': The Paxton Riots and the Coming of the Revolution in Pennsylvania," in *Pennsylvania's Revolution*, ed. William Pencak (University Park: Pennsylvania State University Press, 2010), pp. 7–35.

23. See their epistle urging members to raise money to alleviate "the afflictions and distresses" of the people of New England, in *The Pennsylvania Ledger*, July 22, 1775.

24. Cited in Bauman, *Reputation of Truth*, p. 159.

25. Sharpless, *Quakers in the Revolution*, p. 151.

26. William Penn, *Some Fruits of Solitude, in Reflections and Maxims Relating to the Conduct of Human Life* (London: Thomas Northcott, 1693), pp. 103–105.

27. TP, *Rights of Man*, this volume, pp. 199, 213.

28. TP, *Rights of Man* [in "Observations on the Declaration of Rights"], this volume, p. 235.

29. TP, "Thoughts on Defensive War," this volume, pp. 3, 4.

30. Ibid.

31. PYM, "To the Representatives of the Freemen of the Province of Pennsylvania, in General Assembly Met" (Philadelphia, October 27, 1775), p. 1.

32. Ibid.

33. "The Memorial of the Officers of the Military Association of the City and Liberties of Philadelphia," in *Pennsylvania Archives,* 8th ser., 8 vols. (Philadelphia: J. Severns, 1931–1935), vol. 8: pp. 7337–7339. See also pp. 7334–7337 and 7339–7343.

34. PYM, "To the Representatives," p. 2.

35. I am using the term "civil disobedience" in its modern, technical sense. See Calvert, *Quaker Constitutionalism,* pp. 6–7.

36. TP, *Common Sense,* this volume, pp. 24, 25.

37. PYM, *Ancient Testimony and Principles of the People Called Quakers* (Philadelphia, January 20, 1776), pp. 2, 3, 4. It should be noted that, before *Common Sense,* although colonists disputed the authority of Parliament and had begun to question the authority of the king, they had not entirely abandoned the notion that the colonies might be united through the king's authority. See Jack P. Greene, *Peripheries and Center: Constitutional Development in the Extended Polities of the British Empire and United States, 1607–1788* (New York: W. W. Norton, 1986), pp. 94–95.

38. TP, "To the Representatives of the Religious Society of the People called Quakers . . . ," in *Common Sense,* this volume, pp. 48, 49, 51, 48.

39. TP, *The Crisis,* "Number III" (April 19, 1777), this volume, p. 92.

40. TP, "To the Representatives of the Religious Society of the People called Quakers . . . ," in *Common Sense,* this volume, pp. 51, 50, 51.

41. Penn, *Some Fruits of Solitude,* p. 104.

42. TP, "To the Representatives of the Religious Society of the People called Quakers . . . ," in *Common Sense,* this volume, p. 49.

43. Ibid.

44. John Adams to James Warren, March 21, 1776, in *Letters of Delegates to Congress,* ed. Paul H. Smith et al., 24 vols. (Washington, DC: Library of Congress, 1976–2000) [hereafter *LDC*], vol. 3: p. 422.

45. TP, "Letter IV. To the People," *Pennsylvania Journal; and Weekly Advertiser,* May 8, 1776.

46. Ibid.

47. A 1764 campaign by a few Pennsylvanians to abolish the charter and place Pennsylvania under a royal government had been opposed by a majority of the inhabitants, who most certainly saw their constitution as permanent. See James H. Hutson, *Pennsylvania Politics, 1746–1770: The Movement for Royal Government and its Consequences* (Princeton, NJ: Princeton University Press, 1972).

48. TP, "Letter IV."

49. *Journals of the Continental Congress, 1774–1789,* ed. Worthington C. Ford et al. (Washington, DC, 1904–37), vol. 4: p. 342. The resolution passed on May 15.

50. On May 29 he wrote to Benjamin Hichborn that "The Proprietary Governments, are not only incumbered with a large Body of Quakers, but are embarrassed by a proprietary Interest. Both together clogg their operations a little: but these cloggs are falling off, as you will Soon see," in *LDC,* vol. 4: p. 96.

51. Ryerson, *The Revolution Is Now Begun*, p. 212.

52. Ibid., p. 219.

53. Cited in Gordon S. Wood, *Creation of the American Republic, 1776–1789* (Chapel Hill: University of North Carolina Press, 1969), p. 229.

54. *Journals of the Continental Congress*, vol. 4: pp. 208–209; Committee of Inspection and Observation, "In Committee Chamber . . ." (Philadelphia: William and Thomas Bradford, May 16, 1776).

55. TP, *Crisis*, "Number III," this volume, p. 89.

56. Keane, *Tom Paine*, p. 136; Brunhouse, *Counter-Revolution*, p. 28; Selsam, *Pennsylvania Constitution*, p. 208.

57. John Dickinson et al., *Pennsylvania Gazette*, October 23, 1776.

58. See Bauman, *Reputation of Truth*, p. 161.

59. The constitution was technically amendable, but not for seven years, and not by the people themselves but by a Council of Censors. The moderates found such an arrangement unacceptable. See Brunhouse, *Counter-Revolution*, p. 15, passim.

60. PYM, "To Our Friends and Brethren in Religious Profession" (Philadelphia, December 20, 1776).

61. "To the Honorable the Council of Safety of the State of Pennsylvania," reprinted in TP, *Crisis*, "Number III," this volume, p. 91. This was not the only time the Quakers words would be manipulated by their opponents. Quakers complained that *The Pennsylvania Packet* published their missives "with transpositions and the interposition" of entire paragraphs and introductions not their own. They also noted that their publications were of the same tone and content as the Olive Branch Petition, issued by Congress in 1775. See Society of Friends, *A Short Vindication of the Religious Society Called Quakers* (Philadelphia, 1780),vol. 2: p. 1.

62. TP, *Crisis*, "Number I" (December 23, 1776), this volume, p. 53.

63. TP, *Dissertation on First-Principles of Government* (1795), this volume, pp. 519–520.

64. TP, *Crisis*, "Number II" (Jan. 13, 1777), this volume, p. 65. It should be noted that in *Crisis*, "Number III," Paine mistakenly refers to it as the epistle "of the 20th of November."

65. *Crisis*, "Number III," this volume, p. 89.

66. Ibid., p. 80.

67. TP, *Rights of Man. Part the Second*, this volume, p. 360.

68. TP, *Crisis*, "Number III," this volume, p. 76.

69. See Edward Larkin, "What Is a Loyalist?: The American Revolution as Civil War," *Common-Place* 8, no. 1 (2007); available at: http://www.common-place.org/vol-08/no-01/larkin/.

70. TP, *Crisis,* "Number III," this volume, p. 88. On King George's Quaker mistress and possibly his first wife, Hannah Lightfoot, see Michael Kreps, *Hannah Regina: Britain's Quaker Queen* (Fredericksburg, VA: Cardinal Press, 2003).

71. TP, *Crisis,* "Number III," this volume, pp. 91–92, 82, 92.

72. Ibid., pp. 89, 76.

73. Ibid., p. 95. Notice Paine's use of Quaker language here. To be "read out of meeting" was to be disowned by the Quaker meeting.

74. Ibid.

75. Ibid., p. 91.

76. Cited in Sharpless, *Quakers in the Revolution,* p. 183.

77. The Meeting for Sufferings reported at least £35,000 by the end of the war (Sharpless, *Quakers in the Revolution,* p. 176).

78. Committee of Inspection and Observance, "In Committee Chamber . . ."; Sharpless, *Quakers in the Revolution,* pp. 172–206.

79. Edward Rutledge to Robert R. Livingston, October 2, 1776, in *LDC,* vol. 5: p. 295.

80. Henry Laurens to John Lewis Gervais, August 5, 1777, in *LDC,* vol. 7: p. 424.

81. A collection of primary documents on this episode is Thomas Gilpin, *Exiles in Virginia* (1906; repr., Bowie, MD: Heritage Books, 2003). See also Society of Friends, *A Short Vindication.* In addition to work on Quakers in the Revolution in general, see Robert F. Oaks, "Philadelphians in Exile: The Problem of Loyalty during the American Revolution," *PMHB* 96, no. 3 (1972): pp. 298–325.

82. Richard Henry Lee to Patrick Henry, September 8, 1777, in *LDC,* vol. 7: p. 637.

83. Bauman, *Reputation of Truth,* p. 164.

84. William Hooper to Joseph Hewes, November 16, 1776, in *LDC,* vol. 5: p. 499; Elbridge Gerry to Unknown, Sept. 10, 1777, in *LDC,* vol. 7: p. 641.

85. Henry Laurens to John Lewis Gervais, September 5, 1777, in *LDC,* vol. 7: p. 613; Richard Henry Lee to Patrick Henry, September 8, 1777, in *LDC,* vol. 7: p. 637.

86. John Adams to Abigail Adams, March 7, 1777, in *LDC,* vol. 6: p. 409.

87. Adams to Adams, September 8, 1777, in *LDC,* vol. 7: p. 627.

88. *Pennsylvania Packet,* September 9, 1777.

89. New Hampshire Delegates to Meshech Weare, September 2, 1777, in *LDC,* vol. 7: p. 596.

90. Oaks, "Philadelphians in Exile," p. 316.

91. Elbridge Gerry to James Warren, October 6, 1777, in *LDC,* vol. 8: p. 66.

92. Gouverneur Morris to George Clinton, February 17, 1778, in *LDC,* vol. 9: p. 68.

93. Hampden, "For the *Pennsylvania Ledger," Pennsylvania Ledger,* May 9, 1778.

94. Henry J. Young, "Treason and Its Punishment in Revolutionary Pennsylvania," *PMHB* 90, no. 3 (1966): pp. 287–313, 304–305.

95. Nicholas Waln, "Appeal to Pennsylvania Assembly," August 5, 1778, in Sharpless, *Quakers in the Revolution,* p. 180.

96. Samuel Adams to Peter Thacher, August 11, 1778, in *LDC,* vol. 10: p. 421.

97. TP, *Dissertation on First-Principles,* this volume, p. 519.

98. Joseph Reed to John Armstrong, October 5, 1778, in *LDC,* vol. 11: p. 26.

99. Young, "Treason and Its Punishment," 306. See also Peter C. Messer, "'A Species of Treason & Not the Least Dangerous Kind': The Treason Trials of Abraham Carlisle and John Roberts," *PMHB* 123, no. 4 (1999): pp. 303–332.

100. Messer, "'Species of Treason,'" 326; Rosswurm, *Arms, Country, and Class,* p. 157.

101. John Adams to Benjamin Rush, October 12, 1779, in *Letters of Benjamin Rush,* ed. Herbert L. Butterfield, 2 vols. (Princeton: Princeton University Press for the American Philosophical Society, 1951), vol. 1: p. 240.

102. On Dickinson's political Quakerism, see Calvert, *Quaker Constitutionalism,* esp. pp. 189–192.

103. Parkinson, "'Manifest Signs of Passion,'" passim.

104. TP, *Age of Reason. Part the Second,* this volume, p. 419.

105. Ibid., p. 495.

106. On French idealization of Pennsylvania Quakers, see Edith Philips, *The Good Quaker in French Legend* (Philadelphia: University of Pennsylvania Press, 1932) and Durand Echeverria, *Mirage in the West: A History of the French View of American Society to 1815* (Princeton, NJ: Princeton University Press, 1968).

107. Miers Fisher, *A Reply to the False Reasoning in the "Age of Reason"* (Philadelphia: Henry Tuckniss, 1796).

108. Stephen Grellet and Benjamin Seebohm, *Memoir of the Life and Gospel Labours* (Philadelphia: Henry Longstreth, 1862), pp. 163–164.

109. TP, "The Will of Thomas Paine," in Conway, *Writings of Paine,* vol. 4: p. 509.

110. "Thomas Paine. A Sketch of his Life by William Cobbett," in Conway, *Life of Paine,* vol. 2: pp. 433–459, 451.

Thomas Paine amidst the
Early Feminists

EILEEN HUNT BOTTING

This essay traces the place of Thomas Paine amidst the feminist[1] discourse of the late eighteenth century in Europe and the United States. Because of Paine's radical critique of monarchy and other forms of hereditary power, support of the American and French Revolutions, and defense of the "rights of man," it has been assumed that he was also an advocate of women's rights.[2] For decades, the main evidence for Paine's feminism was his supposed authorship of the 1775 articles "An Occasional Letter on the Female Sex" and "Unhappy Marriages," published in *The Pennsylvania Magazine*.[3] Scholars have more recently debunked both the claim of Paine's authorship, as well as the feminist character, of these texts.[4] Is there, then, any room left for Paine – the leading exponent of the "rights of man" in the revolutionary era – amidst Enlightenment advocates of the "rights of woman"?

Paine – like many male radicals of the late Enlightenment – was neither a steady nor consistently direct advocate of the rights of women, particularly women's equal civil and political rights with men. In this way, he was no different from William Godwin in London, Bishop Talleyrand-Périgord in Paris, or Charles Brockden Brown in America. Early in his career, from *Common Sense* (1776) to *Rights of Man* (1791), Paine was silent on the issue of women's rights, and sometimes slipped into using derogatory, patriarchal language to describe women's inequality with men. The shift from the republican-based discourse of *Common Sense* and *The Crisis* series (1776–1783) to the rights-based language of *Rights of Man* seems to have pushed Paine toward a deeper philosophical consideration of women's possession of the same natural rights as men. Much of what Paine argued in the later part of his career, especially in *Rights of Man. Part the Second* (1792) and *Agrarian Justice* (1797), either explicitly or implicitly endorses women's equal rights with men, especially welfare rights but also political rights such as suffrage.

Several potential explanations for Paine's relative disregard of women's rights, especially in the first part of his writing career, have been proposed, including latent or overt misogyny, or the prioritization of other causes and projects above it.[5] I will not speculate on the reasons for Paine's early neglect of the issue of women's rights, since he left no written discussion of the matter. This essay will rather set forth the first extended account of the evolution of the place of women's rights in his political thought and his reception within women's rights discourse through the mid-nineteenth century.

Paine was the major promulgator of the transatlantic doctrine of the "rights of man" through his works *Rights of Man* and *Rights of Man. Part the Second.*[6] As such, he exerted vast influence on the rise of rights discourse in the late Enlightenment. Rights discourse– which became prominent in eighteenth-century Britain, America, and France–promoted the individual rights of subjects or citizens, which generally meant white male landowners. But in some cases, the language and logic of rights discourse was extended to other groups, including African slaves and women. This extension of the "rights of man" doctrine to other groups became more prominent around the time of the American and French revolutions. The liberation of the masses through political rebellion became a philosophical model for the liberation of people oppressed by their social status.

Some of the earliest extensions of the "rights of man" doctrine to women are found in the French tradition; Condorcet's "On the Admission of Women to the Rights of Citizenship" (1790) and Olympe de Gouges's "Declaration of the Rights of Woman and Citizen" (1791) asked for women to be granted the same civil and political rights as men in the new French republic. The phrase "rights of woman" was bandied about in Anglo-American public discourse–more often humorously than seriously–in the early 1790s. In 1791, *The United States Chronicle* published a poem "To a Young Lady, who sent to the author for 'The Rights of Man,' written by Mr. Paine." The poem mocked the young lady's desire to apply the ideas of Paine to the subordinated condition of her sex, by invoking the age-old patriarchal idea that women were in fact the arbitrary, sexually manipulative rulers of men:

But have not women greater rights than these;
Do they not rule and govern as they please?
The servile men of every age and nation,
Are always slaves to female legislation. . . .
Tho' "Common Sense," may suit the sons of Freedom,
The lovely ladies will not deign to read him;
Full well they are convinc'd his reasoning's vain,
And that their charms will rule in spite of PAINE.[7]

Until the publication of Mary Wollstonecraft's *A Vindication of the Rights of Woman* in London in 1792, the use of the idea of women's rights was more often than not in the joking mode above. Wollstonecraft's book helped propel the development of an international discourse on women's rights, however, that took the issue seriously as a logical extension of the "rights of man" doctrine. Yet even into the mid- to late 1790s, the norm was to understand the rights of man as literally pertaining to men, not to see them as universal rights grounded in human nature. Paine followed this trend until early 1792, when he composed his most radical work to date, *Rights of Man. Part the Second.*

Although Paine socialized with some of the leading women's rights advocates of the era, including Benjamin Rush in Philadelphia, Condorcet and Théroigne de Méricourt in Paris, and Mary Wollstonecraft in London and Paris,[8] he did not follow their lead in direct advocacy of women's rights prior to his exposition of women's welfare rights in *Rights of Man. Part the Second.* Following Condorcet, de Gouges, and Wollstonecraft, Paine may have picked up on the early 1790s shift toward a serious public discourse on women's rights and developed his own views accordingly. The simple yet elegant internal logic of the emergent "rights of man" doctrine – which at least implicitly suggested that people have rights by virtue of their nature as humans – was another likely reason for Paine's growing consideration of the rights of women.

The *Rights of Man. Part the Second*'s exposition of universal human welfare rights – and their specific application to women – was composed soon after the publication of Wollstonecraft's *Rights of Woman* in London. Paine's gradual move toward defending women's human rights, including a right to property, suffrage, and welfare, evolved during his stay in Paris during the most extreme stages of the Revolution. *Agrarian Justice,* his boldest feminist text, shows how his political thought was revolutionized while in France. Unfortunately, Paine's radical turn in matters of religion and politics led to his public vilification by the anti-Jacobins in Britain and America in the late 1790s. After *Rights of Man. Part the Second* – which occasioned his trial and conviction for sedition by the British government in 1792 – and especially after the publication of his harsh critique of Christianity and revealed religion in *The Age of Reason* in 1794, his public reception took a decided turn for the worse.

Agrarian Justice, his last major published work, felt the brunt of this misfortune through its relative neglect by the public, and has since remained an understudied text. Although its philosophical contributions to modern theories of liberal property rights, basic income, and social security have been explored,[9] *Agrarian Justice* also contains a creative argument for women's human right to suffrage that builds on Paine's proposal for universal human welfare rights. I interpret Paine's 1797 proposal for universal human welfare rights as entailing the national government's provision of the basic monetary means of personal independence to each adult citizen, according only to the criteria of age and disability.[10]

In conclusion, I argue that Paine's neglect of the women's rights issue, prior to the publication of *Rights of Man. Part the Second* and *Agrarian Justice,* contributed to the "gendering" of human rights discourse in the public sphere of 1790s Britain and America. Paine came to symbolize the "rights of men," while Wollstonecraft came to symbolize the "rights of women." This gendered reception of their rights doctrines was soon overturned by the sexualized attack on their personas and ideas by the anti-Jacobins. Paine's posthumous reputation recovered more quickly than Wollstonecraft's, leading to his resurrection as a leading icon of universal human rights in nineteenth-century America. I explore the ironies of this gendered, sexualized reception of Paine and Wollstonecraft in the public sphere of the postrevolutionary era, especially in light of Wollstonecraft's and the later Paine's defense of universal human rights. This gendering and sexualizing of human rights discourse has colored the trajectory of both liberalism and feminism to the present day, posing complications for the realization of egalitarian political goals within either tradition.

The Presence and Absence of Women in Paine's Early Writings

Since 1892 – when Moncure Conway attributed to Paine the anonymous articles "Occasional Letter on the Female Sex" and "Unhappy Marriages" from the 1775 *Pennsylvania Magazine* – it often has been repeated that Paine was one of the first feminists in America.[11] Scholars have subsequently shown that Paine did not write these articles and, furthermore, that they are not in fact feminist in content. In 1930, Frank Smith was the first scholar to determine that Paine was not the author of the "Occasional Letter."[12] Mary Catherine Moran has recently corroborated this thesis and provided further evidence to support it. They have shown that the "Occasional Letter" is actually the preface of Scotsman William Russell's *Essay on the Character . . . of Women in Different Ages* (1773), which was a loose translation and expansion of a French work by Antoine-Léonard Thomas, *Essai sur le caractere . . . des femmes dans les differens siecles* (1772).[13] Moran and other scholars, such as Mary Trouille and Lieselotte Steinbrügge, have determined that the original *Essai* is best understood as a Rousseauian text, which reinforced the idea of the natural inequality of the sexes, even as it praised many of the virtues of women.[14] Thomas's book was originally critiqued along these lines by the French feminist Madame d'Epinay, who retorted that women's unequal social status was not natural but could be rectified by improved education.[15] Moran likewise argues that Russell's *Essay* supported many patriarchal stereotypes of the day, especially as found in the Rousseauian and Scottish Enlightenment traditions.[16] Some readers have misinterpreted the "Occasional Letter" as feminist because it was excerpted out of context and associated with the progressive politics of *The Pennsylvania Magazine* and Paine. Once in context, it reads as a flowery, patronizing defense of women's continued dependency on men.

Scholars have also questioned Conway's and others' attribution of "Unhappy Marriages" to Paine solely on the basis of stylistic parallels between it and his early works.[17] In 2001, Edward Pitcher provided the first conclusive evidence that the work could not have been Paine's, by showing that it was first published in 1739, when he was but two years old. The 1739 text was reprinted verbatim in the 1775 *Pennsylvania Magazine,* without citing its original publication in a London literary journal.[18] Beyond some coincidental similarities with Paine's early marital difficulties, the content of "Unhappy Marriages" has no relation to Thomas Paine.[19] While the text mocks the conventions of eighteenth-century marriage, it is not particularly attentive to the issue of the patriarchal oppression of women within marriage – thus it has no strong relation to the feminist tradition, either.

One reason why these two essays were linked with Paine was their stylistic similarities to *Common Sense.* But their shared background of eighteenth-century republican discourse – grounded in Rousseau, *Cato's Letters* (1720–1723), and the Scottish Enlightenment – is the likely source for this similarity in style. The republican tradition has been criticized for its exclusion of women from its political doctrines, despite its defense of popular sovereignty and other aspects of what today is known as democratic government.[20] Not until the early 1790s do we find explicitly feminist republican works – by Condorcet, de Gouges, and Wollstonecraft – that argue for women's equal citizenship with men.

Paine's *Common Sense* and *The Crisis* series generally follow the Anglo-American republican tradition in their political arguments, including the use of gendered metaphors and masculine language to advocate for republican government – for *men. Common Sense* begins by leaving women out of its account of "society," or life before monarchical government (and social inequality) is established.[21] "Society" is gendered as a male realm of basic survival where "Four or five united would be able to raise a tolerable dwelling in the midst of a wilderness, but *one* man might labour out the common period of life without accomplishing any thing; when he had felled his timber he could not remove it, nor erect it after it was removed; hunger in the meantime would urge him from his work."[22] Against the background of the Revolutionary War, Paine insinuates that American *men* must bond together to survive outside of government. In such a crisis, Paine treats women as irrelevant except as metaphors for the corruption of society under government. Indeed, woman first enters the argument of *Common Sense* as a symbolic "prostitute," in Paine's pointed analogy between men who associate with whores and men who are "in favour of a rotten constitution of government."[23]

In *Common Sense*'s opening argument against monarchy and hereditary succession, Paine briefly raises the issue of sex inequality – not to challenge it, but to reinforce it. He describes sex inequality as a natural inequality in contrast to the unnatural inequality between "kings and subjects": "Male and female are the distinctions of nature, good and bad the distinctions of heaven; but how a race of men came into the world so exalted above the rest, and distinguished like some new species, is worth enquiring into, and whether they are the means of happiness or of misery to mankind."[24] In this passage, Paine's contrast of "male and female" with the "kings and subjects" shows that his use of masculine language, such as "race of men," is not generic but rather pertains only to males. Moreover, his contrast of the natural inequality of the sexes with the unnatural inequality of a monarchical society strongly implies his unquestioning acceptance of the former despite his belligerent attack on the latter.

Rogers Smith and others have noted Paine's use of patriarchal familial and gendered metaphors to inspire sympathy for the Revolutionary cause.[25] What is also clear is that he uses such language to particularly cultivate sympathy in American men. His intended male audience is obvious in such queries as "Are your wife and children destitute of a bed to lie on, or bread to live on? . . . But if you have, and can still shake hands with the murderers, then are you unworthy the name of husband, father, friend, or lover."[26] Rhetorical questions such as these pepper *Common Sense,* clearly demarcating its audience as male colonists who seek the full benefits of republican government for themselves, not for their wives or daughters.

By the end of *Common Sense,* Paine has reduced women entirely to a metaphor. America is a virtuous mother, who needs to be defended by her chivalrous sons, so that she can "provide for herself" rather than "granting away her property, to support a power who is become a reproach to the names of men and christians."[27] Although this metaphor in isolation could suggest an independent woman, supporting herself and her family, it is clear that Paine deploys it as an argument for America's being "separated from Britain" not for women's actual independence. Even after putting such gendered metaphors and language aside, there is no direct reference to women's rights in *Common Sense*. The few nonmetaphorical references to women only reinforce Paine's neorepublican acceptance of women's natural (and thus social) inferiority to men. When the text ends with a rousing call to fight for "*the* RIGHTS *of* MANKIND," we can only interpret Paine in the most literal sense.[28]

The Crisis, "Number I" (1776) follows the same pattern. Addressing the work to "he that stands it NOW"–the brave man who is neither the "summer soldier" nor the "sunshine patriot"–Paine promises the reward of "the love and thanks of man and woman."[29] The concluding lines of the essay reinforce his intended audience as male. To them he threatens the prospect of "homes turned into barracks and bawdy-houses for Hessians, and a future race to provide for whose fathers we should doubt of."[30] If American men do not courageously go to war, their homes will become houses of prostitution and they will forever distrust the paternity of their children. Here, Paine suggests that women's virtue is not as stable as men's virtue; female virtue is in fact dependent on male virtue winning the war. The social, if not natural, inequality of women is reinforced by such rhetorical threats toward the men he seeks to summon to war.

Arguably the only text from Paine's early writings that addresses the condition of women in any serious, sympathetic way is his private letter to Catherine "Kitty" Nicholson Few, a daughter of a New York republican politician, in January 1789.[31] Paine was living in London and moving in the same social circles as Few, who stood on the eve of her marriage. Despite his sense of "loss" at the prospect of seeing another "female friend . . . drop off by matrimony," Paine wished her the best in her nuptials and expressed his hope that he could remain friends with her.[32] He asked that she and other women see him as "not the churlish enemy of their sex, not the inaccessible coldhearted mortal nor the capricious tempered oddity, but one of the best and most affectionate of their friends."[33] Although the letter does not address the question of women's rights, it shows Paine's desire to be recognized as a friend of women who was open to understanding their feelings. The letter also reveals Paine's recognition of some men's reputation as "churlish enemies" of women, especially among women themselves. His attempt to distance himself from such a perception suggests, at the very least, a desire to critically assess eighteenth-century gender relations from a woman's perspective. Yet the letter is a "sentimental" and "emotional" piece of personal writing, as Jack Fruchtman, Jr., puts it, not an explicitly political work.[34]

The Rights of Men versus the Rights of Women

The publication of Paine's *Rights of Man* in 1791 launched a transatlantic debate on the nature of human rights.[35] It was also the first published response to Edmund Burke's *Reflections on the Revolution in France* (1790) to generate an international following across Britain, Europe, and the United States.[36] With this book, Paine became strongly associated with the concept of the "rights of man," to be henceforth contrasted with Burke's conservative critique of such "political metaphysics."[37] For example, a 1793 British song parodied Burke's elitism by ironically berating Paine: "To conclude, then, no more about Man and his Rights,/Tom Paine, and a rabble of Liberty-lights."[38] Another song from the same book straightforwardly declared Paine the champion of the rights of man: "Monarchs tremble at the sound/Freedom, freedom, freedom, freedom/Rights of Man and PAINE resound."[39]

Yet Paine's *Rights of Man,* like *Common Sense* and *The Crisis* series, treated woman as a metaphor in the rhetorical presentation of its arguments for the rights of males, rather than directly advocating for the rights of females. The press duly noted the book's neglect of women's rights, but only to mock the issue. A 1792 Philadelphia newspaper published an article entitled "The Rights of Woman," which contended that "Mr. PAINE, has ushered into the world a dissertation, which he calls, The Rights of Men; and, in the course of the whole performance, he has not bestowed a glance or hint respecting the Rights of Women; whence it may be fairly implied that he supposes we are not entitled to any."[40] The article, by the pseudonymous Susannah Staunch, proceeded to declare a satirical list of rights of wives – including retaliatory adultery and an "unquestionable and uncontrollable right in the kitchen, the laundry, and the dairy" – which implicitly derided the concept of the rights of man as it explicitly ridiculed the idea of the rights of woman.[41]

Such wholly ironic approaches to the topic of women's rights stood in contrast with Mary Wollstonecraft's *A Vindication of the Rights of Woman.* Published in early 1792, it was both the first book on women's rights and the first internationally renowned work on the subject.[42] Wollstonecraft frankly argued that women were entitled to the same "civil and political rights" as men on the basis of their common moral and rational natures as human beings.[43] In her dedicatory letter to Talleyrand-Périgord, the former Catholic bishop turned French revolutionary, Wollstonecraft challenged him and the French republic to address the issue of women's rights: "If the abstract rights of man will bear discussion and explanation, those of women, by a parity of reasoning, will not shrink from the same test."[44] Later in the work, she confronted the British public's amusement at the idea of women's rights: "I may excite laughter, by dropping an hint, which I mean to pursue, some future time, for I really think that women ought to have representatives, instead of being arbitrarily governed without having any direct share allowed them in the deliberations of government."[45] By anticipating the public's laughter, she preempted it. Wollstonecraft thus opened the door to serious consideration of what had been heretofore a joke in her homeland of Britain: extending representation and suffrage to women and other disenfranchised groups.[46]

As fellow republicans, Paine and Wollstonecraft both reject Burke's traditionalism, use Rousseau to undermine the legitimacy of aristocratic civilization, and deploy the revolutionary rhetoric of the "rights of man." Yet the early Paine uses the language of the "rights of man" in a pseudo-universal sense, only to defend the rights of males. In the dedication to *Rights of Man,* he tells George Washington "That the Rights of Man may become as universal as your Benevolence can wish."[47] Instead of obsequiously asking a male leader to define the scope of the rights of men, Wollstonecraft demands that a male leader (Talleyrand-Périgord) recognize women's rationality and consequent participation in the "natural rights of mankind."[48] Although Paine's book is replete with tantalizingly universal rhetoric concerning the rights of individuals and humans, Paine never specifically applies these rights to women; in contrast, the *Rights of Woman* pointedly complains of the confinement of the "rights of humanity" to "the male line from Adam downward."[49] Paine also examines the Genesis account of the creation of mankind, but unlike Wollstonecraft, does not challenge the "distinction of sexes" that it established in the Western tradition. Rather, he contrasts the Mosaic "distinction of sexes" with unfair social distinctions that have robbed men of their God-given natural rights.[50] As with *Common Sense,* this affirmation of the "distinction of sexes" as natural and God-given implies a lack of concern with reform of women's unequal social status.

Women thus function mainly as metaphors and similes, not rights-bearers, in *Rights of Man.* For example, Paine mockingly compares an aristocratic title to a girl who calls attention to her "fine *blue ribbon*" and "*garter.*"[51] He concludes that such titles render men "the counterfeit of women" and instill "a foppery in the human character which degrades it."[52] This metaphor treats women and girls as inferior members of the human race whose behavior, when appropriated by men, "degrades" them. Paine extends the metaphor, claiming that France's abolition of titles means that it has "outgrown the baby-cloaths of *Count* and *Duke,* and breeched itself in manhood."[53] Following the patriarchal rhetoric of the neorepublican tradition, Paine implies that to be a self-governing man or nation entails the rejection of the trappings and influence of women and mothers.

There is one moment in *Rights of Man,* however, when Paine appears to briefly express concern for the rights of girls and women. Partway through the text, he addresses the oppressive practice of primogeniture. Like Wollstonecraft, Paine critiques primogeniture for favoring eldest males, who "begin life by trampling on all their younger brothers and sisters."[54] He praises the French revolutionaries for abandoning the practice of primogeniture and approves it as an essential step in establishing a genuine republic. Yet Paine does not explore how women's enjoyment of greater property rights, once primogeniture is abolished, might entail other civil and political rights for them. Indeed, he upholds the *Declaration of the Rights of Man and Citizen* (1789) as a constitutional model for other nations, without questioning the French republic's exclusion of women from the enjoyment of the same "human rights" as men.[55] It is not until *Agrarian Justice* (1797) that Paine picks up this provocative line of argument concerning women's property rights and finally explores it to its logical conclusion.

Paine's Feminist Turn: Universal Welfare Rights and Universal Suffrage

The first half of *Rights of Man. Part the Second* is much like *Rights of Man:* Paine wavers between the bold use of universalistic rights language and a narrow, patriarchal application of it. Yet a serious turn in Paine's political theory occurs in the latter half of *Part the Second,* with his radical advocacy of a human right to welfare provided by the state. Scholars have shown that this is one of the earliest arguments in the Western tradition for a national system of state-provided welfare entitlements without requirements of labor, demonstrated economic need, or parish residency.[56] In many ways, this radical turn runs parallel to the shift in political emphasis between Wollstonecraft's 1790 response to Burke's *Reflections, A Vindication of the Rights of Men,* and her early 1792 book *A Vindication of the Rights of Woman.* Alongside

Wollstonecraft in 1792, Paine moves from the use of more generic rights discourse to the specific and urgent defense of the human rights of women.

What has not yet been explored fully enough is the feminist dimension of Paine's proposal for human welfare rights in his homeland of England.[57] Near the end of *Rights of Man. Part the Second,* he argues that poor people – male and female, young and old – have a right to welfare payments from the state to help them escape the snares of poverty. To support his case for poor people's equal right to welfare, regardless of sex or age, Paine cites the fact that women and children are taxed, just as men are, as part of the English system of household taxation.[58] He argues that the state consequently owes *all* taxed persons protection against poverty. Paine then proceeds with an analysis of the demographics of England in the early 1790s, which calls attention to the lower socioeconomic status of women and children. He states that most of the poor in England are either elderly men and women, or families with young children.[59] Paine's latter point addresses the relation between female fertility and poverty, and paves the way for his advocacy of welfare rights for mothers.

Paine argues that the state must provide welfare rights to certain segments of the population that are vulnerable to poverty. He contends that "this support . . . is not of the nature of charity, but of a right."[60] In this way, he distinguishes his political proposal from the private "benefit clubs" that sought to assist the poor through charity in late-eighteenth-century England.[61] His proposal was also different from the extant Poor Laws in Britain. Such parish-based systems of poor relief, dating to the late-medieval and Tudor eras, determined eligibility for state provision of welfare (whether monetary or in-kind) through residential status (in a parish, poorhouse, and/or workhouse), proven (not potential) poverty, and/or mandated labor.[62] Paine abandoned the traditional eligibility requirements and in-kind benefits in his vision for a national system of welfare for adults distributed according to the criteria of maternity, marital status, age, and disability. In short, *Rights of Man. Part the Second* imagined a new system of state provision of exclusively monetary welfare that was national in jurisdiction and not conditional on labor, poverty, or local residence.

For Paine, welfare is a "right" because every person has earned such assistance from the state through the lifelong payment of taxes to it. He calculates the benefit owed to each person, in order to justify the state's granting of the right: "Every person in England, male and female, pays on an average in taxes two pounds eight shillings and sixpence *per ann.* from the day of his (or her) birth. . . . Converting . . . his (or her) individual tax into a tontine, the money he shall receive after fifty years, is but little more than the legal interest of the nett money he has paid."[63] Notably, in the above passage, Paine twice added a female pronoun ("(or her)") to remind the reader that he was speaking of both males' and females' right to welfare based on their shared burden of taxation by the state. According to this tax-based formula, Paine proposes state welfare payments to persons over the age of fifty who are "husbandmen, common labourers, journeymen of every trade and their wives, sailors, and disbanded soldiers, worn out servants of both sexes, and poor widows."[64] Specifically, they should receive six pounds per year after age fifty and ten pounds per year after age sixty, all paid out of surplus taxes.[65]

Because the poor tend to be not only the elderly but also members of large, youthful families, Paine offers a feminist analysis of women's rights with regard to fertility and maternity. To relieve the "instant distress" and economic burden that befalls families upon the birth of a child, he proposes that twenty shillings be given to "every woman immediately on the birth of a child" and "every new-married couple."[66] In the context of late-eighteenth-century mores about the restriction of female sexual activity to marriage, Paine's former proposal is quite progressive, as it does not require the woman to be married to receive the payment. The latter proposal, however, could institutionalize an economic incentive to marry prior to childbirth, as a mother's payment would double in that case. A radical aspect of both proposals is the granting of welfare rights to mothers and the newly married in general, regardless of class, in order to *prevent their* descent into poverty upon the birth of their children.

A limit to the feminist dimension of Paine's proposal for welfare rights is in his discussion of the right to state-sponsored education. He begins with a promising argument, suggesting that the state allot four pounds per poor child for their parish-sponsored education.[67] He immediately calls into question the universality of this right, however, by emphasizing how poor boys need access to such a state-sponsored education: "Many a youth, with good natural genius, who is apprenticed to a mechanical trade, such as a carpenter, joiner, millwright, shipwright, blacksmith, &c. is prevented getting forward the whole of his life, from the want of a little common education when a boy."[68] Later in the book, Paine expands his proposal to include working-class as well as poor children; the state should additionally allot ten shillings for the tutelage of each child from a working-class family that cannot afford to pay for the full cost of education in the local parish.[69] Although he does not specifically limit the latter proposal to boys, Paine never discusses the rights of girls to the same education as boys at any point in *Rights of Man. Part the Second.* His neglect of the issue of female education stands in striking contrast to Wollstonecraft. Her *Rights of Woman* had, but a few months earlier, argued for an equal right to primary and secondary schooling for girls and boys of all classes, paid by the state through the age of eighteen.[70]

Paine also differs from Wollstonecraft in that he supports the extant parish school system, whereas she envisions the development of a national system of free, mandatory, coeducational day schools.[71] He assumes that because rural villages do not currently have public schools, new and better forms of education will not be initiated in these underprivileged areas. He also presumes that there will be persons of "both sexes" as well as "distressed clergymen's widows" in these villages who will be willing to work as parish teachers at the rate of ten shillings per poor child.[72] Paine patronizingly assigns the female sex the role of teacher, not student, in his scheme for delivering the right to education to the poor and working class. This proposal built on the broader eighteenth-century English cultural assumption that girls received enough informal education in the home to adequately function as (usually primary) schoolteachers while adults. Wollstonecraft's life fell into this pattern, as she lacked a formal education but still worked as a schoolteacher and school mistress in 1780s London.[73]

Most importantly, Paine's neglect of female education is a striking flaw in his republicanism. According to Paine, monarchies and aristocracies depend on the ignorance of their subjects, but "a nation under a well regulated government, should permit none to remain uninstructed."[74] Following this logic, equal education for the sexes should be required in any "well governed" republic. Moreover, female education would ameliorate many of the conditions of poverty that he sought to address through his system of welfare rights, by rendering women more skilled and self-sufficient. By pigeonholing women in the roles of mothers, teachers, and widows–whose identity is defined by service to and dependency on males–Paine misses the opportunity to realize the full egalitarian potential of his argument for welfare and education rights.

Agrarian Justice, a short pamphlet published in 1797, is Paine's most radical statement on human rights and social justice. It is also his most explicitly feminist work, insofar as it specifically makes a case for women's entitlement to the same rights as men. It is here that Paine contends that women have rights not because they are mothers, wives, widows, or are among the elderly poor, but simply because they are human.[75]

Paine grounds his argument for universal human rights on an account of nature and society before government is established. Appealing to the book of *Genesis* to dismantle Bishop Watson's contention that economic status is divinely ordained, Paine writes that "It is wrong to say God made *Rich* and *Poor;* he made only *Male* and *Female;* and he gave them the earth for their inheritance."[76] Unlike *Common Sense* and *Rights of Man, Agrarian Justice* does not use scripture to support the natural basis of the social inequality of the sexes. It rather uses scripture to contend that women and men equally share a natural right to "the COMMON PROPERTY OF THE HUMAN RACE," or "the earth, in its natural, uncultivated state."[77] Paine then makes a counterfactual argument for the partial restoration of humans' natural rights to the earth and its bounty. If private property had never been established by corrupt governments and civilizations, then humans "would have been born to property."[78]

Paine thus pleads for a "right" to welfare, paid by the state, to ensure that every person – male or female – receives partial compensation for the loss of "*his or her natural inheritance,*" which was unjustly taken as a result of the cultivation of the earth and the development of "landed property" under government.[79] He proposes the establishment of a "national fund," generated by a 10 percent estate tax, "*out of which there shall be paid to every person, when arrived at the age of twenty-one years, the sum of* Fifteen Pounds sterling."[80] Moreover, "*every person now living of the age of fifty years, and . . . all others as they shall arrive at that age*" will receive "Ten Pounds *per annum.*"[81] This welfare program moves well beyond the scope of the one set forth in *Rights of Man. Part the Second,* both in its financial generosity and in its explicitly universal application to all adult persons regardless of sex, marital status, or fertility.[82] According to *Rights of Man. Part the Second,* a couple should receive twenty shillings upon marriage; according to *Agrarian Justice,* each male and female should receive "fifteen pounds" at the age of twenty-one, independent of marital status, to partly redress the loss of "*his or her natural inheritance.*"[83]

The most important departure of *Agrarian Justice* from the logic of Paine's earlier political works is its strong implication that adult humans have a right to suffrage, regardless of class or sex. Because "all individuals have legitimate birthrights in a certain species of property" – namely, the originally "common" property of the earth – they have an equal right to suffrage so that they can vote on how their governments regulate access to land and other forms of property.[84] Although he never specifically applies the right of suffrage to women, Paine concludes the dedication of *Agrarian Justice* with a call for the French republic to realize "equality in the sacred right of suffrage."[85] His revolutionary political proposals for universal welfare rights and universal suffrage rest on the same philosophical assumption that humans, both male and female, were originally entitled to the same natural right to property in the earth. With this philosophical genealogy in mind, we can reasonably infer the later Paine's commitment to women's political incorporation as full citizens alongside men in the French republic and beyond.

Paine, Wollstonecraft, and the Gendering
of Human Rights Discourse

The early Paine's divorcing of rights language from the woman question stood in noticeable contrast with Wollstonecraft's direct connection of the two in both the title and content of *A Vindication of the Rights of Woman*. In 1790s Britain and America, Paine and Wollstonecraft were used as foils for each other's political ideas – such that Paine was quickly associated with the rights of men, and Wollstonecraft with the rights of women. In London in 1792, a satirical pamphlet thanked "Mrs. Mary with the hard German name" for her ideas on "the general rights of girls," and exclaimed "Oh! Mr. Paine, what do we not owe you" on the matter of "the general rights of boys."[86] Without any such irony, Miss Ann Harker gave a 1794 commencement address at the Young Ladies' Academy of Philadelphia, in which she defended girls' education in the traditional male fields of rhetoric and oratory; putting her feminist conception of rhetoric into practice, she proclaimed, "In opposition to your immortal Paine, we will exalt our Wollstonecraft."[87] A 1794 Boston newspaper stated that "Thomas Paine, the author of the rights of Man, and Mrs. Wolstoncraft [*sic*], authoress of the Rights of Woman, who were both imprisoned during Robespierre's Influence, have both been liberated" – misreporting Wollstonecraft's incarceration alongside Paine while reinforcing the gendered contrast between their rights doctrines.[88] A 1797 Philadelphia newspaper praised the women of Elizabethtown, New Jersey, for using their right to vote in local elections, saying:

> The *Rights of man* have been warmly insisted on by TOM PAINE and other democrats, but we outstrip them in the science of government and not only preach the *Rights of Women,* but boldly put it into practice – Madame Woolstencrafts [*sic*] has certainly the merit of preaching the subject, and as women are now to take part in the jurisprudence of our state, we may shortly expect to see them *take the helm* – of government.[89]

In the latter case, the symbolic opposition of the two radicals leant credibility to the nascent cause of women's civil and political rights. Yet the
rhetorical trope also buttressed the idea that the "rights of men" and the
"rights of women" were separate and distinct issues, rather than jointly
rooted in a deeper conception of human rights.

In the late 1790s, Paine and Wollstonecraft were targeted by anti-
Jacobins as symbols of the dangerous excesses of the French Revolution.
Scandalous biographies of them only supplied more ammunition to their
political enemies.[90] *Memoirs of the Author of A Vindication of the Rights
of Woman* (1798) William Godwin's posthumous biography of his wife,
who died after giving birth to their daughter, Mary Shelley, in 1797 – was
too open in disclosing the details of Wollstonecraft's early fascination with
the married Henry Fuseli, the breakdown of her first marriage to Gilbert
Imlay, and her premarital sexual relationships with each of her two husbands. In the context of British and American anti-Jacobinism, Wollstonecraft's life quickly became a morality tale for how revolutionary ideas such
as the "rights of woman" caused the breakdown of sexual morality and
femininity. This backlash against her was strongest in her homeland of
Britain, driving engagement of her ideas underground for the bulk of the
Victorian era.[91] By contrast, in the United States, Wollstonecraft exerted
both public and private influence throughout the early national period. In
her study of women and politics in the early American republic, Rosemarie Zagarri identified a cultural and ideological turn toward "biological es-
sentialism" as partly responsible for a downward trend in positive, public
references to Wollstonecraft and the egalitarian idea of women's human
rights during the first two decades of the nineteenth century. But even then,
Wollstonecraft remained a highly visible if often vilified political symbol
of the nascent feminist cause in the United States. She even grew in both
elite and broad popularity as the abolitionist movement – led by many of
her passionate American readers, such as the Quaker preacher Lucretia
Mott – gained steam alongside the women's rights cause from the 1830s
forward.[92]

At the turn of the nineteenth century, Chalmers's and Cheetham's slanderous biographies of Paine perpetuated rumors of his physical abuse of his
two wives, his first wife's death from a miscarriage caused by his abuse, his
sexual deviancy in refusing to consummate his second marriage, his abandonment of his second wife, and his supposed affair and fathering of a child
with a married Frenchwoman with whom he resided for spells near the end
of his life.[93] Anti-Jacobin works used these insinuations to portray Paine
and the supporters of the "rights of man" as hypocrites who supported the

reform of law but violated the law themselves: "When you hear a man loud against the severity of the laws, set him down as a rogue."[94]

Wollstonecraft and Paine's public reputations thus suffered a similar reversal of fortune in early nineteenth-century Britain and America: both were victims of sexual slander that cast them as symbols of how radical politics led to immorality, especially in the relations between men and women. Their unconventional domestic decisions, especially living with the opposite sex outside of formal marriage, were as disturbing to the public eye as they were fitting to the culture of their fellow British radicals. These lifestyle choices combined with their publications made them targets of a salacious kind of political criticism. An annotated American edition of Richard Polwhele's 1798 poem "The Unsex'd Females" drew a causal link between the "infamous publications of Paine and others" and the "licentious love" practiced by "Wollstonecraftian" women.[95] Likewise in London in 1799, an anti-Jacobin satire dryly noted that "the restraints on the natural desires of the sexes was one of the greatest violations of the rights of man and the rights of woman, which Thomas Paine and Mary Wollstonecraft so ably and successfully vindicated."[96]

Ironically, Paine and Wollstonecraft's sexualized reception by the anti-Jacobins called attention to the philosophical unity beneath their doctrines of the "rights of man" and the "rights of woman." No longer gendered as separate political causes, the "rights of man" and the "rights of woman" were seen as dangerous because they sought the equal treatment of the sexes in all areas of life. The posthumous fates of Wollstonecraft and Paine continued in a gendered direction, however. Wollstonecraft's notoriety as a "fallen woman" persisted through the late Victorian era, especially in Britain,[97] while Paine, as a man, unsurprisingly fared much better in the recovery of his personal reputation after his death in 1809.

As nineteenth-century biographers discredited the sexual slanders of Chalmers and Cheetham,[98] Paine was upheld as an icon of both the rights of man and the rights of woman. Celebrations of Paine's birthday were held in New York City, Providence, and Cincinnati in the mid-nineteenth century.[99] Before hundreds of people, songs, speeches, and toasts honored Paine's role in advancing the cause of both men's and women's rights. At the 1832 birthday party in New York, a song about romantic love, attributed to Paine, followed a toast to "The Fair—may they soon enjoy equal rights and equal privileges with man."[100] Although Wollstonecraft was sometimes mentioned in such freethinker events, the center stage was often given to Paine. At the "Paine Festival" in Cincinnati in 1856, held just a year after a women's rights convention in the same city, a medical doctor professed:

"The most advanced reformer of this day does no more than to extend, to a wider and more comprehensive sphere, the application of the principles of the 'Rights of Man,' as stated, and in the statement demonstrated, by Thomas Paine. It was this work that excited Mary Wollstonecraft to write her noble 'Vindication of the Rights of Woman.'" [101] His speech reduced Wollstonecraft to philosophical sidekick to Paine on the issue of women's human rights, despite the fact that her *Rights of Woman* was the first major philosophical book on the topic in the wake of the French Revolution. This nineteenth-century institutionalization of Paine as the great theorist of universal human rights was correct in light of *Agrarian Justice* but ironic in light of his early neglect of women's rights and Wollstonecraft's groundbreaking treatise on the subject. Prejudices about the natural abilities and proper roles of men and women, derived from centuries of patriarchal culture and law, seem to have driven this ideological trend of treating the issue of human rights in gendered and sexualized terms. Paine and Wollstonecraft became convenient symbols in the public fitting of the new liberal ideas in old patriarchal clothes. [102]

Rights discourse continues to be gendered and sexualized, often hindering the realization of universal human rights. Liberalism, while embracing Paine's idea of equal rights for equal citizens, has not always used this idea to address the injustices that women face. Feminism, while following in the footsteps of Wollstonecraft, has sometimes focused on women's issues to the point of missing opportunities for broader human rights advocacy. In the spirit of Wollstonecraft and the later Paine, feminist theorists such as Susan Moller Okin, Martha Nussbaum, and Catharine MacKinnon have recently emphasized the value of a human rights approach to political justice that encompasses and addresses the rights and needs of women as well as other historically oppressed groups. [103] We would do well to remember the lesson Paine learned late in life and incorporated into *Agrarian Justice:* women have rights because they are human, not because they are weaker, poorer, or more vulnerable than men. With this conception of universal human rights in mind, we can avoid the pitfalls and prejudices of narrow views of the rights of men and women.

NOTES

I thank the Institute for Scholarship in the Liberal Arts at the University of Notre Dame, the staffs at the Massachusetts Historical Society and at the New England Historic Genealogical Society, Ian Shapiro, William Frucht, Jane Calvert, Rogers M. Smith, David Armitage, Richard Bernstein, Jonathan Clark, and Andrew Haley – a class of 2012 and Glynn Family Honors Program student at the University of Notre Dame – for their assistance with this project.

1. Following Offen, I use the term "feminist" to refer to "a system of ideas and a movement for sociopolitical change based on a refusal of male privilege and women's subordination within a given society" and apply it to historical cases before the term "feminist" was coined and widely used in this sense at the turn of the nineteenth century. See Karen Offen, *European Feminisms, 1700–1950: A Political History* (Stanford, CA: Stanford University Press, 2000), pp. 19–20.

2. This argument dates to Moncure Conway's *The Life of Thomas Paine* (New York: G. P. Putnam's Sons, 1892), vol. 1, p. 45.

3. William M. Van de Weyde, *The Life and Works of Thomas Paine* (New Rochelle, NY: Thomas Paine Historical Association, 1925), vol. 2, pp. 73, 85; Frank Smith, "New Light on Paine's First Year in America, 1775," *American Literature* 1, no. 4 (Jan. 1930): p. 368; Augusta Violette, *Economic Feminism in the United States prior to 1848* (New York: B. Franklin, 1971), p. 24; John Harbison, "Thomas Paine: Eighteenth-Century Feminist," *The Social Studies* 69, no. 3 (May/June 1978): pp. 103–107; Michael S. Kimmel and Thomas E. Mosmiller, eds., *Against the Tide: Pro-Feminist Men in the United States, 1776–1990* (Boston: Beacon Press, 1992), pp. 16, 56, 63.

4. Frank Smith, "The Authorship of 'An Occasional Letter on the Female Sex,'" *American Literature* 2, no. 3 (November 1930): pp. 277–280; Lieselotte Steinbrügge, *The Moral Sex: Woman's Nature in the French Enlightenment,* trans. Pamela E. Selwyn (New York: Oxford University Press, [1992] 1995), pp. 35–40, 90–99; Mary Trouille, "Sexual/Textual Politics in the Enlightenment: Diderot and d'Epinay Respond to Thomas's Essay on Women," *British Journal for Eighteenth-Century Studies* 19, no. 1 (1996): pp. 1–15; Mary Catherine Moran, "L'Essai sur les femmes/Essay on Women: An Eighteenth-Century Transatlantic Journey," *History Workshop Journal* 59 (Spring 2005): pp. 17–32.

5. Jack Fruchtman, Jr., *Thomas Paine: Apostle of Freedom* (New York: Four Walls Eight Windows, 1994), p. 160; Marc E. Kann, *The Gendering of American Politics: Founding Mothers, Founding Fathers, and Political Patriarchy* (Westport, CT: Greenwood Press, 1999), p. 7.

6. Fifty thousand copies of *Rights of Man* (the first part) were sold upon its publication in 1791. The book inspired British working-class people to establish clubs to discuss it. See Christopher Hitchens, *Thomas Paine's Rights of Man: A Biography* (New York: Atlantic Monthly Press, 2006).

7. Anonymous, "To a Young Lady, Who Sent to the Author for 'The Rights of Man,' Written by Mr. Paine," in *The United States Chronicle,* vol. 8, no. 412 (Providence, RI: Bennett Wheeler, 24 November 1791), p. 4. The heading for the poem states that it was reprinted "from the *New-York Daily Advertiser.*"

8. Lyndall Gordon, *Vindication: A Life of Mary Wollstonecraft* (New York: HarperCollins, 2005), pp. 188–189; Iain McLean and Fiona Hewitt, trans. and eds., *Condorcet: Foundations of Social Choice and Political Theory* (Northampton, MA: Elgar, 1994), p. 16; Eric Foner, *Tom Paine and Revolutionary America* (Oxford: Oxford University Press, 2005), p. 73.

9. For example, see James R. Miller and Hugh M. Ayer, "*Agrarian Justice*–Thomas Paine's Social Security Program of 1797," *Educational Gerontology* 7, no. 4 (1981): pp. 375–382; Judith Buber Agassi, "The Rise of the Ideas of the Welfare State," *Philosophy of the Social Sciences* 21, no. 4 (1991): pp. 444–457; Adrian Little, "The Politics of Compensation: Tom Paine's *Agrarian Justice* and Liberal Egalitarianism," *Contemporary Politics* 5, no. 1 (1999): pp. 63–73; Jack Fruchtman, Jr., *The Political Philosophy of Thomas Paine* (Baltimore, MD: Johns Hopkins University Press, 2009), pp. 119–133; Robert Lamb, "Liberty, Equality, and the Boundaries of Ownership: Thomas Paine's Theory of Property Rights," *The Review of Politics* 72, no. 3 (Summer 2010): pp. 483–511. Among these scholars, only Agassi and Fruchtman are attentive to Paine's prescriptions for women's welfare rights.

10. In her excellent study of Paine's theory of welfare rights, Agassi assumes rather than demonstrates that Paine includes women in his argument for universal suffrage. See Agassi, "Rise of the Ideas," p. 456.

11. See Conway, *The Life*, vol. 1, p. 45; Violette, *Economic Feminism*, p. 24; Harbison, "Thomas Paine"; Kimmel and Mosmiller, *Against the Tide*, pp. 16, 56, 63; Gordon, *Vindication*, p. 130. Anthologies misattributed this text to Paine well into the 1990s, contributing to the misperception of his early feminist advocacy; for example, see Myra Jehlen and Michael Warner, eds., *The English Literatures of America, 1500–1800* (New York: Routledge, 1997), p. 865; Winston Langley and Vivian Fox, eds., *Women's Rights in the United States: A Documentary History* (Santa Barbara, CA: Praeger, 1998), p. 15.

12. Smith, "Authorship of 'An Occasional Letter,'" p. 277.

13. Moran, "L'Essai."

14. Steinbrügge, *The Moral Sex*, p. 35; Trouille, "Sexual/Textual Politics," 2; Moran, "L'Essai," p. 20.

15. Trouille, "Sexual/Textual Politics," pp. 7–9.

16. Moran, "L'Essai," p. 27.

17. In November 1930, Frank Smith was the first to cast doubt on the attribution of "Unhappy Marriages" to Paine, since his discovery of the real author of the "Occasional Letter" undermined his previous thesis that the stylistic similarities between the two texts suggested that Paine authored both; see Smith, "New Light," p. 368, and Smith, "Authorship of 'An Occasional Letter,'" p. 277. See also Arnold K. King, *Thomas Paine in America, 1774–1787* (Chicago: University

of Chicago Press, 1951), pp. 43n33, 54; A. Owen Aldridge, *Thomas Paine's American Ideology* (Cranbury, NJ: Associated University Presses, 1984), p. 287; John Keane, *Tom Paine: A Political Life* (New York: Grove Press, 1995), p. 551.

18. The *Pennsylvania Magazine* version of "Unhappy Marriages" was taken from London's *The Gentlemen's Magazine* 9 (May 1739). *The Gentlemen's Magazine* version was taken from London's *Universal Spectator* 552 (5 May 1739). See Edward W. R. Pitcher, *The Pennsylvania Magazine, or American Monthly Museum, 1775–1776: An Annotated Index of Sources, Signatures, and First Lines of Literary Sources* (Lewiston, NY: Edwin Mellon, 2001), p. 97; W. Andrew Haley, "Thomas Paine and the Authorship of 'Reflections on Unhappy Marriages'" (2010), unpublished manuscript, p. 8.

19. A recent edition of Paine's works includes "Unhappy Marriages" partly on the basis of parallels between it and Paine's early life. See Thomas Paine, *Common Sense and Related Writings,* ed. Thomas P. Slaughter (New York: Palgrave Macmillan, 2001), p. 69.

20. Linda Kerber, "The Republican Mother: Women and the Enlightenment – An American Perspective," *American Quarterly* 28, no. 2 (Summer 1976): pp. 187–205; Joan Landes, *Women and the Public Sphere in the Age of the French Revolution* (Ithaca, NY: Cornell University Press, 1988).

21. Thomas Paine, *Common Sense,* this volume, p. 8.

22. Ibid., p. 9.

23. Ibid., p. 12.

24. Ibid., p. 13.

25. Rogers M. Smith, *Civic Ideals: Conflicting Visions of Citizenship in U.S. History* (New Haven: Yale University Press, 1997), pp. 75–76; Kann, *Gendering,* p. 7.

26. Paine, *Common Sense,* this volume, p. 25.

27. Ibid., p. 42.

28. Ibid., p. 47.

29. Paine, *The Crisis,* this volume, p. 53.

30. Ibid., p. 60.

31. Fruchtman, *Thomas Paine: Apostle,* p. 194.

32. As quoted in Harbison, "Thomas Paine," p. 103.

33. Ibid., p. 104.

34. Fruchtman, *Thomas Paine: Apostle,* p. 194.

35. David A. Wilson, *Paine and Cobbett: The Transatlantic Connection* (Montreal: McGill-Queen's University Press, 1988), pp. 7, 82–84.

36. Fruchtman, *Thomas Paine: Apostle,* p. 222.

37. Edmund Burke, *Reflections on the Revolution in France,* ed. J. G. A. Pocock (Indianapolis, IN: Hackett, 1987), p. 51.

38. R. Thompson, *Tom Paine's Jests* (Philadelphia: Matthew Carey, [1793] 1796), p. 43.

39. Ibid., p. 58.

40. Susannah Staunch [pseud.], "The Rights of Woman," *Supplement to Dunlap's American Daily Advertiser,* no. 4280 (October 13, 1792), p. 4.

41. Ibid.

42. Janet Todd estimates that fifteen hundred to three thousand English copies of *A Vindication of the Rights of Woman* were sold between 1792 and 1797. This may be an underestimation, as Susan Branson points out that fifteen hundred copies of the book were printed in Philadelphia alone in 1794. In addition to two further editions in London and reprintings in Boston and Philadelphia, the book was also published in Dublin in the 1790s. Editions or selective translations in German, French, Danish, Dutch, and Spanish appeared in the 1790s, expanding the audience for *A Vindication of the Rights of Woman* well beyond the English-speaking world. See Janet Todd, *Mary Wollstonecraft: A Revolutionary Life* (New York: Columbia University Press, 2000), p. 185; Susan Branson, *These Fiery Frenchified Dames: Women and Political Culture in Early National Philadelphia* (Philadelphia: University of Pennsylvania Press, 2001), p. 38; Sally Ann Kitts, "Mary Wollstonecraft's 'A Vindication of the Rights of Woman': A Judicious Response from Eighteenth-Century Spain," *Modern Language Review* 89, no. 2 (April 1994), pp. 351–359; John Windle, *Mary Wollstonecraft Godwin. A Bibliography 1759–1797* (New Castle, DE: Oak Knoll Press, 2000); Eileen Hunt Botting, "Wollstonecraft in Europe, 1792–1904: A Revisionist Reception History," *History of European Ideas* 39, no. 4 (May 2013), pp. 503–527.

43. Mary Wollstonecraft, *A Vindication of the Rights of Woman,* in *A Vindication of the Rights of Men and A Vindication of the Rights of Woman,* ed. Sylvana Tomaselli (Cambridge: Cambridge University Press, 2005), p. 69.

44. Ibid.

45. Ibid., p. 237.

46. Ibid.

47. Paine, *Rights of Man,* this volume, p. 172.

48. Wollstonecraft, *A Vindication,* p. 69.

49. Ibid., p. 167. Although Paine would later write one of the most radical Enlightenment critiques of the supernatural character of the Bible–*The Age of Reason* (1794)–it did not occur to him to critique its patriarchal rhetoric and symbolism along the feminist lines of *A Vindication of the Rights of Woman.*

50. Paine, *Rights of Man,* this volume, p. 197.

51. Ibid., p. 208.

52. Ibid., p. 208.

53. Ibid., pp. 208–209.

54. Ibid., p. 211.

55. Ibid., p. 233. Paine also used the term "human rights" in *Rights of Man. Part the Second,* this volume, p. 282.

56. Miller and Ayer, *Agrarian Justice*; Agassi, "Welfare State"; Little, "Politics of Compensation"; Fruchtman, *Political Philosophy,* pp. 119–133; Lamb, "Liberty, Equality."

57. Agassi and Fruchtman provide helpful overviews of Paine's specific prescriptions for women's welfare rights but do not address how they fit into the evolution of his views on women's rights over time or stand in relation to the feminist tradition. I build on their analyses to tackle the latter two points. See Agassi, "Welfare State," and Fruchtman, *Political Philosophy,* pp. 119–133.

58. Paine, *Rights of Man. Part the Second,* this volume, p. 296.

59. Ibid., p. 334.

60. Ibid., p. 337.

61. Ibid., p. 334.

62. Amir Paz-Fuchs, *Welfare to Work: Conditional Rights in Social Policy* (Oxford: Oxford University Press, 2008), p. 88; Paul Slack, *The English Poor Law, 1531–1782* (Cambridge: Cambridge University Press, [1990] 1995), pp. 33–36.

63. Paine, *Rights of Man. Part the Second,* this volume, p. 337.

64. Ibid., p. 336.

65. Ibid., p. 337.

66. Ibid., p. 339.

67. Ibid., p. 339.

68. Ibid., p. 335.

69. Ibid., pp. 338–339.

70. Wollstonecraft, *A Vindication,* p. 263.

71. Ibid.

72. Paine, *Rights of Man. Part the Second,* this volume, pp. 338–339.

73. Gordon, *Vindication,* pp. 47–48.

74. Paine, *Rights of Man. Part the Second,* this volume, p. 338.

75. In a similar vein, Martha C. Nussbaum reads *Agrarian Justice* as an important philosophical precursor to contemporary theories of welfare rights as part of universal human rights. See Nussbaum, *Creating Capabilities: The Human Development Approach* (Cambridge, MA: Harvard University Press, 2011), p. 140.

76. Paine, *Agrarian Justice,* this volume, p. 553.

77. Ibid., p. 555.

78. Ibid., p. 555.

79. Ibid., p. 557.

80. Ibid., p. 557.

81. Ibid., p. 557.

82. Paine allots welfare on the basis of age and disability in *Agrarian Justice,* whereas in *Rights of Man. Part the Second* he prescribes it on the basis of sex, age, and disability. In *Agrarian Justice,* the "blind and lame" receive ten pounds per year until they reach the age of fifty, when they subsequently qualify for the generic age-based benefit. See *Agrarian Justice,* this volume, p. 561. *Agrarian Justice*'s proposal for universal human welfare rights, based solely on age and disability, moved well beyond even the British Speenhamland system of poor relief that began during the grain-price crisis of 1795–1796. The Speenhamland system required means-testing of poverty in order to receive a top-up of pay gauged by the current price of bread. See Paz-Fuchs, *Welfare to Work,* p. 88.

83. Paine, *Agrarian Justice,* this volume, p. 557.

84. Thomas Paine, *Political Writings,* ed. Bruce Kuklick (Cambridge: Cambridge University Press, 1997), pp. 320–321.

85. Ibid., p. 322.

86. Anonymous, *A Sketch of the Rights of Boys and Girls. By Launcelot Light, of Westminster School; and Laetitia Lookabout of Queen's Square, Bloomsbury* (London: J. Bew, 1792), pp. 5, 14.

87. Ann Harker, "The Salutory Oration," in James Armstrong Neal, *An Essay on the Education and Genius of the Female Sex* (Philadelphia: Jacob Johnson, 1795), p. 17.

88. Untitled, *The Mercury* 4, no. 44 (Boston: November 25–28, 1794), p. 2. Wollstonecraft was never incarcerated in France during the Revolution, but Paine was jailed during the Reign of Terror, from December 28, 1793, to November 4, 1794. See Fruchtman, *Thomas Paine: Apostle,* p. 317.

89. "Rights of Women," *General Advertiser,* no. 2127 (Philadelphia: October 20, 1797), p. 3.

90. George Chalmers [Francis Oldys], *The Life of Thomas Paine, the Author of Rights of Man, Age of Reason, Etc.* (Boston: David West, [1791] 1796); William Godwin, *Memoirs of the Author of A Vindication of the Rights of Woman* (London: Joseph Johnson, 1798); James Cheetham, *The Life of Thomas Paine* (New York: Southwick and Pelsue, 1809).

91. Barbara Caine, "Victorian Feminism and the Ghost of Mary Wollstonecraft," *Women's Writing* 4, no. 2 (1997). pp. 261–275

92. Rosemarie Zagarri, *Revolutionary Backlash: Women and Politics in the Early Republic* (Philadelphia: University of Pennsylvania Press, 2007), pp. 164–180; Nancy Isenberg, "'To Stand Out in Heresy': Lucretia Mott, Liberty, and the Hysterical Woman," *Pennsylvania Magazine of History and Biography* 127, no. 1 (January 2003), p. 15; Eileen Hunt Botting, "Making an American Feminist Icon:

Mary Wollstonecraft's Reception in U.S. Newspapers, 1800–1869," *History of Political Thought* 34, no. 2 (Spring 2013), pp. 273–295.

93. Chalmers, *The Life,* pp. 4–13; Cheetham, *The Life,* pp. 28–33, 238–248.

94. William Cobbett, *The Political Censor* (Sept. 1796), p. 9.

95. Richard Polwhele, "The Unsex'd Females" (New York: William Cobbet, 1800), pp. 15, 25n, 34. Polwhele's poem was originally published in London in 1798.

96. Robert Bisset, "The Adventures of Timothy Newlight, A Votary of Godwin' s Philosophy," in *The Historical, Biographical, Literary, and Scientific Magazine,* ed. Robert Bisset (London: G. Cawthorn, 1799), p. 29.

97. Caine, "Victorian Feminism." Wollstonecraft was always more warmly received in the Americas and continental Europe during the nineteenth century than in her homeland, where the Romantic-era scandals surrounding the Godwin-Shelley circle exacerbated the public perception of the immorality of her teachings. See Botting, "Wollstonecraft in Europe, 1792–1904."

98. Anonymous, *The Life of Thomas Paine* (New York: George H. Evans, 1835); Gilbert Vale, *The Life of Thomas Paine* (Boston: J. P. Mendum, 1859).

99. John Morrison, "An Oration Delivered in Tammany Hall, in Commemoration of the Birthday of Thomas Paine: And an Account of the Celebration" (New York: Evans and Brooks, 1832); N. C. Rhodes, "An Oration, Delivered before the Society of Moral Philanthropists, at the Celebration of the Ninety-Sixth Anniversary of the Birth Day of the Hon. Thomas Paine, Together with an Account of the Proceedings of the Festival" (Providence, RI: Published by Request of the Committee of Arrangements, 1833); Anonymous, *The Paine Festival: Celebration of the 119th Anniversary of the Birth-Day of Thomas Paine at Cincinnati, January 29, 1856* (Cincinnati, OH: Valentine Nicholson, 1856).

100. Morrison, "An Oration," p. 28.

101. Anonymous, *The Paine Festival,* p. 15.

102. My reading of the reasons behind the "gendering" of human rights discourse diverges from scholars such as Carole Pateman, who interpret patriarchy as inherent to liberalism, rather than its outdated, superadded dress. See Pateman, *The Sexual Contract* (Stanford, CA: Stanford University Press, 1988).

103. Susan Moller Okin, "Feminism, Women's Human Rights, and Cultural Differences," *Hypatia* 13, no. 2 (Spring 1998), pp. 32–52; Martha Nussbaum, *Women and Human Development: The Capabilities Approach* (Cambridge: Cambridge University Press, 2000); Catharine MacKinnon, *Are Women Human? and Other International Dialogues* (Cambridge, MA: Belknap, 2006).

Index

Chronicles, books of, 430–31, 440,
441–46, 454, 456
Chrysostom, John, 486n15
churches: national institutions of,
373; oppression of, 5
church and state: connection between, 498; as idol, 200; union
of, 214, 215
citizenship, 215, 527, 529–30, 590
City of God (Augustine), 571
City Tavern (Philadelphia), 144
civil disobedience, 605, 609
civil government, 201, 223, 228, 245,
310–11, 316, 331, 513–14
civilization, characteristics of, 554;
commerce and, 311–12; first principle of, 555; government and,
310; injustice in, 564; organizing,
on charitable principles, 561; preserving, 554–55; universal, 315
civil religion, 579, 583, 622
civil rights, 198–99
civil society, purpose of, 516
Clark, Jonathan, xxi
class divisions, 584
Clemens, Samuel (Mark Twain), xxi
clergy: condition of, 211–12; salaries
of, 351
Clootz, Anacharsis, 419
Cobbett, William, xii
Collins, Henry, 581
colonial governments, replacement
of, 612
colonialism, 584, 585
colonies: infant state of, 37–38;
temper of, 29
commanders in chief, 131
commandments, 375, 427
commerce: advantages of, 314–15;
effect of, on patriotism and

defense, 38; foreign dominion and, 314–15; importance
of, 595; as means to universal
civilization, 311–13; peace and,
312–13; promoting and extending, 156; protection of, with
navies, 314; taking care of itself,
158
Committee of Public Safety, 530,
533, 540–41n6
committees of inquiry, 148
common cause rhetoric, 603
commons, 10, 11
Commons. See Tiers Etat
Common Sense (Paine), xiii, xiv, xv,
xvi, xvii, xix, xxii, 86n4, 582;
contesting British colonialism,
584; influence of, 594; liberal vision of, 582; masculine language
in, 634–36; publication and distribution of, 588–89; publication
of, 402–3; Quakers responding to,
609–10; reaching the threshold
of socialism, 581; scripture used
in, 588; significance of, 581;
style of, 634; success of, 317n13;
universal values of, 583; women
in, 635–36
Commonwealthmen, 593
communism, xx
commutation tax, 343, 344, 346
Condorcet (marquis de; Marie Jean
Antoine Nicolas de Caritat), 631,
632, 633
Confucius, 376
Congress: Charter of, 161–62;
choosing members for, mode of,
40; formation of, 30
conquest, government arising from,
200

government: abolished, 273; absolute, 10; allegiance to, 527; altering, right of, 226; arbitrary power of, 238; beginning at the right end, 38; budgetary plan for, 332; changing opinions about, 239; characters of, 311; checks and balances in, 11; civilization and, 310; components of, 300; contempt and, 241; continental form of, 28; as contrivance of human wisdom, 244; defects of, exposing, 266; distinct from constitutions, 289, 294–95; evil of, 8; first principles of, 10, 200–201, 241, 526; forms of, 256, 283–84, 504; foundation for, 210, 271, 297; greediness of, 270; insolvency of, 253–54; interest of, different from nations', 260; mixed, 256–57; as national association, 275, 302–3; nature of, 258; object of, 309; obsolescence of, 261; old system of, 278–80; reason applied to, 308–9, 331; reform of, 355–56; religion as duty of, 38–39; representative (new) system of, 278–79 (*see also* representative system of government); revolution in system of, 270; rights of, 199–200, 292; security as true design and end of, 8, 10; society and, 8–9, 274; source of, 38, 238, 292; strength of, 10; study of, 503–4; systems of, prejudices toward, 267
Greeks, schools of, 397–98
Greene, Nathanael, 55, 318n
Grenville, William, 537–38, 543
Grogan, Claire, 581

Hammond, George, 533
Hanover, house of, 252, 296, 327, 591, 593, 594
Harker, Ann, 644
heads, stuck on spikes, 190
heathen mythology, 375, 400–401n4, 410, 470
Henry, Patrick, xxvi
Henry IV (France), 259–60
Henry VI, 18
Henry VII, 18
hereditary crown, 241–42. *See also* hereditary government
hereditary estates, 348
hereditary government, 237, 242–44, 256, 504–5, 587–88; civil wars resulting from, 281; evil of, 16–18; lacking right to exist, 505–10; problems with, 278–80, 282–83, 285; as slavery, 302; wars resulting from, 18–19. *See also* monarchy
hereditary powers, 242–43, 248
hereditary principle, Paine's zeal against, 591–92
hereditary rights, 237
hereditary succession. *See* hereditary government
hereditary system. *See* hereditary government
hereditary wisdom, 237
Herodotus, 424
Hill, Samuel, xi
History of England (Smollett), 593
History of the Revenue (Sinclair), 326, 330, 333
Hitchens, Christopher, xxi
Hobbes, Thomas, xvi, xviii, xx

Rethinking the Western Tradition

Groundwork for the Metaphysics of Morals
By Immanuel Kant
EDITED BY ALLEN W. WOOD

Sesame and Lilies
By John Ruskin
EDITED BY DEBORAH EPSTEIN NORD

"The Social Contract" and "The First and Second Discourses"
By Jean-Jacques Rousseau
EDITED BY SUSAN DUNN

Discourse on Method and Meditations on First Philosophy
By René Descartes
EDITED BY DAVID WEISSMAN

Culture and Anarchy
By Matthew Arnold
EDITED BY SAMUEL LIPMAN

The Idea of a University
By John Henry Newman
EDITED BY FRANK M. TURNER

The Prince
By Niccolò Machiavelli
TRANSLATED BY ANGELO CODEVILLA